W9-BAE-352

To Kent,

Fondly remembering
our lynx restoration effort
and the Adirondack
adventures that went
with it!   Best,

Rainer

# THE GREAT EXPERIMENT IN CONSERVATION

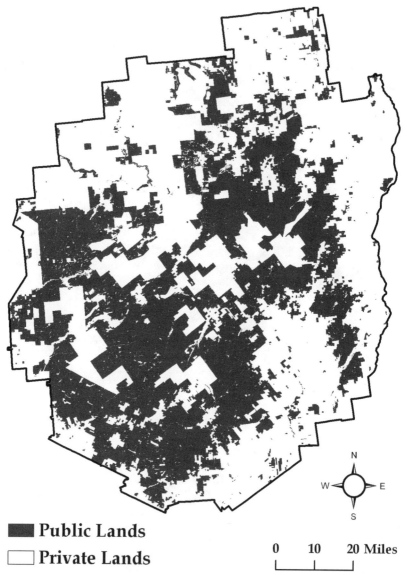

Public Lands

Private Lands

0    10    20 Miles

Public and private lands in Adirondack Park. Courtesy of Stacy A. McNulty, Adirondack Ecological Center.

# The
# GREAT EXPERIMENT
# *in* CONSERVATION

## *Voices from the*
## ADIRONDACK PARK

*Edited by*

William F. Porter,

Jon D. Erickson,

*and* Ross S. Whaley

SYRACUSE UNIVERSITY PRESS

Copyright © 2009 by Syracuse University Press
Syracuse, New York 13244–5160

All Rights Reserved
First Edition 2009
09  10  11  12  13  14      6  5  4  3  2  1

The paper used in this publication meets the minimum requirements
of American National Standard for Information Sciences—Permanence of Paper
for Printed Library Materials, ANSI Z39.48–1984.∞™

For a listing of books published and distributed by Syracuse University Press,
visit our Web site at SyracuseUniversityPress.syr.edu.

ISBN-13: 978-0-8156-3231-3
ISBN-10: 0-8156-3231-2

**Library of Congress Cataloging-in-Publication Data**

The great experiment in conservation : voices from the Adirondack Park /
edited by William F. Porter, Jon D. Erickson, and Ross S. Whaley.—1st ed.
   p. cm.
Includes bibliographical references and index.
ISBN-13: 978-0-8156-3231-3 (hardcover : alk. paper)
ISBN-10: 0-8156-3231-2
   1. Conservation of natural resources—New York (State)—Adirondack Park.
   2. Adirondack Park (N.Y.)—Environmental conditions.   I. Porter, William F.
II. Erickson, Jon D.   III. Whaley, Ross S.
S932.N7G74 2009
333.7209747′5—dc22
                              2009011313

Manufactured in the United States of America

*In memory of David J. Allee and Richard W. Sage, Jr.,
who were catalysts for this book. Their voices were not
captured because they were gone too soon.*

# Contents

# Figures

# Tables

# Foreword

*Connecting Means and Ends in the Study of Place*

HERMAN E. DALY

This book's organization is both bottom-up and top-down. It begins with ultimate means, low entropy matter-energy, that without which we can accomplish nothing and for which we are totally dependent on the natural world. No substitutes are available.

But how should we use the means at our disposal, what are the ends they should serve, and because scarcity prevents us from satisfying all ends, which should have priority and which should be sacrificed?

Framed in this holistic way, the problem is so large that it defies solution, however intellectually satisfying the overall vision may be.

To be operational we have to move from ultimate means to intermediate means, from the too-low common denominator of low entropy to its higher specific expressions in terms of solar radiation, photosynthetic capacity, water availability, mineral deposits, surface gradients, food webs, and all the other specific funds and structures determining life's metabolic flow through a particular place. In this book, that place is the Adirondack Park. It is the specificity of place that tethers abstract concepts of ends and means to the real world and its concrete problems.

Even less are we able to reason operationally in terms of the ultimate end, even though our ranking of intermediate ends implies an ultimate criterion by which to prioritize good things. So we reason in terms of intermediate ends—timber supply, housing, water catchment, wildlife preservation, recreation—balancing them as best we can, but without having a clear picture of the ultimate criterion of value by which we measure their relative worth at the ever-shifting margins. This lack of clarity forces continual reconsideration of our implicit vision of the ultimate end. We should have by now learned at least one important thing about the ultimate end—it cannot be growth forever, not for the Adirondacks, not for the earth.

The editors and contributors deserve hearty congratulations for having put together in a unifying and helpful framework so much ecology, history, economics, ethics, policy, and analysis about such an important place. May other important places receive the same careful and caring study!

# Acknowledgments

We gratefully acknowledge Mary Selden Evans, Kay Steinmetz, John Fruehwirth, and D. J. Whyte at Syracuse University Press for their support and encouragement and for their editing, and De Ann Porter for her assistance with the book. Many of the ideas presented in this book had their genesis in discussions at meetings of the Adirondack Research Consortium and at an early meeting of many of the authors. We especially thank the family of Barbara McMartin for their help to ensure that her voice was part of our project, even with her death in the middle of the effort. Finally, all book projects take enormous portions of personal time, and we appreciate the inspiration, indulgence, and patience of our families as we brought this project to completion, especially De Ann, Pat, and Beverly.

# Contributors

PETER BAUER is executive director of the Fund for Lake George and past executive director of the Residents' Committee to Protect the Adirondacks, and served on the staff of the state Commission on the Adirondacks in the Twenty-First Century. He has been one of the leading environmental advocates for the Adirondack Park since the early 1990s.

DONALD BEHREND is professor emeritus in the Department of Environmental and Forest Biology at the State University of New York College of Environmental Science and Forestry in Syracuse. He was executive vice president and provost of the statewide University of Alaska system and retired as chancellor emeritus of the University of Alaska–Anchorage. Don spent more than twenty years engaging conservation issues in the Adirondacks and then another twenty years confronting many of those same issues in Alaska.

RUSSELL D. BRIGGS is a professor in the Department of Forest and Natural Resource Management at the State University of New York College of Environmental Science and Forestry in Syracuse. Russ is among the foremost soil scientists in the northeastern United States and is a skilled educator.

RAINER H. BROCKE is professor emeritus in the Department of Environmental and Forest Biology at the State University of New York College of Environmental Science and Forestry in Syracuse. Rainer arrived in the Adirondacks about the time the Adirondack Park

Agency was being formed and spent a career conducting research on wildlife in the region and teaching wilderness ecology.

STUART BUCHANAN is former director of Region 5 of the New York State Department of Environmental Conservation, headquartered in Ray Brook. During his tenure with the DEC, Stu was known as a skillful administrator. He brings thoughtful observations of the interplay of public agencies.

CHARLES D. CANHAM is a forest ecologist with the Cary Institute of Ecosystem Studies in Millbrook, New York. Charlie's graduate work was completed in the Adirondack region and he has spent more than twenty years studying forest dynamics in the Northeastern United States and throughout the world.

CHRISTOPHER P. CIRMO is professor and chair of the Geology Department at the State University of New York College at Cortland and directs its environmental science programs. Chris completed his doctoral research in the Adirondacks and has a long history of research on wetlands, hydrology, and biogeochemistry in the region.

GRAHAM L. COX is the forest and open-space coordinator for Audubon New York, headquartered in Albany. Graham completed his doctoral research on sustainable forest management and policy in New York and has had a long career working within both state government and environmental organizations in the Adirondacks and Northern Forest.

HERMAN E. DALY is a professor in the School of Public Policy at the University of Maryland in College Park. Herman is a cofounder of the field of ecological economics and the international journal of the same name. He was formerly senior economist in the Environment Department of the World Bank, where he helped to develop policy guidelines related to sustainable development.

ROBERT A. DANIELS is curator of ichthyology at the New York State Museum in Albany. Bob's work at the State Museum contributes to the largest repository of information on fishes of the region and a collection of regional importance.

GEORGE D. DAVIS is former director of planning at the Adirondack Park Agency in Ray Brook. George provided much of the vision for the ideas behind the legislation that established the regulatory authority of the Adirondack Park Agency and its land classification system for public and private lands in the Park. He was on the staff of Governor Rockefeller's Adirondack Study Commission and was executive director of Governor Cuomo's Commission on the Adirondacks in the Twenty-First Century. George was awarded a MacArthur Fellowship for his work in the Adirondacks.

CHAD P. DAWSON is professor and former chair of the Department of Forest and Natural Resources Management at the State University of New York College of Environmental Science and Forestry in Syracuse. Chad has more than thirty years of experience with issues relating to wilderness and recreation on a national scale and a long history of engaging those issues in the Adirondack region.

CHARLES T. DRISCOLL is university professor in the Department of Civil and Environmental Engineering at Syracuse University. He has been studying the effects of air pollutants on forest and aquatic ecosystems in the Adirondacks and their recovery in response to decreases in emissions for the past thirty-five years.

KIMBERLEY M. DRISCOLL is a research scientist in the Department of Civil and Environmental Engineering at Syracuse University. Kim is involved in research on the effects of acidic deposition on forest and aquatic ecosystems in the Adirondack region.

ROGER DZIENGELESKI is manager of woodlands for Finch Paper LLC, headquartered in Glens Falls, New York. Roger had responsibility for management of more than 160,000 acres of forest land in the central Adirondacks and for more than thirty years has been an advocate on behalf of the forest industry in the region.

JON D. ERICKSON is associate professor of ecological economics at the Rubenstein School of Environment and Natural Resources and the Environmental Program, and Fellow of the Gund Institute for Ecological Economics at the University of Vermont in Burlington. He helped found the Adirondack Research Consortium and is current executive editor of the *Adirondack Journal of Environmental Studies.*

DAVID GIBSON is executive director of the Association for the Protection of the Adirondacks, located in Niskayuna, New York. David has written extensively on the history of the Forest Preserve and has worked tirelessly for the association, which is among the nation's oldest environmental organizations, to protect the New York Forest Preserve for more than a century.

CRAIG GILBORN is the former director of the Adirondack Museum in Blue Mountain Lake. Craig served on the Governor's Commission on the Adirondacks in the Twenty-First Century and has written extensively about the history of the Adirondacks.

ROBERT GLENNON is former chief counsel and executive director of the Adirondack Park Agency in Ray Brook. Throughout his career with the Park Agency, Bob was involved in the debates over land planning, including the forest industry, real estate developers, environmental organizations, and state agencies.

ROLAND W. KAYS is curator of mammals at the New York State Museum in Albany. Roland is internationally renowned for his work with mammals and is especially known for his research on the mammals of the Adirondacks.

DEAN LEFEBVRE is former president of the Adirondack Association of Towns and Villages headquartered in Mayfield, New York. Dean played a key role in organizing the many Adirondack communities into a cohesive and more powerful group to advocate within state government on behalf of local communities within the Park.

RICHARD LEFEBVRE is former chairman and executive director of the Adirondack Park Agency in Ray Brook. Dick brought his experience as an educator and local organizer to the Park Agency, where he sought to change the tenor of the debate among traditional adversaries to one that was more open and constructive.

ROBERT MALMSHEIMER is associate professor of forest law and policy in the Department of Forest and Natural Resources Management at the State University of New York College of Environmental Science and Forestry in Syracuse. Bob teaches environmental law and draws on his legal training to present the foundation and challenges to Article 14 of the New York State Constitution.

TERRY DEFRANCO MARTINO is executive director of the Adirondack North Country Association in Saranac Lake. Terry offers the perspective of someone who had spent much of her career championing the cause of community development within the Park.

BILL MCKIBBEN is an author of international reputation who offers exceptional insight to his explorations of the relationship between humans and the natural environment. His roots are in the Northern Forest of New York and New England, and few people possess the ability he commands to engage the minds, as well as touch the hearts, of those who value the wilderness.

JAMES MCLELLAND is Charles A. Dana professor emeritus in the Geology Department at Colgate University in Hamilton, New York. Jim brings more than forty years experience studying the geochronology and structural geology of the Adirondacks and the evolution of rock and mineral resources making up this terrain.

BARBARA MCMARTIN was a prolific author of all things Adirondack. She lived in Caroga Lake, New York. Barbara was a very active voice in helping to shape the interpretation and management of the Adirondack Park and the Forest Preserve for the past four decades, before passing away during the preparation of this book. Her voice is captured here with permission from her family and publisher in a reprint of a commentary from one of her many books pertaining to the Adirondacks.

MYRON J. MITCHELL is distinguished professor in the Department of Environmental and Forest Biology at the State University of New York College of Environmental Science and Forestry in Syracuse. Myron had led numerous research projects pertaining to the impacts of air pollutants and climate changes on forest watersheds for more than thirty years.

JOHN PENNEY is the former managing editor of the *Adirondack Daily Enterprise,* the only daily newspaper published in the Adirondacks. John brings to the book his keen insights on local politics during an era of heated debates around the findings of the Commission on the Adirondacks in the Twenty-First Century. Penney is the Community Conversation/Editorial Page editor of the *Poughkeepsie Journal.*

WILLIAM F. PORTER is professor of wildlife ecology at the State University of New York College of Environmental Science and Forestry in Syracuse. He has been director of the Adirondack Ecological Center since 1981. Located in the heart of the Adirondacks, this facility is one of the largest field stations dedicated to ecological research in the eastern United States.

DUDLEY RAYNAL is distinguished teaching professor emeritus and former dean of instruction and graduate studies at the State

University of New York College of Environmental Science and Forestry in Syracuse. Dudley is among the foremost experts on the plant communities of the Adirondacks and led the group that included Charley and Kimberley Driscoll, Myron Mitchell, and Karen Roy on researching atmospheric deposition issues in the Adirondacks.

KAREN ROY is a research scientist with the Division of Air Resources of the New York State Department of Environmental Conservation. Karen's early work with the Adirondack Lake Survey Corporation contributed to the definitive research on lake acidification in the region, joined by the team of Charley and Kimberly Driscoll, Myron Mitchell, and Dudley Raynal.

BRUCE SELLECK is H. O. Whitnall Professor in the Geology Department of Colgate University in Hamilton, New York. Bruce joined Jim McLelland to write the chapter on geology, bringing special expertise with geomorphology and glacial geology of the region.

PHILIP G. TERRIE is professor emeritus of American Culture Studies, Environmental Studies, and English at Bowling Green State University in Bowling Green, Ohio. Phil has authored several books on the Adirondacks, including *Contested Terrain,* and offers keen insight on the interplay of culture and nature in the history of the region.

ELIZABETH THORNDIKE is a visiting lecturer at the Department of City and Regional Planning at Cornell University in Ithaca, New York, and former board member of the Adirondack Park Agency. Liz brings to the book the voice of a long-time commissioner of the Park Agency and the broader perspective of nationwide efforts to preserve wilderness.

AMY VEDDER is past vice president of the Wildlife Conservation Society, headquartered in Bronx, New York. Amy, together with Bill Weber, was able to look at the Adirondack Park from afar given her many years of international conservation experience.

BILL WEBER is former director of the North America Program for the Wildlife Conservation Society, Bronx, New York. Bill, together with Amy Vedder, brings a lifetime's experience with conservation issues on an international scale as well as a personal familiarity with the Adirondacks through recent work of the North America Program.

ROSS S. WHALEY is emeritus president and professor of the State University of New York College of Environmental Science and Forestry in Syracuse, and former chairman of the Adirondack Park Agency, Ray Brook. He served as a member of the Governor's Commission for the Adirondacks in the Twenty-First Century. He lives in the Adirondacks.

ANNE M. WOODS is a biologist and education specialist at the Adirondack Ecological Center, a research station of the State University of New York College of Environmental Science and Forestry located in Newcomb. Annie was statistical analyst for the community-focus-group research conducted by Graham Cox, Jon Erickson, and Bill Porter.

# Introduction

*The Cornerstones of Conservation*

ROSS S. WHALEY, JON D. ERICKSON,
AND WILLIAM F. PORTER

The Adirondack region of New York State is, in many respects, America's cauldron of conservation. It was here more than a century ago that wanton exploitation of forests first aroused concern and action about human impact on the environment. It was in the Adirondacks that political leaders in 1885 made the decision to establish a forest preserve and shortly thereafter drew a line around both the state and intervening private lands and declared it a park. And it was here that the citizens in 1894 protected the Forest Preserve as "Forever Wild" by means of a constitutional amendment. Nearly eight decades went by before the prospect of rapid development of private lands within the park boundary for residential homes and commercial enterprise aroused concern once again. The result was the establishment of the Adirondack Park Agency and strict regulatory controls over use of private land, new planning guidelines for the Forest Preserve, protection for wild and scenic rivers, and enhanced protection for wetlands. The cauldron continued to boil as those wanting greater protection of the land battled with those who saw regulations as unwarranted invasion of their private property rights, but the decisions were sustained into the current era.

Here we have the genesis of a most unusual park. The Adirondack Park is big—bigger than the more well-known U.S. national parks of Yellowstone, Yosemite, Grand Canyon, Glacier, and Great Smoky

Mountains combined. The Adirondack Park boundary is inclusive of a geologically defined bioregion, the Adirondack uplift, separate from the neighboring Appalachian chain. The Adirondacks is largely ecologically intact, with few species missing from pre-European settlement, and the many once extirpated have since found their way back into a land that sits on the transition from temperate forests to the south and boreal forests to the north. Among the forests are 2,800 lakes and ponds, 1,200 miles of rivers fed by 30,000 miles of brooks and streams, and 42 peaks over 4,000 feet. The ecological success story alone does not make the case for the Adirondacks as particularly noteworthy among U.S.-style land conservation, nor among efforts in park management worldwide. However, the inclusion of human communities, which are excluded in many protected areas, makes the Adirondack Park one of the great experiments in conservation in the industrialized world, and certainly the great American experiment in rural wildlands management. Public lands are protected by constitutional prohibitions and managed along a continuum from wilderness preservation to active recreation, and the intermingled private lands are zoned to complement environmental conservation and provide for economic development.

To set the stage for the Adirondacks as worthy of study, reflection, and perhaps a source of vision as we rush through the current century, consider this sketch of history. While much of the northeastern United States was seeing widespread agrarian and urban development during the eighteenth and early nineteenth centuries, the Adirondack region of New York was largely a place to be avoided. The soils were shallow and the climate harsh. The Algonquin chose to stay farther north in the St. Lawrence Valley, and the Iroquois stayed south in the Mohawk Valley. The state had little success in finding developers who wished to buy land on which to live or raise crops. By the mid-1800s, however, timber and minerals tempted early entrepreneurs. Anticipating the impact of the exploitation of resources on the quality and quantity of water supplied to the southern reaches of the state and the potential decline in future supplies of timber, the state legislature in 1885 enacted a law creating the Forest

Preserve, protecting the forest lands for future supplies of timber and clean water. In 1892 a line was drawn on the map around the Forest Preserve—the Blue Line—and the land within was called the Adirondack Park. It included both public and private land. Two years later the public lands within the Blue Line were put under the protection of the state constitution and declared "forever kept as wild forest lands," with the state holdings not allowed to "be leased, sold, or exchanged, or be taken by any corporation, public or private, nor shall the timber thereon be sold, removed nor destroyed." The land was protected, but not for future supplies of timber. Since then, the state has acquired substantially more forest preserve, expanding the land base protected by the constitution.

If we fast-forward several decades to the 1960s, the U.S. economy was flourishing, and the interstate highway system brought the Adirondacks to the masses. The pressure on the region was no longer just exploitation for resource extraction, but recreation demands by the burgeoning American middle-class and an expanding appetite for second homes. One proposal for protecting the park from the prospects of rapid private development was made by Laurance Rockefeller, the brother of the governor of New York State. He suggested the creation of an Adirondack National Park. This proposal seemed to be uniformly disliked by the citizens of the state, whether they lived in the park or not, and its subsequent defeat was one of few actions that ever generated widespread agreement between upstate and downstate interests. The possibility of a national park, however, did bring attention to the fragility of the Adirondacks to development and the need for the state to come to terms with the loosely defined relation between state and private lands within the park boundary. Governor Nelson Rockefeller established the Temporary Study Commission, which ultimately recommended the creation of the Adirondack Park Agency. The agency would have substantial regulatory authority over both public and private lands. The controversy that emerged was rooted in a new agency that was given land-use control responsibilities over private lands more commonly associated with local government, as well as authority to establish public land-planning guidelines that would have to be adhered to by another government agency, the Department of Environmental Conservation.

These two watershed moments—the protection of land as Forever Wild provided by Article 14 of the state constitution and the creation of a state planning agency that flew in the face of an American tradition of home rule—are the crucibles of the Adirondack experiment. In fact, the decisions that form the foundation of Article 14 and the Adirondack Park Agency Act have produced a body of experience that underlies the very concept of American conservation. Cast with visionary aspirations, the decisions were implemented day-by-day and issue-by-issue by people who brought not just talent and energy, but passion. The lessons learned set the stage for far-reaching policy that brought conservation into the American vernacular and government. Theodore Roosevelt's experience with the Adirondacks provided the impetus to establish the national forest system and the national parks. Adirondack lessons were antecedents for environmental legislation of the 1960s, most notably the 1964 Wilderness Act. It was the Adirondack Forest Preserve that first demonstrated the economic value of maintaining natural ecosystems, the spiritual value in protecting wilderness, the ecological value of including people within the boundaries of a large, relatively intact ecosystem, and the political value to managing natural resources of a region for multiple uses. Today this unusual park offers lessons for policy makers worldwide who struggle with protecting the natural environment while attending to the immediate problems of developing vigorous communities and viable economies.

This book proposes to capture the wisdom born of the experience since the creation of the Adirondack Park Agency more than thirty-five years ago by drawing on scholars to explore the ecological, cultural, and economic cornerstones of the park; practitioners to bring insight based on direct experience; and activists who have been fighting over the right blend of private interests and public control since the park was created over a century ago. We place that experience within a backdrop of the natural and human history that forged its foundation. We focus on the Adirondack Park because of its rich history in shaping conservation, and because it is in the study of *place* that the diverse viewpoints on conservation and development can best be teased apart and then re-aggregated into lessons for the future. We seek to understand how the Adirondack experiment has proven to be important for New York, the nation, and the world at large. We aim to understand the duality of the human relationship with the natural system: the influence of nature on culture and culture on nature. We hope to draw wisdom from the recognition that although there are ultimate means available to achieve humanity's ultimate ends, the success of conservation is determined by those who struggle with the social processes in between.

The book is organized into three sections, each tackling a portion of the continuum from physical means to metaphysical ends. The first focuses on the foundations of the Adirondack ecosystem and the human activities that the very rocks, soil, water, wildlife, and forests afford. Here we learn principally from the scientists who define the biophysical boundaries of what makes human culture and economy possible in the Adirondacks; the building blocks of natural capital that allow Adirondack towns and villages to prosper and form ties with regional, national, and international communities. The Adirondack ecosystem has shaped human activity and culture, but economic uses have, in turn, affected the integrity and resilience of the environment. In the Adirondacks, this is both a story from *within* the park boundary as the landscape has been shaped by wildlife exploitation, forestry, mining, recreation, and housing and business development, and from *outside* the park through impacts of acid and mercury deposition, climate change, downstate energy and water demand, and the voracious appetite for second homes and outdoor recreation of over ninety million American and Canadian consumers within a day's drive of the Adirondacks.

The middle section of the book describes the cultural history, institutional mechanisms and political economy that set the social cornerstone of the park. Here we draw lessons from the cultural context of major shifts in the political landscape of the park and from the history of managing the interface between humans and our sustaining environment. The role of institutions is sandwiched between the biophysical realities of the human-dominated environment and the equally constraining goals of individuals and society, including economic vitality, social well-being, and environmental sustainability. We learn of the legal instruments designed and political compromises met from the voices of those in various positions of responsibility in the Adirondacks, from staffers of government agencies and environmental advocates to industry representatives and local businesses. Each voice reflects on the evolution of political economy in the Adirondacks and on the imposition of controls and limits on the system to meet higher goals.

The final section brings together many voices that reacted to the political conflict of the park agency years, but also sought resolution through the balancing act between conservation and development. At the dawn of the twenty-first century we are witnessing a maturation of the Adirondack experiment, and perhaps an era of reconciliation is upon us. There are many lessons to draw from the Adirondack experiment. Each insight should be chewed on and etched into a vision of the Adirondack ecosystem and economy that is prepared for new ecological and social realities—trends that the framers of Article 14 and the Adirondack Park Agency Act could not have foreseen. The top-down demands for conservation in the Adirondacks have not always matched the bottom-up pleas for economic development. In the broader scope of things, the Adirondacks is but a small experiment among the thousands of daily choices over development and conservation worldwide. But each of the authors in this section inherently struggles with the notion that if we cannot strike a balance in the Adirondacks—given all the far-sighted choices and accidents of history that have made the Adirondack experiment possible—then where on earth can we get it right? While the opinions on how to strike balance are diverse, their goals are similar. In the end, conservation must mean an enduring livelihood of the human species and the web of life on which we depend, and development must mean a sustained quality of life within the

limits of the sustaining ecosystem and pursuant to hard-won principles of justice and fairness.

In the concluding chapter we use the contrasting images of a
development philosophy grounded in an empty world versus a full
world, from which we summarize the lessons of the Adirondack
experiment in the context of the current national and international
discussion of sustainability. The struggles between the allocation of
public and private rights to land serve as a useful jumping point into
the many lessons that emerge from over one hundred years of policy
debate, institutional reform, and visioning exercises. Ultimately,
what does the Adirondack experiment to date have to say about the
future of rural wildlands in the United States? What of the future
of protected areas worldwide? What of the tension between public
and private lands and uses? And could the patchwork quilt approach
of integrated Adirondack ecosystems and economies be extended to
large landscapes, creating the kind of ecological connectivity that
will be needed to face the environmental and social challenges of
the current era?

We hope you enjoy the book and make relevant the voices herein
for your own communities.

PART ONE | *Foundations of the Adirondack Ecosystem and Economy*

# Introduction

*A Dark Spot in a Sea of Lights*

WILLIAM F. PORTER

As we look at the Adirondacks at night from space, we see a dark spot in a sea of lights. Those who have a sense of the geography of eastern North America know that this is the Adirondacks, a remarkable mix of wilderness and small towns in the midst of one of the most heavily developed regions in the world. How could this dark spot still be here? More to the point, how did the Adirondack landscape moderate the influence of human activity with such dramatic results? Of course, the Adirondack region is not completely dark, so the complementary question is: how has human activity affected the Adirondack ecosystem? And in the end, what is working toward and against striking balance between economic development and environmental conservation?

The intent of part one is to begin to answer these questions. To the natural scientist, part one is a description of the biological and physical attributes of the natural ecosystem that first greeted Native Americans and, later, European immigrants. To the social scientist, part one is defining the *ultimate means* for human enterprise, the natural capital that enables human communities to prosper and form ties with larger national and international economies. To those interested in both nature and culture, part one is a look at how humans began to exploit this landscape, turning the ultimate means to *intermediate means,* and at which of these actions produced lasting environmental change.

*3*

This opening essay is an overview designed to give the reader a sense of the place and the issues. It is followed by a series of voices that enrich the story of the region as told by people who have spent their careers working in it. We first hear from James McLelland. He brings to this work more than forty years experience studying the geochronology and structural geology of the Adirondacks, and the evolution of rock and mineral resources making up this terrain. He collaborates with Bruce Selleck, who lends his expertise in geomorphology and glacial geology. Then, we hear from Christopher Cirmo. Cirmo conducted his doctoral work in the central Adirondacks and southwestern Adirondacks and has many years of experience studying the hydrology and biogeochemistry of the regions wetlands and streams.

Next we move to the soils and hear from one of the nation's foremost soil scientists, Russell Briggs. Charles Canham extends the story of soils to tell us about the changing faces of Adirondack forests. Canham, like Cirmo, conducted his doctoral work in the Adirondacks, and he has since spent more than twenty years investigating the dynamics of forest systems in the Adirondacks and throughout the world.

With this foundation of natural attributes in place, we begin to explore the dualism of nature and human culture as these forces interacted to shape one another over four centuries. We begin with two chapters on fish and wildlife and their attraction to humans. Here we get our first exposure to the exploitation of the region's natural resources. Roland Kays and Robert Daniels review the history of mammals and fishes inhabiting this region of lakes and forests, and they examine the role of humans in not only removing species from the system but adding exotic species to the region. Then I examine the resilience of the wildlife populations in the face of exploitation. In the short term wildlife proved vulnerable, and many species were quickly eliminated completely from the system, but the long-term picture is not quite so dark. Indeed, as we attempt to use wildlife as a measure of how far we may have moved the ecosystem from its natural state, we are seeing ongoing changes. We proceed through a sequence of human encounters with the region, hearing again from James McLelland and Bruce Selleck as they describe the mining in the region. I take on the challenge of relating the story of the exploitation of the Adirondack forest and draw on nearly thirty years of learning from extraordinary foresters and ecologists like Ralph Nyland, Dick Sage, and Jerry Jenkins.

Next we explore less direct but equally important human impacts. First is the influence of the acid and mercury pollution that rains down on forests and lakes. It is the story of an enormous amount of science that is nicely summarized by the multiple voices of Charles Driscoll, Kimberley Driscoll, Myron Mitchell, Dudley Raynal, and Karen Roy, who are among the world's top scientists on acid rain and mercury pollution. Their research, which was among the first efforts to quantify the effects of these pollutants, has been ongoing in the Adirondacks since the mid-1970s. Next is the influence of recreation. Chad Dawson examines the importance of recreation to the history of the region and the wilderness ethic that arose from it. Dawson offers the perspective of someone whose thirty years of research on recreation and contributions to wilderness issues has earned national respect. Peter Bauer then guides us through the numbers on residential development in the region. He is probably the person who has studied development in the park most over the past twenty years.

The debates over development are crystallized in the natural world by the debates over restoration of the large predators, and perhaps no one is better equipped to lead us through those debates than Rainer Brocke. He has spent more than thirty years examining the possibilities that the Adirondacks might once again be populated by lynx, cougars, and wolves, and he is among the few scientists in history to attempt the restoration of a major predator.

The most obvious and defining qualities of the Adirondack Park arise from its size and location. As a frame of reference, the park is about 100 miles by 100 miles. The 9,375 square miles, or 6 million acres, that constitute the Adirondack Park encompass an area that is greater than the size of the Commonwealth of Massachusetts and is three times the size of Yellowstone National Park, the largest of our national parks outside of Alaska. The southern boundary of the park lies just north of 43° N latitude and spans 73°30 W to 75°30 W longitude. Geographically, the Adirondack region is isolated by water courses: Lake Ontario and the large areas of lowland to the west, the St. Lawrence River and its broad valley to the north, Lake Champlain and Lake George to the east, and the Mohawk River on the southern periphery. These water bodies present important barriers and also travel corridors for wildlife. And, as we will see, they were crucial to shaping how both Native Americans and European immigrants used the region.

We begin with the geology of the region because in a real sense we can trace the origins of the black void on the satellite image to the geological history of the Adirondacks. Whereas Yellowstone National Park lies within an enormous and currently active volcanic caldera, the Adirondack Mountains represent a domical, deeply eroded remnant of a 1.3–1.0-billion-year-old mountain range of Himalayan scale that was created by the collision of massive tectonic plates. By 500 million years ago the range had been eroded to sea level, submerged beneath those ancient waters, and blanketed by flat-lying sedimentary strata. The neighboring Appalachian chain formed ~450–250 million years ago and, except for small inliers of billion-year-old Precambrian core, is much younger than the bedrock of the Adirondacks. The present-day Adirondack dome and mountain topography are perhaps no older than 20 million years and appear to be due to very recent, and relatively mild, crustal warping followed by erosion. McLelland and Selleck note that unraveling the origin of this ancient bedrock and younger dome has been a product of combining long-established geological methods with the tools of modern technology. The history that emerges, as they describe in more detail, is one of a region in which extreme pressure and heat created rock of a crystalline structure and mineral content that proved exceptionally resistant to weathering and erosion. As late domical uplift occurred, these resistant materials became especially prominent in the eastern portion of the region that underlies the

High Peaks, where there are more than 100 peaks rising in excess of 3,500 feet above sea level and 42 mountains that reach above 4,000 feet elevation. Mount Marcy and Algonquin each exceed 5,000 feet. Many of these mountains appear less impressive to the casual observer because they rise from a plateau of 1,500 feet.[1] Elevations fall rapidly from the High Peaks down into the Lake Champlain valley to the east and more gradually to the west.

Today, if we look at the Adirondacks from space during the day-light, we see that the lakes and rivers, and also the principal ranges of the Adirondacks, are generally oriented in a southwest to north-east direction. Long Lake and Indian Lake, and the Gothic Mountain Range and MacIntyre Ranges, are good examples. McLelland and Selleck show that this orientation is a result of the faults and fractures that occurred during the uplift, which occurred along a southwest-to-northeast axis. Although the crystalline rock structure is resistant to erosion, once it fractures it becomes much more vulnerable. In contrast to the nearby Green Mountains of Vermont, the fractures did not result in any significant lowlands that traversed the dome from one side to the other. As we will see, the landform had profound influences on human activity in the region.

Christopher Cirmo talks of the aquascape, describing the hydrology we would expect for a region shaped like a dome. Precipitation is evenly spread throughout the year but the cold temperatures throughout winter mean that the snow accumulates to a depth that gives purpose to snowshoes. During the winter, areas of the western Adirondacks receive an average of 200 inches of snow per year, while the eastern periphery gets about 80 inches. Snowfall accumulates rapidly in early winter until Lake Ontario freezes over to the west. In average winters, snow depths in the geographic center of the Adirondacks reach 15 inches by about January 10, but that is highly variable. Snowpacks reaching 40 inches are common and persist 80 days on average. Snowmelt in the spring brings depths below 15 inches by April 1 with greater regularity.

Fourteen rivers drain radially from the center into five major watersheds. To the north and west a large region of wetlands drains into the St. Lawrence valley via the Grass and Raquette River systems. To the north and east, the Saranac and Ausable Rivers drain to the Lake Champlain basin from the High Peaks. To the southeast is the Hudson River system, the largest in the park, draining south to Albany and New York City. To the southwest is West Canada Creek flowing into the Mohawk River. Finally, to the west are the Oswegatchie and Moose Rivers flowing into the Black River and on to Lake Ontario. Except in the immediate vicinity of the High Peaks, the rivers tend to run slowly from the center of the dome, picking up the pace as they reach the periphery and drop down into the surrounding lowlands.

What is unexpected is the more than 10,000 lakes that dot the landscape. Indeed, the Adirondack region is unusual in its combination of mountains, lakes, and hardwood forests. As McLelland and Selleck and Cirmo relate, this combination is a product of glacial activity. The glaciers deposited rocks and soil at their margins as they retreated, leaving a thin veneer in most places and larger accumulations in the valleys. These larger accumulations dammed up water, producing many of the lakes, especially in the western Adirondacks. Many of the lakes are elongated because they occur in the original fractures produced as the dome uplifted. Where the topography is flatter, glacial moraines and eskers cause poor drainage, leaving lowland soils that have been perpetually waterlogged. Where the water drained more completely, melting glaciers washed the clay and silt particles, leaving behind sandy soils. The glacial lakes that surrounded the Adirondacks to the east, north, and west were recipients of significant depositions of sand, silt, and clay and formed much more fertile soils on their floodplain terraces.

Russell Briggs and Charles Canham pick up the story and show how the variation in the soils, the growing seasons, and natural disturbance events are central to understanding the forests of the Adirondacks. When we look down upon the Adirondacks from space during the daylight, we see a landscape covered primarily by temperate, broad-leafed deciduous forests known collectively as northern hardwoods. But we also find boreal species, the conifers or softwood. The Adirondack region contains this unusual diversity because it is located geographically on a transition zone between two major North American forests. The temperate forests to the south grade into the boreal forest of the north, and the variation in elevation creates climatic conditions common to both.

Growing seasons, those summer intervals that are frost free, vary with elevation. First frost occurs between September 10 and September 20 throughout much of the park; it comes later in the periphery, even to the north, as elevation drops down below 1,000 feet, and earlier in areas above 2,000 feet. In low elevations, the last frost is generally recorded before May 10. Average freeze-free intervals through the summer are 110 to 130 days throughout much of the park and 130 to 140 days at lower elevations.[2] July temperatures in 2002 averaged 63–65° Fahrenheit, and overall summer temperatures are about 2° warmer than in 1900. January temperatures average about 13–15° Fahrenheit, and winter temperatures are about 4° warmer than 1900.[3]

Over the Adirondack landscape, we find thirty-four species of trees, exceptionally diverse among mountainous regions of the world. The distribution of these species is dependent on soil depth and mineral content, moisture, and length of the growing season. The influence of these gradients is most obvious when we look at the forests in the northeastern Adirondacks, an area of the park known as the High Peaks because of the abundance of mountains whose elevation exceeds 4,000 feet. At the top of the mountains above 4,000 feet in the Adirondacks there are no trees at all. This is the *alpine zone,* where soil is so limited that there is little to capture moisture or make basic minerals available to trees. The wind scours these exposed areas so severely that soil cannot accumulate and, consequently, no forest can grow. By comparison to other mountains of the world, there is relatively little of this treeless alpine zone in the Adirondacks—only eleven mountain tops comprising about eighty-five acres.

In the sub-alpine forest are mountain paper birch, black spruce, and balsam fir, species able to grow in the organic duff that overlies thin soils. This organic duff is composed of dead vegetation that decays slowly in the cold climates of higher altitude. The trees growing at this altitude are stunted and misshapen unless protected from the wind. Farther down the mountain, at about 4,000 feet elevation, the soil is deeper though generally not fertile because it contains few clay and silt particles. Moisture seeps through almost continuously, and the growing season is a little longer. Red spruce and balsam fir begin to share the crevasses with paper and yellow birch. From 4,000 down to about 2,500 feet, the sandy and rocky soils are increasingly deeper and mixed with silt and clay, so fertility and moisture conditions of the soil improve. Growing season lengthens, and here the birches and spruce are mixed with sugar maple, American beech, and eastern hemlock.

The transition continues on the lower slopes, where sugar maple, birch, and beech grow alongside white ash, black cherry, red maple, white pine, and red spruce. Much of the Adirondack dome lies within this zone of 1,000 to 3,000 feet elevation, where hardwoods are abundant and conifer species (softwoods) are more scattered. It is these midslope forests that give the Adirondack region its rich array of fall colors. And this is the reason that our satellite view suggests a region dominated by hardwoods.

In the river valleys and lowlands, we encounter areas of glacial till and other areas of sandy outwash soils. The mineral-rich till soils that developed in the large valleys surrounding the Adirondacks—Lake Champlain, the Mohawk River and the St. Lawrence River—supported hardwood forests of great stature. In contrast, the sandy soils of the major river valleys lack the mineral richness and are prone to drought. These areas are typically dominated by pines, especially white, red, pitch, and jack pine. White pine reaches greatest abundance and its 130-foot stature in the southeastern Adirondacks. Jack pine occurs on the sand barrens of the northeastern Adirondacks and the St. Lawrence River valley and pitch pine on sandy outwashes north of the capital city of Albany. It is in these same peripheral regions of the park, where growing seasons are longer, that the only significant stands of oak occur.

In the lowest areas, where soils are frequently saturated with moisture, we find yet another transition. Sugar maple, beech, birch, cherry, and white ash drop out, and where hydrology produces moving water red spruce and balsam fir persist, mixed with red maple and hemlock. The floodplain areas of rivers that exist just a few feet above the water table produce the large areas of red spruce forest. As soils become completely saturated and water is stagnant, the forest grades into black spruce, white cedar, and tamarack. These are the forests most common in western regions such as the Raquette and Oswegatchie River systems.

We tend to think of these forests as unchanging. In fact, as Canham points out, they are continually undergoing change because trees are continually dying and new individuals are growing to take their place. The change becomes more obvious, though, when there is a significant disturbance. As much as the forests are a reflection of the kinds of soils on which they grow, they are a product of disturbance. Fire nearly always comes to mind as a disturbance factor, and certainly fire has been important in the Adirondacks, especially in the early 1900s. However, large-scale fire is not a common occurrence in the region. With 30 to 40 inches of annual precipitation supporting a forest dominated by hardwoods, the region is just too moist to permit large burns. More common to the Adirondacks is disturbance due to wind storms. To flatten large areas of Adirondack forest requires wind speeds of 100 to 200 miles an hour. These are winds of tornadoes or hurricanes. While hurricanes are associated with the southeastern United States and the Gulf Coast, they periodically reach into the Adirondacks. The last one occurred in the fall of 1950, and it blew down forests over 800,000 acres, mostly in the western part of the park. Smaller areas of forest are flattened by tornados or derechos (gusting straight-line winds) associated with summer storms. In 1995 a derecho blew down about 130,000 acres in half an hour.

More subtle, but of greater impact to forests, is disturbance caused by insect outbreaks and disease. The Adirondack region is not prone to large-scale insect outbreaks, in part because there are no large expanses dominated by one or two species of trees, like the spruce-fir forests of Maine and eastern Canada. Nevertheless, disease is an important player in the Adirondacks. Disease can completely eliminate tree species of great importance to the forest community. Beech scale disease, a combination of an insect, *Cryptococcus fagisuga,* and a fungus, *Nectria coccinea,* has attacked American beech since its arrival in the central Adirondacks in 1965. By the late 1990s, 90 percent of the trees six inches in diameter or larger were dying. The loss of beech has wide-scale implications because it comprised almost half of the mature hardwood trees in the Adirondack hardwood communities, which produced a nut crop that was important as a food for many forms of wildlife from grouse to squirrels to black bears.

Just as the tree species of the Adirondacks reflect the fact that the region lies on the transition zone of the temperate and boreal biomes, so too do the species of wildlife. Animals such as spruce grouse and moose represent boreal species and white-tailed deer and wild turkey the temperate species. Most species are not abundant because Adirondack land is either at the southern or northern edge of the ecological tolerance of boreal and temperate species. Spruce grouse and moose number a few hundred but are much more abundant to the north. White-tailed deer, perceived by many people to be truly at home in the Adirondacks, actually occur at relatively low densities in comparison to populations farther south. Some species, like the chipmunk, span both biomes and number in the tens of millions. Others, like the wild turkey, may actually be beyond their native range and probably number fewer than a thousand.

Thus biodiversity in the Adirondacks is a reflection of these countervailing ecological forces and, as Roland Kays and Robert Daniels argue, a lot of recent human intervention. Of 384 terrestrial species of wildlife, 55 are mammals, another 40 are reptiles and amphibians, and 197 are birds. The 92 fish species reflect the broad reach of the Adirondack Park, particularly the inclusion of Lake Champlain and Lake George. Our knowledge of the losses of species from the Adirondacks and invasion by exotics is limited to fish and wildlife, trees and flowers. This number is changing as we learn more about insects, lichens, and other forms of life. A total of 61 species are known to have been lost or purposely extirpated: 14 fishes, 1 reptile, no amphibians, 5 birds, 7 mammals, and 34 plants. A somewhat smaller number, 45 species not native to the Adirondacks have arrived or were consciously introduced: 25 fishes, perhaps 1 reptile, no amphibians, 3 birds, 1 mammal, and 15 species of plants.

Biodiversity is a common and important measure of the health of an ecosystem. However, the number of different species in a park such as the Adirondacks is only one measure, and ecologists recognize that it can be a misleading indicator. For instance, the presence of exotic species adds to the biodiversity but at the same time is indicative of degradation of the ecological system. In the Adirondacks, most exotic species are common in two of the five major private land-use classes, Hamlet and Rural, but still rare in Wilderness, Wild Forest, and Resource Management lands. Hamlet and Rural lands constitute about 21 percent of the park, so native populations are still largely intact.

A second important measure of the health of an ecosystem is resilience to human impacts. A resilient ecosystem is one in which populations of native species that have been severely reduced or extirpated are able to recover or return. This ability reflects the size of the region and its degree of connectedness to other ecosystems containing similar complements of species. Size is important because it increases the possibility for species to persist in isolated pockets and then rebound when conditions improve. Connectedness is important because greater connectedness increases the potential that a species will find its way back into the region.

With this sketch of geological base and biotic systems as a backdrop, we then begin to examine how European explorers, entrepreneurs, and settlers attempted to harness the resources of the Adirondacks. It is a history that is largely one of uncontrolled exploitation resulting in economic booms and busts but, interestingly, little permanent ecological damage. Mining, lumbering, and trapping begin the story, but contrary to expectation, prove not to be the undoing of the biological integrity of the Adirondacks.

Indeed, Canham observes that what makes the Adirondacks particularly interesting is that while harvest was extensive, the region escaped the fate of so much of the rest of eastern North America. Despite widespread disturbance in Adirondack forests, their composition today is largely the same as in presettlement times.

The impact of human settlement and natural resource exploitation was ameliorated early on by the harsh Adirondack environment. Much can be read into the observation that from the date of the first European encounter with the region, it was more than three centuries before the Adirondack Mountains were mapped.[4] Then, through much of the next 150 years to the present, only the wealthy or those providing direct service to the wealthy could afford to live in the region. Most communities in the Adirondacks were built around mining and forest industries, and came and went with the fluctuations of supply and demand and the cost of transporting the resources to urban markets.

Mining was among the first activities to attract large investments of capital. McLelland and Selleck point to the region as providing major iron ores to our war efforts from the American Revolution through World War II as well as fueling U.S. industry through the nineteenth century and up until the 1960s. Beginning in the early twentieth century, and continuing until the 1970s, titanium ore from Tahawus was utilized for both industrial and military purposes. Closely associated was the timber industry. The local impact of these industries was huge. As much as two million acres of the eastern Adirondacks were cleared, and operations penetrated the region. Mining was limited by lack of easy transportation, and much of it collapsed by the 1850s. With the exception of the large open-pit iron-titanium mine at Tahawus, few scars are evident to the casual observer. Those people who are more discerning can find the influence in relics now rapidly becoming overgrown and in the mix of tree species inhabiting a site. Even there, natural change continues to restore original conditions.

Timber harvest continued to grow owing to the demand for construction material following the Civil War. And as with mining, the long-term impacts of lumbering were relatively small. The one lasting mark of these enterprises that is likely to affect the Adirondacks well into the future is the infrastructure of roads they created. Built initially to allow extraction of wood fiber, they facilitated other human pursuits, especially recreation and residential development, and became corridors for invasive species. Roads are a two-edged sword. On one side, they prove valuable because they enable the public to enjoy the Adirondacks, although at the same time they raise concerns about too much development. On the other side, they prove a harbinger, if not direct cause, of a downward trend in the biological integrity.

Still more subtle has been the change that has come from without, the pollution of acid rain and mercury. The Adirondack region is located downwind of a high concentration of coal-fired power plants in the Midwest and so receives doses of acid precipitation on a continuing basis. As Charles and Kimberley Driscoll, Myron Mitchell, Dudley Raynal, and Karen Roy relate, the ecological impacts of these airborne pollutants raise questions about the future of the very essence of the Adirondacks, the health of the ecological processes that support it.

One might argue that truly lasting effects have been those that brought permanent human presence to the landscape. Chad Dawson chronicles the importance of the Adirondacks to recreation and the emergence of a romantic image of wilderness as a source of renewal in the face of an industrializing society. Artists and writers promoted the Adirondacks, and entrepreneurs like William West Durant recognized the opportunity to bring the Adirondacks to the attention of those with wealth and time. Durant, the son of a railroad tycoon, was a visionary who saw the potential to push railroad lines to the interior of the Adirondacks to develop tourism. His initial clients were the economic elite of America's Gilded Age: the Vanderbilts, Whitneys, Morgans, Rockefellers, and Huntingtons.

Beginning near Raquette Lake, Durant built what would come to be known as Great Camps. Craig Gilborn suggests that in these initial recreational investments by the wealthy were the seeds of an American wilderness ethic. Summer homes of the rich brought politically connected people into contact with the pleasures of seclusion amid the beauty of the region. They became a manifestation of the cynic's definition of a conservationist: a person with *his* cabin on a lake to himself. At the pivotal points of the establishment of the Forest Preserve, and later the Adirondack Park, they wielded political and economic influence to favor protection.

The pace of development began to increase after World War II. The postwar years brought three dramatic changes that influenced the Adirondacks with increasing intensity. First was the movement of a large portion of society from rural environments to urban areas. These were people whose formative years had been spent outdoors and who had strong ties to the philosophy of self-sufficiency. So, while they earned a livelihood in the city, they sought recreation elsewhere in hiking, camping, fishing, and hunting.

Second was the rapid improvement and expansion of the transportation infrastructure. National security interests and expanding business persuaded the government to develop the Interstate Highway System and improve roads everywhere. This made it possible for people to leave the city and travel to the Adirondacks for a weekend. Completion of Interstate highways I-87 and I-90 meant that more than one third of the human population in the United States and Canada was within eight hours drive of the Adirondacks.

Third was the accumulation of wealth that permitted the ownership of second homes, which, since the late 1990s, has spurred the park's largest sustained period of residential growth. Peter Bauer laments the negative impacts on the social fabric of the community because the associated land speculation has priced many people out of the communities in which they grew up. The limitation to permanence remains the availability of jobs, and today that is the central issue confronting most communities. However, the internet and fax service, and the transition from manufacturing to a service economy, are enabling businesses to consider establishing themselves in more distant locations from urban centers. This is a park within which there are 103 communities.

The irony, and the challenge, is that the major attractions for residential development are the rural character of the communities, the clean air and water, and the beauty of the wild forest. The magnitude of development may change that vitality from within. A new limit may be imposed by economic costs of ownership. Peter Bauer observes that the Adirondack region is becoming a place where whole neighborhoods and even towns are dominated by second homes, and the large wild areas are increasingly surrounded by developed areas.

The Adirondack region has moved from a position where extractable natural resources were the main economic engine to one where conservation of those same natural resources is the engine of tourism. Private ownership that was once dominated by the forest industry is now moving to major conservation organizations, and eventually to the public, because of the value society places on open space. This recognition of the economic value of wild lands may not be new, but the scale of its impact is likely to be profound. Just as the Adirondack experience with unbridled exploitation set a cornerstone for conservation a century ago, so may the experiment with highly regulated regional land management provide another.

We come full circle to our original question of why the wilderness character of the Adirondacks is still there and realize that the question is not that simple. A reasonable person might ask, is it? A measure of wilderness is the presence of the top predators in the ecosystem, and the Adirondack region has lost all of those we associate with wilderness: the lynx, the cougar, and the wolf. Rainer Brocke takes a hard look at the prospects for restoring these species. People and roads, and all that they bring with them, are encircling the Adirondacks to the point of limiting the connectivity of wild areas to the north and east. The loss of connectivity can limit the natural return of predators. Active management efforts have tried to overcome these limits, and restoration programs have successfully reestablished the bald eagle and peregrine falcon. However, Brocke describes how an attempt to restore the lynx met with an uncertain fate and says that the prospects of restoring the cougar are dim. The wolf holds special interest because mere mention generates so much debate and because the story is complicated by the coyote.

The voices of the chapters that follow add important detail to the overview presented here. Geology, hydrology, and soils may sound esoteric, but the stories are as fascinating as they are important. And the history of how the natural environment shaped human enterprise in the region is as much about the soils and the weather as it is about the forests and the wildlife. But the great experiment is about the impacts of human activity, especially in the past two centuries, that motivated creation of a Forest Preserve, an Adirondack Park, and a stringent set of land-use regulations. In each case, the story is told by observers whose experience and exposure to the Adirondacks sets them apart.

# 1

## Geology of the Adirondack Mountains

*Like an Egg with Its Major Axis to the North*

JAMES McLELLAND AND BRUCE SELLECK

In his *Survey of the Second Geological District,* Ebenezer Emmons captured an Adirondack vision that holds today and poses questions that remain objects of scientific research:

> That portion of New York which is north of the Mohawk Valley may be considered one of the great natural divisions of the state. . . . [It] is a territory which is unsusceptible to farther [*sic*] subdivision; it may be considered as an insulated portion of the State, bordered by three great valleys; the valley of the Champlain on the east, that of the Mohawk on the south and the St. Lawrence on the west, northwest and north. . . . Geologically considered, it is one great uplift with gradual but unequal slopes on all sides, which, if we leave out of view minor irregularities, may be compared to an egg with its major axis to the north. [While] the Green Mountains of Vermont run onward through Lower Canada as far as the eye can trace them in the distant horizon, those of the Adirondack rise suddenly from the Mohawk and Hudson valleys, and terminate equally abrupt either upon the lakeshore or in the levels of Lower Canada. . . . We have indubitable evidence of this mighty and concentrated force in the magnificent cliffs and precipices, which are continually arresting to the attention of travelers.[1]

The Adirondack Mountains (fig. 1.1), although positioned in proximity to the Appalachian Belt, are clearly not part of that

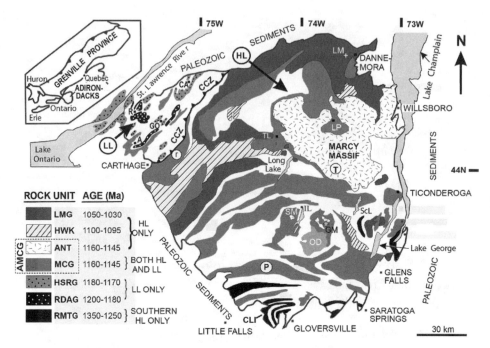

1.1. Generalized geological and geochronological map of the Adirondacks. Published with permission of the Geological Society of America.

linear chain but belong to an older, deeper, and more profoundly deformed part of North America. Their insularity, ruggedness, and impenetrability remain as barriers to human development, just as when Emmons wrote his report on the first geological expedition to the Adirondacks almost 170 years ago. Since Emmons's pioneering work, the tools of modern geology have allowed us to know quite precisely the origins and ages of the rocks constituting the Adirondacks and to develop realistic explanations for the complex patterns in which the rocks occur. We now understand this ancient terrain as a product of global plate tectonic processes that gave rise to the continents and ocean basins of planet Earth. In this chapter we describe the current understanding of the geological origin and history of the Adirondacks. These findings are summarized in figure 1.2, which presents a series of age-designated, schematic NW-SE cross sections through the upper ~60 miles of the earth. The vertical sections are

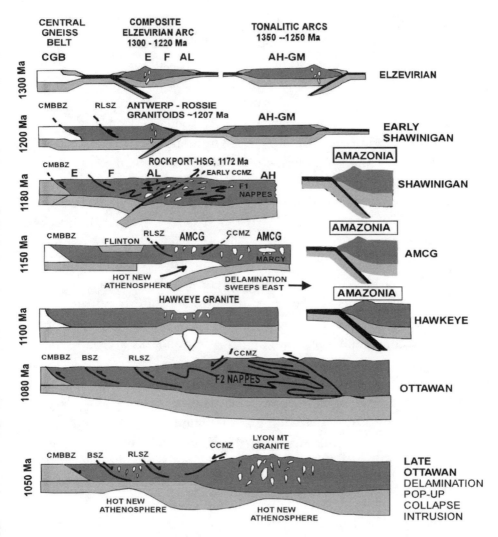

1.2. Cross-sections of continental crust. Published with permission of the Geological Society of America.

anchored on the east by Rutland, Vermont, and on the west by Bancroft, Ontario, a distance of ~300 mi. The cross sections are subdivided into continental crust; oceanic crust; and cool, rigid upper mantle. Together, these three units compose the lithospheric plates that slide along the underlying hot, ductile athenosphere (A, fig. 1.2) thereby giving rise to plate tectonics. These and other subdivisions are identified on figure 1.2 where the heavy black arrows indicate the relative motions of plates and melts. New oceanic crust (gabbro/basalt) is added to oceanic lithosphere by volcanism at mid-ocean ridges, and old, cold oceanic lithosphere is consumed at subduction zones where new continental crust is created by arc volcanism.

As Emmons aptly described, the Adirondacks form a slightly elongate, domical uplift of 1,300–1,000 million-year-old (henceforth designated as Ma) Precambrian rocks that rises from an elevation of 100 feet along the Lake Champlain shore to the summit of Mount Marcy at 5,348 feet. An ancient fault zone known as the Carthage-Colton Shear Zone (CCZ, figs. 1.1, 1.2) separates the Adirondack Highland (HL, fig. 1.2) and the smaller Lowland (LL, fig. 1.2) topographic sectors. The Adirondack Park lies entirely within the Highlands, which are largely underlain by erosion-resistant igneous and metamorphic rocks. In contrast, the Lowlands are dominated by less-resistant marble (metamorphosed limestone) that yields a more subdued topography. Surrounding the Adirondacks are flat-lying, softer Paleozoic sedimentary marine sandstone and limestone deposited about 550–450 Ma. These younger rocks either lie on top of the older, deformed basement or are down-faulted against it along large faults (mostly NE-SW trending) that bound the eastern Adirondacks. The most important regional rock units are shown in figure 1.2 and are divided on the basis of composition and age.

The age and origin of the present-day Adirondack dome are enigmatic. However, the uplift is certainly younger than ~350 Ma, which is the last time that the region was beneath sea level. Fission-track dating that determines the time at which rocks have risen from deep in the crust to approximately 1.2 miles below the surface suggests that the High Peaks were uplifted to these levels about 150 Ma, whereas the southeastern Adirondacks were uplifted about 100 Ma. These ages are related to the breakup of the supercontinent Pangea and the opening of the modern Atlantic Ocean. Locally, the breakup resulted in steep NE-SW faults that are readily visible on satellite imagery and that define the orientation and shape of Lake George, Lake Champlain, Long Lake, Indian Lake, and the Ausable

Lakes as well as the orientation of the major mountain ranges in the Adirondacks (e.g., Gothics, MacIntyre, and Great Ranges). A magnificent view of the Long Lake fault system can be seen from the summit of Ampersand Mountain.

A problem with sustaining the domical Adirondack uplift is the absence of a low-density crustal root extending into the upper mantle so as to buoy up the region like an iceberg. Accordingly, the topographic dome would not rise as its surface was eroded and would be rapidly reduced to sea level. We can calculate how long it would take to erode the current topography to sea level: approximately 18–20 million years, which is much younger than the fission-track ages. Two possible resolutions to this enigma are: (1) an upper mantle hotspot is holding up the dome, or (2) the dome is supported by broad crustal compression that arches up this sector of the North American continent. A difficulty with the hotspot model is that rocks beneath the Adirondacks today are cooler than normal, yet a hotspot would produce hotter than normal rocks. The compression model, however, is consistent with the numerous small earthquakes that occur in the Adirondack region, particularly in the Blue Mountain Lake and northeastern Highlands regions. Active, recent compression could also account for the region's radial drainage system, which is characteristic of young uplifts. This recent crustal compression could have produced the final mile of uplift in the region as well as its current topography.

Although the topography of the Adirondack region may be young, its bedrock is ancient and is best understood on a regional scale. The Adirondack Mountains constitute a southwestern outlier of the much larger Grenville Province that consists of approximately 1,750–1,000 Ma igneous and metamorphic rocks extending throughout southeastern Canada from Lake Huron to the coast of Labrador (fig. 1.1, inset). The region was affected by several mountain-building events that extensively deformed and metamorphosed the bedrock. Similar rocks with similar ages are found in eastern North America from Newfoundland to Alabama and westward through Texas to California, and even in Australia. The scale of this ancient belt of mountain building rivals the great Himalayan-Alpine chain of Eurasia and was surely equally as spectacular.

## Early Evolution of the Adirondack Mountains

Unraveling the origin of complex ancient mountain belts requires knowing the ages of their constituent rocks, and modern geochronology has provided major advances in our understanding of the history of the earth. In the Adirondacks, the most important results have involved the mineral zircon, which is present in small amounts in most rocks. When zircon crystallizes, it incorporates tiny quantities of the radioactive element uranium but almost no lead. Uranium undergoes spontaneous radioactive decay into lead and does so at constant rates. When zircons are analyzed, they are found to contain lead that formed by the radioactive decay of uranium. Because the decay rates of the uranium/lead series are constant, and because zircon neither gains nor loses lead or uranium, the absolute age of the igneous rock can be determined by calculating the length of time required for the uranium to produce the quantity of lead found in the zircon. While this core strategy appears simple, the method requires highly expensive and sophisticated instrumentation and technology not available until about 25 years ago.

The oldest igneous rocks (1,350–1,250 Ma) in the Adirondacks are granites and granitelike tonalites in the southern and eastern Highlands (RMTG, fig. 1.1) that intrude garnetiferous metamorphosed sediments (originally shale and muddy sandstones). Similar assemblages characterize modern volcanic island arcs (e.g., Aleutians, Indonesia, Lesser Antilles), suggesting that the proto-Adirondacks originated as a sequence of volcanic island arcs with igneous material produced by melting of the upper mantle in the wedge overlying subducting lithosphere, including its thin skin of oceanic crust (Fig. 1.2, left). Assembly of this arc-derived crust occurred over a 200-Ma interval, and began to be accreted to what was then eastern North America by about 1,220 Ma (accretion along CMBBZ, fig. 1.2). Subduction then stepped eastward with the downgoing plate descending to the west beneath the Adirondack Lowlands and resulting in tonalites and granites that were emplaced into the overlying Lowlands continental margin (RDAG, H, HSRG, fig. 1.1). By ~1,200 Ma, the Adirondack–Green Mountain terrane collided with the subduction zone and the powerful Shawinigan Orogeny ensued (fig. 1.2). Accretion continued until about 1,160 Ma and resulted in metamorphism and strong deformation across the entire Adirondack region (Shawinigan Orogeny, fig. 1.2). Similar events occurring at the same time in the Blue Ridge of Virginia, in Texas, and in Australia document that this was a global-scale event.

At about 1,160 Ma (fig. 1.1), the Adirondack region had become thickened by collision, and a deep mass of relatively cool, dense lithospheric mantle (density about 3.5 gm/cm³) was driven down into warmer, less dense athenosphere (density about 3.3 gm/cm³). Density differences of this magnitude commonly lead to the breaking off and sinking of the denser rocks into the deeper mantle. This process is known as delamination and causes the overlying crust to rebound upward, just as a ship will float higher when its heavy keel is detached. As the rebounding mountain belt rises, its own weight causes it to collapse outward along gently sloping detachment faults. Similar delamination-related faults are currently causing large portions of the Himalayas to collapse outward as the range continues to rise following delamination. The process causes the deep, hot cores of active mountain belts to ascend rapidly to the surface, thereby preserving the high temperature rocks and mineral assemblages (about 1,475° Fahrenheit and 15 miles depth) such as those we now find in the Adirondacks. At the surface it is common for basins to form in the extending crust and then to receive erosional detritus that lithify into sedimentary rocks. This is the origin of the Flinton basin (fig. 1.2).

Delamination at about 1,160 Ma caused hot, deep athenosphere underlying the lithosphere to rise and fill the potential void at the base of the crust (fig. 1.2). As the buoyant athenosphere ascended, it underwent melting that formed gabbro, which is the intrusive equivalent of basalt lava flows such as those that erupt in Hawaii or Iceland. Owing to its high density, the gabbro was trapped at the base of the less dense continental crust. Upon crystallizing, it formed large gray crystals of plagioclase feldspar that floated in the denser melt and collected into crystal-rich mushes that eventually ascended to form large masses of the rock anorthosite (fig. 1.2) that underlie the entire High Peaks region (i.e., Marcy Massif, figs. 1.1, 1.2) as well as the Oregon dome (OD, fig. 1.1). Anorthosite consisting of ~95 percent plagioclase feldspar is magnificently exposed in a series of rock cuts along Route 3 from Tupper Lake to Saranac Lake. Heat derived from the crystallization of the deep gabbroic magmas melted large portions of the overlying continental crust, giving rise to a spectrum of granitic melts that rose together with the plagioclase-rich crystal mushes to form the 1,150-Ma anorthosite-granite suite (AMCG suite, figs. 1.1, 1.2d) that accounts for the greatest volume of Adirondack bedrock. AMCG rocks of 1,150 Ma age are found in large volume throughout the Grenville Province (fig. 1.1) and are thought to have formed by the same processes as those described for the Adirondacks.

The Adirondacks experienced quiescence until about 1,100–1,090 Ma, when small volumes of Hawkeye granite (HWK, figs. 1.1, 1.2) were intruded. At about this time Amazonia (fig. 1.2), an Australia-size continent that now underlies most of Brazil, drew close to North America, and a continent-to-continent collision ensued at about 1,090 Ma (fig. 1.2). The collision resulted in intense deformation and metamorphism that by 1,050 Ma yielded a Himalaya-style mountain range. Thick slabs of rock were stacked up to produce double crustal thicknesses of 37–44 miles (fig. 1.2). Temperatures of ~1,475° Fahrenheit and pressures corresponding to 15–19 miles depth resulted in intense deformation that generated large refolded sheets of rock and ribbonlike rock fabric and caused partial melting of many Adirondack rocks. This major collision is known as the Ottawan Orogeny, and it occurred throughout the Grenville Province, as well as in the Appalachians and west Texas. Outside of North America, evidence of the Ottawan is present in southern Scandinavia, Australia, and Antarctica, supporting the existence of a Late Proterozoic supercontinent known as Rodinia.

Late in the history of the Ottawan Orogeny a delamination event resulted in buoyant rebound of the mountain belt (fig. 1.2g). Large, low-angle detachment faults developed, and portions of the mountain belt collapsed outward under its own weight. The most significant of these faults in the Adirondacks is the Carthage-Colton Zone, along which the Lowlands were down-faulted to the west (CCZ, figs. 1.1, 1.2). To the northwest in Ontario, a series of similar collapse faults formed and dropped crustal blocks back to the southeast (fig. 1.2).

At the same time, the emplacement of hot new athenosphere at the base of the crust caused partial melting of older, deeply buried AMCG-rich crust. This melting produced pink granite intrusions referred to as Lyon Mountain Granite (LMG, fig. 1.1, 1.2) and are dated at 1,050–1,030 Ma. The map distribution of Lyon Mountain Granite (fig. 1.1) and its age relationships suggest that it may have locally intruded into and lubricated the detachment fault zones related to collapse of the mountain range. This granite event extends through the Precambrian core of the Appalachians at least as far south as the Blue Ridge Mountains and resurfaces in central Texas.

Following the Ottawan Orogeny, relative quiescence returned to the Adirondack Mountains, and they, together with related terranes to the northeast and south, were reduced by erosion until inundated by seas some 550 million years ago. The Adirondacks would remain subdued until uplifts at ~150 Ma and ~20 Ma brought them to near-surface and surface positions, respectively.

## Glaciation and Recent Adirondack History

It is a commonly held misconception that glaciers formed the mountains. Glacial ice is a powerful mechanical agent but not nearly powerful enough to form significant mountains. During glaciation, ice sheets modify and round V-shaped water-carved valleys; this is a secondary effect and has little impact upon relative elevations, which are primarily determined by running water. However, ice certainly modifies the landscape by sculpting the final nuances of landforms. Thus glaciers round—but rarely deepen—the V-shaped valleys cut by running water. They pluck away at mountaintops to produce the converging amphitheater-like cirques that converge on Whiteface Mountain to form a classic horn (e.g., Matterhorn) at its summit.

Glacial meltwaters deposit sediment, including well-washed sand and gravel that accumulate in deeper, broader valleys and are sources of sand and gravel for construction and road building, as well as aquifers for domestic and municipal water wells. Many Adirondack lakes are the result of glacial deposits that dammed what otherwise would have been river valleys. For example, Long Lake exists as a lake because glacial sediments dammed the Raquette River at the north end of a long and wide stretch of its fault-controlled valley.

During maximum advances of the last ice age, the Pleistocene, glaciers extended as far south as Kansas and Nebraska, where their southerly advance is marked by piles of sedimentary debris known as terminal moraines. Although these earlier ice sheets passed through and covered the Northeast, the last great Pleistocene advance (i.e., Wisconsin glaciation) has largely obscured the effects of earlier advances. In fact, most of what we know about Wisconsin glaciation comes from features left behind during its retreat. The advance reached its maximum southerly terminus about 21,000 years ago and upon retreat left large terminal moraines whose eastern extent passed through central Pennsylvania and created both Long Island and Cape Cod. At its maximum the ice was about 1 mile thick and must have covered most of the Adirondacks, with the possible exception of the highest summits. About 21,000 years ago the ice began to melt northward, and meltwaters formed proglacial lakes (i.e., lakes in front of the glacier) that were dammed to the north by the glacier itself and to the south by earlier glacial deposits through which the impounded waters cut outlets to the sea.

One of these lakes occupied the Hudson Valley, and its size increased as the ice continued to melt back to the north. This lake, known as Glacial Lake Albany, ultimately extended through the Lake George region and into the Champlain Valley to form Glacial Lake Vermont, which extended to the Canadian border, where it was blocked by another large lobe of ice that extended eastward to the Atlantic. The latter glacial mass had dammed its own meltwater to the west, thus forming a large precursor of Lake Ontario known as Glacial Lake Iroquois (about 16,000–13,000 years ago) that submerged the St. Lawrence Lowlands almost to Lake Chateaugay and the present-day town of Ellenburg on the northeast and reached southward to present-day locations of Rochester and Rome.

When the Hudson Valley ice sheet retreated north of present-day Schenectady, the great mass of water to the west broke through ice and earthen dams near the area that is now the cities of Barneveld, Rome, and Little Falls. The water cut a channel that drained into the western Mohawk Valley and flowed eastward to join Glacial Lake Albany. Much of this outflow involved large bursts of water (called jokulhlaups) whose erosional effects were catastrophic, carrying huge boulders and cutting deep gorges.

By about 13,350 years ago, the northeastern arm of Glacial Lake Iroquois breached its ice impoundment north of present-day Ellenburg and debouched into Glacial Lake Vermont, whose northern terminus lay only a few miles to the east in the Champlain Lowland. As catastrophic floods rushed downhill, they scoured soil and overburden from the underlying Potsdam Sandstone, leaving clean, bare pavement and gave rise to the Flat Rock area (about 12 by 2 miles) that extends southeastward from Covey Hill, Quebec, to the Champlain Valley and is well exposed in the town of Altona.

The conjoined Glacial Lake Iroquois–Lake Vermont waters burst southward into the Hudson Valley system and broke through the terminal moraine at Hell's Gate and the Narrows near Staten Island. The immense volume of water carried huge boulders to the edge of the continental shelf, which was then exposed because of a lower global sea level. The flood also deposited enormous lobes of sediment on the shelf and carved much of the Hudson Submarine Canyon.

Subsequently, the ice lobe impounding the northern terminus receded into the St. Lawrence Lowlands (about 12,000 years ago) and then opened drainage to the Gulf of St. Lawrence. Enormous volumes of water rushed northward and into the Atlantic. The cold, fresh waters from these jokulhlaups interrupted flow of the Gulf Stream thermal conveyor belt, and that, in turn, resulted in brief repetitions of glacial climate (i.e., Inter-Allerod and Younger Dryas events). As the lake waters emptied, sea water moved in to take its place, forming the Champlain Sea about 13,000–12,900 years ago. Marine waters extended throughout the St. Lawrence Lowlands to Lake Ontario and north to Ottawa and persisted until about 10,000 years ago. A postglacial rebound led to an uplift of the crust and draining of the sea. Numerous fossils (e.g., whales) testify to this incursion by marine waters at the end of the Wisconsin glacial event.

As the Wisconsin-age glacier withdrew to the north it thinned, so that Adirondack summits became exposed at about 14,000 years ago. The first place that this happened was along the Hudson–St. Lawrence River Divide in the vicinity of Blue Mountain Lake. As the ice receded, a series of proglacial lakes formed in the easily erodable valley from Blue Mountain Lake through the Marion River, Raquette Lake, the present-day Fulton Chain of Lakes, and then on to the Moose River. During periods of slower retreat the ice dumped debris at its terminus and formed moraines that would serve to impound its meltwaters. The result was the series of eight partially connected lakes that extend from Old Forge to a few miles southwest of Raquette Lake.

By about 13,000 years ago, melting had removed all ice from the Chain of Lakes and the Moose River basin. At the same time that this ice lobe was retreating, lobes along the western margin of the Adirondack Mountains were also undergoing meltback. The result was that a sequence of proglacial lakes waxed and waned between Tug Hill and the western margin, sometimes reaching 20–30 miles farther east into the Adirondacks. Periodically these lakes broke out through low spots in rock and/or ice (e.g., Cedarville, Barneveld) and disgorged southeastward into the Mohawk-Hudson drainage system. During the lifetime of these lakes, they deposited significant thicknesses of sand and gravel in stream valleys, lake deltas, and shorelines, especially throughout the Black River drainage basin.

On the northeastern side of the Adirondack region, a lobe of glacial ice retreated northward (about 13,000 years ago) along the Keene Valley from St. Huberts to Ausable Forks and formed a proglacial lake with numerous terrace deposits, deltas, wave-formed beaches, and outbreak channels. Ultimately, the Keene Valley proglacial lake connected with related bodies extending from Ausable Forks to Keeseville. During the incursion of the Champlain Sea, marine waters extended to St. Huberts, and marine fossils can be found there in local terrace deposits.

The highest peaks of the Adirondacks retain tundra ecosystems as vestiges of the former cold-climate ecology. The warming of the region following deglaciation is recorded in pollen buried in lake sediments. Pollen records indicate that the earliest postglacial forests were adapted to cooler climates, but that the climate warmed to nearly modern temperatures by 7,500 years ago and by 4,500 years ago may have been warmer than today. More subtle cycles of warming and cooling in the last 4,500 years likely caused shifts in the geographic boundaries of some plant and animal species.

Globally, the earliest vestiges of recognizable civilization appeared about 10,000 years ago, coinciding with emergence from the Wisconsin glaciation. The coincidence is no surprise, for the warming climate brought with it a far gentler and more abundant way of life. As sea level rose, valleys filled with water and commerce by watercraft became viable, thereby facilitating trade, commerce, and the emergence of civilization. On the other hand, the advent of farming, clearing of forests, and animal husbandry may have helped to reverse an otherwise decreasing temperature regime and thus prevented a slide back into the glacial icehouse.

## Suggested Readings

Donnelly, J. P., N. W. Driscoll, E. Uchupi, L. D. Keigwin, W. C. Schwab, R. E. Theiler, and S. A. Swift. "Catastrophic Meltwater Discharge Down the Hudson Valley: A Potential Trigger for the Inter-Allerod Cold Period." *Geology* 33 (2005): 89–92.

Emmons, E. *Survey of the Second Geological District.* Albany: Appleton, Wiley and Putnam, 1842.

Karlstrom, K. E., S. S. Harlan, M. L. Williams, J. M. McLelland, J. W. Geissman, and K-I. Ahall. "Refining Rodinia: Geologic Evidence for the Australia-Western U.S. Connection in the Proterozoic." *GSA Today* 9, no. 10 (1999): 1–9.

McLelland, J., J. S. Daly, and J. M. McLelland. "The Grenville Orogenic Cycle (ca. 1350–1000 Ma): An Adirondack Perspective." *Tectonophysics* 265 (1996): 1–28.

Roden-Tice, M. K., S. J. Tice, and I. S. Schofield. "Evidence for Differential Unroofing of the Adirondack Mountains, New York State, Determined by Apatite Fission-track Thermochronology." *Journal of Geology* 108 (2000): 155–69.

Ruddiman, W. F., "How Did Humans First Alter Global Change?" *Scientific American* 292, no. 3 (2005): 46–53.

# 2

## Water Resources

*The Unique Adirondack Aquascape*

CHRISTOPHER P. CIRMO

What catches the senses most upon entering the Adirondack region is the seeming superabundance of water! In the soils; on the foliage; covering the roads; in ponds, lakes, and streams; in wetlands and rivers; on the trees, and in the sky! In winter, it is difficult to look down on the Adirondacks and find a point not associated with water in the form of snow or ice. Any discussion of the resource means by which the Adirondack region fulfills its anthropogenic ends must include the water that drives the engine of recreation, development, industry, art, resource extraction, wealth, well-being, ethics, and, in the end, value. From wildlife resources and fisheries, to mining and industry, to human consumption and aesthetics, the Adirondack region of the past, present, and future depends on both water quality and water quantity for its human valuation. Water can be thought of as the fundamental template for such lightning-rod issues as wetland protection, shoreline development, air pollution control, stream bank erosion, fisheries viability, drinking water supply, recreation . . . the list includes almost all issues at the intersection of conservation and development. The interaction and abundance of water as a manifestation of geography allows us to combine the words *aquatic* and *landscape* into a resource called the *aquascape*. The base of critical food chains in the region is maintained directly by the aquatic conditions in wetlands, springs, streams, lakes, and rivers, and indirectly by the saturated conditions presented by soil water and groundwater. It is therefore incumbent upon all caring for this magnificent resource to have a modicum of understanding of the water resources that give the Adirondack region much of its unique character.

## Inputs and Climate: Why Does It Seem to Rain So Much Up Here?

The Adirondack region gets a mean annual precipitation of 40 inches, somewhat unevenly distributed through the year. The geographic location of the Adirondacks, as the first major mountainous region east of the Upper Great Lakes, guarantees abundant orographic precipitation, with more falling in the west and southwestern areas, and relatively less in the east and northeast. Over 30 percent of total annual precipitation is in the form of snow, resulting in up to 40 percent of the total annual flow of most rivers and streams occurring during the short period of springtime snowmelt known as the vernal flush. Snow has been observed on the highest peaks as late as July. The snowpack can accumulate 3 to 4 feet deep in an average year.

Up to 38 percent of input precipitation evaporates from the surfaces of water bodies, soil, rock, and vegetation or is transpired through plant leaves and tissues, as part of the water transport system of plants (these processes are collectively called *evapotranspiration*). That means that up to 62 percent of input water must either reside in surface water pools, enter the ground to recharge groundwater and soil water, or be lost as surface runoff from the region in its major rivers. Local industry, tourism, recreation, and water for human consumption rely on this balance from year to year. It can be a mixed blessing for local residents when a "dry" year results in fewer blackflies and at the same time compromises the output of their private groundwater wells.

## The Geologic and Geographic Template of Water Distribution

Adirondack bedrock, largely shaped, scoured, and coated with glacial debris from the most recent glacial period, is responsible for the location and diversity of surface and groundwater resources in the

Adirondacks. The ancient metamorphic and largely crystalline bedrock is relatively impervious to water, but it is fractured by thousands of geologic fault lines trending mainly northeast–southwest. A cursory look at a map of the region shows these major northeast–southwest trending valleys, many containing large bodies of water. Examples include Indian Lake, Long Lake, Schroon Lake, and Catlin Lake.

Water generally moves away from the central highlands in what is referred to as a radial drainage pattern. Locally, however, there seems to be little symmetry in the distribution of water features (e.g., wetlands, streams, ponds, beaver ponds, and vernal pools). The distribution of material deposited from glacial meltback (collectively called glacial drift) is largely responsible for these local features. Sinuous linear hills of sand and gravel (eskers) alternate with mounds and benches on hillsides (kames and kame terraces) in proximity to large, flat plains of sand and peat (outwash plains). When one considers the action of beavers, along with anthropogenic influences in the form of dams, reservoirs, roads, bridges, culverts, and other human infrastructure, it is evident that the water resources of the region are hardly in pristine condition. In addition, there is much more water that is not visible; it exists below the surface in the form of soil water and groundwater. The water resources of the region include (a) channelized and flowing surface water such as streams, rivers, and spring outlets, which create unique lotic (flowing) habitats; (b) standing or nonchannelized surface water, including ponds, lakes, and reservoirs, or lentic habitat; (c) wetlands, including beaver ponds and vernal pools; and (d) groundwater and soil water. Each of these resources has peculiarities, sensitivities, and importance in creating the unique Adirondack aquascape.

## Flowing Water on the Surface

Streams begin in areas considered "ephemeral" or "zero-order," where tiny channels appear and disappear with each hydrologic event or storm. These tiny, ephemeral channels are the site of the initial interaction of water with soil, vegetation, surface deposits, and bedrock. Springs normally flow continually from a break in slope or from a geologic source exposed by a landslide or geologic discontinuity. Springs are normally cold and only dry up under regional drought conditions. Tiny rivulets become larger and more permanent first-order streams, which can be either "intermittent" or "perennial," depending on local groundwater inputs. These tiny channels are rarely mapped or named but make up the ultimate source of all downstream waters. Many springs and spring channels were historically impounded or diverted by pipes to residences or camps.

Springs, rivulets, and ephemeral and intermittent streams coalesce in the landscape to form perennial streams on lower slopes. Eventually these waters become large enough to be the brooks and streams we find named on maps. In these environments, populations of invertebrates, amphibians, and young fish interact to create the classic Adirondack stream so celebrated in folk and fishing lore. Many streams are cold and oxygen rich as water tumbles in and out of pool and riffle habitats. Great communities of invertebrates flourish in the rapidly moving water, and surface algae on rocks and insect larvae serve as food for many Adirondack game fishes. Ironically, the very presence of clear, cold, flowing water creates the perfect habitat for the blackflies of May and June that many find so intolerable.

As water flows from steeper channels to more level ground and valley bottoms, it slows, deposits sediments (called alluvium), warms, becomes less oxygenated, and begins to take on the characteristics of ponded water. Vegetation begins to take hold of bottom sediments, and fish are able to forage, spawn, and deposit eggs. As streams coalesce in the lowlands, they take on the characteristics of rivers, creating a combination of flowing and standing water habitat. It is estimated that there are 30,000 miles of streams and rivers in the Adirondacks. There are five major river drainage basins and fourteen major river systems. These rivers include the Black, Moose, Beaver, Oswegatchie, Grass, Raquette, St. Regis, Salmon, Saranac, Ausable, Bouquet, and the Lake George/Lake Champlain system, which all drain to the St. Lawrence River. The Schroon, Upper Hudson, Sacandaga, and West Canada all drain to the Hudson River. Flow in these major rivers ranges from only a few cubic feet per second in the driest times to thousands of cubic feet per second during snowmelt and major weather fronts. The United States Geological Survey (USGS) maintains twenty-seven hydrological gauging stations on these major rivers for long-term observation of ranges, extremes, and anomalies in flows to allow better predictions of flood conditions to protect human health and infrastructure.

### Wetlands, Vernal Pools, and Beavers

Undoubtedly the most ubiquitous of water resources in the Adirondack region are the saturated soils, shallow standing water, and expansive wet areas between contiguous lakes. These areas are collectively called wetlands. It is difficult to view an Adirondack scene without some sense of this ever-present saturated zone. Indeed, up to 15 percent of the total area of the Adirondacks may be considered wetland. We use many names to characterize these systems in the vernacular, including swamps, bogs, marshes, mires, and beaver meadows. Wetlands have been variously identified and classified by many criteria, including vegetation, hydrology, geographic location, and peat content.

The presence of saturated conditions leads to changes in the biogeochemical soil environment because of a condition called *anoxia,* or lack of oxygen. The depletion of soil oxygen gives rise to unique bacterial soil populations that use specialized anaerobic metabolic pathways in the decomposition of organic material. This decomposition process leads to byproducts in the soil (e.g., red and orange mottling, concretions of metals, reddish-orange halos around fine plant roots, the odor of hydrogen sulfide, methane production) that give wetland soils their features and their odor. The cycling and chemical transformation of many nutrients (including nitrogen, sulfur, phosphorus, and iron) depend on anoxic conditions. The shiny, oily surface of some wetland waters is due to the presence of certain iron-oxidizing bacteria (often mistaken for petroleum spills). Many beaver ponds, marshes, and bogs bleed red iron deposits to downstream waters, causing iron accumulations known as "bog iron deposits." Wetlands have also been shown to be potential sinks for acid-rain chemicals (like nitrate and sulfate), reducing acid rain impacts on downstream waters, and they have been implicated in the transformations of acid-rain-related mercury found ubiquitously in soils and sediments (see chapter 9).

Swamps are perhaps the most widespread wetland type in the Adirondacks. They are characterized by shrubs, willow and alder thickets, and trees (either deciduous or conifers). Swamps have a limited depth and duration of flooding, such that they can seem at times quite dry, but have soils covered with mosses and ferns adapted to moist conditions. The dark Adirondack "conifer swamp" is a classic example of this type of wetland. Marshes are more likely to be observed by the public because some of the largest (such as the Tupper Lake Marsh) are crossed by roads or bridges and are associated with the edges of large lake systems. They have standing water at most times, are very wet in comparison to swamps, and may have some small bushes but no trees. They are home to muskrats and beaver and are important to a plethora of songbirds, wading birds, and other waterfowl. Marshes are nearly always flooded but can dry at times to reveal muddy flats or wet meadows. Areas of shallow water along and between many large lake systems labeled on Adirondack maps as "flows" are actually marshes. Examples include the Cedar River Flow, the Grass River Flow, and the Flowed Lands in the High Peaks region. Access to these wetlands is limited, and they may represent some of the least disturbed areas of the park.

Peatlands (bogs and fens) can range in size from small bogs to valley-wide systems with deep accumulations of peat. This peat can eventually control the hydrology, nutrient status, and wildlife habitat of these systems. Bogs are peatlands that have been effectively sealed off from groundwater by the relatively impervious nature of peat. They are nutrient poor, have a unique vegetation type adapted to low nutrient conditions, and are normally acidic owing to lack of groundwater input. Sundews, pitcher plants, and other "carnivorous plants" that are uniquely adapted to low nutrient, acid conditions are found in bogs. Fens also accumulate peat but are not isolated from groundwater. They are still somewhat nutrient poor but develop richer vegetation, including unique sedges and ferns. Classic examples of large peatlands are the Spring Pond Bog and the Bloomingdale Bog.

Peatlands are of ecological and historical interest because the peat and sediments located within them may have been developing since the end of glaciation and may hold keys to understanding the climates of the past. As we zoom to an aerial view of these large peatlands, we get a greater sense of their "connectedness" with other seemingly disconnected wetlands. Peatlands are also being studied as systems that are uniquely sensitive to climate change. If boreal zones do begin to warm and dry, there exists the potential for the oxidation of their massive peat deposits, with subsequent releases of additional carbon dioxide to the atmosphere. Regional scientists are studying these ideas by observing the layers in cores drilled down through the peat and identifying significant signs of paleo-events such as soot from fires, pollen from vegetation, and other particulates from the atmosphere.

Of recent interest to wildlife managers, ecologists, and hydrologists are the smallest and most transient of wetlands called vernal pools, which appear and disappear within forested areas as small pools of water found in depressions. Vernal pools have standing water for part of the year but are not permanent, and their dynamics are thought to be controlled by snowmelt, rainwater, and groundwater, in some combination. Short-cycle pools dry up soon after spring snowmelt, not later than June in the east, while long-cycle pools dry in mid- to late summer. Vernal pools are normally predator (fish) free, and amphibian larvae (a favorite fish food) can more successfully survive to adulthood. One estimate puts the density of these pools in the uplands of the Adirondacks at approximately 13 per square mile. If vernal pools prove to be as ubiquitous in the Adirondacks as in other parts of the northeastern United States, they may be responsible for a huge portion of amphibian habitat.

Any discussion of water in the Adirondacks would be incomplete without touching on the workings of the North American beaver (*Castor canadensis*). Beavers not only create temporary ponds with dams, but also, with dam collapse, a succession of sedge and beaver "meadows" can develop. The flood-and-collapse cycle of beaver ponds has dramatic implications for wildlife, creating stagnant shallow water conditions in an otherwise relatively dry upland. Beaver ponds can store water from spring runoff and major storms, somewhat dampening downstream effects of high flows, and can also be sources or sinks for nutrients and other chemicals related to acid deposition. Sediments are also entrained, building up alluvial and organic sediments that might have otherwise washed directly into a nearby lake. It has been estimated that in areas of the Adirondacks and Canada, up to 40 percent of streams and lakes are affected by beaver activity.

## Lakes: Aquatic Jewels of the Adirondacks

In both folklore and scientific literature, it is Adirondack lakes that hold the imagination of the public. The Adirondack region was one of the first places where acid rain effects on lakes were studied, and many discoveries about the role of lake ecosystems in the landscape were a direct result of these studies. Lakes form mainly in low-lying areas where there tend to be accumulations of glacial drift, or in pockets and depressions formed by irregular ice buildup and melt-back from Pleistocene glaciation. Many of the larger natural lakes in the Adirondacks formed along major fault zones (e.g., Catlin Lake, Long Lake, Schroon Lake, and Lake George). The many linear valleys and close ridges of various basins in the region led to a spurt of dam building and reservoir creation during the early part of the twentieth century. Over 50 percent of the settled-shoreline lakes in the park are artificial, and their water levels are carefully managed. These impoundments include large lakes such as Cranberry Lake, Tupper Lake, Stillwater Reservoir, and Great Sacandaga Lake.

Attempts to classify Adirondack lakes issued from the need to understand their hydrology and water sources for management of water quality, and to address acid rain issues. An often used classification was created by Newton and Driscoll in 1990.[1] They proposed a model whereby all lakes could first be classified as either "seepage" or "drainage," depending on the presence or absence of inlet and outlet streams. Drainage lakes represent systems where small geographic basins are connected to each other via streams or the large marsh-like "flows" characteristic of wide and level plains between basins. Seepage lakes are not connected to other surface waters by inlets or outlets and are either isolated from groundwater or fed only by groundwater. Additional classification is based on thickness of surface geological deposits, effects of road salt, presence of calcium-bearing rock influence, and the level of organic "color" in the water (DOC, or dissolved organic carbon).

Ecologically, lakes provide protected and deep aquatic environments with quiescent waters for fish, otter, and many other animals to flourish. They also create shallows (called littoral zones) which resemble wetlands with rooted and emergent vegetation. If lakes are deep enough, the water column can be divided into an upper portion of warmer water (epilimnion) and a deeper portion that is colder and more isolated (hypolimnion). Sediments and organic matter in this deep zone can play a critical role in the recycling of nutrients and the maintenance of overall lake water quality.

Lakes and the habitat they provide for fish and wildlife are most endangered by shoreline development. There are many lakes and ponds with little or no disturbance of shore zones in the publicly owned portions of the park. However, few privately owned lakeshores are undisturbed, and old and sometimes failing septic systems and waste discharges near these shores have created degraded water quality, nuisance vegetation, and reduced fishing and recreation value.

All lakes, whether on public or private lands, may be affected by acid rain and associated mercury pollution (see chapter 9). Some lakes have proven to be more sensitive to this impact than others because of their geographic location and underlying geology. Weather fronts hit the western and southwestern Adirondacks first, dropping much of their acid-laden precipitation. Some lakes are underlain by deep glacial deposits, which help neutralize acids, and others exist in areas where the bedrock is rich in marble or other calcium-bearing materials, which leads to generally higher pH values. Recent concern regarding mercury levels has centered on some of the larger reservoir systems (e.g., Stillwater Reservoir; see chapter 9).

## Groundwater: The Unseen Water Resource of the Adirondacks

Historically, groundwater has not been routinely used for human consumption in the Adirondack region because it was easier just to tap into available lakes and rivers. However, the jumble of rocks, sand, silt, and clay materials left on top of the bedrock by glaciation provides for substantial groundwater resources. There are three types of groundwater resource in the Adirondacks: (a) that found in the overlying regolith, including soil, sand and gravel, weathered bedrock, or glacial drift; (b) water found in fissures, joints, and fractures of the metamorphic crystalline bedrock of the Adirondack highlands; and (c) water found in the sedimentary units of the bordering lowlands. Water-bearing strata and deposits of sand and glacial drift form aquifers that can produce enough water for human consumption.

Exploitation of sand and gravel aquifers for water supplies or consumptive uses is not easily accomplished because of the heterogeneity of these deposits and their impermeability in places. Stratified (layered) sands and gravels are more productive for groundwater, but often exist in broad valleys that are inaccessible, or that are thin and cannot be exploited for consumptive use. These aquifer resources may also be isolated from the surface by ancient lake silt and clay layers, or by "hardpans" developed in iron-rich soils. The chemistry of any of these groundwater pools is dependent on the mineral makeup of the rock or sediment, and on the relative "residence time" of water in the medium.

A major factor driving interest in groundwater in the Adirondacks is the recent U.S. Environmental Protection Agency regulation that is part of the Safe Drinking Water Act. The regulation applies new water-quality standards for water supplies using surface water for drinking. This rule requires expensive filtration of most municipal water supplies that come from lakes and rivers. This regulation has forced many localities and hamlets within the park to seek access to groundwater supplies, which do not require filtration. In addition, pressure has been placed on local Adirondack aquifers because of the popularization of bottled water and the perceived water quality of Adirondack supplies.

## The Future of Adirondack Water Resources

Throughout this discussion, the unique distribution and quality of water in the Adirondacks allows us to consider it a "resource." We should not restrict our use of this word to the dictionary definition, "a natural source of wealth or revenue." The wealth and revenue of the water resources of the Adirondacks arise from the combination of its consumer, wildlife and fishery, and aesthetic and recreational value. There are critical concerns for the protection of water resources as a most important "ultimate means" within the Adirondack region. For example, we have little knowledge of the functional role of vernal pools, the long-term recovery of lakes from acid deposition, and the connection of surface water to groundwater resources. Our knowledge of the hydrologic linkage between lakes, streams, wetlands and groundwater is rudimentary at best. In addition, beaver management has direct implications for flooding and loss or gain of sensitive wetlands, and little is known about long-term groundwater depletion owing to increased municipal demand.

Issues under human control include reductions in atmospheric emissions of acid rain precursors, shoreline development, wetland protection and designation, the conservation of groundwater and surface waters, and the disposal of solid refuse and wastewater. To those who live elsewhere, these water resources have mostly aesthetic and recreational valuation, but for Adirondack residents they are crucial to everyday life and livelihood. It is at once critical and timely that we explore ways to value water in the Adirondacks as possibly the most critical "ultimate means" for valuation of Adirondack resources.

## Suggested Readings

Baker, J. P., S. A. Gherini, S. W. Christensen, C. T. Driscoll, J. Gallagher, R. K. Munson, R. M. Newton, K. H. Reckhow, and C. L. Schofield. *Adirondack Lakes Survey: An Interpretive Analysis of Fish Communities and Water Chemistry, 1984–1987.* Ray Brook, N.Y.: Adirondack Lakes Survey Corp., 1990.

Driscoll, C. T., R. M. Newton, C. P. Gubala, J. P. Baker, and S. W. Christensen. "Adirondack Mountains." In *Acidic Deposition and Aquatic Ecosystems,* ed. D. F. Charles, 133–202. New York: Springer-Verlag, 1991.

Jenkins, J., and A. Keal. *The Adirondack Atlas: A Geographic Portrait of the Adirondack Park.* Syracuse: Syracuse Univ. Press, 2004.

Jenkins, J., K. Roy, C. Driscoll, and C. Buerkett. *Acid Rain and the Adirondacks: A Research Summary.* Ray Brook, N.Y.: Adirondack Lakes Survey Corp., 2005.

Roy, K. M., et al. 1997. Influence of Wetland and Lakes in the Adirondack Park of New York State: A Catalog of Existing and New GIS Data Layers for the 400,000-Hectare Oswegatchie/Black River Watershed. Ray Brook, N.Y.: Adirondack Park Agency, 1997.

# 3

## Soils of the Adirondacks

*Out of Site, Out of Mind*

RUSSELL D. BRIGGS

The variable nature of vegetation in space and time, which reflects a combination of soil conditions and plant-life history coupled with disturbance, is often apparent. However, the dynamic role of soil in forest ecosystem function is seldom recognized. The adage "out of site, out of mind" (spelling intended) aptly describes this situation. Soil, which is normally shielded from view, occupies the space between three systems: atmosphere, lithosphere (the solid portion of the earth's crust), and hydrosphere (streams, lakes, and groundwater). This juxtaposition confers a unique role on the soil system; it functions as an interface, mediating exchanges of energy, water, and gases among atmosphere, lithosphere, and hydrosphere.

The topography and parent material in which Adirondack soils formed reflect glacial activity on coarse-grained igneous and metamorphic rocks that underlay the region. The continental glacier extended southward through present-day Canada to the northern portion of the United States before receding approximately 12,000 years ago. The underlying bedrock was plucked and scoured by an ice sheet that was several thousand feet thick, transporting materials ranging in size from finely ground rock flour to large boulders.

Till, a heterogeneous mixture of rock and soil particles, was plastered across the landscape. The composition of the till reflects the properties of rocks ground up and carried by the ice. As the ice receded, glacial meltwater transported and deposited parent material in the valleys. Unlike the heterogeneous till, water-deposited materials tended to be well sorted. Particle size distribution of water-deposited materials is a function of the rate of meltwater flow. Coarse sands and gravels were deposited by fast-moving water in glacial meltwater streams, while fine sands and silts were deposited by slow-moving water in glacial lakes that occupied the valleys.

Eskers, long sinuous ridges consisting of coarse sands and gravels, resulted from deposition of sand and gravel carried in meltwater streams flowing within the glacier. These north–south-oriented landforms are a common feature throughout the region. One of the most notable eskers, the Massawepie, located in the town of Colton in St. Lawrence County, is home to the Massawepie Boy Scout Camp. The nature of the coarse-textured material is revealed in many road cuts and gravel pits.

Outwash plains, consisting of coarse sands and gravels in extensive plains of limited relief, are another common feature of the Adirondack landscape. Sand and gravel transported by braided streams at the melting front of the glacier formed extensive plains. One of the most prominent is the Pack Forest Plain near the mouth of the Hudson River at Warrensburg. The area is famous in forest soil science as the first place in North America where potassium deficiency was identified in red pine.

Bedrock geology has an equally important influence on Adirondack soil texture as well as on soil fertility. Coarse-grained igneous and metamorphic rocks such as granite, syenite, amphibole, and feldspar are common. Weathering of these rock types by glacial action and by chemical processes generated sand-sized particles and some coarse silt. Limestone, a sedimentary rock high in calcium carbonate, is absent. The few instances where marble, a calcium-bearing metamorphic rock, is encountered are confined to some of the valleys. The paucity of such fine-textured rocks high in carbonates limits fertility of Adirondack soils. Fine-textured soils are uncommon in the Adirondacks.

What exactly is soil? Soil can be defined as a natural, dynamic, four-phase system consisting of mineral particles, organic matter, air, and water. The system supports an array of organisms ranging in size from macro- to microscopic. These organisms are part of an intricate food web that processes remains of plants and animals, converting them to humus (the highly decomposed, stable form of organic matter in soil), carbon dioxide, and water. In the process, nutrient elements required by plants are released from the dead tissue and made available to plants, a process that is referred to as mineralization. Metabolic byproducts of organisms involved with organic matter decomposition contribute to mineral weathering, enhancing soil formation and development.

The role of soil as an interface is analogous to that of a biogeochemical membrane. Solar radiation strikes the forest canopy and drives the process of photosynthesis, which converts carbon dioxide to sugars. Radiation that passes through the canopy strikes the soil surface and is conducted downward, raising soil temperature and increasing rates of biogeochemical reactions. Precipitation from the atmosphere passes through the canopy and infiltrates and percolates through the soil. A portion of soil moisture is returned to the atmosphere via evapotranspiration. The remaining soil water is either stored or makes its way to streams, lakes, and groundwater, becoming a component of the hydrosphere. Atmospheric oxygen diffuses into the soil atmosphere, where plant roots and organisms utilize it for respiration. The carbon dioxide produced during respiration diffuses outward from the soil to the atmosphere. The rates of exchange of energy, water, and gases through the biogeochemical membrane are greatest at the soil surface and diminish with depth.

These rates of transfers ultimately constrain biological activity, dictating species composition and growth rate. Soil organisms require water and energy. In the absence of water, biological production is greatly restricted. Similarly, when energy inputs are low (cold soil temperatures), biological activity is reduced. Many organisms inhabiting the soil, plant roots included, are aerobic; they require oxygen for respiration. Under conditions where the transfer of water is restricted and water collects, oxygen is depleted. Only those organisms that do not require oxygen (anaerobic) persist, and thus biological activity is drastically reduced. The rate of organic matter production through plant growth and development is very slow and confined to a few species of plants and organisms that are able to tolerate poor aeration. Red spruce and balsam fir, for example, are able to persist in wet, poorly aerated soil, whereas species such as sugar maple cannot. Although spruce and fir can persist, their growth rates under those conditions would be very slow; it may take 100 years to attain a stem diameter of 6 inches. Growth rates are much higher for spruce and fir on better-drained upland sites.

The rate of organic matter decomposition is also greatly reduced under conditions of poor aeration. Organic matter builds up; plant nutrients contained in organic matter are stored or "locked up," making them unavailable for plant uptake. The rate of nutrient cycling is greatly reduced, further constraining biological productivity. One of the consequences of poor aeration is the development of organic soils, defined as soils with an organic carbon content exceeding 20 percent. Organic soils, commonly referred to as peat or muck, are a common feature throughout the Adirondacks in topographic positions where water collects.

The physical properties of soil influence the size and distribution of pores. Pores effectively constrain the transfer of energy, water, and gases through the soil system. Large pores that allow water to move through the soil under the force of gravity are termed macropores. Conversely, small pores that hold water against the force of gravity are called micropores. While we sometimes think of soil as a solid, ideally, half of the total volume of the soil would consist of pores, and these pores would be evenly divided between macropores and micropores, simultaneously allowing for both drainage and water storage. Consequently, pore size distribution is a fundamental physical attribute influencing biological productivity.

Pore-size distribution is a function of soil texture and organic-matter content. Sandy soils are commonly referred to as coarse textured. Sand-sized particles do not stack very efficiently, and the spaces between particles are relatively large, allowing rapid water movement. Clay soils represent the other end of the spectrum.

Micropores dominate, and water is held against the force of gravity. Silt-sized particles are intermediate in size between sand and clay. Loam-textured soils, which consist of a mix of sand-, silt-, and clay-sized particles, have a wide distribution of pore sizes that simultaneously facilitate water storage in the small pores and rapid drainage through the large pores.

Knowledge of soil texture provides important interpretations of how rapidly air, water, and gases move through the soil system (table 3.1). These fluxes directly affect vegetation growth and development. Sandy soils are dominated by macropores, so water flows freely when drainage is not impeded. The rapid exchange of carbon dioxide and oxygen between the soil and the atmosphere does not impede root growth. However, macropores do not store water, so the soils tend to be droughty. Clay soils, on the other hand, hold large amounts of water in the micropores and do not readily drain; they tend to be poorly aerated. Loam-textured soils tend to have a mixture of macropores and micropores, allowing for rapid drainage from the large pores and adequate storage in the smaller pores.

Vegetative production is greatest when plant roots are continually supplied with water and nutrients while maintaining an adequate influx of oxygen and efflux of carbon dioxide. Trees, shrubs, and annual crops attain their highest growth rates under those conditions. The capacity of a site for vegetative production is referred to as site quality. High-quality sites produce the greatest amount of

TABLE 3.1. **Relative rating for soil properties related to soil textural class**

| | Soil Textural Class | | |
|---|---|---|---|
| *Soil property* | *Sand* | *Loam* | *Clay* |
| Internal drainage | High | Medium | Low |
| Plant-available water | Low | Medium | High |
| Runoff potential | Low | Low-medium | High |
| Aeration | High | Medium-high | Low |

vegetation in the shortest time. The ideal soil from an agricultural perspective is a deep, well-drained loam with some limestone or marble influence and without an excessive volume of rock fragments. Soils of this type are not very common in the central Adirondacks, for reasons that will become apparent in the following sections. When these soils are encountered in the central Adirondacks, they are generally found in the valley bottoms. In those instances when the early settlers attempted to grow crops on the less-productive sites, the results were usually poor. The land was ultimately abandoned, and it reverted back to forest.

The interaction of physiography and vegetation provides a means to understand the distribution of soils across the Adirondacks. The ecological land-classification system developed by the U.S. Forest Service provides an excellent framework. Physiography and vegetation differentiate the six subsections for the Adirondacks. The highest elevations and the widest ranges in elevation occur in the Adirondack Peaks subsection (M212Dd; see fig. 3.1, table 3.2). The feature common to each of the six subregions is the presence of coarse-grained igneous and metamorphic rocks (i.e., gneiss and schist). The till derived from grinding and transport of crystalline rock is high in sand with lesser amounts of silt; clay-size particles are rare. Consequently, Adirondack mineral soils tend to be relatively coarse textured (i.e., sandy).

Another consequence of till composed largely of ground-up coarse-grained igneous and metamorphic rocks is relative low fertility. Mineral weathering of coarse-grained materials occurs at relatively slow rates. Essential plant nutrients are released very slowly; fertility limits potential plant growth as well as poor water-holding capacity. Nutrient cycling and plant nutrition in coarse-textured soils are highly dependent on soil organic matter; clay-sized particles, which play an important role in nutrition, are largely absent. Levels of soil organic matter are limited in coarse-textured soils by high rates of oxidation. The low amount of clay places further importance on soil organic matter for fertility and nutrient cycling in Adirondack soils.

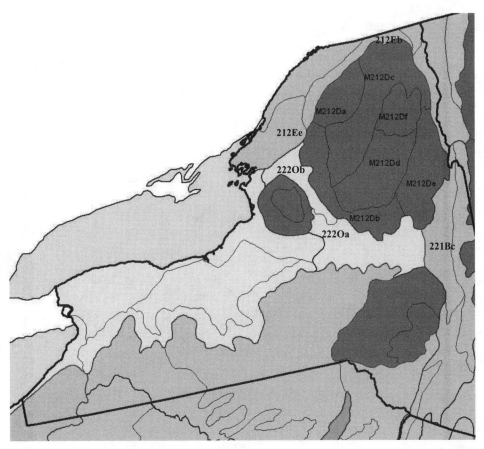

3.1. Map illustrating ecological subregions in the Adirondack region and immediate vicinity. Courtesy of the USDA Forest Service.

The coarse texture of Adirondack soils contrasts strongly with the finer-textured soils surrounding the region in the lower elevations (see fig. 3.1, table 3.2). The St. Lawrence Glacial Marine Plain and the St. Lawrence Till Plain to the northeast are occupied by fine-textured soils that were deposited in lake and ocean water following glacial retreat. Many of those soils are high in carbonates that originated from shells of marine creatures that populated the ocean. The Champlain Glacial Lake and Marine Plain and the Champlain Hills to the northeast, are composed of fine-textured soils resulting from lake and marine deposits. The Hudson Glacial Lake Plains to

TABLE 3.2. Physiography and rock type associated with ecological land types in northern New York

| Ecological subregions | Physiography | Height (ft.) | Parent material | Rock type |
|---|---|---|---|---|
| Adirondack Hills and Flats, M212Da | Plains with hills, glaciated peneplain | 900–2,518 | Coarse loamy sandy till, outwash lake deposits | Gneisses-schist |
| Western Adirondack Foothills, M212Db | Plains with hills, glaciated peneplain | 800–1,800 | Sandy till | Gneisses-schist-calcsilicates-marble |
| Adirondack Highlands and Lakes, M212Dc | Open hills and high hills, glaciated peneplain | 1,500–2,500 | Sandy till, outwash–delta deposits, alluvium | Gneiss-anorthosite |
| Central Adirondack Mountains, M212Dd | Open low mountains, glaciated, block-faulted | 1,600–3,900 | Sandy till, alluvial inwash | Gneisses-schist |
| Eastern Adirondack Low Mountains, M212De | Open low mountains, glaciated block-faulted | 400–2,600 | Variable textured till | Gneisses-schist |
| Adirondack Peaks, M212Df | Open low and high mountains-glaciated | 1,000–5,344 | Variable textured till, glaciofluvial valley deposits | Anorthosite |
| St. Lawrence Glacial Marine Plain, 212Ea | Irregular plains | 300–1,200 | Marine silt-clay-sand–gravel, sandy till | Sandstone, carbonates |
| St. Lawrence Till Plain, 212Eb | Plains with hills, ground moraine | 400–1,200 | Silty clay, silt loamy till | Sandstone, siltstone, dolostone |
| Champlain Glacial Lake and Marine Plain, 212Ec | Plains with hills | 100–1,000 | Marine–lake silt-clay, delta sand–gravel | Metasedimentary rock |
| Champlain Hills, 212Ed | Plains with high hills, ground moraine | 400–1,900 | Loamy-sandy loamy till, delta sand–gravel | Dolomite, quartzite, slate, schist |
| St. Lawrence Glacial Lake Plain, 212Ee | Irregular plains | 300–800 | Lake sand–gravel, sandy till | Carbonate, limestone |
| Hudson Limestone Valley, 221Ba | Rolling hills, glaciated, ice-molded | 100–1,000 | Loamy-sandy loamy till, ice contact delta deposits, lake silt-clay | Limestone, shale |
| Hudson Glacial Lake Plains, 221Bc | Level to rolling glacial lake plain, dunes | 100–900 | Lake silt-clay-sand–gravel, loamy till, alluvium | Shale, siltstone |

the southeast hosts fine-textured silt and clays, as well as coarse-textured sands and gravels. The contrast in parent materials between the Adirondacks and the surrounding lowlands are highlighted in table 3.2.

The current distribution of working farms as one proceeds to the Adirondacks from any of the surrounding lower elevations reflects the combined differences in soil and climate. In addition to finer-textured and more fertile soils, the lower elevations of the surrounding regions provide a climate more conducive to crop production. Reduction in temperature and growing-season length associated with increasing elevation combines with poorer soil conditions to create marginal (at best) conditions for agricultural production.

The soils of the Adirondacks have been mapped by field soil scientists of the Natural Resource Conservation Service (NRCS). On the basis of their mapping experience, several generalizations can be made beyond that of relatively coarse texture. Smooth back slopes on the southeastern sides of mountains tend to be occupied by basal till, characterized by a layer that was compressed under the weight of the glacier. The dense layer restricts roots and downward movement of water, resulting in a perched water table on gently sloping to flat topography. Ablation till, consisting of material that settles out of the ice as it melts, lacks the dense impermeable layer of basal till. Ablation till tends to occupy complex topography. Organic soils and alluvial (water-deposited) soils tend to occupy positions at the bottom of slopes. These landscape relationships and others are used to map the soils by extrapolating observed relationships among topography, vegetation, and soil properties.

On a more local scale, soil distribution over the landscape is strongly influenced by topography. Topography further constrains how fast water drains or accumulates in the soil profile. This latter feature is expressed directly as soil-drainage class, which ranges from very dry (excessively drained) to very wet (very poorly drained).

Excessively drained soils drain so rapidly and hold so little moisture that they tend to be droughty. These may be either deep sandy soils in a variety of landscape positions or thin soils on ridge tops that receive minimal or no lateral flow. Well-drained soils, characterized by a rooting zone free of a seasonally high water table, occupy landscape positions that shed water, such as convex slopes. These sites have roots that penetrate more deeply into the soil compared to poorly drained soils, which have a perched water table within 4–8 inches of the soil surface. Poorly drained soils occur on lower portions of the landscape where water collects. The shallow water tables prevent root growth and development, restricting roots to the surface layer and limiting plant productivity.

The strong influence of topography on soil-drainage class gives rise to a catena—a group of soils of similar parent materials and age that differ in drainage class as a function of topography. One of the common catenas in the Adirondacks consists of the following soil series formed in sandy sediments: Adams (well to excessively well drained), Croghan (moderately well drained), Naumburg (somewhat poorly to poorly drained), and Searsport (very poorly drained). As drainage becomes restricted because of lower landscape positions or an impermeable layer that impedes water flow, these soils form a group where a perched water table is increasingly closer to the soils' surface, limiting plant productivity.

Soil-drainage class has a strong influence on species composition. Conifer species such as red spruce and balsam fir dominate in the uppermost and lowermost topographic positions. The excessively drained soils on mountaintops do not provide sufficient water and nutrients for most hardwood species. The lower landscape positions are characterized by poorly and very poorly drained soils, where poor aeration restricts species to conifers that can tolerate those conditions. In spite of their ability to compete, growth in height and diameter of conifers on those wet soils is relatively slow. The well and moderately well drained soils of the midslope positions support stands of sugar maple, American beech, and other hardwoods.

The complex nature of glacial deposits, coupled with topography, translates to a high degree of variability for soils within the Adirondack region. That variability is reflected in the soil maps of the region. Within the space of a single chapter, it is not feasible to list the soil-map units of the seven main counties that constitute the approximately 6 million acres in the Adirondacks. However, focusing on soil variability within a representative landscape serves to illustrate the variability typically encountered in the region.

The Huntington Forest (HF), an 15,000-acre research and demonstration forest located near Newcomb, provides an appropriate case study for Adirondack soils. The HF soil survey was completed in 1986. The resulting map supports the generalization that Adirondack soils tend to be coarse-textured. The clayey particle size class is absent. The HF map unit legend also reveals the high degree of variability for which Adirondack soils are well known, even within this small portion of the Adirondack Peaks subsection. More than half of the map units consist of complexes and associations of two or more soil series and represent 85 percent of the landscape (table 3.3). Complexes are groups of soils that are so intricately mixed that it is not possible to identify the components individually on the landscape. Individual components of associations, on the other hand, could be identified on the landscape and delineated on a map if there were sufficient resources to devote to the field work.

A number of the map units include soil types that are so variable, and have ranges of properties so far outside of existing soil series, that they are identified at the subgroup level (i.e., Lithic Haplorthods—Ricker complex). There are approximately 19,000 series and 2,500 subgroups in soil taxonomy. Lithic Haplorthods, a classification at the subgroup level, are soils having a spodic horizon (accumulation of sesquioxides) and bedrock within 20 inches of the soil surface. There are several series that fit into this subgroup. For example, Ricker is a soil series characterized by organic matter overlying bedrock within 20 inches, with a thin layer of mineral soil right on bedrock (if it is present at all).

Examination of the map units for the Huntington Forest provides an accurate indication of soil variability at the subregional scale (100–1,000 acres), but it does not convey the degree of variation within map units. NRCS guidelines for mapping accuracy suggest that within a map unit, the named soils should constitute 65 percent

TABLE 3.3. Soil map units[a] for the 15,000 acres of Huntington Forest, 1986

| Soil Series (% area) | Particle size class[b] |
|---|---|
| Adams (0.20) | Sandy |
| Allagash-Madawaska association (1.08) | Coarse-loamy over sandy |
| Becket-Skerry-Croghan association (0.63) | Coarse-loamy |
| Becket (7.10) | Coarse-loamy |
| Berkshire (0.66) | Coarse-loamy |
| Becket-Skerry association (10.98) | Coarse-loamy |
| *Carbondale muck (0.07)* | |
| Croghan (0.07) | Sandy |
| Fluvaquents-Borosaprists association (2.10) | |
| Dysic Typic Borofolists-Ricker-Rawsonville complex (0.06) | Coarse-loamy |
| *Greenwood mucky peat (0.31)* | |
| Hermon (0.40) | Sandy-skeletal |
| Hermon variant–Killington complex (0.12) | Loamy-skeletal |
| Houghtonville (0.14) | Coarse-loamy |
| Hermon variant (0.83) | Sandy-skeletal |
| Killington-Rock Outcrop association (0.08) | Loamy-skeletal |
| *Loxley-Beseman association (0.17)* | |
| Lithic Haplorthods–Lithic Udorthents–Hogback-Ricker-Rock Outcrop complex (1.52) | Loamy |
| Lithic Udorthents–Ricker complex (0.06) | |
| Marlow (0.58) | Coarse-loamy |
| Mundal (3.59) | Coarse-loamy |
| Mundal-Skerry variant association (6.74) | Coarse-loamy |
| Naumburg (0.09) | Sandy |
| Rawsonville-Aquic Haplorthods variant-Skerry variant complex (2.74) | Coarse-loamy |
| Rawsonville–Aquic Haplorthods variant–Hogback complex (2.79) | Coarse-loamy |
| Rawsonville-Mundal association (3.44) | Coarse-loamy |
| Rock Outcrop (0.01) | |

TABLE 3.3. *(continued)*

| Soil Series (% area) | Particle size class[b] |
|---|---|
| Raynham variant (0.02) | Coarse-silty |
| Skerry variant–Aquic Haplorthods variant association (0.28) | Coarse-loamy |
| Sand (0.02) | Coarse-loamy |
| Skerry-Groveton-Madawaska complex (0.29) | Coarse-loamy |
| Skerry variant–Hermon variant association (0.06) | Coarse-loamy |
| Skerry (18.28) | Coarse-loamy |
| Skerry-Westbury variant association (5.59) | Coarse-loamy |
| Sunapee (0.97) | Coarse loamy |
| Skerry variant (1.09) | Coarse-loamy |
| Skerry-Waumbek association (0.56) | Coarse-loamy |
| Skerry variant-Wilmington association (0.31) | Coarse-loamy |
| Tunbridge-Becket association (2.37) | Coarse-loamy |
| Tunbridge-Aquic Haplorthods-Lyman complex (0.28) | Coarse-loamy |
| Rawsonville-Hogback-Rock Outcrop complex (10.57) | Coarse-loamy |
| Tunbridge–Aquic Haplorthods–Skerry complex (2.11) | Coarse-loamy |
| Tunbridge (0.15) | Coarse-loamy |
| Waumbek (0.43) | Sandy-skeletal |
| Waumbek variant (0.85) | Sandy-skeletal |
| Water (8.57) | |

*Source:* Soil survey completed by Dr. Robert Somers as part of his Ph.D. dissertation, SUNY College of Environmental Science and Forestry, Syracuse, N.Y., 1986.

[a] Organic soils shown in italics do not have a soil texture. Entries that do not have a particle size and are not italicized are soil classes within the series but are not mineral-soil based, so particle size is not meaningful.

[b] Particle size classes: Skeletal classes have > 35 percent rock fragments; sandy classes have a texture of sand or loamy sand; coarse loamy classes have 18–35 percent clay; loamy classes have < 35 percent clay; clayey classes have > 35 percent clay.

of the area and dissimilar soils should not exceed 25 percent. In reality, that level of accuracy is not often attained in complex forest landscapes.

One of the most interesting results of the Huntington Forest soil survey was the recognition of the high degree of variation within individual map units in this forested landscape. The variation in microtopography, owing to the presence of hummocks and hollows, sometimes results in a complex array of well- and poorly drained soils within the distance of 10–100 feet. After developing the soil map for Huntington Forest, Dr. Robert Somers of the State University of New York College of Environmental Science and Forestry examined soils on each of 5 transects located on Catlin and Goodnow Mountains, proceeding from the valley bottom to mountaintop. Plots were established every 200 feet along each transect, and 3 soil pits (50 feet apart) were examined along the contour at each plot (a total of 267 soil pits). Only 11 percent of the plots had all 3 soil pits along the contour classified into the same soils series. Forty-eight percent of the plots had three different soil series. Placed in the context of each of the map units, 66 percent of the plots along the contour had soils that were identified in the map unit. This work quantified the variability of soil types within map units on landscapes typical of much of the Adirondack region.

Diversity of soil conditions within map units is associated with species diversity. Sugar maple and American beech growing on elevated sites in these landscapes exhibit vigorous growth. Species such as yellow birch and red maple, more tolerant of excess soil moisture, grow vigorously on the adjacent somewhat poorly drained soils in the local hollows in the same map unit. Consequently, productivity of these forests, as indicated by production of wood, is relatively high. Productivity drops off significantly for the very poorly drained soils in the lower landscape positions and for the thin, excessively well drained soils on the ridge tops. Ecosystem function is strongly influenced by soil properties.

In summary, biological activity is constrained by the fluxes of energy, water, and gases through the soil system. Those fluxes are effectively regulated by pore-size distribution. The size and con-figuration of the pores determine water storage capacity and rate of movement, which directly affects soil aeration. The most productive soils (from the perspective of plant roots) are medium textured, deep, and well to moderately well drained without an excess of coarse fragments. As a result of glacial dynamics, those types of soils are generally confined to the valleys in the Adirondack region. Con-sequently, agricultural production in the Adirondacks is restricted to the valleys because of the combination of better soil conditions and more favorable climate. Soil and air temperatures decrease with increasing elevation, and exposure to wind and ice increases, which effectively reduces growing season length for agricultural crops.

# 4

## Upland Forests of the Adirondacks

*Reflections of Soils and a Record of Disturbance*

CHARLES D. CANHAM

Upland forests are the fabric of the Adirondack landscape. They occupy a broad spectrum of terrestrial environments and vary widely in composition, structure, and function. With the exception of the Champlain Valley, current forest cover within the Adirondack Park is remarkably similar to levels that occurred prior to European settlement, about 85 percent of the landscape. Although European settlement profoundly affected the Adirondack forests, they have largely recovered. Today, the Adirondack region represents one of the world's most important temperate deciduous forests.

Naming forest types has been a quagmire for forest ecologists for over seventy years. The most common names applied to the temperate forests of eastern North America—"temperate deciduous forests" or the closely related "temperate broad-leaved forest"—reflect the importance of deciduous species of angiosperms, but they do not do justice to the importance of evergreen species of conifers. Over the much broader sweep of evolutionary time, the conifers have gradually given way to the evolution of angiosperms. In temperate regions with distinct cold seasons, the angiosperms are typically deciduous. Evolutionary biologists still debate the reasons for the apparent competitive displacement of conifers by angiosperms, but it is clear that in broad terms, conifers have been displaced from the most productive soils and environments by angiosperms and are now most abundant in cold regions and on infertile soils that are excessively dry or wet.

The Adirondack Mountains display this evolutionary drama in microcosm. The high-elevation and least productive environments are dominated by spruce-fir forests. The sandiest soils, and therefore the most drought prone, infertile, and fire prone, are typically dominated by white, red, or jack pine. The particular species depends on fire frequency and severity. The more fertile soils support the deciduous angiosperms, or what we call hardwoods. As is true for many regions, the most fertile soils within the park were the ones converted most thoroughly to agriculture, but the evidence from presettlement records indicates dominance by hardwood forests. The agriculture of the Lake Champlain valley is an example of fertile soils that once supported a hardwood forest.

Conifers may have been more abundant in presettlement times than is apparent from looking at the canopies of Adirondack forests today. Dr. Ed Ketchledge, who spent a career as a forest ecologist at the State University of New York College of Environmental Science and Forestry, is among the most perceptive observers of old-growth forest. When I asked him to help me locate old-growth forests in the park many years ago, he pointed out that one of the easiest ways to identify stands without a history of logging was to look at an aerial photograph. When taken in winter, the photos of old-growth stands had the distinctive salt-and-pepper look of mixtures of conifers and hardwoods. The conifers were the first species to be harvested, in part because they could be floated down rivers more easily than hardwoods. Until railroads were available, the hardwoods were largely spared. It is likely that conifers are still under-represented in the canopies of many forests within the park, even after 100 years. A walk through the often dense understories of balsam fir and red spruce in Adirondack forests would suggest that natural regeneration will rectify this disparity soon.

The notion of the presettlement forest as a benchmark for natural conditions is ubiquitous in the American conservation movement. There are many reasons to question the value of the concept as a target for conservation. It implicitly assumes that Native Americans had little impact on the forested landscape, despite much evidence to the contrary. It also ignores the well-documented and constant change in forest composition that has occurred over the past 13,000 years following the retreat of the Pleistocene glaciers and the recolonization of the landscape by plants and animals. Nonetheless, providing a sketch of the nature of Adirondack forests prior to the arrival of European trappers, loggers, and farmers allows us to document the nature and extent of the changes wrought by humans over the past 300 years.

At the landscape scale, variation in both bedrock geology and surface deposits of glacial till and outwash gave rise to gradients in soil fertility and moisture that translated into predictable differences in forest composition and structure. Among the late successional shade-tolerant trees, sugar maple was most abundant on higher pH (less acidic) and higher fertility soils. Beech was most abundant on the more ubiquitous acidic and relatively infertile soils derived from granitic till. The two late successional conifers, eastern hemlock and red spruce, also tended to segregate along soil drainage and fertility gradients. The early and mid-successional tree species show similar degrees of niche differentiation, as do forest understory species.

Superimposed on these soil gradients was a complex mosaic of stand ages, structures, and compositions reflecting patterns of natural disturbance. The cultural memory of the widespread fires in the northern Adirondacks during the early 1900s is still strong in the region, but there is ample reason to conclude that those fires were the product of the extensive logging and human sources of ignition from railroads that characterized that period. Fire was clearly a feature of the presettlement landscape but appears to have been restricted to the most drought-prone soils. Fire was almost certainly responsible for the presettlement white pine forests on coarse-textured eskers and sandy outwash soils throughout the park, but it is unlikely that fire was common in the more typical upland forests.

Although fires may have been localized disturbances in the presettlement landscape, severe windstorms were likely to have been the dominant natural disturbance over much of the park. The region is subject to extreme winds from a number of distinctly different sources, each with a characteristic signature in terms of spatial scale and intensity. Tornadoes and thunderstorm downbursts can create strong but localized disturbance. At the other end of the spectrum of sheer size, hurricanes and high winds associated with more generic severe low-pressure systems appear to have periodically blanketed large swaths of the park. Wind damage is highly variable in the Adirondacks, not just because of the variable nature of storms, but also because of the effects of the topography and forest structure of the region. The windstorms of 1950 and 1995 in the western Adirondacks provide a vivid example of the spatial scale and potential degree of damage that can occur in these storms.

For the Adirondacks, there is no rigorous analysis of the pre-settlement frequency of windstorms. However, such studies have been done both east (Maine) and west (Wisconsin) of the park. We can infer that the average interval between catastrophic storms that killed nearly all of the trees at any one location exceeded 1,000 years in the Adirondacks. Far more common were storms of intermediate severity that selectively snapped off or uprooted some fraction of the canopy trees in a stand. These return with a frequency of one for every 10 to 100 years.

Severe winds have fundamentally different effects on forest dynamics than do fires. While fires often reset successional dynamics by creating ample opportunities for colonization by pioneer and shade-intolerant tree species such as aspen and paper birch, even the most severe winds generally remove just the canopy trees, while sparing many understory seedlings and saplings. In this case, wind disturbance can actually accelerate succession by releasing the understory of shade-tolerant species. Nonetheless, it is clear that wind disturbance has historically been an important contributor to the diversity of Adirondack forests by providing opportunities for regeneration by tree species of intermediate shade tolerance such as white ash and black cherry. The paper birches that many associate with the modern Adirondack forest landscape are largely a human artifact of the widespread postlogging fires of the early 1900s. In contrast, it is likely that yellow birch—the most shade tolerant of the

Adirondack birch species—was the most common birch in the pre-settlement landscape. It is unmatched among Adirondack tree species in its ability to withstand severe windstorms and then disperse seeds to exploit the soil disturbance and high light levels present in the aftermath of a storm.

Both the 1950 and 1995 storms stirred a great deal of debate over the pros and cons of salvage logging. There are clearly social and economic aspects to the debate, but the ecological issues are clear. The soil disturbance and woody debris left by a storm represent important resources for a wide range of plant and animal species. Wind-throw was and is an important natural process in the Adirondack landscape and contributes to the overall diversity of plant and animal species in the park.

This portrait of Adirondack forests 300 years ago captures just one snapshot in the waxing and waning of tree species abundance since the retreat of the Pleistocene glaciers approximately 13,000 years ago. Much of that variation is attributed to post-Pleistocene climate change, with periods even within the past 1,000 years that were substantially warmer (the Medieval Warm Period, about 900–1300 AD) or colder (the Little Ice Age, about 1350–1850 AD) than conditions 150 years ago. As global temperatures began to rise at the end of the Pleistocene era, and the glaciers began to recede from the Adirondacks, the region paradoxically entered a relatively cold period that lasted over 1,000 years (the Younger Dryas period). The arctic tundra communities present immediately following the retreat of the glaciers gave way during this period to spruce forests. The end of the Younger Dryas period saw a remarkably rapid rise in temperature (on a timescale of several decades), and a correspondingly rapid replacement of spruce forests by pine (on a timescale of a century or so).

One of the most dramatic events recorded in pollen samples from lake sediment cores throughout the northeastern United States is the nearly synchronous and abrupt decline in the abundance of hemlock about 4,800 years ago. There is no obvious climatic cause, so the decline is usually attributed to the appearance of a novel pest or pathogen. Indeed, remains of a hemlock-feeding insect can be found in lake sediments from that period. Prior to European arrival, this is the only known case of such an abrupt and regional decline in the abundance of a native tree species during the past 10,000 years of Adirondack forest history. Hemlock needed more than 1,000 years to recover its previous abundance, perhaps a telltale sign of time needed for recovery of the many other native tree species that have been decimated by pests and pathogens introduced by humans during the past 100 years.

One of the most salient features of the modern ecological history of the Adirondack Park is the resilience of its forests. The eastern United States as a whole has seen a remarkable increase in total forest cover over the past 100 years, as the early waves of intensive logging and agriculture swept westward and forests have reclaimed clear-cuts and abandoned agricultural lands. In many parts of the eastern United States, however, the resurgence in total forest cover masks striking differences between the new forests and presettlement conditions. While the trees may have returned, postagricultural forests are often lack many other taxa, particularly native forest wildflowers.

In many regions south of the Adirondacks, presettlement fires (particularly ground fires) appear to have been instrumental in maintaining dominance by species of oaks and hickories. Fire suppression during the past century is likely to have been one of the major reasons the oaks have given way to more fire-sensitive species, particularly red maple and sugar maple. As a result, the mixes of tree species in forests that have reclaimed old clear-cuts and abandoned farmlands often bear very little resemblance to presettlement forests.

Adirondack forests, in contrast, have tended to avoid these fates. The Adirondacks had much less clearing for agriculture than many regions of the eastern United States, and Adirondack logging practices appear to have had far less impact than agriculture on long-term biodiversity. Fire suppression in the park has generally eliminated a human-induced disturbance rather than an important natural ecological process. For all of these reasons, the current

forested landscape of the Adirondacks is probably closer to presettlement conditions than any other major forest region of the eastern
United States. There seems little doubt that the region has the largest expanses of old-growth forest of any region in the eastern United
States, and it is quite likely that it has the largest remaining tracts of
old-growth temperate deciduous forest left anywhere in the world.

The old-growth forests owe their continued existence to the
Forest Preserve and Article 14 of the New York State Constitution,
discussed at length in part two of this book. They provide distinctive habitat for many species but are probably most notable simply
because human activities have made them so rare in other parts of
the world. It is worth remembering, however, that in presettlement
times, old-growth forests dominated the Adirondack landscape, and
areas recently disturbed by wind or fire would have been considered
diversity hot spots, home to many early successional plant species
and critical habitat for many animal species.

The list of current threats to Adirondack forests is quite long,
and by and large the threats originate outside the Blue Line. They
are typically not the result of deliberate actions such as logging or
clearing for development. Rather, they are the inadvertent impacts
of the dramatically accelerating pace of global change driven by
human activities. Their cumulative effect has been continued degradation of the structure and function of Adirondack forests. Some
of the threats can be addressed at a local and regional scale, but
others require national and international efforts. Anyone who studies the ecology of the Adirondacks will have their own ranking of
the threats, but the top four on my list are (in order of increasing
concern): invasive plant species, air pollution, introduced pests and
pathogens, and climate change.

## Invasive Species

By national or global standards, it might seem anomalous to list
invasive plants as a major concern within the Adirondack Park. By
comparison with many other parts of the country, the upland forests
of the park have remarkably few invasive species of either plants or

animals. This relative lack is in contrast to aquatic ecosystems within the park, where introduced plants and animals are a mounting concern. The park is blessed with a remarkably sparse road network, and transportation corridors are notorious as avenues of invasion by exotic plant species. Once an invasive species becomes widely established, control options generally range from exorbitantly expensive to impossible. However, it is precisely because of the relatively "invasive-free" status of Adirondack forests that I consider invasive plants an important issue for the park. Unlike many regions of the country where invasive species have become an overwhelming problem, the park has a good chance of controlling this threat, through vigilance and diligence by both state agencies and NGOs.

## Air Pollution

While the local economy of the park generates some amount of homegrown air pollution, the park has the misfortune of being located downwind from one of the continent's major industrial regions. Concern about apparent "forest decline" throughout the northeastern United States, beginning in the mid-1970s, led to an immense amount of research on the potential effects of air pollution on Adirondack forests. It is clear that the cocktail of pollutants to which Adirondack forests are or were exposed can have complex, interacting effects on both plant performance and ecosystem function. For example, acid deposition leads to soil acidification and can deplete essential nutrients such as calcium from Adirondack soils. The decline in calcium availability appears to be particularly critical for the growth and survival of young sugar maple trees. Nitric acid is a major component of acid deposition and continues largely unabated, unlike sulfuric acid loading, which has declined in recent years because of the effects of the Clean Air Act amendments of 1990. Nitric acid contributes to both acidification and nitrogen loading. When nitrogen is supplied to terrestrial ecosystems in excess of their demand for that nutrient, the ecosystems eventually become saturated with nitrogen, with a host of cascading and generally detrimental changes in ecosystem function.

One of the most worrisome consequences of nitrogen saturation in the Adirondacks is an apparent link to the prevalence of a major insect pest and pathogen complex, beech bark disease. Research in the western part of the park has shown that the disease is more severe in old-growth forests than in second-growth forests. This increased severity is linked to the greater nitrogen saturation of the old-growth stands, which did not need nitrogen fertilization, unlike the second-growth stands, where logging and burning depleted stocks of nitrogen from the ecosystem, allowing the forest to take up the input coming in from air pollution. Nitrogen pollution is a precursor to the formation of ozone, and high-elevation forests of the park appear to be exposed to particularly high levels of ozone, with a host of detrimental physiological effects on trees.

There is no question that important strides have been made in reducing levels of critical air pollutants affecting Adirondack forests. However, it is equally indisputable that current levels of deposition continue to pose a significant threat to the forests, and arguably an even greater threat to aquatic ecosystems. Recent studies suggest widespread mercury contamination of both terrestrial and aquatic ecosystems within the park. The direct effects of mercury toxicity will be manifested in animals rather than plants, but with the potential for cascading changes in ecosystem structure and function.

## Introduced Pests and Pathogens

Although land clearing has been perhaps the most visible transformation of the forested landscape of eastern North America, many ecologists would argue that insect pests and pathogens have produced the most profound changes in eastern forests over the past century. The litany is long and almost too depressing to recite: chestnut blight, Dutch elm disease, beech bark disease, and the hemlock woolly adelgid have all caused major, long-term changes in the abundance of native tree species in eastern forests. Of these, beech bark disease has had the most devastating impact within the Adirondack Park. Other pests and pathogens such as the emerald ash borer have not reached the park but appear poised to do so.

There is every reason to believe that new pests and pathogens will continue to be introduced, largely as an inadvertent consequence of human commerce. There is also good reason to be concerned that climate change will allow the northward spread of pests and pathogens that were previously limited by low winter temperatures. Because trees represent such a major component of the structure of a forest, and because different species of trees can have very different effects on ecosystem function and habitat quality, declines in the abundance of native tree species have cascading effects on a host of other plant and animal species. Responding to the threat posed by pests and pathogens is particularly problematic within the park, where the strict legal protection of Forest Preserve lands will have to be taken into account.

### Climate Change

There seems little question that climate change poses the greatest long-term threat to Adirondack forests. Current models of climate change over the next 50 years predict conditions in the Adirondacks that would be too warm to support forests of sugar maple, beech, hemlock, and red spruce. Although analyses have not been done for all of the other plants and animals that live in forests dominated by those species, it is fair to assume that many of them would be displaced, too. Presumably these species would be replaced by new species migrating northward, but there is growing evidence that tree species are not capable of migrating as fast as the climate change would dictate. The exact nature and pace of the ecological transformations will be influenced by a host of highly unpredictable events, particularly processes like the emergence of new pests and pathogens or changes in the frequency of fire or storms with severe winds that kill adults of existing tree species and create opportunities for displacement by new colonists.

Change has been a constant feature of the Adirondack landscape since the retreat of the glaciers 13,000 years ago, but the pace of change that is likely under current scenarios is so rapid relative to the response times of forest ecosystems that it seems inevitable that there will be significant disruptions to Adirondack species and eco-systems, and to the services that they provide us. Given the inherent inertia in the earth's climate system, some degree of disruption due to climate change seems inevitable even if dramatic measures to reduce greenhouse gas emissions are implemented today. For 200 years we have been transforming the forests of the Adirondacks, often inadvertently. The challenge in the next 50 years is likely to be to find ways to mitigate the effects on the Adirondack forests of our pervasive changes to the global environment.

## Suggested Reading

Jackson, S. T., and D. R. Whitehead. 1991. "Holocene Vegetation Patterns in the Adirondack Mountains." *Ecology* 72 (1991): 641–53.

Jenkins, J., and A. Keal. *The Adirondack Atlas: A Geographic Portrait of the Adirondack Park.* Syracuse: Syracuse Univ. Press, 2004.

McMartin, B. *The Great Forest of the Adirondacks.* Utica, N.Y.: North Country Books, 1994.

Reschke, C. *Ecological Communities of New York State.* Albany: New York Natural Heritage Program, New York State Department of Environmental Conservation, 1990.

Woods, K. D., and C. V. Cogbill. "Upland Old-growth Forests of Adirondack Park, New York, USA." *Natural Areas Journal* 14 (1994): 241–57.

Ziegler, S. S. "Composition, Structure, and Disturbance History of Old-growth and Second-growth Forests in Adirondack Park, New York." *Physical Geography* 25 (2004): 152–69.

# 5

## Fish and Wildlife Communities of the Adirondacks

ROLAND W. KAYS AND ROBERT A. DANIELS

For millions of years Adirondack animal communities were determined solely by the physical environment and the rules of evolution. Only in the last four centuries, geologically a mere moment, has man sought to dominate these communities. As is evident in earlier chapters, the Adirondack Mountains have been swept clean by glaciers many times over the past 100 millennia, essentially giving the region a clean slate when the glaciers of the Wisconsinan period began to recede only 10,000 years ago. Thus, on a geologic timescale, all animals in the Adirondacks are relatively new immigrants. There has been little time for the evolution of specialized endemic species, although there are a few. New arrivals to this freshly thawed and uncovered earth have found a rough, rainy landscape—conditions good for animal life.

The glacial ice was replaced by tundra, then boreal forests, and finally the mixture of boreal and temperate forests we know today. Animals followed the plant communities. Today the mix of species mirrors the mixture of plant species, being midway in character between the temperate and boreal biomes. There are 55 mammal species occupying the Adirondack Park. Most of these are cosmopolitan eastern species found throughout the region, such as the American black bear, deer mouse, cinereus shrew, and big brown bat. The cold-climate and higher-elevation habitats encourage northern species, some of which reach their southernmost limits in the park, including the American marten and moose.

The same trends are seen in the park's birds, reptiles, amphibians, and fish. Most of the 197 bird species in the park are common to the forests across northeastern North America. The exceptions are the mountaintop specialist Bicknell's thrush and a suite of boreal birds that reach their southeastern limit in the park: spruce grouse, gray jay, and three-toed woodpecker. Eighteen amphibians are reported from the region, but only the mink frog is a species largely confined to the Adirondacks. All other species are widely distributed throughout northeastern North America. The situation for reptiles is similar. Nineteen species of reptiles are reported from the region, but all are found throughout the Northeast, even though many have a limited or disjunct distribution.

Although many wildlife species found suitable habitats in the region, the human species did not. In fact, the Adirondack Mountains first distinguished themselves in the eyes of humans as unfertile and inhospitable. Native Americans never established permanent settlements of any size in the area, preferring the more fertile surrounding lowlands. Likewise, European colonists were stymied by poor farming conditions. Despite exponential population growth throughout northeastern North America, the human population of the park has never exceeded 150,000 year-round residents (16/mi²), with little change over the last 70 years.[1]

Still, this region felt the hand of man. Despite its reputation for wildness, the makeup of the wildlife communities of the Adirondacks has been the direct product of human action for the last 200 years. Initially guided by accident and instinct, and later by government decree, the humans have been the major force directing animal life of this region, primarily for the purposes of exploitation. Despite this harsh treatment, most wildlife populations are stronger now than they have been in 150 years, excepting the extinct top predators and passenger pigeon. In contrast, most species of native fish have suffered declines during this period, even though a few favored species of native and exotic fish are artificially maintained through stocking. Four factors directed these dynamics in the past and continue to challenge those charged with their management today: land-use change, pollution, direct exploitation, and species introductions.

Land-use change is a catch-all term to describe the different ways humans try to make a living off the land, ranging from selective logging to farming to parking lots. Because the Adirondack region has never been heavily populated, the rate and scale of land-use change has been relatively minor and has involved relatively little pavement. This low rate of change has allowed animal populations to shift and recover from human insults and has allowed forests to recover (fig. 5.1).

Land-use change can affect different wildlife species in a variety of ways. The replacement of Adirondack forests with regenerating clear-cuts, farm fields, roads, and hamlets will drive some wildlife out, have little effect on some species, and help others move into an area for the first time. Native species adapted to wilderness areas

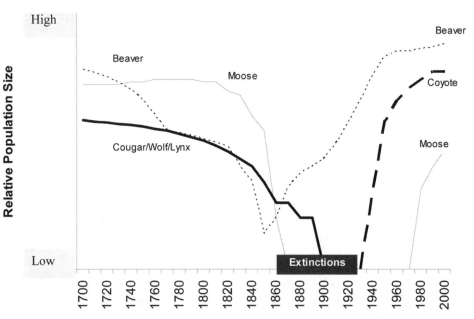

5.1. Broad trends for the Adirondack population size of seven wildlife species. Primary references used were DeKay 1842, Merriam 1884, Kogut 1990, Terrie 1993, Jenkins and Keal 2004, and recent harvest records and discussions with staff at the New York State Department of Environmental Conservation.

are typically those that decline, while exotic species or others that have adapted to take advantage of towns and agriculture are those that increase. The biological integrity of an area (measured by the presence of native birds) is affected by the increased road density associated with development, but not by different strategies of logging.[2] Although this measurement is specific to birds, the pattern is generally true for all wildlife and fish groups. Mosaics of different forest types and ages can sustain healthy natural communities, while human development can have big impacts at its lowest level, even a single road through the middle of nowhere.

Although natural communities can retain their integrity in the face of forest management, some individual species notice and respond to these changes. Over the past 200 years, the cutting of the Adirondack forest has certainly had a negative impact on other forest-dependent species. That appears to be the case for spruce grouse, which has yet to recover from a population crash at the end of the 1800s. When its preferred coniferous trees were targeted by timber companies, spruce grouse populations declined rapidly. Although some of this habitat has recently recovered, many of their previous population centers remain flooded (e.g., Lows Lake, Stillwater Reservoir, Spruce Grouse Pond). Unfortunately, even apparently good habitat has not been recolonized in the last few decades, possibly because spruce grouse do not typically travel much and therefore are slow to discover new habitat.

Compared to logging, the conversion of forests to pavement and cities is more difficult for animals. The spread of 5,000 miles of paved roads and houses over the natural landscape is a concern. On one hand, the large lots (5–40 acres) typical of Adirondack houses are usually covered mostly with forests; on the other hand, many wildlife species could still be affected by this level of human disturbance. Although such disturbance clearly can affect animal communities, there are few hard data to evaluate the specific threat to different wildlife species.

Although land-use change is highly visible, invisible pollutants have had equally important effects on the region's animals since the first tannery and mill were constructed in the early decades of the nineteenth century. The most famous modern example of this problem is the effects of the acidification of Adirondack waters on fish, and the cascade effect this loss of fish has had on other wildlife. Declines in game fish, indeed the complete loss of fisheries in several lakes, became obvious in the late 1960s, but records of fish declines date back to the 1940s in some lakes. By the 1970s acid deposition was identified as the cause of many fish declines. Indeed, one study determined that 8 percent of 120 lakes were fishless because of acid rain.

Pollution from coal plants and incinerators also was deposited in the wildest sections of the Adirondacks by snow, rain, and dust. Mercury, in particular, can be dangerous even at relatively low levels. Levels are high enough in the Adirondacks that the New York State Department of Health has implemented a limited ban on human consumption of fish from all Adirondack waters. Unfortunately, some animals do not have the option of skipping a fish dinner, and they are being poisoned. Loons primarily eat fish and are suffering the effects of decreased reproductive success and low survival across New England. In the Adirondacks, 17 percent of 93 loons tested between 1998 and 2000 had dangerously high mercury levels.[3]

Distant factories have not been the only source of pollutants affecting wildlife and fish within the park. In the 1960s pesticides, especially DDT, took their toll on predatory birds and fish around the country, leading to widespread declines in falcon, osprey, eagle, and loon populations. The effect of DDT is indirect. It accumulates in the bodies of predators as they consume contaminated prey, and although adult birds can survive high levels of DDT in their body, relatively low levels have serious effects on their eggs. Before the use of DDT the park hosted at least 30 pairs of nesting bald eagles, 18 pairs of peregrine falcons, and 12 pairs of golden eagles.[4] By the 1970s all were extirpated. The banning of DDT and careful reintroductions in the 1980s and 1990s returned bald eagles and peregrine falcons to the park.

The third factor, human exploitation of wildlife, has produced the most dramatic ups and downs. Humans have always exploited the fish and wildlife of the Adirondacks, but Native American populations were never large, and their hunting and fishing probably had relatively little impact on Adirondack species. European fur trappers were the first to exploit wildlife in the Adirondacks as a source of cash. The first trappers entered the mountains in the early 1600s, targeting traditional furbearers, beaver, fisher, and marten, as well as deer and moose for meat and skins. By the end of the century deer, moose, and beaver were virtually eliminated from most of the state, surviving only in remote corners of the Adirondacks.

White-tailed deer brought over-exploitation to the attention of government. They were the first New York species to be managed by the state, with the implementation of a deer-hunting season in 1741. For the first 200 years these game laws were impossible to enforce and largely ignored. Declines in the Adirondack deer herd at the turn of the century produced the political pressure for increasing enforcement as well as respect for the laws. By 1910 the region was reputed to have the best game laws in the country and more deer than anytime in the last 100 years. Although the details of deer management still stir lively discussion, the tradition of respect for game laws has been passed on through generations of hunters. Modern deer populations are affected more by hard winters and limits of available browse than by direct exploitation.

These experiences with deer fluctuations taught hunters and wildlife managers the importance of implementing and respecting game management laws to keep enough wildlife around to continue hunting. Unfortunately, these lessons were learned too late for the five Adirondack mammals and one bird hunted to extinction in the area. It is not surprising that wolverines were the first to go. Their fur is prized for resisting frost, they are relatively easy to catch, and they naturally live at low densities and range over enormous areas. They were never common and are rarely mentioned in early anecdotal Adirondack literature. The first comprehensive account of the region's wildlife was published by DeKay in 1842,[5] and he was the last to mention the presence of wolverine, declaring them rare in districts north of Raquette Lake. Forty years later C. Hart Merriam could not find any hunters or trappers who had ever seen a wolverine in the Adirondacks.[6]

The second half of the nineteenth century was a bad time to be a large predator in the Adirondacks. Following on the heels of the wolverines, wolves, lynx, and cougar also were extirpated, with the last animals being killed in 1890, mid-1890s, and 1908, respectively. The threat of having man-eating beasts in the forests drove many communities to institute local bounties as early as 1811. Killing predators became a community service, and there was money, and political gain, to be had in their persecution. In the mid-1800s predator populations crashed hard and fast, but the fear and money remained. Even though there were probably only a few dozen of each of these species left in the park, the state joined the hype by offering bounties against them in 1871.[7] Most of the killing had already been done, and the state only paid 46 cougar and 45 wolf bounties over the next 11 years.

All furbearers in the Adirondacks were hunted or trapped, down to the smallest weasel. Luckily, these smaller species withstood the persecution long enough for wildlife managers to recognize their decline and regulate their harvest. Fisher, marten, otter, and beaver all declined in parallel to their larger cousins but never to regional extinction. Although fragmented and full of hunters and trappers, the forests within the Adirondacks were one of the only natural areas left at the turn of the twentieth century. Along with the remotest parts of Maine, these were the only places where most of these furbearers survived in the northeastern United States. A statewide ban on trapping, lasting from the 1930s to 1970s, allowed many of their populations to recover (fig. 5.1). Marten have not expanded past the core of the park, but otter and fisher are now expanding into areas well beyond the Adirondacks.

The extinction of large predators is not the end of their story in the Adirondacks. Today there is little fear of tooth and fang, and fewer chicken coops, and the trapping and hunting are well regulated to avoid overkill. Smaller carnivores thrive, and reintroduction for all large carnivores has been considered at one time or the other, although only attempted once (Canada lynx; see chapter 13). The idea of reintroducing wolves was raised again in the 1990s but then shelved because of sociological and biological uncertainties.[8] In the wake of wolf extinction coyotes colonized eastern North America, reaching the Adirondacks by way of Ontario between the 1930s and the 1950s.[9] Adirondack coyotes are larger than their western cousins and may be hybrids, having bred with wolves in Canada.[10] With wolf populations in the Great Lakes region increasing, and small populations surviving nearby in Ontario, some believe that full-sized wolves will find their own way to the Adirondacks.

Hans Kruuk suggests that the more dangerous an animal is, the more humans are fascinated by it and attracted to it.[11] That idea helps explain the abundance of cougar (also called mountain lion or puma) sightings in the Adirondacks over the last 50 years. This secretive, solitary hunter was persecuted with the same fervor as wolves, with the last animal shot near Elk Lake in 1908. Despite its nearly 100-year absence from the state, many New Yorkers are still fascinated by this lion, and sightings are reported every year. However, there is no evidence of a breeding population, no physical evidence from nearly a century worth of hunters and speeding cars. Most sightings are probably bobcats or released pet cougars. Indeed, the only two cougars turned into the state were escaped domestic animals.[12]

Finally, the human intervention is evident in species introductions, and perhaps most apparent are the changes in fish assemblages in the Adirondack Park. A total of 92 species of fish are reported in the park, including the species found in Lake Champlain and its low-elevation tributaries.[13] Approximately half of these species are present only in the two large lowland lakes and their tributaries (tables 5.1 and 5.2), but because these systems are not typical of the Adirondacks, we will confine our discussion to the species of the upland lakes and streams of the park.

The upland fish fauna is similar to that of surrounding areas. Only round whitefish, lake chub, and finescale dace are prevalent in the Adirondacks and largely absent from surrounding areas.[14] Still, even these species are widely distributed in northern North

TABLE 5.1. Stocking of fish by NYS Department of Environmental Conservation into lakes and streams of three counties in the Adirondack Park, 2004

| County | No. species stocked[a] | No. fish stocked | No. stocking events | No. bodies of water stocked |
|---|---|---|---|---|
| Essex | 2 native species | 143,490 | 137 | 119 |
| | 5 exotic species | 516,490 | 141 | 86 |
| | 2 hybrids | 2,590 | 3 | 3 |
| Hamilton | 2 native species | 193,890 | 126 | 123 |
| | 4 exotic species | 72,675 | 52 | 47 |
| | 2 hybrids | 15,000 | 2 | 2 |
| Warren | 2 native species | 45,060 | 41 | 41 |
| | 3 exotic species | 67,613 | 45 | 36 |

*Source:* Records reported by NYS Department of Environmental Conservation at *http://www.dec.state.ny.us/website/dfwmr/fish/foe4clst.html*

[a] Native species are brook and lake trout; exotic species include brown trout, Atlantic salmon, rainbow trout, muskellunge, northern pike, and walleye; hybrids are tiger muskellunge and splake.

America. Round whitefish is the only species in the Adirondacks that is managed as an endangered fish.[15]

Historically, upland Adirondack waters contained the fewest number of species in the region. In total, there were few species within the park (i.e., low species richness) and there was little variation in species encountered between different sites within the park (i.e., low β-diversity or community richness). Native fishes entered upland areas after the retreat of the last glaciers, 5,000 to 10,000 years ago. The species with most generalized habitat requirements and better dispersal abilities were the ones that could best capitalize on new areas as glacial ice retreated. Mather[16] recorded only 25 species in 1890 and many were exotic species. The native fauna of the upland sites he surveyed comprised only 17 species. Mather's survey was cursory and relied heavily on anecdotal information, but he argued that common species, like yellow perch, golden

TABLE 5.2. **Summary of fishes of the Adirondack region of New York**

| | Moore 1929[a] | Mather 1890[b] | Bean 1902[c] | Moore 1930, 1932–35[a] | George 1980[d] | Smith 1985[e] | Gallagher and Baker 1990[f] | Carlson and Daniels 2004[g] |
|---|---|---|---|---|---|---|---|---|
| Total taxa | 87 | 25 | 11 | 53 | 58 | 49 | 45 | 55 |
| Total native taxa | 75 | 17 | 7 | 30 | 26 | 25 | 24 | 30 |
| Total exotic taxa | 12 | 8 | 4 | 23 | 32 | 24 | 21 | 25 |
| Percentage exotic | 13.8 | 32.0 | 36.4 | 43.4 | 55.2 | 49.0 | 46.7 | 54.5 |

*Sources:* Some data are from published reports dating from 1890:

[a] E. Moore, Biological surveys of the Champlain (1929), Oswegatchie and Black River systems (1931), Upper Hudson Watershed (1932), Raquette Watershed (1933), and Mohawk-Hudson Watershed (1934), supplements to the annual reports of the New York State Conservation Department (Albany: NYS Conservation Dept., 1930–35).

[b] F. Mather, "Adirondack Fish." Supplement to the 18th Report of the Commissioners of Fisheries (Albany: NYS Conservation Dept., 1890).

[c] T. H. Bean, *Catalogue of the Fishes of New York* (Albany: NYS Museum Bulletin 60, 1903).

[d] C. J. George, *The Fishes of the Adirondack Park*, Lake Monograph Program (Albany: NYS Dept. of Environmental Conservation, 1981).

[e] C. L. Smith, *The Inland Fishes of New York State* (Albany: NYS Dept. of Environmental Conservation, 1985).

[f] J. Gallagher and J. Baker. "Current Status of Fish Communities in Adirondack Lakes," In *Adirondack Lakes Survey: An Interpretive Analysis of Fish Communities and Water Chemistry, 1984–87, 3–11–3–48* (Ray Brook, N.Y.: Adirondack Lake Survey Corp., 1990).

[g] D. M. Carlson and R. A. Daniels, "Status of Fishes in New York: Increases, Declines, and Homogenization of Watersheds," *American Midland Naturalist* 152 (2004).

shiner, and fallfish, were introduced into the upland areas of the park even though they are native to the lowlands waters of the Adirondack watersheds. Stocking of lakes, in particular, became a cottage industry in the middle of the nineteenth century. For example, high-elevation lakes supported assemblages that included minnows, suckers, sunfish, and bullheads, but no trout, conditions that have been observed elsewhere.[17] Because stocking of fish in the nineteenth century was largely unreported and often unsanctioned, the presence of fish, even trout, in high elevation lakes above barriers, should not be taken as a certain indication that the population is native.

Government stocking programs began by 1870, and stocking was underway in earnest by the 1880s and 1890s.[18] Annual reports of the Fisheries, Game, and Forest Commission published lists of localities where fish were stocked. By the 1930s other non-native species were routinely stocked into the waters of the park, including northern pike, Atlantic salmon, kokanee, and largemouth and smallmouth bass.[19] Stocking remains an important part of the management program in the Adirondacks today, with a variety of species stocked throughout the Adirondacks each year. Stocking has increased the species richness of the park but has had little effect on increasing the diversity of fish communities in the region as a whole. Rather, stocking has homogenized the fish fauna across the park.

The motive of these incredible stocking efforts is to satisfy public demand for game species. In this goal, stocking has succeeded: the diversity, distribution, and abundance of game species within the park is higher now that at any point in history. Unfortunately, only two of the important games species in the park, brook and lake trout, are native to the Adirondacks. A third native species potentially important as a game fish is the round whitefish, and it is endangered. The downside of introducing species for exploitation is that it has completely changed fish assemblages throughout the Adirondacks in two different but related ways. First, the assemblages are artificial, often temporary, creations—species mixed and matched for the moment. Second, the new mix contains many exotic species.

Because several fish surveys have been conducted in New York over the last 80 years, we have the opportunity to compare fish assemblages in 436 Adirondack lakes sampled in the 1930s by the Department of Conservation[20] and again in the 1980s by the Adirondack Lake Survey Corporation.[21] The results are striking. In only 11 lakes were the fishes present in the 1980s the same as those present 50 years earlier. The assemblages in 62 percent of the lakes had more than a 70 percent change in species composition. In 87 lakes (20 percent), the changeover was complete; all species present in the 1930s were replaced by others by the 1980s. In 44 percent of the lakes, a change in species composition resulted from the loss of a native species. In 82 percent of the lakes, a change in composition resulted from the introduction of an exotic species. Obviously, many lakes lost native species while gaining one or more exotic species.

Exotic species had been reported from throughout the Adirondacks in the nineteenth century, which means that even when the lakes were first surveyed in the 1930s many assemblages were already compromised by the presence of exotic species. Another way to assess the engineering of fish assemblage in Adirondack lakes is to look at the percentage change in the number of exotic species across the 436 lakes surveyed. Only 13 percent of the lakes had no change in their exotic-species count in the half century between samples. The number of exotic fish increased in 61 percent of the lakes and declined in 26 percent. Clearly, the spread of exotic species has been promoted.

These raw numbers do not show the link that exists between the spread of exotic species and the decline in native species. Throughout the Northeast, the introduction of exotic predators, particularly largemouth bass and northern pike, has led to a rapid decline in numbers of native minnows and other species in those lakes.[22] Despite knowing that the introduction of exotic predators has a negative impact on local biodiversity, there has been little effort to curb the desire to introduce exotic game fish. Except in the case of smallmouth bass and walleye, the percentage of Adirondack lakes with game fish present has remained relatively constant from the 1930s to 1980s (table 5.3).

TABLE 5.3. Percentage of lakes with game fish present

| Game fish species[a] | 1930s | 1980s |
|---|---|---|
| *Esox lucius,* **northern pike** | 13.0 | 9.3 |
| *Esox masquinongy,* **muskellunge** | 2.0 | 0.2 |
| *Esox niger,* **chain pickerel** | 2.5 | 4.4 |
| *Coregonus artedi,* cisco | 0.5 | 0.4 |
| *Coregonus clupeaformis,* lake whitefish | 8 | 1.2 |
| *Oncorhynchus mykiss,* **rainbow trout** | 2 | 2.8 |
| *Prosopium cylindraceum,* round whitefish | 3.5 | 0.4 |
| *Salmo salar,* **Atlantic salmon** | 4 | 1.2 |
| *Salmo trutta,* **brown trout** | 4.5 | 5.5 |
| *Salvelinus fontinalis,* brook trout | 60.0 | 51.6 |
| *Salvelinus namaycush,* lake trout | 20.0 | 4.7 |
| *Micropterus dolomieu,* **smallmouth bass** | 39.5 | 8.7 |
| *Micropterus salmoides,* **largemouth bass** | 9.5 | 10.0 |
| *Pomoxis nigromaculatus,* **black crappie** | 1.0 | 1.0 |
| *Perca flavescens,* **yellow perch** | 32.5 | 30.8 |
| *Sander canadensis,* sauger | 0.5 | |
| *Sander vitreum vitreum,* **walleye** | 9.0 | 1.1 |

*Source:* Data from the 1930s are based on the 200 lakes sampled in Warren, Essex, and Hamilton Counties during the Watershed Surveys of the Upper Hudson, Raquette, and Lake Champlain. Data from the 1980s are from surveys of the same lakes conducted by the Adirondack Lake Survey Corporation.

[a] Species in bold are exotic to the upland areas of the Adirondack Park.

In another way, stocking programs have also promoted protection of biodiversity. These programs are not completely blind to fish origins, and they have been extremely important in preserving the nine remaining native Adirondack strains of heritage brook trout.[23] This active management program includes hatchery and stocking components as well as habitat preservation of lakes known to harbor these strains. This program has successfully preserved populations, in part by extending their ranges into non-native lakes. Of course, the widespread stocking of brook trout in the nineteenth and early twentieth centuries is the reason that there are only nine heritage brook trout stocks remaining—any others that might have existed were lost to competition or interbreeding caused by careless stocking.

Preservation of the threatened round whitefish in Adirondack waters is a second example of the potential value of stocking programs. Round whitefish, abundant during the 1880s, showed a dramatic decline late in the nineteenth century. By 1910 it was present in only 25 lakes and is confirmed in only seven lakes today.[24] For round whitefish, over-harvesting, toxic poisoning, habitat loss, and the introduction of exotic species all help explain the declines. The species has recently been introduced into five lakes to assess its ability to establish itself. Like the heritage strains of brook trout, round whitefish declined in the park because of historic efforts to develop new populations of exotic game fish. Ironically, both are being protected by the same program that almost destroyed them—stocking.

Despite the large wilderness areas, human activities have had major effects on Adirondack biodiversity over the last 200 years. By physically altering habitats, introducing toxic substances, exploiting natural populations, and introducing exotic species, human activity has accelerated biological change throughout the region. In short, humans manage all aspects of the park, even large Forever Wild areas. Initially the forces behind our impacts were unregulated, and many species fell to the tragedy of the commons. However, the modern Adirondack Park is governed by rules, and these have saved the fish and wildlife of the region from some of the worst problems faced by other species around the world. The extraordinary result is that changes in land use are not now pushing many Adirondack species to extinction. This is astonishing because six of the top ten causes for endangered species in North America are related to changes in land use.[25]

In the past 200 years, the most tremendous forces affecting Adirondack fish and wildlife have been those associated with direct exploitation. Hunting and trapping initially drove a number of species to local extinction, eventual harvest restrictions let surviving species recover, and over 130 years of fish stocking have radically altered almost every fish community in the park. Although fish and wildlife are apparently managed for the same purpose, exploitation by sportsmen, the results of this management has had strikingly different effects on terrestrial and aquatic systems.

On land, wildlife managers have restricted harvests of rare species to allow their populations to recover naturally. In some cases they have supplemented the populations of native wildlife with introductions (e.g., beaver), but introductions of exotic species have been few and have had little impact. The results not only are attractive to sportsmen, but also represent healthy native wildlife communities. Into the lakes and rivers of the Adirondacks fisheries managers and have stocked fish from dozens of species, most of which were not native to the park. The result is fish communities made up of exotic game fishes that meet the needs of many anglers, but at a great cost to native biodiversity.

Unfortunately, it often takes a great tragedy to change conservation policy. The Adirondack Park itself was created as a response to the incredible destructions of forests across the rest of the Northeast at the end of the 1800s. Our country's pollution crisis was finally recognized when Rachel Carson's *Silent Spring* shocked the world in 1962 by highlighting the damage that had already been done.[26] The tragic crash of over-harvested wildlife populations at the turn of the nineteenth century led to the first effective game management laws in the country. These laws saved dwindling populations (e.g., beaver, fisher) from extinction and set the stage for a remarkable recovery that produced the secure populations of bear, deer, moose, and other species that symbolize the Adirondack region today. Government-funded fish stocking continues today across the Adirondacks, even in Forever Wild areas. To hard-line conservationists, the loss of native aquatic biodiversity and scrambling of communities are a tragedy that deserves recognition and should be halted immediately. To sportsman the spread of game fish across the region is a blessing, but even anglers recognize that the stocking programs require constant monitoring and funding. Will this issue rise to the surface and change fisheries management policy? As the history of the Adirondacks shows, attitudes can be slow to change, but nature can recover if managers and the public recognize and respect a problem.

# 6

## Wildlife Exploitation in the Adirondacks

*From Beavers to Biodiversity*

WILLIAM F. PORTER

The exploitation of wildlife resources, like the exploitation of timber resources, was driven by economics. Wildlife populations of importance to Native Americans and European immigrants were those that were related to food, clothing, barter, or danger. The Adirondacks had them all, but for the most part, the region's populations were so low that they attracted little attention by Native Americans. Beaver populations estimated by some as in the millions, probably numbered fewer than 100,000. Deer populations were estimated at two to three per square mile of northern hardwood forest.[1] Deer are not well adapted to prolonged periods of deep snow, so the Adirondack region might have supported fewer than 25,000 deer. Moose are better adapted for deep snow and were probably more common than deer. Elk were not present in the Adirondacks, and neither were wild turkeys. The Adirondacks may have supported about 1,000 bears.[2]

Why were wildlife populations so meager? The answer lies with the forests of the region, and the infrequent disturbance of those forests. Moose, deer, elk, wild turkeys, and bears, species of particular importance to Native Americans, thrive in areas where young forest is common. The Adirondack Mountains were dominated by mature forests for long periods; lack of disturbance by fire and disease or insect outbreaks, and the low frequency of large-scale windstorms, meant that young forest was uncommon. These species also depended on nut and berry crops as food resources. The short growing season limited oaks and chestnuts to the periphery, so the region had only one important mast (nut) producer, American beech.

It is therefore not surprising that despite the fact that hundreds of thousands of Native Americans occupied the Mohawk, Champlain, and St. Lawrence Valleys when European explorers arrived in 1609, the Adirondack region was largely vacant and unused. The unreliability of finding sufficient game and the poor soils and short growing seasons for horticulture or agriculture made starvation too likely for Native Americans to see much point in living in the Adirondacks. Indeed, it is claimed by some that the name *Adirondack* originated as a derisive term applied by the Iroquois to their enemies among the Algonquians who hunted the region, and were commonly thought to eat the bark of trees out of necessity.

Beavers provided the first strong economic motive for Native Americans to begin using the region more heavily. The fur of beavers was highly valued by Europeans because of the qualities it brought to the manufacture of felt used in making hats. Advances in metallurgy of European manufacturing provided knives and hatchets highly valued by Native Americans. The demands on both sides of this equation drove one of the most dramatic exploitations of a wildlife resource in North American history. The region quickly became known as *Couchsachrage* to Native Americans—the beaver-hunting country. The Dutch, and later the British, arriving via the Hudson River to the south of the Adirondacks, allied with the Iroquois. The French arrived via the St. Lawrence to the north and allied themselves with Algonquin peoples. Together they exploited first the periphery and then the interior of the Adirondacks, and by the 1620s trading posts were well established in Beverwyck (later, Albany) and Montreal. With no regulation of the harvest, the beaver population was nearly eliminated from all but the most remote portions of the Adirondacks within about 30 years.[3] By 1650, trappers and traders were moving west beyond the Great Lakes.

The next wave of exploitation of wildlife arrived when the farmers, miners, and loggers entered the interior a century later. Wildlife surrounding each new locale was a source of food for men burning 4,000 calories a day. Market hunting to supply logging camps and mines took a rapid toll. Moose, described as abundant in 1840, were completely extirpated by 1861.[4] Cougars and wolves were not common through the eighteenth and nineteenth centuries because their primary prey of beaver was gone and deer were scarce. That left moose, and the wolf. Which wolf is still uncertain. Some taxonomists believe it was *Canis lycaon*,[5] which is a smaller wolf than the timber wolf, *Canis lupus*, the species that occurred in western North America. Nevertheless, both cougars and wolves were a threat to farmers' livestock, and bounties were levied for their removal. The last of these two species to inhabit the Adirondacks were killed in 1894 (cougars) and 1899 (wolves).[6]

Perceptions of the relatively infinite wildlife resources of the seventeenth and eighteenth centuries gave way to a growing realization of the exhaustibility of all wildlife in the nineteenth and early twentieth centuries. The recognition that wildlife populations were being harvested to the point of complete extirpation drove a demand for active management. Moose and beaver were reintroduced into the region, and a concerted effort was made to establish elk. Of these efforts, the restoration of the beaver was the only success. Adirondack beaver populations were never completely eliminated but had been reduced to just two known colonies by 1895. Beavers were translocated to the Adirondacks from Canada and from Yellowstone National Park, and from 1902 through 1909, 35 beavers were released. In less that 20 years, beaver populations had expanded to the point that foresters were expressing concern over the amount of timber being flooded. Regulated trapping began again in 1924.[7]

Efforts to restore moose began in earnest in 1900 with the release of five moose. In 1901, the New York State legislature authorized funds to support moose restoration and passed a law protecting moose from killing. In 1902, 15 moose were released near Uncas Station, west of Raquette Lake. Of these, several were killed illegally by hunters, others were killed in collisions with trains. No calves were born, and the project was deemed a failure in 1908. Retrospective analysis suggests that a parasite may have played a role, and by the 1950s biologists believed that the presence of the parasite precluded the restoration of the moose. This parasite, brainworm or *Parelaphostrongylus tenuis*, is known to occur in deer without causing death, but in moose it is fatal.

Moose populations began to grow in neighboring regions in concert with heavy logging of the forests during the 1970s and, contrary to expectations, were thriving in areas where deer and the parasite occurred. A reevaluation of the earlier studies of brainworm raised questions about the methods of the earlier studies and the role of brainworm as a major factor affecting moose populations. At the same time, young bull moose dispersing out of Vermont and Quebec were finding their way into the Adirondacks in increasing numbers. A plan was devised to translocate cow moose from Algonquin Park to supplement those that had come in on their own. A combination of economic and political challenges eventually killed the plan, but the moose kept coming on their own. Increasing reports of cows with calves prompted a regionwide survey in 1998 and 67 moose were tallied.

Introduction of elk was occurring about the same time as the initial releases of moose in 1900, but it followed a more aggressive path. Elk were released in several locations, but especially in the Raquette Lake area. A release of 20 elk resulted in successful reproduction. Releases continued until 1907, when there were an estimated 350 elk in the central Adirondacks. However, by 1910, elk numbers were declining, apparently because of illegal hunting, and they were largely gone by 1920.

Driving the interest in moose and elk was a dramatic natural increase in the deer population and a concomitant emergence of sport hunting as a serious recreational pursuit. Deer populations had been extirpated from all of New York except the Adirondacks. There, deer populations were expanding rapidly. Three factors drove this expansion. First was dramatic and widespread increase in food supply as a result of vast acreages of regenerating hardwoods created by logging and fires. Second, deer populations were living in an environment without their principal predators, wolves and cougars. Third, regulation of hunting beginning in 1912 limited the harvest to bucks only. While mortality among bucks was significant, the other half of the population was surviving without predation or harvest pressure. Furthermore, only a few males were necessary to breeding all of the females, so the reproduction continued unabated.

Winter proved to be the limiting factor for deer populations. Not well adapted to deep snow, deer migrated from their summer range to spend the winter in areas of low-lying stands of spruce and hemlock along river drainages. The spruce and hemlock acted as a blanket, providing a slightly warmer microclimate by reducing the wind and heat loss by the deer and by intercepting much of the snow before it reached the ground, allowing the wind enough time to blow the snow elsewhere. Unfortunately, the canopy also limited the amount of vegetation growth in the understory and so there was little food for deer in these wintering areas. Deer spent the summer accumulating fat reserves so that they could survive in these wintering areas. Most adult deer can accumulate fat reserves to meet their needs for more than 100 days. However, most fawns cannot accrue more than about 80 days of reserve. So, when winters were relatively short, deer survived and populations grew. Unfortunately, the Adirondack region is known for long, not short, winters.

Winter in the world of a deer is defined by the accumulation of 15 inches of snow on the ground because at that depth travel becomes exceedingly costly. Interestingly, the snowpack in much of the Adirondacks diminishes with regularity about April 1, and deer begin to return to their summer range. Counting back from April 1, 80 days means that if 15 inches of snow accumulates on January 10, then deer are on winter range for exactly 80 days. In average winters, snow depths reach 15 inches or more by the end of December. That means that most fawns do not survive the average winter. Deer populations can only expand if fawns survive, and that necessitates a milder than normal winter. Records show that severe winters caused heavy losses in 1892–93, 1894–95, 1903–4. These declines spurred action to conserve deer population through shortening hunting seasons and developing winter feeding programs. Mild winters from 1905–6 through 1909–10 allowed growth, a severe winter in 1910–11 caused extensive mortality, and then 15 years of mild and average winters allowed expansion of the population. From the perspective of a deer, during the twentieth century one or two winters in ten have been mild, and three to four in ten have been severe.[8]

In the absence of substantial deer populations in the remainder of the state until the mid–twentieth century, the Adirondacks became the traditional destination for deer hunters. Beginning in 1954, the Fish and Game Commission began experimenting with regulated harvest of deer of either sex. However, deer populations in the region proved unable to sustain any significant harvest of females. A harvest of females, in concert with a series of severe winters in 1969 through 1971, caused such a dramatic decline in the deer population that the state legislature took action to limit harvest to bucks once again.

The fact that an unmanaged Adirondack wilderness did not support great herds of deer was used repeatedly as a justification for managed timber harvests on the Forest Preserve instead of promoting large areas of old-growth forest. This argument was especially strident in the early part of the twentieth century, when deer populations were abundant only in the Adirondacks. However, as deer populations returned to the Adirondack periphery and then began to occur throughout the state in ever-increasing numbers, the political appeal of the argument declined. Since the 1970s, deer populations throughout the interior of the Adirondacks have been in general decline, while those on the periphery have been increasing.

This brings us full circle. Game regulations have largely eliminated the loss of wildlife to over-exploitation. However, changes in wildlife populations are likely to continue, depending on the future of the forest. The legacy of an old debate continues. If more of the Adirondack forest moves from active management by forest industry to Forest Preserve and inactive management by home owners, then we will continue to see wildlife move toward the original complement of species and their relatively low abundance. If another wave of forest harvest crosses the region, then the wildlife will shift toward greater abundance of species suited to forest disturbance.

We must be cautious about this old debate and about using the larger wildlife community as justification for either more preservation or more forest management. Much of what we see in the Adirondack wildlife community today is a product of its location on the transition zone of temperate and boreal forest biomes, the large size of the area, and its connections to a larger landscape that still contains large areas that are undeveloped. A comparison to national parks of similar character gives us an indication of the richness of the Adirondacks (table 6.1).

What we really seek is a measure of the degree to which the integrity of the ecosystem is being maintained. Species richness has been used in the past, but a better measure may be the *index of biotic integrity,* which captures the presence and absence of various animals

TABLE 6.1. Comparison of biodiversity of Adirondack Park to four of the largest U.S. national parks

| Park | Adirondack | Acadia | Great Smoky | Shenandoah | Yellowstone |
|---|---|---|---|---|---|
| Amphibians | 21 | 15 | 43 | 21 | 6 |
| Birds | 197 | 364 | 254 | 192 | 320 |
| Fish | 92 | 44 | 71 | 37 | 18 |
| Mammals | 55 | 53 | 70 | 53 | 70 |
| Reptiles | 19 | 11 | 40 | 26 | 6 |
| All vertebrates | 384 | 487 | 478 | 329 | 420 |

*Sources:* Adirondack reptiles and amphibians from NYS Amphibian and Reptiles Atlas Project (includes mudpuppy, western chorus frog, five-lined skink, black rat snake, common musk turtle, spotted turtle, and eastern box turtle); mammals from website of the Adirondack Ecological Center at the State University of New York College of Environmental Science and Forestry; birds from *1980 Breeding Bird Atlas;* fish from Kays and Daniels (chap. 5 in this book) and includes Lake Champlain. Acadia, Great Smoky, Shenandoah, and Yellowstone data based on e-mail from Beth Johnson of NPS, Dec. 9, 2005, and Jan. 17, 2006, and *NPS Species,* the National Park Service Biodiversity Database at https://science1.nature.nps.gov/npspecies/ (accessed Aug. 1, 2003).

filling important roles in ecosystem processes. The idea for indexing biotic integrity comes from biologists assessing stream quality. More specifically, they sought to measure the capability of maintaining an integrated community of organisms that can adapt to environmental fluctuation. Birds are an especially good group of species with which to apply this index to terrestrial ecosystems because they are so diverse and because many species have specific habitat requirements. When environmental stressors cause changes to occur in the vegetation, birds respond with varying degrees of sensitivity, depending on the specificity of their habitat requirements. The measurement is more refined than just an enumeration of the variety of birds. Instead of counting exotic species and native species, and specialist and generalist species, equally, the index of biotic integrity counts the number of species in each of the important ecological groupings. Ecosystems are better able to carry on essential processes if they have cavity-nesting birds, shrub-nesting birds, freshwater bottom-feeding birds, forest canopy–feeding birds, and so on.

The Adirondack region is an especially good place to use birds as a measure of biotic integrity. Not only are there many species with specialized habitat requirements, but we also have especially good data on the distribution of birds in the region. Two breeding-bird atlases have been completed in which every bird species was recorded, one in 1985 and another in 2005.[9] Analyses of these data have shown that the index of biotic integrity is sensitive to human development: as development increases, biotic integrity declines. Among the strongest predictors of change in biotic integrity is the abundance of roads. It is likely that roads are representative of the broader human impact because with them comes opening of the forest and presence of homes with their associated gardens and lawns.

The Adirondack region has proven resilient to the effects of human activity, as is evident in the return of the moose, the peregrine falcon, and the bald eagle. Yet today the region is facing human disturbance of a different kind. Although in the past the human influence was largely associated with forest harvest, today that influence is related to development. Roads, gardens, lawns, and other activities represent a human footprint on the landscape that is more permanent and ecologically more powerful than harvesting the timber. The question is, when does that footprint get so large as to completely disrupt the ecological processes that are the cornerstones to the resilience of the wilderness ecosystem? In more concrete terms, when will the footprint eliminate groupings of birds and the broader ecological processes they represent? How will those losses affect those natural processes that enable the symbols of wilderness to persist: the loon, the moose, and the wolf?

While research has shown that development is affecting the biotic integrity, the wilderness quality of the Adirondacks is intact. We know that shoreline development is affecting the behavior of loons, but current levels do not appear to be affecting their ability to survive and reproduce.[10] We know that moose populations in the Adirondacks number about 200 and are continuing to double every five years or so.[11] We suspect that wolves will return to the Adirondacks but wonder if there is enough room left for a self-sustaining population. If not, is the habitat connecting the Adirondacks to Ontario, Quebec, and Vermont suitable for continued immigration? Are there ecological thresholds that when passed will result in rapid change, or will continued development cause a gentle decrease in biotic integrity? Will clustering development on the landscape minimize our impacts on the surrounding wilderness? How far into an adjacent wilderness does the influence of development extend? We have much to learn.

# 7

## Mining the Adirondacks

JAMES McLELLAND AND BRUCE SELLECK

Mining in the Adirondacks began no later than the mid-1700s. Although far removed from major population centers, the eastern Adirondack Mountains were well connected to markets via waterways such as Lake Champlain, and the ores within them gave rise to a vigorous mining industry that persisted for nearly 250 years. Much of the region's mineral value can be attributed to three major ores that are found in three different igneous rock types: (1) magnetite in Lyon Mountain Granite (LMG, fig. 1.1, chapter 1); (2) ilmenite in anorthosite (ANT, fig. 1.1, chapter 1); and (3) garnet in gabbro (bodies too small to be shown in fig. 1.1). Marbles host other significant important deposits (i.e., wollastonite, talc, and zinc). Historically, the Adirondack mining enterprise was world-class with respect to iron, titanium, wollastonite, and garnet. Although the iron and titanium mines are now closed, the nonmetallic minerals and the zinc ores continue to be worked, but their deposits are approaching exhaustion. The geology of each of these ores is summarized below, together with local history where warranted.

Historically and economically, low-titanium iron oxide (i.e., the mineral magnetite) has been the most significant ore in the Adirondacks and occurs within, or in proximity to, the distinctive red and pink Lyon Mountain Granite of the Highlands. Hot, chemically corrosive subsurface waters whose circulation was driven by heat from crystallizing granite magma scavenged iron from enclosing rocks and redeposited it within the granite or near its perimeters.

The earliest magnetite mines lay in the vicinity of Port Henry and were first worked during the French and Indian War. During the War of Independence, these and other nearby ores were refined at a forge owned by Philip Skene along the shore of South Bay near the present village of Whitehall. Iron from this forge was used to make the fittings for the first vessels of the just-created United States Navy. This fledgling fleet was intended to keep the British from making their way south along Lake Champlain and was under the command of Benedict Arnold. At one point, Nathan Hale and his Green Mountain Boys commandeered Skene's ore barges to make their daring raid on Fort Ticonderoga.

In the mid-1800s large discoveries at Mineville, Benson Mines (outside the park), and Lyon Mountain led to an iron industry that ranked among the largest and finest in the world. The mines continued to operate until the late 1960s, when they became economically uncompetitive with ores from the Great Lakes, Brazil, South Africa, and Australia. Today tens of millions of tons of high-grade magnetite ore remain underground but are unlikely to become profitable again in the foreseeable future. If the United States needs to produce its own raw ore, the easily accessible open-pit iron ore ranges of Minnesota and Wisconsin contain hundreds of years of reserves, and many more sources are located within Canada.

A sideline of the iron industry concerns the calcium phosphate mineral apatite (our teeth are made of this material) that occurs together with the magnetite deposits. In the eighteenth and nineteenth centuries it served as source of phosphorous for fertilizer. When better fertilizers became available, apatite concentrates were discarded in spoil heaps that grew to the size of hills. One of these is present at Mineville and can be seen from the highway leading to the Crown Point Bridge. Several years ago a French corporation purchased this spoil heap because it is now known that apatite contains high concentrations of Rare Earth Elements (REE), which are actually not as rare now as when they were first discovered. These are exceedingly useful in electronics, photovoltaics, telecommunications, and a wide variety of other technological arenas. Until recently, this once-useless throwaway mineral commanded a higher price than the iron ore ever did. In the 1980s China began to develop large, easily mined deposits of REE. Today China provides about 95 percent of global consumption, has cut the price by a factor of ~60, and claims over 1,000 years of reserves. Should the Chinese source evaporate, the huge, mothballed Mountain Pass mine in California contains REE deposits that could provide our needs for decades, and many more undeveloped deposits are known in the United States and Canada. It would be nice to get rid of the spoil pile at Mineville, but nobody is likely to put any money into it.

In 2003 the Tahawus–Sanford Lake properties were sold to the State of New York and divided into Forever Wild, parkland, and commercial tracts. Today at least 50 million tons of ore remain in place, especially in the undeveloped Cheney Pond deposit. Future demand for titanium could conceivably make these ores once again profitable, and, if so, the Adirondack Park Agency will have to decide whether or not to permit development. For the moment, there is virtually no prospect of a resumption of mining at Tahawus. The vast ilmenite-magnetite deposits at Lac Allard, Quebec, are of higher quality, of greater volume, and far easier to deal with economically.

Open-air roasting of both magnetite-ilmenite and low-titanium iron ores resulted in intense site-specific pollution in the nineteenth and early twentieth centuries. The need for firewood and charcoal during the on-site smelting period led to significant deforestation that roused public opinion and contributed to the establishment the Adirondack State Park in the late nineteenth century. The population increase in eastern Adirondack settlements associated with iron mining in the mid–nineteenth century represents one of the most significant population growth periods the region has experienced.

Zinc has a long history of production in the Adirondack Lowlands, and large mines have yielded high-grade ore in marbles at both the Balmat and Pierrepont mines. Unfortunately these deposits now appear to be almost played out, and prospects for new discoveries are not good, although small new concentrations have been located at Balmat. No economically valuable deposits of zinc occur in the Highlands. Numerous and very large zinc mines exist across the United States and Canada.

Large talc deposits in marble are located in proximity to the zinc mines at Balmat and are operated by the Gouverneur Talc Company. The material mined not only contains the mineral talc but includes a fibrous or needlelike substance known as tremolite that is considerably harder than talc and is referred to as "industrial talc." It is used in the ceramic industry and not for talcum powder.

The world-famous garnet deposits formed in gabbro on Gore Mountain were developed by H. H. Barton in the 1880s and have remained in the family since then. The garnets average 10 inches across and can reach basketball size. Because the garnet crystals are highly fractured, they are of limited value as gemstones. However, as Barton discovered, they can be ground into a wide variety of excellent abrasives. The earliest application was sandpaper, which brought Barton a fortune. Eventually fine rouges were developed and are still used to polish optical lenses, telescope mirrors, and television screens. Not only is Gore Mountain the world's largest garnet mine, it is also the site of the world's largest garnets. Similar deposits are mined at Thirteenth Lake. At present, the Barton Corporation is partnering with Australian firms to develop the production of garnet from beach sands in Australia and elsewhere.

Wollastonite is a white, fibrous, nonmetallic mineral that forms during the metamorphism of limestone and was known in the Adirondacks for over 150 years before it became economically attractive in the 1950s. Initial operations began near Willsboro, but these deposits were exhausted by 1980, and a surface strip mine was opened at Lewis, near Elizabethtown. These rich deposits are now approaching exhaustion, and a site has been opened at nearby Oak Hill. Both the Lewis and Oak Hill deposits are limited by abutment against state land. Another major deposit in production is the Valentine mine near Lake Bonaparte in the Lowlands. The world's largest wollastonite deposit is located in Mexico, but its quality is inferior to Adirondack ore.

Initially wollastonite was used as a coating for welding rods, but subsequently applications were developed in the ceramic industry, for use as a binder in resins, as a paint thickener, and as a fire-retardant and insulation substitute for asbestos. Today this versatile mineral is in great demand, and the Adirondack deposits are among the highest quality in the world. All of the deposits are localized in metamorphosed limestone situated along the margins of large, high-temperature igneous rocks: anorthosite in the Highlands and the Diana complex (granitic) adjacent to the Valentine mine.

Finally, we note that sand and gravel deposits throughout the Adirondacks are very important economic assets. These were formed during the last glacial retreat (~15,000–10,000 years ago) and represent deposits in glacial lakes, deltas, and streams.

Obviously the presence of mining creates environmental dilemmas for any region, but fortunately for the Adirondacks, both past and future problems are greatly diminished by the important fact that the major ores within the park contain very little sulfur. That means that mine waters and runoff from waste and spoil heaps will not produce the sulfuric acid that ravages so many terrains in proximity to coal mines as well as sulfide-bearing metallic mines (e.g., pyrite in many copper deposits). Moreover, Adirondack rocks are essentially devoid of gold and the dangerous cyanide and mercury pollution associated with gold production. The only real problems associated with Adirondack mining are: (1) despoiling the landscape, and (2) incursion into the wilderness. The landscape problem is especially pronounced at large open-pit mines such as those at the Tahawus and Benson mines. Smaller open-pit operations such as those at Gore Mountain or Lewis are removed from sight and easier to manage and reclaim. Both the Tahawus and Benson mines' open pits are now filled with water and should remain that way as long as they are securely gated off from the public until water quality, drainage, inflow, and general safety factors are clarified. There are no good or reasonably inexpensive ways to reclaim the terraced slopes resulting from hard-rock mining, but it can be argued that they provide an awesome landscape feature in their own right. In

addition, the open pits and the terraces provide unparalleled expo-
sures for geologists to investigate these unique mineral deposits.

The issue of incursion into the wilderness is moot with regard
to the already existing mine sites, but it could become significant if
new mines were developed in the western Highlands, where mag-
netic anomalies from Stillwater Reservoir to McKeever strongly
suggest the presence of subsurface iron ore. However, this possibility is exceedingly remote because the world is awash with cheap iron
ore, and, as mentioned, the United States itself still has vast reserves
in the iron ranges of Minnesota and Wisconsin. Similar considerations apply to zinc, talc, garnet, REE, and wollastonite, so there is
very little prospect that new, economically attractive deposits will
be found in the Adirondacks.

Like anything else, mining is a trade-off between what we need
to function and what we would like to preserve. In the mid-1900s
Newcomb, Mineville, Lyon Mountain, and Benson were bustling
towns where a good living was to be had by those engaged in the
mining business. Now these places are almost ghost towns, and the
region is left with more pockets of poverty and scars upon the landscape. Yet the ore was essential at the time and not to use it would
have been self-defeating. Perhaps the future will bring "clean" mining methods, but those prospects are dim and largely incompatible
with conservation of wilderness anyway. Perhaps the ultimate sal-
vation for the Adirondacks is this: to be pursued, mining must be
economically attractive, and, except for sand and gravel, most Adirondack ores (and potential ores) are no longer in the attractive category and/or are almost exhausted. Current policies within the park
should suffice to deal with this diminishing problem. By now Adirondack mining is almost completely history, and conservation can
proceed unimpeded by the extraction of Earth's mineral riches.

# 8

## Forestry in the Adirondacks

*An Economy Built on a Handful of Species*

WILLIAM F. PORTER

That the great debates over the Adirondacks *could* take place can be attributed to the opportunity created by the unusual geology of the region. That they *did* take place is because of the forests. What we have today began, after all, with establishment of the Forest Preserve in 1885. The economic boom of the post–Civil War period created huge demands for products of the forest, and the Adirondack region was a resource at hand. We think of that demand principally in terms of lumber and the exploitation of stands of old-growth spruce and pine. The pictures of the men with axes standing next to enormous trees seem indelible in our minds. Yet the harvest of big trees is only one facet of a much richer story. Lumber and tannins, potash, and wood fiber for paper were valuable commodities to the wider economy, and their extraction had an immediate ecological impact. The long-term indirect influences may be much more important, however. For as with mining, exploitation of the forest drew people and investments in transportation systems into the interior of the region.

A cursory look at the Adirondacks reveals 34 different species of native trees that fall into two basic kinds of forests. Hardwood forests contain species such as maple, birch, beech, and cherry. These are trees with dense wood that proved hard to cut with ax and saw. The softwoods—pines, spruce, and firs—proved easy to cut and to transport by waterways. In forests, these species form predictable mixtures that occur across the landscape. Hardwood forests tend to dominate the more fertile soils and softwoods the poorer soils.

Among these 34 species, a handful of species are central to the story of human exploitation: white pine, eastern hemlock, red spruce, American beech, sugar maple, and yellow birch. Certainly a few others have played a role, but these were species that provided products in demand, and they were among the most abundant in the region in the eighteenth and nineteenth centuries. Early on, white pine was the prize species because its tall stature, lightness, and straight grain made it of exceptional value for constructing masts of sailing ships. It was also easy to cut and plane, making it desirable lumber. White pine grew especially abundant in the southeastern region of the Adirondacks and along Lake Champlain and so was close to established commerce and waterways. However, white pine was not abundant regionally, probably occurring on less than 3 percent of the Adirondack landscape, and much of that was scattered and largely inaccessible. What pine was accessible was gone by 1830.

Ecologically, the long-term impact of the harvest of white pine was localized to those areas where large stands of pine had existed. The origin of such stands depended on a rare coincidence of factors. Regeneration of the stands with all the characteristics of large, old-growth pine would require centuries. Across the broader Adirondack landscape, however, the removal of scattered individuals had minimal impact because younger, smaller individuals were not taken, and they replaced those removed over the next few decades.

In contrast, eastern hemlock was abundant. In a short span of 40 years, more than a million acres was cleared to obtain hemlock, and the process had profound economic and ecological impacts. Eastern hemlock, like white pine, grew abundantly along the eastern edges of the Adirondacks, where it could be easily exploited from the transportation corridor of Lake Champlain and Lake George. Hemlock is a species that grows well across a wide range of ecological conditions and is widely distributed across the region. It seeds under established forests and grows slowly beneath the canopy of other species. Once it attains a position in the overstory, it can persist for centuries. In the southeastern portion of the Adirondacks, hemlock represented 15 percent of all trees as deduced from records of land surveyors who marked witness trees for property lines.

The value of hemlock was its bark, which is rich in tannin. The trees were cut and the bark stripped and transported back to tanneries, where it was ground and leached. The tannin was used to treat cowhides, shipped in from outside the region, and turn them into shoe leather. Hemlock became an important part of the economy beginning in about 1850. Tanneries required substantial capital investment and, like all industry in the nineteenth century, were labor intensive. Communities developed around the tanneries. The need for transportation to bring cowhides in for tanning anchored the development of this industry to the periphery of what is now the Adirondack Park, and largely to the Lake Champlain and Lake George valley. The need to carry the hemlock bark to the tanneries promoted the development of rough roads that allowed access toward the interior. The industry declined in the Adirondacks in the 1890s as local supplies of hemlock were depleted and more profitable opportunities opened up in southern New York and Pennsylvania.

Ecologically, the harvest of the hemlock and the tannery industry had lasting effects. The development of the tannery industry coincided with mining and early harvest of spruce for lumber. Hemlock and spruce, and the hardwoods from which charcoal is made, often grow together in the same stands and grow best on the soils that are also the most productive in the region for agriculture. Consequently, every tree in the best stands was valuable to the growing economy, and the best stands occupied land that itself was valuable for agriculture. The complete removal of the forest cover and conversion to agriculture over large portions of the eastern Adirondacks caused substantial ecological change to the Lake Champlain–Lake George basin. As the best stands were depleted, the harvest moved north and west. The tannery industry, like mining, was limited to transportation networks along the eastern periphery of the Adirondacks. Although the ecological impact was intense, and the geographic scale was large, its overall impact was limited to the periphery of the

Adirondacks. At the moment exploitation of the interior might have expanded dramatically, a sudden shift in business drew the industry away from the Adirondacks.

What drove forest exploitation into the interior of the Adirondacks was spruce. Two species of spruce are especially abundant in the Adirondacks: black spruce, which grows in areas of waterlogged soils, and red spruce, which grows well on a wide range of soil conditions and elevations. Red spruce was the resource of desire because, like white pine, it has a straight grain, is easily cut and planed, shows moderate strength, and floats. What red spruce lacks in stature in comparison to white pine—80 feet tall and 24 inches in diameter versus 150 feet and 48 inches in diameter—it more than made up for in abundance, constituting as much as 25 percent of the Adirondack forest. Like hemlock, red spruce reproduces best under the deep shade of an existing overstory of another species, often balsam fir but also hardwoods. It can spend a century living beneath a canopy and then emerge to dominate the canopy for 250 years. Early loggers exploring up the river drainages found extensive stands of spruce on floodplains. These "spruce flats" were especially attractive to loggers because the trees were large, abundant, and immediately adjacent to a ready means of transporting them to a mill.

Logging of the spruce occurred in two separate waves. The initial pass began in the 1830s and reached its peak in 1890. Loggers sought trees that would provide 40 to 50 feet of merchantable timber with a diameter at the small end of 19 inches, and they sought trees that were close to rivers. While the largest stands of spruce occurred in the western Adirondacks, early exploitation was relatively limited because rivers were few and their flow was highly variable from one year to the next. Most of the harvest in the western Adirondacks fed into Forestport, by way of West Canada Creek. A connector to the Erie Canal reached Forestport.

Heavier exploitation occurred in the eastern part of the region throughout the Hudson River system and the Lake Champlain–Lake George valley. Here the harvest fed into Glens Falls, and from 1850 through 1890 the community burgeoned with saw mills. Just

south of Glens Falls on the Hudson was Albany, where the confluence of the Hudson River and the Erie Canal provided access to
markets demanding all the lumber the Adirondacks could produce.
Once the large trees were removed from the stand, loggers moved
farther up the drainage, and farther into the interior. When all of the
easily accessible stands of large trees were gone, the industry began
exploring west into the Great Lake states.

The initial pass caused little overall effect on the ecological
integrity of the Adirondacks. The trees removed were the largest
individuals in stands that also contained many smaller spruce, so
those trees removed were soon replaced. Where spruce was harvested in conjunction with hemlock and hardwoods, the impact was
significant because large areas were cleared and the regeneration of
spruce would take a century. However, when viewed on a regional
scale, ecological impacts were largely benign. Much of the spruce
was on rough terrain or too distant from transportation to justify
the expense of harvest. By 1885 more than 2 million acres remained
untouched. The estimated 25 million cords of spruce that had been
cut was an enormous volume, but most of this came from lands also
affected by hemlock removal and the cutting of hardwoods for charcoal and agriculture.

The second pass through the Adirondacks for spruce was the pivotal event. The first pass just attracted the attention of the financiers;
in the second pass they invested in infrastructure. Improvements
in technology for sawing lumber and the invention of a process by
which paper could be made from softwood provided a demand for
smaller spruce trees. This time, the ecological impact of the exploitation was limited by a quirk of fate in ownership. After the initial
pass through the region for large spruce, those owning the land
could see little value in holding title and paying property taxes when
there was land with large spruce farther west. However, no one else
wanted the land, so many large landowners simply left, defaulting
on taxes owed on their lands after the first cut. The land reverted to
state ownership. While some of this land was purchased by payment
of back taxes, an emerging public debate about forest management

practices coalesced with political action in 1885 to establish a forest preserve. This political sentiment continued with the creation of the Adirondack Park in 1892 and then an amendment to the New York State Constitution declaring that all public lands in the Forest Preserve "shall be forever kept as wild." The important point is that when the demand for smaller spruce erupted, the state-owned land was not available for harvest and once again the cut was limited.

The large stands of spruce we see today, and those large individuals on higher slopes, are there because so much land fell into state ownership before the cutting of spruce was complete. By 1910, much of the industry was gone from the Adirondacks. While logging of the spruce was geographically limited and did not bring families that put down roots for permanent communities into the interior of the Adirondacks, it laid a lasting foundation. It brought people to cut trees and haul the logs to rivers and then drive down to the mills. The movement of thousands of men and horses up and down the rivers required trails and roads. The logging also brought railroads. The demand for spruce was so great that investors began building railroads into the interior to gain access to the stands that previously had been considered economically inaccessible. By 1875, rail lines completely encircled the park, and four penetrated the interior; by 1892 rail lines were crossing the region and more than 30,000 people were employed in the industry. The rail also brought families, and with women and children came the schools and churches and businesses that create permanent communities. As the rail lines expanded, communities in the interior began to grow into major centers of commerce, and the heart of lumber milling began to shift away from the periphery.

At the turn of the century, spruce was giving out in the Adirondacks. Forest managers were realizing that while the spruce appeared to have regenerated from the initial pass through the region to provide a new crop, there was no regeneration from the second pass. That aroused concern and ultimately resulted in the development of the science of forest ecology and silviculture. Today, the reason for failure of the spruce to regenerate is well understood. However, in the early 1900s, industries based on spruce were faced with either moving or shifting to hardwoods. Hardwoods appeared to hold a significant advantage over spruce because they regenerated easily. Indeed, hardwoods captured sites where spruce had been removed. They had not been considered valuable in earlier generations because they did not float and thus could not be transported to mills via river drives.

The rail lines solved that problem. The transportation infrastructure was already in place for another pass through the same stands that had been the source of spruce, this time for the hardwoods. In 1890, relatively little hardwood was harvested, but by 1905 railroads were being extended and mills built specifically to exploit the hardwood resource. The stands that could be accessed by railroads were cut with an intensity unparalleled in the experience of Adirondack forests. By 1914, cutting of Adirondack forests was estimated to be occurring at five times the rate of growth. The intensity declined sharply by 1920 as the entire logging industry contracted.

In one sense, the ecological impact of this intense harvest was probably not much different from that of a generation earlier in the eastern edges of the Adirondacks. The intensity of removal of both the spruce and the hardwoods in corridors of clear cuts created by the railroads caused local ecological changes that were probably no more substantial than been seen in the removal of spruce, hemlock, and hardwoods on the eastern edge of the Adirondacks several decades earlier. Both were patchy, with areas of complete removal of forest cover adjacent to areas that were mostly still intact.

What made it different was the aftermath. First, the effects of the railroads and the intense logging were expanded dramatically by fire. Logging practices at the time left the tops of the trees on the ground, creating piles of fuel for fire. Sparks from railroad steam engines and careless cigarettes and campfires, as well as lightning strikes, were always sources of ignition. In an extraordinary coincidence, the period of greatest expansion of the railroads and most intense cutting occurred in the same decade as a general drought that included two years of particularly serious drought, 1903 and

1908. Nearly 700,000 acres burned, most of it in the northwest, where rail lines were most abundant and cutting was heaviest. The forest responded with abundant natural regeneration, but there was a pronounced shift in the composition away from mixtures of spruce and hemlock and toward a forest with a much heavier composition of hardwood. We would expect this change because spruce and hemlock regenerate from within an existing forest, not on open ground. Reclaiming the original composition of the forest will take several centuries.

The quirk of fate that limited the extent of the ecological impact of the second cut also limited the fires. Relatively little of the Forest Preserve lands burned. Although these lands, too, had once been logged, the removal was so light and so distant in time that the fuel was not sufficient to carry the fire. Even in drought, stands of living hardwoods are difficult to ignite. Thus, the lands in the Forest Preserve are as much as half a century ahead of the private lands on the timeline to achieve the historic forest composition.

The cutting continued, but not the expansion of the railroads. The heavy financial investments required to run rail lines could not be justified, and they began to be supplanted by roads. The last trees were hauled out of the forest by railroad in the 1940s. The last log drive by river hung on until 1950. Trucks and heavy equipment became increasingly available and networks of roads began reaching farther into the forest.

While spruce remained the most economically valued species, markets were developing for large-diameter hardwoods, especially sugar maple and yellow birch. In the late 1950s a new process for making paper from hardwood pulp created a new demand for smaller diameter trees. Once again, loggers went back into stands they had previously harvested. By the 1960s papermaking relied on the Adirondack hardwood forests to provide 60 to 70 percent of the pulp.

The development of pulp paper as the primary product of the region meant that the forest industry became increasingly tied to the land. Pulping and papermaking required much greater capital investment than did sawmills, and that meant the forest industry would need a strong return on that investment over a longer period of time. Hardwoods were growing rapidly across the Adirondack landscape and afforded a prime resource. While large portions of the Adirondacks were in Forest Preserve by the 1960s, the forest industry held title to more than 600,000 acres. The pulp process could consume all trees down to small size classes, and trucks and mechanized equipment made nearly all forested stands accessible for logging. Once again, the potential impact was limited by a coincidence. This time it was a combination of political and economic decisions.

In 1971, the Adirondack Park Agency (APA) was formed with a mission of regulating land-use practices on private as well as public lands throughout the park. While the motives for creation of the park agency were complex, among them was a desire to influence how the forest industry managed its lands. Key regulations included a provision to limit the size of clear cuts to 25 acres. This encouraged the forest industry to adapt to a selective harvest system in which only a portion of the trees on a site are harvested at one time and the remaining trees allowed to grow for 10 to 30 years before another harvest occurs. However, the unintended consequence on many stands was "high-grading," taking the best stock and leaving the undesirable and often genetically inferior stems to meet the regulations for basal area.

Where the forest industry found the regulations onerous, environmental advocacy groups found them inadequate. The APA provided a focal point for what had been a century-long debate about the impacts of humans on the ecological integrity of the region. Much of the debate was based on perception and values, with little scientific evidence to buttress any contention. By the end of the twentieth century, however, science began to suggest that the regulations and the debate surrounding them might be producing dramatic and unexpected consequences.

Selective harvest of hardwood produced two long-term changes to the forest. First, it created more permanent roads into the forest stands. The repeated harvest of stands on relatively short time intervals meant that investment in roads was cost effective. The ecological effects of these roads appeared to be limited in the short term because they were narrow, not open to the public, and used infrequently. Second, when done according to sound silvicultural guidelines, each harvest promoted a good distribution of tree species and age classes that maintained a diversity of wildlife. The application of sound silviculture was debatable, but the increased presence of regenerating patches of hardwoods important to many species of wildlife was not.

In practice, roads and regeneration were setting the stage for a very different forest. Protracted and vociferous debate was waged over the differences among lands classified by the APA as *Wilderness, Wild Forest, Resource Management, Rural,* and *Hamlet*. The Wilderness and Wild Forest designations were for Forest Preserve lands. Resource Management lands were managed by the forest industry. Rural and Hamlet classifications represented increasing amounts of residential and commercial development. A central argument of the debate was the impact of the forest industry on the ecological integrity of the Adirondack region. As science began to find ways of measuring ecological integrity, it became apparent that the distinction between Resource Management land and Wild Forest and Wilderness was minimal. The more important demarcation was between Resource Management and Rural land-use classes, the latter being more open to development. The key factor proved to be the amount of road open to the public. With increased roads on the landscape came increased numbers of exotic species and loss of native species from important segments of the natural community.

Regeneration under selective harvesting was not adding to the diversity of tree species but subtracting from it. The forest industry was heavily criticized for continuing to allow market forces, instead of sound silviculture, to drive harvest decisions, but it almost did not matter. Selective harvest resulted in removal of enough of the overstory to stimulate regeneration in the understory. The regeneration was being shaped by the reproductive strategies of the suite of species on the site, and by how well each species could withstand browsing by deer. Hardwood species regenerating were those from seeds buried in the soil and seedlings present at the time of harvest that respond to increased sunlight. Beech proved to be the exception. When cut, it sent up scores of shoots from its root system. These shoots carried a decided advantage over the seedlings of other species because they could draw on the energy stored in the root system of their parent as well as from photosynthesis, whereas seedlings were dependent on just photosynthesis.

The advantage to beech extended further because of browsing by deer. Regenerating hardwoods were a favorite food of white-tailed deer, again except beech. Deer prefer to nibble on the birch, maple, ash, and cherry and leave the beech alone. So each day as deer wandered through these stands taking a bite here and there, they gave the beech a small competitive edge. The cumulative impact was that hardwood forests throughout much of the Adirondacks were showing a shift toward beech. From the perspective of black bears, ruffed grouse, squirrels, and many species of small mammals, beech was valuable because it produced a nut crop that is high in energy. From the perspective of the forest industry, beech provided limited marketability beyond pulp for the dwindling number of paper mills.

The real change occurring in stands with increasing abundance of beech proved not to be beneficial to wildlife, and it portended even greater financial constraints on the forest industry. For at the same time the forest was shifting increasingly to beech, a disease began to cause high mortality among larger beech trees. Beech bark disease is caused by a combination of an insect that bores holes in the bark of the tree and a fungus that invades and kills the tree. The scale insect was introduced to Nova Scotia in 1890 from Europe. The fungus may be native to North America. The disease arrived in the central Adirondacks in 1965 and by 1980, 80 percent of the trees larger than 16 inches in diameter were infected. As those died, the insect appeared to shift to smaller diameter trees and by 2000, 90 percent of the beech trees 6 inches in diameter and larger were infected. Each death of a large tree produces the same effect as cutting it: a profusion of shoots sprout from the roots.

What might the future forests hold? Will they have economic value? In many stands, the future hardwood forest appears unlikely to have few large trees of any species other than beech because these shoots so dominate the understory, and it is unlikely to have large beech because of the disease. Dense thickets of small beech trees may be just what is needed to drive the next major exploitive wave across the region: the demand for wood fiber as a source of biofuel. Much of the land that was forest industry could be quickly brought on line with sufficient economic incentives. The real question is, how strong will those incentives become? Indeed, will New Yorkers seek to maintain the Forest Preserve and the Forever Wild status of those lands? Or will acid rain make the argument moot?

# 9

## Human Impacts from Afar

*Acid Rain and Mercury Deposition in the Adirondacks*

CHARLES T. DRISCOLL, KIMBERLEY M. DRISCOLL,
MYRON J. MITCHELL, DUDLEY J. RAYNAL,
AND KAREN M. ROY

Air pollution is an important disturbance affecting forest and aquatic ecosystems in the Adirondacks. Two particularly important components of air pollution disturbance are acidic deposition and mercury deposition. These two components have a common origin (i.e., fossil-fuel combustion) and important linkages within the environment. The Adirondack region receives elevated acidic and mercury deposition compared to both preindustrial conditions and areas far removed from atmospheric emissions and deposition. The Adirondack Mountains are inherently sensitive to acidic and mercury deposition because of their high precipitation and cool climatic conditions, forest-wetland-surface water landscapes, acidic soils, and shallow surficial geologic deposits that are derived from rock and minerals that slowly break down. The response of Adirondacks to air pollution inputs is closely linked to the structure and function of forests (see chapter 4), soils (chapter 3), wetlands (chapter 2), and aquatic ecosystems. An important future issue is the extent and rate of recovery of Adirondack ecosystems

This contribution was supported by the New York State Energy Research and Development Authority through the Adirondack Lakes Survey Corporation.

in response to ongoing and potential future air pollution control programs.

## A Primer on the Science of Acid Deposition and Its Impacts

Over the past 30 years, scientists have gained considerable insight into the ways that air pollution and atmospheric deposition have altered ecosystems. When it was first identified in North America in the early 1970s, acidic deposition was viewed as a simple problem that was limited in scope. Scientists now know that acids, acidifying compounds, nutrients, and toxins of atmospheric origin are transported through soil, vegetation, and surface waters and have deleterious effects on interconnected ecosystems.

Acidic deposition is composed of various atmospheric inputs including the wet deposition of sulfuric and nitric acids and ammonium, as well as the dry deposition of sulfur dioxide, nitrogen oxides, and ammonia. These compounds are largely emitted to the atmosphere by the burning of fossil fuels and by agricultural activities. The term "acidic deposition" encompasses all the forms in which these compounds are transported from the atmosphere to the earth, including gases, particles, rain, snow, clouds, and fog.

Most total acidic deposition generally occurs as wet deposition (i.e., deposition from precipitation such as rain, snow, sleet, and hail). Wet deposition is relatively easy to measure. Substantial inputs also occur as dry deposition, the deposition of particles and gases. Dry deposition is difficult to measure and poorly quantified. Cloud deposition can be the largest input of acidity at elevations above 2,100 feet. Like dry deposition, cloud deposition is difficult to measure.

Acidity can be characterized by measurements of pH. With the inputs of sulfuric and nitric acids to precipitation and surface waters, there generally is an increase in acidity and a decrease in pH. Wet deposition of sulfate and nitrate is highest in the southwestern portion of the Adirondacks, with deposition values decreasing toward the northeast (fig. 9.1).

Acidic deposition trends in New York and other areas of the Northeast mirror emission trends in the atmospheric source area or

9.1. Wet deposition of sulfate in the Adirondacks in kilograms per hectare each year. Reprinted from *Atmospheric Environment* 36, no. 6, "Spatial Patterns of Precipitation Quantity and Chemistry and Air Temperature in the Adirondack Region of New York," 1051–62, Copyright 2002, with permission from Elsevier.

airshed that extends to the Midwest, the source of the greatest emissions in North America. Sulfate in wet deposition is largely derived from sulfur dioxide emissions, which are largely associated with emissions from coal combustion used by electric utilities and industrial processes. Long-term data from the Adirondack region show declining concentrations of sulfate in wet deposition since the late 1970s owing to the air quality controls associated with the Clean Air Act. Based on these data, it is evident that a strong positive relationship exists between sulfur dioxide emissions in the source area and sulfate concentrations in wet deposition. Similar relationships have been developed at other sites in New York and New England. It is expected that sulfate concentrations in wet deposition will decrease in a direct linear response to anticipated future decreases in sulfur dioxide emissions in the source area. Emissions of nitrogen oxides largely are derived from transportation sources (e.g., automobiles and trucks) and electric utilities. Wet deposition of nitrate has remained relatively constant in the Adirondacks over the last 20 years, and this observation is consistent with the relatively constant nitrogen oxide emissions in the source area for the northeastern United States. It is notable that in recent years there have been decreases in emissions of nitrogen oxides from electric utilities that have coincided with some decreases in wet nitrate deposition.

The Adirondack region is among the most acid-sensitive and acid-impacted in North America. Acidic deposition alters soils, stresses forest vegetation, acidifies lakes and streams, and harms fish and other aquatic life.

Over the last century, acidic deposition has accelerated the loss of large amounts of available calcium and magnesium from acid-sensitive soils in the Adirondacks and other acid-sensitive areas in the Northeast. Depletion occurs when calcium and magnesium are displaced from the soil by acidic deposition at a rate faster than these nutrients can be replenished by the slow breakdown of soil minerals (i.e., weathering) or atmospheric calcium and magnesium inputs. This depletion of available calcium and magnesium fundamentally alters soil processes, compromises the nutrition of some trees, and hinders the capacity for sensitive soils and surface waters to recover from acidic deposition.

Aluminum is often released from soil to soil water, lakes, and streams in forested regions with high acidic deposition, low stores of available calcium and magnesium, and high soil acidity. High concentrations of dissolved aluminum can be toxic to forest vegetation, fish, and other organisms. Concentrations of toxic forms of aluminum in streams in the Adirondacks and in other acid-sensitive portions of the Northeast are often above levels known to have adverse effects on fish and much greater than concentrations observed in surface waters draining forest watersheds that receive low inputs of acidic deposition. Although there have been decreases in acidic deposition over the past 30 years, soils in the Adirondacks continue to exhibit depletion of available calcium and magnesium under currently lower deposition conditions.

Elevated atmospheric deposition increases the transport and accumulation of sulfur and nitrogen in forest soils. If this soil sulfur is released in response to decreases in atmospheric sulfate deposition, it will contribute to the ongoing acidification of streams and lakes. The recovery of surface waters of the Adirondacks in response to emission controls has been delayed by the release of soil sulfur left by the legacy of acidic deposition.

Similarly, elevated atmospheric nitrogen deposition appears to have increased nitrogen availability in soil in excess of the amount needed by the forest, resulting in nitrate leaching into surface waters in the Adirondacks and many other parts of the Northeast. Although forests require nitrogen for growth, several recent studies suggest that in some areas of the Northeast, such as the Adirondacks, nitrogen levels are above what forests can use and retain, a condition known as nitrogen saturation. In contrast to sulfur, there has not been appreciable change in atmospheric nitrogen deposition in recent years.

Research has shown that acidic deposition has contributed to the decline of red spruce and sugar maple trees in the eastern United States. Symptoms of tree decline include poor crown condition, reduced tree growth, and unusually high levels of tree mortality. Declines of red spruce and sugar maple in the Northeast have occurred during the past four decades. Factors associated with declines of both species have been studied and include important links to acidic deposition.

Significant growth declines and winter injury to red spruce have been observed throughout its range in the Northeast. Acidic deposition is believed to be a contributing factor in red spruce decline at high elevations in the Northeast. Red spruce decline occurs by both direct and indirect effects of acidic deposition. Direct effects include the leaching of calcium from needles of trees, whereas indirect effects refer to changes in the underlying soil chemistry.

Recent research suggests that the decline of red spruce is linked to the leaching of calcium from cell membranes in spruce needles by acid mist or fog. The loss of calcium renders the needles more susceptible to freezing damage, thereby reducing the tolerance of trees to low temperatures and increasing the occurrence of winter injury and subsequent tree damage or death. In addition, low calcium and elevated aluminum concentrations in the soil may result in a reduction in biomass and limit root uptake of water and nutrients, contributing to decline.

The decline of sugar maple has been studied in the eastern United States since the 1950s. Sugar maples are typically found in soils with high levels of calcium availability and high microbial production of nitrate. Extensive mortality among sugar maple stands appears to have resulted from deficiencies of calcium and magnesium, coupled with other stresses such as insect defoliation and drought. Studies suggest that the probability of the loss of sugar maple crown vigor or incidence of tree death increases on sites where the supply of calcium and magnesium to soil and foliage is low and stress from insect defoliation and/or drought is high. Low levels of calcium and magnesium can cause a nutrient imbalance and reduce the ability of a tree to respond to stresses such as insect infestation and drought.

Forests in some areas in the western Adirondacks contain sugar maple with foliage having low calcium and magnesium concentrations. Sugar maple in these forests may be susceptible to decline. Other research has suggested that regeneration of sugar maples has declined markedly over the last 60 years in the calcium-poor soils of the western Adirondacks and other areas of the Northeast. This pattern is in contrast to more calcium-rich areas in the eastern Adirondacks, where the density of sugar maple seedlings is greater. There have also been field experiments that suggest that decreases in sugar maple regeneration are linked to soil calcium depletion.

Acidic deposition also degrades water quality by lowering pH (i.e., increasing acidity); decreasing acid-neutralizing capacity, and increasing concentrations of toxic forms of aluminum. Acid neutralizing capacity is a measure of the ability of the water to neutralize inputs of strong acids and is an indicator of the sensitivity and impacts of waters to acidic deposition. A comprehensive survey of lakes greater than 0.5 acres in surface area in the Adirondack region of New York was conducted by the Adirondack Lakes Survey Corporation to obtain detailed information on the acid-base status of waters in this region. Of the 1,469 lakes surveyed, 27 percent were highly acidic throughout the year (i.e., chronically acidic), and an additional 21 percent could experience acidic conditions for short periods during the year. Of these acid–sensitive lakes (48 percent of total), 45 percent (265 lakes) were characterized by relatively low concentrations of dissolved organic carbon (less than 5.0 mg C/L). These lakes had a chemical composition that suggested their acidity was largely derived from sulfate associated with acidic deposition. In contrast, 55 percent of the lakes (320 lakes) were characterized by high concentrations of dissolved organic carbon (greater than 5.0 mg C/L) and naturally occurring organic acids (associated with wetlands and the decomposition of organic matter). These lakes are probably naturally acidic. While naturally occurring organic acids contribute to the low pH values of these lakes, their overall acidity has been greatly enhanced by acidic deposition.

Seasonal acidification is the annual increase in acidity and the corresponding decrease in pH and acid-neutralizing capacity in streams and lakes during winter and spring. Episodic acidification is caused by a sudden pulse of acids and/or a dilution of bases (e.g., calcium, magnesium, sodium, potassium) by spring snowmelt or large rain events throughout the year. Increases in nitrate in stream and lake water are generally important to the occurrence of acid episodes in the Adirondacks, especially when trees are dormant and therefore uptake of nitrogen by vegetation is low. Episodic acidification also often coincides with pulsed increases in concentrations of toxic forms of aluminum. Short-term increases in acid inputs to surface waters can result in conditions that are lethal to fish and other aquatic organisms.

Decreases in pH and elevated concentrations of toxic forms of aluminum have decreased the species diversity and abundance of aquatic life in many streams and lakes in the Adirondacks and other acid-sensitive areas of the Northeast. Fish have received the most attention to date, but entire food webs have also been adversely affected. Other impacts include diminished species diversity and abundance of plankton, invertebrates, and fish in acid-impacted surface waters in the Northeast (table 9.1). In the Adirondacks, a significant positive relationship exists between the pH in lakes and the number of fish species present in those lakes. Surveys of 1,469 Adirondack lakes conducted in 1984 and 1987 show that 24 percent of lakes (346) in this region do not support fish. These lakes had consistently lower pH and acid-neutralizing capacity, and higher concentrations of aluminum, than lakes that contained one or more species of fish. Experimental studies and field observations demonstrate that even acid-tolerant fish species such as brook trout have been eliminated from some waters in the Adirondacks.

Although chronically high acid levels stress aquatic life, acidic episodes are particularly harmful because abrupt, large changes in water chemistry allow fish few areas of refuge. High concentrations of dissolved aluminum are directly toxic to fish, and pulses of aluminum during acid episodes are a primary cause of fish mortality. High acidity and toxic aluminum levels disrupt the salt and water balance of blood in fish, causing red blood cells to rupture and blood viscosity to increase. Studies show that the viscous blood strains the heart, resulting in lethal heart attacks.

## Atmospheric Mercury Deposition

There is widespread contamination of mercury in the Adirondacks and elsewhere in the United States. In remote forested regions such as the Adirondacks, the source of mercury contamination is largely atmospheric deposition associated with air pollution. There is limited information on historical changes in mercury deposition to the Adirondacks. However, studies using lake sediment cores suggest that mercury deposition to the Adirondacks has increased approximately fivefold since 1900, peaking in the 1970s and 1980s. Mercury emissions in the United States have decreased during the 1990s because of controls on medical and municipal waste incinerators associated with implementation of federal regulations. Conversely, electric utility emissions have remained largely unchanged,

TABLE 9.1. **Effects of surface water acidification on aquatic biota**

| pH range | General biological effects |
|---|---|
| 6.5–6.0 | Small decrease in species richness of phytoplankton, zooplankton, and benthic invertebrate communities resulting from the loss of a few highly acid-sensitive species, but no measurable change in total community abundance or production. Some adverse effects (decreased reproductive success) may occur for highly acid-sensitive species (e.g., fathead minnow, striped bass). |
| 6.0–5.5 | Loss of sensitive species of minnow and dace, such as blacknose dace and fathead minnow; in some waters decreased reproductive success of lake trout and walleye, which are important sport fish species in some areas. Visible accumulations of filamentous green algae in the littoral zone of many lakes and in some streams. Distinct decrease in the species richness and change in species composition of the phytoplankton, zooplankton, and benthic invertebrate communities, although little if any change in total community biomass or production. |
| 5.5–5.0 | Loss of several important sport fish species, including lake trout, walleye, rainbow trout, and smallmouth bass; as well as additional nongame species such as creek chub. Further increase in the extent and abundance of filamentous green algae in lake littoral areas and streams. Continued shift in the species composition and decline in species richness of the phytoplankton, periphyton, zooplankton, and benthic invertebrate communities; decrease in the total abundance and biomass of benthic invertebrates and zooplankton may occur in some waters. Loss of several additional invertebrate species common in oligotrophic (low productivity) waters, including *Daphnia galeata mendotae, Diaphanosoma leuchtenbergianum, Asplanchna priodonta,* all snails, most species of clams, and many species of mayflies, stoneflies, and other benthic invertebrates. Inhibition of nitrification. |
| 5.0–4.5 | Loss of most fish species, including most important sport-fish species such as brook trout and Atlantic salmon; few fish species able to survive and reproduce below pH 4.5 (e.g., central mudminnow, yellow perch, and, in some waters, largemouth bass). Measurable decline in the whole-system rates of decomposition of some forms of organic matter, potentially resulting in decreased rates of nutrient cycling. Substantial decrease in the number of species of zooplankton and benthic invertebrates and further decline in the species richness of the phytoplankton and periphyton communities; measurable |

TABLE 9.1. (continued)

| pH range | General biological effects |
| --- | --- |
| | decrease in the total community biomass of zooplankton and benthic invertebrates in most waters. Loss of zooplankton species such as *Tropocyclops prasinus mexicanus, Leptodora kindtii,* and *Conochilis unicornis;* and benthic invertebrate species, including all clams and many insects and crustaceans. Reproductive failure of some acid-sensitive species of amphibians such as spotted salamanders, Jefferson salamanders, and the leopard frog. |

*Source:* J. P. Baker, D. P. Bernard, S. W. Christensen, M. J. Sale, *Biological Effects of Changes in Surface Water Acid-base Chemistry* (report SOS/T 13). Washington, D.C.: National Acid Precipitation Assessment Program, 1990.

and their contribution to total U.S. emissions has increased from 25 percent to 40 percent over the past decade. It is anticipated that mercury emissions from these sources will be controlled in the future. Other important emissions include industrial, commercial, and institutional boilers and process heaters. Identifying the specific sources of atmospheric mercury deposition is difficult. Nevertheless, recent research points to the sources in the United States as being an important contributor to mercury deposited in the U.S., in addition to global sources.

Forested regions are among the most sensitive areas for mercury inputs. In contrast to acidic deposition, mercury inputs to forests largely occur as dry deposition (i.e., particles, gases). Canopy trees filter mercury from the atmosphere, greatly enhancing deposition. Shallow soils allow for the transport of mercury to surface waters. Wetlands, which are a prevalent component of the Adirondack landscape, are critical for the conversion of ionic mercury deposited from the atmosphere to methyl mercury, the form of mercury that bio-accumulates in the aquatic food chain. Unproductive lakes, like many in the Adirondacks, show particularly high bio-accumulation of methyl mercury in fish. In the Adirondacks, methyl mercury bio-accumulates from water to fish by a factor of a million to ten million. In the Adirondacks, 34 percent of the yellow perch collected have concentrations of mercury above the 0.3 parts-per-million action level suggested by the EPA, and 96 percent of the lakes surveyed have at least one fish with mercury concentrations greater than 0.3 parts per million. The western and central Adirondack region has among the most severe mercury contamination in fish and wildlife observed in eastern North America and recently has been identified as a biological mercury "hotspot." This area is also severely affected by acidic deposition.

Several research studies suggest a linkage between acidic deposition and mercury concentrations in fish. Atmospheric deposition of sulfate associated with sulfur dioxide emissions provides the necessary substrate for bacteria that produce methyl mercury. Experimental addition of sulfate to wetlands and lakes increases the production of methyl mercury by bacteria and concentrations of methyl mercury in water. Through these experiments, researchers have inferred that reducing sulfur dioxide emissions and sulfate deposition would result in decreased methyl mercury in the fish of receiving waters. Many studies across eastern North America, including the Adirondacks, have also reported increases in fish mercury concentrations with decreases in surface water pH. Acidification of lakes by acidic deposition apparently has enhanced fish mercury concentrations. As a result, concentrations of mercury in fish are likely to decrease with decreasing acidic deposition.

Exposure of humans and wildlife to mercury largely occurs through consumption of fish. Approximately 8 percent of women of childbearing age have mercury levels in blood exceeding the value at which most people could be exposed without risk. Children who are prenatally exposed to high levels of methyl mercury are at increased risk for neurological behavior problems. Indigenous people and local residents who consume large quantities of fish may be exposed to high mercury concentrations. In aquatic ecosystems, methyl mercury causes neurological, behavioral, and reproductive changes and at extremely high levels may cause death in fish and wildlife such as loons, mergansers, mink, and otter. Although most studies of mercury to date have focused on the aquatic food chain, recent research suggests that mercury can also bio-accumulate through the terrestrial food chain and affect songbirds and bats.

It is expected that mercury in fish would decrease in response to future reductions in mercury emissions. Moreover, mercury that is recently deposited from the atmosphere is in a reactive form and is more readily taken up by aquatic organisms than mercury that already exists in the ecosystem. As a result, there is likely a benefit associated with a shorter timeframe for controls on mercury emissions.

## Recovery of Adirondack Surface Waters from Acidic and Mercury Deposition

Adirondack lakes have exhibited marked decreases in concentrations of sulfate, which coincide with decreases in atmospheric sulfur deposition. While sulfate concentrations in lakes and streams have decreased over the last 30 years, they remain high compared to preindustrial background conditions. Concentrations of nitrate have also decreased in several Adirondack lakes. As atmospheric nitrogen deposition has not substantially changed over this period, the mechanism contributing to this apparent increase in lake/watershed nitrogen retention is not evident but may be related to vegetation changes in the watershed. Decreases in concentrations of sulfate and nitrate have resulted in increases in acid neutralizing capacity and pH and a shift in dissolved aluminum from toxic inorganic species toward less toxic organic forms in some lakes. Extrapolation of current rates of increases in acid-neutralizing capacity and forecasts using computer models suggest that the time frame of chemical recovery of Adirondack lakes at current rates of decreases in acidic deposition will be many decades.

Several factors account for the slow recovery in chemical water quality in the Adirondacks, despite the decreased deposition of sulfur associated with the Clean Air Act. First, levels of acid-neutralizing calcium and magnesium in streams and lakes have decreased markedly owing to a loss of available calcium and magnesium from the soil and, to a lesser extent, a reduction in atmospheric inputs of calcium and magnesium. Second, atmospheric nitrogen inputs continue to affect acidic episodes (i.e., springmelt and heavy rainstorms).

Sulfur has accumulated in the soil and is now being released to surface water as sulfate, even though sulfate deposition has decreased. Finally, several Adirondack lakes have shown long-term increases in concentrations of dissolved organic carbon. Increases in dissolved organic carbon may be the result of changing climate or a decrease in the retention of naturally occurring organic acids associated with decreases in acidic deposition. These changes have partially offset decreases in acidity associated from sulfate and nitrate from acidic deposition. In addition, Adirondack soils continue to lose available calcium and magnesium under current inputs of acidic deposition.

It is anticipated that there would be increases in the diversity of aquatic biota in response to increases in pH and decreases in concentrations of toxic form of aluminum. Unfortunately, there have not been many published reports of the response of aquatic biota to decreases in lake acidity in the Adirondacks.

Although much less is known about ecosystem response to changes in mercury emissions, studies from lake sediment cores suggest there has been an approximately 30 percent decrease in mercury inputs to the Adirondacks since the 1970s and 1980s. Despite these decreases, mercury concentrations remain elevated in fish and other wildlife, particularly in the western and central Adirondacks. Additional monitoring of biota is needed to assess how ecosystems will respond to anticipated future decreases in mercury emissions.

## Suggested Readings

Baker, J. P., D. P. Bernard, S. W. Christensen, and M. J. Sale. *Biological Effects of Changes in Surface Water Acid-base Chemistry.* Report SOS/T 13. Washington, D.C.: National Acid Precipitation Assessment Program, 1990.

DeHayes, D. H., P. G. Schaberg, G. J. Hawley, and G. R. Strimbeck. "Acid Rain Impacts Calcium Nutrition and Forest Health." *BioScience* 49 (1999): 789–800.

Driscoll, C. T., C. Yan, C. L. Schofield, R. Munson, and J. Holsapple. "The Mercury Cycle and Fish in the Adirondack Lakes." *Environmental Science and Technology* 28 (1994): 136A–143A.

Driscoll, C. T., G. B. Lawrence, A. J. Bulger, T. J. Butler, C. S. Cronan, C. Eagar, K. F. Lambert, G. E. Likens, J. L. Stoddard, and K. C. Weathers. "Acid Rain Revisited: Advances in Scientific Understanding since the Passage of the 1970 and 1990 Clean Air Act Amendments." Hanover, N.H.: Hubbard Brook Research Foundation, Science Links™ Publication (www.hubbardbrook.org), 2001.

Driscoll, C. T., D. Whitall, J. Aber, E. Boyer, M. Castro, C. S. Cronan, C. Goodale, C. Hopkinson, K. F. Lambert, G. Lawrence, and S. Ollinger. 2003. "Nitrogen Pollution: From the Sources to the Sea." Hanover, N.H.: Hubbard Brook Research Foundation, Science Links™ Publication (www.hubbardbrook.org), 2003.

Driscoll, C. T., D. Evers, K. F. Lambert, N. Kamman, T. Holsen, Y.-J. Han, C. Chen, W. Goodale, T. J. Butler, T. Clair, and R. Munson. *Mercury Matters: Linking Mercury Science with Public Policy in the Northeastern United States.* Vol. 1, no. 3. Hanover, N.H.: Hubbard Brook Research Foundation, Science Links Publication, 2007.

Jenkins, J., K. Roy, C. T. Driscoll, and C. Buerkett. *Acid Rain and the Adirondacks: An Environmental History.* Ithaca, N.Y.: Cornell Univ. Press, 2007.

Likens, G. E., C. T. Driscoll, and D. C. Buso. "Long-term Effects of Acid Rain: Response and Recovery of a Forested Ecosystem." *Science* 272 (1996): 244–46.

United States Environmental Protection Agency. *2003 Progress Report.* EPA Acid Rain Program, EPA 430-R-04–009, Clean Air Markets Division, U.S. Environmental Protection Agency, (www.epa.gov/airmarkets), 2004.

# 10

## Recreation and Tourism in the Adirondacks

CHAD P. DAWSON

The Adirondack Mountains were largely unexplored and unknown before 1800 and were a blank area on the early European maps of the region. In 1806, Lewis and Clark were making more detailed maps during their expedition with the Corps of Discovery in the northwestern United States than existed for the Adirondacks. Some of the first recorded travels in the Adirondacks were made in 1837–41 by the explorer and geologist Ebenezer Emmons, who reportedly suggested the name "Adirondack" for the mountainous region following a guided trip there with a native American named Sabael Benedict.[1] Although some trappers and hunters were making a living in the Adirondacks at that time, few had reported about their travels there. When reports began to emerge, the future themes for recreation and tourism in the Adirondacks took shape—a retreat to primitive nature for renewal and the preservation of a wild mountainous and forested landscape.

Emmons's published reports of his explorations and observations in the Adirondacks reached Henry David Thoreau, who marveled at the wild region of the Adirondacks, even though the region surrounding the Adirondacks, after 1800, was generally settled and developed for agriculture, forestry, and mining in the rich resources of northern New York. Thoreau often focused in his writings on the romantic notion of wild lands and their capacity to bring renewal to an industrializing society. His commentary on Emmons's travels with Benedict caught the national attention: "New York has her wilderness within her borders; and though the sailors of Europe are familiar with the soundings of her Hudson, and Fulton long since invented the steamboat on its waters, an Indian is still necessary to guide her scientific men to its head-waters in the Adirondac [*sic*] country."[2]

This emphasis on and promotion of a wild landscape, in contrast to the rapid human habitation and industrialization of the United States, caught people's attention at that time and has continued to do so to the present, as seen in the policies and management of the Adirondack Park. There was a countertheme among those who wanted to transform the wilderness into prosperous communities and places of commerce. The tension between those who wanted to protect the wilderness and those who wanted to develop the wilderness persists today in Adirondack communities. Conservationists and the recreation and tourism industry have attempted to balance these two themes, with some consensus that the Adirondack region, through protection and preservation of wildlands, is the place of and backdrop for recreation and tourism experiences.

## Tourism Begins

The extensive waterways of the Adirondacks formed the transportation network that allowed early exploration and development of settlements. Much of the travel was on rivers and connecting lakes and ponds. Travel involved either leaving larger or heavier boats on a body of water and changing to another boat on the next waterway, or carrying canoes or lighter boats over portage trails to the next waterway. The need for light boats that could be carried by hand to another water body and that could transport guides, hunters and anglers, tourists, large game, and other goods and supplies resulted in much experimentation in boat building. The result was a type of boat that was unique and began to be seen in the central Adirondack region in the 1820s. The Adirondack guide boat could be built from local wood, could carry a guide and a customer with gear for the day, could take the extra weight of harvested fish or game on the return trip, and could be carried across a portage to extend the range of hunting and fishing trips and other exploration.[3]

With the expansion of the railroads and the opening of the Erie Canal in New York, public transportation began to make tourism affordable and popular prior to the Civil War. By 1850, transportation consisted of railroad terminals at the periphery of the Adirondacks that were connected with stage roads and log-drive river and dam systems. That era of forest resource harvesting made the Adirondacks the largest producer of lumber in the United States, which led to investment in and expansion of the peripheral railroads around the Adirondacks by 1875, and commercial and passenger service to most major interior communities by 1900.[4] After 1900, railroads lines for mines and logging began to decline, and passenger transportation to hotels, resorts, summer home colonies, and private parks increased. In some locations, horse-drawn stages and steamboat service lines were created to link up with the rail lines, providing transportation to more remote public and private tourism destinations.

The spark that started considerable interest in rustic camping and guided sport hunting and fishing trips was born of a series of popular articles and well-known paintings that captured the romantic notions of the era in stories and imagery about the Adirondack landscape and rugged mountain ranges. Some of the more well-known authors of that time and their popular books included: *Wild Scenes in Forest and Prairie* by Charles Fenno Hoffman in 1839; *The Adirondack; or, Life in the Woods* by Joel T. Headley in 1849; *Woods and Water* by Alfred Billings Street in 1860; and *Adventures in the Wilderness* by William H. H. "Adirondack" Murray in 1869.

Numerous other authors wrote travelogues and adventure stories that were published in popular magazines and newspapers of that time. The articles caught the imagination of those who would one day go to the Adirondacks and those who would just share in the folklore. The stories they related about real and romanticized travels with local guides through a rugged and forested landscape while exploring, hunting, fishing, and hiking elevated the Adirondack guide to the level of legend and mythology.[5] Those early travelers set the theme, the setting, and some of the characters that would be part of culture and public image of the rustic and rugged Adirondack tourism experience. These themes and the imagery in this genre of Adirondack nature stories was picked up and used by tourism businesses like railroads and hotels and resorts in marketing materials to further promote travel to the Adirondacks for a wide variety of recreation and leisure experiences.

Artists of that time included painters of the Hudson River school such as Thomas Cole and Asher B. Durand, as well as romantic landscape painters such as Winslow Homer and Frederic Remington. Many artists flocked to the Adirondacks and hired guides or joined groups to go out to study and paint the natural features— waterfalls, ponds, lakes, river valleys, cliffs, mountains, and forested landscapes. These images were reproduced and distributed regionally and nationally in books, magazines, and other printed materials that, in combination with all the published stories, set the stage for attracting more tourism. The stories of hunting deer, moose, and bear and fishing for lake trout and brook trout from rugged camps set the stage for those tourists who would follow in the popular expansion phase of Adirondack exploration and development. The Adirondacks stood in stark contrast to the declining environmental conditions in cities as urbanization and industrialization became more evident and served as a push away from post–Civil War–era cities toward the redemption of nature. The opening of tourism within the Adirondacks was met with enthusiasm because it was a unique experience in relatively close proximity to urban areas, and the periphery was increasingly accessible by train, even though travel in the interior was largely by stage coach, boat, and trail.[6]

## Tourism Develops Mass Appeal

It was not until 1872 that the state legislature authorized Verplanck Colvin to make a survey and map of the Adirondack area. In spite of some recorded explorations and preliminary compass survey notes, the Adirondack region was often depicted as a blank spot on maps of the state, or settlements were not correctly located or described.

Colvin spent years and many surveying trips to various regions of the Adirondacks. He was able to comment in his surveying reports about how the landscape was rapidly changing with increasing human habitation and tourism development. In his seventh written report to the New York State legislature, Colvin noted that during 1875–79 many new changes could be seen:

> I find following in the footsteps of my explorations the blazed-line and the trail; then the ubiquitous tourist, determined to see all that has been recorded as worth seeing. Where first comes one—the next year there are ten—the year after full a hundred. The woods are thronged; bark and log huts prove insufficient; hotels spring up as though by magic, and the air resounds with laughter, song, and jollity. The wild trails, once jammed with logs, are cut clear by the axes of the guides, and ladies clamber to the summits of those once untrodden peaks. The genius of change has possession of the land; we cannot control it. When we study the necessities of our people, we would not control it if we could. This change—this new revelation of fresh, exhilarating mountain summer life—is having too important and beneficial an influence upon society at present, not to demand the sympathy of government. To the wealthy dwellers of cities, debilitated by a tainted atmosphere, the breezes and the mountain springs bring life, while the free, joyous exercises of their children in these summer homes, lay for them the foundations of continued health.[7]

Colvin also saw the tremendous growth of tourism in all types of lodgings as he notes in his surveying reports. These changes he viewed as good and appropriate for human health and welfare, but he also foresaw the need for preservation of what was yet undeveloped:

> Where in 1870 and '73, the small bark shanty of our hunter guide stood solitary—our only shelter—near the sand beaches of Blue Mountain Lake, now stand here and there the comfortable

woodland hotels, with semi-rustic grounds, and bright Concord coaches. . . . And, so elsewhere; a thousand new resorts are
found. . . . The region is already the summer home of untold
thousands—a public pleasure ground—a wilderness Park to all
intents and purposes. . . . Already private clubs have separated
large areas. . . . So elsewhere in the forest the task of preservation
is beginning.[8]

As demand increased, tourism services and accommodations
became more developed and widely available in small settlements
and communities in the central and peripheral Adirondacks. The
emphasis of the tourism experience remained on the natural appearance of the forested landscapes and mountains as well as the buildings for human habitation and equipment for transport. Although
it was no longer necessary to endure a long, rugged, and physically
difficult hike or canoe with the prospect of sleeping in a bark lean-to
and hunting and fishing for provisions, those primitive recreation
elements were retained during shorter and less demanding travels
on day trips from the resorts and lodges by guide boat or hiking.
Now tourists could choose how and when to experience the wild
landscape and to what degree to immerse themselves in recreation
activities within a primitive forested landscape.

Adirondack camps for hunting and fishing became more common as land was resold to groups of sportsmen following forest
harvesting. Many railroads originally built for transporting logs to
mills or markets were turned to passenger service or removed. Some
wealthy businessmen and their families from New York City bought
up large tracts of land as preserves and built what became popularly
known as "great camps," so named because of the number and size
of the log buildings and lodges. Some of these estates were meant to
be self-sufficient and were often designed to be primitively elegant
summer homes for wealthy people who hired large staffs to maintain
the remote settlements throughout the year.[9]

During the late 1800s, the primitive recreation and tourism experience and the culture of the Adirondacks flourished and evolved into

definable elements: the Adirondack guide boat and twig furniture; human habitations like the great camps and the three-sided log and bark lean-to; notable characters like the Adirondack guide; physical transportation like canoe and boat travel on waterways and hiking to mountain vistas; and experiences like remote and primitive hunting and fishing. The wilderness landscape was rapidly becoming a special place for recreation and escape from urbanized environments with unhealthy living conditions.

## Preserving the Landscape

The wilderness preservation movement began in New York with the legislative creation of a forest preserve in 1885 to protect watersheds for water supply and transportation use, to conserve lands after the extensive harvesting of forests, and to provide a future supply of lumber. The public perception that the environmental conditions in urban and rural areas had declined fostered support for the idea that public ownership and conservation of natural and forested landscapes could be used for public enjoyment and human health and welfare.[10] The citizens of the state passed a referendum in 1894 to add constitutional protection to the Forest Preserve lands in the Adirondacks. The most often quoted passage of that legislation is in Article 14, which states, in part, "The lands of the state, now owned or hereafter acquired, constituting the forest preserve as now fixed by law, shall be forever kept as wild forest lands."

The Adirondack Park was created in 1892 and encompassed about 2.8 million acres, of which only about 700,000 were state-owned Forest Preserve lands. The original intent of the legislature was to purchase all the lands within the "Blue Line" to complete the park. However, the mixture of state and private lands was to become the future of the park with the unifying goal of preserving the forested landscape and allowing the environment to be restored to its pre-lumbering and pre-mining conditions. The Adirondack Park contains the only constitutionally protected wild forest lands in the fifty states. Never again did New Yorkers want the Adirondacks to be so heavily disturbed. Rather, the majority voted for the protection and preservation of these forested landscapes. Eventually, in 1971, the Adirondack Park Agency was formed by the legislature to set the policy for development and use of private lands and the Department of Environmental Conservation's management of the Forest Preserve lands.

The wilderness preservation movement that later spread across the nation had its beginnings in the Adirondacks. The Adirondacks mirrored on a regional scale the change in public sentiment and legislation about wild places in the United States: when there were few wild places left, they were valued as important places to protect because of their regional uniqueness, ecological services, and as a place to remind us of our heritage and what the country had been like before European settlement.

The forever-wild concept, the ecological recovery of the forests landscape, and the personal experiences in the Adirondacks of state residents like Bob Marshall and Paul Schaefer affected their wilderness vision and advocacy at both state and national levels.[11] In the 1950s and 1960s, Howard Zahniser wrote many drafts of the federal legislation that became the U.S. Wilderness Act of 1964 from a small cabin in the Adirondacks near what is now the Siamese Ponds Wilderness, a unit of the state Forest Preserve lands. The state and national wilderness preservation movement was strongly influenced by the efforts of these men and others who wanted wild lands as a place for experiencing wild nature and as a scenic backdrop for restorative recreation and tourism experiences away from urbanized environments.[12]

The state designation of some of the Forest Preserve lands in the Adirondacks as wilderness was first proposed by the state legislature in 1960 and finally adopted in 1972. The New York State definition of wilderness is nearly identical to the federal wilderness definition. By 2005, there were 17 wilderness management units in the Adirondack Forest Preserve, totaling more than one million acres. The definition clearly states the need to preserve and maintain wilderness character and ecological integrity while providing for the historic types of nonmotorized recreation that would have existed—hiking, hunting, fishing, boating, camping, primitive travel, and exploring.

## Automobiles Foster More Recreation and Tourism

The common use of the automobile increased the mobility of the public by the 1920s, and recreation and tourism activity began spreading away from railroads and their supporting transportation networks in the Adirondacks. As interest in nature and the availability of automobiles increased, family travel and camping along roads and in developing campgrounds became a new form of recreation. Camping provided a lower-cost way to experience the Adirondacks for many families who could not afford to stay at a resort or to own a summer home or great camp. Camping provided a base from which one could pursue some common recreation activities without guides. A new era of public access to recreation and tourism experiences was opened.

At the turn of the nineteenth century, the state began developing primitive recreational access. The Adirondack Trail Improvement Society began working on foot trails in the High Peaks region in 1897, and their volunteers have constructed and maintained many miles of trail since that time. Almost 70 miles of hiking trails had been constructed by state efforts in the Adirondacks by 1914, and hikers found hiking old logging roads and trails to lookout towers to be a convenient way of traveling in the woods. The 134-mile Northville-Placid trail was completed by the Adirondack Mountain Club in 1924 and donated to the state. Foot trails were developed and marked to many scenic overlooks and summits throughout the Forest Preserve, often requiring permission to create access across adjoining private land holdings.

The state encouraged use of these trails and Forest Preserve lands by granting permits for volunteers to construct Adirondack-style three-sided log lean-tos based on the historic hunting shanties and lean-tos of Adirondack guides. By 1919, the state was also building trailside and waterfront lean-tos for hikers and people traveling by boats on the waterways.[13] Rustic campsites along trails and at the waterfront were created during this era, including the start of camp-sites on state land on the islands in Lake George.

The construction of rustic public campsites for "car camping" began in the 1930s with the Civilian Conservation Corps work-force.[14] These campgrounds were intended to provide a small open site for pitching a tent, a fire ring or fire place, drinking water, and sanitary facilities. The demand for these experiences grew over the decades, and interest in increasing the level of development at the campgrounds fostered the construction of rustic and primitive boat launching sites on waterways, small boat docks, small swimming beaches, and sanitary facilities. Some open ski trails were constructed along mountain routes in the High Peaks region and became popular long before the advent of modern cross-country skiing. Horse trails were mainly horse-drawn wagon trails on abandoned logging roads; horse riding trails would not become common until the 1970s.

Visitors to the Adirondacks could now have brief experiences like that of early explorers and guides by using primitive camping and travels skills. Whether camping, hiking, or traveling by canoe and boat, they saw the landscape as forests grew and vegetation recovered from mining and logging operations of the previous dec-ades. This new recreation approach allowed for more independence when canoeing, camping, hiking, hunting, and fishing, with the help of equipment rented at tourism businesses as well as maps and information supplied by the state and local tourism organizations. It was no longer necessary to rely on guides and resorts for back-to-nature experiences, and one did not have to be wealthy and join the hunting clubs and landowner organizations, or own a great camp. Automobile transportation made recreation and tourism more open to all and less segregated by class—and it gave a means for more to have the freedom to enjoy restoration in nature.

Demand for recreation led to numerous proposals to open the Adirondack Forest Preserve lands to building "closed" cabins (not three-sided lean-tos) in resort-type complexes as had been done in many western national parks.[15] Proposals to build larger state camp-grounds with more capacity and more services and amenities were also debated and defeated. Equally controversial were squatters who built camps without permits on state lands and tent-platform permit holders who increased their structures until they were more like cabin complexes than platforms for canvas tents. Both the squatter and tent platform users would grow in number and abuses until they were largely eliminated by the late 1970s in very controversial and public programs to restore the intent of recreation access to be Forever Wild without human habitation.

Proposals for large recreation developments like downhill ski areas and Olympic competition facilities on state Forest Preserve lands were sometimes defeated and sometimes approved depending on public perception and political interests. In planning for the 1932 Olympics, a proposal to build a bobsled run on state lands was defeated. Judge Harold J. Hinman handed down a judicial opinion that such developed recreation facilities were against the Forever Wild intent of the Forest Preserve:

> We must preserve it in its wild state, its trees, its rocks, its streams. It was to be a great resort for the free use of the people in which nature is given free rein. Its uses for health and pleasure must not be inconsistent with its preservation as forest lands in a wild state. It must always retain the character of wilderness. Hunting, fishing, tramping, mountain climbing, snowshoeing, skiing, or skating find ideal setting in nature's wilderness. It is essentially a quiet and healthful retreat from the turmoils and artificialities of a busy urban life.[16]

Some projects, such as the Whiteface and Gore Mountain ski areas, were approved and constructed. These and other winter recreation facilities built for the Olympic competitions in 1932 and 1980 are the more obvious exceptions to protecting the Forever Wild lands of the Adirondacks. The various interests within preservation organizations and the recreation and tourism industry have attempted to balance protection of the wilderness with interest in developing the wilderness. In many cases, the result has been constructing larger and intensive developments on private lands in

Adirondack communities and constructing more rustic and primitive facilities and access on state lands. However, tension and conflict are inevitable when two such goals must be balanced and when different parties interpret their rights and what constitutes the proper balance in different ways.

## Conflicts in Recreation

After World War II, motorized vehicles like jeeps, snow machines, and powerboats began to appear on the lands and waters of the Forest Preserve. Although at first expensive and slow moving, the machines evolved dramatically in the following decades into versatile, highly technical, and powerful motorized vehicles that could move through difficult terrain and across large land and water distances at high speeds. With more disposable income and mass-produced vehicles of all types, many visitors could afford to purchase and use the equipment to access and traverse landscapes or waterways that previously had required considerable human effort, skill, and time. Canvas-covered wood canoes gave way to lighter and affordable aluminum canoes. State jeep and truck trails, as well as old logging roads, became the access paths for jeeps, four-wheel-drive trucks, dirt bikes, motorcycles, snowmobiles, and all-terrain vehicles of all types. While early state policies prohibited vehicular use on hiking trails, the legal and policy questions about who controlled motorized vehicles became a serious question that continues today. For example, town and county roads exist on some public lands, and that raises questions about which government agency can control which types of motorized vehicles and under what conditions.

Private development on lakes and public-access waterways opened these bodies of water to public use for human-powered boats and canoes, and later for powerboats. Like the recreation-use situation on land, conflicts emerged because the experiences sought by human-powered watercraft users were being negatively affected by powerboats and their operation. Float planes offered another popular means of sightseeing and access to remote bodies of water within the Adirondack Forest Preserve. Historically, primitive forms of recreation had been human powered, and the general level of recreation and tourism use had been small. While transportation had shaped the recreation and tourism industry and experience in the Adirondacks, now the experience itself was being directly shaped by the transportation. Instead of immersing themselves in the wilderness and nature experience on its terms, visitors were quickly traveling through the landscape as the background to a more luxurious or comfortable experience. Of course, there were those who still traveled and explored by the more rustic and primitive methods, but it was the sudden change in equipment, and the transformation of the experiences, that caused the conflict in feeling and ideology. For those who were attempting to leave the civilized life behind in urban areas, there were others who tended to bring all the equipment of a fast-paced life style with them on vacation.

The conflicts in use, activities, and equipment among different types of visitors and residents were exacerbated by the growing number of visitors in the Adirondacks and their use of the Forest Preserve lands. Seeking the restorative powers of nature was becoming difficult, and those who had grown used to and expected the human-powered activities and immersion in a quiet, remote environment began to feel neither quiet nor restored. State management of recreational use and users began in the 1960s to restrict what, when, and where certain activities could be enjoyed and the number of people participating.

Since the 1960s, there has been a steady increase in the diversity and types of equipment and activities in which people engage, along with their wide array of interests and levels of ability. The large numbers of people concentrating in some facilities, using some areas, and enjoying some rapidly growing sports became a concern to conservationists and the public. Some believed that current recreation and tourism demands were having a negative and lasting impact and endangering the Forest Preserve land and resources. These fears were further fueled by the proposed recreation and tourism development projects being discussed at that time. The fears of others were that restrictions on tourism and housing development would further increase unemployment and local dependence on limited seasonal tourism employment.

A new limited access highway, I-87, was completed between Albany and the Canadian border in 1967, opening up the eastern Adirondacks to more pressure for summer homes and vacation interests of all types. Affluent middle- and upper-class families all wanted to enjoy the park whether by powerboat or a remote multi-day canoe trip, or whether for camping in a recreational vehicle in a campground or backpacking through the wilderness for brook trout fishing. Numerous proposals for resorts, theme parks, tract housing, and second-home developments raised serious concerns among con-servationists and the public about the future of the wild character of the Forest Preserve lands and the entire Adirondack Park.

The tension between those who want to protect wild forested landscapes and rustic human-powered transportation with primitive travel methods and skills and those who want to develop the for-ested landscape for more tourism-based employment remains high in most Adirondack communities. How people view nature, the Forest Preserve lands, and the interrelationship between public and private lands depends on the perspectives they hold when they look upon that landscape—and these conflicts and tensions have been part of the Adirondack culture and region for over 150 years. Within the legal context of the Adirondack Park a wide range of recreation and tour-ism experiences can be provided either on public or private lands, as long as the ecological integrity and forested landscape are protected.

## Trends in Provision of Recreation

In the last 150 years, the Adirondack region has gone from a mature forest to a heavily harvested and disturbed ecosystem and back to a largely intact forested landscape that represents the mixed north-ern hardwood and conifer forest that is reminiscent of the former landscape. The recreation and tourism experiences of permanent and seasonal residents and visitors have been largely defined in the Adirondacks by the protection and preservation of wildland land-scapes. Adirondack history, culture, and the biophysical landscape have shaped what recreation and tourism are as a uniquely an Adirondack experience. Overall there are four trends that are worth noting because of how they will affect recreation and tourism in the next decades:

1. Transportation has shaped recreation and tourism through time and will continue to shape it and be shaped by it. For example, the first railroad to traverse the Adirondacks from Remsen to Malone, which hauled forest products and later passengers, was not operated during the 1960s and 1970s. That railway has reopened as what is now the Adirondack Scenic Railroad service for tourism excursions along a route that will one day extend from Utica to Lake Placid. Transportation is now part of the tourism attraction as well as offering a service.

2. Adirondack resources shaped the recreation experience, and, in turn, those experiences are directly and indirectly shaping the resources and their management. For example, brook trout fishing was historically one of the unique and rewarding recreation activities that could be found throughout most Adirondack waters. A series of environmental changes and fishing pressure caused brook trout fishery to be significantly reduced to some lakes and ponds and small higher-elevation streams with good gradient, water temperature, and flow volume. Since the 1940s, about 150 of the possible 3,100 water bodies that could support brook trout populations have been reclaimed with seven heritage strains of Adirondack brook trout.

3. The relationship between the public and private sectors is an important component of the Adirondack Park and is one of its greatest attributes, and yet it can be a cause of conflict. One example of compatibility and cooperation is the attempt by state, county, and local officials and snowmobile clubs to create a parkwide snowmobile trail system that crosses public lands where legally allowed and is connected across private lands through landowner agreements and leases. These trails are planned as a trail system that can be maintained by volunteer organizations and financially supported by the users and the state through a variety of funding mechanisms. Thus, this system is safer and more enjoyable as predominantly a

single-use trail for this user group with the support of the public and private sectors.

4. Conflicts in use, goals, and activities will continue to occur as the diversity and number of users and their interests, activities, and equipment increases. One of the mechanisms to help manage visitors and their experiences on public lands is through the completion and implementation of the Unit Management Plans for the Forest Preserve areas by the state Department of Environmental Conservation under the policies provided by the Adirondack Park State Land Master Plan.

The "sense of place" in the Adirondacks held by recreationists and tourists, especially permanent and seasonal residents, is strongly influenced by public and private sector land ownership and management. Having more developed facilities on private lands and fewer developed facilities and programs on public lands allows for a wider spectrum of recreation opportunities.

## Suggested Readings

Bond, H. E. *Boats and Boating in the Adirondacks.* Blue Mountain Lake, N.Y./Syracuse: Adirondack Museum/Syracuse Univ. Press, 1995.

Brown, E. *The Forest Preserve of New York State: A Handbook for Conservationists.* Glens Falls, N.Y.: Adirondack Mountain Club, 1985.

Brumley, C. *Guides of the Adirondacks: A History.* Utica, N.Y.: North Country Books, 1994.

Durant, K., and H. Durant. *The Adirondack Guide Boat.* Blue Mountain Lake, N.Y.: Adirondack Museum, 1980.

Gilborn, C. A. *Adirondack Camps: Homes Away from Home, 1850–1950.* Syracuse: Syracuse Univ. Press, 2000.

Glover, J. M. *A Wilderness Original: The Life of Bob Marshall.* Seattle: Mountaineers Press, 1986.

Jamieson, P. *The Adirondack Reader.* Glens Falls, N.Y.: Adirondack Mountain Club, 1983.

Jenkins, J. and A. Keal. *The Adirondack Atlas: A Geographic Portrait of the Adirondack Park.* Syracuse: Syracuse Univ. Press, 2004.

Schaefer, P. *Adirondack Explorations: Nature Writings of Verplanck Colvin.* Syracuse: Syracuse Univ. Press, 1997.

————. *Defending the Wilderness: The Adirondack Writings of Paul Schaefer.* Syracuse: Syracuse Univ. Press, 1989.

Schneider, P. *The Adirondacks: A History of America's First Wilderness.* New York: Henry Holt, 1997.

Terrie, P. G. *Contested Terrain: A New History of Nature and People in the Adirondacks.* Blue Mountain Lake, N.Y./Syracuse: Adirondack Museum. Syracuse Univ. Press, 1997.

Thoreau, H. D. *The Maine Woods.* Princeton, N.J.: Princeton Univ. Press, 1972.

Zahniser, H. *Where Wilderness Preservation Began: Adirondack Writings of Howard Zahniser.* Utica, N.Y.: North Country Books, 1992.

# 11

## Great Camps and Conservation

CRAIG GILBORN

In 1972, when my family and I were new to the Adirondack region, the larger camps were by no means a secret, but because of their inaccessibility in a region bigger than the neighboring state of Vermont, the particulars about them and their importance in the aggregate were not understood. Having studied the building arts at museums in Delaware and Virginia, I soon began visiting camps in the vicinity of Blue Mountain Lake, one being Camp Pine Knot on Raquette Lake, built between 1875 and 1900 and regarded as the spiritual father of "great" camps in the Adirondacks.

These villagelike enclaves were outposts for sheltering and feeding a dozen or more people in remote places that are no easier to reach today than they were more than a century ago. Constructed almost wholly from trees cut and milled on the preserve, the wood buildings needed attention almost from the start, by repairing wind damage and removing snow from roofs. Asked the number of buildings at Nehasane Park, the superintendent gave 87, each having to have snow shoveled off its roof.

The Great Depression and two wars led many owners and managers to see the day when the camp and its preserve would be unaffordable. Labor was scarce in wartime, and luxurious camps, which

This article is dedicated to the late Harold A. Jerry, Jr., with whom the writer served as a member of Gov. Cuomo's Commission on the Adirondacks in the Twenty-First Century, in 1989–90.

depended on workers, cut back, partly out of necessity but also out of sensitivity for idle talk about life at the camp at a time of rationing. Descendants became alarmed as expenses rose every year on vacation homes occupied at most for two or three months out of the year. Then there were property taxes. Young adults coming out of the war wanted alternatives to the sedentary (stodgy) vacations of their parents and grandparents.

It is important to recall that the stringency of life and credit in the 1930s and 1940s carried into the postwar era. Easy credit and grants from foundations and government agencies were phenomena that peaked in the years of a booming economy, starting with the Reagan administration. It was about that time, in the 1980s, that the outlook for camps began to brighten, as owners learned that the Adirondack Nature Conservancy and other organizations would help them find ways, such as conservation easements, for keeping properties intact.

The 1980 Winter Olympic Games in Lake Placid are a convenient benchmark marking the rediscovery of the Adirondacks by men and women whose year-end bonus exceeded the lifetime earnings of nearly all residents. Where to put that embarrassment of cash? One place was a cottage on a lake, a perfect investment, since it could be enjoyed as it appreciated in value. The oil embargos of 1973–74 and 1978–81 raised questions about transportation and keeping some camps heated in winter, but those perturbations were brief, forgotten as the cost of gasoline and heating oil fell.

It took years before people grasped that a second Gilded Age had been returning to the Adirondack Park, a renaissance of the rich analogous to the titans of commerce and industry whose sojourns in the Adirondacks began about 1890. Their names are identified with many educational and charitable institutions: Huntington, Webb, Morgan, Vanderbilt, Whitney, Guggenheim, Rockefeller, Durant, Lewisohn, Hochschild. What the new wealth of today leave as a legacy remains to be seen.

An 1893 inventory of preserves in the Adirondack Park, in Roger Thompson's dissertation, "The Doctrine of Wilderness,"[1] lists 45 "estates" ranging in size from the 267 acres of the Saranac Club to the 116,000 acres of the Adirondack League Club, still the holder of the biggest private preserve in the Adirondack Park. In extent the preserves averaged more than 21,000 acres, with the 8,752 acres of the Greenshue Club being midway.

Some preserves were purchased at tax sales, the earliest example being Township 39, purchased in its entirety in 1851 by Benjamin Brandreth for 15 cents an acre. Brandreth Park's holdings, while not as extensive today, still belong to the descendants of Dr. Brandreth. A literary and artistic group from Boston and Cambridge purchased a 22,000-acre tract for $600 in 1858–59, but soon gave it up, in part because of the Civil War. The tract, or a portion of it (14,472 acres), was acquired from its owner in 2008 by the Adirondack Nature Conservancy, which will hold it until the state pays the $16 million purchase price.

Several designated "estates" on Roger Thompson's list—all of Township 6, most of Township 5, and part of Township 34—likely were concessions made by the state to the Adirondack Railroad years earlier. Constructing roads and railroads was necessary for settlement and economic growth, which made it a legitimate function of government to offer land and exemption from taxes to investors and builders. William West Durant acquired many of the railroad's lands as a consequence of his selling the railroad—which his father had built—to the D&H Railroad in 1889.

Durant carved the Uncas Preserve out of Township 5, the Sagamore Preserve and Kill Kare Preserve in Township 6, and a country club and golf course on three connecting lakes in Township 34. He also set aside three preserves in Newcomb, all or most of which were acquired by Archer Huntington. Durant's need for money forced him to ask the state's Game and Forest Commission to buy the bulk of those townships that he still held; the three-man Forest Commission authorized the purchase of nearly all of Township 6, or 24,000 acres, in October 1897. Questions and eyebrows were raised in Albany when it was learned that the lieutenant governor, who was commission chair, owned 1,030 acres now surrounded by state land, a private in-holding.

Scouting councils have sometimes treated purchases and gift of land in the Adirondacks as investments, demonstrating the limits of stewardship when business considerations are given precedence. Camp Uncas was purchased from a nonprofit medical organization as an investment by a trust acting on behalf of the Rockland County Boy Scout Council. The buildings were neglected when I visited them in 1973, and most of their furnishings had been sold or carried away. My escort boasted of bathing in a bathtub in which J. Pierpont Morgan presumably had sat. The state acquired the preserve at the time it also was acquiring the Sagamore Preserve, in 1975, thereby consolidating the adjoining two tracts for the first time since 1895. The couple behind the organization that acquired Sagamore Lodge were allowed to buy Uncas's camp and farm buildings.

A wake-up call for preservationists occurred in 1975 when Syracuse University announced it was selling its conference center and preserve on Sagamore Lake. It owned two other Adirondack camps, one being Minnowbrook Conference Center, on Blue Mountain Lake, and it needed the money and relief from the expenses of the facility. The university had gotten the property, including some 1,526 acres, from Margaret Emerson, the widow many years earlier of Alfred G. Vanderbilt. She gave the property with the understanding that it would be part of the school's continuing education program.

Perhaps mindful of the continuing problem of Santanoni, the DEC separated the land with the chalet and service buildings at Sagamore, approximately 10 acres, retaining the farm buildings. (The university cut the trees on the preserve and held a public auction at which many furnishings were sold.)

The buildings at Santanoni had been part of the 1971 purchase by the state for inclusion in the Forest Preserve, making the disposition of the buildings—which now were nonconforming structures under the Forever Wild provisions of the state constitution—a dilemma. Had there been a constituency for preserving structures of architectural and social importance, the several parties engaged in negotiations might have searched for a buyer for the site, with its lodge and ancillary buildings. Historic preservation had not yet gained a following inside the Adirondack Park, and little was known about the architectural importance of the camp and its model farm and dairy operation. No one in state government wanted to be blamed for destroying the camp at Santanoni, as the law ordained. It locked the buildings but did nothing otherwise, leaving climate and nature to bring them down. Environmentalists were not happy, one adherent of Forever Wild warning against any effort to blacktop the road to the camp, which no one had ever proposed. But they maintained a discreet silence, since they sympathized with the residents of Newcomb, the population of which was declining due to cutbacks at the mine and mill at Tahawus.

Given that experience at Santanoni, the DEC allowed the land under Sagamore's Swiss chalet lodge and its satellite cottages and service buildings to be used as before. However, the agency held onto the farm and staff buildings adjoining the camp complex. The nonprofit owner needed the farm to interpret the property and appealed, thereby beginning a lengthy and costly exchange of some 10 acres of land under the farm buildings for a tract of equal or greater value elsewhere in the Adirondack Park.

As effective as Great Camps were in taking basic human needs and magically turning them into wants, the camps still harkened back in time to their antecedents, the military garrisons or forts of colonial America, in which the residents were sustained in remote but strategic locations by foraging, light farming, and resupply from the outside. Closer in time to the Great Camps were logging camps, which were staging areas in the woods where loggers ate and slept in bunkhouses.

Going from the dank shanties of loggers to the woodland lodges of the rich is admittedly a challenge for the imagination, remembering the historic appeal of the Adirondacks and places like it for leisure classes who had never held an ax or leghold trap. Informality governs the dress code today, sandals and shorts replacing the jackets and dresses of the 1940s, which in turn were compromises for suits and gowns before the First World War, when gentlemen and ladies dressed for dinner, a reminder to everyone, including the help, that privilege entailed responsibility.

Donations of camps and preserves began in the 1930s. Archer and Anna Hyette Huntington (she was a noted sculptor) gave the former lands of the Caughnawauga Club in 1931, and their camp and preserve on Arbutus Lake in 1939, to the College of Environmental Science and Forestry in Syracuse, which acquired thereby 15,000 acres of contiguous forest land. Another prewar gift came in 1937, when a married couple gave Eagle Island to a Girl Scout Council in New Jersey. Built for Levi P. Morton on Upper Saranac Lake in 1903, it included the island and a parcel on the mainland. The property, like others on the Saranac Lakes, lacked a large preserve, probably because wealthy buyers on the lakes were not interested in land for farming or management purposes, fresh food being available by a developed delivery system that now included daily arrivals of trains to Saranac Lake.

In 1948 Camp Pine Knot was given to Cortland College by Archer Huntington, whose father, Collis P. Huntington, had died at the camp in August 1900. Except for a caretaker, the camp had unoccupied for forty-seven years. Since 1948 generations of teachers and students have used the camp as a classroom and jumping-off place for learning about nature and outdoor recreation. Summer is the busiest period, but winter sessions are held when the ice on Raquette Lake is strong enough to allow a truck to keep open a road to the camp from the mainland.

An option to buy 25,000 acres of forest land imperiled by logging led to the establishment of the Adirondack Mountain Reserve in 1887, the stockholders of which generally belonged to the Ausable Club, at St. Hubert's. Some of that land, in the High Peaks area, was purchased by the state. The Kildare Club divided 10,000 acres into two roughly equal sections, one where occasional cutting was allowed and the other left untouched. Kill Kare's 1,000 acre preserve was purposely left uncut by Mr. and Mrs. Francis P. Garvan. The Adirondack League Club has managed its very extensive holdings more adroitly than any other entity in the Adirondack Park.

For example, it sold 14,000 and 22,000 acres to the state in 1897 and 1900, respectively, thereby assuring that there would be a buffer of Forest Preserve land on its flank. Long a supporter of scientific research of fish in its lakes, the club owned 53,000 acres in 1990, the year of its centennial.

The state began acquiring land at tax sales beginning in 1871, in response to critics who saw the state's declining stake in a region with recreational potential. New York's confiscation of Crown and Loyalist property in 1781 had given it most of the land in the region. But by 1873 it had only about 39,854 acres. It began peremptorily claiming lands at tax sales, so that by 1883 it held an estimated 750,616 acres. At a tax sale in 1877, Dr. Thomas Clark Durant fumed when an official of the state removed 19,434 acres of Township 40 from public bidding. Most of the land around Raquette Lake is in state hands today, a consequence of what Dr. Durant said was the state's "building title" at tax sales in 1871, 1877, and 1881.[2] A law in 1883 prohibited the sale of state lands in the ten (now eleven) Adirondack counties, followed two years later by a law that established the Forest Preserve and a three-person Forest Commission as the replacement for the Land Office.

Despite the tension inherent between parties with very differing private and public accountabilities, preserve owners and state officials found it in their interest to cooperate. The impression that the state and private owners are adversaries derives from stories that newspapers like to run, but history tells a different story, in which the state is potentially a willing buyer of select tracts of land owned by willing sellers. Those in government know that the great majority of New Yorkers have always applauded additions to the Forest Preserve.

Legislation sanctioning private preserves, passed in 1871, allowed owners to post their land and apprehend trespassers, a sanctioning of property rights by the state in a region where people had hunted and camped pretty much where they wanted. It was reminiscent of the privileges and rights of land ownership claimed by monarchs and their favorites in Europe and Great Britain. Posting previously open land was unpopular in Adirondack towns, although enforcement was difficult and easily evaded, as everyone knew.

Greatly influencing both the state and private estate owners were university-trained specialists in forestry and wildlife management. Science, as in "scientific forestry," was often intoned, and if errors were made, they could be rationalized as part of the learning curve: game birds and elk were unsuccessfully introduced at Litchfield Park and Nehasane Park, fingerlings from a hatchery outside the region died by the time they reached Newcomb, and a fish hatchery constructed at Kamp Kill Kare had a brief life. But then also did Gifford Pinchot draw up a management plan for the forests at Dr. William Seward Webb's Nehasane Park, and a model farm was designed by Edward Bennett, an agricultural planner, for Robert C. Pruyn at Santanoni.

Hundreds of men and women found useful employment at the camps. Seasonal work for men included construction jobs that often required that they live at or near the site. Lists of names and destinations were posted for local readers in the weekly newspapers. Much of the furniture and all of the ironwork was done during the reconstruction and expansion of Kamp Kill Kare, between 1915 and about 1923. The men who did the carpentry and stonework were praised for their ability to improvise rustic effects at the site, according to architects in the Manhattan offices of John Russell Pope.

William West Durant, in a letter to Alfred G. Vanderbilt, said that five employees were needed at Sagamore Lodge: a caretaker and his wife, a teamster, and two laborers. That was the number, he wrote, "without entertaining,"[3] implying that Vanderbilt would need to augment the five with five or six more—a housekeeper, two cooks, and a couple more for doing the fourteen hours of work each day, in the kitchen, waiting table, and making and changing beds.

Camps were visible evidence of occupancy in the wilderness. The lumber barons had hunting and fishing camps, but their stake in the region was tenuous, always subject to commercial conditions. Preserves, which were sometimes logged and sometime not, or a little of both, anchored their owners to the Adirondacks and an environmental ethic.

Skeptics might agree to a point, but such superfluities as bowling alleys (Sagamore, Bluff Point, White Pine Camp), squash court (Kill Kare), Norman chapel (Kill Kare), and the like, which were among the hallmarks of Great Camps, had nothing to do with conservation, any more than did chefs and personal secretaries from the city (Wildair, Kill Kare) or the politically powerful of Washington, carried by private plane, square dancing in country costume in Mrs. Post's dacha (Topridge).

For the late Anthony N. B. Garvan, whose mother delivered him at Kamp Kill Kare, the charm of the Great Camps was that they made difficult things look easy in an unbroken forest. Silver and crystal at dinner, commonplace at his mother's other homes, in Manhattan and Millbrook, were magical in the Adirondacks.[4] Diversions like those were indulgences, but then so were the preserves surrounding the camps.

The owners, for all their wealth, can be seen to have been adopting an environmental ethic. They saw the beauty and value of nature and most likely could see the harm that had been done by industry, even as some undoubtedly had profited from it. Nature is savored all the more from the safety and fellowship afforded by the camp. Doing good in the end may require a little sinning along the way; what appears to us as supercilious may be a kind of investment in the camp and the preserve around it, adding human lore to the beauty of place.

We might note the antipathy in western civilization for a visually unbounded land, or what John Brinkerhoff Jackson called the "vernacular landscape,"[5] a large amorphous territory lacking visual signals about underlying ownership. A New York law in 1784 referred to the region's lands as "waste and unappropriated," implying opprobrium and the kind of legal legerdemain that allowed European nations and the American government to claim territories of indigenous peoples who lacked recorded traditions of land ownership.

Common law recognized squatter's rights to land if its owner failed to mark his property or visit it. There were squatters in the Adirondacks, some on lands owned by logging companies, which generally did not object to cabins because they did not hamper their operations. Alvah Dunning had shanties at three locations, two on Raquette Lake and a third on Eighth Lake. His claim to the last was not upheld, but the Raquette Lake properties remain in private hands, although the state has never relinquished its claim, which dates from the tax sales of the 1870s. Osprey Island's owners trace their title back to the late 1860s or a little later, when Dunning occupied shanties abandoned there by writer William "Adirondack" Murray. In 1880, the hunter and trapper signed the island over to the Durant family for $100.

Whether modest or "great," buildings on preserves sustained the owner and his workers, but, as seen, they were evidence of an underlying ownership of the territory on which they stood. That may not seem important until we see what happened to the forest without resident stakeholders: lumbermen harvested the marketable timber and then let the cutover land to be sold for back taxes. Lumber interests held an estimated 1.2 million acres in 1892, so they remained an influence in Albany despite public criticism of the wasted and drowned lands left behind by their operations.

Great Camps have not always been saved from destruction. In 1978 the state acquired by purchase Lake Lila and 14,644 acres of land, the Webb family retaining about 18,000 acres in the western part of the preserve. The shingle-style lodge, with dormers and a porch that in summer had awnings of striped canvas shading a wide front porch, slept twenty-five, although the family in time came to prefer the cottages on the lake. But the lodge was not unique, a plainer version (especially inside) of country estate houses elsewhere, including the Webb home in Shelburne, Vermont, which is now part of Shelburne Farms. No one defended the lodge when it was dismantled, in part because it had been an island of exclusivity whose only connection to the outside world was by railroad. When rail service ended in the 1960s, the Webb family had to buy additional land and build a road to the highway.

Santanoni was significant architecturally, although the reasons for that were not apparent in the Adirondacks in 1971, where historic preservation had yet to gain an informed foothold. That year saw the preserve purchased in its entirety, its buildings now part of the Forest Preserve and theoretically subject to destruction. For Newcomb, already suffering from cutbacks by its biggest employer, NL Industries, the prospect was a bleak one. Decision makers in Albany, as if aware, postponed an execution date, perhaps in hope of a compromise down the road. It was an instance of good coming out of foot-dragging by a bureaucracy.

A succession of events subsequent to the formation of Adirondack Architectural Heritage (AARCH), chiefly by Howard Kirschenbaum, who had support from George Canon, the town's supervisor and longtime resident, secured the future of the camp and farm buildings at Santanoni. The lodge was unique in the Adirondack Park, a "veranda camp," in which the unifying features were the porch and its roof, or, as explained in the Forest Commission Report of 1893, "There is so much rain in the Adirondacks and life indoors is so unnatural, that provision against confinement was made by adding 5,000 square feet of piazzas." The porch, which extended across the entire front of the lodge, or 265 feet, constituted a matrix that enclosed five cottages, the biggest in the middle, flanked by two cottages on each side that were used for sleeping and personal time.

Americans today know more about the Adirondacks because of the region's claims to the forested hideaways of the rich and famous than from knowledge about the cornerstone of wilderness preservation, the Forever Wild protections in New York's constitution. This is due to the flood of illustrated stories about large Adirondack camps that began appearing a year or two before the 1980 Winter Olympics in Lake Placid, principally on television followed by the Internet.

I close this article on an ironic note: the proposal to build what proponents call "Great Camps," up to 25 in number, each on lots of 50 to 100 acres, south of Tupper Lake Village. "Great" is a marketer's lure that seeks to trade on the glamour of the camps and an era gone by. Having written about the camps, I am an accessory to the meretriciousness to which I now object.

But what is proposed for Tupper Lake Village repeats what was evident in Westchester County in the 1950s, when I cleared branches from telephone lines in what had been farmland north of White Plains that had been divided into estates with houses set back from the road by expansive green lawns and partly concealed by shrubbery. The gentrification of suburban New York does not belong in the Adirondacks. Already the waterfronts of too many Adirondack lakes are overdeveloped, and while "44-acre zoning" around each "Great Camp" sounds ample, it still represents the slice-and-dice strategy inimical to wilderness, wildlife, and open space.

# 12

## Development Rates and Patterns in the Adirondacks

*Paradise Lost*

PETER BAUER

Of all the forces that will change the Adirondack Park in the years and decades ahead, it is residential development, and all that supports and follows it, that threatens the park most of all. Even as we face such monumental challenges from global climate change, which could substantially change the flora and fauna across the Adirondack Park, development will determine whether or not a truly wild landscape exists at all. Development threatens the ecological integrity of the Adirondacks as it fragments forest systems and changes aquatic systems. Development also threatens not just the vast, unbroken forested landscape that today dominates the Adirondack Park, but the wild aesthetic character of the Adirondack Park as highly visible houses are built on hilltops, ridgelines, lakeshores and on formerly vacant lands across the Adirondacks. Both the wild aesthetic and wild ecological landscape are at stake for the Adirondack Park.

In the early years of the twenty-first century, the impacts of development are being talked about outside a few lone voices in the Adirondack environmental community. The impacts of development are now squarely on the agenda of park residents, policymakers, and elected officials. Beyond the ecological impacts from forest fragmentation, degraded water quality, and denigration of the wild character of the park, development is also tearing apart the historic social fabric and traditional culture that dominated many Adirondack communities over the past century. Development has made many Adirondack communities unaffordable for those most likely to live there—those who grew up there—as well as working-class and middle-class families wishing to move here, as the housing market is skewed toward luxury recreational housing. Further, the social institutions that are dominated by local residents, such as fire and rescue squads, are struggling to enlist adequate numbers. Hospitals and school districts complain that the high cost of housing limits their ability to attract professional positions. Major tourism facilities have resorted to foreign labor as the local labor supply cannot meet their demands.

In 2007, neither the futures of the natural resources of the Adirondack Park nor of Adirondack communities are secure. The northern hardwood forest and high- and low-elevation boreal forests that dominate the Adirondack Park today once covered 600 million acres across the central and eastern United States, southern Canada, and western Europe. The Adirondack Park is the best representative large landscape that remains of this once-great forest and is recognized as such across the world by scientists and policymakers. While nothing in the future is ever guaranteed or ever secure, if present trends continue through the next several decades, the internationally significant landscape that exists today in the Adirondack Park will not exist in the future. Nor will the park have viable human communities that allow people skilled and unskilled, imaginative and enterprising, as well as disadvantaged and uneducated, to sustain themselves economically. Rather, we will have sprawling communities akin to parts of Colorado, where there are more houses than year-round residents.

Continued public land acquisition and accelerating housing development are cementing parts of the Adirondack Park that have been suspended in a state of flux since 1892. We know that Mount Marcy will be wild Forest Preserve in the future and that the Main Streets of Lake Placid and Old Forge will be downtown, commercial village areas as well. But, while there are many other parts of the Adirondack Park that could go either way, there are fewer in

2007 than there were 25 years ago on both sides of the ledger. What will be the final composition of public and private lands within the Adirondack Park? It is safe to say that either lands will be protected through acquisition of conservation easements and by addition to the Forest Preserve or lands will be developed into housing.

## Background on Development Trends

In any discussion of development in the Adirondack Park, there are several facts to keep in mind. From 1990 to 2004 over 13,500 new houses were permitted across the Adirondack Park. In the years 2005–6, another 1,500 were added. This represents a rate of growth of just over 1 percent annually. Growth was uneven; the busiest 10 towns saw 30 percent of the development (just under 4,000 houses). Development was high in 1990 (1,150 new houses), largely spurred on by public concern that development might be restricted after the appointment in 1989 by Governor Mario Cuomo of the Commission on the Adirondacks in the Twenty-First Century and its report two years later, but development has been highest of all in the years after 2001 (over 1,200 new houses in 2004). Other indicators of growth–real estate transfers, jurisdictional inquiries to the Adirondack Park Agency (APA), property values, population, growth in buildings, new lots and subdivisions–all trend up. The most important fact to note is that the APA regulated just 34 percent of the development in these years. The rest was regulated unilaterally by the 103 towns and villages in the Adirondack Park.

There have been five significant research efforts on development in the Adirondack Park since the late 1960s, but relatively little research on the impacts of development or the limits of growth in the park. A brief review of these five efforts sets the stage for what we know about development in the Adirondack Park and what we do not know.

### 1970: Temporary Study Commission on the Future of the Adirondacks

The Temporary Study Commission was appointed by Governor Nelson Rockefeller in September 1968 and made its report to the governor in December 1970. In its Technical Report 1A, "Public and Private Land," the commission inventoried private lands across the Adirondack Park. The commission found that 40 percent of the park was public lands. Of the private lands, 55 percent was private forestlands, 12.6 percent in agriculture, and 12 percent in "urban-like uses including single-family residences, vacant residential lots, commercial, industrial, utilities and railroads." The report found that 80 percent of the park was in open space, but the areas in which development had occurred represented the areas of highest values.

In addition to analyzing land uses, the commission's real historic value was its work to analyze land ownership patterns across the Adirondacks. For both sets of data, the commission's work represents an important benchmark in our collective understanding of development in the park. The commission found some 626 landowners of 500 acres or more whose ownership was nearly two million acres combined, some 53 percent of the total private land area studied. The commission also provided an analysis of landownership by residents and nonresidents. The park would benefit by a replication of this research.

*1988: Adirondack Park Zoning: Property Values*
*and Tax Bases, 1963–1983*

In 1988, the New York State Office of Equalization and Assessment published a report by Peter Wissell on the impact of the APA Act and creation of the Adirondack Park Agency in 1971 on property values in the Adirondack Park. The report studied 4,300 individual land transactions of unimproved parcels from 1963 to 1983. The report found that boom and bust cycles affected land values both within and outside the park; that legislative action that created the APA initially increased values in the park, but that lands outside the park caught up after a few years; that factors of proximity to water, distance from improved roads, and distance from Albany all shaped the value of a property more than its zoning; that there was a rough parity between lands in Hamlet, Rural Use, and Resource

Management areas with comparable lands outside the park; and that Low Intensity lands seemed to possess a higher value than comparable lands outside the park. The report concluded that the real-estate market in the Adirondack Park was cyclical and was strongly influenced by national economic forces.

*1990: Commission on the Adirondacks in the Twenty-First Century*

The commission researched development trends in the Adirondacks and prepared technical reports about this issue. Technical Report 38 (1990) sought to track development trends through analysis of a variety of indicators, including subdivisions recorded with county clerks (8,400 new lots added between 1969 and 1989); State Department of Health, APA subdivision applications (applications for 16,000 new lots between 1974 and 1988); assessors' annual reports (2,490 new lots created between 1981 and 1988); post office delivery statistics (133 zip codes had 15 percent increases in new postal addresses between 1985 and 1989); and electrical customer information statistics (hookups increased by 1,700 in 1988 and 1989). The report showed an upward trend in development activity in the Adirondacks from the late 1960s through the late 1980s.

This report relied upon a variety of indicators because centralized data were limited in the late 1980s. It attempted to analyze building permits issued by the towns and villages, but most towns and villages in the Adirondacks only had such records going back a few years. The report concluded,

> Among the most important findings in this study is the fact that a great deal of effort is required to gather any useful data relating to the overall amount of subdivision and development activity occurring in the Park. The fragmentation of jurisdiction over these matters has resulted in a record-keeping system that is too disjointed and incomplete to yield useful information in a timely fashion. Furthermore, the statutes which require the review and filing of records related to, subdivisions contain gaps and ineffective sanctions that contribute to the lack of good information.

*1993: Growth in the Adirondack Park*

In 1993, the APA summarized important information for the period 1967–92 based on tax-roll data from Adirondack towns and villages (table 12.1). During that 25-year period, the total number of residential tax parcels (200 classification series on tax rolls) in the Adirondack Park grew from 45,886 to 72,269. The study is an important benchmark and is useful for showing the dramatic increase in residential development in the Adirondack Park between 1967 and

TABLE 12.1. **Adirondack Park residential growth, 1967–1992; net additions to tax rolls**

| | Taxable parcels | | | | 5-year totals, 1987–1992 | | |
|---|---|---|---|---|---|---|---|
| County | 1967 | 1987 | 1992 | Total | Total | Resource management | Rural use |
| Clinton | 2,810 | 4,251 | 4,735 | 1,925 | 484 | 45 | 232 |
| Essex | 11,245 | 15,999 | 17,095 | 5,850 | 1,096 | 192 | 251 |
| Franklin | 5,462 | 6,497 | 7,108 | 1,646 | 611 | 23 | 307 |
| Fulton | 4,697 | 6,360 | 6,707 | 2,010 | 347 | -5 | 104 |
| Hamilton | 3,627 | 5,152 | 5,794 | 2,167 | 642 | 60 | 114 |
| Herkimer | 2,995 | 3,775 | 4,143 | 1,148 | 368 | 28 | 65 |
| Lewis | 806 | 1,111 | 1,274 | 468 | 163 | 24 | 68 |
| Oneida | 556 | 694 | 705 | 149 | 11 | 1 | 17 |
| St. Lawrence | 2,290 | 2,756 | 2,893 | 603 | 137 | 113 | 94 |
| Saratoga | 2,968 | 4,590 | 4,810 | 1,842 | 220 | -6 | 71 |
| Warren | 7,424 | 13,108 | 14,993 | 7,549 | 1,885 | — | — |
| Washington | 1,006 | 1,704 | 2,012 | 1,006 | 308 | 80 | 43 |
| Total | 45,886 | 65,997 | 72,269 | 26,383 | 6,272 | 555 | 1,366 |

*Source:* J. S. Banta, "Growth in the Adirondack Park," Adirondack Park Agency, Oct. 7, 1993. 1967 tax roll data were compiled by the NYS Division of Equalization and Assessment for the Temporary Study Commission on the Future of the Adirondacks. 1987 and 1992 tax rolls were adjusted to exclude all parcels with centerpoints outside of Adirondack Park. Land-use classifications are based on the location of the centerpoint of the parcel.

1992. It is the most important study we have for development over that period of time.

## 2001: Growth in the Adirondack Park

In the late 1990s, the Residents' Committee to Protect the Adirondacks (RCPA) set out to analyze development in the Adirondack Park from 1990 to 1999. The RCPA selected 1990 for the year to begin this research for two reasons. First, 1990 marked the publication of the final report by the Commission on the Adirondacks in the Twenty-First Century, and the RCPA was interested in seeing how much new development had occurred in the ten years after the report. Second, from 1990 forward, building permit records were largely maintained and intact by the local governments across the Adirondack Park, which enabled a better survey of building activity than was available for previous research efforts. The key findings of the RCPA study over this period are as follows:

• Adirondack towns and villages issued 47,762 total building permits, of which 8,589 were for new residential, commercial, or industrial structures;

• The APA issued 3,242 permits, which authorized 3,731 new residential, commercial, or industrial structures and a total of 9,647 total activities;

• The APA regulated 43 percent of new development within the Adirondack Park, and local governments regulated 57 percent;

• 8,268 new residential tax parcels were added to tax rolls in the Adirondacks in the 1990s. The RCPA found that residential tax parcels (200 class) increased from 67,249 to 75,517 in the 103 towns and villages;

• In the 103 towns and villages of the Adirondack Park, 15 had APA locally approved land-use plans, 29 had sanitary codes, 61 had subdivision ordinances, 60 had zoning ordinances and zoning boards of appeals, 60 had comprehensive plans, and 72 had planning boards;

• Development was heaviest along roadsides and lakeshores and was occurring at a lighter rate in nonindustrial Resource Management areas. Overall, development was occurring at a significantly lighter rate in Resource Management Areas (areas with a zoning density of a maximum of one dwelling per 42.7 acres under the APA Act). The RCPA did see additional development in Resource Management areas that were not owned by large corporations.

• Stable land ownership limits development in Resource Management areas. The top 30 landowners in the Adirondack Park together own over 1.2 million acres, mostly zoned Resource Management.

Since publication of *Growth in the Adirondack Park* in 2001, the RCPA has continued to update this information. The RCPA has now assembled the best long-term database to analyze growth in the Adirondack Park. The RCPA has worked with code officers, town supervisors, and assessors across the Adirondack Park to analyze building permits issued from 1990 to 2004. As previously discussed, it is unfortunately not possible to analyze building permits for all the towns and villages across the park prior to 1990. Under the New York State Uniform Fire Prevention and Building Code law passed in the early 1980s local governments were only then required to standardize issuance of building permits. The RCPA found that building permit records from 1990 to date are mostly in good order across the park. The RCPA performed counts of building permits in the early and mid-1990s for the towns and villages across the park, but since that time the overwhelming majority of data collected has been provided by code officers, clerks, or other government officials, who have performed the counts and provided the information to the RCPA.

From 1990 to 2004, the towns and villages across the Adirondack Park issued 73,972 building permits (fig. 12.1). These permits were for every conceivable type of development from a new chimney, new septic system or furnace, or a new roof, to a new single-family or multifamily residence. Of these 73,972 building permits issued, the RCPA calculated that 13,509 were for new single-family or multifamily residences or were commercial or industrial buildings. Growth across the park in these years was not uniform. Often

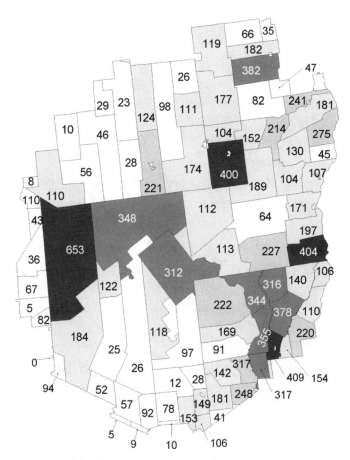

12.1. Total building permits issued by towns across the
Adirondack Park for new residential, commercial, and
industrial structures, 1990–2004. Source: RCPA data.

Adirondack communities are described as monolithic, but a town
such as Webb that issued over 4,300 building permits in 15 years and
permitted 653 new houses is very different from the town of Benson,
which issued 67 building permits and permitted 12 new houses.

Of the 91 Adirondack towns included in the latest analysis, 63 are
completely within the Adirondack Park and 28 are split by the Blue
Line. Population trends are different between the "split towns" and
the towns completely within the Adirondack Park ("full towns").

The split towns saw much more robust growth, from 50,357 people in 1910 to 110,206 in 2000, a 110 percent increase. This compares with the full towns population of 90,101 in 1910 and 110,754 in 2000, an 18 percent increase. The split towns grew at a rate roughly equal to the rest of New York, while the full towns grew at a much slower rate.

Property values have also risen dramatically in the Adirondack Park in the last two decades, though this growth was not equal (table 12.2). Generally, growth in property tax values follows growth of new development, as most of those with the greatest growth–Bolton, Webb, Queensbury, Long Lake, Horicon, and North Elba–include some of those that also experienced high new development rates. Growth was less in some of the more remote areas of the park, such as towns in St. Lawrence, Fulton, and southern Herkimer counties.

While some have benefited from the rapid rise in values, and a wave of speculators have made out well in these years, the high value of property is changing Adirondack communities. Simply put, those who grew up here often cannot find housing that they can afford. The high prices also limit families that desire to move into and live year round in the park. A comparison of the median family income from the U.S. Census to the median residential property value in each town shows that 12 of the 103 towns and villages are not affordable for families with median incomes.

There are national forces at work, including the vast wealth created since 1990, tax laws favorable for second-home development, historically low interest rates, weak stock market and strong land values market, the Bush tax cuts for the wealthiest Americans, and the resultant vacation-home boom as the first wave of baby boomer generation retires (the wealthiest generation in American history, if not the history of the world). The real-estate boom that the Adirondack Park has experienced from 2000 to 2004 is likely only the beginning of a sustained period of high development rates and increasing land values. Unfortunately, most Adirondack communities are not prepared to protect their chief long-term interests during this boom. Although a few may make out well financially in real

TABLE 12.2. **Increases in land values in Adirondack towns, 1984–2004**

| Town, county | 1984 | 2004 | % increase |
|---|---|---|---|
| *12 Adirondack towns with greatest total land values increases, 1984–2004* | | | |
| Bolton, Warren | $122.5 million | $741.4 million | 604 |
| Webb, Herkimer | 170.1 | 1.022 billion | 601 |
| Newcomb, Essex | 38.6 | 230.5 | 596 |
| Putnam, Washington | 26.3 | 145.3 | 552 |
| North Elba, Essex | 187.8 | 1.035 billion | 551 |
| Hague, Warren | 55.9 | 306.8 | 548 |
| Fort Ann, Washington | 64.6 | 348.8 | 539 |
| Horicon, Warren | 52 | 278.1 | 534 |
| Edinburg, Saratoga | 39.7 | 211.1 | 531 |
| Long Lake, Hamilton | 96.4 | 503.1 | 521 |
| Providence, Saratoga | 19.9 | 101.8 | 511 |
| Queensbury, Warren | 391.1 | 1.993 billion | 509 |
| *12 Adirondack towns with smallest total land values increases, 1984–2004* | | | |
| Ephratah, Fulton | $25.7 million | $50.9 million | 197 |
| Hopkinton, St. Lawrence | 26.5 | 58.2 | 219 |
| Fine, St. Lawrence | 43.2 | 95.7 | 221 |
| Oppenheim, Fulton | 24.4 | 56.1 | 229 |
| Caroga, Fulton | 44.1 | 108.6 | 246 |
| Stratford, Fulton | 21.5 | 52.5 | 247 |
| Parishville, St. Lawrence | 54.2 | 138.8 | 256 |
| Waverly, Franklin | 17.5 | 45.2 | 257 |
| Bellmont, Franklin | 32.7 | 84.5 | 257 |
| Crown Point, Essex | 29.2 | 75.4 | 258 |
| Jay, Essex | 44.4 | 116.5 | 262 |
| Clare, St. Lawrence | 8.4 | 22.4 | 266 |

*Source:* Office of the State Comptroller.

*Notes:* Totals are for entire town areas, both for towns completely within the Adirondack Park and for towns that straddle the park boundary. For towns with the greatest increase, the Town of Greenfield, Saratoga County, experienced a 547% increase in the Total Tax Levy since 1984 ($67.4–369.1 million) but was not included in this chart because only a small portion of its total geographic area is within the Adirondack Park. Similarly, the Town of Lawrence, St. Lawrence County, was not included in the towns with the smallest increase (247%, $15.5–38.5 million).

estate or construction, many others will be displaced and find they have no future in the Adirondack Park.

## Concluding Thoughts

The key challenge in the next 25 years, and that's probably all the time we have, will be to protect the great northern forest of the Adirondack Park in perpetuity through a larger Forest Preserve, more state purchases of conservation easements, a serious program to support private open space stewardship, and serious community preservation through planning, affordable housing programs that will change the current market dynamics, and investing in and building community infrastructure and capacity that can support a local tourism, small business, and forest-products economy.

The Adirondack Park will truly be a model to replicate around the globe if we can figure out a way to create a shared landscape of viable rural communities, public wilderness, and public/private managed forests that enables a great forest to dominate the landscape. A great forest dominates the Adirondack Park today, but if current trends continue, a great forest dotted with small communities will not dominate in the future.

# 13

## Wildlife for a Wilderness

*Restoring Large Predators in the Adirondacks*

RAINER H. BROCKE

It was an unusual gathering by Arbutus Pond's scenic shore in the central Adirondacks—a mix of university professors and their graduate students, agency biologists, administrators, and lay naturalists. This was the first conference of the Adirondack Wilderness Fauna Program (AWFP) at the Huntington Lodge of the State University of New York College of Environmental Science and Forestry, August 4 and 5, 1977. The agenda featured progress reports and discussions of fully operational wildlife studies within the Adirondack ecosystem. Presentations covered the status and ecology of the loon, raven, goshawk, spruce grouse, coyote, bobcat and yellow-nosed vole (rock vole); the role of the brainworm parasite in the coexistence ecology of the moose and the white-tailed deer; the potential restoration of the lynx and cougar in the Adirondack Park; and historical perspectives on Adirondack wildlife.

There was excitement in the air as meeting events were boldly colored by the magical word "Adirondack." New and fresh was a focus on wildland values rather than on game management. And there was the opportunity for graduate-student researchers and their professors to interact with agency professionals in a Great Camp setting. This meeting was notable for another reason—it hosted representatives of two feuding agencies with overlapping jurisdictions—the brand new Adirondack Park Agency (APA) and the reconfigured New York State Department of Environmental

Conservation (DEC). Attending professionals of these organizations were afforded this rare opportunity to visit with each other—the only such occasion that year. Antagonism between these agencies was so acute that merely inviting representatives of both to the same meeting was viewed with suspicion. As AWFP coordinator and program chair, I recall being asked by one agency chief, "Whose side are you on?" In truth my dedication was to both. Eventually, agency differences would be resolved, but they were very real at the time.

The meeting at Arbutus Pond and the formation of the AWFP gave new impetus to Adirondack wildlife research with seemingly little to becloud the future of individual studies. But for those of us contemplating wildlife restoration it was clear the scientific road ahead would be long and hard, with a feasibility study possibly ending in an officially negative decision by the DEC or eventual failure if the effort went forward. Restoration efforts worldwide have often been unsuccessful, while numerous introductions of nonnative species have ended in biological disasters. For wildlife restorations, such past episodes pointed to a need for thorough research, conservative decisions, and careful preparation—thoughts very much in our minds as my graduate students and I contemplated research on potential restoration of the lynx.

It was clear that the bobcat, current Adirondack resident, should merit special attention as potential competitor for the lynx. Adirondack country variously hosted either one or both of these lynxes over geologic time. Following glacial retreat northward, the lynx was the only species here for a while, superbly adapted to cold winter landscapes with its ample gray-spotted fur coat and large furred "snowshoe" feet. The advent of warmer climes brought the bobcat north, and for a time these species coexisted. In the mid-1800s, DeKay observed, "The lynx is not uncommon in the northern district of the state."[1] But that was soon to change—the last resident lynxes apparently persisted in the Adirondack High Peaks (northeastern region) until the 1880s, and extinction followed soon afterward.[2] Individual sightings were occasionally reported in the eastern Adirondacks, apparently wanderers from a remnant population that held out in New Hampshire's White Mountains and from a currently existing population in Canada's Gaspé Peninsula and adjacent northern Maine.[3]

Where their ranges meet, research has shown that these two handsome bobtailed cats are strong competitors—for good reason. They are both similar in appearance and behavior, weighing up to 30 pounds and sometimes more, and have been known to interbreed—a testimony to their close kinship. They often feed on identical prey, although the lynx specializes in killing snowshoe hares in their typical northern conifer habitats. Where the outcome of competition has been observed, it favors the bobcat. For example, on Canada's Cape Breton Island, where the lynx originally occupied the entire area, bobcats crossed onto the island (apparently via a man-made bridge) and in 25 years colonized the lowlands, displacing the lynx population into the island's snowy highlands. This displacement suggests that bobcats are behaviorally the more aggressive species. Elsewhere in Canada, a similar competitive pattern has been observed. Areas penetrated by bobcats have been simultaneously vacated by lynxes, a sequence resembling that in the Adirondacks.

A key question for us was what gives the bobcat its competitive edge over the lynx where their habitats bring them into contact with each other? Researchers have reported that northern winter-stressed bobcats lacking smaller prey do kill deer. In contrast, lynxes rarely attack such large prey. We hypothesized that in the Adirondacks, intensive logging during the 1800s was the principal factor triggering lynx population decline. Logging probably affected lynxes as a double-edged sword by degrading the conifer habitat essential for its snowshoe hare prey and by creating ideal habitat conditions for white-tailed deer, the critical winter prey for competing bobcats. We also hypothesized that unlogged, high-elevation, conifer-clad mountaintops and ridges supporting snowshoe hares, but lacking deer, had served as the last refuges for Adirondack lynxes, extending their tenuous coexistence with bobcats. Finally, trapping most probably pushed the lynx population to extinction, as had been documented in New Hampshire's White Mountains.[4] Adirondack woodsmen were a tenacious lot who derived their livelihood from commercial trapping, hunting, and guiding. These men, unconstrained by weak or nonexistent regulations, were effective far beyond the abilities of most trappers and hunters today.

If logging had indeed degraded lynx habitat while favoring bobcat competition, what hope was there for a successful restoration? Several possible factors seemed to favor restoration: (1) regrowth of conifer habitat during the last century, particularly on lands acquired by the state; (2) enhanced deer habitat at low elevations, attractive to bobcats, especially on logged private lands, potentially leaving a high elevation niche for lynxes; and (3) recent colonization of the Adirondacks by a steadily expanding coyote population, perhaps further depressing the bobcat population by competing for deer prey. These possibilities had to be verified by research. As part of a possible lynx restoration, study of the bobcat was timely because both species had been nationally listed in appendix 2 (a category of concern) of the Endangered Species Act. The lynx restoration feasibility–bobcat ecology studies were a package funded by the DEC.

Results of the lynx restoration feasibility study were encouraging. Satellite maps showed a large tract of conifer habitat subject to long winters and heavy snowfalls, centered on the northeastern High Peaks region—roadless, mountainous land classified as Wilderness. Most of the region had not been logged. We termed this area the Potential Lynx Restoration Area (PLRA), encompassing 670 square miles, with mean elevations above 3,000 feet. Graduate student Lloyd Fox[5] found that his telemetered bobcats ranged exclusively below 2,000 feet, potentially leaving a high-elevation niche for lynxes, relatively free of competing bobcats.

Deer prey is key to the survival of Adirondack bobcats, as Fox discovered. He examined stomach contents of 169 bobcat carcasses contributed by trappers, showing deer as the most important prey item. Analysis of femur bone marrow showed that Adirondack bobcats were physically stressed compared to those of southern New York. The importance of deer prey was also reflected in the fate of five telemetered cats in the Adirondacks—three of them known to have fed on deer prey survived the winter of 1979–80. It is remarkable that a bobcat can kill prey as large as deer, even though most deer kills are subadults. Following telemetered cats in winter, Fox observed dramas of predation written in the snow. In one case, a whitetail had paused to feed on some fallen green boughs under a large hemlock tree. Given this opportunity, a stalking bobcat had leaped on the whitetail's back from an overhanging rock, killing it with a bite to the throat; this cat stayed with its kill for a week, picking the bones clean. On another occasion, marks in the snow revealed an epic struggle where an attacking bobcat had ridden the whitetail's back as it tried desperately to throw off the cat, eventually succeeding. A bite to the throat is the usual killing technique, as Fox recorded for 13 deer carcasses located by snow tracking. He verified bobcat predation in each case by skinning out the carcass neck, revealing the cat's fang marks on the throat. Put into a larger perspective, the bobcat's Herculean predatory feat is accomplished at a predator-to-prey weight ratio of 1 to 4, equivalent to that of a lion killing a cape buffalo, although several lions often work together to accomplish that task.

By the late 1970s, however, the bobcat's predatory prowess would no longer grant it uncontested access to deer prey. The coyote population had increased steadily, becoming firmly established in the Adirondacks, and as the "new wolf on the block" it would prove to be an effective predator on deer, as later studies would affirm. The effects of apparent competition with the bobcat were reflected in the Adirondack trapper harvest, showing a simultaneous decrease in bobcats as coyotes increased. This positive evidence favored lynx restoration. Virtually any small animal is potential lynx prey in summer—a generous season for the cat. However, in winter snowshoe hares are the preferred prey—this hare and its feline predator usually occur together in their far northern boreal habitats. In the Adirondacks, hare densities were assessed at high elevations using fecal pellet counts in meter-square quadrats; these data were collected by squads of student technicians. Mountains sampled included Santanoni, Marcy-Skylight, Whiteface, and the Seward Range, with elevations ranging from 2,360 to 4,800 feet. Pellet counts were converted to hare population densities based on my previous research at Huntington Forest, yielding an estimated mean winter hare population density of 420 hares per square mile, judged adequate to support a population of 70 lynxes in the PLRA.

I submitted the lynx restoration feasibility study to the DEC, with the recommendation to attempt reintroduction. However, it was clear that success was not assured. There were several caveats, namely: (1) successful restoration would depend on released lynxes colonizing the Adirondack high country, thereby providing a critical mass of interacting and reproducing lynxes; (2) should lynxes move into lower elevations, they would be exposed to bobcat competition and highway mortality; (3) unintended mortality caused by hunting and trapping was possible, especially at lower elevations; and (4) the restored lynx population would have to be self-sustaining because the Adirondack ecosystem is surrounded by broad water barriers and dense human populations, largely precluding future lynx immigration from the nearest northeastern population in northern Maine and adjacent Canada. Additionally, the scientific literature provided little guidance, as restoration of any wild predator had rarely been attempted anywhere in the world. Hence, whatever its outcome, a lynx restoration effort in the Adirondacks would have important scientific value.

Upon receiving the necessary permits from the DEC and the U.S. and Canadian governments, preparations for lynx restoration began in 1986. The Yukon Territory in northwest Canada became our source for lynx release stock, although this far-flung location was not our first choice. We had hoped to acquire animals from nearby Quebec, but there the lynx population cycle was at its 10-year low point, eliminating that possibility. The city of Whitehorse served well as our base for lynx shipments south. A graduate student, Andrew Major, purchased lynxes from cooperating trappers for around $1,000 each, arranging collection points with enclosures for caged lynxes ready for truck shipment to the Whitehorse airport. Lynxes were inspected by a local veterinarian prior to their

3,000-mile air journey south in transport kennels to Toronto. Captaining the lynx restoration was Kent Gustafson, a graduate student and experienced wildlife biologist. Gustafson shepherded most lynx shipments from Toronto through the U.S. border inspection point at Niagara Falls, armed with U.S., New York, and Canadian permits. From there, it was on to Huntington Forest, our main operations base, where cats were held in a quiet wooded compound, carefully tended and fed, immunized for three cat diseases, and radio-collared for later telemetry.

January 6, 1989, dawned cold and clear in the central Adirondacks as our procession of autos and trucks wound its way through the snowy landscape from Huntington Forest to a mountain trailhead north of Newcomb. There we would assemble for the hike into high country near Lake Colden—final destination for release of our first five lynxes! From a biologist's standpoint, this was a gala event attended by a happy staff, smiling students, important well-wishers, and reporters from every major newspaper in the state—an appropriate sendoff for this signal event. The cheers of the crowd were soon left behind as a safari line of 15 students and staff tackled 6 miles of snowy trail, climbing 1,000 feet to our destination—normally a comfortable hike. But on this occasion pairs of carriers were burdened with portable cages, dubbed kitty litters, each containing a lynx and three domestic rabbit carcasses, enough to feed each cat for a week, adding an extra 30 pounds per person to the weight of winter camping gear.

It was a cheerful but exhausted gathering at our lean-to camp that evening, but merriment was short, and everyone was soon asleep deep in their sleeping bags by the dying embers, oblivious to the occasional lynx growls issuing from the cages behind the log shelter. That night temperatures plunged to -20° Fahrenheit. The next morning, all five cages were relocated to a spruce thicket appropriately surrounded by the High Peaks and crisscrossed by snowshoe hare trails. Lynxes would remain in their cages for five days in keeping with our soft-release strategy, to acclimate them to their new home. It was truly a thrill to watch these gorgeous cats march off unhurriedly into the snowy wilderness, animals we hoped would permanently reclaim their ancestral range.

The "lynx pipeline" operated smoothly during the winters of 1989, 1990, and 1991, as we transported and released respectively 18, 32, and 33 lynxes—49 females and 34 males totaling 83 animals. Females were more difficult to get and therefore fetched a premium price for Yukon trappers (exceeding $1,000). We insisted that animals be caught in mid- to late winter so that younger lynxes (kittens of the previous year) had developed their predatory skills (young lynxes learn to hunt following their mothers) before shipment to New York. We were especially pleased to acquire a whole lynx family—a female and her two grown young, who were released in the Elk Lake area where they remained for some time. As the lynx is normally a solitary animal, such a social grouping is the only one for the species. All lynxes were released in the park's northeastern high country, but after the first release subsequent transports to release sites were made by DEC helicopter.

Soon after the first releases, telemetry data began telling a story we did not like. Too many animals were traveling widely while too few were inclined to settle down. We had expected to see longer than normal travel distances as freshly released lynxes explored their new environments, but the scale of reality truly surprised us. Data for the first two years showed that lynxes (50 animals) traveled up to 2 miles daily, averaging a total distance of 88 miles from the release point for females and 106 miles for males. To put this into perspective, the PLRA has an approximate diameter of 30 miles and the Adirondack Park is about 90 miles wide. Some animals traveled generally in one direction, while others crisscrossed the PLRA hunting conifer patches for hares. These "exploration areas" were large, averaging 680 square miles for males, 162 square miles for females, or 398 square miles for all animals. In comparison, home-range areas of settled lynxes are much smaller, namely 18 square miles for the Yukon, 23 square miles for Washington, and 54 square miles for Minnesota.[6]

Most lynxes soon moved to lower elevations where they were more prone to human-induced mortality—19 animals were killed by autos and 8 were shot. Additionally, 2 starved, 2 were killed by other predators, and 6 died of unknown causes. We were particularly anxious to find evidence of reproduction, but neither telemetry nor field searches yielded den locations or any signs of kittens. A few animals traveled far afield; one was killed raiding a chicken coop in New Hampshire, 290 miles from the release site, and another was shot in New Brunswick, Canada, 450 miles away. Others traveled to Pennsylvania, New Jersey, Massachusetts, Ontario, and Quebec. In view of excessive movement distances and dispersals from release sites and lack of evidence for reproduction, we decided to end releases in 1991, still hoping for positive results. But they never came.

Several factors contributed to the biological failure of our lynx restoration effort.[7] Principal among them was the inadequate extent of the PLRA's "safe space." Large as it was by eastern standards (670 square miles), it was apparently inadequate to contain the extensive explorations of freshly released lynxes. Without a critical number settling down there to attract others, lynx reproduction did not occur. Such reproduction would have been the only factor offsetting emigration. Once lynxes wandered outside this safe zone, they were subject to excessive highway mortality and accidental killings by humans. The project clearly showed that in today's world, where human-caused mortalities are usually common, even in the Adirondack Park, colonizing lynxes could not outlive their initial vulnerability of extensive exploration. These results also support the proposition that conserving a vulnerable but established population will be more effective in terms of effort and expended funds than reintroducing a new one, which (as in our case) may be impossible under marginal circumstances of habitat quality, human penetration and use, and available space.

For us, the lynx project was truly an exciting adventure in conservation—a privilege granted to biologists perhaps once in a lifetime. However, we did not expect much public enthusiasm for this predator-restoration effort. Indeed, we experienced hostility in some quarters, indifference in others, and a residue of modest support among most of the rest. Attempting to pave the way, we sold the project to the public as part and parcel of the Adirondack Wildlife Program, successor to AWFP, with all its other appealing components.[8] We all made presentations to lay audiences, service clubs, village audiences, hunter and trapper organizations, school groups, legislative staffers, and many others. In retrospect, we underestimated the large reservoir of public goodwill toward the lynx project and toward conservation in general. Indeed, the positive reaction was truly astounding. With the initial flurry of newspaper articles, radio announcements, and TV programs congratulatory letters arrived almost daily, many with donations. Individual donations ranged from 75 cents to $1,700; small organizations donated as much as $10,000. While the state legislature covered most the funding, the Baird Foundation of Buffalo became a major and steady contributor. A particularly touching contribution was that of the Roxboro Road Middle School in North Syracuse, whose students developed a fund drive led by their enthusiastic teacher. The students sold $27,000 worth of chocolates to the community, donating a check of $11,000 to the lynx project in front of TV cameras at the State Capitol Building, while congressmen looked on. Students sang their own composition, *And the Lynx Came Back,* followed by an illustrated presentation on lynx ecology.

There are parallel findings from wildlife research elsewhere in the country. In the American West, lessons learned from historical mismanagement of Yellowstone's wildlife resources and associated political experiences led to the realization that management actions for wildland values, particularly for large wild animals, had to be coordinated over a large region. Not long ago, biologists sought to determine in study after study what specific habitat features might "save" this or that large carnivore species. They learned that many of these predators, incarnated in one genetic subset or another, are quite unspecific in their habitat requirements. For example, the cougar ranges from North America's subarctic region to Patagonia in South America—across mountains, deserts, wetlands, savannahs, brushlands, tropical forests, and conifer woodlands. Like other large predators, its key requirements are catchable chunks of

protein—whatever large prey is locally available—and most important, an area within its potential range where deaths due to human
causes are minimal. The survival value of this safe space—the core
area—cannot be overstated. Studies of wolves in Minnesota and
wolves and grizzlies in the West have confirmed that, given some
legal protection, the safe space of core areas can insure expansion
of such populations, continually replenishing higher losses in surrounding human-dominated landscapes. Ecologists refer to such a
population as a *source-sink metapopulation,* where excess animals produced in the core *source* areas emigrate and establish new subpopulations in habitats where deaths exceed births (the *sink* areas). These
sink areas need constant replenishment, although some may eventually become self-supporting core areas. The network of sources and
sinks forms a weblike metapopulation. These are not uncommon,
but they have rarely been studied for carnivores. Minnesota's wolf
population is a developing metapopulation, as is a cougar population in Utah where cougars in core areas of the Wasatch Mountains
emigrate and replenish surrounding sink habitats subject to cougar
losses from managed hunting.[9]

A key concern for carnivore survival is the presence of roads.
Simply put, roads of any type intersecting the landscape enhance
human access, thereby increasing the risk of human-caused deaths,
intentional or not. And, as large carnivores tend to travel extensively—20 miles or more in a single night—they are likely to encounter
roads within their home ranges. It is ironic that dirt roads in wildlands actually attract large cats such as cougars, leopards, and tigers,
who use them at night as quiet pathways to travel and to stalk prey.
Given careful species management in the context of a law-abiding
citizenry, moderate road or trail densities may not be a critical problem. However, it is useful to remember the various causes of death
for large predators. Human-induced mortalities, usually the largest component, include legal hunting, management culling, illegal
killing, accidental kills because of misidentification, disease brought
into wildlands by pets, and road kills. Natural deaths include old
age, malnutrition, starvation, and intraspecific predation when

either adult males or females kill others of their own kind, often juveniles. Indeed, the last-mentioned cause of death can be substantial, ranking second after kills by humans; it accounts for 10 percent mortality annually among wolves[10] and 17 percent mortality for cougars in Utah.[11] Road kills are often underestimated because animals struck by autos may wander away dying some distance from the highway—a fact we painfully learned for our transmitter-equipped lynxes. Without transmitters, such animals would normally not be found. Collisions with vehicles accounted for 49 percent of documented cougar deaths in Florida.[12] In a 9-year Utah study, 74 percent of all cougar mortality was due to various human causes,[13] a serious loss because the reproductive rate of cougars is lower than wolves. In a rural area near Plattsburgh, adjacent to the northeastern end of Adirondack Park, 88 percent of all documented deaths in a coyote population in a 2-year study were human-caused.[14] Road densities in this area are higher than in the Adirondack Park, on average 1.85 miles of road per square mile within coyote home ranges.

Road density is perhaps the single best index for a wide spectrum of potential human-induced mortalities, as road density is directly proportional to the degree of human presence. Black bear population density related to road density in the Adirondacks illustrates this point.[15] As hunter success is directly related to bear population density, and bear population density is inversely related to road density, we related Adirondack road densities for 12 counties against black bear harvest per 100 square miles in those counties. Representative values show 6.46 bears harvested per 100 square miles each year at a road density of 0.2 miles per square mile versus 0.66 bears harvested per 100 square miles each year at a road density of 2 miles per square mile. These values represent a tenfold increase in bear kill (or bear population density), with a tenfold decrease in road density. These road densities are for highways, graveled roads, municipally maintained forest roads, and some private roads. While the Adirondack black bear population is healthy and relatively stable at around 5,000 animals, these values illustrate the regional effect of bear vulnerability owing to human predation mitigated by vehicular road access.

In 1981, prior to this lynx restoration effort, I completed a study for the Department of Environmental Conservation on the potential restoration of cougars in the Adirondack Park. My recommendation was not to reintroduce cougars. This negative conclusion was primarily based on data showing the lack of survivable space for these animals because densities of humans and roads (primary and secondary roads and major forest roads) in the park's wildest area—encompassing the High Peaks, West Canada Lakes, and Five Ponds regions—are considerably greater than for areas where cougar populations are known to exist. In what we'll call the "Adirondack Wildest Area" (AWA), average road and human densities are respectively 0.67 miles per square mile and 3.35 people per square mile. Although we tend to think of Florida as a crowded state, a cougar population survives there (with difficulty), largely within Everglades National Park and adjacent Big Cypress National Preserve in the state's southern end. This isolated cougar range includes 3,400 square miles of wetland, where average road and human densities are respectively 0.06 miles per square mile and 0.5 people per square mile. In the West, we studied cougars in southern Utah near Boulder and Escalante, an area of 500 square miles, primarily brushlands and desert and pine habitat on public lands and private ranchlands, where road and human densities were respectively 0.36 miles per square mile and 1.60 people per square mile.

Although human and road densities in the AWA are low by eastern standards, they are much higher than the values of Florida and Utah where cougars exist. Indeed, the average road density within the AWA, 0.67 miles per square mile, is 1.9 times as high as that of Utah's Boulder-Escalante area, and 11.9 times as high as that of southern Florida's Everglades. Likewise, the AWA's human density, namely 3.35 people per square mile, is twice as high as that of the Boulder-Escalante study area and 6.7 times as high as that of southern Florida's cougar range. These high critical densities for AWA's potential cougar habitat are too great to permit cougar survival in the Adirondack Park. These differences also explain why viable cougar populations do not exist in the East, north of Florida and Texas.

TABLE 13.1. Predator home range areas (in mi²) in northern U.S. wildlands compared to home range areas elsewhere (Adirondack lynx utilization areas appended)

| Species | A. Northern U.S. wildlands; northern soils of low productivity | | B. More southern or better soil areas | | Ratio A/B |
|---|---|---|---|---|---|
| Bobcat | 79 | Adirondacks, N.Y.[a] | 13 | Catskills, N.Y.[a] | 6.0 |
| Lynx rufus | (n = 8) | | (n = 3) | | |
| Lynx | 54 | Northern Minnesota[b] | 23 | Washington[c] | 2.3 |
| Lynx canadensis | (n = 4) | | (n = 7) | | |
| Eastern coyote | 44 | Adirondacks, N.Y.[d] | 15 | Champlain Valley[e] | 2.9 |
| Canis latrans | (n = 10) | | (n = 11) | | |
| Wolf | 210 | Isle Royale, Mich.[f] | 45 | North Central Minnesota[g] | 4.7 |
| Canis lupus | (n = variable) | (pack territory) | (n = 33) | | |
| Black bear males | 664 | Northern Maine[h] | 169 | Central Maine[h] | 3.9 |
| Ursus americanus | (n = 5) | | (n = 6) | | |
| Black bear females | 17 | Northern Maine[h] | 8 | Central Maine[h] | 1.9 |
| Ursus americanus | (n = 9) | | (n = 5) | | |
| *Adirondack lynx utilization areas* | | | | | |
| Lynx males | 679 | Adirondacks, N.Y.[i] | | | |
| Lynx canadensis | (n = 21) | | | | |
| Lynx females | 162 | Adirondacks, N.Y.[i] | | | |
| Lynx canadensis | (n = 29) | | | | |

n = sample size

*Note:* Male and female samples are combined, unless listed separately.

[a] L. B. Fox, "Ecology and Population Biology of the Bobcat (*Felis rufus*) in New York," Ph.D. diss. SUNY College of Environmental Science and Forestry, Syracuse, 1990.

[b] L. D. Mech, "Age, Sex, Reproduction and Spatial Organization of Lynxes Colonizing Northeastern Minnesota," *Journal of Mammalogy* 61, no. 2 (1980): 261–67.

[c] G. M. Koehler, "Population and Habitat Characteristics of Lynx and Snowshoe Hares in North-Central Washington," *Canadian Journal of Zoology* 68 (1990): 845–51.

[d] G. C. Brundige, "Predation Ecology of the Eastern Coyote (*Canis latrans var.*) in the Adirondacks, New York," Ph.D. diss., SUNY College of Environmental Science and Forestry, Syracuse, 1993, 12–34.

[e] D. K. Person and D. H. Hirth, "Home Range and Habitat Use of Coyotes in a Farm Region of Vermont," *Journal of Wildlife Management* 55, no. 3 (1991): 433–41.

[f] L. D. Mech, "The Wolves of Isle Royale," U.S. National Park Service, Fauna Series 7, Washington, D.C., 1966.

[g] T. K. Fuller, "Population Dynamics of Wolves in North-Central Minnesota," *Wildlife Monographs* 105 (1989): 1–41.

[h] D. R. Hugie, "Black Bear Ecology and Management in the Northern Conifer-Deciduous Forests of Maine," Ph.D. diss., University of Montana, 1982.

[i] R. H. Brocke, K. A. Gustafson, and L. B. Fox, "Restoration of Large Predators: Potentials and Problems," in *Challenges in the Conservation of Biological Resources: A Practitioners Guide*, ed. D. J. Decker, M. E.Krasny, G. R. Goff, C. R. Smith, and D. W. Gross, 303–15 (Boulder, Co.: Westview Press, 1991).

Cougar populations may eventually become established in northern portions of Minnesota, Wisconsin, and Michigan, with invaders reaching this area from the West, particularly from South Dakota, currently the easternmost outpost of the western population.

Another perspective on carnivore survival in the Adirondack Park is apparent from home ranges spatially related to a map of land ownerships, settlements, and roads. Average home ranges can be mentally moved around on the map, but no area will be found where they do not intersect private (probably roaded) lands, highways, and secondary roads, exposing these theoretical animals to human-induced mortalities. As noted previously for wolves, such mortality does not preclude population survival, as long as births exceed deaths in the metapopulation system. Indeed, the checkerboard pattern of Adirondack Park land ownerships suggests acceptable prospects for carnivore metapopulation survival, as long as the reproductive rate is high, as it is for the gray wolf. A hypothetical minimum core area, one of several needed to serve a metapopulation, is represented by an area of 400 square miles. There are no equivalent uninterrupted public land areas in the park, but some are close. Ranges of individual animals can be extremely large, such as that of a male black bear tagged with a radio collar in northern Maine. This home range, superimposed on a like-scaled map of the Adirondack Park, would extend from Cranberry Lake to Old Forge, covering an area one-fourteenth as large as the entire park!

A surprising feature of carnivore home ranges in northeastern forested wildlands (Maine to Minnesota, including the Adirondack Park), is that northern home ranges are apparently larger than those to the south or elsewhere. Comparative home ranges are given in table 13.1. Northern home ranges for various species are from 1.9 to 6 times as large as those farther south. It is noteworthy that a variety of predator species show this trend. Factors causing these differences may be (1) sparse prey populations in the north caused by infertility of northern podzol soils, forcing predators to search more extensively for prey; (2) long, harsh winters, depressing prey abundance; (3) a lack of early successional habitats on Adirondack Forest

Preserve lands, reducing prey densities; or (4) some combination of these factors.

## The Future of Carnivore Restoration in the Adirondack Park

In view of the park's many positive esthetic and cultural values, it is difficult to dwell on negatives—namely, the park's ecological short-comings—because reflecting on the realities of nature may often run counter to our desires. What are these ecological shortcomings? How might they be addressed to enhance the park's existing wildlife complex and its benefits to humans, possibly preparing the way for a future predator reintroduction, if such is considered?

To assess the quality of the park's ecosystem for wildlife, comparison with the Greater Yellowstone Ecosystem (GYE) is revealing. Encompassing 18 million acres, the GYE is recognized as the largest remaining wildland in the "lower 48" and today hosts a dazzling array of large, wide-ranging mammals, including moose, elk, white-tailed deer, mule deer, bighorn sheep, mountain goat, pronghorn antelope, buffalo, gray wolf, coyote, cougar, black bear, and grizzly. This conservation success story played itself out over many decades of political strife. Compared to Adirondack Park, the GYE's management jurisdictions are complex. The GYE is located in three adjoining states—Wyoming, Montana, and Idaho—and includes Yellowstone and Grand Teton National Parks, six national forests, three national wildlife refuges, several Bureau of Land Management (BLM) holdings, and is surrounded by state and sparsely populated private lands. The GYE's core, as large as Adirondack Park (6 million acres), is continuous federal land managed as wilderness, of which Yellowstone National Park (YNP) constitutes just 2.2 million acres. These lands are administered by the National Park Service and U.S. Forest Service). The next "ring" of wildland, largely continuous with the core, is managed by the Forest Service and BLM for multiple uses, including logging, mining, grazing, and recreation. Private lands (6 million acres) complete GYE's outermost extension. In terms of public lands alone, the GYE's relatively continuous 12 million acres contrast with Adirondack Park's 2.5 million public Forest Preserve acres, scattered in large and small blocks across the park.

Compared to the GYE, Adirondack Park's wildlands are small and poorly distributed to meet the survival needs of umbrella species such as the moose and wolf. I have concentrated here on large mammals because ecological conditions robustly support them; such wildlands will also harbor more complete complexes of all organisms, including plants, small mammals, reptiles, amphibians, fish, and invertebrates. First on the list of the park's ecological shortcomings is its geographic position—isolated on three sides by substantial bodies of water and by rural development on the fourth. These circumstances largely eliminate immigration to bolster survival of any aborning carnivore population within the park. Hence, predator populations must be self-sustaining. A habitat corridor extending toward the park's northern border from Canada has been proposed. However, that is an impractical idea given the settled countryside, and even if it could be achieved, the St. Lawrence Seaway would remain as a barrier. Then, there is the park's relatively small size, its lack of a secure central core of public lands, the lack of a buffer zone surrounding it, and substantial road penetration even within the hypothetical Adirondack Wildest Area. All these factors increase potential mortality, enhanced by the unusually extensive predator movements in the Adirondack environment reflected in their large existing and projected home ranges.

Two related measures could go far toward mitigating these ecological shortcomings. First, there is a need to strengthen state tax policies encouraging industrial forest management on private lands, possibly by additional tax relief as proposed by the Northern Forest Lands Council. The problem is that the market value of the land exceeds the income-producing value of the land as forest. Tax relief, if attained, could increase the extent of successional forests in rotated stands, enhancing populations of herbivores and predators and opportunities for related outdoor activities such as hunting, wildlife viewing, and camping. As these successional forest stands interface with older growth on private and public lands they maximize biodiversity on transitional forest gradients. Enhanced productivity would boost the park's ecological self-sufficiency, reducing wildlife movements, emigration, and associated mortality, and would better support metapopulations, distributed patchily in the park's checkerboard land distribution. These private lands distributed throughout the park would provide ecological benefits (such as early biotic successions) similar to the large buffer zone surrounding Yellowstone Park within the GYE, albeit in its less-than-ideal patchwork configuration. Second, New York's current policies emphasize land acquisitions for increasing the extent of Forest Preserve acreage in the park. This policy needs reexamination and fine-tuning. Large private land tracts might best remain under forest management, rather than being sold to the state by industrial landowners seeking to move elsewhere. Once sold to New York, these lands are removed from forest management and classified as Forest Preserve. Rather, conservation easements purchased by the state would better serve the park's ecological potentials through continued forest management, while also precluding development and supporting local economies. Such changes will require political backbone, particularly the support of Adirondack conservation groups.

Finally, if there is a large carnivore that might successfully be restored in the park, what could it be? It is not the cougar. The perception that it was once common in the park is an illusion based on fraudulent bounty collections. In the West, where this great cat thrives, its subpopulations are centered on large, rugged mountain masses, often public lands in federal or state ownership. Such country, alternating with broad settled valleys, serves as a system of connected refuges supporting cougar metapopulations—habitat termed *coarse grained* by ecologists. Cougar mortality is highest in valley ranchlands and near settlements. Because cougars are occasionally encountered in peopled areas there is a perception that they can readily coexist with humans, when in fact their population survival depends on adjacent mountains. In the East, even in the Adirondacks, human presence tends to be denser and more evenly distributed—a *fine-grained* environment lacking large refuges, thereby increasing chances for cougar mortality. This eastern land pattern is probably why cougar populations are absent north of Florida, and why cougars have not survived even in the Great Smoky Mountains. Although it is currently unoccupied, potential cougar habitat does exist in the northern Midwest.

We are left with possible restoration of the wolf, an issue posing complex biological and political questions. Restoring this predator is not now ecologically urgent as the coyote has very successfully invaded its relinquished niche. Functionally, the eastern coyote is an effective deer predator—a miniwolf, complete with some wolf genes and a pack structure similar to that of the wolf. Eventually, when moose are common in the park, a process that may take many years, according to models,[16] control of the moose population can be partly accomplished by hunting. Then wolves may be needed to complete the job. Moose over-population would soon be noticed as their collisions with autos have severe consequences, including death for drivers.

Restoring wolves to the Adirondack Park would probably not increase the current level of deer losses to coyote predation as wolves will displace coyotes, even while wolves occur at lower densities. Wolf predation on deer tends to be most severe in winters with deep snow. Within the park, wolf depredation on pets and livestock would probably not exceed that of coyotes. However, wolves emigrating from the park are likely to cause local livestock depredation, requiring strong control measures. Legal hunting of wolves would have little effect, as it is difficult at best; in Minnesota wolves shot illegally were killed opportunistically. Trapping individual nuisance animals has been effective, as has education of farmers in the disposal of livestock carcasses that might habituate wolves to livestock predation. Wolves kill a variety of domestic animals, but young cattle and sheep are taken most often. In farm country, wolf control cannot be relaxed as the wolf population grows, expanding its colonized range, and as wolves may learn to prey on livestock.[17]

Closely intertwined with wolf politics are knotty biological problems facing any prospective wolf restoration in Adirondack

Park. Which wolf should be reintroduced—the gray wolf (*Canis lupus*) or the eastern wolf (*Canis lycaon*)? And, given the existing coyote population, is wolf-coyote hybridization acceptable? These questions need some explaining. Recent DNA analysis has shed much light on wolf ancestry, literally turning previous conceptions of wolf relationships upside down. It appears that the gray wolf (*Canis lupus*) evolved in Eurasia—the common wolf of western North America, ranging across Canada into Alaska. DNA data show that this wolf is not related to the eastern wolf (*Canis lycaon*), formerly named the eastern timber wolf. Rather, the eastern wolf is closely related to the red wolf (*Canis rufus*) and the coyote (*Canis latrans*) and all three species evolved from the same ancestral stock in North America, about 200,000 years ago. This close evolutionary relationship explains why these three wild dogs may hybridize and why the western coyote does not interbreed with its more distantly related cousin, the gray wolf. When the western coyote migrated east through southern Ontario, it hybridized with the eastern wolf. Some of these hybridized coyotes moved into New York's Adirondacks and points further south, establishing the populations we have today. Hybridization between eastern wolves and coyotes has been so intense in Ontario's Algonquin Park region that there is now a range of sizes for these wild dogs and their hybrids, for which the term "canid soup" has been coined. The name "tweed wolf" has been given to some of these hybrids.[18]

In the Adirondacks, the wolf population was most probably that of the eastern wolf or some variant, now extinct. Hence, in the strictest sense, the Endangered Species Act (ESA) no longer applies in the Adirondacks because there is no local wolf population left to save. If the closest relatives were selected, they could be eastern wolves from Ontario, possibly wolf-coyote mixtures themselves that are likely to hybridize further with resident coyotes in the Adirondacks—not a desirable outcome. If gray wolves moved in of their own accord, or were artificially introduced, they would be unlikely to hybridize with coyotes, judging from DNA data. Since gray wolves are not native to the region they would not be protected under the ESA, nor would the population qualify for federal monies to finance damage control. Hence, any wolf control efforts to curb depredation and reimbursements for livestock loss would have to be funded by New York State or private organizations. Clearly these are disadvantages. New Yorkers would have to opt for wolves on esthetic grounds, as other grounds apparently do not apply.

Currently, the U.S. Fish and Wildlife Service and various conservation organizations and interest groups for and against wolf restoration, as well as U.S. Circuit Court judges, are sparring over ESA's legal technicalities regarding probable identities of wolf stocks, wolf population presence or absence, wolf distributions real or imagined, and funding responsibilities of ESA—each to gain legal advantage for its own agenda. Whatever the solution, it is likely to be a muddy one.

Would wolves survive in Adirondack Park? Recent experiences in the West and Minnesota strongly suggest that wolves would thrive, given initial protection. The most effective stock might be that of the gray wolf (Midwestern population), unlikely to hybridize with coyotes. Whether wolves enter the park on their own or are introduced artificially, firm control measures, including hunting and trapping, may eventually be necessary—a possibility of which all interest groups should be thoroughly aware. If New Yorkers decided to foster a wolf population in the Adirondack Park, I believe they would not be disappointed. If reintroduction is "voted down" and natural immigration does not occur, we would still have our mini-wolf as a consolation prize—a wild dog whose interesting ways and musical howls are a good stand-in for the Top Dog. But consolation prizes are just that—there is nothing like the real thing.

We have learned much since that day at Arbutus Pond in 1977. Clearly, predator restoration faces special challenges in the densely populated eastern United States. But large predators are constantly evolving toward survival with humans, while humans are evolving culturally to accommodate their presence. Perhaps some day these trajectories will cross—a day of hope for Adirondack Park.

PART TWO | *Institutions and Management of the Adirondacks*

# Introduction

*The Park in Perspective*

JON D. ERICKSON

Part one of the book aptly describes the means of the Adirondack experiment in conservation. The very rocks, trees, and rivers provided the base from which to build human communities and economies. Their study has traditionally been the realm of the natural scientist. As "nature" takes on the name "natural resource," the door to the social sciences is open, and inquiry turns away from the "what" of describing the evolution and ecology of the natural resource base to the "how" of allocating resources toward meeting desirable ends of human communities. Human choice now enters the equation, and so do such fields as economics, sociology, and political science.

From rock to ore, trees to timber, and rivers to waterways, part one also places the transformation of nature to resource in the context of recent human history in the Adirondacks. The pre-history of the park's formation followed a course familiar to students of anthropology worldwide. As hunting, fishing, and farming to sustain local populations gave way to mining, logging, and construction, the Adirondack economy developed through exporting natural resources. First raw resources were exported by water, then by rail and road. But not long after, the very beauty of the Adirondacks was exported through a burgeoning tourism industry. The early Adirondack story mirrors the story of natural resource depletion worldwide—with the northeastern United States as no exception—fueled wherever labor and energy is cheap and access to resources is open.

But something happened along the way. New York snapped out of it. Why? Why then, and why in New York amid the excesses of the Gilded Age? What else was happening in the world? What is so special about the Adirondacks?

Part two focuses on this portion of the Adirondack experiment. We turn our attention squarely on the evolution of Adirondack institutions and both their success and failure in striking a balance between economy and ecology and seeking genuine development in Adirondack communities. The periods surrounding first the creation of Article 14 of the New York State Constitution in the late nineteenth century and second the Adirondack Park Agency Act of the late twentieth divide the institutional history into a handful of "before" and "after" segments. And, as we will see, we might further divide the APA era into before and after the Commission on the Adirondacks in the Twenty-First Century.

To begin, before the passage of Article 14, there were a number of conditions that led to significant state landholdings, calls for a State Forest Preserve, and then the "Forever Wild" constitutional amendment itself—one of the strongest protections of land in the world. These conditions include a low opportunity cost of preservation, a high amount of conservation dollars on the table, and a fortunate geography.[1] The hammering of the landscape was part of what led to the protection of the Adirondacks. During the initial years of state land acquisition in the nineteenth century, much of the land that became the Forest Preserve had long since lost its value as a material resource. In fact, by 1885 the state owned nearly 800,000 Adirondack acres—what would become the core of the Forest Preserve—essentially by accident. Most of these lands were lumbered, abandoned, and then purchased by the state from local municipalities at the cost of unpaid taxes.[2] It was not until 1890 that the state was authorized to purchase land to add to the Forest Preserve created just five years earlier.

The resources and political will to continue public acquisition were also part luck, as the wealthy accumulated cheap land for summer retreats, but also in part a sign of the changing culture of the time. An elite conservation effort fueled by deep pockets and political prowess was on the move, creating a rather ironic tension between a rising romanticism of the era and the utilitarian realization of the economic value of watersheds. In the late nineteenth century, wealthy aristocrats were reinventing nature by bringing the luxuries of city life to the woods through the Adirondack Great Camp, and other extravagant bondings with nature. In 1893, 45 private preserves totaled over 940,000 acres.[3] By 1897, ownership of the nearly 3-million-acre Adirondack Park was in close to equal thirds between the state, individuals and companies, and private preserves and parks. These private playgrounds were protected primarily for fishing, hunting, summer retreats, and limited lumbering. As decades passed and the interests of these families changed, they began selling their land holdings, and more often than not they provided a significant source for continued low-cost state land purchases (or gifts) through the twentieth century.

Finally, the geography of the Adirondacks served to protect the landscape both before and after Article 14. If the Pacific Ocean began at the edge of the Adirondacks, we would likely be telling a very different story today. The rugged terrain and short growing seasons of the Adirondacks kept these mountains from the agrarian fate of its New England neighbors early on, and the western frontier secured the Adirondacks against a wholesale liquidation once rail and road arrived. Today's Adirondack Mountains, and the northeastern United States more generally, are a "second-chance" forest in part because there was more land and timber to be had elsewhere, and in part because public land protections were in place once the twentieth-century development pressures arose.

The first chapters of this section explore the before and after of Article 14. Historian Philip Terrie addresses the changing cultural landscape that contributed to the foresight of the New York legislature, including the dynamic between romanticism and utilitarianism. Legal analyst Robert Malmsheimer lays out the original foundations of and the rising challenges to Article 14. Throughout the twentieth century, the development and lumbering restrictions set forth by Article 14 withstood many challenges from timber interests and hydropower projects, and more recently, large-scale tourism development interests.[4] Any change to the New York State Constitution requires the passage of amendments in consecutive state legislatures followed by a statewide public referendum. In fact, the significance of Article 14 has extended well beyond the park's boundaries. It is widely recognized that its language and the decades of legal experience in its defense laid the foundation for the U.S. Wilderness Act of 1964.

However by the 1960s, amid the population and economic growth of postwar America, the Adirondack Park was nothing more than a patchwork quilt of state land that could not be timbered. "Forever Wild" had little substantive meaning against the unresolved issues of recreation intensity on Forest Preserve lands and the vast development potential of intermingled private lands within the park boundary. In particular, the completion of the four-lane Adirondack Northway (I-87) through the park's eastern portion in 1967 opened the Adirondacks to millions of new visitors and thousands of new summer residents. An era of "after Article 14" gave way to "before the APA."

As Article 14 reflected the back-to-nature romanticism of the late nineteenth century, so did the Adirondack Park Agency Act reflect an awakening of the American environmental consciousness of the 1960s and early 1970s. A decade of progressive national environmental legislation—sandwiched between the Wilderness Act of 1964 and the Endangered Species Act of 1973—set a backdrop for the APA Act. Terrie stresses the importance of the U.S. environmental movement to the momentum behind the APA Act, as well as a renewed interest (however brief) in state and regional planning, most notably in Vermont, Oregon, Florida, and California. A 1967 proposal to forge a national park from the center portion of the Adirondacks—from 1.1 million acres of Forest Preserve and 600,000 acres of private land—also had a significant influence on how the APA Act was to take shape. The public demanded that the forest preserve remain in state ownership and that the public and private lands complement one another toward both ecological end economic ends. The Adirondack region was to become something more than isolated pockets of public land among haphazardly developing private land. As with the framers of Article 14 eighty years before, there was little precedent to follow, particularly at a scale of nearly 6 million acres, an area larger than five of the biggest national parks combined.

The next chapter of this section, by coeditors Porter and Whaley, provides a sketch of the politics leading up to the APA Act, the early years of implementation, and a more detailed description of both the State Land Master Plan (SLMP) and the Adirondack Park Land Use and Development Plan (APLUDP) that the act required. The chapter draws on the early history of the APA from interviews with Peter Paine and Dick Persico—the creative forces behind the state and private land plans—as well as the more recent perspective of Ross Whaley, chairman of the APA from 2003 to 2007. What follows is a more personal account of the politics and personalities that led to the act's creation and a candid assessment of the APA at year 5 from a transcribed 1976 interview with George Davis, a visionary behind the Temporary Study Commission that led to the drafting of the APA Act, the leader of the planning staff in the early years of the APA, and later executive director of the Commission on the Adirondacks in the Twenty-First Century. Complementing this chapter is the pre- and post-history of the APA Act from the perspective of the New York State Department of Environmental Conservation (DEC) by Stu Buchanan, as well as a more contemporary perspective on management of state lands from his position as director of Region 5 of the DEC from 1995 to 2007, the region encompassing the eastern portion of the Adirondack Park.

While politics, personalities, and interagency arm wrestling perhaps define how the APA Act was ultimately forged, debated, passed, and implemented, the act provides a foundation (or perhaps more accurately a dart board) from which to evaluate loftier ideas of what is often described under the banner of sustainable development. The work of the Temporary Study Commission on the

Future of the Adirondacks preceded the famed 1987 World Commission on Environment and Development's report, *Our Common Future,*[5] better known as the Brundtland report, by nearly two decades. Yet together with Article 14, the resulting APA Act sets forth a framework that looks and feels like sustainable development—a living example of the balancing act between environmental conservation and economic development—at least on a regional scale.

The ideas behind the state and private land-use plans were actually a test of then contemporary ideas from landscape architecture representative of Ian McHarg's seminal work *Design with Nature.*[6] In the McHargian tradition, land characteristics were to be inventoried, and development in the park was to be based on site-specific constraints (e.g., slope, soils, water impact) as well as landscape goals (e.g., natural beauty, watershed protection, recreation access). The resulting parkwide zoning map represents a system of concentrated development, linked via transportation corridors, buffered by natural beauty, and designed to protect water, forests, wildlife, and recreation resources. The private land plan was based largely on residential development intensity, while the public land plan was based largely on recreational use intensity.

Today we might evaluate the successes and failures of the APA Act, at least on the merits of environmental conservation, through the interdisciplinary lens of conservation biology that emerged in the 1980s.[7] A mirror image of the McHargian foci of towns and cities, habitat becomes the core area in this model, circling outward to increasingly human-impacted buffers, until areas of intensive use are reached.[8] Core preserves are then linked via buffered migratory corridors. Space is allocated not to its highest economic use, but rather a scale of substitution is defined from total preservation to compatible economic use to total human development.

Again, perhaps the APA Act was ahead of its time. While the conservation biology model was designed with very large landscapes in mind—with the Adirondacks more often viewed as a core to a conservation network that stretches up the eastern seaboard of the United States[9]—the SLMP and the APLUDP together provide the sort of interlaced quilt of development and recreation intensity that might be evaluated against this view. The SLMP classifies Forest Preserve land into four main categories according to compatible recreational uses ranging from foot traffic only to various forms of motorized access and public recreation facilities. Private land is zoned into six main categories, ranging from least intensive use (forestry, low-density housing) to most intensive use (mining, high-density housing). Many Forest Preserve areas would satisfy as core preserves in the conservation model, where current, direct human impact is limited. Inner to outer buffers might include remaining state land and large private holdings, where close to 90 percent of land zoned for resource management and rural use is forested, with much of it now under conservation easements preventing residential or commercial development. The two degrees of intensive land use, hamlets and industrial-use areas, total less than 8 percent of the park, providing for concentrated, dispersed, and buffered areas of intensive use.

However, as with any policy and management endeavor, there is *intent* and then there is *reality*. The intent of the APA Act might be judged favorably against the concepts of landscape design or conservation biology, but to judge the realities of application requires a bit more pragmatism. For our purposes—to evaluate the great conservation experiment of the Adirondacks—lessons should be drawn from the good, the bad, and the ugly. Enter Bob Glennon, longtime counsel to the APA and executive director of the agency during very tumultuous years. Here we are witness to the professional frustrations and what Glennon felt were significant compromises to the spirit of the APA Act. Written law comes up against practiced ideologies and the politics of the times. As the APA pendulum swayed between pro-preservation and pro-development agendas, Glennon concludes that the APA has always had "a state government that could not decide whether preservation, or development, or both, were best for the park, so it backed both half-heartedly and got neither."

Criticizing the APA Act, the park agency, and the DEC in the 1970s and 1980s had become a full-blown sport in the Adirondacks.

The chapters by Davis and Glennon attest to the lawsuits, threats to staff, and politic compromises that defined the early years of the APA. By the mid-1980s, and precipitated by some very large shifts in land ownership in the Adirondacks and eastward through Vermont, New Hampshire, and Maine, it was clear that the Adirondacks had become a political hot potato. Sales of subdivided property in the park tripled in 1982–85 and then doubled again by 1988. Developers were not happy about the slow pace and constraints on development. Environmentalists were not happy about the fast pace and lack of constraints on development. The forest-products industry was losing its grip on the region, selling off large tracts of land to conservation organizations and land speculators alike. And local governments were not happy about losing any of their historical home rule.

So nearly 20 years after the APA Act, Governor Mario Cuomo did what all politicians do when they need to make tough decisions: he appointed a study commission to pose recommendations. Of course, many feel the real intent was to deflect the issues. The years of *before* and *after* the Commission on the Adirondacks in the Twenty-First Century were here. Glennon recalls the many deficiencies in the original APA Act that led to the work of the Twenty-First Century Commission. But the next chapter by John Penney, managing editor of one of the region's main newspapers during the commission's study and then during the period of public reaction to their 245 recommendations, puts a fine point on much of the local sentiment surrounding these years. The APA plan recognized "the complementary needs of all people of the state."[10] However, as Penney captures, the local view was one of the state government protecting the land conservation interests of tourists and downstate residents at the expense of local Adirondack residents' economic interests and private property rights.[11]

The work of the Twenty-First Century Commission was to fuel the many critics of the APA and DEC, but this time advocacy groups were prepared for battle on both sides of the development-versus-conservation debate. The environmental groups had long been well-organized, with financial and lobbyist support drawing from both state and national organizations. In fact, the chairman of the commission, Peter Berle, had most recently been the president of the National Audubon Society. To many locals it was a forgone conclusion that the commission was already in the hands of the downstate environmentalists—what Penney calls the "back-room agenda." But unlike the years surrounding the Temporary Study Commission that led to the APA Act, this time the pro-development and home-rule crowd had the changing winds of national sentiment on their side.

The 1980s and early 1990s were the Reagan and Bush years, and the environmental debate was in full force on the national scene, epitomized by battles over protecting gray wolves and grizzly bears in the Rocky Mountains, and over land for timber or habitat for owls in the Pacific Northwest. The Endangered Species Act lapsed in October 1992 (and has not be reauthorized since) and the Republican sweep of the 104th Congress in 1994 was due in no small part to a growing national private-property-rights platform. Closer to home, in the face of the commission's recommendations to the governor, and unlike the early 1970s, local opponents were not speeding down the Northway to block legislative proposals at the eleventh hour. This time the home-rule groups were blockading I-87 and organizing protests at the capital.

The commission's tenure marked a time when citizens of the Adirondacks and downstate New Yorkers alike began to rein in a state government that many felt had overstepped its bounds. In 1990, for the first time in state history, New York voters failed to pass an environmental bond issue that would have provided funds for significant additions to the Forest Preserve. The message was not lost on politicians throughout the state. Legislation based on the Twenty-First Century Commission's recommendations was defeated in the New York State Senate in four consecutive years. In 1994, New York's three-term democratic governor was defeated by a Republican, pro-business platform, with the help of a high voter turnout in the northern New York counties. A major theme for the years following the commission would be the erosion of a longtime top-down planning process in the park.

Ross Whaley, a member of the Twenty-First Century Commission, reflects on the events leading up to its formation, summarizes the recommendations made, and offers some lessons learned from the experience. Although the recommendations on park administration, economic revitalization, open space conservation, and other matters were never formally adopted, the public backlash from these years did lead to substantive changes in the political landscape of the park. As Whaley observes, "The commission made a mistake in not appreciating the difference between public input and public involvement." The new citizens' groups that emerged in the 1990s were no longer going to let the state government set the policy agenda for the region. For example, the Adirondack Association of Towns and Villages (http:// aatvny.org) formed to give locally elected officials a voice at the planning table, and the Residents' Committee to Protect the Adirondacks (http://www.rcpa.org) formed to give a voice to local environmentalists, giving balance to what had long been viewed as a downstate-only environmental agenda. An era of nearly universal top-down planning that began with the APA Act was coming to a close.

The new paradigm was to be tested almost immediately. In the wake of the defeat of the 1990 Environmental Bond Act, New York citizens demanded a more clearly defined rationale for land and water conservation needs and a stronger local voice in state land acquisition. In response, in 1992 the state produced the first statewide Open Space Conservation Plan with input from nine Regional Advisory Committees jointly appointed by the state and local governments. The plan was to be revised every three years and provide for the rationale and public process to guide state land conservation efforts.[12] The Forest Preserve was to expand throughout the 1990s and into the twenty-first century under new Bond Acts, and an annual State Environmental Protection Fund was created in 1993—accomplishing one of the more controversial recommendations of the commission for more open space protection. But the politics of land acquisition was to find greater balance between local and state agendas, as well as between outright state land acquisition and purchase of development rights.

The growing use of conservation easements was to help define the state conservation agenda through the 1990s and into the twenty-first century. With easements, the state and conservation organizations such as the Nature Conservancy could buy development rights on private lands in return for public recreation access and sustainable forestry plans. Easements offered a way to keep large parcels of forest in timber production and reduce the expense of outright purchase and tax and overhead costs on protected land. The organizing principle in the northeastern United States had become the concept of the "working forest"—emerging from a U.S. Forest Service–funded study of the Northern Forest of New York, Vermont, New Hampshire, and Maine—and easements became a tool of compromise between outright preservation and outright development. Special resources such as waterways and recreation-access corridors continued to be added to the Adirondack Forest Preserve, but conservation easements resulted in the protection from development and continued timber output of the vast private forest holdings of Lyons Falls, Champion International, International Paper, and, most recently, Finch-Pruyn.

The forest industry perspective reflects on regional, national, and international trends and challenges, including this recent spate of conservation easements. Roger Dziengeleski presents the perspective of the manager of woodlands for Finch Paper LLC, a privately held pulp and paper mill that for more than a century was one of the largest private owners of managed timberland in the park. He outlines the economic climate of a rapidly changing forest-products industry in the northeastern United States that has led to the sale of hundreds of thousands of acres in the last few decades, and homes in on the shared threat of parcelization to both the preservationist and forest management agendas. Parcelization to a forest-products manager is not just the threat of home and large-lot owners no longer interested in active timber management. It also means parcelization because of state land purchases. Dziengeleski the optimist sees the emergence of third-party certification of sustainable forestry and the potential of easements to keep land in timber production as an indication of "a social tolerance for local forest-products manufacturing." But his skeptical side wonders if it is all too little, too late for a forest-products industry that has lost much of its historic infrastructure, faces an ecological crisis from beech bark disease and other threats to forest health, and is today left with a legacy of regulation on private lands that unwittingly lead to much "high-grading" and consequent degradation of stand quality and resilience.

The move away from purely top-down management of the park—as reflected by these new tools for land conservation and new dialogues with the public and forest-products industry—also found its way to the changing face of the Adirondack Park Agency. Richard Lefebvre was one of several agency commissioners in the 1990s who were hand-picked by the AATV, representing the rise of the influence of locally elected officials. Lefebvre went on to chair the APA over a period that he calls the years of reconciliation, communication, and education. As he observes, "Right or wrong, the locals of the park felt disenfranchised, and there was now a chance to bring them into the process." In the final chapter of this section, Lefebvre brings an insider's view to the changing tone of Adirondack politics. Whether one agreed or disagreed with the policies or day-to-day management decisions of those years, Lefebvre brought a much-needed civility, openness, and inclusiveness to the debate. The pendulum was to swing more toward an economic development agenda for the region, an agenda many feel the APA Act promised but never delivered.

In the end, sustainable development calls for both ecological and economic strength and resilience. If the Adirondack experiment is to be successful, it will ultimately require a balanced approach. It is neither a park only for people, nor a park only for the rest of nature, but a vision for integrated conservation and development. But can the Adirondacks be all things for everybody? Can conservation and development ultimately coexist? What visions of the future are grounded in the realities of both our biophysical constraints and our evolutionary upbringings as social beings? Although parts one and two of the book help to tell the story of the ecological and social underpinnings of this great experiment in conservation, we will turn to these much more difficult questions in part three, considering perspectives on the future of the Adirondacks, as well as lessons that this special place might provide for the rest of the world.

# 14

## Cultural History of the Adirondack Park

*From Conservation to Environmentalism*

PHILIP G. TERRIE

During the nineteenth century, the Adirondacks became one of America's sacred places. The process by which certain American places came to enjoy special significance was a complex cultural phenomenon, born of the confluence of European romanticism, the rise of industrial capitalism, the emergence of a professional class with leisure time, and the increasing wealth of many (but hardly all) Americans.[1] After the Civil War, as transportation arteries improved and comfortable hotel accommodations became widely available, the vacation became an annual ritual for American families of means. And places where the nation's natural heritage remained relatively unchanged were especially appealing.[2] At these sacred places, affluent Americans could restore body and soul via the beneficent powers of nature and by observing the rituals of touristic performance that became well understood among the professional classes. American tourists visited the springs of Virginia, the coasts and mountains of New England, and the Adirondack Mountains. Later, as transcontinental transportation improved, tourists discovered the spectacular scenery of the great American West.[3]

This chapter contains material, revised and expanded, originally presented at a conference observing the 30th anniversary of the Adirondack Park Agency, Lake Placid, New York, Oct. 3, 2003, and published in the *Adirondack Journal of Environmental Studies* (Spring/Summer 2004); it is republished here with permission.

Beginning in the 1840s, a rich literature of travel and sport, of which Joel T. Headley's *The Adirondack: or, Life in the Woods* (1849) is the best example, portrayed the Adirondacks as a scenic and spiritually redemptive retreat from the stresses of a country rapidly becoming urbanized and industrialized.[4] In the Adirondacks, as with a few other sacred places, the holiness of the place led to early calls for protection against the ravages of an increasingly despoiling industrial culture, the primary manifestation of which in the Adirondacks was an apparently insatiable appetite for lumber and other wood products.[5] Albany journalist Samuel H. Hammond considered the combination of fragility and sacredness of the Adirondacks in the 1850s and concluded,

> The old woods should stand here always as God made them, growing old until the earthworm ate away their roots, and the strong wind hurled them to the ground, and new woods should be permitted to supply the place of the old so long as the earth remained. There is room enough for civilization in regions better fitted for it. It has no business among these mountains, these rivers and lakes, these gigantic boulders, these tangled valleys and dark mountain gorges.[6]

This romantic conviction that the Adirondacks merited protection for scenic and spiritual reasons was one of two major threads in the drive toward preservation. The other was the widely held belief that healthy Adirondack forests were essential to the reliability of the water flowing to critical transportation arteries like the Erie Canal and the Hudson River. First promoted by Vermonter George Perkins Marsh in his international best seller, *Man and Nature* (1864), the fundamental connection between intact mountain forests and the watershed vital to both agriculture and transportation in the valleys below became a key element in the arguments advanced for protecting Adirondack forests. In *Man and Nature,* Marsh had presented prodigious evidence showing how clear-cutting or otherwise removing mountain forests interrupted the gradual release of rain and snowmelt and led to cycles of flood and drought, and his warnings resonated profoundly with New Yorkers alert to developments in the state's northern forests.[7]

The utilitarian argument advanced by Marsh and the psychological or spiritual position so eloquently expressed by Headley, Hammond, and many others combined to inspire a growing constituency advocating protection of Adirondack forests. A critical contention in the protectionist arsenal—the idea of the Adirondacks as somehow different from the rest of New York, worthy of special concern—appears throughout the documentary record. In 1872, the New York legislature, slowly becoming aware of the threats to the state's northern forests posed by uncontrolled logging and the fires that so often followed in the loggers' footsteps, established a citizen commission to examine the possibility of creating a public park in the Adirondacks. A year later, when this commission reported to the legislature and recommended the establishment of such a park, it observed, "After a careful consideration of the projected forest park, with its practical bearing upon the interests of the people of the whole State, we are of the opinion that the protection of a great portion of the forest from wanton destruction is absolutely and immediately required."[8]

In the expansive, exploitative Gilded Age, the idea that the state could even contemplate removing a large part of its natural wealth from the hands of cut-and-run loggers or the other handymen of contemporary industrial capitalism was remarkable. At that point, the state could not muster the legislative momentum to effect any sort of protection. But only ten years later, in 1883, as concern about threats to the environmental stability of the region's forests and the watershed that depended on them mounted, the state went so far as to declare that it would no longer sell any Adirondack lands still in its possession.[9] And two years after that, in a move of lasting and monumental importance, the state established the New York State Forest Preserve, comprising publicly owned land in both the Adirondacks and the Catskills; at the time the Adirondack total was about 681,000 acres. The 1885 Forest Preserve law contained the clause, "the forest preserve shall be forever kept as wild forest lands";

these words have become an indelible feature of not only Adirondack but the nation's environmental discourse.[10] It is important to note that this law focused on the land, not the trees; that is to say, it prohibited the alienation of the land of the Forest Preserve from the state's public domain, but it did not explicitly prohibit the removal of trees. Indeed, within only a few years, the state was undertaking to permit logging operations on its Forest Preserve.[11]

The tentative steps toward protection of the northern forests, moreover, focused on the idea of regional forest and watershed stability. From the start the state assumed, though imprecisely, that what happened on private land occurred within its purview. The park commissioners of 1872 noted, "When we find individuals managing their property in a reckless and selfish manner, without regard to the vested rights of others, it becomes the duty of the State to interfere and provide a remedy."[12]

In its *Annual Report* for 1890, the Forest Commission, charged by the legislature to administer the recently created Forest Preserve, observed the importance of protecting a contiguous, viable forest, what it envisioned as "one grand, unbroken domain." In this report, it submitted a map to the legislature delineating with a blue line the forested area it believed the state should protect in an Adirondack Park. If such a park were to be created, the commission acknowledged that the state might not be able to buy the large private clubs, most of which had only recently been established. In that case, the commissioners hoped that some legal instrument could be devised to secure public access to the clubs' lands and forests.[13] In addition to anticipating one of the uses of scenic easements, this expectation confirms the early existence of the state's assumption that private land in the Adirondacks possessed special significance.

It was precisely this concern for protecting the northern forest in a regional sense—regardless of current ownership—that led, in 1892, to the establishment of the Adirondack Park. In 1891, the Forest Commission had again pushed its proposal for a park, suggesting that the legislature create a park of some 2,847,000 acres in Essex, Franklin, Hamilton, Herkimer, and Warren Counties.

The commission, moreover, requested that it be empowered to purchase all the private land within the bounds of the proposed park.[14] When the legislature met the following year and finally established the park (though without funding to buy private land), its intent was to mark the contiguous area of the northern forest where the state had an interest. The park included "all lands now owned or hereafter acquired by the state" in specified Adirondack towns. It was to be dedicated to public use, watershed protection, and a "future timber supply."[15]

A crucially important feature of the park legislation was that it still did not explicitly distinguish between public land, already defined as part of the Forest Preserve, and private lands. The park boundary indicated an ideal more than a reality. It surrounded an extensive, contiguous part of northern New York—2,807,760 acres—considered vital to the state's welfare, both for its role in regulating watersheds and for its potential for recreation.[16] But the park law did not provide any strategy outlining what the state intended to do with respect to the vast expanses of private land within its bounds.

The final element in this era of intense conservation activity was the extension of constitutional protection to the state-owned Forest Preserve. By the early 1890s, New Yorkers still concerned about the watershed supplying water to transportation arteries were becoming increasingly alert to the insufficiency of the Forest Preserve law, which was widely interpreted to permit logging in the Forest Preserve. The state bureaucracy, moreover, seemed to be entirely too cozy with the regional lumber barons.[17] A state constitutional convention was scheduled for the summer of 1894, and the New York Board of Trade and Transportation saw this as an opportunity to effect stronger protection for the Forest Preserve, this time for the trees in addition to the land on which they stood. After lengthy debate, the convention adopted a provision submitted by the Board of Trade and Transportation:

> The lands of the state, now owned or hereafter acquired, constituting the forest preserve as now fixed by law, shall be forever kept

as wild forest lands. They shall not be leased, sold, or exchanged, or be taken by any corporation, public or private, nor shall the timber thereon be sold, removed, or destroyed.[18]

This provision has been included, in precisely the same language in every subsequent New York constitution, proposed or adopted, most recently in 1967.[19] It makes the New York State Forest Preserve one of the best-protected landscapes on the planet.

The rigorousness of the constitutional protection, coupled with the vagueness behind the park law of 1892, led in unanticipated directions. State land was now unambiguously defined. With the authority of the constitution behind it, the public domain suddenly achieved a significance it had not previously enjoyed. At the same time, private property also came to be seen in new ways, and the first no-trespassing signs appeared in the Adirondacks.[20] For decades New Yorkers, both local and downstate, had thought of the Adirondack region as a vast, forested place; they hunted and fished, collected firewood, and moved freely about, mostly unconcerned with the details of ownership. In a period of a few years, that changed dramatically. There was the Forest Preserve, where anyone could hunt, fish, or camp. And there were private lands, some owned and exclusively used by wealthy club members (e.g., the Adirondack League Club, near Old Forge, founded in 1890); some owned and logged by woods products companies; and some, mostly in or near the villages, owned as the year-round homes, farms, or businesses of Adirondack residents. The Adirondacks had been split into separate domains—intricately intermixed, but nonetheless distinct.

It took many decades of ambivalence and uncertainty—until the 1960s, in fact—before the state seriously addressed the importance of private land in the Adirondacks. But from the start, there was this clear understanding: whether for protection of an adequately functioning watershed or for saving a recreational retreat, New York, as a collective polity, showed its concern with maintaining the forested character of the Adirondacks, irrespective of whether the land was owned by the state or by private individuals, clubs, or corporations.

Of course, it was the very failure to decide what to do if and when the state abandoned its intent to own all the Adirondacks that presented New York with the need to take another look at private property in the mid–twentieth century.

Throughout the activity of the 1880s and 1890s, moreover, the fate of the Adirondacks was almost exclusively discussed and settled by people from outside the region. Governors, journalists, legislators, and tourists all had opinions about what should be done, but seldom was the voice of a year-round Adirondack resident heard. In the process of legislating protections for Adirondack Forests, local practices—including hunting and fishing for food rather than for sport and gathering firewood—were severely restricted, or even prohibited, by a growing state bureaucracy.[21] A pattern of resentment of what seemed like outside indifference to local needs was established.

For half a century, the distance separating Adirondack reality, where the region was rigidly divided between Forest Preserve and millions of acres of private land, from the Adirondack dream of one contiguous, protected Adirondack Park, was mostly ignored. During this time, most of what was interesting in Adirondack legal and judicial history flowed almost exclusively from efforts to establish the constitutional status of the Forest Preserve—what did "Forever Wild" really mean?—as a series of court decisions and opinions from attorneys general meandered toward clarity.[22] At the same time, the Forest Preserve was growing, as the state slowly added to its acreage. The summit of Mount Marcy, for example, did not become part of the Forest Preserve until 1919.[23]

There were, to be sure, important developments on private land, but they were incremental and largely ignored. Logging continued, though subject to state regulations that for the most part eliminated the threat of massive fires like those that raged across hundreds of thousands of acres just after the turn of the century.[24] The critical change, barely noticeable at first, was the construction of vacation homes for middle-class families. In the late nineteenth century, two kinds of people came to the Adirondacks in the summer. Millionaires built the famous Great Camps, while the middle class lodged at hotels and boarding houses or camped in the woods. Beginning after World War I, developers discovered the profits to be made in selling relatively small lots, especially along lake and river shores, to families of comfortable means but not in the same class as the Vanderbilts and Rockefellers, who for a generation had been rusticating snugly in their opulent wilderness retreats.[25] Over the next several decades, hundreds of miles of previously undeveloped shorelines were lost to second-homes. This process was so slow that until mid-century it did not appear to threaten the regional, forested landscape that the park legislation of 1892 had declared was vital to the state's welfare.[26]

Finally, in the 1960s, an era of broad-spectrum political protest led, in part, to a new environmental consciousness, including a concern about the nation's remaining expanses of relatively undeveloped open space. The reinvigorated environmental movement gave birth to Earth Day, April 22, 1970, wherein 20 million Americans participated in an eclectic combination of teach-ins, guerrilla theater, street fairs, and environmental protest.[27] This was the same year that legal scholar Joseph Sax, writing in the *Michigan Law Review,* argued that the historic Public Trust Doctrine, which traced its roots to the sixth century and the Code of Justinian and which had been used for a millennium and a half (though certainly sporadically and with mixed results) to protect those features of the natural heritage vital to the common welfare, should be reinterpreted and expanded to embrace all the things "so particularly the gifts of nature's bounty that they ought to be preserved for the whole of the populace."[28]

Sax was, among other things, concerned about unregulated development, and New York State saw this issue as especially pressing as it contemplated, finally, what was happening to private land in the Adirondacks. Two years earlier, in 1968, Governor Nelson Rockefeller had appointed the Temporary Study Commission on the Future of the Adirondacks and charged it to examine threats to the integrity of the northern forests.[29]

In the middle of December of 1970, the Temporary Study Commission sent 181 recommendations to the desk of Governor Rockefeller. These recommendations constituted the beginning of the modern era for the Adirondacks. While the completion of the Northway (I-87) in 1967 helped bring this region closer to the population centers downstate, and while a recreation boomlet had begun a few years earlier, it was the bombshell at the heart of the Temporary Study Commission's plan for the future—the establishment of an Adirondack Park Agency and the delegation to it of parkwide planning authority for private lands—that made the Adirondack Park what we know it to be today.

The work of the Temporary Study Commission, the establishment of the Adirondack Park Agency and, especially, the very idea of regional planning were part of the new environmental consciousness of the 1960s and 1970s, which the report of the Study Commission explicitly acknowledged: "The concern is nationwide. Significant action has been instituted in many state capitals. Can New York afford to ignore its Adirondacks?"[30] In addition to concern about clean air and water and the many other issues that galvanized the first Earth Day, the notion of regional planning was gaining momentum.

In large part, the drive to effect regional planning was a response to rapid, mostly uncontrolled loss of open space to sprawling post–World War II suburbs, of which Long Island's Levittown is perhaps the best-known example. Around virtually every urban center in the United States, Americans, abetted by miles and miles of the new interstate highway system, were building uncountable new houses; eventually, some people began to ask whether this was altogether a good thing.[31] This skepticism about uncontrolled development and the consequent implementation of more effective zoning eventually became known as the "Quiet Revolution," following a report summarizing its tenets drafted for the Council on Environmental Quality in 1971 by Fred Bosselman and David Callies, attorneys and experts in American land-use law. In addition to the well-known and path-breaking Hawaii Land Use Act of 1961, other important examples were both state-wide applications—for example in Vermont, Oregon, and Florida—and regional efforts, as in the New Jersey Pine Barrens, the California coast, and Lake Tahoe.[32]

The tentative steps toward regional land-use regulation and planning depended on a new understanding of the term "land."[33] As Bosselman and Callies noted, up until the years immediately following World War II, Americans clung to a fundamentally nineteenth-century notion of the meanings of this much-freighted word. "Land" nearly universally implied something that enabled its owner to make money, either through some sort of resource extraction or use or through sale or development. The postwar change of sentiment that introduced wetlands into the classification of "land" and gave them "value" was thus a remarkable step. Obviously, this change was at least partly a function of the emergence of the science of ecology, which dramatically helped to expand our awareness of just what constitutes such a slippery concept as "value."[34] Where to the nineteenth-century farmer, value derived from the crops a parcel of land could produce, or where to the logger value depended on board feet of lumber, by the mid–twentieth century value could also mean how a specific place fit into complex webs of interdependence, including its capacity to support wildlife, filter water, or add to the value of often distant other places. In other words, something that nearly everyone understands today—that places, just like all of the natural world, are interconnected—entered the culture of planning and land-use decisions and encouraged protecting, or at least planning for, regions as opposed to individual lots or neighborhoods.

At the same time that land came to be understood as more than what it might produce or sell for, its finitude also penetrated the public consciousness. When people see land as something finite, then the value of land is both increased and complicated. The culture of abundance that had characterized American thinking since the arrival of Europeans in the New World finally came to be challenged.[35] All of this is part of the shift to seeing land as a resource as well as a commodity. So long as land was merely a commodity, zoning existed only to protect the commodity value of those land owners sufficiently powerful to exercise their will on local politics. Once it became a resource (while never really losing its commodity value), then environmental and social concerns entered into the realm of zoning. Where those responsible for zoning had previously asked only what would protect or enhance the economic value of this land, they now began to ask, "What is the best use for this land?" These new ways of understanding land manifested themselves from coast to coast: what happened in Hawaii or Oregon also came to pass in the Adirondacks.

These tectonic changes in what zoning meant constituted the context for the Temporary Study Commission and its recommendations. Locally, we had the construction of the Northway, an explosion in second-home development in Vermont, the growing affluence of a mobile and acquisitive middle class, and the same concern with enjoying and protecting nature that gave us the Quiet Revolution. Joining the regional-zoning movement constituted the latest chapter in the long saga of New York's efforts to protect the forested character of the Adirondacks.

"A crisis looms in the Adirondack Park," wrote the commissioners. "Throughout this country unplanned development of both public and private land is despoiling resources once considered limitless." Noting that the Adirondack Park's capacity to be a sanctuary from modernity, in other words a sacred place, had largely escaped the worst of post–World War II sprawl, they further observed, "Whether it will continue to be one depends on the foresight and resolve of all New Yorkers."[36] Widespread development of second-home villages, the construction of garish theme parks, strip mines— these and a host of other environmental disasters were possible and even likely, given the laissez-faire attitude of the state toward the 60 percent of the Adirondack Park it did not own.

The Study Commission's solution was clear: "A massive state action program is necessary to make the Adirondack Park a viable and lasting entity. This program must be concerned with both the private and the public lands." They went on to note, "The key to maintaining the Park as a *lasting* entity lies in the avoidance of misuse by all landowners, large and small."[37] The commission's charge boiled down to a twofold thrust: use regional zoning to limit inappropriate development on private land and promote careful expansion and consolidation of the Forest Preserve.

The Temporary Study Commission recommended the establishment of an Adirondack Park Agency, to be housed in the executive branch of state government, with zoning powers over private land and authority over how the Department of Environmental Conservation managed the Forest Preserve. The New York legislature created the park agency in 1971. In 1972, the agency submitted its Adirondack Park State Land Master Plan to the governor, and in 1973 it released its Adirondack Park Land Use and Development Plan. According to the terms of the legislation creating the agency, the State Land Plan required only approval by the governor, while the Adirondack Park Land Plan required the imprimatur of the legislature.

The key element of both plans was zoning. Both the Forest Preserve and all private land were classified into a wide variety of categories, on the basis of, among other things, historic uses, ecological conditions, and scenic or recreational value. The zoning of private land proved immediately and explosively controversial, as the APA strove to limit development on millions of acres of previously undeveloped land. The story of how the Adirondack Park Land Plan works, how its original intent was blunted by the legislature, how it has been amended and implemented over the last three and a half decades, and whether or not it has been successful is the primary subject of the remainder of this section.

# 15

## Legal Structure and Defense
## of the Adirondack Park

ROBERT MALMSHEIMER

The Adirondack Park's public and private lands are governed by a unique constitutional and statutory legal structure. This framework attempts to balance the conservation, protection, preservation, development, and use of the park's unique natural resources and open space.

The size and location of the Adirondack Park and the use and disposition of New York State's lands within the Forest Preserve is governed by Article 14 of the state's constitution. Since the location of these lands and the Forest Preserve's land-use controls are constitutionally based, any changes to these provisions require an amendment to the New York State Constitution, an onerous process that requires the New York State Assembly and Senate to pass the amendment in two consecutive terms and the state's voters to then approve it. In contrast, the size, location, and use of withdrawn federal lands, such as national parks, national forests, national wildlife refuges, and wilderness areas, and most states' parks and protected lands, are statutorily governed, which means that their size, location, and use can be amended by a subsequent statute—a significantly less arduous task.

The Adirondack Park Agency (APA) Act and other statutes supplement the park's constitutional provisions. The APA Act includes a requirement for a comprehensive land-use system for the park: the Adirondack Park Land Use and Development Plan, which governs the preservation, use, and development of the park's private and public lands. Like the statutory provisions that govern federal lands and most state lands, the APA Act (and the other statutes) can be amended by legislative and executive action. However, the APA Act has remained relatively stable for more than thirty years, with the last amendments being enacted in 1986.

This chapter describes the constitutional and statutory framework that governs the Adirondack Park's public and private lands and legal challenges to this framework. It begins with an analysis of the constitutional provisions governing the Forest Preserve and then examines the park's statutory framework, focusing on the Adirondack Park Agency Act.

## The Forest Preserve's Constitutional Prohibitions

As the previous chapter describes, on November 6, 1894, New York's voters approved a revised state constitution that included two sections of Article 7 (later renamed Article 14) that govern the use and disposition of the state's Forest Preserve lands. These sections can be enforced by the attorney general or a private party (who has notified the attorney general and received the consent of the Supreme Court in Appellate Division).

Section 1, the much more important and famous "Forever Wild" section, originally contained only two sentences. Those two sentences, which have not been changed since they were enacted, continue to introduce the section today:

> The lands of the state, now owned or hereafter acquired, constituting the forest preserve as now fixed by law, shall be forever kept as wild forest lands. They shall not be leased, sold, or exchanged, or be taken by any corporation, public or private, nor shall the timber thereon be sold, removed, or destroyed.

Since its enactment, more than 130 proposed amendments have been introduced in the state legislature to change this section. Only twenty-one of these have been successful. Among other things, these amendments have authorized the construction of ski centers and trails (Whiteface Mountain, 1941 and 1987; Gore, South, and Pete Gay Mountains 1947 and 1987) and the construction and maintenance of roads (eliminating dangerous curves and grades on state highways, 1957; and the Northway, 1959) on Forest Preserve lands. Most amendments have authorized the exchange of Forest Preserve lands for lands owned by local governments and private parties (e.g., Village of Saranac Lake, 1963; Town of Arietta, 1965; International Paper Company, 1979; Sagamore Institute, 1983; and Town of Keene, 1995).

As of January 2005, the Westlaw Legal Database reports that 15 state court cases and 50 New York Attorney General Opinions have interpreted this section. These cases and opinions have addressed controversies involving the removal of timber, sand and gravel, top soil, minerals, gas, and oil; construction of highways, ski trails, pipelines, camps, campsites, and power and telephone lines; and the state's legal rights, such as adverse possession claims, and the conveyance of easements and other rights. These cases and opinions reveal that courts and the state attorney general strictly enforce the section's lease, sale, and exchange provisions. However, judges and the attorney general have not interpreted the section's timber removal, sale, and destruction prohibitions absolutely. For example, cases have allowed the cutting of trees to: construct new trails and parking areas (*Balsam Lake Anglers Club v. DEC,* 1991, 583 N.Y.S.2d 119); maintain trails and lessen soil compaction, erosion, and destruction of vegetation (Attorney General Opinion 86-F3); provide deer with food (1948 Attorney General Opinion 159); protect human safety and life (1935 Attorney General Opinion 308); and build roads (*D'Angelo v. State,* 1951, 106 N.Y.S.2d 350). The most controversial of these decisions, and most contrary to the section's language, was an Attorney General's Opinion (1950 Attorney General Opinion 154; see also chapter 6 of the Laws of 1950) that, in the name of fire protection, authorized the salvage and sale of Forest Preserve trees destroyed by a hurricane.

Section 2 of Article 14 also addresses the use of the Forest Preserve. It limits the construction and maintenance of reservoirs for municipal water supplies and canals to 3 percent of Forest Preserve lands. The section has been amended only once, in 1953, when the legislature's power to use lands for the construction of reservoirs to regulate the flow of streams was revoked. The section has been the subject of only two published court cases and four Attorney General Opinions, all of which were decided more than fifty years ago.

## The Adirondack Park's Statutory Structure

The Adirondack Park Agency was created in 1971 by the APA Act. The agency is charged with administering the APA Act (Executive Law Article 27); the Freshwater Wetlands Act (Environmental Conservation Law (ECL) Article 24) within the park; and the Wild, Scenic, and Recreational Rivers System Act (ECL Article 15, Title 27) on the park's private lands. The APA Act has been amended nine times since its enactment, most recently in 1986.

In 1973, the agency fulfilled one of its legislative directives and developed a comprehensive land-use system for the park. The Adirondack Park Land Use and Development Plan (APLUDP) governs the preservation, use, and development of the Park's private and public lands.

The APA Act primarily addresses the development and use of the park's private lands. The APLUDP and its associated map classify the park's private lands into six land-use areas: Hamlet, Moderate Intensity use, Low Intensity use, Rural, Resource Management, and Industrial use. For each area, the APA specifies a character description; purposes, policies and objectives; guidelines for development intensity (except for industrial-use areas); classifications of primary and secondary uses (except for hamlets); and Class A and Class B regional projects. The agency must review and approve (by permit) all proposed Class A and Class B regional projects, except those proposed Class B regional projects situated in localities that have adopted a local land-use plan approved by the agency.

The land-use areas define the type and amount of development, with hamlets allowed the most variety of development at the greatest density. The APLUDP regulates development more restrictively as one proceeds through the land-use areas from hamlets to moderate intensity use areas to low intensity use areas to rural use areas to resource management areas. Hamlet areas serve as the park's service and growth centers. All land uses and development are compatible with a hamlet's character, purposes, and objectives, and they have no intensity guidelines. Moderate intensity use areas are adjacent to hamlets or along highways and accessible shorelines with existing development or those with deep soils and moderate slopes. Development intensity in these areas should not exceed 500 principal buildings per square mile (one principal structure per 1.3 acres). Low intensity use areas are areas with fairly deep soils, moderate slopes, and no critical biological importance. No more than 200 principal buildings per square mile (one principal structure per 3.2 acres) should be erected in these areas. Rural-use areas' natural resource limitations and public considerations require more stringent development constraints to protect intolerant natural resources and to preserve open space. Development intensity in these areas should not exceed 75 principal buildings per square mile (one principal structure per 8.5 acres). Resource Management areas protect forest, agricultural, recreational, and open-space resources. No more than fifteen principal buildings per square mile (one principal structure per 42.7 acres) should be erected in these areas. Industrial-use areas are lands with existing industrial or mineral extraction operations or lands local and state officials have identified for new industrial development. The APLUDP does not define development intensity guidelines for industrial-use areas.

While the majority of the APA Act addresses the use and development of private lands, it also addresses the use of the park's public lands. Section 816 directs the Department of Environmental Conservation to develop individual management plans for land units classified in the Adirondack Park Master Plan, which was approved in November 1987 and updated in 2001. These Unit Management Plans must conform to the master plan's guidelines and criteria. Once completed, these management plans guide the unit's development and management.

As Ginsberg and Weinberg describe in the Adirondack Park Agency section of their treatise *Environmental Law and Regulation in New York,* early published cases established the constitutionality of the APA Act. More recent cases have addressed the agency's administration of the act and its implementation. The agency has been very successful in these lawsuits, and courts have upheld "Agency determinations that have gone beyond the literal wording of the [APLUDP] . . . when the exercise of the Agency's discretion was necessary to achieve the purposes of the Act."[1]

Despite the often vocal criticism of the APA Act and the agency, it is surprising how few published court cases the statute and its agency have produced. As of January 2005, the Westlaw Legal Database reports that 28 state court cases and three New York Attorney General Opinions have interpreted the APA Act. More than half (54 percent) of these cases were litigated in the 1990s, which documents the act's controversy during that time. The courts addressed fewer cases in the decades before and after the 1990s. Six (21 percent) were litigated in the 1970s, four (14 percent) in the 1980s, and three (11 percent) in the first five years of the first decade of the twenty-first century. Table 15.1 lists the APA Act's sections and the number of published cases that have referenced each of those sections. The number of cases listed in table 15.1 exceeds the total number of cases because cases can address more than one act section. Only six sections generated more than two cases. The most litigious section was section 809 (Agency Administration and Enforcement of the Land Use and Development Plan), which generated nine cases; two-thirds of those cases were litigated in the early 1990s. These cases litigated the section 809's constitutionality, the agency's powers, jurisdiction, public hearing requirements, and the agency's adverse impact, aesthetic considerations, and wetlands project determinations. The agency's administration of section 806's shoreline restrictions generated six cases, which addressed the section's purpose, public hearing requirement, and APA's boathouse, lodging, or residency exemptions, mean high-water mark, and setback determinations. Section 818's judicial review requirements generated six cases, all but one of

TABLE 15.1. **Number of published court cases referencing the Adirondack Park Agency Act sections**

| Section | Title | Number of cases |
|---|---|---|
| 800 | Short title of act | 0 |
| 801 | Statement of legislative findings and purposes | 4 |
| 802 | Definitions | 1 |
| 803 | Adirondack Park Agency | 1 |
| 803-a | Adirondack Park Local Government Review Board | 1 |
| 804 | General powers and duties of the agency | 2 |
| 805 | Adirondack Park Land Use and Development Plan | 3 |
| 806 | Shoreline restrictions | 6 |
| 807 | Local land-use programs | 0 |
| 808 | Administration and enforcement of approved local land-use programs | 1 |
| 809 | Agency administration and enforcement of the land-use and development plan | 9 |
| 810 | Class A and Class B regional projects | 1 |
| 811 | Special provisions relating to agency project review jurisdiction and the shoreline restrictions | 4 |
| 812 | Public hearings | 0 |
| 813 | Penalties and enforcement | 2 |
| 814 | State agency projects | 1 |
| 815 | Interim development controls | 0 |
| 816 | Master plan for management of state lands | 0 |
| 817 | Activities of the United States in the Adirondack Park | 0 |
| 818 | Judicial review | 6 |
| 819 | Applicability | 2 |
| 820 | Severability | 0 |

*Source:* Westlaw Legal Database, Jan. 2005.

which was decided after 1990, that determined courts' jurisdiction over APA Act–based claims and litigation limitations. Four cases, one every decade, litigated the special provisions relating to agency project review jurisdiction and the shoreline restrictions. These Section 811 cases examined adverse possession claims and agency existing nonconforming use and preexisting subdivision determinations. All but one of the cases involving section 801 (statement of legislative findings and purposes) was decided during the 1970s. These cases determined the APA Act's constitutionality, construction, and purpose.

## Conclusion

The Forest Preserve's constitutional provisions have protected the park, especially the conveyance prohibitions, which courts and the attorney general have strictly interpreted. The constitution's tree protections have been interpreted to balance human use and protection of the Forest Preserve resources. Most courts and attorneys general have reached the same conclusion as the New York Supreme Court in *Balsam Lake Anglers Club v. DEC* noted, the "framers of the New York State Constitution intended not to prevent or hinder public use of the forest, but to allow forested areas to revert to their natural or wild state without human interference with natural succession of different types of trees, selective cutting or thinning to 'improve timber' or harvesting of any mature timber. There is no indication of any intent to maintain the forest in an 'absolutely' wild state with no organized human alteration or intervention at all."[2]

Despite the often vocal criticism of the APA, the APA Act has seen few amendments and produced surprisingly few published court cases. The act's stability and the agency's success in court defending and protecting the APLUDP demonstrate the act's successful balancing of use, development, and preservation.

The Adirondack Park's unique constitutional and statutory legal framework, and the framework's success, can serve as a model for landscape-scale mixed-use parks in the United States and in other countries, especially in the developing world. Although the framework has sometimes been controversial, it has allowed the Adirondack Park to balance human use and natural resources conservation for more than a century and to withstand the increasing development pressures of the past thirty years.

## Further Reading

Readers can find additional information on the Adirondack Park's legal structure at the APA's website (http://www.apa.state.ny.us) and in:

Adirondack Park Agency. *Adirondack Park State Land Master Plan* Ray Brook, N.Y.: Adirondack Park Agency, 2001.

Commission on the Adirondacks in the Twenty-First Century. *The Adirondack Park in the Twenty-First Century.* Executive summary and vols. 1 and 2. Albany: State of New York, 1990.

Ginsberg, William R., and Philip Weinberg. *Environmental Law and Regulation in New York.* §12.3. St. Paul, Minn.: West Publishing Co., 1996.

Graham, Frank, Jr. 1978. *The Adirondack Park: A Political History.* Syracuse: Syracuse Univ. Press, 1978.

# 16

## Public and Private Land-Use Regulation of the Adirondack Park

WILLIAM F. PORTER AND ROSS S. WHALEY

In politics, as in chemistry, a catalyst is often the secret to getting a process moving. For the Adirondack Park, the catalyst was a proposal offered by Laurance Rockefeller. In 1967, Rockefeller was chairman of the New York State Council of Parks. Concerned that the Adirondack Park existed in name only, and recognizing that protection of 40 percent of the park as Forever Wild left the majority of the region open to runaway development, Rockefeller hit upon the idea of creating a national park. He proposed enlisting the federal government to amalgamate about 1.1 million acres of Forest Preserve and 600,000 acres of private land to form the Adirondack Mountains National Park. News of his idea reached the *New York Times* on July 30, 1967, and the reaction was strong. Almost no one liked the idea.

Whether the idea was intended as a serious proposal or as a political catalyst is uncertain, but its effect was dramatic. While the

The description of the creation of the Adirondack Park Agency that follows draws on interviews with Peter Paine, a member of the Temporary Study Commission, original member of the Adirondack Park Agency, and principal author of the State Land Master Plan; George Davis, a staff member of the Temporary Study Commission and the first employee hired by the park agency; and Richard Persico, the executive director of the APA at the time the Adirondack Park Land Use and Development Plan was approved by the legislature and principal author of the legislation.

many Adirondack constituencies seemed to have little in common, all were united in their opposition to inviting the federal government into the mix. Many also agreed that something needed to be done about the Adirondack Park. Some advocates sought to provide protection for more than 5 million acres and saw the Rockefeller proposal as a retreat to a smaller core area. Others sought to prevent the loss of their own land to the future park. Still others wanted to forestall any further discussion of federal involvement. Nelson Rockefeller, brother of Laurance and governor of New York, saw a political opportunity in this brief consensus. He channeled the political will into a Temporary Study Commission on the Future of the Adirondacks. He brought together the public interest in wilderness and the growing societal interest in land-use zoning. Specifically, he asked the commission to explore ways to create a novel park: a single entity where both public and private lands were essential elements. Nowhere had such an idea been attempted. Certainly there were parks containing appreciable amounts of private land as in-holdings, or where adjacent private land was important to the welfare of the park. However, nowhere (at least in the United States) had there been attempted the creation of a park where the private land was considered part of the park and constituted the majority of the land within the park's boundaries.

Nelson Rockefeller charged the commission with formulating recommendations on long-range policies for ensuring protection of the park. The charge recognized two important political pressure points. First was the rising concern about lack of attention to management of the Forest Preserve. Since the inception of the Forest Preserve, the Conservation Commission had sought authority to bring the Forest Preserve into active silviculture programs for purposes of both forest stewardship and wildlife management. The authority, consciously removed from the Conservation Commission by constitutional amendment in 1894 after some scandal, was never restored, and the Forest Preserve languished. Rockefeller asked if there should be more active oversight and greater safeguards for the Forest Preserve in the form of wilderness designation. Further, he asked if additional lands should be purchased by the state for inclusion in the Forest Preserve. Second, there was concern about impending development of private lands. Entrepreneurs were looking to the Adirondacks as a site for communities of second homes, and the magnitude of the developments being planned alarmed many people. In an unusually bold political step, Rockefeller asked the commission to consider how to assure that development of private lands was done in a manner appropriate to the long-range well-being of the park.

The Temporary Study Commission conducted its work within a context of two conflicting societal trends. First, the environmental movement of the 1960s was culminating in major federal legislation to protect wilderness, endangered species, and environmental quality from destructive effects of development. Second, the emerging wealth of American society was driving a development boom in remote regions with construction of second homes and outdoor recreation venues such as ski areas. The commissioners heard this clash of values as they were lobbied by the contrasting voices of preservationists and developers in the Adirondacks, and they saw it firsthand as they looked across Lake Champlain at Vermont. The commissioners recognized that the relationship between private and public land in the Adirondacks was crucial and that the future of the park would be determined largely by what transpired on private lands. Specifically, maintaining the qualities of a wilderness park required that much of the private land remain open space in perpetuity.

Given that the commission's membership included strong representation by a mix of industrialists, downstate attorneys, and Adirondack landowners, its recommendations contained a remarkable environmental ethic. At the heart of the recommendations was a simple philosophical conclusion: without specific planning and zoning, development on private land posed "a grave and growing threat to the entire park." Delivered in 1970, the report detailed 181 recommendations that addressed issues of managing public and private lands, including the natural resources and economic opportunities, as a coherent whole. The commission's most significant recommendation was its first: "An independent, bipartisan Adirondack Park Agency should be created by statute with general power over the use of private and public land in the park." Among its primary charges, the Adirondack Park Agency was to prepare a comprehensive plan for the park. The agency was to have authority for planning for not only public lands within the park, but powers to control use of private land in the park as well.[1]

Government is notorious for shunting political issues aside by sending them to a committee, accepting the report of the committee with fanfare, and then ignoring or watering down the recommendations to the point that almost nothing happens. The fact that this report of the Temporary Study Commission, with its bold recommendations, was approved is probably a testament to its chairman, Harold Hochschild. Some people claim that the governor did not fully appreciate what he was doing when he appointed Hochschild to the commission. Hochschild was a retired international industrialist who had made a fortune in mining. He had spent summers for much of his life living in the Adirondacks and commuting to New York City. He was accustomed to socializing with those in the highest levels of industry and government, at one point advising President John Kennedy on foreign policy in Africa. It is said that with the raise of an eyebrow, he could put people in motion.

When the recommendations of the commission came to the legislature, the language was changed, resulting in removal of most of the bold strokes that would give the Adirondack Park Agency its power. In what was expected to be a late-night negotiation, Hochschild refused to bargain. He simply told the Speaker of the Assembly, "no." The governor was intent on creating the State University of New York, passing more severe drug laws, and protecting the Adirondack Park. It was also an election year, and the Speaker decided not to test Hochschild's fortune, friends and reputation. In one of those extraordinary moments in history, the Adirondack Park Agency was established with its powers intact.

The Adirondack Park Agency was to share responsibility for management of the park with a sister agency, the Department of

Environmental Conservation. The DEC was a new super-agency that combined the old Conservation Commission with other environmental agencies into a single administrative entity. In a move destined, or perhaps designed, to create debate, the APA was given responsibility for long-range planning and the establishment of guidelines for the management of state lands. The DEC maintained its historic responsibility for preparing management plans and supervising ongoing management. The APA was authorized to determine whether land-use activities were in compliance, and the DEC was responsible for enforcement.

Within a year, the agency fulfilled its first charge: to prepare a State Land Master Plan (SLMP) for the management of public land within the Park. By the end of the second year, 1973, the APA had created the Adirondack Park Land Use and Development Plan (APLUDP). While the SLMP for management of public land was approved by executive order of the governor, the APLUDP required approval by the legislature. The legislators made substantive changes to the standards for development recommended by the APA in just three areas: shorelines, thresholds for triggering the permit process on subdivisions, and jurisdiction in Critical Environmental Areas. Perhaps most important, and ironic, among these was a dramatic increase in density of development allowed along shorelines, areas most vulnerable to environmental degradation due to development. Still, the Master Plan and the Development Plan claimed extraordinary authority over regional land management for the APA.

The APA was so controversial that there were continual attempts over the decade following its creation to rescind the legislation. Even the Ogdensburg Diocese of the Catholic Church publicly decried the agency. The New York State Senate voted to abolish the APA, but the Assembly, with a solid downstate majority, did not support this vote. Stories of attempts to burn the park agency headquarters, manure dumped on the front lawn, and APA automobiles shot at are legendary.

The APA was to survive, and in many ways the APA Act, the State Land Master Plan, and the Adirondack Park Land Use and

TABLE 16.1. **Adirondack Park Agency land-use classification, 2007[a]**

| APA classification | | | Compatible human uses |
|---|---|---|---|
| *State land (49.10%)* | *Private land (50.90%)* | *% of park[b]* | |
| Wilderness | | 18.81 | Camping, hiking, canoeing, fishing, trapping, hunting, snowshoeing, ski touring |
| Primitive & Canoe | | 1.44 | Similar to wilderness uses |
| Wild Forest | | 22.11 | Similar to wilderness uses with the addition of some motorized vehicle access |
| Other | | 6.73 | Water (5.74%), pending (0.61%), state administration (0.03%), historic (0.01%), and intensive use (ski centers, public camp-grounds, developed beaches, boat launching; 0.34%) |
| | Resource Management | 26.09 | Forestry, agriculture, game preserves, recreation, very low density development (42.7-acre average lot size) |
| | Rural Use | 17.34 | Similar to resource manage-ment; low density development (8.5-acre average lot size) |
| | Low Intensity | 4.62 | Low density residential develop-ment (3.2-acre average lot size) |
| | Moderate Intensity | 1.71 | Concentrated residential develop-ment (1.3-acre average lot size) |
| | Hamlet | 0.92 | Many uses compatible; no APA development intensity limit |
| | Industrial | 0.21 | Existing industrial uses (e.g., min-ing), future industrial development |

[a]In addition there are approximately 599,600 acres (10.30% of total acreage) of private land and water with conservation easements, NYSDEC, March 2008, www.apa.state.ny.us/gis_assets/EasementLandClassOverlay.pdf.

[b]Percentages are from March 28, 2007, APA estimates, available at http://www.apa.state.ny.us/gis/stats/colc0903.htm.

Development Plan documents are today among the most important in American conservation history. They are the first to lay out a regional planning agenda that promotes sustainability of both wilderness character and economic vitality. These documents have proven extraordinarily prescient about the key challenges that would face the Adirondacks and resilient to the shifting economic, social, and ecological threats to the park. In legal form, these are long and complex documents, but their essence can be captured in their description of the land-use classification and management guidelines. Table 16.1 provides a snapshot of all the public and private land use classifications in the Adirondack Park, the percentage of land in each category as of August 28, 2007, and a brief description of each. In the following two sections we provide more detail on both public and private land-use classifications and their intent.

**State Land Master Plan**

The premise of the SLMP is that human use of public lands is to be encouraged as long as physical and biological resources, and social or psychological attributes, are not degraded.[2] The SLMP focuses primarily on the Forest Preserve in the Adirondacks, which "shall be forever kept as wild forest lands" by order of the state constitution. With few exceptions, all public lands in the park fall within this protection. While there have been challenges to the specific constitutional language protecting these lands, its central language has remained unchanged for more than a century.

The enabling legislation for the Adirondack Park Agency requires that the agency evaluate all public lands and classify them for ongoing management. The fundamental determinants of land classification are the physical, and biological characteristics of the land, and the associated capacity of the land to support human use. For instance, alpine communities are fragile because of the physical and biological conditions of high altitude. Social and psychological factors such as scenic quality or the opportunity to experience remoteness are also evaluated. Finally, classification acknowledges existing facilities, such as highways or ski areas.

The touchstone for the SLMP is wilderness and the plan incorporates specific language directly from the federal Wilderness Act of 1964: "A wilderness, in contrast with those areas where man and his own works dominate the landscape, is hereby recognized as an area where the earth and its community of life are untrammeled by man, where man himself is a visitor who does not remain." The SLMP proceeds from this definition to classify all public lands in the park into nine categories by comparing their qualities to those of wilderness.[3]

*Wilderness.* These are areas of at least 10,000 acres of contiguous land and water. Management guidelines for Wilderness are to perpetuate a natural plant and animal community where human influence is not apparent. All human improvements, such as cabins, roads, fire towers, and electric or telephone lines are removed. The only improvements allowed are hiking trails. Public use of motorized vehicles, including all-terrain vehicles and snowmobiles, and even all-terrain bicycles, is prohibited. Acceptable uses include hiking, mountaineering, tent camping, hunting, fishing, trapping, snowshoeing, ski touring, birding, and nature study. Management plans for each Wilderness area prescribe administrative procedures to ensure that degree and intensity of use does not threaten the resource. Procedures include allowing use by permit, closing areas to public access, and education programs to minimize impacts. In total there are 15 Wilderness areas containing all the major ecosystems from alpine to wetlands. The Wilderness class occupies nearly 1.1 million acres and 18.8 percent of the park. To appreciate the significance of this land, the Adirondack Park includes 20 percent of the wilderness areas east of the Mississippi River and 85 percent of wilderness areas in the northeastern United States.[4]

*Primitive.* This class is intended to capture two types of land. First, a Primitive designation is assigned to areas that can be upgraded to Wilderness when nonconforming qualities can be corrected, or when future amalgamation of lands can reach the 10,000-acre threshold. It is also the category for areas of wilderness character where upgrades are not possible, such as one containing a public highway that cannot be removed. Management guidelines call for maintaining Primitive areas in a condition as close to Wilderness as possible. All-terrain bicycles may be used on existing roads, but no public access via motorized vehicles is permitted. Acceptable uses are the same as those for wilderness areas.

*Canoe.* This class is essentially a wilderness setting focused on water resources. A Canoe area is composed of rivers and lakes that make possible a remote and unconfined type of water-oriented recreation. Management priorities are the quality of the water and fishery resources and the wilderness character on the adjacent lands. All-terrain bicycles are permitted on existing roads. Acceptable uses are the same as those for wilderness areas with special emphasis on canoeing, fishing, winter ski touring, and snowshoeing. Canoe areas represent 0.03 percent of the park.

*Wild Forest.* This category is an important step away from wilderness character. Wild Forest areas are less fragile than wilderness or primitive areas and can withstand greater human impact. Management guidelines allow public access via motorized vehicles on roads and snowmobile trails. Motors on boats are allowed but limited by the carrying capacity of the lake. Limited structures are allowed, including fire towers and communication facilities for official state purposes. Currently, there are nearly 1.3 million acres of Wild Forest, or 22.1 percent of the park.

*Wild, Scenic, and Recreational Rivers.* Wild Rivers are sections of rivers that are free of diversions and impoundments. They are free of human development except footbridges and are managed in accordance with Wilderness standards. Scenic Rivers are sections of rivers that are accessible via road and are managed in accordance with Wild Forest standards, except that motorboats are not permitted. Recreational Rivers are sections of rivers that may have undergone diversion or impoundment in the past and may still have development in the river area. They are administered in accordance with Wild Forest areas and motorboat use is permitted. Stream improvement structures for fisheries management are permissible in Scenic and Recreational Rivers. There are 1,200 miles of Wild, Scenic, and Recreational Rivers in the Adirondacks.

*Intensive Use.* These areas support high density recreation such as camping and downhill skiing. The state manages two major ski areas that fall within this category, Gore and Whiteface Mountains. Winter Olympic venues at Mount Van Hoevenberg and visitor information centers are also included. Management guidelines call for campgrounds without utility hookups, but vehicle camping is permitted. Boat launching sites are allowed on lakes greater than 1,000 acres. The total land area in the category is nearly 20,000 acres.

*Historic.* These areas have buildings, structures, or sites owned by the state that are significant in history, architecture, archeology, or culture. They may be designated as state historic sites or listed on the National Register of Historic Places. Management guidelines seek to preserve the quality and character of historic resources in a setting and on a scale in harmony with the relatively wild and undeveloped character of the park. There are three designated sites: Crown Point, John Brown's Farm, and Santanoni.

*State Administrative.* This category accommodates facilities for government purposes and for public use. Management guidelines call for facilities to be in a setting and on a scale that is in harmony with the wild and undeveloped character of the park.

*Travel Corridors.* This category is for strips of land that are the roadbed and right-of-way for state, federal, and interstate highways and rail lines in the Adirondack Park. Management guidelines recognize roadsides as central to the experience of visitors to the park and seek to preserve scenic vistas and ensure uniformity and high quality of signage and minimal intrusion of utility lines for power and telephone. There are 5,285 miles of public roads in the Adirondack Park.[5]

The State Land Master Plan also provides guidance on criteria for acquisition of private lands by the state for inclusion in the Forest Preserve. The intent is to acquire lands that would protect Wilderness areas where development might jeopardize their ecological integrity, or lands that would enlarge Primitive areas to greater than 10,000 acres, a size sufficient to qualify as a Wilderness area. Priority in acquisition is also given to protecting key habitats and rare species or natural communities. Finally, priority is given to lands that would improve public access to Forest Preserve lands, canoe routes, and fishing.

The SLMP identifies types of lands that should not be targets for acquisition. Perhaps most significant, acquisition of highly productive forest lands is to be avoided unless these lands are threatened by development. To reduce the threat of development while promoting continued sound forest management on these lands, the Master Plan encourages the purchase of the development rights through conservation easements.

Finally, the SLMP requires that formal management plans be prepared for all of the units of public land within the park by the Department of Environmental Conservation. Updates of these plans are scheduled at five-year intervals. The planning process involves submission of draft plans to the APA staff for review and comment on the plans' compliance with the Master Plan requirements, and presentation to the public for comment. After revision and further public comment, the final plan is presented to the APA board for review and confirmation that the plan conforms to the State Land Master Plan. Agency requirements for these Unit Management Plans stipulate that they contain inventories of natural, scenic, and cultural resources, as well as actual and projected public use. The plans are also to provide an analysis of the ecosystems and an assessment of the degree to which public use was consistent with the capacity of these ecosystems to sustain that use. Special attention is to be given to areas threatened by overuse or where rehabilitation is needed. To ensure that management planning is done in the context of a park that contain both public and private lands, plans must be integrated with the characteristics and management objectives of adjacent public and private land.

## Adirondack Park Land Use and Development Plan

The Adirondack Park Agency Act required that the APA prepare a land-use plan for all lands in the park, other than those owned by the state. Specifically, the plan was to contain a map showing a series of categories of acceptable land use. For each category, the plan was to contain a narrative describing the type, character, and extent of land use allowed, and a description of any limitations to be imposed on development and the purpose of the restrictions. The plan was to focus attention on shorelines, setting standards for lot widths, the distance buildings and septic systems would be set back from lakes, and cutting of vegetation along the shoreline.[6] The intent of the Development Plan was to channel commercial and residential construction into areas where it already exists or where environmental impacts can be minimized.

The APA accomplished this charge, classifying private land into a series of six categories of acceptable use. The primary distinction among these categories is the density of development.

*Resource Management.* Resource Management is the most restrictive private land class, but compatible uses include forestry, agriculture, and residential development. The management guidelines call for maintaining as much of this land in open space as possible. Purposes of regulations are to encourage sound economic management of the natural resources and to discourage strip development along travel corridors. Much of the land in the park within this class is owned by the forest industry, and regulations focus on limiting the size of clearcuts and the proximity of cuts to shorelines. Where residential development occurs on this land, the number of principal buildings allowed is 15 per square mile (average lot size of 42.7 acres).[7] As a category, Resource Management areas constitute 26.5 percent of the Park.[8]

*Rural Use.* Rural Use is a transitional class between large tracts of open forest and the residential and commercial areas within the park. Management guidelines call for maintaining a rural character by allowing density of residential or commercial buildings of not more than 75 per square mile (average lot size of 8.5 acres). Like Resource Management areas, the purpose of regulation in Rural Use areas is to encourage preservation of open space and discourage strip development. Rural Use areas make up about 17.4 percent of the park.

*Low Intensity Use.* For this residential and commercial land-use class, the density of principal buildings is limited to a maximum of 200 per square mile (average lot size of 3.2 acres). These areas are intended to serve as space for expansion of residential development, especially seasonal homes. Regulations are intended to promote an orderly development. Low Intensity Use areas constitute 4.6 percent of the park.

*Moderate Intensity Use.* This is a residential and commercial land-use class where the density of principal buildings is 500 per square mile (average lot size is 1.3 acres). Guidelines anticipate these areas to be primarily developed as residential areas on the periphery of towns and along transportation corridors and accessible shorelines. As with Low Intensity areas, regulations are intended to promote an orderly development. Moderate Intensity use areas include about 1.7 percent of the park.

*Industrial Use.* In these areas of industrial and commercial use there is no limit to density of buildings. The purpose of regulation is to encourage development of existing industrial and mining operations in a manner that contributes to economic growth of the park without detracting from its wilderness character. Industrial Use areas occupy about 0.2 percent of the park.

*Hamlet.* In the Adirondacks, hamlets are what much of the rest of society calls small towns, including commercial and residential areas, industrial and recreational sites, and government centers. There is no limit to the density of buildings. Hamlet areas are intended to absorb the greatest portion of future expansion of housing, business, and recreational services in the park. Consequently, original maps delineated Hamlet areas to include space for expansion. Within Hamlet areas, regulation is largely done by the local town government. The APA plays little role in regulating development in hamlets except for subdivision developments of more than 100 units or structures higher than forty feet. There are 103 towns and villages in the park. Hamlet areas comprise 0.9 percent of the park area.

The APLUDP includes particular restrictions on lakeshore development, including minimum lot widths, set-back requirements, and restrictions on tree cutting. However, the framers of the APA Act view the weaknesses in shoreline protection as the biggest political compromise. According to Peter Paine, the legislative language recommended by the APA was not as strong as it should have been, and the final legislation was even worse.

## The Role of Local Government

Local governments also play an important role in regulating development on other land-use classes within their borders: Moderate Intensity, Low Intensity, Rural, Industrial, and Resource Management. To exercise this authority, towns are required to formulate a comprehensive plan for development, and their plan must be approved by the APA. Once approved, the plans allow for a distinction between projects that remain under the jurisdiction of the APA and those that are deemed to be the jurisdiction of the local government. Larger projects, such as subdivisions of more than 100 lots, are defined as Class A and remain within the primary jurisdiction of the APA. Smaller subdivisions and projects, such as multiple family dwellings, public buildings, and tourist attractions, are defined as Class B and regulated by local government. Regardless of whether the APA or local government is deemed to have regulatory jurisdiction, the same environmental standards apply.[9]

A key exception to this division of responsibility occurs for areas considered to be especially sensitive to human impact. These areas are designated Critical Environmental Areas, and when a project shows potential impact, jurisdiction is maintained by the APA. Critical Environmental Areas include wetlands, higher elevations (above 2,500 feet), and land in close proximity to state land. Given the abundance of wetlands, land above 2,500 feet, and the checkerboard arrangement of state lands throughout the park, the APA plays a large role.

In addition to the regulatory authority offered to local government by the legislation, it also called for the creation of a Local Government Review Board, with advisory responsibility for the APA. According to Dick Persico, creation of a citizen review board was another of the compromises necessary for approval of the Adirondack Park Land Use and Development Plan. But unlike the compromises reached over shoreline development, agreeing to a citizen review board was easy, because the board has no teeth. The review board concept was also less than successful because the early members did not recognize that by working with the APA they could accomplish more than by railing against it.

## Conclusion

The importance of the State Land Master Plan and the Adirondack Park Land Use and Development Plan is that these laws captured a paradigm shift, a fundamental change in society's view of an old debate. The impetus for environmental planning, impact assessment, and public involvement during the 1960s and 1970s drew bipartisan support and resulted in federal legislation such as the National Forest Management Act (1974), the Forest and Rangeland Renewable Resources Planning Act (1974), the Endangered Species Act (1973), and the National Environmental Policy Act (1970), in addition to the Wilderness Act (1964). In a sense, New York was simply following a national trend that brought environmental quality and public involvement in land-use decisions to the fore.

Yet New York appears to have been well ahead of society in initiating a much more comprehensive change in the paradigm for land management. What is unique is that the Temporary Study Commission and then the Adirondack Park Agency are the extension of public interest for the environment beyond public land into private land. Under this paradigm, the public could stipulate acceptable uses of not only all public land, but all private land within the park. Furthermore, regional government planning could take precedence over local government interests.

When one considers that there was virtually no regulation of private land in the Adirondack Park prior to 1971, it is not hard to understand that the shift wrought controversy. The regulation of private lands produced two immediate legal challenges. The Horizon Adirondack Corporation and the Ton-Da-Lay Association sued the APA. In both cases, the courts ruled that regulations imposed by the APA were legally comparable to those that would affect any urban, suburban, or even rural landowner as part of zoning laws. Perhaps most significant in these court decisions was an affirmation of the philosophical basis for the regulation as originally cast by the Temporary Study Commission. The intent of preserving open space and environmental quality were judged to be valid bases for regulation. The preeminence of planning on a geographic scale such as the Adirondack Park was also accepted. While the courts acknowledged that local governments should always have a voice in the decisions about land use, local interests could not justify impairment of strong state interests.[10] Without question, the legal decisions in support of the Adirondack Park Agency, the State Land Master Plan, and Adirondack Park Land Use and Development Plan, transformed the Adirondack Park and our thinking about sustainable development. Although the legislation allows for economic growth, protection of the rural economy was not central to the mandate of the agency. According to Peter Paine, our failures to this day relate to our inability, still, to understand sustainability, whether economic, ecological, or social.

# 17

## The Early Years of the Adirondack Park Agency

GEORGE D. DAVIS

*Editors' Note: In our conversations with Dick Persico, the second executive director of the Adirondack Park Agency, he observed that both visionary thinkers and pragmatists were enormously important in the early days of the agency. Among the visionaries was George Davis. He was a gifted advocate for wilderness and regional planning. Davis came to the Adirondacks initially as a member of the staff of the Temporary Study Commission on the Future of the Adirondacks. When the Adirondack Park Agency was formed, he was its first employee. Later, he would also play a key role in Governor Cuomo's Commission on the Adirondacks in the Twenty-First Century. His ideas are found throughout the commission reports, the enabling legislation for the agency, and the State Land Master Plan and Adirondack Park Land Use and Development Plan. What follows is an edited version of an interview of George Davis by Bill Verner, curator of the Adirondack Museum in Blue Mountain Lake. The interview was conducted in April 1976. The Adirondack Park Agency was just five years old, and the legislation giving it power to regulate all activities on both public and private land was still younger. The debate was hot, and Davis's ideas were at the center of nearly every issue.*

Taken from a transcription of a George Davis interview by Bill Verner, Apr. 5, 1976, at the Adirondack Museum, Blue Mountain Lake, N.Y. The interview was recorded on reel-to-reel tape and the transcription was made by Davies Associates of Ogdensburg, N.Y. Copyright to this transcript is held by George Davis. Publication is with permission. For further information, contact the Adirondack Museum at 518–352–7311.

I think we ought to begin on June 30, 1967. As I recall, this was the date the Adirondack Mountains National Park proposed plan hit the front page of the Sunday *New York Times*. I was in Colorado at that time, working for the U.S. Forest Service, and even there I had heard of the national park proposal for the Adirondack Mountains. It delineated about 1.7 million acres of the 5.7 million that was New York State's Adirondack Park as a national park. The report was drawn together by three individuals under the auspices of Laurance Rockefeller. It created quite an uproar. Most people, regardless of their interest in the Adirondacks, did not like the idea of a national park for a variety of reasons. One, it involved the purchase of practically all of the land in the 1.7-million-acre area, except for a few of the hamlets and small areas already developed. Two, hunting would not be allowed, and hunting was a long-standing Adirondack tradition.

But, the main reason for the wide opposition to this proposal was that it was "big brother," the federal government, coming in. Also, I think the people of the state were confused and believed the New York State Constitution's Forever Wild provision, which protected the 2.3 million acres of state lands in the Adirondack Park, protected the entire 5.7-million-acre park. So, they thought, if we have done such a great thing by adopting the Forever Wild provision, why should "big brother" now come in and take over here in the Adirondacks? All of a sudden diverse groups such as the Sierra Club and other preservation interests were in bed with the private land owners, the timber industry, the mining industry, and everyone else with an interest in the Adirondacks. All seemed to agree there should not be a national park in the Adirondacks. There were supporters of the concept, but they were few and far between. Probably wisely, for their own sake, they did not speak up.

The national park proposal created some problems for Governor Nelson Rockefeller, who was an astute politician. He recognized that Laurance Rockefeller, his brother and principal conservation advisor, was suggesting a national park while most of the people of New York State were adamant about keeping the federal government out of the Adirondacks. The governor, as does many a politician with a hot issue, appointed a commission to study the proposal. The motive may have been to allow the subject to cool off, but I don't believe Nelson Rockefeller thought he was just sweeping the issue under the rug. He was much too intelligent for that. If that is what he wanted, he would not have picked the 13 people he did as commissioners. The creation of the Temporary Study Commission on the Future of the Adirondacks was announced in September 1968.

Most study commissions are established with certain members appointed by the governor and certain members appointed by the leaders in the legislature. Rockefeller could not be bothered by this kind of nonsense. He established the commission by executive order and appointed all of the commissioners himself. He chose Leo O'Brien, a former congressman and a Democrat to head this commission. He chose Harold Jerry, his trouble shooter from the Conservation Department, as executive secretary and chief of staff to the commission. On the commission itself, he appointed a mix of Republicans and Democrats. It was not a partisan commission. Members included Julien Anderson, Henry Diamond, Bob Hall, Stewart Kilborne, Howard Kimball, Dick Lawrence, Lowell Thomas, Jim Loeb, Fred O'Neal, Peter Paine, Senator Watson Pomeroy, and Fred Sheffield, along with a man from Blue Mountain Lake, Harold Hochschild. Hochschild was a captain of industry and a respected advisor at all levels of government. He would become the chairman of the commission.

At the first meeting of the commission, the governor had assured the commissioners they had wide latitude. They could concern themselves with anything in the Adirondacks. He charged the commission with addressing seven questions concerning the Adirondacks. I won't reiterate the questions, except to say they were general enough they could have included anything the commission wanted to study. This commission was to operate out of the executive chamber, right out of the governor's office, which proved to be very wise. It made practically anything we wanted possible.

In December 1970, the final report of the Commission was published with 181 specific recommendations, backed by 7 technical reports. The actual press release date was January 3, 1971. We had to hit the Sunday *New York Times,* and we made the front page. That report, over the next month or so, received editorial support from every single daily newspaper in the State of New York. Sometimes there would be a qualification, specifying some minor disagreement. But it is amazing that any government report could receive the amount of support as that study commission report.

We went down to New York from Albany and had meetings with Nelson Rockefeller. I was just amazed at his authority. It was almost dictatorial. Being very naïve, and knowing how the democratic system was supposed to work according to text books, I was shocked that one person in state government could have so much authority. I did not really like it, at least until I met the state legislators. After I saw that cast of characters, I was very thankful that a man with the vision and the intelligence of a Nelson Rockefeller essentially ran the show. He was not a conservationist, he was a developer. On the other hand, he was a rather open-minded individual. If people came in with ideas, and if they pointed out the values and the shortcomings, you could sell Rockefeller. I think this was the case with the commission report. The first recommendation of the report was to establish an Adirondack Park Agency. Rockefeller was a very innovative man and here was an idea that, in terms of land use policy at the state level, had not been tried elsewhere in the country. With the governor behind it, the legislature created the Adirondack Park Agency in March 1971.

The agency was originally to consist of nine commissioners. At the insistence of the members of the Study Commission, Chairman Hochschild recommended to the governor that none of the staff be considered for appointment to a permanent Adirondack Park Agency. Those of us who were not commissioners, however, thought that was untenable. You had to have some continuity. I think the final decision was very good, in terms of bringing two of the Study Commission people on board, Dick Lawrence and Peter Paine. That gave the agency the continuity it needed, and yet these people did not constitute a majority.

I was hired as the first staff member, and I immediately began hiring additional staff. We had three jobs before us. First, we had to write a State Land Master Plan for the management of state lands (Forest Preserve) in the Adirondack Park and deliver it to the governor in 1972. Second, we had to write a private land use and development plan and develop a map categorizing all the private lands and formulate zoning. This we had to submit to the legislature in 1973. And third, we had to specify interim powers for the park agency so destructive development didn't happen during the planning process. The agency began to take shape in late 1971. So, we didn't have much time to do all of this.

The Study Commission had done a great deal of work on the State Land Master Plan and, with its recommendations, which took up an entire volume of the 7 technical reports, one could almost say that the plan, in essence, had been worked out. Transforming any idea into specifics is always difficult, but the idea of the various land categories and where they ought to be was essentially done. Clarence Petty and I developed the State Land Master Plan Map, delineating which areas of Forest Preserve should be Wilderness, Primitive, Wild Forest, and Intensive Use Areas. Our counsel, Bill Kissel, and I went to New York City to Peter Paine's Wall Street office to write the State Land Master Plan in about four days. Peter Paine was the final word.

Our biggest problem with the State Land Master Plan, of course, was not with agency members and certainly not with the public, who were very supportive. Our problem was with the Department of Environmental Conservation (DEC). These people had been managing or administering the state lands in the Adirondacks for nearly one hundred years. All of sudden, this new agency that is less than a year old is mandated by law to come up with and set policies for how the DEC was to administer these lands in the future. I think that the Department personnel in the Division of Lands and Forests viewed us as finding fault with the way they had managed lands in the past. That was not the intent of the plan. The intent was to answer the question, how should these lands be managed in the future?

We went as far as we thought we could in the plan. Although we worked with DEC personnel in developing it, because of the short time we could not convince them and win them over. I am not sure if we'd had three or four years, it could have been done. We had to smooth the waters as best we could. The educational process had to take over in following years. As I look back, I don't think we could have established the types of management tools the state land required by spending dozens of years convincing people.

Our second task, a plan for the 3.5 million acres of private land in the park, had to be completed in about a year and a half. A lot of people said this was not nearly enough time, when it typically takes at least two to three years to develop a local town or village zoning ordinance. But we were looking at something that was more general and regional. We weren't looking at specific property lot lines and specific problems that a town had to face. Those problems really take the time.

The park agency had a professional and paraprofessional staff of about 10 people. The staff began by developing a series of overlays depicting physical, biological, and social constraints using the methodology for an inventory of private land capabilities I had developed at Cornell (1970). It was based on McHarg's *Design with Nature.* The compilation of overlays indicated how much development the land could take and what would be the appropriate land-use category. To develop the critical Adirondack Park Land Use and Development Plan Map, I realized we couldn't have all of them divvying the park up, or we'd lose the needed continuity. You really have to have an overall mechanism, so you're sure, for example, that Clinton County is done the same as Franklin County. Dick Estes and I divided the counties into just two groups. Dick, along with Bill Curran, did Clinton, Franklin, St. Lawrence, and Lewis Counties, and I, along with Anita Riner, did the other eight counties. Others assisting for long hours each day in the development of the map were Clarence Petty, Greenie Chase, Gary Duprey, Gary Randorf, and John Mills. As we finished, the really key step was that we insisted on field checking these areas. We wanted to make sure they made sense on the ground. Is this really *resource management?* Is it really *moderate intensity development?* We conducted the field check strictly by road. There's darn little development that we couldn't drive to. We drove every single road, and we checked, often with a commissioner along, and corrected these draft maps. There are some mistakes in the final map, but we have really been amazed, when you stop to think of all the considerations that went into it, how few there are.

Existing use proved to be a real bugaboo because we were trying to look at the land capabilities and not existing development. So, we mapped land capabilities first and then superimposed existing use and other social and political considerations. For instance, if a village already existed on what ought to be *resource management,* you couldn't very well make the village *resource management.* Where existing use really hurt was along lakeshore areas. In the Adirondacks, where there's an accessible lakeshore, it's generally built up. We had to classify many lakeshores as *moderate intensity* largely because they were already built up, even though they should have been *rural use* or *resource management* according to their capabilities.

We took every single land-use area in each county and described exactly why it was classified as it was. We identified the good things and the bad things and went right down the list for every area. This was really good training because it made your mind work. You could explain your decision making. Then we invited every town supervisor in to review the map and suggest revisions, most of which we made.

Next we had to get this plan through the legislature. Governor Rockefeller deserves the credit. Once he was sold and made up his mind that this was a popular and innovative program, that's all there was to it. If he said let's go with it, he was not going to accept defeat. The governor signed the legislation on May 22, 1973, with a strong statement and a rather large ceremony to emphasize the fact that he thought this was an important accomplishment. When the governor resigned from office to run for president, he listed 10 accomplishments he was most proud of in his 15- or 16-year tenure, and the Adirondack Park Agency program was number 3 on that list.

The law said that as of August 1, 1973, the land use and development plan and map would take effect. In other words, these mapped categories would be how the land is classified. There was to be a system set up so that all projects would be reviewed to make sure they didn't create an adverse environmental impact and to make sure they would meet the constraints of the plan. By August 1, however, we discovered we didn't have a plan for implementing all of this. When a land owner came into the office to propose something on his land, we didn't even have a form for him to complete. We did not know what we wanted to ask him. The guy wants to do something on his land, and now the law says he has to go through us. We can't just tell him to come back next month. We were so geared toward getting this plan through the legislature that we hadn't focused on implementing it. Now once again we had to really scramble and get a project review mechanism set up.

Local governments were supposed to take care of things below the threshold of regional impact, and there was to be a local assistance program set up to try to get local governments involved in planning and land-use regulation at the local scale. The law defined areas of state concern and those of purely local concern. For those areas where there were both state and local concerns, you were to sort things so that everyone was in agreement. The plan was politically wise, and environmentally and socially good. The problem was that the law laid out some very specific criteria that local governments had to meet in order to gain agency approval for their local plan. We encouraged local governments to come in and work with us toward a local land-use plan that the agency could approve. But the law failed to recognize a clear fact of life: most Adirondack communities didn't have the personnel, the experience, the finances, or anything else, to come up with their own land-use plan. The law did not set up a graduated system through which a local government could learn and take on their responsibilities step by step. It was an all-or-nothing system.

As an agency, we should have decided we were going to review them step by step. We could have done everything to help them, for instance, to do a trailer ordinance or simple use zoning for part of their town. We could have helped a little at a time so they could gain experience and an understanding of what land use controls are all about. Many of the local problems were not intricate. Maybe they didn't want junkyards. Well, that can be simply taken care of with an ordinance. But no, we had to look at it as state law specified, and told them they had to have the comprehensive final product before we could help financially and technically.

So we would tell them they're going to get all these grand land-use regulation powers if they come up with an approvable local land-use program. But we couldn't define what it would mean to them for making day-to-day decisions. It was too complex. We found ourselves, after a year or two, with more than 50 municipalities going gung ho. They were spending their time and energy, mostly volunteer, moving toward something that, if they get it, and that is a big if, they aren't going to know what to do with it. Everybody's in their little box, and it's not going to work. It all sounds very nice in Albany, but in practice in the Adirondacks, it does not work.

As an agency now five years old, we face a larger decision. Do we become strictly an agency designed to provide regulatory and service guidelines, or do we start laying groundwork for a park, as a region of New York? What do the people want for the Adirondacks? How do we take advantage of the assets of the Adirondacks? I would submit that if we decided to stay just with a regulatory role and provide service to local government, we would soon be amalgamated into other agencies. Our regulatory powers would be taken by DEC and our planning powers by the offices of the Secretary of State. Yet, the legislature did not do that, and I believe wisely so. I think there was a recognition that one agency needed to look at the park as an entity. Just one agency needed to concern itself with environmental issues and with planning, development and aesthetics, all at once. So, how do we now step back, keeping an eye on the regulatory machinery, and start determining how the state should treat the Adirondacks? We get faced with public pressure and, unfortunately, we let the day-to-day decisions determine future policy courses. We don't plan for the future. I envision the basic purpose of park planning to be to define the qualities of a park we seek at some date in the future. If you can do that, then you give the day-to-day decision makers a very easy question to ask themselves: Which decision is going to lead me in a direction toward those qualities? But to date, we have not defined, either at the staff or agency level, where we want the park to be in future years. This has to be done. Then, let the chips fall where they may.

# 18

## The Evolution of the Department of Environmental Conservation

STUART BUCHANAN

The creation of the Adirondack Park Agency (APA) and subsequent development of the Adirondack Park State Land Master Plan (SLMP) in 1972 had a significant influence on the Department of Environmental Conservation's (DEC) management of the Adirondack Forest Preserve over the next thirty-three years. Between 1885, when the Forest Preserve was created, and the present time, the DEC and its various organizational predecessors have been guided in their management efforts by the New York State constitution, legislation, court decisions, opinions issued by the office of the attorney general, the SLMP, and the rules, regulations and policies that were developed along the way.

The original purpose of the Forest Preserve was to protect the forests from fire and destructive timber practices and to preserve their timber value, sources of water supply, healthful environment for human visitors, and opportunities for passive recreation. This purpose has been variously interpreted over the years by legislative bodies and the Conservation Department as a mandate for forest

The author is indebted to the following retired DEC regional and division directors for their historical perspective and editorial suggestions: Norm Van-Valkenberg, director, Division of Lands and Forests (1977–86); Bob Bathrick, director, Division of Lands and Forests (1987–96); Tom Brown, director, Region 6 (1982–98); and Tom Monroe, director, Region 5 (1977–94).

protection while allowing for public use. Between the First and Second World Wars, demand for more intensive-use recreational facilities, such as picnic areas, camping sites, and ski centers, brought about changes in management policies. The increase in prosperity and the availability of the automobile in the 1920s accelerated the transition of the Adirondack Park from the playground of the very wealthy to a destination for those with lesser means and demonstrated a need for public access and the creation of recreational-use facilities within the Adirondack Park. The availability of a large labor force to work on public works projects through the Civilian Conservation Corps (CCC) in the 1930s made possible the establishment of facilities such as the first formal campgrounds, and scenic/recreational motor-vehicle roads like the Whiteface Mountain Veterans Memorial Highway.

Reconciliation of the apparent conflict between forest protection and public use has been an evolving challenge the department has struggled with for decades. The post–World War II increase in recreational demand and accompanying interest in public land use raised the debate over Forest Preserve protection to a new level. The Conservation Department first called for areas within the Forest Preserve to be set aside as Wilderness in 1952 and began studying this possibility formally in 1960. This led to a prohibition in 1963 of motorized vehicles in parts of the Forest Preserve previously identified as potential Wilderness areas, followed by a formal proposal for the establishment of twelve Wilderness areas within the Adirondack Park in 1965. These early efforts at Wilderness designation and protection by the Conservation Department occurred in the context of a national wilderness debate and passage of the 1964 Wilderness Act. It provided the early blueprint for what ultimately became fifteen designated wilderness areas in the 1972 SLMP and was followed by further protection in the form of a ban on float planes and motorboats on 700 Wilderness lakes and ponds in 1973.

The period from 1967 to 1973 was one of tremendous change for the Conservation Department and its efforts to manage the Adirondack Park. Beginning with Laurance Rockefeller's ill-fated proposal to create an Adirondack Mountains National Park, the Conservation Department saw the formation of the Temporary Study Commission, the creation of the Adirondack Park Agency, and the development and adoption of the SLMP. During this same period, the Conservation Department, with its entire identity and institutional history invested in the management of fish, wildlife, public forest lands, and outdoor recreation, became the Department of Environmental Conservation and was transformed into a comprehensive environmental agency with significant new responsibilities, including a strong regulatory mission focused on implementation of clean air, clean water, and solid and hazardous waste rules, in addition to its traditional natural resource management focus. This transformation necessitated an internal shift from a military-type organization with a relatively narrow mission and clear chain-of-command to a matrix organization that relied on cross-program coordination to function effectively.

It is important to understand the organizational mind set of the department or, at least, of the staff within the department at the time of these changes. As noted, the main functions of the Conservation Department were centered in two disciplines—fish and game, and lands and forests—with the latter including responsibility for the Forest Preserve. The Adirondack Park was split among six forest districts, each of which was headed by and staffed with trained foresters who had spent their formative years with the department managing camps of the CCC all across the state. With minimal oversight from the central office (which had no staff or unit directly assigned to Forest Preserve matters), Forest Preserve management varied district to district depending on the personality and beliefs of the forester in charge. The formation of the DEC in 1970 effected some consolidation of management but still left the Adirondack Park split between two regions; however, the same staff remained responsible for care, custody, and control of the Forest Preserve with no increase in central office oversight.

The establishment of two new agencies created a unique and challenging jurisdictional mandate within the Adirondack Park, where the DEC sometimes found itself in the role of both regulator and landowner for projects involving Forest Preserve lands. It also brought in new interests and constituencies to serve and changed the state's relationship with local governments within the park. The agency that had historically managed their state lands and wildlife also became the agency that required them to close their landfills and comply with other environmental quality regulations. All of these changes occurred in the larger context of a growing national environmental movement that added to the climate of increased accountability, public involvement, and process.

The early transition to adapt to these changes was not an easy one for DEC managers and staff who were required to accept a forced collaboration with the APA, while coping with the significant internal adjustments created by the DEC's new programmatic responsibilities. The creation through the APA Act of limitations on private development was welcomed and seemed a logical step forward in protecting the overall integrity of the Adirondack Park without giving up control to a federal agency. Even the concept of a policy document for guiding state land management that gave legal status to the creation of Wilderness areas was something that a few within the old Conservation Department had been advocating for years. However, when the SLMP was developed and adopted with little input from department staff and given to a new Adirondack Park Agency to implement, it adversely affected the DEC's view of its newest sister agency.

The SLMP brought organization to the Adirondack Forest Preserve by classifying land areas into categories based on their character and use. This approach was widely accepted for the Wilderness areas that, for the most part, had long been recognized as the core areas within the park most requiring protection. It also classified other Forest Preserve lands into categories that allowed non-wilderness uses, including motorized access and the creation of facilities to accommodate recreational demand and administrative needs. It effectively closed the door on any proposals to allow active forest and wildlife management, or for private or commercial uses within the non-wilderness portions of the Forest Preserve. It required that

Unit Management Plans (UMPs) be developed for each of the land areas designated by the SLMP. These UMPs were required to be consistent with the classification standards contained in the SLMP and were subject to formal APA review.

The feeling within the DEC (and, arguably, outside as well) was that the Conservation Department had done a pretty good job with its Forest Preserve management responsibilities over the years, given the often conflicting laws and opinions that it relied on for guidance. Why then was there a need for oversight by a small, new, inexperienced agency? The rationale suggested in the original (1972 version) introduction to the SLMP was that an APA-administered State Land Master Plan was necessary as a companion to the private land development master plan authorized under section 805 of the APA Act. The implication was that only by administering the two plans together could the larger issues of increasing recreational use and parkwide infrastructure needs be dealt with in the context of the intermingled private and public land ownership pattern in the park. A clear, if not directly stated, justification was that a higher standard of stewardship and accountability would result and would achieve a new vision for the park. What was left unstated was the view that the creation of the APA was necessary to provide a more effective mechanism of oversight and influence of Adirondack Forest Preserve policies and management practices than was available through the DEC decision-making process, by providing a regular public forum and a board of commissioners representing a range of Adirondack Park interests.

Many within the DEC felt that APA oversight would just add another layer of state government, resulting in waste, overlap, and confusion, and that the resources required to staff a new agency could be much better used to augment the existing DEC organization. This feeling among long-term departmental staff resulted in a resistance to embrace and cooperate with the agency during the early years of its existence. To add to the difficulty, there was a perception among some early DEC managers that agency commissioners and staff were not interested in working with department staff on Forest Preserve policy, assuming instead that the agency would determine management policies and that DEC would carry them out. This inability by both agencies to move forward in a collaborative fashion set the stage for a difficult transition and a lack of significant progress in state land management for the first few years of the SLMP's existence.

Some initial effort was made to establish credibility in the newly formed agency by transferring respected DEC staff like Clarence Petty and Greenleaf Chase to the APA, where their expertise was needed and their relationship with DEC staff could help establish a connection between agencies. The effect of this move was undermined, however, when these key staff were not replaced, nor were additional positions provided to the DEC to handle the new and expanded duties required of it by the SLMP. In addition, the perception was that the APA's function was to watch over the DEC's management of the Forest Preserve with no commitment to assist its sister agency in carrying out that responsibility. It was not until the mid-1970s that serious efforts were initiated by the DEC to recognize that the two agencies needed to work together to realize the vision that led to the inclusion of a state land oversight role in the APA Act. This move toward a more collaborative relationship was facilitated by changes in DEC leadership at several levels and a clear commitment to implement the SLMP through DEC policy and regulation.

As a result of these efforts, DEC staff felt empowered to begin addressing important Forest Preserve management issues, examples of which include the banning of float planes from Wilderness lakes and the removal of privately held tent platforms from Forest Preserve lands. While these actions had the enthusiastic support of agency staff, and efforts were made to improve the joint working relationship between the two agencies, the lack of a clear definition of corresponding roles and responsibilities inhibited any real progress in establishing a cooperative approach between the agencies.

The significance of these actions is considerable when viewed in the perspective of the historic mandate and mission of the

Conservation Department, which had always felt a strong obligation to provide public recreational opportunities, and viewed this responsibility as equal to that of protecting the Forest Preserve. This sense of duty was a reflection of decades of legislative debate over the appropriate use of the Forest Preserve, combined with a direct mandate to provide recreational opportunities on other state lands across the state. The actions taken to restrict human uses, which were publicly supported by the department and carried out and enforced by department staff, demonstrated that the SLMP was bringing about a shift in the DEC's emphasis to an overarching priority for protection of the Forest Preserve, in concert with consideration for public recreation.

Other organizational and policy-related changes were made during the late 1970s and early 1980s in an effort to better align the department with both its historic and new responsibilities. The *Forest Preserve Handbook,* which had been compiled over the years from opinions of the attorney general's office as a guide to Forest Preserve management, was revised into a set of Forest Preserve policies based on the SLMP. A Bureau of Preserve Management was formed within the Division of Lands and Forests and a Forest Preserve Advisory Committee was appointed to give the various interest groups and local governments a forum to discuss Forest Preserve issues. While these actions sent a clear message that the department was serious about its Forest Preserve management responsibilities and that the SLMP would guide Forest Preserve policy, they did not come without a price. The new bureau was created by "borrowing" staff from other bureaus within the division and staff were diverted at both central office and field levels to work on UMPs and to administer the advisory committee. The internal strains created by reassignment of staff to perform Forest Preserve duties contributed to feelings of frustration among DEC managers and ultimately dampened their enthusiasm for the new responsibilities.

In spite of these efforts, Forest Preserve planning at the unit level was slow to evolve. The need to do meaningful planning was recognized and the SLMP was accepted as the guiding document;

however, several obstacles stood in the way of UMP progress. During the mid-1970s an unsuccessful attempt at developing a UMP for the High Peaks Wilderness (HPW) caused some disenchantment in the regions for the UMP planning process. The HPW, with its large geographic size, heavy public use, numerous existing facilities, and strong vocal constituencies, was, in retrospect, a poor choice for an initial attempt at developing a Unit Management Plan that conformed to the definitions of Wilderness contained in the SLMP. This first venture into unit management planning was viewed by DEC staff as being very staff-intensive and, ultimately, unsuccessful as a vehicle for resolving difficult issues. The general feeling among regional managers was that unit management planning required significant staff resources and a firm commitment from Albany in order to complete the task effectively. As a result, there was a reluctance to take on new UMPs. This eventually changed in the 1980s, and a handful of plans were completed.

In addition to a lack of a strong unit management planning mandate and accompanying resources, the 1980 Winter Olympics in Lake Placid consumed much of the department's energy and focus in the late 1970s. As managing agency for the Olympic facilities at Whiteface Mountain and Mount Van Hoevenberg, and with added responsibilities for various logistical planning tasks, the department had little time or resources to deal with other Forest Preserve management demands. The need for Olympic facility construction and upgrades raised constitutional and SLMP issues that some felt were ignored in order to meet the facility needs and deadlines of this high-profile event. The national audience that followed these preparations included Wilderness advocates who maintained a heightened level of interest in the Adirondack Park and spawned a growing environmental constituency that demanded to be included in the Forest Preserve management process after the Olympics were over.

An issue that has been raised at various times since the creation of the DEC in 1970 is the difficulty (both real and perceived) in achieving a coordinated approach to Forest Preserve management when the park is split between two different DEC regions. Some interests feel that the "special place" management recognition deserved by the Adirondack Park cannot be achieved without a single, consolidated administrative park unit. It has been recognized by interests both outside and within the department that DEC Region 5, which is responsible for the eastern portion of the park and headquartered in Ray Brook, and Region 6, which is responsible for the western portion of the park and headquartered in Watertown, have different patterns of historical use, a different balance of local interests, and as a result evolved differing perspectives on policy and administrative direction.

In the late 1970s, and again in 1990, this dichotomy of perspective was considered to be sufficiently problematic to cause the department to investigate the feasibility of combining administrative functions for the Adirondack Park into a single regional unit. However, this proposal failed to gain the support of the legislature and local governments that had developed ties to the existing regional DEC offices and feared that the loss of a regional office in one area or another of the park would affect their ability to work with the department. The department concluded that rather than creating a single administrative unit for the park, unified "special place" administration could be assured under the existing DEC organizational structure through well-defined Forest Preserve policy and direction.

Governor Mario Cuomo's Commission on the Adirondacks in the Twenty-First Century issued its report in 1989. This report included a long list of controversial recommendations aimed at increasing protections for the park. It once again changed the landscape for the department by creating much local animosity toward the two state agencies responsible for managing the Adirondack Park and led to the creation of several new Adirondack interest groups. It also contributed to the defeat of the 1990 Environmental Quality Bond Act, which was proposed to fund ongoing land conservation activities in the park. These events ultimately resulted in greater efforts to involve local government in Adirondack Park state land management, and land conservation in particular.

In 1992 the state's first Open Space Conservation Plan was completed; it provided a set of criteria for open space protection throughout the state and included a list of proposed projects for acquisition. The Open Space Program was especially significant for the Adirondack Park and resulted in the first meaningful response to the eleven acquisition policy recommendations contained in the 1972 SLMP. The new open space planning process also provided local government representatives and other interests an effective forum for meaningful discussion of issues important to Adirondack towns and villages. The regional Open Space Advisory Committees have been invaluable in bringing Adirondack Park interests together and fostering a dialogue that has benefited other planning efforts around the park.

The last decade has been a time of significant progress on many fronts related to Forest Preserve planning and management. In spite of increased pressures on Adirondack Park resources and a challenging fiscal climate, a strong commitment by both the DEC and the APA to work together to address Forest Preserve issues has had results. This cooperation has not happened without some difficulties, and many long-standing uses of the Forest Preserve have not withstood the measure of the SLMP. That has been particularly evident in dealing with motorized uses across the park, which have been severely curtailed over the past ten years through a combination of policy development, unit management planning, increased enforcement, and, in some cases, as a result of challenges from outside groups.

All of this activity and emphasis is reflective of a certain maturity in the relationship between the DEC and the APA and a growing acknowledgment that the two agencies must work together if either is to achieve its mission. This progress is perhaps best exemplified by Governor George Pataki's UMP initiative, which charged the two agencies with completing all of the remaining Adirondack Park UMPs over a five-year period beginning in 1999. Although this goal was not achieved within the proscribed time, it resulted in a significant number of new plans and established a process and momentum that demonstrated that translating the SLMP into UMPs was possible. Today there are Unit Management Plans in place for approximately 56 percent of the Forest Preserve land in the park. Perhaps more important than the tally of completed plans, the initiative resulted in raising the quality of the plans significantly when compared with those previously produced. This effort also resulted in the resolution of numerous difficult issues that had gone unresolved for over thirty years, a well-documented assessment of resources and issues that provide a historical context for future management and planning, the development of a clear set of management actions that lay the foundation for future stewardship activities and investments, and perhaps most important, the creation of a strong consultative process and much improved working relationship between the DEC and the APA.

The past thirty-five years have been incredibly challenging for the DEC and provide a wonderful opportunity to assess what happened, what worked, and what might have been handled differently. The rocky start that characterized the first years of coexisting with the APA could perhaps have been smoother if Conservation Department managers and staff had been more involved in the development of the Temporary Study Commission recommendations, the design of the new Adirondack Park Agency, and the creation of the SLMP. This lack of ownership undoubtedly contributed to feelings of resentment by department staff.

It is also clear that a concerted effort was needed during the first few years to create an atmosphere of collaboration between the two agencies. This collaboration was eventually attempted, but not until much early energy and momentum that should have launched the new state land management team approach was lost. This not only resulted in a lost opportunity, but sent a mixed message to the public regarding the implementation of the SLMP and sowed the seeds of dissension that lasted for years afterward. Much could have been accomplished through strong direction from the leadership of both agencies requiring cooperation and commitment, in addition to a clear delineation of the new roles and responsibilities of the two agencies that emphasized a complementary relationship.

Over the past few years we have begun to realize the promise that the changes of over thirty years ago made possible. True, we still have a ways to go; there are still occasional differences of opinion between the staff of the two agencies, which is to be expected when good people care deeply about their work. The challenge of involving varied interests in land management decisions will always leave issues to be resolved. Nevertheless, we have made much progress in the areas of open space conservation and Forest Preserve planning; while the third leg of the Forest Preserve management stool—stewardship—will require a strong commitment in the future. Meanwhile, the realization that the Adirondack Park is a very special place continues to be rooted deeply within the department and the lessons learned since the APA Act have created a solid foundation for the future management of the park.

# 19

## A Land Not Saved

ROBERT GLENNON

Upon passage of the Adirondack Park Agency Act, Governor Rockefeller is supposed to have said the Adirondacks are saved forever. If he did, he was tragically wrong.

Because I came to the agency in July 1974, when the APLUDP had been in effect over a year, I cannot bear witness to the making of the official map or the drafting of the statute. Part of the lore was that it was all done up in a rush; neither local people nor local officials were consulted. There was some story about the agency engaged in delivering the proposed APLUDP to the legislature and the Adirondack Park Local Government Review Board chasing it down the Northway, trying to serve legal papers to prevent it from doing so. Governor Rockefeller rammed it through, it was said. That was still the view when I got there. It was the view when the load of manure was dumped on the APA's doorstep. It was the view when APA people were hanged in effigy. It was the view when the review board held "speak-outs," kind of like revival meetings, only devoted to hate. And it certainly was still the view about 2 AM one night in 1977 when I caught an arsonist in the log building, black ski mask, two gallon jugs of gasoline. In my darker moments, I have said that today I would hand him a match.

In its early years, 1971 to 1973, the agency developed and gave the park its two most lasting contributions to date: the State Land Master Plan (which was sketched out in the 1960s by the Joint Legislative Commission on Natural Resources, and again in detail in

1970 by the Temporary Study Commission), and the Adirondack Park Land Use and Development Plan. The more we study the soils and other resources, the more we marvel that the APLUDP Map—the one prepared before the political compromises—was right on in both analytic approach and accuracy. Heady stuff for a fledgling agency. Nothing it has produced since has matched these plans, although both have been somewhat improved since and 1,200 miles of Adirondack rivers were added to the state's Wild, Scenic, and Recreational Rivers System in 1975 (Adirondack rivers make up 95 percent of such rivers in the state).

Let me quickly sketch the compromises, so you will know the agency itself substantially weakened and compromised the APLUDP as submitted to the legislature from the preliminary plan first released, and the legislature, if anything itself an instrument of compromise, watered down the APA Act even further on its way to enactment. The allowable density of development (average number of buildings per acre) was increased in all land-use areas. The minimum lot widths and building setbacks on shorelines were lessened. The small amount of use zoning proposed was all but eliminated. A cutoff date by which local governments had to have local land-use programs in place was removed. All performance standards for project approval were eliminated. The number of lots in a project that would trigger APA permit jurisdiction was raised substantially. The "critical environmental areas" along roadsides, where agency permit jurisdiction was pervasive, were substantially reduced in size. The already compromised structure whereby far smaller lots were permitted in shoreline subdivisions and whereby far less development was subject to agency review on shorelines in the first place, was further weakened.

The APA Act accepts as its fundamental premise that over 400,000 new buildings can be built and, as I said, with much of that development unregulated and on shorelines. Also as noted, it contains no use zoning and no performance standards. It does not address the ultimate public/private land mix, or the preservation of the private lands through conservation easement or other nonregulatory means. It does not address remediation, and the private lands in the park need plenty of it: removal of utility lines from roadsides; clean-up of abandoned and derelict buildings; screening of junkyards, gravel pits, electric substations, state and local highway departments and salt and sand storage areas, and all manner of other unsightly uses.

Writing elsewhere I described it as:

> an inordinately complex, yet rather pedestrian land use control statute based upon the police power . . . it is ludicrous to think it could achieve "optimum overall conservation, protection, preservation, development and use" of the unique resources of the Adirondack Park. A comparison of the soaring language of Section 801 [Legislative Findings and Purposes] with the regulatory machinery provided to achieve the stated purposes reveals a sad, flawed, megacephalic statute unworthy of the magnificent natural areas it is supposed to protect.[1]

From 1973 to 1975, the new agency had to get a project review system up and running, write regulations, and resolve fundamental philosophical differences among its members. Its meetings were marked by constant debate between a basically preservationist faction, and the faction that felt pretty much that development and growth are good, local officials know best, and-we-in-the-philosophical-minority-aren't-even-sure-about-this-here-regional-land-use-plan-or-this-here-agency. An agency divided against itself cannot stand, especially one circling its wagons, under attack from all outside quarters. Also, lawsuits were brought against the agency on every possible constitutional ground beginning in 1974.

Let me tell you another amazing but true story. Long about '74 or '75 an attorney from somewhere downstate came to the door and said, "Is this the Adirondack Park Agency?" Told that it was, he said he represented the Wambat—yes, that's how they spelled it—Realty Corporation and he had something for us, and deposited an 18-inch-thick application to develop a large vacation-home community known as Valmont Village on the former J & J Rogers tract in the Town of Black Brook, Clinton County, some of them some-how hanging off the raptor cliffs on Silver Lake Mountain.

Both Wambat and the town eventually sued us over the Home Rule Article, article 9 of the New York State Constitution, saying the Town had been conferred the constitutional right to zone and plan and to be free of state interference in matters relating to its property, affairs or government.

Now the settled decisional law emanating from a lot of home rule litigation is that the legislature is always free to act with regard to matters of statewide concern. Of all the angles of constitutional attack upon the agency's organic act, this was surely the one least likely to succeed, the dumbest case to bring. And in 1977, at the very height of the tumult and shouting, the highest court in New York, the Court of Appeals, came through, in an opinion by the Chief Judge, writing for a unanimous Court. Following are excerpts from that opinion:

> To categorize as a matter of purely local concern the future of the forests, open spaces, and natural resources of the vast Adi-rondack Park region would doubtless offend aesthetic, ecological, and conservational principles.[2]
>
> Turning now to the Adirondack Park Agency Act, applica-tion to it of these principles [that the legislature is free to act in matters of state concern] leads inexorably to its validity. Of course, the Agency Act prevents localities within the Adiron-dack Park from freely exercising their zoning and planning pow-ers. That indeed is its purpose and effect, not because the motive is to impair home rule, but because the motive is to serve a supervening State concern transcending local interests. As ably explained by Mr. Justice JAMES GIBSON at Special Term, pre-serving the priceless Adirondack Park through a comprehensive land use and development plan is most decidedly a substantial State concern, as it is most decidedly not merely 119 separate local concerns. . . . All but conclusive of this aspect of the issue is the constitutional and legislative history stretching over 80 years

to preserve the Adirondack area from despoliation, exploitation, and destruction by a contemporary generation in disregard of the generations to come.[3]

In the face of increasing threats to and concern with the environment, it is no longer, if it ever was, true that the preservation and development of the vast Adirondack spaces, with their unique abundance of natural resources—land, timber, wildlife, and water—should not be of the greatest moment to all people of the State. These too relate to life, health and the quality of life.[4]

The short of the matter is that neither Constitution nor statute was designed to disable the State from responding to problems of significant State concern. In this case, the controversy is between the State and the would-be developer of land for profit, and, in the companion case . . . between the State and a town, which understandably seeks to promote its own development, even, if necessary, at the expense of regional planning for the benefit of all the people and future generations. Such a controversy is not resolvable by the principles designed to encourage strong, decentralized, local government in matters exclusively of local concern and to restrain the State from paternalistic interference with local matters. The issue is much larger. It is whether the State may override local or parochial interests when State concerns are involved. That issue is, and has been, resolved in favor of State primacy. The price of strong local government may not be the destruction or even the serious impairment of strong State interests.[5]

From 1975 to 1978, a number of things took place: I mentioned the passage of the bill to expand the Adirondack Wild, Scenic, and Recreational Rivers System, a kind of last straw, I think, which caused the legislature to put its collective foot down and say "not one more iota of additional land-use control are you characters going to get"—a line to which it has consistently adhered ever since; the APA won *Wambat* and two other very important constitutional lawsuits; the Agency Act was actually improved in 1976; and the Senate voted 32–19 in 1977 to replace the agency with a much more locally controlled entity with far less land-use control powers, although, midst marches in Albany and all manner of hoo-raw, the Assembly Environmental Conservation Committee had killed the bill two months earlier.

Long about 1976 Bob Flacke, supervisor of an Adirondack town, was appointed chairman of the APA by Governor Carey. As I tried to describe, the Adirondack region was still in turmoil over the May 1973 enactment of the APLUDP. The lore goes that the governor's marching orders to Bob were "clip the Agency's wings or I will." Bob set out visibly and publicly to reverse some of the horror stories (turn around and grant previously denied permits); to get rid of two lightning rods, the agency's director of planning and its counsel; and to approve local land-use programs, no matter what their quality, whether or not they strip-zoned every highway, and whether or not they had a sanitary code. I wish some graduate student would tally it, but the staff called the map amendments candy: the official map was amended many, many times and places for reasons wholly unrelated to the merits, for the sole reason that local government wanted more dense development allowed in X, Y, or Z place. A number of poorly drafted, mostly pedestrian local land-use programs were approved, a lot of them in one of the most sensitive, beautiful, important areas of the park: the Lake George basin.

That was bad enough, and it marked the beginning of the decline of the APA that continues to this day, but the 1980 Winter Olympics were yet another coffin nail. The good burghers of Lake Placid wrapped themselves in the American flag, told us they had been told by the governor's people that state government supported the Olympics, warned us we'd better not bring about another Denver (Denver voted down the Olympics . . . democracy in action), and among other things refused to consider alternate sites for their 90-meter ski jump, the tallest structure between Albany and Montreal, with all the architectural grace of a cement factory, which it very strongly resembles. Flacke forbade the staff from putting on a case at the hearings, got six votes (but not that of the governor's own commissioner of Environmental Conservation) and—for there was no evidence as to this in the hearing record—justified the thing by *taking official notice* that the Olympics would bring economic benefits to the area. The ski-jump was constructed on what they called a fast-track process. What they meant was they were designing the top of the thing while the concrete was being poured for the bottom.

I mention Gerald Ford's gift to the Adirondacks, a federal prison that began life as the Olympic Village, only in passing; upon taking over the site in the hamlet of Ray Brook the feds cleared and grubbed about 80 acres; it rained and rained; Ray Brook, the brook, ran brown for days, maybe weeks; and Oseetah Lake Marsh, prime ringneck habitat, silted up.

I also mention only in passing the agency's approval of the Lake Placid Hilton, which for all the world would be perfect in Santa Fe, New Mexico, and which replaced, with a complete city block of dun cement and stucco, a lovely, multiporched and rocking-chaired, clapboard country inn known as the Homestead, once surrounded by vast green lawns and defended by magnificent tall sentry pines.

A brand spanking new and huge unsightly 115-kilovolt power line was built along the railroad tracks between Placid and Saranac, and smaller but even uglier lines appeared on both sides of Route 73 from the Olympic bobsled run to Placid. You've gotta have reliable power.

Carey made Flacke his DEC commissioner, having fired the one who voted against the ski jump around 1978, but the agency never recovered. The staff became even more infected with planners, something I did not think was possible. The next chairman and his executive director tried very hard to force me out, but he had environmental instincts, and he did not give away the store to local government, so he looked worlds better to me than Flacke.

Those pro-development planners (is there any other kind?) pushed very hard to approve a large ski bowl project in a place called North Creek.

Governor Cuomo's first chairman followed, 1984 maybe. He, too, had environmental instincts but he spent an inordinate amount of time on global warming—this is with Bush *père* in the White

House—and some on belugas in the Saint Lawrence. If memory serves, we stuck it to the Patten Realty Corporation, a large-scale, industrial-strength land subdivision machine, during his tenure. A real good guy, lawyer not planner, was his executive director at the beginning of his chairmanship, and that was the first time, 10 years in, I ever felt good about coming to work.

But his term was marked—marred—by the advent of two silly Visitor Centers. The entire agency had a new toy to play with and was probably relieved to waste vast amounts of time playing with it. And boy did they, to the neglect of far, far more important things. Site selection, building design and development, exhibits, they even debated ad nauseam what Adirondack creature should be in the logo (Great Blue Heron won). Today they're nature centers—butterflies, bird-calls, and basket weaving. Go to them and try to find out about how Forever Wild or the Adirondack Park came about. Beyond a small wall display, you can't. Ask who Sam Hammond was. They won't know. Ask them where such Adirondack icons as the Tryon Corner was. They won't know. The Broadhead Gore? No. Watson's East Triangle? Well, maybe.

We blew our chance. I said nothing we have done since the State Land Master Plan and Adirondack Park Land Use and Development Plan had matched them. The Visitor Centers could have been—and what an irony is here!—our greatest contribution, assuring the intellectual concept of the Adirondacks endures in the minds of the people of the state. Instead, butterflies, bird-calls, and basket weaving.

I became executive director, 1988 maybe. A bit later, a new chairman took over, a fifth generation Adirondacker yet a preservationist. Those were fairly decent years, with a fairly solid environmental bench sitting. Others should, can, and no doubt will judge those years.

Let me tell you about the Berle Commission. In 1989, Governor Cuomo appointed another commission, not 20 years after the first reported the park would vanish within a generation. There were four major reasons.

First, Sir James Goldsmith's takeover and subsequent dismemberment of Diamond International Corporation resulted in almost 100,000 acres of timberland, most of it in the park, being put up for sale. In an exact repeat of what had happened to another 100,000 acres or so of Diamond Lands in New Hampshire and Vermont a few months earlier, the State of New York came in with too little, too late, and the state lost the tract to a Georgia businessman named Henry Lassiter. In late 1988 the governor was attacked by John Oakes for this loss on the op-ed page of the *New York Times:* he wrote a letter to the *Times* saying we're gonna get the land, and not too much later the state made a deal for 15,000 acres for the Forest Preserve and put another 40,000 under conservation easement, in the process paying a price per acre far higher than that which it had been accustomed to paying. Perennial criticism of the state's cumbersome acquisition procedures reached a crescendo. (Lassiter's company later went into Chapter 11, and the remaining lands were put back on the market.)

Second, a few of the timber companies in the Adirondacks, long-time good neighbors, I was always careful to call them, made a few cautious steps toward subdividing some of their prime lands or selling them to hunting lessees. Much writing appeared on how timber companies in particular are ripe targets for leveraged buyouts, being worth far more sold off in pieces, and how new cold-eyed accounting methods made each part of a company, timberlands included, pay its own way as a "cost center." In short, the comfortable Potemkin world of long-term stewardship gave way to notions of remote Wall Street bean counters and companies swallowing "poison pills."

Third, the Patten Realty Corporation arrived in the Adirondacks, started digging through land records and sending mass mailings to large landowners, offering finder's fees, acquiring lands—12,000 acres by 1988—much more efficiently than the state and seeking promptly to resubdivide them as wilderness ranchettes if you will, your piece of the vanishing wilderness.

Fourth, more and more people began to realize the flaws in the Adirondack Park Agency Act, most as a result of compromises by both the agency and the legislature. Again, allowing 400,000 new buildings in the Adirondack Park as buildout, encouraging a vast proportion of them on the shorelines of its lakes, ponds, and rivers, many without any review of their environmental impacts, allowing almost any land use of any nature whatsoever anywhere on its private lands, much of it also unregulated, and leaving the activities of one of its largest developers, the State of New York, also unregulated, is most assuredly not the way to achieve optimum overall conservation, protection, preservation, development, and use of the unique scenic, aesthetic, wildlife, recreational, open-space, historic, ecological, and natural resources of the Adirondack Park. Yet that is exactly what the Adirondack Park Agency Act does, as expressed by the legislature.

How much development has occurred since Governor Rockefeller proudly proclaimed the Adirondack Park saved for all time? About 19,000 single-family dwellings between 1967 and 1987, an increase of 43 percent, and proceeding apace around 800 to 1,000 units a year. Every year.

Governor Cuomo first mentioned the idea of another citizens' commission in October 1988. He formally announced it in his January 1989 Message to the Legislature and appointed it shortly thereafter. He asked it to evaluate existing state programs for the Adirondack region and its people, and to articulate a vision for the park in the twenty-first century. Former state assemblyman, former Adirondack Park Agency member, former commissioner of Environmental Conservation (he's the one who voted against the ski jump), and later president of National Audubon, Peter A. A. Berle chaired it.

Also serving on the commission was Bob Flacke, of whom I wrote earlier. For reasons best known to him, Bob took to the hustings during the commission's deliberations, urging Adirondackers to unite against the forthcoming report, saying it would surely result in more state control over their lives. Citizens' groups were formed, poised and angry when the long-awaited report, containing 245 recommendations, was finally released on May 8. Lost in

the tumult, shouting, and general uproar were many recommendations to improve the life and lot of the 130,000 residents of the park.
The most vehement criticism was reserved for the recommendations
that 645,000 acres of Forest Preserve be acquired (the 1970 Commission recommended 600,000); that the APA's land-use control
powers be increased; that a complex scheme of transferrable development rights be enacted to protect backcountry areas; and that a
one-year moratorium be imposed on development of shoreline and
backcountry. The commission was accused by Flacke and others in
the Adirondacks of conjuring up a phony development "crisis," yet
unlike the 1970 Commission, this one never used the word. The
Adirondack Park Agency, perhaps because of institutional memories
of attempted arson and a truckload of manure dumped on its front
stoop in the 1970s, went into its stealth mode and became invisible to the naked eye. Woods-wise Adirondackers sharpened their
tracking skills, found it in Ray Brook where it had always been, and
staged demonstrations in its parking lot. Motorcades slowed traffic
on the Northway and honked their way to Albany to encircle the
Executive Mansion. Before May was out, the governor announced
he saw no need for a moratorium, opened negotiations with a group
representing Adirondack local government, and assured them no
legislation would be introduced until all parties to the debate had a
chance to be heard. Between 1989 and 1991, an APA members' barns
were burned; the offices of an environmental organization known
as the Adirondack Council were vandalized; one of their staff members had an angry mob descend upon his home; strange powdered
substances arrived in the agency's mail; and on July 8, 1991, shots
were fired at a vehicle in which three members of the APA staff,
young fathers all, were riding, striking about three feet from them.
A proposed $1.2 billion environmental bond act was defeated, the
first time in history, and the governor's legislation, watered down
more and more over the next two years, went nowhere.

It all came to an end in 1995. Republicans took the Statehouse in
the 1994 elections. The agency's lowest point since the Flacke years
was its approval of the Oven Mountain project, one of my last acts

at the agency. Its executive staff recommended it be canned, on what we felt were solid legal grounds. The last thing the former bench did was one of the worst things any agency membership has ever done, ski jump included. Big project, maybe 80 lots, Town of Johnsburg, developer putting as many lots as he could around a pristine, lovely, and biologically valuable pond, whacking up the tract in a manner the staff and I were certain was not within the legislative vision for Rural Use areas expressed in the statute, thus in our view unapprovable as a matter of law. The agency members did what they'd done for over twenty years: they blamed the staff and approved it. They fell all over themselves to praise it—read the minutes if your stomach can stand it—it was a Cadillac, no, it was the end of a great horserace, and on and on. I'll tell you what it was: it was a shameful, but not unprecedented, thus not unexpected, failure of will, dereliction of duty, and, in my view, violation of law. It was an abandonment of principle, and it was the last major and most unbefitting act of a fairly decent bench.

If I may be permitted to hold acid rain aside in the foolish belief that positive events are occurring, and if I may be permitted to put constant fragmentation aside in the abysmal despair that nothing will ever be done about it, then I say to you the most important Adirondack issue is the appalling quality of a near majority of the agency members and state agency designees. They don't know history. They don't know the magnificence and uniqueness of this area, public and private lands alike, whose future is at least in part entrusted to them. They don't know how much it is cherished by New Yorkers from every part of the state, including the Adirondacks.

They don't know that more of America is paved than is wilderness. They don't know environmental law, or administrative law. They don't even know the three statutes they administer, and I wish they would read them. They may not know there are sixteen million people in the state, and they own over 40 percent of the park as Forest Preserve, and that those from outside the park own a great deal of the private lands. They may not know there are a large number of Adirondackers who don't want the park further degraded, malled, or sprawled.

They don't know they sit to regulate, not to ingratiate, and they sure as *hell* don't know how to say no. They don't know what sustainable development is. They don't know what cumulative impact is. They don't know what clustering is. They don't know how bad Adirondack soils are for on-site sewage disposal. They act as if they don't know the beauty, the friendliness, the quiet, the human scale, the security, the joy of a small-town, essentially rural way of life; no Wal-Mart, no prison, no mercury vapor lights, no locking your door or your car, no sea of pavement.

They don't know that this can be the alternative place; the one that took the right path, not the herd path; the model; the beacon.

There's a lot they don't know.

I left on August 31, my fiftieth birthday, and left for Vladivostok with George Davis, the first director of planning at the agency, the next day. He had created a not-for-profit with his MacArthur genius money, and his vision was to bring the resource-driven land-use planning the APA Act was originally meant to be to other precious parts of the world.

At least in its general scope and dominant features, the Adirondack private land legislation has merits.

It represented a comprehensive, natural-resource-based approach to a large physiographic region. The Adirondack Park is the largest area in the country subject to a state land-use control scheme.

It boldly occupied legal territory—planning and zoning—ceded to local control almost a half-century earlier, in a state with a very strong home-rule tradition, and, as mentioned earlier, a constitutional provision on the subject.

It increased the amount of state control in direct proportion to the degree of state interest. In a thoroughly settled Hamlet area, state permits are required at 100 units. Extensive state control is in wetlands, highlands, along major roads and rivers, and in the boonies—remote areas where the soils are thin, the habitat plentiful and intact, the open space and natural character of the park most pristine. These controls, I suggest, are appropriate to the largest natural area east of the Mississippi. It obviously sought and failed, but sought, in its quaint 1970s way, to bring about a regime of sustainable use—before Gro Harlem Brundtland used the word—to complement 2¾ million acres of Forever Wild State Forest Preserve.

What were, and are, APA's problems?

A state government that never funded the thing at a level more than about half of what it needed.

It has had, at various times, hot and cold running chairmen—they were all men—some of whom tried with varying degrees of success to kill the thing ideologically, but its pathetic size alone is a good reason for putting the poor thing out of its misery.

It had a state government that couldn't decide whether preservation, or development, or both, were best for the park, so it backed both half-heartedly and got neither.

While, to be sure, it has had a number of brave and stalwart members, most of the time there have been gubernatorially appointed citizen members and even state agency members who neither understand nor believe in it, and get their jollies publicly undercutting it.

It has a mandate that it eventually turn over the vast majority of its land use authority to local government, which is horrendously ill-equipped as to the requisite natural resource expertise and wholly without political or philosophical sympathy for its mission.

It has a situs in a sparsely populated rural area where, let's face it, the prevailing view is that "development" or "growth" is good and what is perceived as the effort of the state to single out the area to halt or slow it, bad. If you accept the state interest argument, and I do, and if you count noses, and I hasten to say this is crudely overstated but I think essentially true, you have an agency serving about 15 million people who live for the most part in sterile urban—or even more sterile suburban—sprawl, who want the park preserved, and you have about 150,000 permanent residents—let's say they're 100 percent opposed—who want that wonderful life, that "development" and "growth" that transforms natural areas into sterile ones. I know I'm overstating—I just said so—but I'll bet my magnitudes are right.

But it's the execution that's flawed, not the idea.

Protected area systems used to be the most practical way to pre-serve the greatest amount of the world's biodiversity and ecological processes. Nope. Not any more. Won't do it. Too late. Not enough of the natural world left to create the protected areas on the scale necessary, and no *will* to create them.

> Recent advances in conservation biology . . . have shown that by themselves the strictly protected [International Union for the Conservation of Nature] categories . . . will not be able to con-serve all—or even most—species, genetic resources, and eco-logical processes. Far greater expanses are required than modern societies are willing to remove from direct production. The best answer to this dilemma is to design and manage different types of protected areas—including very large expanses in the catego-ries that permit, and even encourage, compatible human use of resources—to support among them the overall fabric of social and economic development.[6]

That's someone named McNeily, in a book on conserving biologi-cal diversity put out by the following alphabet soup: IUCN, WRI, WWF-US, and the World Bank.

> Most conservationists . . . recognize that protecting some exem-plary natural ecosystems is not enough. We must look beyond the boundaries of reserves to the ecosystems that form the larger matrix in which reserves are embedded. These are often semi-natural ecosystems—ecosystems that have been modified by human activities such as logging, fishing, and grazing livestock, but which are still dominated by native species.[7]

That's Professor Malcolm Hunter of the University of Maine in his college textbook on conservation biology.

> With growing development and the almost exclusive policy emphasis on economic growth, [saving every component of bio-diversity] will be impossible in the near future. Thus, the best that we can do now is to have biodiversity preservation policies that

have two related, long-term objectives: first, setting aside certain areas and environmental resources that are off-limits to economic exploitation, and second, requiring those areas and environmental resources that will be economically exploited to be used according to policies that will insure their sustainability.[8]

That's John Gowdy and Carl McDaniel, in the journal *Ecological Economics*.

We cannot accomplish our objectives simply by creating preserves; the objectives of maintaining biodiversity must be incorporated into intensively managed temperate landscapes. The bulk of the temperate landscape will be used for production of commodities and for human habitation. We must therefore develop management strategies for forestry, agriculture, water development, and fisheries that incorporate the broader diversity. Most intensive management strategies currently do not take biological diversity into consideration; rather, they emphasize simplifying and subsidizing ecosystems, i.e., organismal, structural, successional, and landscape homogenization.[9]

That's Jerry Franklin of the Forest Service in *Biodiversity,* edited by E. O. Wilson.

That is a lot of brainpower, a lot of gray neural meat at work on a fairly important question—whether the human race, and indeed whether all life on Planet Earth, will survive. And it validates not only Forever Wild, but the APLUDP. Well, no, not exactly; it validates the underlying principles of the plan, not the lame, tame, tainted, medium-grade result of their attempted application. Under those principles, this cherished area could become a worldwide example of sustainable development being put into practice. Under what resulted, there is no chance whatsoever.

From the beginning, the Adirondack Park statute has failed to preserve the Adirondack Park, instead accepting as its organizing principle the park's rational destruction, but fervently hoping that destruction is phased, orderly, clean and well-lighted.

From the beginning, the APA has had to try to administer the unadministrable and enforce the unenforceable. From the beginning, the bean counters—or somebody—have allowed the agency to have about a third or a half of the personnel needed to do the job called for by that statute. And from the beginning far, far too many wholly unqualified, ecologically and historically illiterate, and philosophically biased citizens and state officials have sat on that board, their only purpose to undermine that already flawed statute. We who are about to destroy the park salute you. We are the unqualified, the unbelieving, and the ill-equipped, chosen to shatter a dream, most methodically.

# 20

## Top-Down Regulation
## and Local Economic Autonomy

JOHN PENNEY

"It's called the Commission on the Adirondacks in the Twenty-First Century," reporter Laura Rappaport said patiently, trying to gauge the reaction from her new boss. "Sounds boring to me," I replied. "What do you think you'll have for page one?"

It was the fall of 1989, the commission was holding its public hearings on the future of the Adirondack Park, and I had just arrived as the new managing editor of the *Adirondack Daily Enterprise*. Rappaport was heading to one of those hearings, and I (it seems patently obvious now) was in dire need of getting up to speed on the major issues of the day in the Adirondacks. Little did I know of the hornet's nest of activity the Twenty-First Century Commission report would soon stir up, how its top-down, extreme approach toward government control would enrage many Adirondackers—and how it would dominate the *Daily Enterprise*'s page-one coverage for the weeks and months ahead.

A six-million-acre patchwork of private and public lands (viewed by many as the most valuable environmental treasure east of the Mississippi) the Adirondack Park is a complicated place, pulled in different directions by competing special-interest groups. The state's

Originally published as J. Penney, "My View," *Adirondack Journal of Environmental Studies* 4 (1997): 24–26. Reprinted with the kind permission of the *Adirondack Journal of Environmental Studies*.

appalling view of home rule here was made apparent by the fact that of the dozen or so public hearings held by the commission, only two were located within the boundaries of the Blue Line. And the commission infuriated many with its calls for wholesale changes to the Adirondack land-use map and for a building moratorium in the park until its 245 recommendations could be implemented.

Following the public's furor over these and other matters, the state backtracked, and the Twenty-First Century Commission report proved to be a bust. Much like the Adirondack Park Agency Act itself, the report was replete with vague and subjective terminology; commission members advocated that the APA permit process take into account such nebulous concerns as biodiversity; locally significant scenic vistas; and undue, adverse impact standards. Such terms have been the basis for much of the hostility regarding the Adirondack land-use issue. Even the premise behind why I was asked to write this article—to offer a view of how sustainable development can be achieved in the Adirondacks—is subjective in nature, conjuring up different images for different people. It is all fiendishly difficult to quantify. Yet, from Wal-Mart to the Whitneys, the underlying issues endure in the Adirondacks.

## The Back-Room Agenda

There are members of the APA staff and commissioners who, through words and deeds, have deemed the APA Act insufficient and have charted their own course for how development should take place in the Adirondacks; in essence, the agency is in the bartering business. Most developers realize this when they forge ahead with a project subject to agency review—even if their plans seemingly comply with the APA Act.

For instance, several years ago, the Town of North Elba sought to make improvements to the Lake Placid Airport, including the installation of pilot-activated lighting and navigational aids, construction of a taxiway, and improvements to the existing runway. The Federal Aviation Administration (FAA) approved the plan—but the APA process lingered. First, the park agency made the town pay $8,000 to conduct a nighttime noise study as part of its master plan for the improvements—a study deemed unnecessary by the FAA. Then, APA staff wanted the agency to have oversight over town leases with present and future airport operators, and it called for the formation of a citizens advisory group to advise the town on future issues related to the aviation facility. This should have been a one-shot project review; instead, APA staff was advocating placing the airport under the agency's authority on a continuing basis. Moreover, it was seeking to become involved in such business decisions as lease agreements, an ambitious agenda for a land-use agency, to say the least.

In a more recent example, the agency attempted to exceed its authority over the Whitney land in the Town of Long Lake. The Whitneys wanted to subdivide 15,000 acres of Whitney Park into 40 "great camps" and build a hotel near Little Tupper Lake. They intended to keep 36,000 acres in private ownership for logging and recreation purposes, though they were reserving their right as private landowners to consider other uses in the future. But the agency wanted a detailed accounting of what the Whitneys planned on doing with those 36,000 acres, even though they were not part of the development project before the agency.

Distrust on such park land-use issues runs deep; it is apparent not only in day-to-day battles between developers and the APA, but also in the comments of local officials concerned about proposed state laws—and even the language of existing ones. For example, Governor George Pataki had proposed making payments in lieu of taxes (PILOTs) on state-owned lands not currently subject to taxation. While the plan would not have affected state holdings in the Adirondacks, local leaders were troubled nonetheless. Under the Real Property Tax Law, the state currently pays taxes on Adirondack Forest Preserve lands, but proposed PILOT agreements involving other state holdings would have no such statutory protection. Some local government officials were worried that this would have been a first step toward placing a tax cap on state lands in the Adirondacks.

In another case, although no action toward this end has been taken—or even suggested—several local boards mounted a campaign to ensure the state would not tear down the Mount Arab fire tower in the Town of Piercefield. All indications from the state were that such structures would be preserved and, in some cases, possibly renovated. And state Department of Environmental Conservation officials noted that this particular wooden tower could not be torn down since it is listed on the National Register of Historic Buildings. Still, local officials were unconvinced. They cited the language in the state constitution as it related to Forest Preserve lands, pointing out that those lands were to be kept "forever wild" and, therefore, could be interpreted to mean the fire towers don't belong.

## The Protectors as Perpetrators

While the park requires some form of special protection, I believe such protection is already in place, considering the economic conditions and the environmental regulations in the Adirondacks. True, the park has been carelessly developed in places—but some of the worst abuses have been at the hands of the state itself, whether that be for construction of Olympic venues, prisons, or state agency buildings. Indeed, in many instances, the park has needed protection from, rather than by, the state. For example, a public authority was found to have buried toxic barrels on state land in the Adirondacks. And a state-run fish hatchery was identified as at least one of the causes of a blue-green algae bloom in Upper Saranac Lake several years ago.

The hypocrisy and contradictions are apparent in other ways. Through the Department of Economic Development, the state pumps millions of dollars into "I Love New York" campaigns, in part to promote tourism in the Adirondacks; then, through its environmental agencies, the state complains about overuse in the High Peaks area and seeks public funds to help alleviate the problem. Through such initiatives, the state controls not just the regulatory condition but the economic engine of the park. It is, in essence, a false economy, a place too reliant on public sector jobs—a place where the salary of a typical school teacher draws more envy than sympathy.

Under these prevailing conditions, it is obvious that sustainable development will occur in the Adirondacks only if the state says it should. Based on what I have seen, and especially in light of the aforementioned actions of state government in the park and the move to downsize the public sector in general—I would question the basic fairness and wisdom of this continued direction for the Adirondacks.

## Rectifying the Problem

If the state wants to tightly restrict the park and set it off as a "special place," it must find a way to pay for that privilege. More money should be used for low-interest loans and grants for Adirondack businesses. Seasonal changes are common in most places, but ours are more extreme, affecting both institutional structures and personal attitudes. The terrain and weather conditions already make the Adirondacks less than business-friendly; the onerous land-use regulations merely seem to seal our fate. Now and again, I remember the words of David Petty, the former president of North Country Community College, who lamented that Adirondack children are being raised as second-class citizens. They are essentially steered in the direction of forest- or service-industry jobs if they intend to stay and grow old in the Adirondacks.

Is there hope? Of course. Perhaps as environmental studies become more accurate, land-use data will become clearer and less subject to personal interpretation. Until then, though, environmental groups and advocates of private property rights will continue to push and give a little, depending on the political wills and winds of the day and the most pressing of needs. In the meantime, the Adirondack spirit, coupled by an unfailing sense of community pride, endures. During my tenure as managing editor of the *Adirondack Daily Enterprise,* I witnessed it on many occasions. Those images include hundreds of volunteers gallantly fighting a forest fire in Vermontville, where 400 acres were lost—but only one structure damaged; scores of people gathering to take part in a Crop Walk to raise funds for the hungry; rescuers braving severe weather conditions to search for lost hikers in the High Peaks; volunteers working at break-neck speed in bone-chilling temperatures to build and/or restore the Ice Palace for the Saranac Lake Winter Carnival; and business people, already walking a razor's edge financially, unable to look the other way when a community organization knocks on the door and asks for help.

The Twenty-First Century report said, "Environmental considerations should be set ahead of any other in the Park." I would respectfully disagree. Economies do many things—remaining stable is not one of them. For those raising families here and trying to eke out a meager existence, other factors must have at least equal importance if people are to survive, and development is to be sustained, in the Adirondack Park.

# 21

## Lessons from the Commission on the Adirondacks in the Twenty-First Century

ROSS S. WHALEY

*FOR SALE: Developers are grabbing huge chunks of the Adirondacks, and Albany's bumbling has already put 100,000 acres in jeopardy*

James Howard Kunstler, a novelist who lives north of Albany, used the above statement to grab readers' attention to his June 18, 1989, *New York Times Magazine* piece. In the same article he paraphrases Roger Jakubowski, who had recently purchased Topridge, the Marjorie Merriweather Post estate: "Adirondack real estate was the last nickel bargain in America and . . . he [Jakubowski] intended to buy up the whole goshdarn park, all six million acres of it." While the whole six million acres clearly was not for sale because almost half of it was publicly owned and protected from sale by the Constitution of the State of New York, the statement gives a reasonable caricature of the times. Large estates were being sold to developers who, in turn, would subdivide the property and sell lots to those who wanted a piece of the park. These events raised the question of whether the Adirondack Park Agency established in 1971 had the tools to protect this unique park comprising both public and private lands. This was the setting that prompted Governor Mario Cuomo to establish a commission to study the Adirondack Park in the twenty-first century.[1] In his letter of invitation to the commissioners, Governor Cuomo stated, "Recent developments suggest that we may be entering a new period in the Adirondacks, an era of unbridled land speculation and unwarranted development that may threaten the unique open space and wilderness character of the region."

Applications for subdivisions tripled between 1984 and 1989 and there was a concern that much of the land owned by the for-est-products industry might come on the market. Recent research based on building permits by the Residents' Committee to Protect the Adirondacks indicates that this concern continues (see chapter 12 in part one). Although the pace of subdivision may ebb and flow, the central issues remain the same: how much development, what kind, and where is it appropriate to assure a desirable future for this unique park?

The governor's charge asked the commission to focus on four questions:

1. What kind of park does the commission expect and envision for our children in the twenty first-century? This is interesting wording. Is it the expectations and vision of the commission that is important or the expectations of the citizens of New York, and how do you determine that?

2. Are the existing state programs and policies adequate to achieve that type of park in the twenty-first century?

3. What, if any, new programs or modifications in existing pro-grams are necessary to achieve the kind of park envisioned?

4. How can a strong economic base, compatible with the park be maintained? "Maintained" is an interesting word, when some would argue that that the economic base of the park was not very strong to begin with or at least was deteriorating as the timber and mining industries declined.

The membership of the commission and its staff speaks to the wealth of experience and perhaps the mind-set that influenced the outcome. To mention only a few, Peter Berle, the chairman, had been a state legislator and was instrumental in the passage of the Adirondack Park Agency Act in 1971. Harold Jerry had been the executive director of the Temporary Study Commission in the late 1960s that resulted in the creation of the Adirondack Park Agency. George Davis, the executive director of the Commission on the

Adirondacks in the Twenty-First Century, had been an early employee of the Adirondack Park Agency (APA). Robert Flacke, who wrote a minority report, had been a chairman of the Adirondack Park Agency and was, at the time of the commission, president of Fort William Henry, a major tourist facility in Lake George. Other members of the staff and commission were also significant contributors to the deliberations, but those mentioned significantly influenced the tone.

In response to the governor's charge, the commission developed 245 recommendations falling within the following categories: administration of the park (32); jobs, housing, health, and education (40); revitalizing hamlets (13); open space (41); compatible uses (84); creating greenways (29); and extending the park boundaries (6).

Although serious consideration was given to all these areas, clearly most of the discussion focused on park administration, open space, and compatible uses emphasizing open space, the essence of the park. The limited space in this chapter only allows a summary of the intent of the first four categories of recommendations—the core of the recommendations, not a review of all 245 individually.

*Administration of the park.* Although state law recognized the will of the people in establishing this special park with its combination of public and private lands, the bureaucracy was never organized accordingly. The park includes three different regions of the Department of Transportation, the Department of Health, and Department of Economic Development, and none of the boundaries are coterminous. The Department of Environmental Conservation that manages the public lands in the park has two regions; the headquarters of one lies within the park and the other outside the park. At best this leads to confusion and at worst it suggests that state agencies are not attuned to the special character or needs of a park.

The commission recommended replacing the Adirondack Park Agency with an Adirondack Park Administration that would subsume some of the regulatory responsibilities of other agencies and would be responsible for planning in the park. It further recommended the establishment of an Adirondack Park Service as a unit within the Department of Environmental Conservation. Last, the current Adirondack Park Agency Act offers the opportunity for local government to assume some regulatory responsibilities if they have an approved local land-use plan. The commission suggested requiring local governments to have a land-use plan within three years or the obligation would fall to the county. That is, local planning and regulation would have gone from permissive to required.

*Jobs, housing, health, and education.* The people of the Adirondack Park suffer from many of the same problems that befall the residents of most rural wildland areas, whether in New England or in northern Minnesota. The unemployment rates tend to be higher than in the rest of the state, many jobs are seasonal, per capita incomes are lower than elsewhere, and the delivery of services is expensive in sparsely populated areas. Some residents of the park would attribute their situation to the preponderance of public lands protected by the constitution as "forever wild lands" and the regulations on private land. The commission recognized that for the Adirondack Park to thrive as a unique park that more than 130,000 permanent residents call home, "The state should therefore help create a strong economic base that in no way degrades or depletes the Park's resources."[2]

Since the commission issued its report, the problem of affordable housing that it recognized has only gotten worse. The commission recommended establishment of an Adirondack Community Development Corporation that would be funded by a tax on the sale of "upscale" homes. The corporation would have a responsibility to address the problems of housing for the employees of the region. Health and education suffer from the problems associated with 130,000-plus residents scattered over an area almost the size of Vermont. The diseconomies-of-scale make health and educational services that, in most instances, are substantially supported by local taxes prohibitively costly. The recommendations to offset these diseconomies are based on the premise that a unique state park presupposes a state obligation to compensate for the social costs that are reinforced by a combination of substantial state land ownership and a regulatory environment that precludes rapid population and tax growth.

*Revitalizing the hamlets.* The commission recognized at the outset that the beauty of the expanse of wildlands, the sparkling streams, abundant lakes, and mountainous terrain, and the recreation that these assets offer, attract most visitors to the Adirondack Park. However, the character of the park is also influenced by an impression left by its hamlets—sometimes good and sometimes not so good. The hamlets are also where the local people live, shop, go to church, and volunteer for the fire department. If the park is to reach its potential in the twenty-first century, vital hamlets form a critical part. Maintaining the open space is critically linked to making hamlets the residential location of choice, making business locations affordable, and establishing incentives for the rehabilitation of older (often architecturally more interesting) buildings preferable to building new structures "out-of-town." These goals not only lead to enhancing the character of the park and protecting open space, but most important, add to the quality of life for the permanent year-round residents. The commission once again recommended a palette of solutions ranging from regulatory, to tax incentives, to planning and design standards.

*Open space.* "The essence of the park," open space, was front and center, and received the bulk of the attention by advocates and advisories alike. When the commission was created, the state owned 42 percent of the land in the park. The remainder was in private ownership, with half of that owned by residents of the park. Five hundred sixty four large landowners (holders of more than 500 acres) held a little more than 2 million acres, half of this held by the forest industry. The question facing the commission was: What will the future hold for these private lands? Between 1967 (the time of the Temporary Study Commission that recommended the creation of the APA) and 1987, "some 21,000 single family homes and 6,500 vacant lots including over 4,000 on the waterfront, had been added to the Park."[3] Would this trend continue, increase, or decline, and should it?

The commission presumed that pressures for development would continue, and its recommendations formed a plan with two basic elements: "the addition of land to the Forest Preserve for certain specified reasons; and the protection of privately owned open space from the pressures of development by purchase of conservation easements, zoning changes and the transfer of development rights."[4] Tax policy adjustments that would encourage maintenance of open space were also suggested. The strength of feeling on the protection of open space by the commission members is illustrated by perhaps its most controversial recommendation, number 86: "A one-year moratorium should be enacted to halt subdivision or development of land or changes in land use in Resource Management (RM) and Rural Use (RU) areas to provide time for the State Legislature to consider and enact policy options to protect the Park's working landscape."[5] (More about this controversy later.)

Shortly after release of the commission's report, the critics concerned about invasion of their property rights promoted a motorcade along the Northway (I-87) that stretched from the Adirondacks to Albany, over 100 miles. The criticisms of the commission were many and strongly felt. One thing the commission accomplished was the spawning of many new organizations: the Fairness Coalition, the Adirondack Landowners Association, the Residents' Committee to Protect the Adirondacks, the Adirondack Association of Towns and Villages, and others. Each of these groups had their own perspectives and concerns about the commission's recommendations. Some were concerned about further government intrusion into private property rights. Some were concerned about state acquisition of private land. Some were concerned about the loss of local government authority to the state. And one group wanted it known that there were residents of the park who were supportive of further environmental protection.

In addition to criticisms of the recommendations, there were the expected criticisms of the process. There were those who were convinced that the commission was composed of the same old-guard preservationists that were responsible for creating the Adirondack Park Agency in the first place. I personally found that an interesting comment because I was a relative newcomer to the state, was by education a forester/economist (a group that historically has not been lumped with the preservationists), and had chaired the Governor's Task Force on the Forest Industry, another rather ineffective study committee. There were others on the commission who were quite concerned about the economy, health, and education. The fact that none of the commissioners voted yes on every recommendation is, in itself, an indication that it was not a single-minded group.

The question was often raised, "What right do those people, the commissioners, have to tell us what to do with our land?" "Those people," by statement or implication, were those outsiders, those rich people, those city dwellers, those environmentalists. Yes, there may have been some of each on the commission, but it was not a uniform group by most measures. The answer to the question was, of course, "None!" But by being asked to serve, we had the opportunity and the right to give our best study, thinking, judgment, and conclusions. The report was only that. Implementation would require executive or legislative changes.

This leads to another criticism, however, and that is the question of the state vis-à-vis the individual or local for control over land use. "What right does Albany have to tell us what to do with our land, our home?" This question stems from a difference between culture and law with regard to property rights. In law it is clear that the "rights" to land is a bundle of rights that government (in the United States this means state government) has the responsibility to distribute. Popular opinion is that the land belongs to me, and I can do as I please with it. Most landowners feel passionately about this until their neighbor proposes doing something that they are convinced will devalue their own land. The law is clear that government can regulate the use of land to meet the greatest social good. But this is little understood or accepted by many landowners, and still begs the question of how to determine the greatest social good.

It could be argued that the commission made a tactical error in framing its report in the context of a crisis, and thereby recommending that a moratorium be placed on permitting further development until the legislature acted on the recommendations. Was there really a crisis, or was that an overly used ploy to garner attention? In my opinion, most of the criticisms were not well founded, except the last. But in retrospect, the commission and its report deserved to be criticized, because to a large extent most of the recommendations were ignored.

The crisis mentality did not serve the commission well. The recommendation for a moratorium on approving pending permit applications until the legislature acted on other recommendations was the immediate undoing of the commission. It so inflamed the critics that serious attention was never given to the remainder of the recommendations by the legislature. It would have served the process simply to propose that some kinds of land-use changes are essentially irreversible. Are the irreversible ones consistent with the kind of park we want for following generations? The premise of irreversibility (at least in a reasonable time period) is sound, and thus the question of consistency with a vision for the park essential, and not inflammatory in and of itself. The question of consistency with a vision of the park would require further debate on what the vision is and what the impact of particular kinds of development on that vision would be.

For others considering studies similar to that of the commission, there should be a real client poised to receive the deliberations at the end of the process. With the Temporary Study Commission of the 1960s that recommended the creation of the Adirondack Park Agency, there was a governor and some legislators eager to carry the recommendations on to further debate, refinement, and legislation. For the Commission on the Adirondacks in the Twenty-First Century, the client was hard to find once controversy became heated. Why do we have government tasks forces, commissions, or study committees anyway? It is usually because the problem is too complex for a single person or organization to get their hands around, or the issues transcend the purview of a single government agency, or perhaps it is hopeful to improve the chances of "buy-in" from diverse citizen groups. In all of these instances, it can be anticipated that more often than not the recommendations of such study will be controversial because they challenge the status quo. There may be instances, however, when it is simply a good political strategy to avoid dealing with issues by giving them to a committee in hopes that there will be a hung jury or inoffensive general recommendations. Or if by chance they come up with controversial results, the committee and the results can be ignored. In this instance it can be questioned whether there was a client, governor or legislature, committed to follow through on the recommendations.

The commission also made a mistake in not appreciating the difference between public input and public involvement. It had plenty of public input, but limited public involvement. The reasoning was that there would be plenty of opportunity for further involvement of the public during the legislative process. This presumed, of course that there was a receptive audience to carry significant recommendations to the legislature.

As in all big endeavors, the devil truly is in the details. The commission's report was attractive and thoughtful, but was in some ways offensive, and it included a map that did not accurately portray the actions of the commission. For example, there were pictures in the report that were meant to portray development that was inconsistent with the commission's vision for the park, but these same pictures depicted individuals' homes. The map included in the report represented a recommendation for public land acquisition that was never approved by the commission. The commission recommended kinds of land to be acquired by the public, not specific locations. Yet the map alone resulted in the formation of the Adirondack Landowners Association, many of whose members may have been supportive of much of the report, but who were more concerned about protecting their land from the threat of public acquisition.

Looking back, however, the commission did make a difference either directly through its recommendations or indirectly through the furor that arose from its very existence. There have been encouraging gains protecting the future of this special place:

1. Conservation easements have become commonplace in the Adirondacks. Negotiating the first large conservation easement on

Lyons Falls Pulp and Paper Company lands was a nightmare for all parties. It paved the way, however, for a process that, though never routine, does not call for acts of bravery on the part of the land-owner, the staff of nongovernment organizations such as the Nature Conservancy, or state bureaucrats.

2. Much land has been protected through state Bond Acts and the facilitation of nonprofit groups. Although the controversy over how much land should be protected and at what cost will continue to be debated, the argument today is more over the specifics of a particular deal rather than broad-based ideological arguments over land preservation vis-à-vis jobs. Recent successes in protect-ing sensitive ecosystems or lands with public values that would be reduced by subdivision must be attributed to the governor and the support of organizations such as the Nature Conservancy, but the stage was set by the commission, both through its report and by deflecting the heat through the threat of more radical protectionist measures.

3. The tone of the debate has become more civil in recent times largely because the Adirondack Park Agency and Regions 5 and 6 of the Department of Environmental Conservation have actively reached out for greater citizen input. They have accomplished much in diluting the impression that government is all bad guys.

4. Although it is premature to offer congratulations over progress in planning for community development that is sensitive to aesthet-ics, economics, and protecting special places, there are myriad activ-ities underway that are promising, including: discussions held under the imprimatur of the Gateways Project, the Residents' Commit-tee's expansion into sustainable forestry, the Wildlife Conservation Society's actively pursuing the notion of sustainable development, and citizen involvement and leadership in long-term planning as exemplified in the Town of Webb.

So while the commission itself may not have been a success, the "great conservation experiment" in the Adirondack Park continues and suggests a model that just might be worth exploring in rural wildland areas in North America and abroad.

# 22

## A Perspective from the Forest-Products Industry

ROGER DZIENGELESKI

What would you do if you were placed in charge of growing the size and economic impact of the forest-products industry in New York State? Of making it locally and globally competitive with forest-products industries in other parts of the United States as well as in China, Indonesia, Scandinavia, and South America for at least the next fifty years? Hypothetically, the job title for this position might be Commissioner of Forest Economy. Keep in mind that you are the kind of person who would not turn this job down or cop out by saying that the forest-products industry is a mature industry dying from terminal old age. What would you do?

Perhaps one major item on your agenda would be to ensure that the forest itself is intact, healthy, and accessible for management not just now, but for at least the next fifty years. After all, forest products cannot be manufactured if there is not a dependable, consistent crop available for harvest. To accomplish this task you may seek legislation that would prevent the conversion of forestlands to other uses, such as housing developments. You might also seek legislation or changes in policy that would ensure that publicly owned forests are available for forest management and crop production. Most certainly you would ensure that laws and regulations require all forests to be managed sustainably.

You may vow to fix the property tax system, which for decades has taxed forestland to pay for schools and other public services that are not used by trees, your reasoning being that high taxes lead to the sale and development of forestland. You would look comprehensively at all forest taxes, including capital gains, and ensure that the tax rates did not exceed the income attained under sustainable forest management systems. You would also monitor all other legislation to ensure that new laws did not limit the ability of the forest to produce a crop.

You may authorize funding to prevent the import of forest pests and diseases such as Dutch Elm disease, chestnut blight, hemlock woolly adelgid, Asian longhorn beetle, and beech bark disease. Where these pests and diseases already exist, you would fund research looking for ways to eradicate the pests effectively or at least to minimize their impacts. Another of your agenda items may provide incentives that would encourage industry to invest in new technology, keeping mills modern and competitive. Your incentives may include interest-free loans to corporations when the monies are used to modernize equipment such as computer systems and warehousing or even to purchase state-of-the-art manufacturing machinery. These incentives would be available for existing as well as new forest-products manufacturing facilities.

You may also consider grant programs to fund facility improvements that would help businesses comply with laws and regulations relating to air and water quality—your strategy being to pass these expenses to the broader public, which will benefit from the improvements. You might feel that this is especially important when regulatory costs of compliance with air and water regulations cannot be added to the price paid for the wood product because of global price competition.

Policies that would encourage improvements in energy use and reduce the cost of energy would be a must, as energy is one of the largest costs of forest-products manufacturing. Social infrastructure programs such as employee training programs, workers compensation insurance programs, unemployment insurance programs, health insurance programs, and others that are major costs for manufacturing would be evaluated and monitored with a goal of keeping costs in check. You might even be so bold as to devise an economic credit for New York–made forest products, to ensure that locally produced products are used in local government offices and buildings, something similar to the credit currently allowed for recycled products in governments' competitive bid process.

Last, you may focus some of your attention on the image of forest-products manufacturers by promoting the many social positives of this segment of the economy. You would constantly keep the size of the forest-products industry's payroll and benefits in front of the public's eyes, noting that forest-product manufacturers provide good jobs to those young people who choose not to go to college and would like to continue to live in the rural areas where they grow up. "Made in New York" would be celebrated under your administration. You would point out that every locally made forest product reduces the need to clear more acres of tropical forestland for plantation forestry in Brazil or Indonesia.

Actually, the blueprint for your policies to make and keep the forest-products industry competitive follows many existing publications. Your ideas have already been documented in numerous sources. The Adirondack Park Agency Act addresses the need to protect both the environment and the park's forest economy. The publications of the Northern Forest Land Study and the Northern Forest Lands Council also highlight the necessity of maintaining a competitive forest-products manufacturing sector in all sections of the rural northern forest. The Governor's Task Force on the Forest Industry report gives detailed information on what actions are needed to maintain a healthy forest-products industry.

The fact that forest-products manufacturing enjoys broad and diverse support from many interest groups also bodes well for the success of your policies. Recent New York governors have acknowledged the importance of the industry by naming it a target industry for growth and expansion in the state. Many of New York's environmental groups have supported the forest-products industry for its ability to provide rural area jobs and to protect renewable timber and wildlife resources. Sportsmen's groups support the industry both for the game management that occurs on managed forestlands and for the motorized access and recreational leases that industrial forestlands provide. Landowner groups support the forest-products industry because it provides a source of income for timber harvested from their properties. The income in turn helps pay their property taxes as well as wildlife and recreation management expenses.

Let's fast forward three or four years and evaluate your progress as Commissioner of Forest Economy. Would you be shocked to learn that the forest-products industry is even less competitive now than it was when you accepted your position? That despite your dedication and drive, despite your well-defined blueprint for success, and despite your broad base of government and constituency group support, you have been unable to increase the size and health of the forest-products industry? How could this possibly be the case?

Your hypothetical job parallels what has actually occurred since 1973 in the Adirondack Park. For 32 years the public and private experiment that is the Adirondack Park has stated a goal of preserving land as well as the vitally important rural economy, including forest-products manufacturing. Yet there are fewer sawmills and paper mills in the park now than there were in 1973, and fewer forest-products industry jobs. So far, the experiment is failing. But why?

## Forest Ownership Changes, Sale, and Parcelization

Forest parcelization has received a lot of attention over the last 30 years but mostly in more developed regions of the state, such as the Catskill Park. Although not as well advertised, the impact of parcelization on the forest-products industry in the Adirondacks is even more damaging.

Forest parcelization by definition involves subdivision. For example, a forest-products company subdivides 1,000 acres and sells it to three different individuals. A number of changes occur. First there is the loss of economy of scale. Where prior to the subdivision one road network was maintained by one road maintenance crew, now three road networks are maintained by three completely separate road maintenance operations. Where before there was the expense for one forest management plan, now three are needed. Where before the subdivision one professional timber harvester would move onto the land and harvest the entire 1,000 acres at one time, now three harvesters move on and off three separate properties at different times, increasing equipment moving expenses and downtime. Where before the entire 1,000 acres may have been taxed at a value of $350 per acre, now the three smaller properties may be taxed at a rate of $500 per acre because of the inherent increase in the per-acre value of the smaller parcels.

So what happens to the competitiveness of the forest-products industry? The loss of economy of scale means that the economic efficiency of forest management decreases. Parcelization means that costs for both professional timber harvesters and landowners increase. Ultimately these costs are covered by the wood-using manufacturing plants in the form of higher prices paid for delivered wood. Although one 1,000-acre subdivision may not influence the prices paid for delivered wood, a larger number of subdivisions are certain to have an impact. Over the six million acres of the Adirondack Park, it is not unlikely that 500 small 100- to 300-acre lots are created through subdivision every ten years. It may not be today or tomorrow that the prices for delivered wood will increase, but with the parcelization of the Adirondack forest occurring on a slow and steady basis year after year, the die is cast for ever-increasing wood costs.

Even more troubling is the fact that parcelization of the private Adirondack forest is likely to accelerate in the future as a result of the events of 9/11. A steady real estate market has developed as residents from New York City and other perceived urban terrorist target areas look to "escape" to rural properties. Unlike most refugee populations, this group comes with a wealth that is not deterred by the purchase price of 100-to 300-acre or larger forest lots.

Loss of economy of scale is not the only, nor even the most dramatic impact of forest parcelization. The most dramatic impact to the forest-products industry results from the change in management objectives when a fragmented property is placed under new ownership. As noted above, many of the new forest owners of 100- to

300-acre parcels are migrating out of the cities to more rural locations. Because they bring with them great wealth, they do not feel economic pressure to derive income from the forest property. This economic independence, combined with an urban perception that management leads to forest degradation, often results in a landowner decision not to harvest trees at all, entirely removing the fragmented lots from crop production—the worst-case scenario for forest manufacturing plants.

During the history of the Adirondack Park experiment, many privately owned, large forestland properties have changed hands. In earlier years, before the enactment of the Adirondack Park Agency Act, these transactions did not involve subdivision. Rather, one large-forest owner would sell its property in total to another large-forest owner. Consequently, the forest management and forest harvest plans did not change dramatically. For example, in the early 1900s, mining companies began to sell their excess Adirondack holdings to paper mills in large, intact parcels. It was also common for one paper company to sell its entire land holdings and even its mill to another paper company. These sales did not dramatically impact forest-products manufacturers, as the forest was not parcelized into small holdings that decreased economies of scale.

In the 1960s and 1970s the trend of large properties being sold to other large property owners changed. Several privately held large forest ownerships were purchased by buyers who intended to subdivide them and resell the smaller parcels for second homes or recreational lots. Had that trend continued, the slow, barely perceptible impact on the forest-products industry caused by forest parcelization as described earlier would have resulted. However, the larger public reacted to the possible parcelization of large Adirondack forest properties by demanding that state government take actions to prevent recreational home development from occurring. The public's negative reaction set the stage for the state to become more aggressively involved in the purchase of large blocks of forestland as they were put up for sale. Fueled by the passage of Bond Acts, the state became the preeminent buyer of large forest parcels in the Adirondacks. This policy was very significant and would have long-lasting impacts on the forest-products industry. Instead of a slow parcelization of forest properties into smaller lots, entire multithousand-acre parcels were removed from private ownership and placed into the state Forest Preserve, where timber harvesting is prohibited. As with the small-lot parcelization, the new owner had the wealth to own large properties and to manage them exclusively for wilderness recreation. Thus the threat of parcelization accelerated the withdrawal of private forestlands from crop production.

Another negative impact of the public's desire to buy land to prevent subdivision was the dampening effect the state acquisition programs had on forest-products manufacturing capital investments. The state's steady stream of money for land purchases sent an implied message to mill owners: the goal was to buy all the large private forest holdings in the park for the Forest Preserve. It was like putting signs up at the entrance to the park saying "Forest-products industry not wanted." And some companies read the signs.

Georgia Pacific, which owned two mills in or near the park, made a corporate decision not to invest long-term capital in those facilities. Building a new mill or investing in an old mill in this climate was not justifiable according to GP. The state's "bond act and buy" practice continued into the early 1990s. Then the shape of large-acreage purchases by the public began to change, in part because of the negative impact to rural economies from the loss of forest-products jobs and because of the effect the cost these purchases had on the state budget.

As a result, more recent large-forest property transactions have become more complex, involving a number of different parties. These complex transactions are slowing the transfer of private forest property to public wilderness preserve. For example, as a large forest parcel comes on the market, some portion of the acreage, such as a mountain, river valley, or pond, is deemed to have a high public value and, as such, is subdivided from the property and usually purchased by the public for wilderness recreation. Portions of the property that have potential for resource management are sold to a private concern, often a timber investment management group (TIMO)/real estate investment trust (REIT), but not usually to a forest-products manufacturing facility. Forest-products companies are not typically asked to participate in these complex transactions, likely on the assumption that since so many forest-products companies are divesting their lands they would not be interested in acquiring new lands. That is not the case—forest-products companies do continue to purchase forestland where it is strategically important to their manufacturing plant. Another reason may be that TIMOs/REITs have investment advantages in the form of tax breaks that are not available to forest-products companies, allowing TIMOs/REITs to pay higher prices for forestland. The timber management portion of the property is further subdivided by separating some of the rights of ownership. Development and recreation rights are purchased by the public or a conservation group to allow some public access and eliminate the threat of future development.

These changes were friendlier to forest-products manufacturing than the state's "bond act and buy" policies of the 1970s and 1980s. Fewer forest acres were put into the wilderness preserve. Those not placed in a preserve were managed as income-producing properties, thus making it likely that consistent forest management for timber crops would occur. In addition, the fairly sizable forest properties managed by forest investment groups will be protected in part from further forest parcelization. Finally, this change in policy shows a public interest in allowing the forest-products industry to exist in the Adirondacks, figuratively removing the "forest-products industry not wanted" signs.

On the negative side, the economics of owning easement-encumbered land, where income streams from recreation and value appreciation of development rights no longer exist, are not yet fully understood and may not result in profitability over the long term. Also, easement conditions such as forest management plans, annual reporting requirements, and "no harvest" zones on parts of the property may so negatively affect flexibility and efficiency of management that income suffers. Finally, the combination of public recreational use of easement-encumbered property and private management of the forest may result in conflicts similar to those we experience on publicly owned and managed forestland. If so, the private owner of the timber rights will lose in the resolution of any such conflicts. For example, if the public complains that timber harvest is negatively affecting their hiking experience on the property, it is likely that timber harvest near the hiking trail will be eliminated, further reducing income.

It is too early to tell how complex forestland transactions involving conservation easements will impact the competitiveness of the forest-products industry. It may well be that this change in philosophy regarding how best to prevent forest parcelization has come too late. The size and productivity of the commercial forests in the Adirondacks has been substantially reduced and may no longer possess the advantage that made it a globally competitive place for large-scale forest-products manufacturing. The vast acreage of the Adirondack forest and the great excess of wood available from that forest kept raw material costs competitive with other regions where trees grew faster or taller. Increased regional demand for wood, combined with the shrinking Adirondack commercial forest, may already have eliminated this competitive advantage.

Before forest parcelization can occur, and before forestlands can be acquired and placed into the Forest Preserve, a large-acreage private forest holder must first decide to sell its property. We know that many of the large-forest property owners in the park were forest-products manufacturers or else were strongly connected to the forest-products industry in their need for income from the sale of forest crops. So if the forest-products industry needed the efficiencies of scale provided by a large unbroken forest to stay competitive, why did they offer up their land holdings for sale? As we explore some of the reasons, keep in mind that as forest management objectives differ from one forest owner to another, so do the reasons for selling a forest property.

Forest-products manufacturers who owned land often managed it as though they were going to own the land forever. They managed their manufacturing facility the same way, as though it were going to exist forever. Hence there is a tie between the two assets and often, especially in the early years of the Adirondack Park Agency Act, there was no separation between the two groups of assets—land and mill. The profits and/or losses were reported together on one report as one company. In this structure, even if there were financial losses connected to the management of the forestland (and there often were), they were balanced and dramatically exceeded by profits from the sale of products made at the manufacturing plant.

In later years global competition increased, and the quality of the forest products produced by competitors overseas improved. In addition, the costs of environmental compliance with clean air and water legislation, and other environmental regulations, increased in comparison to similar costs for overseas competitors. As a result, profits from the sale of manufactured goods declined, and the consolidated forest-products manufacturing companies, which depended upon large profit levels to exist, began to look for ways to cut costs and generate income. The hierarchy of ownership demands that the mill, which produces the bulk of the income, be protected first and foremost. So selling land to generate income and reduce the cost of the whole operation made sense, especially when the decision makers believed there was an overabundance of roundwood in the region—a strong belief in the 1960s, 1970s and 1980s. It just made sense to sell the land, thereby shedding cost and generating needed income at the same time. The belief was that wood could be purchased on the open market in more than adequate amounts to keep the mill running. That would have been the case if only one or two companies pursued this strategy. Unfortunately, it was a logical business plan and many companies pursued it, putting a lot of privately held commercial forest acres on the market over a relatively short period of time.

Another dynamic was also occurring during the early days of the Adirondack Park Agency Act. Some publicly traded companies that had consolidated their forestlands and manufacturing plants under a single company became targets for hostile takeover. In many cases the lands owned by the takeover targets had been on the books for so long that they were fully depreciated to a zero book value. Therefore, the corporate raider could borrow money, buy the integrated company, sell the forestland for cash, pay back all or some of the loan and still own the income-producing mills.

This breakup of assets put more forestland on the market during the state "bond act and buy" period. It also forced potential takeover target companies to restructure their assets. Many separated their forestlands from the mills by creating separate landholding companies. These new forestland companies had to make a profit on their timber management and recreation management operations. No longer were land management losses covered by profits made at the manufacturing plants. The term "profit center" was applied to the forest properties, and managers and owners expected the forestland to produce profits of 10 percent or more. Unfortunately, for most properties that was not possible under the property tax structure and the forest growth rates in the Adirondacks. Even with the annual income produced by leasing recreation rights to sportsmen's groups and by various property tax exemption laws, forest managers had a very hard time producing 10 percent profits without actually selling the land. Forest managers took steps to reduce taxes by selling highly taxed parcels with water or road frontage, sometimes at below-market prices. Selling high-value assets such as shorefront property had the added effect of lowering the value of the retained forestland, making it easier to reach a 10 percent target owing to the lower base value of the land. In more recent years, these same forest property companies have pursued the sale of conservation easements in efforts to further reduce forest asset values and to make the 10 percent or greater profit margin more attainable.

Another response made to discourage takeover attempts involved mergers. Mergers allowed a company to be so large that it would be more difficult for corporate raiders to pay off the much larger loans required to leverage a takeover attempt. Once two companies merged, the new company often found that more forestland was owned than could be justified for a given mill. To take advantage of these synergies, nonstrategic forest properties were sold to improve profitability and reduce the debt of the merged company.

We can see that there were a number of reasons that overrode the forest-products industry's need for accessible forestland and resulted in the sale of large forest tracts. Where tracts sold were not purchased by the public for wilderness preserves, TIMOs/REITs often purchased them. Unlike the previous forest-products industry owner who managed the land as though they would be owned forever, the new institutional investors looked at the forestland as ten- to twenty-year investments that would be sold to capture the appreciated value of the asset. This part of the management planning for the institutional investor was called an "exit strategy." Exit strategies ensure that forest properties will continue to be sold on a relatively frequent basis in the Adirondack Park in the future. Each sale will allow potential for additional forest parcelization, change in ownership management objectives and possible loss of raw resources needed for forest-products manufacture.

## Timber-Cutting Practices

The Adirondack experiment is also failing because of past cutting practices, which have had a negative impact on the health and productivity of the current forest. Two of the most-used practices during the late 1800s and early 1900s were clear-cutting and high-grading. Of the two, clear-cutting was the least damaging from a silvicultural point of view because clear-cuts more closely resemble natural occurrences such as wildfire or blowdowns. For example, the 1995 Adirondack microburst blew down nearly 1,000,000 acres of trees in a Swiss-cheese pattern very similar to scattered patch clear-cuts. The forest is well adapted to regenerate after such events, even if large acreages are involved. In clear-cuts and blowdowns, forest regeneration occurs on a relatively clean slate, as all trees from the strongest to the weakest have been removed from the forest canopy. High-grading, on the other hand, does not resemble natural forest occurrences in that the strongest and best-adapted trees are removed from the forest canopy, while the weakest, least competitive trees are left to provide seed for the next forest. High-grading occurred in the early years of forest management because markets did not exist for the low quality and partially rotten stems produced by the weakest trees in the forest. High-grading is the exact opposite of the natural selection process that removes the weakest trees in favor of the strongest. When the strongest occupy the largest space in the forest canopy, they produce the largest volume of seed for regenerating the next forest, contributing to forest health and vigor.

Thus by the time the Adirondack Park Agency Act was made law, the overall productive capacity of the Adirondack forest was already somewhat impaired by past cutting practices. Substantial acreage had been high-graded, for the most part because of inadequate markets for low-grade material.

As mentioned earlier, in the 1970s bond acts combined with advocacy group warnings of potential second-home development to bring New York State into an aggressive forestland buying mode. This seemingly positive step actually had a negative impact on forest harvest practices in the Adirondacks. Forestland owners perceived an opportunity to profit from their lands in two ways. First, they could cut all the trees from their property and profit from the market liquidation of the timber resource. Second, the forestland owners could sell the cut-over lands to New York State, which did not seem to mind buying such heavily harvested property at above-market prices.

Who could blame New York State for purchasing cut-over property? They were under constant pressure from advocacy groups representing public sentiment to increase the number of acres protected in the Forest Preserve. Since the acres were going to be placed in wilderness, the most important criterion was the size of the ownerships purchased and the elimination of the development threat, not the number of standing trees on the property. The trees would grow back even if it took more than one hundred years. Everyone was happy. The forestland owners made profits on their forestland and the size of the Forest Preserve increased.

Even the forest-products manufacturing mill owners were happy. Wood was flowing to their mills at a rapid rate. Cutting exceeded growth on a number of large-forest ownerships, resulting in an excess supply of wood at the mills. The excess supply situation meant the prices paid for wood was very low. Indeed it was a wood buyers' market, which helped the mills to compete both locally and globally.

Concurrent with the "cut and sell to the state" practices of some landowners, another event triggered even heavier cutting on some properties. Beech bark disease (BBD) invaded the Adirondack Mountains and immediately had a dramatic impact. Many forest stands had substantial standing volumes of beech trees. This species, although less valuable than maple and birch, made a great contribution to wildlife via its beechnut crop. Beech was also used by the various pulp and paper mills of the region. Since there were no economical treatment methods that could be used to control the disease, landowners began salvage operations in an attempt to slow or stop the spread of BBD to stands not yet infected. Within a period of only a few years, however, the aggressive spread of BBD forced a change from the surgical removal of infected beech stems to the salvage of all merchantable beech trees in the forest in order to capture the value before they became infected and died. The impact of the disease was so quick that in a matter of just a few years, the beech sawlog harvest in the Adirondacks declined by more than 80 percent. This decline occurred because the beech trees harvested were so damaged by the disease that they could not be used to make lumber. The regionwide salvage of beech helped to sustain excess wood supplies well into the early 1990s.

As a result of the heavy cutting practices of the 1970s, along with the advent of new high-volume mechanical tree harvesting equipment, and the building of a wood-to-energy plant in Burlington, Vermont, the Adirondack Park Agency studied heavy cutting in the Adirondacks and published a white paper that addressed clear-cutting. Although the study found that clear-cutting was not a problem in the Adirondacks, it nonetheless further defined clear-cuts as harvests that left less than 30 square feet of basal area per acre (the cross-sectional area of a tree stem measured 4.5 feet from the ground). Unfortunately, these changes in the rules inadvertently left a loophole that allowed heavy cutting over areas more than 25 acres in size as long as more than 30 square feet of basal area per acre was left in the forest. High-grading allowed forest property owners to remove almost all the trees of economic value from their forests, regardless of how many acres were involved, without the hassle of getting a permit. As mentioned earlier, clear-cuts are less likely to have an impact on the future health and productivity of the forest than the practice of repetitive high-grading.

Another interesting effect of the Adirondack Park Agency's clear-cutting regulations is that they discouraged landowners from dealing more effectively with beech bark disease in the Adirondack forest. Forest biologists suggest that the most effective way to reduce the incidence of beech bark disease is to perform clear-cuts of fifty acres or larger. Part of the theory here is that by creating a large forest opening, shade-intolerant species such as cherry, ash, aspen, and birch will have a competitive advantage and will take over the site. Doing beech salvage operations, on the other hand, will often result in another crop of beech trees on that site, as beech regenerates very aggressively through root and stump sprouts, which grow well in partial shade. This method creates a potentially endless cycle of beech salvage operations followed by beech regeneration followed by beech salvage operations. If the process of getting a clear-cutting permit was less time consuming and expensive, conscientious forest owners might choose this silvicultural treatment over salvage. Since salvage operations do not require a regulatory permitting process, and since salvage operations are not nearly as controversial politically or socially, most forestland owners continue to choose beech salvage operations as the way to deal with beech bark disease. Indeed, a second wave of beech salvage operations is ongoing in the Adirondack forest today.

In the mid-1990s, "sustainable forestry" burst on the scene, as large retailers such as Lowes, Home Depot, Staples, IKEA, and the like became targets of demonstrations by various advocacy groups. The advocates wanted products sold at these stores to come from sustainably managed forests. Their demonstrations were successful, and the managers of these chains demanded that their suppliers provide products that could be certified as coming from well-managed forests. Almost immediately forest-products manufacturers began enrolling their forestlands in certification programs such as the American Forest and Paper Association's Sustainable Forest Initiative and the Forest Stewardship Council's Principles of Sustainable Forest Management. Regardless of the particular standard chosen, third-party auditors evaluated the management of the forest being certified.

This demand had at least two impacts. First, over-cutting growth on large ownerships would have to be justified by showing the need to address diseased or damaged (e.g., by ice storm or wind storm) forests. Over-cutting growth as a strategy to achieve more income in a coming land sale would not pass a certified forest audit. Second, silvicultural treatments had to conform to those well defined in the science of forest management, which meant the practice of high-grading would not be allowed on forests that were certified. These events, perhaps more than any others, reduced over-cutting growth on large forest ownerships in the Adirondacks. From a wood-product manufacturing facility's point of view, the advent of sustainable forestry had both positive and negative impacts. On the positive side, forest productivity and forest growth improved, meaning a stable long-term supply of wood for manufacture would be available. On the negative side, the cost of this wood resource increased because of the costs of compliance with the new standards and the reduced harvests required by the new standards. It remains to be seen if the new sustainable forestry standards will have an overall positive or negative affect on the local forest-products industry.

## The Public

The public has had a tremendous impact on the forest-products industry in the Adirondacks. Sustainable forestry standards were broadly supported in public surveys. Parcelization of the forest is a reflection of the public's strong desire to own forest property, either individually or through government agencies. Even the heavy cutting of sawlogs in the early years of the Adirondack Park reflected the public's strong demand for housing and furniture at affordable prices.

The majority of the public lives in urban, not rural, settings, and in a democracy the majority rules, or at least they do if they vote. So in New York, the urban population rules because it can outvote the rural population. And the urban population makes their decisions to a large extent based upon what they see around them every day. What they see is not enough clean air and too much pollution, not enough open space and seemingly never-ending sprawl. And they see people everywhere. So it is no wonder that protecting the environment is high on their list of things to do. They worry that if something is not done, the entire world will eventually look like their cities.

Elected officials in urban centers understand that to get elected and stay in office, part of their platform must include protection of the environment. One easy way to do that is to purchase forestland and protect it for (or from) the urban public. Usually, the land purchased is in a distant rural area because there is not much open space available to be "saved" in an urban area, and if it was, the purchase price would be very high and might cause local constituents concerned about taxes to complain. The savvy politician will "save" open space far away from local urban constituents, such as forestland in the Adirondacks.

The Adirondack region has been "saved" many times in recent years. Governor Rockefeller "saved" the Adirondacks with the zoning plan that is the Adirondack Park Agency Act. Governor Cuomo tried to "save" the Adirondack Park through his Commission on the Adirondacks in the Twenty-First Century. Most recently, Governor Pataki "saved" the park through the enactment of the Environmental Protection Fund, a budget account funded in part to purchase open space in the Adirondacks. That is what the public wants, and therefore the "saving" of the Adirondacks will continue with each new governor of New York.

Aside from buying land, another popular way to protect the environment is the strict regulation of industries such as forest-products manufacturers. The same public dynamic that requires that the Adirondack Park be "saved" time and again with each new governor and legislature also applies to the environment. Each new set of politicians must establish their own record of "saving" the environment. Thus there is constantly evolving legislation that adds cost to locally manufactured forest products. It is not that environmental regulation is not needed or that it does not accomplish local goals, it is just that in a global economy, these new expenses cannot be passed on to the consumer unless similar regulations govern and increase the costs of competing forest-products manufacturers in other states or countries.

In recent years many New York forest-products manufacturing facilities have closed their plants, and the jobs they provided are now eliminated or substantially reduced. The Champion International mill in Deferiet, New York, is a good example. It produced coated papers used in magazines and catalogs. On a nationwide basis, more than 40 percent of the coated paper used in the United States is now imported from other countries that do not have to follow the same stringent environmental manufacturing requirements the Deferiet mill did. And the paper that was once made locally with wood grown in the Adirondacks is now most likely imported from Western Europe or Asia.

This really is a true "ugly American" policy. We want our forest-products manufacturers and landowners to follow the very best forest management and manufacturing practices but at the same time we purchase lower-priced forest products made at overseas manufacturing facilities that pollute and use wood from clear-cut tropical forests. China, the largest exporting country in the world, is now importing wood chips and logs because there is not enough local forest left to supply its forest-products manufacturing facilities.

## Conclusion

Your efforts as Commissioner of the Forest Economy were valiant, but you never had a chance. Even though you knew what was needed to maintain a healthy forest-products industry in the Adirondacks, current social and economic pressures opposing commercial forest uses were just too large for any policy, or commissioner, to over-come. Society's overall affluence, its urban outlook, and its desire for a perfect Disneyesque world, all conspire for the eventual failure of forest-products manufacturing plants dependent upon trees grown in the Adirondacks. In this climate society may tolerate small mom-and-pop forest-products businesses, but large manufacturers will not be tolerated because of their size and perceived impact.

But that is just for now. The Adirondack experiment is a long-term experiment in adaptive management. There are changes on the horizon that may swing public opinion in another direction and if so, the Adirondack forest may be ready to produce needed forest products.

One such indicator is the change in New York State forestland buying policies. Instead of blanket purchases that place land in a wilderness preserve off-limits to forest management and crop production, the state more recently has placed only small parts of purchased forestland in the Forest Preserve, with the remaining acres being protected from development through the use of conservation easements. Thus land-protection strategies more surgically target development, leaving substantial acreages available for other economic uses, including forest management. The fact that this change is being accepted by the public and various advocacy groups indicates a social tolerance for local forest-products manufacturing. It is interesting to note that there have been no studies that show that further additions to the state-owned Forest Preserve result in corresponding increases in recreational use of the preserve or in a corresponding increase of the tourist-driven economy. Nor is there any conclusive evidence that more Forest Preserve acres are needed to conserve biological diversity beyond that which will be conserved through the use of conservation easements.

The future may also bring a change in the structure of conservation easement documents. Some of the first easements written were very cumbersome and inefficient. New York State's need to control forest management practices on easement-encumbered forestlands in a way that prevented conflict with public recreational use of that land often created management inefficiencies and costs for the owner of the timber rights. As conservation easements have evolved, the state has slowly changed to more hands-off approaches. For example, now the timber rights owner has the option of certifying the forest management of the property under a sustainable forest management standard such as SFI or FSC instead of negotiating a detailed forest management plan with New York State representatives. This option is more efficient both for the timber rights owner and for state government oversight agencies.

Additional improvements in conservation easement documents and administration are still needed. The timber rights owner needs even more assurance that the right to manage the forest for crop production will not be eroded over time by new interpretations regarding public use of the conservation easement–encumbered property. An example of the eroding right to practice forest management activities can be seen in the history of the National Forests. Originally these forests were purchased to ensure clean water and a long-term supply of forest crops for product manufacture. These goals of the National Forests are clearly defined in the Organic Act of 1897: "Forest Reserves are for the purpose of preserving a perpetual supply of timber for home industries; preventing destruction of the forest cover which regulates the flow of streams and protecting local residents from unfair competition in the use of forest and range." Yet today, the use of National Forests for a perpetual supply of timber for home industries is severely threatened by endless lawsuits and conflict. Groups opposed to forest management on the national forests have adopted polices opposing any timber harvest on national forests and favor recreational use only.

Another indicator of the potential for a better future for the forest-products economy is the improvement in the quality of forest management that is taking place in the Adirondacks today. We know that early on in the Adirondacks, high-grading was used to treat many forest acres. The development of sustainable forestry standards that require quality forest management and eliminate the use of adverse practices such as high-grading will lead to increased growth and productivity of the Adirondack forest in the future. This improvement in growth and yield will provide both quantity and quality forest crops for use in local manufacturing—a bumper crop if you will—that will allow forest-products manufacturers to be more competitive.

This bright outlook for the future is diminished somewhat by the continued presence of beech bark disease. Because beech is such a prevalent species in the Adirondacks, the forest-products economy does depend on continued research with the goal of reducing the impact of that disease. We can be encouraged by renewed interest in researching solutions to the beech bark disease problem. In 2004 a symposium helped to focus attention on the disease and the need to find resistant trees or silvicultural applications that limit the impact of the disease. Out of this symposium new research projects have been initiated, some of which will be funded through the United States Forest Service.

Another indicator of potential for a stronger Adirondack forest economy in the future can be found in the area of local zoning. In recent decades the trend in local zoning had been to encourage development and urban sprawl. Residentially zoned lots have grown in size from less than a quarter-acre to one-half acre to one acre to three acres and, in many local Adirondack communities as well as neighboring communities outside of the park, to lots as big as forty-two acres. This increase in lot size resulted in an exponential increase in forest parcelization for development. This trend may slowly change as communities recognize the cost to local government of maintaining dramatically expanded infrastructures. Smart growth, a recently coined buzzword, may become the new wave of local planning. Smart growth emphasizes smaller housing lots located close to community centers, which facilitates easy access to needed services such as groceries and restaurants, often without the need to drive an automobile. One of the goals of smart growth is to reduce pollution associated with our automobile-dependent society. The escalating cost of gasoline should only help public acceptance of this concept.

Another positive sign for the future is adoption of global initiatives by various advocacy groups and forestry associations. As corporations have grown in size and become truly multinational entities, they have become more susceptible to pressure from advocacy groups on a global scale. Such international concerns seldom had systems in place to check the conditions under which the products they bought were produced. For example, illegal logging in tropical forests had been the source of some common products, such as luan plywood, marketed by large retailers in the past. Illegal logging has occurred in many of the world's forests as timber thieves raided those forests for mahogany or other similarly valuable trees. Because the trees were stolen, the end product could be marketed at much less cost than products made from legally managed forests such as those in the Adirondacks. Advocacy and forestry trade groups recognized this problem and have recently worked with larger companies to establish programs that dramatically reduce illegal logging. In fact, prevention of illegal logging is now a component of every major recognized sustainable forestry standard.

The focus on illegal logging is but one small component of a broader effort called "corporate social responsibility" or CSR. CSR strives to place businesses on equal footing throughout the world by establishing goals such as requirements for living wages, adequate working conditions, effective environmental programs, and more. Efforts such as CSR could help to eliminate unfair competitive advantages such as those that exist when environmental regulations are more stringent in one nation than another.

Although there are a number of changes occurring that may lead to a more vibrant forest economy in the Adirondacks, they may not be happening quickly enough. Recent years have seen the closing of a number of forest-products manufacturers in the Adirondack region. Champion's mill in Deferiet has already been mentioned. Other mills closed include Lyons Falls Pulp and Paper; International Paper's Corinth facility; Ethan Allen's Boonville furniture plant, and many small saw mills. As mills close, so do professional timber harvesting businesses. The large maintenance contracting firms that provide labor and expertise to maintain manufacturing plants go out of business, as do many of the smaller support businesses such as fuel suppliers and parts stores. Once the infrastructure of the Adirondack forest economy is gone, it will be very difficult and expensive to replace. Consequently, there is a need to keep existing forest-products manufacturing facilities operating.

One way to help maintain this infrastructure is to improve the working relationships between government and industry. It seems that over the term of the Adirondack experiment a gap has been created between government and forest-products manufacturing. This gap is noticeable in the government's benign neglect of the forest-products economy. It seems the only time the government is concerned about the rural forest-products economy is when a forest-products manufacturer announces that its plant is about to close. Then many political efforts are made to save jobs, but often by that time it is too late. The time to save jobs, and the forest-products forest economy, is before plants become economically challenged. This effort will require constant communication between government and the forest-products groups followed by real solutions to the problems of the day.

For its part, the forest industry must do more than identify the problems of the day. It must constantly promote its positive contributions to the economy and the environment to the broader public. In so doing, government officials will be protected from a public backlash when they go out on a limb to support the forest-products economy. If it were easy to accomplish it would already have been done. If it is not accomplished, eventually the Adirondack experiment to blend park and commercial use will end not in balance, but in a six-million-acre forest wilderness preserve, with an mono-economy based only upon low-paying, seasonal, open-space recreation jobs or jobs with local government.

# 23

## Reflections on the Adirondack Park Agency in the Current Era

RICHARD H. LEFEBVRE

Saying I have served on the Adirondack Park Agency for almost a third of its existence either sounds like a very long time or is a necessary reminder that the Adirondack Park Agency is indeed a very young institution. Although very young, the agency has a legislative mandate betraying its infancy. The decisions made, and the behaviors displayed, are of critical importance, as they involve the variables of our time and, once implemented, are often not reversible. To examine the Adirondack Park Agency (APA) and its leadership, one must have some understanding of the process, or the circumstances of the road to agency membership and the chairmanship. It is with pride that I recall many events demonstrating the perils of politics and of life that I never sought, but I will forever be grateful for their finding me.[1]

I was approached by George Manchester, supervisor of the Town of Bleeker in the southern Adirondack Mountains, asking if I minded if he advanced my name to then governor Mario Cuomo for membership in the Adirondack Park Agency. I recall telling him that I did not mind, but I felt that he might be better off if he found someone with more name recognition. In fact, I told him that I might even be a liability. I was opposed to a plan from Commissioner Thomas Jorling and the Department of Environmental Conservation (DEC) that was looking at land for possible acquisition, and I had even lobbied in Albany against it. My position was influenced, as I was president of the Canada Lakes Protective Association.

Mr. Manchester did advance my name to the governor, and there were no new appointments that year; for many years the membership of the agency did not change. The agency was a lightning rod for political contention, and all gubernatorial nominations also required confirmation by the New York State Senate.

In May, a year and a half later, Bob Bendick, then deputy to Commissioner Jorling, called to ask me to report to the DEC building at 50 Wolf Road, as the commissioner wanted to speak with me about "this park agency thing." I was asked to come after-hours and report to the back door to be escorted to the commissioner's office. I was to say nothing to anyone. At the appointed time, I was met at the back door and escorted to the office, where I met Joe Martens and Dan Luciano of the governor's staff as well as DEC Commissioner Jorling. This meeting was very relaxed and lasted a couple of hours. I was surprised at how comfortable I felt. After all, I was a special education administrator, and the arena that I was talking to them about was so much larger and more complex, with many challenges. As a longtime consumer and resident, I had my visions for the park and felt very comfortable expressing them. I learned in this interview that the commissioner had spoken about me with Neil Woodworth of the Adirondack Mountain Club.

I had known Neil for many years, when he was a young man growing up in the city of Johnstown, where I was teaching. Neil's father, who was the superintendent of the Gloversville School District, had hired me, and I had worked with him for almost 20 years. I learned that Neil had spent considerable time talking about my preparation for the APA position with his father and then reporting to the commissioner and the staff from the governor's office. My point is to remind you that the casting of the net is broad and rather complex. The appointment process has so very many filters, and one never knows from where the next influence may be coming.

I had felt prepared, if I were to be chosen, as I had completed a considerable amount of time in public service. I had sought election to the local Board of Education and had served as the president of that board. I had also administered the Special Education

Department for the City of Gloversville School District. This department had both a staff and budget equal to that of the park agency. My résumé also included service on the Zoning Board of Appeals as well as the Fulton County Planning Board. To further my involvement, I read all that I could on the topic of the Adirondacks. I was on the mailing lists of many groups that ranged from property rights groups to the Adirondack Council. My interest was spurred on when the governor's Commission on the Adirondacks in the Twenty-First Century released its report and it was rumored that property on our lake was targeted for taking. I was not one for joining the motorcades down I-87, but I went to Albany and met with representatives in our government regarding the issue. I was very comfortable in this environment, as I had spent time in the halls of the Legislative Office Building during my tenure as president of the Board of Education.

My "interview" on that night was not only comfortable but also comforting. I was able to ask as many questions as I was asked to answer. I was escorted from the building and asked not to say anything of the meeting. I was told that the governor was going to be making some decisions in the future. As comfortable as I was at that moment, I was unaware of what the next few months would bring.

Toward the end of June of that year, I was nominated by Governor Cuomo to become a member of the Adirondack Park Agency. I was not given any advance notice, and, in fact, I learned of this nomination when a number of reporters converged on my office at school. I learned not only of my nomination, but also of the considerable opposition to my nomination from "environmental groups." I was being declared unfit by some groups because of my interest in property rights. It was reported in the press that I belonged to a fairly conservative property rights group in Bleeker, New York. One must remember that a wide variety of groups sprung up all over the Adirondacks during this period. I also belonged to the Adirondack Landowners Association and the Fairness Coalition. The press started doing a number on the governor for nominating someone unfit to serve in the suggested position.

Confirmation occurred in the middle of the night on July 6, 1993, and I was off to my first meeting the next day. The meeting was in Piseco and held no surprises. The existing membership and members of the public received me graciously; however, the press, and certain interest groups, were not going to let go of my past perceived affiliations. The questions and commentary continued in the press for all of that month and into August, centering on my desire to protect this great preserve and on my feelings regarding development. Governor Cuomo's judgment was questioned as well. Mario Cuomo was preparing to seek reelection against a little-known senator named George Pataki.

I met with then governor Cuomo on the shore of Lake Champlain, and after taking a very deep breath I regretfully offered him my resignation. I had now served for only one month and was concerned about how I was being portrayed in the press as well as how the governor was being condemned for appointing me. The governor just smiled and then turned to my wife, Gay, and asked how she was holding up; he also inquired about our children. I remember Gay responding that the family was doing well. He then turned to me and asked, "What do you know about pottery?" I was flabbergasted because I did not understand the question; it did not seem to be related to this life-altering offer of resignation that I had just given to him. I explained that I was concerned that I was an embarrassment to him, and he again asked me about the pottery. I did respond that I felt I knew a bit about pottery because my wife had a degree in fine arts. He quickly asked, "What do you have if you do not fire clay?" The governor just as quickly answered his own question: "Without heat you will have only sand. Can you take the heat?" With a very quick and affirmative answer from me, Governor Cuomo put his hand on my shoulder and said that we had better get going as we had a good deal of work to get started. Looking over his shoulder, I saw Joe Martens, who had conducted the interview a few months before, smiling. I will say that that moment set the course of my tenure on the agency. I would see the governor two more times during the fall campaign, and he always asked how I was doing. I was fine and, in time, the issues in the press subsided.

Understanding the above route is critical to understanding the Adirondack political landscape. So many people live under the misconception that one wakes up on a given day and seeks the reward of serving. The route is complex and not always meant to be understood. Knowing some of my travels might help to understand what I tried to achieve and my methodology.

*Time Magazine* has characterized those of us born as our nation entered World War II as a "Lost Generation." The essay proclaims that we have been a generation of "bridge builders." My generation has spent their lives filling gaps between ideologies, profound social movements, and trends. I now found myself at the table with the old guard of the agency, and I was again charged with being the bridge builder. This was the period after the issuing of the recommendations of the Commission on the Adirondacks in the Twenty-First Century, and there was so much to be learned from the past. I was fortunate to be sitting with Peter Paine and Arthur Savage, along with Roger Swanson who had sat as Department of State designee for two decades. This period needed to be an evolution and not a revolution. Right or wrong, the locals of the park felt disenfranchised, and here was a chance to bring them into the process.

I soon was reminded of the extremes on both sides and knew that the extremes would never come to the middle. On the other hand, I felt the middle could be defined in such a way that there would be room for many more members at the table. The table needed to have room for local government and the developer as well as those wanting to protect the assets of the park.

I recalled the lessons of a freshman level sociology class that used the theory of Maslow's Hierarchy of Needs to define the basic needs of a person. The basis of the theory is that a person must meet the most basic needs, including physical needs of food, shelter, and water as well as having security, belonging, and purpose before one can attain a status where he/she can view all options as resolutions. I was able to apply this theory when relating to the "old guard" and attempting to advance the idea of moving toward the center in the age-old Adirondack debate.

I took it upon myself to accept speaking engagements in the hope that I might better understand the constituencies as well as to share more about myself and what I stood for. This was an attempt to change some of the press that I had received during the confirmation process. I had always enjoyed public speaking and found it painless and I was comfortable standing before a group to express my feelings on this topic. I asked the APA staff to put together materials, and I was ready as a one-man speaker's bureau.

The first speaking engagement that I accepted was with a serious property rights group, the Blue Line Confederation in the town of Bleeker. I was prepared with land-use maps and the spirit of my new position. I had prepared handouts and a speech that went well. I always looked forward to a question-and-answer period, and this time was no exception. I remember the Q and A going on for a very long time with many good questions coming from a variety of members of the audience in the Town Hall. I remember wanting to be that bridge builder and still respect the needs of this audience. When we left that evening, my wife told me that a female member of the audience came to her, not knowing we were husband and wife, and told her that I was going to have one very sore crotch from sitting on the fence. This was a very true prognostication because it takes a great deal of work to find and maintain the center on these issues. That evening I had placed myself firmly in the center and was very comfortable. I saw myself as offering a hand to explore the center of these issues with me and suggested that it was not threatening to be seen as a moderate. I saw myself as a moderate at the table as well.

There was so very much to learn upon joining the agency. There is a vast landscape that is more complex than the multicolored map of the park. Having driven it for years, I felt that I knew the park; however, the information on soil types and slopes, coupled with water quality issues and access just became a blur. In addition, there were all the issues of economics and governing with all the forces of many interested parties from within the park and around our state and nation. Suddenly, there was a realization that people all around the planet were watching this great environmental and sociological experiment. Never did I realize this more than when I presented at the Millennium Parks Conference in Camerino, Italy. Standing at that podium, I looked out at a sizeable audience of park managers from many countries on five different continents, who were all interested in our Adirondack experiment. The Adirondack Park has one of the most complex constituencies in all of government. This complexity speaks to their passion as well as their preparedness.

The learning curve was immense, and so was the willingness of the staff, the board, and interest groups to share with me all that they knew. The reading was voluminous and always made available upon request. So much of the history was formed in court cases and case law. I was now on the board, and I was not a lawyer. I was not schooled in the physical sciences. To the table, I would hope to bring my past in education and administration; however the most exciting facet of being named to the board was the learning. I enjoyed every topic: law, science, water, cartography, land use, planning, economics, and more.

One year later, then Governor Cuomo lost the election to George E. Pataki, and I was asked to meet with the transition team on a few occasions. The transitioning from one administration to another in our democratic society is a very interesting process. The new governor would start to replace board members, and we could feel his influence as the new people were appointed. My name was mentioned by the press as the front-runner for the position of chairman; to my relief, that was not to be. I have always liked to lead, but I realized that there was so much background to be gained and retained, and I was not ready. The governor named Greg Campbell as chairman, and the new administration was underway. I thought then, and do to this day, that the position of chairman should go to one who has had considerable experience with all of the issues in the Adirondack cauldron. It is not just the obvious issues but also the competing personalities of all of the factions of staff as well as the different interests around the state. The institutional knowledge was being replaced with new board members and new staff as well. Again, I feel that it is incumbent upon the leadership to see that the path to the future is lined with the players to provide for smooth transitions and to avoid loss of institutional memory.

In the next two years, with new board members and new staff, the direction of the agency changed some, but in general the work continued, thanks to a dedicated staff. New people in executive director, deputy director, and agency counsel positions meant that things were to be handled differently. As with all new administrations, it would take some time for the new team to come together and establish itself. Day-to-day events as well as some 500-year environmental events such as a very severe ice storm and the microburst challenged the new administration. All systems were being tested, but the work forged ahead.

On February 8, 1998, I was asked by Governor Pataki to serve as chairman of the agency. This time I felt ready. I felt that I held a better understanding of the issues and the personalities of the constituents and staff. I received the telephone call in the agency headquarters, and within 30 minutes I asked that all staff join me in a meeting. I shared with them my immediate goal of establishing channels of communication to, from, and within the agency. I declared my immediate theme: "it is not what you say but how you say it." I also announced that immediately after the meeting I would start a tour of all of the constituency groups to welcome them into the fold. I was declaring a year of reconciliation.

That was to be my management style for my entire tenure. I would emphasize a single behavior and work to reinforce that behavior for the year. I hoped that it would become not only my goal, but the goal of the board and the goal of the staff as well. A reality is that these goals do not start and stop on a specific date but are carried from one goal period to another, which had a cumulative effect as we worked to modify behavior and product. This process was a fallback to my earliest profession as a speech pathologist in public education. During the period that I was asked to administer the special education department for a city school district, Management by Objective (MBO) was the system that we used to direct our focus. MBO was first outlined by Peter Drucker in 1954 in his book *The Practice of Management.*[2] I had no intention of using the entire management system as outlined by Drucker, but I found it very beneficial to keep a focus on outcomes, which was particularly helpful as I felt that I was being pulled in so many different directions. Concurrent with my efforts, the agency staff would go through the entire *Strategic Planning* process as well.[3]

The strategic planning meetings would go on for almost five years, reflecting a divergent staff and very strong convictions. In time, mission statement and goals were established using a system of consensus statements. A consensus statement was, by mutual agreement, a statement that I might not have wanted but that I could live with. I often used this system of directing discussion to try to bring divergent thinking together. I used this method with staff, the agency board, and with all of the stakeholders in our park.

Year one under my chairmanship was to be a year of reconciliation. The park had long been a place of considerable acrimony. There had always been very strong dictates from all sides but never an attempt to find the center. I spoke of my palette as having much gray color on it. I likened what I had inherited to a palette of black and white but very little mixing of those hues. I started on Monday morning and maintained a full schedule of visits until I felt I had reached out to all constituencies. I visited the Local Government Review Board and the Adirondack Association of Towns and Villages. I told them that I was very much aware that I was not their first choice to be chairman, but that I wished to work with them and hoped that they would feel that they could communicate with me on any subject. I visited the Legislative Office Building and all elected officials. I asked that they make me part of the problem solving. I encouraged the environmental groups to work with me on finding common ground. I felt that the Blue Line Council summed it up best when they offered, "We owe you a chance." I could ask no more of them.

I made a promise to myself that I would try to cover the park and would try to attend meetings whenever invited. I also accepted all speaking engagements and even made it a point to stop in popular spots in each town to talk with the locals. I would often stop for coffee and listen as long as my schedule allowed in many of the local diners or the Stewart's convenience shops. I tried to purchase all that I could in local establishments and also travel through all sections of the park. I was on a mission to see if I could discern where the hurt was and to see if education and communication would lead the way to some degree of reconciliation. I started to feel trends forming from the very first mile of my journey.

My conversations led to an affirmation that groups and individuals alike felt alienated from our park and the landscape that they loved. Even more than an alienation from a place that they loved, individual people and groups were totally estranged from the process of regulating the very place where their homes and businesses reside. I knew that the extremes might not be willing to come to the table, but I did feel that it was worth every effort to offer all considerations to them. The separation of past history and working on the present and future seemed to interest many.

I always was surprised by how I was received. I felt welcomed wherever I chose to hold meetings. I elected to hold "town meetings" in all corners of the park. I found that in some places far away from the High Peaks Region, people had never seen members of the agency, let alone the chairman. They felt totally disenfranchised from the center of the regulatory arm of the park. Meetings were planned and held in each of the counties of the park with board members, members of the staff, local officials, and members of the public. These meetings grew more relaxed as time went along. I also saw to it that agency meetings were moved around the park from time to time. There is considerable work to holding a meeting away from the office in Ray Brook, but the benefits were abundant.

The greatest epiphany of this period was the discovery that we, as the people of the park, really did not have a sense of what this place was or what we wanted it to be other than in our own individual thoughts. I started to fold into my public conversations a question of what it was that brought us together. I was interested in what the people of the park felt we had in common and what our assets were. I quickly found the greatest feeling of commonality was that of dislike for the agency and misunderstanding of the mission of the agency and the designating of this landscape as a park. It just seemed that we were not able to focus on the great place where we lived. We had not looked at our assets other than the ones in the backyard. We had failed to see the whole!

The year of reconciliation was working. People were starting to talk to, and with, each other. The agency now had a recognizable presence in all parts of the park, and needs were being identified for new initiatives. The agency headquarters were a focal point as well. With Dan Fitts, executive director, an exercise in strategic planning was ongoing. This project would take five years and would need to be started twice. However, the staff was determined and completed the project as well as proclaiming a meaningful mission statement. I have always viewed strategic planning as the successor to management by objective.

During this time, plans were made to explore gateway principles. Michael Clarke of Lake Placid and I had been spending a good deal of time talking about the sense-of-place issue. Michael would start talking of a visiting team to study gateway principles and how we might train local governments and interest groups to think of the big picture. Some of the early questions were centered on our relationship to the landscape and the recognition that the state-owned lands were an asset and need to be seen as such. This work was brought to us by Ed McMahon, one of the authors of *Balancing Nature and Commerce in Gateway Communities*. In his book, McMahon and colleagues describe economic strategies, land-use planning processes, and conservation tools that communities from all over the nation have found effective.[4] The authors offer practical and proven lessons on how residents of gateway communities can protect their community's identity while stimulating a healthy economy and safeguarding nearby natural and historic resources.

The traditional thinking has been to think of gateway communities as those communities outside the national parks. Our Adirondack Park team was able to apply many of these principles to our park in establishing a relationship between our communities and the nearby state lands.

Corresponding with the conversations on gateway principles, David Gibson of the Association for the Protection of the Adirondacks and Paul Bray, of Albany, were talking with me about the Abruzzo Park in Italy. The similarities between the Italian park and the Adirondack Park were numerous, including a similar date of establishment. The Italian park and the Adirondack Park were made of a mix of public and private lands and had issues that were analogous. The issues that I had identified during my travels as a lack of big-picture thinking were called "park effect" in the Italian park. During my chairmanship, there would be three delegations sent to visit the Italian park, and as many delegations from the Italian park would visit the Adirondacks. There was a formal twinning agreement signed between the two parks. The park effect initiative summed up what I had found on my tours around the Adirondacks regarding big-picture issues and how to deal with them.[5]

Year two was to become the year of communication. The lines between two given years or two objectives are never clear as there is not a need for a year to end or an objective to be totally met before starting to focus on a new objective. The year of reconciliation included many efforts in communication. I felt it was time to focus on reconciliation of past differences. I was asked to keynote a number of events. I found that when I did one event there were often two more invitations offered to me. I have no recollection of ever saying no to an invitation. I saw this as a way to carry the message of the board of the agency and even more important, the opportunity to show how the group that I was addressing was a part of the whole and how they could help us define the whole and the relationships within this unit.

The effort seemed to increase daily. John Banta and Steve Erman, GIS specialist and economist, respectively, of the agency, were wonderful in keeping me supplied with meaningful information and materials. They had joined me on a number of occasions and soon knew my style and had a natural instinct for my timing and the material needed. I spoke at the Local Government Review Board, Blue Line Council, Intercounty Representatives, Forest Products Industry, Adirondack Association of Towns and Villages, Lake George Association and I even addressed 600 people at the Quality Communities and Smart Growth Conference in Albany. In short, the Adirondack Park Agency had a presence all over the park, and beyond, and was now welcomed as a participant. Equally, the others were now welcomed by us as participants.

I was honored during this period to be named to the Theodore Roosevelt Commission by Governor Pataki. This was a natural fit as Theodore Roosevelt had a long history in the Adirondacks. I was able to attend meetings throughout New York State and communicate the story of the Adirondacks and the work of the agency. This was a newfound opportunity to work with others in the administration and to share the wonder of this great place that I love so deeply. The highlight of this commission was when, with Lucy Popkess of the School of Environmental Science and Forestry in Syracuse and Secretary of State Alexander Treadwell, I was able to plan to bring the Theodore Roosevelt Commission to the Adirondack Park and, with a Paul Smith's College stagecoach, visit Great Camp Santanoni. In addition, we were able to re-create the famous ride from Mount Marcy to North Creek as then vice president Theodore Roosevelt had done on his way to accept the presidency of the United States. The opportunity for meaningful communication was to be found everywhere.

Back at the office, I established two monthly channels of communication. To the staff I wrote "Staff Notes." My desire was to tell the staff what I had done for that month and also to invite them to join me in these efforts. I tried to include some Adirondack trivia and other items of interest, such as births and weddings. On a much larger scale, I introduced "Community Chat" as a monthly mailing. The name was meant to be a play on the internet craze that we were experiencing at the time. I saw it as an opportunity to communicate with each locality in our park, along with many other people each month, regarding the actions of the board and items of interest but always focusing on the whole. I did a feature article entitled, "Spotlight on Staff" and featured the management of the agency and many others on staff. I asked that this communication be reproduced and hung in town barns for the Highway Departments as well as left on the counters of Town Halls. This initially small attempt grew from two pages to four and even six pages some months. The circulation grew as well. We quickly grew to 1,000 mailings each month. Soon we would add a communication specialist to our staff. The timely mailing of the Annual Report of the Agency was another major effort. There was an attempt to upgrade this report and to see that it was not only timely but also distributed to appropriate groups and individuals, an annual project for the communications specialist.

Just by the sheer number of invitations for presentations, I had an indication that the objectives of the period had been exceeded. The addition of a communication specialist and the added pieces that were going out each month had our name in many new places, and we now had a logo! I was appalled to discover that we did not have a logo. I was not encouraged to create one, but I felt compelled to do so. I met with the staff and offered a design contest to see if we could create a logo that would assist me with the creation of name recognition and something that in a quick image would be recognizable all over the Park as well as throughout the State of New York. Henry Savorie, our cartographer, designed a logo that is mostly unchanged to this day. I had it made into lapel pins and started to distribute them on any occasion. The logo was soon on my podium when I spoke and on Certificates of Recognition that I enjoyed passing out at meetings to guest speakers and dignitaries. I felt that I was communicating a feeling of goodwill that showed that all were welcome in the arena of policy development in the Adirondack State Park.

During this time, we also altered the ability of the public to access the board during meetings. I have been privileged to be able to conduct meetings for many organizations over the years, and I feel that government, thus the agency, has a responsibility to conduct its business in public. For that reason, I did not encourage the use of executive sessions, though I am quick to admit that there is an occasional need for them. With that said, I always am swift to remind the public that they are seeing a meeting in public, not a public meeting; the difference is that the public is invited to participate in a public meeting. The agency began working on its rules to let the public speak before the work of the meeting started. This was another attempt to open communication and welcome the disenfranchised. After many months of debate and setting of ground rules, the policy was established.

Communication often leads to transparency and predictability in government. The agency now had a new counsel, Charles Fox. With counsel, I was able to introduce a policy that I first introduced when presiding over a local school board. The simplicity of it was to present for at least three months, in public, a policy that the agency would seek to put in place. Thus, the agency was communicating changes they sought in advance and in public. With public opinion periods at the start and end of each meeting, the public had many opportunities to be heard, and thus the transparency and predictability of the Agency increased.

These small, but substantial, changes led to year three as the year of community. I was always very careful to be certain that people heard the "year of community" and not the "year of the community." I defined community as anyplace where two or more gathered for some common purpose. This was a very focused attempt to see community as more that just those geopolitical boundaries that have traditionally been so engaged in the Adirondack debate. It was my attempt to bring everyone into the discussion. I reminded my listeners that a community might be the Rosary Society, the Cemetery Association, the Lake Sailing Club, or the local chapter of Hadassah. Thus, I had cast the net to another level of participants in the hope that even more thinking would flow into the debate circle. I would try to show that these small communities were in fact a part of larger communities and, as such, were an integral part of the whole.

My outreach was somewhat limited during the winter months, but I did find ski clubs and snowmobile groups very willing to share their thoughts. The church groups were always having gatherings and wonderful suppers. I think I have had more chicken barbeque than any other Adirondacker. The coming of summer brings a resurgence of old groups and new, and I had occasion to visit with many in different areas of the park. This was all part of the plan to cast the net wide and far as we continued to educate and reconcile. If I could encourage individuals and small groups to be involved, then I was confident that the good of the whole would be enhanced. I felt I was gaining in my aspiration to have a very large base involved in the conversations about the park. I was starting to talk with everyone about a "sense of place."

In the boardroom, I was about to try a year-long experiment regarding community. Each month, I would purchase a disposable camera and ask one board member to contribute his or her photos to a "Wall of Pride." I asked that they take pictures of things that they were proud of in the park. I asked that they look at their communities and share them with the public. Again, I reminded them of my definition that community was a gathering of a few people or an idea. The reports to the board each month remained up on the wall, and soon it was evident that the photo essay was to be as varied as all else in the Adirondacks. The most amazing part is that no matter how wonderfully diverse the photo reports were, they were always quite similar.

People have a tendency to pigeonhole the members of the agency into either pro-development or pro-environment groups. To see the diversity grow on the wall of pride was gratifying. Of particular interest to me was the fact that this diversity was within each individual member. The photojournalism presentation from each member showed some of the human-made park as well as the natural park. The members with the "environmental" label were also reflecting upon the wonders of humanity as were the photos of the "pro-development" members. The pictures showed how these could all be compatible and sustained inside the boundaries of the Blue Line. I often saw visitors to our meeting room enjoying this photo montage from all over the park depicting our year of community.

I was able to see many new people engaged in conversations about the park. The spirit of reconciliation and of education had brought new people, and their ideas, to the debate. We were able to talk about this place as a park and to talk about the park effect. Now we were talking about how we could each contribute to the whole, and how, if we see the whole as a park, our actions can only enhance the whole. We were now talking about the community of the Adirondack Park from the perspective of the individual communities to which we all belonged. The goal was to see the value of each other as we contribute to the good of the whole.

The fourth anniversary of my taking the chairmanship was in February 2004. Leadership is not an endless term. I have always felt that the privilege of leadership is earned. Decisions needed to be made on a personal level. I was retired from a very rewarding career in education for ten years and had always had the dream of a trip to Alaska with no time constraints. With the support of my wife, I decided that this would be my last year at the agency. I expressed my desires to the governor's staff, and we all agreed that I would stay on until after the November election.

I was very pleased with these plans as I had no desire to rush away from a position that I was enjoying a great deal. I felt my decision was perfect for me and my family. I was advancing on my sixty-fifth birthday and had not had the best of health. The course was now set, but the execution of that plan was still to be decided. I did not want to be a "lame duck" for ten months. Nor did I want to subject the Adirondacks to the turmoil of having an endless list of favorite sons, or daughters, advance to the governor's office for consideration. The governor needed to focus on the election, and we needed to keep the momentum going for all of the things that were moving forward in the agency.

Thus the year of education would be a wrapping of all we had done so far into one package. Staff would see the benefit of educating and communicating with any community on the issues of the agency and the park. I had long dreamed that the post-secondary institutions that circle the perimeter of our park would see it as a great laboratory in which to place their students for study. I saw no limits to the benefits that would lead to a better understanding of this place. The benefit might be to the participants, but it might spring from the direct participants to many other beneficiaries as well. I envisioned kiosks developed to interpret the local history and also the environment. I envisioned lecture series that would involve local residents and also visitors. All of this could happen and scholarly research could go on concurrently.

During my two visits to the Abruzzo region in Italy, I had focused on the education function of that park. The leaders in Italy had picked themes for different townships and had opened information centers or mini-interpretive centers in a number of towns. I had a vision of similar centers in a number of towns throughout the Adirondacks. Through the energetic leadership shown by Chris Westbrook in the Clifton-Fine area, J. R. Risley in Inlet, and Bill Thomas in North Creek, we had welcomed the openings of three wonderful Adirondack Information Centers. The contents of these centers were researched by the local volunteers, and the themes of the centers were advanced. These centers with kiosks, similar to what we had dedicated on Route 8 in the Town of Ohio and the two Interpretive Centers at Paul Smith's College and in Newcomb, were now all working to fulfill the need of educating ourselves as well as our visitors. So much of what was being done was being done with private money, local funds, and local volunteers. The majority of the contribution from the state was in the form of in-kind help; some monetary assistance was also available, however. Local funds were being advanced in education and advancing the ideals of the gateway principles. We were all examining our relationship to the park and the state Lands that are disbursed throughout.

Our momentum was dealt a blow when the dot-com economy crashed. I was called to Albany to meet with the director of the budget, and I knew what lay ahead. A plan was developed to lead us to a "soft landing" when the economy would slow in its growth. We were all to reduce our budgets by 2 percent each year for the next three years. It was felt that this 6 percent reduction would allow us to offset the loss in revenues as the economy slowed. That was the plan.

The Adirondack Park represents 20 percent of the land mass of the state of New York. The total population of the park is about 135,000 year-round residents, and there are nearly 12,000,000 visitors annually. The park is an integral part of New York State, and all of the decisions made in Albany affect the park. The amount of money for infrastructure, school aid, and local assistance is not only a factor in the more populated areas but in the park as well.

On Tuesday, September 11, 2001, we were reminded of how we were part of a much larger picture. The World Trade Centers were reduced to rubble, and our economy, for which we thought we had a plan, would be in a much more challenged state. We were all reminded that not only what happened in Albany, but also the events of the world, affect our park. The week of the terrorist attacks was the same week as our agency meeting. I received a call from Charlie Fox in Albany. He instructed that we were to convene our meeting and try to proceed as normally as possible. Doug Schelling was there as the designee from Empire State Development, and he brought his son. I asked his ten-year-old son to lead us in the Pledge of Allegiance. I remember being very moved as I saw this young man lead our government in reaffirming our allegiance. This was our youth leading the government officials. This was our hope.

In April of the following year, President Bush would make one of his first trips away from Washington, D.C., since 9/11 and his first trip to the Adirondack Park. My wife Gay and I had an opportunity to visit with the president. President Bush accepted an etching that Gay had made on a fungus from the park. The president admitted that he did not know of this Adirondack folk art form. I had the opportunity to thank the president for the attention that he was bringing to the issues of the Adirondacks in his clear sky initiatives. We spoke of the needs of the Adirondacks and the issue of acid rain. This was a reminder again of how this place, that appears to be so isolated, is really very reliant, and affected, by what the rest of the state, nation, and world are doing.

I feel that there are a number of successes that were a product of this period. I saw local government leaders and others working to educate as well as learn, affirmation that the circle of education was completed. We were not only teaching, we were also learning. I saw many ideas for education growing from the State University of New York (SUNY) system and private schools. The SUNY College of Environmental Science and Forestry, with a campus in the center of the park, was very influential in many educational initiatives. The towns of the park were seeing their place in a different light and were now establishing their relationships to the lands of the state. I also reflect that things had changed because of the economy and the events of 9/11.

My time as leader was drawing to a close. I had not been a lame duck because all parties, my confidants, the governor's office and family had remained silent regarding my retirement. At the close of the October agency meeting, I asked to meet for a minute with the agency board. I told them I would retire after the November meeting and asked that nothing be said. On Election Day, I cast my vote and then went to the post office and sent my request to retire to Governor Pataki. The governor was reelected by a very large margin, so his work with our park would continue. I had been with him during every day of his first two terms, but it was now my time to leave. My last meeting was very emotional for me. Many things were said that were directed to me that should have been directed to the entire team. I had worked with a wonderful agency board, a very dedicated and professional staff, and a constituency of nongovernment organizations, environmental groups, local government, and a population that loved this place in so many different ways. All had come together and had provided me the freedom to do the things that I felt needed to be done. The prism of the park had transformed divergent energies to a single force working for the good of the whole.

PART THREE | *Many Voices, Many Opinions*

# Introduction

*Visions for the Adirondacks and Beyond*

ROSS S. WHALEY

As is clear by now, a major theme of the Adirondack Park story is controversy. Whether it was the creation of the Forest Preserve, the establishment of the Adirondack Park, the protection offered by the New York State Constitution, or the founding of the Adirondack Park Agency, there were detractors who thought that government had overstepped the bounds of what *government of the people, by the people, and for the people* should mean in New York State. At times the acrimony was so deeply felt that the immediate reaction led to more than letters to the editor of newspapers and public demonstrations, but also to threats of violence. While recent debate has been more civil, letters to the editor or critical comments on television are still commonplace, and differences of opinion over the success of this experiment in conservation and development remain strong.

Now that some 120 years have passed since the creation of the Forest Preserve, and the Adirondack Park Agency has been in operation for more than three decades, it is time to reflect back on the Great Conservation Experiment. Did it work or not? What lessons have been learned? What might have been done better? What might be transferable to other areas of the world interested in finding mechanisms for protecting the natural landscape amid communities where people live and work? And ultimately, what does the future hold for the Adirondack ecosystem and its communities?

The reader has already been exposed to some opinions on the success of the conservation experiment. In part two Bob Glennon, for example, is clearly critical that the regulatory mechanism was not restrictive enough, while Richard Lefebvre gives a more optimistic opinion.

This final section of the book continues perspectives and opinions, beginning with three chapters addressing shortcomings and opportunities. Philip Terrie writes on the many shortcomings of the Adirondack Park and its management, with an eye toward the environmental challenges of invasive species, air pollution, and climate change. The voice of David Gibson, long-time executive director of the Association for the Protection of the Adirondacks, gives the perspective of one environmental nongovernmental organization that has been monitoring the protection of the Forest Preserve and compliance with the constitution for decades. Completing this trio of chapters is the voice of Barbara McMartin, one of the most prolific writers about the Adirondack scene, with an edited selection from her book *Perspectives on the Adirondacks*.

The next four chapters give voice to local citizens and organizations who speak out regarding proposals for stronger community development, the need for local governments to strengthen their involvement in planning and regulation in the park, the necessity to grow the economy, and further environmental protection of the park. Their suggestions are not always mutually reinforcing. Priorities for community development are captured in a chapter by ecological economists Jon Erickson and Graham Cox, with ecologists Annie Woods and William Porter, by drawing on a recent survey of the investment priorities of North Country residents and advocacy organizations alike. Chapters by Dean Lefebvre, long-time town supervisor and cofounder of the Adirondack Association of Towns and Villages, and Terry Martino, from the Adirondack North Country Association, then offer their vision for vibrant Adirondack communities and economy from the view of two prominent nongovernmental organizations. Continuing with the theme, Graham Cox of Audubon New York provides a comprehensive view of the history and current agendas of the key environmental groups active in the Adirondacks.

Part three ends with four chapters envisioning different views of a future for the park. Elizabeth Thorndike, longtime APA commissioner and ardent preservationist, shares her thoughts on the future of wilderness. Wildlife ecologist Rainer Brocke proposes a new paradigm for conservation in the Adirondacks, drawing on lessons from his observations of decades of failures in the global conservation arena. The last two chapters give a perspective from afar. From his experience in both the Adirondacks and Alaska, Don Behrend gives his views on the frontier mentality that challenges land-use regulation. He observes that those who live in Alaska and the Adirondacks are there for the same reasons: an appreciation of open space, a desire for employment, and less intrusion by the outside world. He argues that the lesson from Alaska may be that economic forces could trump all noble aspirations. From an international perspective, Amy Vedder and Bill Weber of the Wildlife Conservation Society broaden the scope of comparison further yet, reflecting on the notion of the Adirondacks as a model for conservation efforts worldwide with lessons drawn from what has worked, as well as what has not.

Each of these perspectives are in the voices of those who have experienced living and/or working in the Adirondack Park and feel strongly about its future. Much of the historic criticism of the park stems from it being an institutional model that is contrary to what has been the custom of governmental authority in the United States. The U.S. Constitution vests authority to govern in the states except for those specific items retained as the province of the federal government. The states, in turn, created smaller geographic units of government such as counties and towns and shared responsibilities and authority with them. This is the system that for more than 200 years citizens have grown accustomed to, and thus it seemed right.

The establishment of the Adirondack Park upset this normal pattern. It created a regional entity that would compete with counties, towns, and villages for authority, and in the case of the Adirondack Park Agency vested authority in a governing body appointed by the governor and confirmed by the Senate. That is, it took away some authority that had traditionally belonged to local governmental units and their locally elected officials, and was therefore, controversial. While this redistribution of governmental authority has been challenged, the constitution is clear in a state's right to give or remove authority to smaller units of government. Nevertheless this intervention with the customary resulted in resentment by local government officials and their constituents. This tension was introduced in the chapter by John Penney in part two and is the basis of the chapter by Dean Lefebvre in part three. But was there need for this redistribution of authority?

Two arguments can be presented for the formation of a regional authority to protect ecological and aesthetic integrity. First, counties and town boundaries more often than not bisect ecological units rather than encompass them. That is, these boundaries are more likely to be set by the existence of a river than established to include a watershed. Boundaries of governmental units were established more to ease transportation within a governmental unit than for the protection of the natural resources and environment that transcend governmental units. Second, protection of the environment is often relegated to a higher level of government because the benefits of such protection fall to a larger group of citizens than those who live within or near the geographic boundaries in which the protected environment falls. This is the rationale for establishment of national or state parks, for passing laws such as the National Environmental Policy Act or its state equivalents, or for creating interstate transportation systems. The Adirondack Park was viewed as a statewide resource for the benefit of all the state's citizens and therefore logically became partly the responsibility of state government. The unrest of local governments was certainly understandable, but the logic of creation of the park and its regulation by a state agency was rational.

The strength of the economy as measured by unemployment rates or average incomes of people who reside in the park lags well behind the rest of the state. Searching for an explanation, the regulatory environment created by the Adirondack Park Agency and the abundance of public land is often blamed. In fact, the park mirrors the economy of most rural wildland areas in the United States. Rural incomes and employment have not kept pace with metropolitan areas. Jared Diamond, in his book *Collapse,* described Montana's Bitterroot Valley, but he could be describing a county in the Adirondacks:

> Within the past decade the number of Ravalli County residents in their 50s has increased steeply, but the number in the 30s has actually decreased. Some of the people recently establishing homes in the valley are extremely wealthy . . . but Ravalli County is nevertheless one of the poorest counties in the state of Montana, which in turn is nearly the poorest state in the U.S. Many of the county's residents find that they have to hold two or three jobs even to earn an income at U.S. poverty levels.[1]

Later in the same chapter, Jared again describes Montana in a way that we could substitute the word "Adirondack" for "Montana": "Hence Montana's history consists of attempts to answer the fundamental question of how to make a living in this beautiful, but agriculturally non-competitive land."[2]

The economic growth of urban areas has served as an attractant for young people, resulting in slower population growth or even a decline in population in many rural areas. The seriousness of this problem should not be minimized, but neither should it be blamed here on the existence of the park. Rather, the underlying problems need to be realistically assessed and dealt with. One could reasonably speculate that in the future the economy might prosper. If the principle infrastructure needed for a small business is electronic connectivity with the rest of the world, and if this connectivity is available via satellite, then what better place to move your small business than a place where nature is minimally disturbed, outdoor recreation abounds, and where regulations exist that will assure that the place will be much the same in the future as it is today? That is, the character of the place will be protected rather than joining the ranks of those regions that have lost their unique identity to ubiquitous housing developments and strip malls of chain stores with their ubiquitous sameness and oversized logos that scream for attention.

Similar to a floundering economy, a growing concern for affordable housing is often blamed on the lack of available land for homes because about half of the land within the park is in public ownership, and much of the remainder has limits on the density of dwellings allowed. For the property owner who screamed about government "taking" value from their land through restrictions on the density of development: time has shown that the screamers have done extremely well. The demand for land relative to the supply simply raised the price, and the profits have been good indeed. However, this imbalance between supply and demand is less the product of regulation and more the shortage of land located on water, or in close proximity to outstanding recreation opportunities, or with outstanding views, as evidenced in wild rural areas throughout the United States.

In contrast to those individuals who lament the restrictions on land use and development in the Adirondack Park, there are those who are concerned that existing regulations and recent interpretations of the constitution are inadequate to protect this special place. They cite the amount of development that has occurred rather than the uncontrolled development that was prevented or the development that was improved through the regulatory process. They raise concerns about intrusions from outside the park, such as acid deposition or invasion by exotic species. They worry about possible accommodations to advancing technology that may result in invasion by man-made exotics such as cell towers or wind farms. And they point out wear and tear on the land from over use by recreationists, who individually have little impact but collectively take a toll on natural ecosystems, particularly when they are in large numbers or participate in motorized recreation that depend on snowmobiles, all-terrain vehicles, or personal water craft.

Those who think the park is inadequately protected are right, of course, if their expectations for the park lean toward wilderness alone or if their measure of success is no change at all. And those who think the park has not provided for enough economic activity are right as well, if their expectations are for the Adirondack economy to follow the course of the larger state or national economy. If, on the other hand, the expectation includes both wilderness and active recreation, both residential communities with their supporting businesses and a forest-products industry, then their concerns are debatable.

The complex story of the Adirondack economy and its sustaining ecosystem falls somewhere in between the often contrasting views of preservation and development.[3] Seasonal unemployment in the park is a real and current burden on local lives, but jobs "in-season" are more plentiful than many rural American communities have been able to muster. The tourist industry has grown, but growth has been mainly in low-wage employment. The state government does heavily subsidize the park through jobs, seasonal unemployment benefits, and tax payments on state land, but local tax revenues still fall short of expenses and local economies may be left to bear the burden of nonlocal tourist demands. Adirondack per capita income ranks as the lowest in the state, the percentage of people living below the poverty level is the highest, and the number of active physicians per 1,000 residents is the lowest; but the park region has the highest public recreation acreage per capita, the lowest number of hazardous waste sites in the state, and the lowest number of felony indictments per 10,000 residents.[4]

These contrasting sides of the Adirondack experiment stem from its unique mix of public and private land. There will be continuing debate on how much land should be public and how much private, and how each should be managed and regulated. If the debate is to be encouraged, then the important question is whether there is an adequate forum and whether there is sufficient flexibility in our government institutions to change if that is the will of the residents of the park and is affirmed by the citizens of the state. Past amendments to Article 14 of the state constitution and changes or refinements to the policies and regulations administered by the Adirondack Park

Agency or the Department of Environmental Conservation would suggest that the flexibility does exist to modify the management and regulation of the lands within the park. Is change in these governing policies easy? No, but nor should they be. Laws of the land should be well thought out and changeable only through careful deliberation not the ephemeral will of the moment.

The following chapters will expand the critique of the park and its regulation by those who have been close observers of this experiment. Those looking to borrow from the Adirondack experience will be served well by listening to their voices. As you read the following chapters you will see the tension and complementarities between a prosperous economy and the protection of wildlands. While there are those who blame the rigid regulatory environment for the economic woes of the park, there are also those who lament that the regulations did not go far enough and that we risk losing the special landscape that constitutes the Adirondack Park. As a recipe for sustainable development for other ecosystems, the Adirondack region has a unique history that would be difficult to match, but also an experience with balancing conservation and development that the world needs to hear.

The Adirondack region does not project a vision of sustainability compatible with long-standing goals of the U.S. growth economy.[5] The most often reported socioeconomic conditions of the park economy are not typically held as attractive regional assets. They include government subsidy dependence, low incomes, high unemployment, low-wage jobs, a declining manufacturing base, and inequitable tax burdens. Together with private conservation, these very real limits on economic growth have made wilderness preservation and compatible use in the park possible. Limits on economic growth, particularly when imposed from outside forces, do not sit well with many people. Yet striking a balance between *realistic* human needs and *minimum* environmental protections requires a certain degree of sacrifice in material growth.

Sustainability, however, must not mean "unchanging" or else the unique character of the Adirondacks will surely wither. The region provides an exquisite story of the coevolution of culture, economy, and ecosystem. Studies of coevolving systems are helping to redefine progress, illustrate examples of sustainability, and share valuable lessons from places such as the Adirondacks. The challenge conveyed by the Adirondack experience questions a faith in unfettered growth in material consumption. But the environmental successes have come at the heavy hand of top-down governance. And the economic successes can only be measured in alternative indicators to income and employment growth.

The first one hundred plus years of the Adirondack experiment have been truly unique, shedding some much-needed light on the application of sustainable development at a regional level. Parts one and two of the book have set the stage for the ecological economic evaluation of sustainable development and the Adirondack experience to date; however, the next era of initiatives would seem to be overdue. This final section of the book looks toward this future. Learn from these many voices and opinions.

# 24

## Compromise, Continuity, and Crisis in the Adirondack Park

*Shortcomings and Opportunities in Environmental Protection*

PHILIP G. TERRIE

When Nelson Rockefeller signed the 1973 law approving the Adirondack Park Land Use and Development Plan, he declared, "The Adirondacks are preserved forever."[1] Seven years later, Richard Booth and Ted Hullar, academics writing about the park agency's impact for *Amicus,* the quarterly journal of the Natural Resources Defense Council, maintained, "By any standard the APA act is a major positive accomplishment in regional land use planning and control." They went on to say that the Adirondack Park Land Use and Development Plan provided a "powerful and imaginative tool to control the level of human use" in the park.[2] Were Nelson Rockefeller, Richard Booth, and Ted Hullar right? Had the Adirondacks been preserved "forever?"[3] Not quite. As Booth and Hullar proceeded to acknowledge, the plan was a bundle of compromises from the start, before it even arrived at the New York State Legislature,

This chapter contains material, revised and expanded, originally presented at a conference observing the thirtieth anniversary of the Adirondack Park Agency, Lake Placid, Oct. 3, 2003, and published in *Adirondack Journal of Environmental Studies* (Spring/Summer 2004); it is republished here with permission. A later version of some of the same material appears in the 2008 edition of Terrie, *Contested Terrain,* also published by Syracuse Univ. Press.

where it was further compromised in the battle between environ-mentalists and entrenched interests determined to see as little con-trol as possible imposed on local land use.[4]

The critical question here, of course, is whether the Quiet Rev-olution, the mid-twentieth-century, nationwide movement toward regional zoning, in fact produced the results its advocates hoped for, in the Adirondacks or anywhere else. We know that many states and regions established some form of regional planning. We know that commissions were set up, maps drawn, professional staffs appointed, and budgets approved. We know that regulations and bureaucracies proliferated. But was the sprawl contained? Was open space pro-tected to the extent that environmentalists and other concerned citi-zens anticipated? Did the Quiet Revolution accomplish anything?[5]

In addition to asking whether the Adirondack Park Land Use and Development Plan preserved the Adirondacks "forever," we must also acknowledge the environmental threats that were not on the minds of the plan's advocates in 1973 and that it was never designed to confront. From trail-ripping ATVs to whining jet skis, from invasive species to acid precipitation and global climate change, today's Adirondack region, notwithstanding the protections afforded by regional planning, is subject to a host of environmental assaults. More than at any time in the past, the fate of the Adirondacks lies not—or not solely—in the hands of New Yorkers or their legisla-ture. Rather, the environmental health of this park is increasingly a function of global patterns of commerce and industrialization. The coal-burning power plant in Michigan or Indiana is just as impor-tant to the future of the Adirondacks as a recommendation of the Adirondack Park Agency staff on a housing development, sewage disposal, or Forest Preserve classification.

When the newly established park agency sent the draft of the Adirondack Park Land Use and Development Plan to the legislature, the commissioners knew it would generate heated opposition.[6] They were right. As a result of the legislative tussle, for example, the plan permits over-development of the shorelines, where we have lots of an acre and a half on previously undeveloped lakeshores, often with only 100 feet of shoreline (often casually measured).[7] Where the plan submitted to the legislature recommended—generously, one might say—minimum lot widths of 200 feet in low intensity areas, 250 feet in rural use, and 300 feet for resource management, the plan approved by the legislature and signed by the governor relaxed these to 125 feet for low intensity, 150 feet for rural use, and 200 feet for resource management.[8] On most of the lakeshores that remained relatively undeveloped in 1973, this change has made an enormous difference, and three decades later the saturation point has been reached. Likewise, the rules for setback, on-site sewage disposal, and felling trees allow further deterioration of some of the park's most sensitive areas. Formerly natural shorelines, a three-mile stretch of the west shore of Long Lake for example, are now lined with houses and septic systems.

There are exceptions to the picture of overdeveloped riversides, but whether they will remain undeveloped remains uncertain. For example, in the northwestern Adirondacks, GMO, an investment company specializing in forest management, bought 55,000 acres of prime forestland in St. Lawrence County in 2004, including long stretches of the North Branch of the Grasse River, "one of the great meandering, wild and still undeveloped rivers in the Adirondack Park." GMO has expressed an interest in selling a conservation easement to the state protecting the river. Similarly, parts of the East Branch of the St. Regis River, owned by another investment company, remain undeveloped, while thousands of acres along the North Branch of the Moose River, in the western Adirondacks, are also in good shape.[9] The fate of these and other river and lake shores will do much to determine the future character of the Adirondack Park.

In some popular areas, where the shoreline has been developed about as far as the plan permits, the houses are moving up the slopes. Mountainsides that for generations have presented forested slopes of unbroken green to canoeists, hikers, and motorists are now becoming pockmarked with opulent palaces of ostentation. This has been the case around Lake George, for example, where houses have been built on slopes visible from the lake and nearby peaks. One of the most egregious of these clusters of houses is the Green Harbour development opposite Pilot Knob. These structures violate the spirit of the Adirondack Park Land Use and Development Plan and demonstrate the weaknesses incorporated in it from the start. Similar eyesores can be spotted along the Northway, in Keene Valley, and around the Saranacs and Lake Placid.[10] Recently, in a display of park agency concern over the aesthetic intrusion represented by such houses, the commissioners demanded that a house overlooking Lake Placid, built in violation of the terms of the permit authorizing its construction, be moved and its roofline lowered.[11]

We have areas of sprawl—in Warren County, for example—zones where moderately priced homes in previously undeveloped wood lots are becoming de facto subdivisions, through the cumulative impact of individually approved single-family dwellings constructed year after year.[12] The cumulative impact of developments on a watershed, a forest, or a shoreline is, many observers believe, inadequately addressed by the Adirondack Park Land Use and Development Plan. The cumulative impact of one septic tank after another on an Adirondack pond, especially when on-site sewage disposal occurs in soils unable to handle it, can reach unacceptable dimensions, even though each house is permissible according to the plan's stipulations and may seem to offer little threat to water quality.

As ecologists Barbara Bedford and Eric Preston have pointed out, efforts to measure the impact of development projects on wetlands, among the most sensitive and significant of common ecosystems, have traditionally assessed the impact of individual projects. They suggest that planners need to assess the history of "all projects and activities affecting a particular wetland."[13] Dr. Bedford addressed the Adirondack Park Agency in 1991. Moving from wetlands to open space in general, she succinctly expressed the need to assess cumulative impact: the most difficult sort of impact to assess, she observed, is "nibbling—three acres here, five acres there, a roadbed through here, a transmission line through there, and finally you've got a significant impact." The key to assessment, she further noted, can be presented in relatively simple terms: "The context for decision making in cumulative impact assessment means that you have to characterize your existing resource in terms that are meaningful and determine the historic rates of change in that resource. In other words, what did we have, what have we got, and how fast are we losing it?"[14]

Notwithstanding the concern of Bedford and others, the terms of the Adirondack Park Land Use and Development Plan have militated against considering cumulative impact. In 2000 and 2001, permits for over 1,500 new houses were issued in the Adirondack Park. Of these, only 15 percent needed to receive a permit from the Adirondack Park Agency. This followed a decade—the 1990s—during which over 8,500 new dwellings were authorized throughout the park, most of which did not fall under the purview of the park agency.[15] In three decades, the number of houses inside the Blue Line has increased by 50 percent. The Adirondack Park Land Use and Development Plan addresses projects, not parkwide impact.

At the same time that certain critical lands—chiefly river and lakeshores—have been intensely developed, much of the vast backcountry, millions of acres of forest, remains largely undeveloped. Of the 3.1 million acres of private land, about 2.6 million remain "woods or sparsely settled." About a half million are developed, with about 80,000 homes for 130,000 year-round residents and the same number of seasonal homes.[16] A key element in the story of protecting the backcountry, in addition to Article 14 and the Adirondack Park Land Use and Development Plan, is the use of conservation easements, whereby a private landowner sells to the state or a third party, such as the Nature Conservancy, the development rights on a tract of private land. In an era of rising real property taxes and with an uncertain market for woods products, this practice allows forestlands to keep producing lumber and fiber, thus protecting local jobs; the alternative, before the adoption of the Adirondack Park Land Use and Development Plan and the use of conservation easements, was selling such lands to developers of vacation homes. Easements have proved particularly useful to the efforts of then governor George Pataki to protect open space.[17]

A recent—and a dramatically important—example of the positive features of the conservation easement involves over a quarter million acres of forest and wetlands owned by International Paper and spread across nine Adirondack counties. In April, 2004, Governor Pataki announced that the state had worked out a deal with International Paper to protect, in the words of a reporter for the *New York Times,* "some of the most magnificent landscape in the Adirondacks, a striking blend of wild rivers, hidden lakes and vast stretches of trees—spruce and fir in the northern sections; birch, oak and other hardwoods in the south." Brokered by the Conservation Fund, a not-for-profit, Virginia-based environmental group, the complex arrangement provides that International Paper will continue to harvest woods products through selective cutting and will pay reduced taxes to local governments; the state will make up the difference in tax payments. And the public gains recreation rights.[18] A *Times* editorial deemed the $25 million price for this deal a bargain.[19]

In addition to land protected through easements, for thirty years the state has aggressively secured fee-title acquisitions to enlarge the Forest Preserve; these constitute monumental contributions to the century-long effort to protect forest integrity in the Adirondacks. The Temporary Study Commission made it clear that enlarging the Forest Preserve was high on its agenda, declaring in one of its recommendations (number 27), "Priority should be given to the acquisition of forest preserve land within the Adirondack Park." By the time of the study commission, hopes to enlarge the Forest Preserve, having departed from the dream of owning the whole park, focused on key parcels of environmentally and aesthetically significant forestlands, lake and river shores, and high elevation slopes and summits. In 1972, the state bought the Santanoni Preserve, a 12,500-acre gem of lakes and forests in Essex County, just south of the High Peaks. In 1978, the state acquired just over 9,100 acres in the High Peaks from the Adirondack Mountain Reserve. In 1979, the Adirondack Nature Conservancy helped the state to protect some 15,850 acres of spectacular lakes and forest in the Nehasane tract. In 1982, 5,900 acres of the Wilderness Lakes Tract north of Stillwater passed to state ownership. In 1997 came the purchase from the Whitney family of 15,000 acres in the Town of Long Lake, including the lovely Little Tupper Lake and nine other ponds along with thousands of acres of forest. The following year, again aided by private money, the state worked out an intricate scheme for protecting, via a combination of outright fee acquisition and conservation easements, 139,000 acres owned by the Champion International Corporation. And in 2003, the Open Space Institute orchestrated the sale of critical lands owned by National Lead abutting the southern flank of the High Peaks Wilderness Area.

This is a stunning, and far from complete, list of Forest Preserve acquisitions, accomplished by cooperation between state government, with the involvement of both main political parties and private capital. They remind us that we really have two Adirondacks. The Forest Preserve is getting better and bigger through major additions, and other extensive portions of the backcountry are protected by easements, while significant parts of our private land, subdivided and developed, slowly degrade. This continuing bifurcation of the park perfectly illustrates the fundamental American ambivalence toward nature: we want wilderness and profits, nature and exploitation of nature.[20] In the Forest Preserve we have nature, and on some of the private land we have often unfettered, laissez-faire individualism.

The foregoing discussion of land-use and land-ownership issues, inevitably structured by the difference between public and private Adirondack lands, emphasizes only a certain cluster of environmental concerns. While these are obviously critical, we must also examine other features of environmental health and degradation. With the rapid growth of a second-home culture added to the existence of established villages and towns, for example, water quality throughout the park has increasingly become the focus of environmental concern. Except for localized industrial developments such as tanneries, lumber mills, or mines, the primary threat to Adirondack water has always been untreated or inadequately treated human sewage and other household and business wastewater. Along the region's hundreds of miles of river and lakeshores, most homes and businesses use individual septic systems; many of these were installed decades ago, and effluent is inevitably leaching into otherwise clean water, both surface and ground.

Unlike many states, New York does not currently inspect or otherwise monitor on-site sewage disposal. Even when a town does have a sewage treatment facility, it may not be functioning at an appropriate level. In the summer of 2003, for example, the Town of Wilmington had to close a beach on the Ausable River after inadequately treated sewage from Lake Placid, ten miles upstream, apparently polluted the river. This was the second year in a row for such trouble; in 2002, the same beach was closed for three weeks because of unacceptable levels of fecal coliform and E-coli bacteria.[21]

A recent report from the Residents' Committee to Protect the Adirondacks spells out with precise detail the inadequacies of New York State's regulation of septic systems, finding that New York ranks 33 out of the 50 states in the "regulation and management of onsite wastewater treatment systems." Indeed, New York "has one of the weakest programs in the U. S., devoid of balances commonly used by the great majority of other states to ensure proper siting, design, installation, operation and maintenance" of on-site septic systems. In addition to the obvious problems of the pollution of ground and surface water with the disease-causing constituents of human waste, badly functioning septic systems also release phosphorus and nitrogen into nearby waters.[22] With tens of thousands of aging septic systems, operating without adequate inspection or maintenance, New York faces an environmental crisis; many of these systems line Adirondack lake and river shores.

In March 2004, a bill to regulate on-site sewage disposal throughout the state was introduced in both the Assembly and the Senate. If passed, it would have, among other things, required that all new septic systems be designed by a professional engineer and that they be inspected every five years. Local governments throughout the state objected to the bill. The Hamilton County Board of Supervisors unanimously passed a resolution, declaring "Now, therefore, be it resolved, that the Hamilton County Board of Supervisors does staunchly oppose passage of Assembly Bill (A04080) and Senate Bill (S00887) in their entirety, or in any form, the passage of which would be devastating to the economy of Hamilton County and all of rural New York state."[23]

Further threats to environmental stability and health have appeared. Snowmobiles, for example, have been used for recreation in the Adirondacks since the middle of the twentieth century. Their popularity has steadily increased despite criticism from environmentalists concerning their noise and impact. As early as 1954, the Conservation Department began to prohibit their use on trails and other inappropriate corridors in the Forest Preserve, and in 1968 they were prohibited throughout the Forest Preserve except for designated snowmobile trails. After a decline in snowmobile ownership, snowmobile use spiked dramatically in the 1990s: in the winter of 2000–2001 about 150,000 machines were registered in New York State. This represented a 300 percent increase in a decade. With popularity at an all-time high, with pressure from snowmobile enthusiasts to open up increased mileage of trails in the Adirondacks, but with serious concerns from environmental groups about impact on wildlife and fragile terrain and conflict with quieter forms of recreation, the state found itself facing conflicting demands over how both to protect the Adirondack landscape and to satisfy demands for recreational use of that landscape.[24] When it released a draft plan for planning the future of snowmobile use in the park (in late 2003), environmentalists predicted increased levels of air pollution and degradation of the land as trails are widened and become de facto roads.[25]

The conflict over snowmobiles in the Adirondacks provides a paradigm of a certain type of land-use conflict in the United States today. Local government and business interests see snowmobilers as the answer to chronic winter economic woes and demand bridges and more trails to lure them to their towns, while environmentalists resist such improvements as violations of the open-space spirit of the Forest Preserve.[26] The Adirondack economy is seasonal and highly dependent on warm-weather recreation; an influx of outside cash is sorely needed during cold-weather months. Defenders of the Forest Preserve cite a litany of damage to trails and forest and other environmental harms and suggest that a forest undisturbed by gasoline engines may be even more likely to attract winter tourists.

A further motorized threat to the aesthetic integrity of state land in the Adirondacks comes from the growing incursion of all-terrain vehicles (ATVs) into the Forest Preserve. It is illegal to use an ATV in the parts of the Forest Preserve designated as Wilderness (though this restriction does not prevent some people from violating the law), but much of the remaining Forest Preserve, designated Wild Forest, has been seriously impacted by ATV use. In the 1990s, the DEC opened selected dirt roads to ATV use, and elsewhere ATV drivers have trespassed on roads and trails not officially designated for their use. The result has been degraded roads and bridges, deep ruts and mud pits, roads and trails that become wider and wider as ATV drivers avoid the deepest of the mud holes they have created, noise and pollution, the haphazard creation of new ATV corridors, and vandalism of gates set up to prohibit their passage. Because of the damage they cause, ATVs pose a threat to forest integrity far more severe than that of other off-road vehicles like snowmobiles.[27] In the spring of 2004, the DEC, responding to complaints from New Yorkers concerned about the rising level of damage to trails and forest aesthetics, announced that it would no longer permit ATVs anywhere in the Forest Preserve. This decision involved interpretation of existing law and court rulings and thus did not require legislative action.[28]

On land and in water, invasive plants from outside the Adirondacks, often from outside North America, threaten the stability of Adirondack ecosystems. This problem, a function of increased trade and movement around the world, is a local manifestation, according to biologist Hilary Oles, of a "global ecological crisis." In the United States, only habitat loss poses a greater threat to ecological stability and the maintenance of native biotic communities. According to Oles, program coordinator for the Adirondack Park Invasive Plant Program, the Adirondack region is especially "vulnerable to invasive species," but "there is still opportunity to preserve or restore vast areas of the Park and avoid the costly ecological and economic impacts caused by invasive plants." The key to protecting the Adirondacks from the worst harm from invasives is early detection.[29]

Plants that have hitchhiked to the Adirondacks on boats and boat trailers are clogging Adirondack waters and threatening native species. Some Adirondack lakes and ponds, for example, have become the new home for an especially troublesome species: Eurasian watermilfoil. This aquatic plant, which grows rapidly and is widely disbursed when shredded by boat propellers, has infiltrated lakes across the United States. Once established, it can grow as much as 20 feet above a lake floor, with long, feathery branches that eventually form dense mats on the water's surface.[30]

Unchecked, it can completely occupy calm lakes and ponds, destroying indigenous habitats and disrupting the reproductive and life cycles of native fish and amphibians. On Lake Flower, it has repeatedly clogged the intake pipes for the Saranac Lake hydroelectric station.[31] Lake George has been especially hard hit by this invasive: it has clogged whole bays, interfering with both boat motors and swimmers. Not only are these species disrupting fragile environments, but their very presence is seen by some as just cause for advocating the application of chemical herbicides, the long-range and likely deleterious effects of which—especially on fish, amphibian, and invertebrate life—are little known. In 2002, the park agency denied a permit for the application of the aquatic herbicide SONAR to the waters of Lake George.[32] Whether allowed to spread or controlled with herbicides, Eurasian watermilfoil, which has been found in all twelve Adirondack counties, presents a major threat to Adirondack waters. Other aquatic invasives requiring vigilance include curlyleaf pondweed, fanwort, and water chestnut.[33]

Terrestrial plants—like purple loosestrife, Japanese knotweed, common reed grass, and garlic mustard—present a similar threat on land. These plants have appeared inside the Blue Line; Japanese knotweed is commonly found in the hamlets of the central Adirondacks, including Long Lake, Blue Mountain Lake, Indian Lake, and Tupper Lake. It colonizes areas that have been disturbed by other forces, like logging or blowdown, and is especially a problem on river and lake shores. Garlic mustard thrives on shaded ground and thus could present a serious problem in the wilderness back country. Purple loosestrife and common reed grass threaten Adirondack wetlands.[34]

Emissions of sulfur dioxide and oxides of nitrogen enter the atmosphere, often hundreds of miles away, and end up acidifying Adirondack waters and soils. The result is depleted fish populations and threatened forests. And even though New York State has taken serious steps toward decreasing the acid precipitation attributable to in-state sources and although the federal Clean Air Act Amendments of 1990 led to further reductions in total emissions of sulfur, "we have not observed the large scale improvements in the acidity of Adirondack lakes and streams that we anticipated."[35] The result is continuing threats to fish, amphibians, and insects, even zooplankton and algae. Animals up the food chain—like loons, eagles, and otters—are affected. Forest composition and health are also affected by acid precipitation. Upper elevation spruce-fir forests are highly stressed by acid precipitation, and annual growth is retarded. As noted ecologist Jerry Jenkins observes, "Sugar maple reproduction is almost absent over large areas of the western Adirondacks."[36]

During the period 1998–2000, the ozone levels in Essex County exceeded national standards on eight separate days, which led the American Lung Association to give the county a grade of "D" for air quality, the same grade it gave the Bronx. It is only slightly reassuring to note that Hamilton County, where ozone levels exceeded those standards less often, received a grade of "C."[37] Elevated surface ozone threatens the health of both humans breathing it and trees, which show diminished photosynthetic capacity.[38]

Yet another air-borne pollutant is mercury, sent up Midwestern smokestacks as an unwanted byproduct of burning coal and carried to the Adirondacks by the prevailing winds. Much of the mercury ends up in Adirondack lakes and ponds, especially ponds susceptible to acidification, where bacteria convert it to methylmercury. Then it enters the food chain, builds up in the tissue of fish, and eventually contaminates the creatures that prey on fish; these include eagles, loons, and mink. In any of these animals—and in humans who might also consume the fish—the mercury can lead to neurological disease and even death. The New York State Department of Health has issued advisories for many Adirondack lakes and recommended that anglers limit their consumption of fish to no more than one per month.[39] In 2003, the DOH added Tupper Lake to the list of Adirondack lakes where mercury levels in fish had reached dangerous levels. Tupper Lake anglers were warned to limit their intake of walleye of any size to one meal per month.[40]

The climate of the entire planet is changing, with at least part of the cause attributable to human action, mostly the release of $CO_2$ and other greenhouse gases from the combustion of fossil fuels. The day when politicians and corporate interests could insist that the science on climate change is ambiguous and unreliable is over. The earth's climate is in an indisputable warming phase; what remains uncertain is how fast the planet is warming and what the specific consequences will be for different regions around the world.[41] In the Adirondacks, winters are getting warmer and drier, with less change apparent in the summer; with warmer, drier winters, the portion of the year with reliable snow cover decreases.[42]

With a 5-degree rise in average temperature, many Adirondack tree species will no longer be able to live here, or at least live well. As Jerry Jenkins laments, "We may be the last generation to see spruce-covered mountains or walk through the great spruce-tamarack bogs." Species like sugar maple and yellow birch will still be here but much less widespread; species more suitable to warmer climates, like oaks and hickories, now found only on the Adirondack periphery, will become more widespread.[43] An additional consequence of climate change will be further deterioration of air quality, with increased ozone levels and acid precipitation. The range for the deer tick, which carries Lyme disease, will expand.[44]

In fifty years, will we have Adirondack winters without snow? If so, we will have a dying forest, with most species unable to cope with warmer weather. Eventually, trees from warmer climes will immigrate and occupy the region, but the period of transition will be characterized by death and blight.[45] The animals, birds, and reptiles we cherish today will vanish.

Clearly, despite the manifest (though incomplete) recovery of the forest from the excesses of nineteenth-century logging and the fires that often followed and despite the recent dramatic additions to the Forest Preserve and the added protection of open space through conservation easements, the Adirondack land is reeling from a host of assaults. The efforts of New York State have been generally positive. The combination of the Adirondack Park Land Use and Development Plan, the constitutional protection of the Forest Preserve, and an aggressive campaign to purchase both back country lands and conservation easements has created an island of well-protected open space, although much of the best lake and river shores has been lost. The state is grappling, somewhat hesitantly, with motorized recreation and with pollution from septic systems.

But what the state cannot do—and what threatens the hopes of all who love the Adirondacks—is control the continuing degradation of the planetary environment by twenty-first-century industrial capitalism and global trade. Greenhouse gases, acid precipitation, and the worldwide movement of non-native plants and animals, to name a few pressing concerns, are unintended side effects of the modern global economic system, and they threaten the Adirondacks no less than they do any other part of this deteriorating world. Both the mercury and the Eurasian watermilfoil in Adirondack waters reflect the pervasive reach of the global consumer economy and the failure of a genuine land ethic to spread through a polity sufficiently widespread and powerful to make it a principle guiding human behavior.[46] Unless a global effort to address these and many other problems emerges soon, the next 50 years may see catastrophic change throughout the Adirondacks.

Over the last 30 years, we have often heard about how the Adirondacks could be a model for the world, a place where protected wilderness exists side by side with human culture—in healthy, productive, mutually supportive ways. Much has been accomplished. The Forest Preserve is a treasure. On lands both private and public, forests have substantially recovered, and the reliability of the watershed is no longer in doubt. The essential idea of regional planning, inspired and encouraged by the Quiet Revolution and inscribed in the Adirondack narrative by the legislature more than three decades ago, is now accepted as a permanent feature of Adirondack culture. If former Long Lake supervisor and long-time critic of the Adirondack Park Land Use and Development Plan Tom Bissell can acknowledge that at least some of the agency's efforts to protect open space have been appropriate, as he did in 2003 to a Syracuse reporter, then it looks like the premise of regional planning has reached its critical (in both senses of the word) constituency.[47] And it is crucially important to note that the backers of Ton-Da-Lay and Horizon, examples of massive, large-scale development, proposed but not built in the early 1970s, have not knocked again on the Adirondack door.[48]

There is much to be proud of when we consider the history of the Adirondacks. Thanks to the foresight of the people of New York, acting through their elected representatives (both in the state legislature and at state constitutional conventions), the forests of this region have largely recovered from the abuses of cut-and-run loggers active in the late nineteenth and early twentieth centuries and from a series of cataclysmic fires. Adirondack forests are among the healthiest and best protected in the eastern United States. The waters of many Adirondack rivers and lakes are potable. The regionwide zoning plan that guides development on private land has for three decades been considered a model of progressive land-use planning. A marvelous diversity of wildlife and plants inhabits our forests and waters.

At the same time, however, Adirondack forests, waters, wildlife, and air reflect the profound consequences of human impact: dramatically altered forest communities, overdevelopment, acid precipitation, the loss of native species, invasive plants and animals, lost wetlands and lake shores, and the catastrophic threat of climate change. The Adirondack land is exposed to degrading impacts from near and far, from leaking septic systems and the terrain-scarring effects of ATVs to the pollution released from smokestacks many hundreds, even thousands, of miles away.

# 25

## Renewing Adirondack Park Mission Through an Educational Forest Preserve

*Shortcomings and Opportunities in Wilderness Preservation*

DAVID GIBSON

Alas, said the great Adirondack ecologist and teacher Ed Ketchledge in 1994, "we merely play with the Forest Preserve."[1] Ketchledge was telling his audience that planning and management of our publicly owned "Forever Wild" lands predominantly for recreational pleasures is a historical trend that showed little sign of abatement in 1994. Nor does it in 2009. Managing the Forest Preserve for multiple use—be it hiking, running, racing, snowmobiling, snow grooming, mountain biking, hang gliding, ice climbing, snowboarding, motorized wheel chairing or whatever the next generation of "severe" or "survivor" recreation may be—will erode the Forest Preserve as surely as the great glaciers rounded Adirondack valleys.

Note how often since 2000 public information meetings on Unit Management Plans have devolved into state-sponsored contests among user groups—pitting recreational users against each other for state attention to their particular sport and recreational outlet. Note how rarely in these settings do the state agencies responsible—the Department of Environmental Conservation and Adirondack Park Agency—work in harness to enlighten those in attendance about their common and joint mission under the constitution and Adirondack Park State Land Master Plan (SLMP) to manage the Forest Preserve for educational, ethical, spiritual, and symbolic values.

It is important that we attempt to transcend the 90-year-long dominant "world view" (I date this to the first state bond of 1916 to acquire new lands and to simultaneously produce pamphlets and trail guides to promote their use) and strongly to incorporate into Unit Management Plans a more diversely humanistic as well as eco-centric set of management principles, assessments, measurements and management tools. Viewing lands that have been uniquely pro-tected as Forever Wild since 1895 purely for their recreational or experiential values severely limits their potential to meet the multi-plicity of human and more than human requirements and desires of the twenty-first century.

Ketchledge was advocating for a diversity of educators and edu-cational principles and management objectives to drive a new edu-cational mission for the Forest Preserve. Of course, "Ketch" is one of those rare scientist-educators who have learned to move almost effortlessly between scientific, educational, sociopolitical, and spir-itual realms. Ketch is the last person to decry recreational pleasures on the forests, meadows, summits, and waterways of the Adiron-dacks. Nor do I. But outdoor recreation should be more than a cer-tain modality of movement through space, satisfying our appetites for speed and adventure. It is a critical pathway to greater human sympathy with all life, personal enrichment, and enrichment of the lives of others. And in the world we now inhabit, many people grow up alienated from the wild and from any direct, positive interaction with natural environments around their neighborhoods. Ultimately, the status and quality of parks and protected areas like the Adi-rondacks are most threatened by a populace that lacks the affective emotions and sympathies instilled by direct and positive interaction with the natural environment early in life.

I love fire towers—and fire wardens—for this reason. They remind me of my youth climbing Boarstone Mountain in Maine and the excitement of finding a fire tower and fire warden tend-ing it. Now, in retrospect, I think of the amazing cultural shift we found there on the mountainside that made our storytelling around the campfire those nights in the late 1960s less about ghosts and more about the fire warden living on the flanks of the mountain, whom we had encountered and had actually spoken to that day. Interpreting Adirondack cultural and environmental history from a fire tower would be a dream assignment for me—well, maybe for a week or two. I claim no special toughness for mountaintop living or ridge running.

But I embrace the educational potential of the Forest Preserve and share Ketch's belief that we must do everything we can to encourage it. I equally embrace the State Land Master Plan as the imperfect way that we humans attempt to undertake wildlands management in our time. One can embrace both fire towers—cultural history—and wilderness in the whole Adirondack Park, but to keep these thoughts in mind at one time requires a clearer sense of park mission for education and stewardship than our appointed and elected state officials manifest today.

For instance, our DEC did us all a disservice by shrugging off their responsibilities as Wilderness stewards and recommending that the Adirondack Park Agency reclassify the summit of St. Regis Mountain from Canoe to Historic in order to permit the fire tower there to remain.[2] By so doing, the authors of that draft dismiss the most important values behind Wilderness designation, the symbolic values (Canoe areas are to be managed as Wilderness under the State Land Master Plan). By symbolic values, I mean those values of Wilderness where human presence is not dominant, where humans acknowledge their lack of knowledge to manage or manipulate landscapes. Wilderness was first designated in this nation and in the Adirondack Forest Preserve as places where people are most likely to exercise humility and restraint in their relationship to their environment. In effect, Wilderness values and the exercise of humility and restraint are merely an extension of the ethics we would like to think we display for our fellow human beings. We need to exercise those ethical muscles for our environment as well as in our personal relationships or we will lose them!

Wilderness designation is, then, the active choice of placing humility and restraint in our relations with the environment uppermost in our priorities. Why would we ever do that? Well, on 95 percent of our nation's landscape we do not, and the results on the quality and integrity of our air, biota, atmosphere, soils, ground and surface waters, oceans, and neighborhoods are telling and dramatic, if we have eyes to see.

Maintaining the fire tower in a designated Canoe Wilderness means that DEC values the means necessary to renovate, maintain, and reach that fire tower for all time—helicopters, mechanized tools, vegetative cutting, and mass hiking to a destination—as a higher priority than the symbolic values of Wilderness, places where as Howard Zahniser, the author of the National Wilderness Act, stated, we most keenly feel our interdependence with all life. From St. Regis peak spreads in all directions the scintillating canoe country of the Adirondacks. This Canoe Wilderness deserves to be expanded, not reduced and trammeled by a 90-year-old fixation on recreational destinations that in this case, thanks to a history of forest fire, already afford marvelous views of the mountains and lake country—without a fire tower. One hopes, and groups like the Association for the Protection of the Adirondacks will work to assure, that our Adirondack Park Agency rejects this part of the St. Regis Draft UMP and requires DEC to do what it must: remove the fire tower to a place out of the Canoe Area where it can continue to serve an educational purpose, perhaps at one of the park's Visitor Interpretive Centers.

On the other hand, our DEC acts in the spirit of an educational and interpretive force for the park by participating actively in the restoration and educational use of fire towers such as the Bald Mountain Fire Tower in the Wild Forest above Old Forge and Inlet. As a member of the Adirondack Park Agency told me in January 2006, too many children native to the Fulton Chain of Lakes region have never beat a path up Bald Mountain and have never appreciated what they can learn of their own home place from the fire tower atop that marvelous hogsback hill overlooking the Fulton Chain. That is now changing thanks to the community, including local government, citizens of the area, and the DEC. I am also proud of the work the DEC, local people in Hadley, the Adirondack

Mountain Club, International Paper, Stewart's (a business with convenience stores throughout the park) and other partners have done to restore and interpret the Hadley Mountain fire tower in Hadley, Saratoga County, the tower nearest my home. These pioneers in fire-tower restoration and education recognized that merely restoring the tower was only the first step. Staffing the tower, training that staff to the mountain and its environment, and introducing that trained staff to the hiking public was critical to the goal of furthering an educational Forest Preserve, even for a few weeks or months out of the year.

There is a unity in the Forest Preserve's wild forest lands protected by Article 14, described by the great twentieth-century constitutional watchdog and park wilderness campaigner Paul Schaefer as lands

> over which nature has full reign and man is of little more consequence than the deer, which come to these pure waters from surrounding wooded ridges. For a moment his hand is stayed, as it were, and he neither destroys nor constructs. He has left time behind him . . . for a moment he becomes as a pebble on the beach and before the exquisite beauties and awesome forces of nature submits himself, to a greater or lesser degree, to these ageless things which link him with the dim and distant past.[3]

There is a unity in the Forest Preserve, Schaefer is telling us, a unity that is constitutional and educational and spiritual. It derives from Article 14, Section 1 of the New York State Constitution, which, as we know, did not and does not today distinguish between what we know as Wilderness, Canoe, Primitive, or Wild Forest lands—or even Intensive Use lands. All are part of the Forest Preserve. The State Land Master Plan is the way we humans implement Article 14 on the ground. As Howard Zahniser often asked of New Yorkers, and I paraphrase: you have inherited a magnificent wilderness in law, but can you keep it? His son, Ed Zahniser, challenged all of us in 1997 during a speech at St. Huberts: Wilderness management is Wilderness preservation in your time.

Imperfect it may be, but the State Land Master Plan remains the best legal tool we have for unifying the 2.7 million acres of publicly owned Adirondack wildlands into a coherent management scheme of which other states and nations are envious. While strictly banning public use of motor vehicles in Wilderness, the authors of the State Land Master Plan (SLMP) did everything in their power to authorize higher levels of certain human uses that remain highly regulated or circumscribed, especially for the use of motor vehicles in Wild Forest. While the plan expands recreational access to retained historical structures like fire towers in Wild Forest, it also contains numerous limits to intense recreational demands on the Wild Forest. For instance, take the following SLMP guideline:

> Although the nature of most wild forest areas indicates that potential recreational overuse will not be as serious as in wilderness, primitive and canoe areas, care must nonetheless be taken to avoid overuse, and the basic wilderness guidelines in this respect apply also to wild forest lands. The relatively greater intensity of use allowed by the wild forest guidelines should not be interpreted as permitting or encouraging unlimited or unrestrained use of wild forest areas.[4]

Such conditional treatment of Wild Forest is replete throughout this guiding document. As difficult as the task was in the drafting 37 years ago, it is even more difficult in the interpretation of these guidelines so many years later. That fact notwithstanding, I believe other park managers around the United States value the SLMP's relatively clear guidance for managing human use so as not to damage the park's wild-forest character and its organizing principle—that the protection of the natural resources of these Forever Wild lands is paramount. Discerning and mission-driven policymakers will read and recognize these limits, understand that the basis for the limitations derives from Article 14 of the constitution, and assure this and future generations that we take opportunities to expand our opportunity and receptivity for education in Wild Forest while continuing strictly to contain and regulate our mechanized appetites, not only in designated Wilderness, but throughout the Forest Preserve.

Stephen Woodley, the chief of science for Parks Canada, Canada's version of the U.S. National Park Service, had this to say about mission-centric, unified, and systematic administration of the Adirondack Forest Preserve at a conference in Lake Placid in 2001:

> Why are the planning principles underlying your management targets and indices for a historically unified system, such as the Adirondack Forest Preserve, not made clearer in a master plan that allows each unit plan to address the few exceptions, deviations or special management needs? Do you really want to debate over and over the same planning principles in thirty or forty different unit plans within the Forest Preserve?[5]

As an observer of the region, Woodley sensed that planning for each unit of Forest Preserve varied greatly depending on the planner's background, training, attitudes toward Forever Wild lands, and predilection for interpreting master plan guidelines. He was right. He was also right that managing for ecological integrity demands that the manager target ecological variables and select measurable indexes by which to measure achievement towards those targets. It requires that state land planners erase today's artificial boundaries between large units and allow separate plans to integrate and "speak to each other." None of this is easy. It requires better recruitment, new civil service positions, the best training that money can buy, and new human resource investments in the Adirondack Park. It requires a new sense of park mission.

Efforts at establishing a strong educational mission for the Adirondack region complement initiatives to manage the Forest Preserve as a true system of wildlands. For example, given their illustrious history dating to 1885, the NYS DEC Forest Rangers in the Adirondack Park ought to be at the very nerve center of the park's educational and interpretive program—in addition to the rangers' role in Forest Preserve law enforcement and public safety. The public holds the uniformed forest rangers in great respect, both in the field and in the backcountry. The potential for this group to add to their current emergency-rescue and forest-fire responsibilities is great. With better recruiting, incentives, and encouragement they could grow to become the most respected information dispensers in the entire 6-million-acre park.

Unfortunately, morale among the rangers today is at a very low ebb. Regardless of how good they may be at emergency rescue, public service, and communications in the backcountry, rangers are treated by DEC administrators as the poorest cousins of the law enforcement family. And, hoping for better pay and benefits, rangers have invited such poor treatment by voting to become part of the law-enforcement office of the DEC in the 1990s. However, if their administrators in Albany had any imagination and a better sense of park mission, imagine what could be accomplished by a highly motivated, well compensated cadre of rangers committed to an educational Forest Preserve. Imagine their service not only in the wilderness, but at the edges of our Forest Preserve in hamlets, villages, and community centers helping to orient, inform, educate, and inculcate a receptive, and paying park visitor? After all, the number of people whose Forest Preserve experience is limited to the edges exceeds those who routinely undertake interior hikes by tenfold, or more. Imagine a ranger role in enhancing heritage tourism in Adirondack communities. Imagine their role in recruiting paid assistant rangers from a well-educated and motivated park resident population who may have just graduated from high schools in the park, or Paul Smith's College, the State University of New York at Plattsburgh or Potsdam, the Ranger School at Wanakena, North Country or Adirondack Community Colleges, or St. Lawrence University. Imagine their involvement in parkwide scientific projects, such as a biological inventory.

An equally great educational and interpretive potential exists at the local community level. For example, the Adirondack Curriculum Project is helping teachers throughout the park's school districts to key into teaching tools and techniques that utilize the Adirondacks as a student laboratory. The idea sprang out of a 1998 conference sponsored by the Association for the Protection of the Adirondacks called "The Adirondack Park: An Educational Laboratory" at Paul Smith's College. Small and underfunded as it is, the Curriculum Project is attempting to bring students directly to appreciation of their Adirondack home through creative use of curricula. Area high schools and colleges are also working against the odds to place their students in new Adirondack study and work programs that could make a great difference to their own outlooks and job opportunities in their home region, as well as to park stewardship. Museums and historic locations open to the public (the Natural History Museum in Tupper Lake, the Adirondack Museum in Blue Mountain Lake, and Sagamore Great Camp in Raquette Lake, e.g.) and other non-profits will over the next decade work together to market the park's cultural and natural history to new generations like never before.

Along the way, there will be many setbacks. For instance, I was saddened to learn in 2005 that Inlet's community information and interpretive center had closed for lack of funds. This center was only established a few short years ago in a former service station at the heart of the village. In efforts to attract tourists interested in regional history and heritage, residents had adopted a theme for the center to reflect their waterway heritage, created a fine centerpiece exhibit, and manned the center with volunteers. This and other centers sprang up in the Adirondacks (in North Creek, Star Lake, and perhaps others) thanks to a partnership between town supervisors; nonprofits; then chairman of the APA, Dick Lefebvre; and regional director of the DEC, Stu Buchanan. All were inspired by a cooperative agreement that the park agency and DEC signed with Italy's Abruzzo National Park, Italy's oldest park, in 1997, and its then director, Franco Tassi.

Tassi directed Abruzzo from the late 1960s until early in the twenty-first century. He is a strong believer in "park effect," meaning directing the impact of the park's natural world, its extraordinary wildlife, to "go to work" for the betterment of the Apennine mountain economy and its villages. He went about this in several ways. First, he protected the wildlife with strict laws and regulations for the first time in the park's history and permitted the slow recovery of long-lived species like the Marsican brown bear, the park's symbol. Second, he established village-based interpretive centers utilizing the Apennine wolf, the Marsican brown bear, the lynx, the chamois, and even his own vast insect collection, as interpretive themes that would draw tourists, educate young Italians about the world they share with nature, make linkages to local businesses, and employ local residents. He was justifiably proud of the hundreds of young people that worked in Abruzzo each year helping the small professional staff to greet visitors and implement park effect. Third, he assured villages that embraced park effect and enforced strict protection of wildlife inside the park's borders that they would receive funds from the European Union for deteriorating infrastructure—water, sewer, road, and community improvements. In fact, a few skeptical border villages just outside the park were convinced by Tassi to embrace the park mission and annex themselves within its borders.

In his later years as park director, Tassi toured parks and protected areas around the world preaching park effect and establishing partnerships such as the one with the Adirondacks. In strictly protecting wildlife and placing his personal stamp on the future of the park and this remote Italian region for decades, Tassi made many converts and also many enemies in Rome and among those who would exploit park resources.

Could the Adirondack Park achieve a common vision, mission, and unifying management direction under a single park director for even ten years, much less forty? Even with Article 14, a State Land Master Plan, and a 38-year-old Adirondack Park Agency, park regional directors, APA commissioners, administrators, and policy emphases change with every new governor. The Adirondack Park remains as it was when the APA was first created: highly balkanized, with multiple state agency jurisdictions that divide the park's human as well as natural communities and that implement contradictory policies and practices in just about every area of management. The APA's interpretation of the unifying elements within the State Land

Master Plan, for instance, has historically been implemented very differently by the two DEC regions within the park, and by DEC's Albany headquarters. Expand this fragmented authority to other state agencies such as the Olympic Regional Development Authority and the Departments of State, Transportation, Economic Development, and Health, and the results hurt the park's ecology and economy. The lack of accountability for "mistakes" in the park, and for the double standard whereby the state is allowed to get away with environmental damage that private residents never could, is legendary. The cutting in 2005 of 5,000 so-called hazard trees on Forest Preserve land along State Route 3, a designated scenic highway linking the park's communities of Tupper Lake and Saranac Lake, is just the latest example of the absence of accountable administration and enforcement that springs from ever-fluctuating views of park priorities and mission in the governor's office and at the heads of all state agencies operating in the park.

More than twenty years ago, I attended my first conference in the Adirondacks at the Adirondack Mountain Club's Adirondack Loj in Lake Placid. The conference featured the park's educational work and its potential for a regionwide system of information and interpretation. One of those leaders who envisioned a parkwide interpretive system was Adirondack resident Joan Payne, who, along with Sue Beck of Inlet, founded and led Adirondack Discovery. For 25 years, they pursued the genius of placing interpretive programs and walks in just about every community in the park. The State of New York must build on these initiatives and invest in the Adirondack Park's educational potential. This call for a parkwide system was echoed by Tom Cobb in his report for the Commission on the Adirondacks in the Twenty-First Century.

Ketch's clarion call for an educational park and Forest Preserve can not be realized without a park agency charged with that mission by a state governor and willing to lead. The Commission on the Adirondacks in the Twenty-First Century recommended an Adirondack Park Service be created for this purpose, with a park service director and investments of time, money, personnel, and teamwork with private-sector partners. It was one of their best recommendations, and I cannot help but believe that some governor soon will embrace it as an economic benefit to the region and the inevitable and logical consequence of numerous independent actions throughout the 6-million-acre region.

There will be stumbles and losses as well as gains in this slow, incremental growth of partnerships toward an educational park and Forest Preserve, with attendant benefits for heritage tourism and regional economies. What is needed is acceleration through mission-driven investments of political and financial capital, a new park service with a renewed mission of public *service,* and management of the Adirondack Forest Preserve and key private lands as a system of ecologically important and linked wildlands managed primarily for ecological integrity, with recreation and experiential values in a secondary, but still important, ranking.

If you say this is an impossible dream, an unrealistic vision, I urge you to think about the people you know in the Adirondacks with the potential to contribute toward an educational park, an educational mission for the region. You know them. So do I. They are your neighbors; they are the unemployed or underemployed young or retired person burning with a desire to affect positively the place in which they live, to make a difference in other people's lives and be paid for it, to "build receptivity in the still unlovely human mind," to quote Aldo Leopold. What the Adirondack region needs is their service married with a park service director with vision and political tenure, patience and resources—a Franco Tassi who, over the course of several decades, can instill a sense of renewal in our state agencies and stronger partnerships with the educators and private institutions without which the park can not achieve its potential and would be a much less exciting and vibrant place.

# 26

## The Role of the People in Wilderness Preservation

*Shortcomings and Opportunities in Governance*

BARBARA MCMARTIN

There is no doubt in my mind that support for Article 14 of the New York State Constitution should be paramount and its intent should guide in all we do with respect to the Adirondack Park. But translating the concept of Forever Wild into rules and regulations that reflect all the changes in the modern world has proven very difficult. The environmental groups have been very important in keeping government on track. But for all the activity of the past thirty years, for all the real accomplishments, I believe many mistakes have been made. Further, we are missing a guide for the future.

Naïvely, I once thought that focusing on just how much has been accomplished in the park, how little remains to be done in comparison, would put any discussions of what else is needed in perspective. The battles that are left are not very exciting; they are difficult to characterize, mired in bureaucracies, consumed by details, and lacking an icon around which to generate support. Peter Bauer wrote me, "On some level the park works despite the dysfunctional way it is managed." But we cannot ignore the problems that keep appearing.

This chapter is an edited version of "Final Thoughts," from B. McMartin, *Perspectives on the Adirondacks* (Syracuse: Syracuse Univ. Press, 2002), 341–48, and is reprinted with permission. Barbara McMartin died in 2005.

I asked many of those with whom I talked what they thought would ensure a positive climate for working together in the Adirondacks. Frank Murray was one of the first people I contacted, and he struck a theme I heard over and over: "Dialogue is essential, but I do not see it in the Adirondacks unless sides get together. There are extremes on both sides and if the extremes dominate, they succeed in stopping any action." Roger Dziengeleski worried about the emotional level of the debate in the park. He faulted the different groups whom he believed depend for their existence on generating emotion; "they are monsters to be fed," he said.

I think the solutions are much more subtle, and they involve bringing people together to appreciate what has been done in such a positive and uplifting way that the differences can fade and we can work together to address modern problems. And to that end, civility, humility, and mutual respect, as Liz Thorndike tried to generate, are the foundations of that cooperation.

Are we inevitably reduced to the problem of figuring out how to balance zealots in our democratic society? Polarization persists; admittedly some of it has origins in the extremes of environmentalism as well as in extremes of opposition to governmental regulation.

Why do I believe the environmentalists have been less successful than I think they should have been? In the Adirondacks there is a tremendous overlap of membership among environmental groups. While there is a commonalty of purpose, it is overshadowed by the rhetoric each group expresses in order to stake out a special role in the environmental arena. Certainly that is a way of building constituencies. James C. Dawson has commented that environmentalists have all too often *not* reached out, but have said, "we know what is right." Jim Cooper compared both poles as representatives of a kind of thinking of true believers like the Jesuits—true believers who leave no room for compromise. Environmental thought has become a "secular religion for some people," he says, and it treats every square inch of the Adirondacks as unique.

Mark Dowie, in *Losing Ground,* concludes his analysis of the environmental movement nationally by suggesting that those groups have lost their grassroots touch. That is equally true in the Adirondacks, where a few of these groups are so far from grass roots that they have become bloated, huge, and nonresponsive except to the members of their moneyed constituencies. And money plays a huge role in what they do. Each group strives to be broadly environmental, lest any other group get ahead, but outstandingly different in some respect in order to justify their ever-increasing need for funds.

For most environmental groups any outreach goes as far as a group of sycophants; leadership "talks to the choir." The failure of environmentalists to reach out to groups that do not share their views has far-reaching consequences. How can environmentalists expect to lead if they do not even talk to all the constituents of the park? And, of course this is a two-way street.

Peter Bauer believes that the environmental groups work differently because there is no clear vision of public policy toward the park. They work independently because they have separate interests and goals and varying tactics to achieve them. But their diversity is no excuse for the cacophony of their voices; I believe they would be more successful if they worked toward a common park vision.

When environmental organizations do agree, their joint efforts and press releases are noticed and effective, but another level of cooperation is needed. The different groups have individually focused on a narrow set of problems: Adirondack Council on acid rain, Residents' Committee to Protect the Adirondacks on quality of life, the Association for the Protection of the Adirondacks on the Forest Preserve. No organization, and certainly not a group of them, is exploring the questions of what the park should be like in a way that addresses all the park's components. Adirondack Council and Residents' Committee to Protect the Adirondacks come closest, but Council's preservationist picture does not encompass local concerns, the economy, tourism, or Department of Environmental Conservation's management problems. These organizations do not seem to recognize that it is the sum of their efforts *and* of the many local projects that can define a vision for the park.

The groups tend to react to problems and governmental misdeeds rather than taking a proactive approach to planning. As Peter Bauer has said, the environmentalists are not talking together or with others about the big issues. Why are they not focusing on the big issues? A good part of the reason is that they have had to spend so much time and effort correcting governmental problems such as insufficient legislative appropriations and administrative budgets, DEC's failures to create adequate policies to reflect the State Land Master Plan or to manage the Forest Preserve according to existing policies, Adirondack Park Agency's inability to perform the required oversight with respect to DEC's activities, and DEC's inability to manage itself or lead public participation.

Could an individual or organization lead public dialogue to a vision for the park? Ross Whaley believes that none of the major players of 2000 could do it. "Consensus," he believes, "needs more subtle advocates than today's environmental leaders."

I started out believing real public participation could be the way to arrive at policy, that closed government or closed groups could not bridge the disparate views of the Adirondacks. I became convinced that the openness of the recent past decade has not been successful because it led to fragmentation and the dominance of certain interest groups. I am aware of how challenging it is to create a framework for rational public decisions. Robert Bendick came to believe that "it is very difficult to arrive at a consensus adopting major priorities and let people have a say in the process."[1]

Could an existing government agency play a leadership role in managing public participation? DEC's attempts have been deficient; the department has listened and responded favorably to all sorts of special interest groups. APA's task forces have made the agency's outreach more successful than DEC's. But APA's efforts to update its methods have been narrowly focused and occasionally without adequate follow-through. They have been largely technical responses, operational functions, too swept up in legal details, and generally inadequate for long-range planning. Having all interests represented can't happen at agency level; there is no time. The agency's permitting and enforcement activities have prevented members from engaging in true planning.

Three decades ago, much of the opposition to regulation came about not simply because Adirondackers felt no one was listening, but because they believed that they had no access to government.

The lack of access is symbolized in the repeated calls for Adirondackers to be able to choose representatives to the park agency. The Local Government Review Board, Adirondack Association of Towns and Villages, and others continue raising this symbol, despite current representation by Adirondack residents.

Stories and rumors of special access to the governor's staff or of closed-door negotiations have reawakened a belief that Adirondackers have no access. What they want in representation is really access to higher-ups, to decision-making. That is what most of the groups wanted that sprang up after the Commission on the Adirondacks in the Twenty-First Century. The environmentalists had access all along. The new groups were unable to gain acceptance partly because they were unsophisticated in the ways of politics. The parochialism among residents, which can be attributed to lack of exposure to the larger world, has made groups and individuals seem to harden positions before they understand issues. Those aspects have changed, but the level of access remains unbalanced.

Environmentalists see Adirondack Park Agency representation by Adirondackers as a symbol of losing control—and today the fear of losing control in the environmental movement is so great that no one wants to revisit the State Land Master Plan, despite the fact that the plan is fourteen years beyond its scheduled revision. However, there is much more to their not wanting to update the plan: Environmentalists fear that government will compromise with those asking for widening of snowmobile trails or permitting more motorized access, for instance, just to prevent confrontation.

There are many issues that a revision of the State Land Master Plan ought to address, and these issues will continue to appear: They include what new land to add to the park; numerous new problems concerning easements; proposed long-distance trails and corridor development; questions of snowmobile trail networks; motorboat use in areas that are part private, part wilderness; DEC use of motorized vehicles; and development of real opportunities for the disabled.

The persistent deep-seated distrust points out how easy it would be to rally opposition to almost anything related to the park, and how difficult it is to bring people together. The radicals—the fringes—are quiescent, but there is no middle ground with concerns for the whole park.

The most amazing thing to come out of all the turmoil of the early 1990s is how many of the goals of the Commission on the Adirondacks in the Twenty-First Century have been accomplished, but not necessarily by using the specific recommendations of their 1990 report. The "score card" on achieving recommendations from the Twenty-First Century Commission includes many of those directed at nongovernmental organizations or local governments and only a few of those directed at parts of state government: roads have been improved, tourism outreach is better, sustainable forestry has been included in easement agreements, many towns are renewing local planning, community housing projects have been started, towns are really cleaning up eyesores, Residents' Committee to Protect the Adirondacks and the agency are working on water quality issues, hamlets and villages are building local parks and tourist information centers, education has improved and there is a renewed interest in an Adirondack curriculum. The list of accomplishments is even longer. What is missing is anything that required actions by the legislature and enhanced budgets. These have been the major stumbling blocks. The achievements have come from people working together on a grassroots level.

Another reason for the relative quiet at the end of the century was that many of the groups that sprang up to fight the Twenty-First Century Commission had reason to believe someone was listening. Richard Lefebvre . . . made listening a hallmark of his term as a chairman of Adirondack Park Agency, and he [did] not [respond] inappropriately to special interest groups.

[E]veryone, from APA economist Steve Erman to local businessmen to realtors, noticed the real improvement in the 1990s. Undoubtedly the most significant factor of all was the fact that the nation enjoyed a period of prosperity and growth all through the 1990s, although an improved economy nationally does not necessarily mean the park will prosper proportionately. . . .

In the past, the state economic agencies often seemed to operate in a rarified sphere that failed to appreciate the variety of community offerings within the park. They looked for big projects. Communities looked for handouts, for businesses to drop on their doorsteps.

The synergism of three different events was required to bring about the changes of the 1990s. First, the state had created the Department of Economic Development in 1987 and enlarged its regional office. The state became much more realistic in its economic goals for the park. DED recognized that new large manufacturing operations, even those tied to Adirondack resources, were unlikely. It sought out small businessmen and entrepreneurs by encouraging people who wanted to live in the park. Jean Raymond, Edinburg supervisor, still wished the governor would get as excited about a business that adds two employees in the park as he [did] about two hundred new jobs in the capital region. DED shifted from emphasizing businesses on the fringe of or just outside the park to encouraging them in the park.

Second, many local Industrial Development Authorities (IDAs) appeared or matured and began to promote the beauty and quality of life in the park as the basis of economic development. For many years, the nay-saying of opposition to [the] Adirondack Park Agency, bolstered by a few bad stories repeated over and over, had created a climate in which businesses did not look to the park. It was not any change in regulations that improved the climate in the 1990s, it was the positive promotion of the park's values by local groups. (Essex County now advertises itself as "A Healthy Place to Grow.") The park is seen as an economic asset.

The third positive, according to Erman, is the political climate, more positive for business now under Pataki, much more positive under APA Chairman Lefebvre, who . . . created a more buoyant image for the park. "He has put misperceptions to rest," said Erman. Now the agency has an economic team, not just Erman, to focus on stewardship of the environment and economics.

From big to small, business is slowly growing in and around the park. Bombardier Corporation, producer of subway cars, is an anomalous heavy industry located in Plattsburgh. It has brought in many support businesses to the area. Several businesses have grown within the park simply because their owners want to live there: Lake Placid Industries, Inc. has expanded by producing close-tolerance machinery; Wilt Industries in Lake Pleasant has a specialty business producing machinery for glass production; General Composites of Westport started with ultra-light canoe paddles and expanded from other plastic sports equipment to medical applications. Bed-and-breakfasts have proliferated.

There have been setbacks, the biggest in the Newton Falls area, where Appleton Coated Papers struggled to keep the former Newton Falls Paper Company alive. It closed, and there are no prospects that it will be resuscitated. This happened despite the fact that there are all too few secondary wood products companies, manufacturers of furniture, and the like. Adirondack North Country Association is trying to stimulate this segment of the economy because the resource could support many more than currently exist.

Also helping improve the economic scene is the Adirondack Economic Development Corporation (AEDC), a not-for-profit, started in 1984. Under Ernest Hohmeyer, AEDC has funneled loans to small businesses and entrepreneurs and offered technical assistance. For a time it was an example of a large project that failed, partly because AEDC was trying to do too much, to expand too far, to be everything for everyone, and as a result the organization faltered and lost major funding. It recovered somewhat by becoming smaller and leaner, and in 2001 was focusing on training entrepreneurs.

Such entrepreneurs are dependent on high-speed communications, and making this kind of communications possible while at the same time protecting the resource is going to be a big challenge. Fiber-optic cables are expensive and the region's towns too spread out, so that placing cables along major road corridors or railroad corridors just does not reach enough people to become economically viable.

What I found most encouraging was the fact that the Forest Preserve, with its mountains, lakes, and all kinds of opportunities, was finally considered as part of the economic base of the park. People are at least talking about economic solutions in the context of the park's natural resources.[2]

The Adirondack climate is so outwardly serene that it seems inappropriate to disturb it. Given the extraordinary birth of the Adirondack Forest Preserve and park, it is sad how one of the brightest preservation efforts in the United States descended into such a pandemonium of competing "supporters" near the end of its first century. Translating the governance of the park into modern terms and creating a structure that adapts to future change are necessary but very difficult steps, steps that would be impossible without leadership and public discussion focused on the larger issues.

Much could be accomplished by creating a special region within DEC to oversee the natural resources of the Adirondack Park. The regional structures of DEC, Department of Transportation, and Department of Health need to be recombined so that their boundaries coincide with that of the park. Those needs are obvious. But the way the park suffers within DEC's management has meant that the Forest Preserve has never been integrated into the economy of the region, and I predict it never will be unless DEC's structure and mission are changed.

It would be a monumental leap to go from analyzing the problems to deducing what else ought to be done in the Adirondacks. Besides, concluding specific recommendations seems like putting the cart before the horse. I would like to think for a while on *who* ought to be making recommendations for the future; what kinds of governmental structures are needed so people can be heard; how the public can participate and do so in a way that all voices are heard, yet consensus and action result. Determining who speaks and how they speak and are heard is essential because since 1970 no broad-based forum and no planning agency has addressed the issues affecting the park as a whole. Even when the commissions, task forces, planners, or thinkers have addressed issues, they have failed to move effectively from the general or ideal to be realized to the specifics of how to do it.

Could a new agency play a leadership role? Tom Ulasewicz reminded me of the role of planners in the Rockefeller era. A planning commission or agency for the Adirondacks might work. But it would have to be an independent, long-lasting, ongoing, regularly reinvigorated, charismatically led agency, practiced in civility, open, and responsive to all points of view but not subservient to anyone. An Adirondack planning agency might consist of a small group of planners, based on the Rockefeller Office of Planning Coordination, made up of professionals, people with vision, full-time workers. They would not work in a vacuum, but would regularly consult all sorts of public groups. They would use what they hear to make decisions based on their knowledge and judgment in order to meld opposing views. Three to five people with long, fixed, but rotating terms and a director would suffice, if they were isolated from political whims of the legislature and changing administrations. They would have backgrounds in law, economics, forest resources, recreation planning, and above all in the values of the Forest Preserve. They would be charged with melding public and private lands, local interests and state interests; ensuring that state agencies work together; doing the impossible. Such a separate planning group needs to be independently funded, to be able to draw funds toward the park, and to oversee the work of existing agencies.

They would need a strong leader. Rockefeller focused on environmental responsibility, Pataki on fiscal responsibility. What is needed is a new leader who would be a champion for Forest Preserve and constituent responsibility. With strong leadership and a trained staff, such a group could lead to better government. Perhaps what I have envisioned is really a park service, another layer of government. It would not be an unwarranted addition if all the agencies within the park had regional boundaries that coincided with the park boundary. It would not be an intrusive layer, if it made all existing agencies and private groups more responsive, better able to integrate public participation with bureaucracies.

Experience has shown that reform has rarely made government simpler, more efficient, or effective. That has to be a goal, for Adirondack governance is mired in complexity as this history documents. I admit that there is no guarantee that any new agency can avoid bureaucratic lethargy.

Who will the planning agency listen to? Adirondack North Country Association, environmental groups, statewide concerns, the watchdogs of the Forest Preserve, towns, counties, villages, Local Government Review Board, Adirondack Park Agency, Department of Environmental Conservation, everyone. With someone listening, there will be no need for groups to pontificate because the listeners will be most responsive to constructive ideas. The listeners will define the goals for the park, and participants will need to agree on consensus building.

There will be side benefits: Giving equal footing to all voices before an unbiased planning agency would help dispel social ills, the sense of discrimination, and class divisions, which are felt by some. That should enhance a needed sense of civility among groups. As the summary of the 1990s shows, every conceivable issue has been taken up by some watchdog group. Organizations are specializing more and more. What they are studying is wonderful, but their output must be viewed as pieces of the puzzle that when completed will spell out a way to manage the park for all, to put people in a place of protected natural resources.

To make this work people will have to step back and give proposals for structural change a chance without stumbling over the details. The planning commission will only be as effective as the support it receives from all branches of government. It will take a strong executive to make sure it stays independent and that its recommendations are adopted.

Many of the good ideas that have been developed over the years faltered because they have not reached down to the people they were meant to help. Besides planning, such a planning group must use education so that all groups can encourage their members to adopt common goals. Lots of efforts have generated good ideas, but the next step, keeping them going and bringing them to fruition, is difficult, but not impossible for such a planning group.

The failure for thirty years (1970 to 2001) to include humans in wilderness preservation philosophy has been the source of many governmental shortcomings. Only in the last decade of the twentieth century has concern for people become important. That concern has appeared in numerous small instances but not within the context of a much-needed philosophical discussion of the role of people in wilderness.[3]

# 27

## Public Opinion and Public Representation

*Strategies in Bio-Regional Development*

JON D. ERICKSON, GRAHAM L. COX,
ANNE M. WOODS, AND WILLIAM F. PORTER

Coordination of local, regional, and state policies is largely recognized as a necessary goal to conserve the Adirondack environment, our resource-based economies, and quality of life of our citizenry. Similar efforts in the past have often been deemed "top-down"—with recommendations largely stemming from discussions between representatives of state, regional, and national environmental, industry, and policy groups. These recommendations were then typically presented to local constituencies for "public comment" and "input." However, a common critique was that local interests were not adequately represented at the outset, only as an afterthought of already well-defined agendas. Consequently, the support (or buy-in) of local interests during implementation has often been weak and could serve as a significant barrier to conservation and development in the Adirondacks into the current century.

In this chapter we review the legacy of top-down planning in the park and contrast it with the emergence of recent participatory processes. Research on agenda-setting in the Adirondack North Country and the larger Northern Forest region highlights areas of agreement as well as disconnect between community-level and parkwide or regionwide interests and priorities. This work points to a new era of participatory planning in the Adirondacks and the potential to solve coordination problems brought on by economic and environmental trends that were beyond the grasp of the drafters of now decades-old legislation that defined the Adirondack experiment.

## The Legacy of Top-Down Planning[1]

The modern era of the Adirondack Park began with the enactment of the Adirondack Park Agency Act in 1971. The act established an agency within the executive branch of the state government responsible for zoning and enforcing land uses compatible with public and private interests within the Adirondacks. Although the act resulted in master plans for both public and private land use, it is the private use plan and an accompanying parkwide zoning map that has stirred the most controversy since its inception. With intent to balance preservation and development, this landmark legislation recognized: "the complementary needs of all people of the state for the preservation of the park's resources and open space character and of the park's permanent, seasonal and transient populations for growth and service areas, employment, and a strong economic base, as well."[2]

In practice, however, the local view was largely one of state government protecting the preservation interests of tourist and downstate residents at the expense of local Adirondack residents' economic interests and private rights. For instance, in the large areas classified as Resource Management a 43-acre parcel of land that once could have been subdivided into numerous plots for sale or construction was suddenly limited to just one principal building. Private local landowners' rights were dramatically limited for the sake of the larger social good.

The drafters of the APA Act recognized and partly addressed this conflict between private and public interests through concessions to the local government voice. The APA commissioners consist of the state commissioner of environmental conservation, the state commissioner of commerce, the secretary of state, and eight members appointed by the governor.[3] Among the eight appointees, five must be full-time park residents and three must not be park residents. The act also called for the establishment of an Adirondack Park Local Government Review Board consisting of twelve members, each representing one of the twelve counties fully or partially located within the park. The purpose of the review board was to advise and assist the APA in carrying out "its functions, powers and duties."[4] Most significantly, the APA Act provided for agency review and approval of "any local land use program proposed by a local government and formally submitted by the legislative body of the local government."[5] Approval was subject to meeting a number of criteria, in essence assuring that local programs were at least as strong as APA regulations.

Despite such efforts to flavor the makeup of the APA with some local input, the magnitude of its centralized decision-making authority and power sentenced the agency to tremendous local animosity from its inception. The perception early on was one of outside experts talking down to local people. Appointments to the APA are highly political. The Local Government Review Board has always acted in only a review capacity, with no voting power. Only a handful of Adirondack towns have taken the necessary steps to write and seek APA approval of local comprehensive plans and zoning laws. Those towns interested in superseding APA regulations with their own have argued that the legal and administrative expenses are prohibitive. Local governments were also reluctant to enact their own land-use plans so that they could blame the APA for any controversial decisions. Thus, as much as the APA Act has been an unprecedented story of zoning over 3 million acres of private land, the result has also led to a lesson in polarizing stakeholders.

This polarization was magnified by the active participation of national environmental groups, such as the National Audubon Society and Sierra Club, in designing park policy. Many well-organized, well-funded groups such as the Association for the Protection of the Adirondacks had been involved in park politics throughout the twentieth century. The organizations lobbying against environmental regulations were largely formed in the modern APA era. Groups such as the Adirondack Solidarity Alliance, the League for Adirondack Citizen's Rights, and the Adirondack Minutemen were formed with the sole mission of abolishing the APA. Their tactics were not limited to political discourse. Incidences of personal threats, rock throwing, and spray painting were common among first-generation APA commissioners.

Amid the hostility, and defending numerous legal challenges to their zoning authority, the APA was able to slow property subdivision pressure in the 1970s and 1980s, but the practice of top-down planning left a legacy of distrust in the park that subsequently hampered new top-down plans from the state, most prominently the highly charged 1990 recommendations of the Commission on the Adirondacks in the Twenty-First Century. Following some time for public review and comment, at times witness to violent public outbreaks against the commission's work, the 245 recommendations were released. The backlash from Adirondack property-rights interests was considerable. For instance, a group calling themselves the Adirondack Liberators was formed, whose mission was to write threatening letters anonymously to commission members.[6]

Twenty years after the APA Act was passed, Adirondack citizens and downstate New Yorkers aligned in a collective sentiment that the state had over stepped its bounds in environmental protection. In 1990, for the first time in state history, New York voters failed to pass an environmental bond issue that would have provided the funds for significant additions to the Forest Preserve. Next, legislation based on the Twenty-First Century Commission's recommendations, which passed the Assembly in four consecutive years, was never introduced in the New York State Senate. In 1994, New York's three-term democratic governor, who had created the Twenty-First Century Commission, was defeated by a Republican, pro-business platform with the help of a high voter turnout in the northern New York counties. The dominant top-down planning process in the park was seriously challenged. The regulatory and planning activities of the APA and Department of Environmental Conservation have continued as before, but they have been made much more sensitive to local opinion.

## The Emergence of Participatory Processes

Given the tensions, controversies, and political shake-up that resulted from the top-down protection efforts during the first two decades of the APA, decision makers gradually came to terms with the need for a more open and participatory process to guide the park's future development and conservation strategies. For example, in the wake of the defeat of the 1990 Environmental Bond Act, New York citizens demanded a more clearly defined rationale for land and water conservation needs, and the means and strategies for their obtainment. In response, in 1992 New York produced the first statewide Open Space Conservation Plan with the input of Regional Advisory Committees jointly appointed by the state and local governments. This plan also gave Adirondack local governments veto power over unpopular land acquisition projects using funds from the Environmental Protection Fund and insisted on a "willing seller" provision in the state's actions to conserve land by full fee purchase.

Throughout the remainder of the decade, new approaches to conflict resolution emerged with a decidedly more inclusive, bottom-up approach. Examples included the formation of the Adirondack Association of Towns and Villages in 1992, a vocal nongovernmental organization represented by locally elected town officials.[7] In 1994, the academic and research community formed the Adirondack Research Consortium[8] to promote interdisciplinary research in the region and open dialogue between the information producers (e.g., colleges, universities, nongovernment organizations) and the information users (e.g., state agencies, county and town planners), a process that led in part to the broad collaboration represented in this book. Environmental advocacy groups in the region also began to take a more inclusive approach to conservation, bringing the voices of local development interests, the forest-products industry, and local government to the table. A prime example has been the Oswegatchie Roundtable meetings initiated in 1996 by the Wildlife Conservation Society to identify and implement ecologically and economically sound forest, water, and land management policies and practices, with particular focus on the large, relatively undeveloped northwest corner of the Park.[9]

The most recent example of this more inclusive era of conservation and development planning has been the drafting of the

"Blueprint for the Blue Line" in 2006. This strategic vision for the Adirondacks has been endorsed by dozens of municipal governments, nongovernmental organizations, and both development and conservation interests. Major impetus came from the Adirondack North Country Association, Adirondack Council, Adirondack Association of Towns and Villages, and a commission member of the APA. Topics under the theme environmental quality include air pollution, climate change, and invasive species. Under sustainable communities, the strategies range from land-use planning and main street revitalization to investment in broadband access, affordable housing, water and sewer infrastructure, and regional energy development. And under the theme of governance and policy frameworks the "Blueprint" calls for renewed support for local planning, consolidation of state agency responsibilities into units that better reflect the park boundaries, and broader public input into park management and policy.

These consolatory processes have made great strides toward arriving at broad agreement on general principles amongst diverse interest groups. The final section of this chapter reports on research on agenda-setting at various scales, ranging from town-level, to parkwide, to northeastern United States perspectives. The success of these participatory processes will ultimately depend on the degree of agreement between local priorities and regional representation of the various constituencies in the park and the larger Northern Forest region.

## Top-Down versus Bottom-Up Agenda Setting[10]

Research conducted in 2006 by the University of Vermont and State University of New York College of Environmental Science and Forestry aimed at better understanding the degree to which political agendas were in alignment between community-level interests and representative agents at the park and Northern Forest scale. Focus group and e-mail respondents in the Adirondack Park, Tug Hill, and the three neighboring Northern Forest states were asked to consider the following question: "If new and additional investment funds were available to help stimulate a sustainable economic and environmental future for your community, what investment choices would you make?"

The premise of the overall study was to understand the ideas and priorities of local communities, the Adirondack North Country region of New York State, and the four-state region as the basis of a vision for the economic, social, and environmental well-being of the larger Northern Forest region (stretching from northern New York, across the northernmost counties of Vermont and New Hampshire, and into the state of Maine).

Discussions and the resulting survey were developed in a three-step process. First, a series of meetings was held with each of the New York groups in which ideas and visions for the future of the North Country were developed. Participants were asked to think about their communities a generation from now (about 30 years into the future) and not to concern themselves with existing resources or existing local, state, or federal government programs. Next, a survey was developed based on focus-group discussions. The survey was then mailed to all these participants, with 53 percent of those contacted responding. The survey was also mailed and e-mailed to interested people in the neighboring Northern Forest states, and their results were tabulated separately; this resulted in a 27 percent response rate from these three states.

The focus groups were purposely selected from people active in community leadership, using a snowball method of sampling. The intent was to capture the community-active voice and not necessarily a representative sample of the Adirondack North Country citizenry. The respondents were older (average age of 53) with families, grew up in small towns or rural communities, had lived in their communities for an average of 21 years, and the great majority (80 percent) had a bachelor's degree or higher level of education. As a group, they also had a higher-than-average household income compared to Northern Forest communities overall.

Results strongly suggested that overall the respondents wanted to maintain and nurture a strong rural character as crucial to their future. Among all survey participants, 88 percent agreed that traditional rural values were important, 87 percent agreed that a strong rural identity was an important community quality and that maintaining the community's rural character ranked as a top social and cultural investment project. Survey respondents also rated encouraging a diverse local economy very highly and collectively voiced the opinion that protecting the environment as the basis for improving their quality of life is important. Opinions on the role and future of the forest-products industry in their communities were somewhat mixed. When asked to choose between five types of investment the respondents, across the board, rated physical infrastructure as the top priority, and within that broad category improving telecommunications, electric services, and cell-phone service as most important. Overall, the respondents rated investment in the economy and planning capacity as the second priority, followed by investment in environmental projects, and then investment in people and social and cultural projects.

Although the survey respondents agreed on many issues and priorities, there were some significant disagreements on issues between the three broad groups—namely local communities in New York; the larger group representing multiple communities and specific interest groups in the park (i.e., the "North Country" group); and the respondents in Vermont, New Hampshire, and Maine (i.e., the "Northern Forest" group). There were key differences in opinion, for example, on whether "a generation from now I would like my community to be much the same as it is today." Among the Northern Forest group 56 percent disagreed, 48 percent of the North Country group disagreed, while just 23 percent of the local respondents disagreed. When asked whether year-round tourism should be the main economic engine of their community, overall, respondents were split with 38 percent agreeing, while 39 percent disagreed. However, when broken down, 50 percent of respondents from local communities agreed with the statement, while 33 percent of the North Country group agreed, and only 22 percent from the Northern Forest states agreed. There was a major split in opinions about the role of agriculture in the economy. Within the three-state Northern Forest group, 93 percent of respondents agreed that their community should "promote local agriculture and agricultural-based businesses." The North Country group also supported this statement, with 73 percent of respondents agreeing, but only 47 percent of the respondents from local communities agreed with the statement. Overall, opinions were split about the role of second-home development, but differences between groups emerged when asked about the effects of second-home development on property taxes. When presented with the statement, "second-home development is completely compatible with the character of my community," 38 percent of all respondents agreed and 38 percent disagreed. However, when presented with the statement, "second-home development is largely responsible for the rising property taxes in my community," the majority of the Northern Forest group disagreed (56 percent), while 33 percent of the North Country respondents disagreed, and only 26 percent of the local community respondents disagreed. There were also differences in priorities on the role of chain stores in local economies and improving centralized sewer and water services.

The survey results were presented and discussed at a workshop in Saranac Lake on November 30, 2006, organized by the Adirondack North Country Association (ANCA). The results are discussed in greater detail in the first issue of the 2007 volume of the *Adirondack Journal of Environmental Studies.* Issues that garnered broad consensus and split opinions emerged because the survey provided information on participants' values, preferences, investment priorities, and attitudes toward sustainable futures for their respective communities, all of which resulted from meaningful input from community-active individuals. Consequently, requests for a much broader survey have come from participating organizations and institutions, namely to expand the survey sample base and establish a survey instrument that can be widely applicable to the broader Northern Forest community. Additional requests have surfaced for a project to be initiated that assesses existing local, state, federal, and private programs and resources that address the issues discussed in the survey results and, where needed, suggest new or modified programs that help communities as they envision and strive for a productive and sustainable future. A follow-up study based on random phone surveys across four states was completed in 2008 and is available from the authors.

These two recent efforts at seeking to identify the critical issues facing the Adirondacks from the bottom up are instructive because they show us that residents are beginning to realize that to be effective, they need broader-based organization. The history of reacting to top-down management spawned a large number of advocacy organizations, most never achieving the size and political clout to effect change. The Blueprint meetings show strong recognition of the need to find common ground across a wide spectrum of opinion. Identifying common values that can be supported by many people is the first step, and often the perception of common threats provides the motive. The central issues that appear to garner ready agreement are threats from the outside: acid rain and climate change. Where opinions differ the most are around the issues of local economic development. Here the focus groups suggest that residents are conflicted. Both the Blueprint meetings and the focus groups identify improvement of communication, transportation, and drinking water as high priorities for the future. Both recognize that those improvements will not only improve the daily life of current residents but will also spur economic development. At the same time, they recognize that preservation of the quality of life associated with small, rural communities is important. With economic development comes a critical threat: fundamental change in the rural character they seek to preserve.

With all societal issues, there comes a time when those on the bottom tire of the fighting and lack of action and recognize that the path to a solution to long-standing problems is to take the initiative. They turn inward, organize, marginalize the idealists, and construct a new vision for the future that will capture broad agreement. Astute leaders see the opportunity and emerge to move the vision forward. We may be at that moment in the history of the Adirondack Park.

People are listening to one another and searching for constructive solutions to long-standing issues. If there is a solution to the dilemmas of preserving wilderness and building a quality of life for residents, perhaps active listening is the first step to finding it.

# 28

## The Adirondack Association
## of Towns and Villages

*Strategies in Local Governance*

DEAN LEFEBVRE

Within the Adirondack Park, among the beautiful mountains and along the lakes and rivers, are 103 towns and villages either wholly or partially located within its boundaries. Most of these towns and villages belong to the Adirondack Association of Towns and Villages (AATV). The credibility of the AATV is considered to be second to none. Why? Because it is representative of the residents of the Adirondack Park in that it is the only group made up exclusively of local elected officials, and as such it is the organization that truly represents the people who reside within the Adirondacks.

Many people who live outside the Adirondack Park wonder how the AATV came to be. In 1992, following the demise of the Commission on the Adirondacks in the Twenty-First Century and another failed attempt by Governor Mario Cuomo to pass more restrictive Adirondack legislation, I wrote a guest editorial that first appeared in the *Adirondack Daily Enterprise* of Saranac Lake, New York, and shortly thereafter in the *Plattsburgh Press Republican*. Subsequently it

This chapter is based on an article originally published by D. Lefebvre, "A.A.T.V.—A Definition, a Direction," *Adirondack Journal of Environmental Studies* 1 (1994): 13–19.

was printed in several other newspapers throughout the Adirondack region in an abbreviated form.

The main thrust of my article was that the people of the Adirondacks, we who live here year-round, should become proactive. Actually, I suggested that at first there be regional meetings among the towns and villages of the Adirondacks and from these meetings would come a consensus on various issues of concern to those of us who live here. I also suggested the coming together of the various economic groups from throughout the park to try and develop an overall economic profile of where we are and where we should be headed economically. Shortly after the publication of my guest editorial, I also sent out personal requests to all supervisors and mayors throughout the Adirondacks to see what, if any, interest was there for us to do anything for ourselves.

The response started out slowly, with Supervisor George Canon of Newcomb being the first, followed by others who became the core group to form the AATV, including supervisors Jean Raymond of Edenburg, Jean Olsen of Horicon, Andy Halloran of Minerva, Fred Monroe of Chester, and Maynard Baker of Warrensburg. Without the help of these other supervisors and the many hours they put into this cause, the AATV would not exist to benefit our people. I believe December 12, 1992, will always be remembered as the day when the residents of the Adirondacks decided the time had come to unite and begin speaking with a unified voice. On that date at the Visitors Interpretive Center in Newcomb, the AATV was born. Following the December 12 meeting came the first official delegate meeting, held in Tupper Lake on January 30, 1993. At that time, the bylaws were approved and our officers elected. Also, on January 30, the association debated and passed several resolutions.

The AATV divided the Adirondack Park into five regions at its January 30 meeting. Each of the five regions is represented on the Executive Committee of the AATV by one regional director. The remainder of the executive committee is composed of a president and five directors at large from throughout the Adirondack Park. The total number of elected officials on the executive committee is 11, and they represent a good cross-section of the Adirondacks' elected local officials.

Early on, the AATV passed a number of resolutions that helped to define the direction of the group. One resolution passed by the AATV following four official meetings called for new local APA commissioners to be chosen from regional lists provided by the AATV. The AATV held four regional conventions in four of the five regions. One region, Region A (Clinton and Franklin Counties), did not hold a convention to select nominees for the post of APA commissioner. Commissioner James Frenette of Tupper Lake was from the region and had only shortly beforehand been appointed by the governor and confirmed by the state Senate. Following the four regional conventions, I personally provided to the Governor's Office a list of three people from each of the four regions for a total of twelve potential nominees. Fortunately for the AATV and the people of the Adirondacks, the governor saw fit to select two of our nominees. So, of three new local commissioners nominated by the governor in June 1992, two came from our list—Barbara Sweet of Newcomb and Richard Lefebvre of Caroga Lake. The governor later named Mr. Lefebvre chairman of the APA. Their appointments are something of which I and the entire AATV are proud.

Many people here in the Adirondacks feel that those two appointments are perhaps the most significant changes at the park agency since its inception on behalf of the people who reside here year-round. There was a need for a true local perspective, and it seems as if that may have been accomplished to a degree with the Sweet and Lefebvre appointments, following Frenette a year earlier.

Another association resolution called for state reimbursement of taxes on forestlands under real property tax laws 480 and 480A. This resolution served two purposes. First, it would provide additional and much needed tax revenues to our Adirondack towns, counties, and school districts. Also, the more land that is kept as timberlands that produce forest products, the more our economy is helped through the vast number of local jobs provided. Finally, and of great importance to all of us, is that these lands under 480 and 480A definitely help to maintain the "open space" character of our region. They are in no way harmful to the environment, while acting as a part of our heritage as well as offering lumbering opportunities. Interestingly enough, the environmentalists have a fear of overdevelopment within the Adirondacks. I personally do not believe the environmentalists' fear of overdevelopment to be credible because over half the land in the park is protected from development—3 million acres is in the Forest Preserve, and substantial additional private acreage has conservation easements prohibiting development. The maintenance of large or small tracts of lands as timberlands would also help to eliminate that fear because the landowners would not develop these lands, but would maintain them as a working healthy forest. The simplest way to do this is by having the state reimburse local governments for the lost tax revenue. More lands will be placed under these tax programs by landowners once they know that their municipalities will not lose any of the much-needed tax dollars for which the state would reimburse them.

There is a need for legislation. The legislation that I believe is needed is not the same old type of legislation that has been proposed previously, calling for more land restriction upon the Adirondacks. The first type of legislation that I propose would establish a special fund to provide monies to the Adirondack towns and villages for infrastructure. Infrastructure, which is water and sewer lines as well as roads, is badly needed by many towns and villages throughout the Adirondacks. Infrastructure funding is very important to economic development. What company or business wants to locate where there is no infrastructure in place? Without this much-needed infrastructure it is cost-prohibitive for a company or business to locate within the Adirondacks and create new jobs and an increased tax base.

I believe that this type of legislation should have a wide base of support from all sides in the Adirondack debate because everyone says how important economic development is to our region and to the people who live here. I foresee the bill as something that would provide grants to our Adirondack local governments to provide the needed infrastructure for economic development. The money would be maintained each year at a certain level, and that level would be maintained year after year to allow the various Adirondack towns and villages the advantage of the grant allotment. One must remember that our region is already hindered somewhat more than other areas of our state because of our regional state-implemented zoning, the Adirondack Park Agency. The agency should also support this type of infrastructure grant funding because some of their environmental concerns with regard to development would definitely be diminished if towns and villages here in our region could provide proper sewer and water and the like to its people, not only those who now own homes, but especially where there might be new construction. I would hope that all environmental factions would agree.

The next piece of legislation that would benefit the towns and villages within the Adirondacks should deal specifically with economic development. There is need for a meeting to take place among the various economic development groups. The purpose of the meeting would be to garner a consensus as to exactly what type of economic development would best serve the residents of the Adirondack region. Particular concern should be given to trying to enhance some of our already existing industries such as the forest-products industry.

I would suggest that perhaps manufacturers of wood products be granted certain incentives, whether it be through taxes or outright grants for construction, in return for the guarantee of badly needed new jobs for the Adirondacks. It has never made much sense to me that although we have an abundant supply of raw material (wood), we ship it outside our region to be processed or used in the construction of many wood products.

The Adirondack Economic Development Corporation in Saranac Lake could serve as the overall catalyst in this procedure, setting up the meeting of all the various groups. Although those of you who live outside the Adirondack Park may not fully understand this, again I believe that because of the Adirondack Park Agency, if even by perception only, we lag behind other areas in economic development, and yet we should not. There is a perception of great difficulty in anyone trying to establish any type of economic venture within the Blue Line or park boundaries.

I believe that the AATV should push hard to follow through on my ideas and that the other executive committee members must try to do as I originally intended—put aside what is best only for them or their own towns and look at what is best for the entire region. That was my original premise when I started out, and lately I feel that the AATV has strayed from it. It will not benefit any of us if we become self-centered; it will benefit us all if we work together for the overall economic well-being of the region's people.

The final piece of legislation would provide financial aid to local governments to defray the costs of cleaning up or revitalizing many of the lakes in the Adirondacks. Our beautiful lakes play such an important role—not only from an aesthetic viewpoint, but also as a part of our own socioeconomic benefit. I envision this program as grants made available to the towns and villages that can show a need. I believe that this type of legislation should receive widespread support from all of the various groups involved in the Adirondack debate.

Local government and its leaders are long overdue in asking for these three pieces of legislation. If we can unite behind these types of legislation, we can all benefit greatly not only in the short term but definitely over the long term. We must become proactive and not just criticize or complain about our plight here in the Adirondacks under the APA. We must do something to benefit our area and the people who live here and are often forgotten. For far too long we as a people have not been united, and now with the Adirondack Association of Towns and Villages we have found a very strong and unified voice for the people of the Adirondacks. The association has proven our credibility in Albany, and we should use that to our advantage and the advantage of our area and people. We must remain forward-thinking and positive.

We need to recognize that big changes will be needed if we are to have economic development. The Adirondack Park Agency map needs to be revisited because it has been over 30 years since its creation. Certain areas such as Rural Use (8-acre zoning) should be changed or amended to 3½-acre zoning to allow for a somewhat sustainable growth in tax base, while at the same time not causing any adverse environmental impact. Take into account what I have said earlier about infrastructure and grants, and there would be no negative environmental impact. If you were to divide the total number of residents here in the Adirondacks (130,000) into the number of acres of land (6 million) you would find that it works out to one person (man, woman, or child) for every 46 acres of land. Does that seem as if we are overdeveloped or becoming overcrowded, or endangering the environment?

The Adirondack Park Agency policies also need to be revisited. A good example is a requirement that is placed on landowners who plan to develop some of their land. Although their development plans may meet all APA criteria, the agency often places an undue requirement upon those landowners in the form of asking for a master plan of the future uses of the lands. Why? This is not set forth in any statute of the agency or anywhere else. For the agency to require these master plans is just another method by which to prohibit the development or use of private lands by their owners. If an owner does not submit a master plan, he or she is often refused an original permit for a qualifying plan or subdivision. It is almost a form of blackmail on the part of the APA.

Among the biggest issues facing economic development in the Adirondacks is the ongoing sale of private land to the state. No one should come between a willing seller and a willing buyer. I do, however, feel that in the interest of our area, its people, and our way of life, great concern should be taken by anyone who intends to sell land to the state of New York. Although New York State does pay property taxes on lands it owns within the Adirondacks, there is no guarantee that it will continue forever. Until there is a guarantee on the permanent payment of taxes, all towns and their residents should have a concern. What would happen to certain towns if the state stopped paying taxes on the lands it already owns? Some towns would go bankrupt. This is an issue that the AATV has addressed in one of our resolutions. Resolution number 3 of 1994 calls for the Amendment of Real Property Tax Law Section 532 to add a new subsection (h), which would read as follows:

> 532 (h) No law repealing subsection (a) here of shall be effective unless enacted by the legislature at two successive regular sessions by a two-thirds vote of the Senate and the Assembly.

Resolution 3 of 1994 also supports the Amendment of Article 7 of the New York State Constitution to provide a new additional Section 20:

> The State Budget shall include the amount necessary to pay the real property taxes on wild or forest lands owned by the state within the forest preserve.

Any timberland owner, whether owners of large or small parcels, should consider selling only the development rights if any rights at all. Further, if they decide to sell these development rights, then they should consider selling them not in perpetuity, but in blocks of perhaps 15 or 20 years. My reasoning is simple: no one knows what the future holds or what value those same lands may have 15 or 20 years from now. It also keeps the landowner somewhat in control over these lands, not only from an economic standpoint—that is to say that the value of those development rights will or should increase—but also the development itself of the property. Environmentalists fear overdevelopment. That is why the purchase of development rights only makes sense and seems logical. If this approach is taken, then there could be less animosity among all parties. This would then be a win-win situation, since the landowner would gain much-needed revenue to help offset the expense of maintaining the land, and the open space character for which some seem so concerned would also be guaranteed for a time.

I believe that the AATV could act as a vehicle to help bring about a meeting between the state and various owners of crucial pieces of Adirondack forestlands. The purpose of the meeting would be to discuss the proposed idea of selling only the development rights to these properties for a specified amount of time, since none have a crystal ball to see what the future might have in store.

How much is enough? As stated previously, the state of New York owns approximately 50 percent of the 6 million acres known as the Adirondack Park. Why does anyone own land? What purpose is served by the state owning approximately 3 million acres here in our Adirondack region? Is it for the public good, or is it as Theodore Roosevelt once said, "so we would have a future timber resource"? I am not sure, but I do believe the time has come for the state of New York to take a look at the management policy of its forestlands here in the Adirondacks. I believe that the state should talk to some of its own foresters at the Department of Environmental Conservation (DEC) and see if they do not agree that maybe the time has come to consider some timber harvesting of specific sections of the Adirondack state forestlands. Why? Because as with any forest, timber harvesting creates new growth, which in turn revitalizes the forest, both environmentally and with regard to habitat and wildlife.

As any environmentalist may know, new young trees are actually more beneficial to our environment than are the much larger, older ones. Young trees definitely give off more oxygen than older trees, which would serve to benefit us all. Also, I believe that there would be more wildlife on the state lands than there has been for some time because new growth means more food and timber harvesting produces better habitats for many varied kinds of wildlife. For example, I believe that hunting would improve on state forestlands, and that is another benefit for the many hunters who cannot hunt the private lands, where there is definitely more game to hunt. Why? Because good forestry management has provided the necessary food and habitat to sustain wildlife.

I propose that the state should seek support of a constitutional amendment that, if presented properly, would allow them to timber harvest its Adirondack lands. The project as I see it would involve the DEC and foresters from the SUNY College of Environmental Science and Forestry. It would be a very selective program, with perhaps only certain areas to be cut each year over a five-year period or longer. The trees to be cut would be selected by the foresters and hauled out by horses rather than machines so as not to unduly impact the environment.

The entire program could be considered as part of a course of study for the forestry students. It should not merely be looked at as a teaching experience, nor should it be looked at as a money maker. However, that is not to say that the state could not realize some economic benefit. The true long-lasting benefit would be that some state forestlands would be revitalized with new growth and more wildlife. What better benefit for our future generations than to know that there would always be growing vital state forestlands with an abundance of wildlife for them to enjoy? We should not sit by and watch much of our state forestlands here in the Adirondacks go to ruin. Once again, all sides should see that this type of very selective timber harvesting is to the benefit of all and should support such a measure. I believe that only the most extreme environmental groups would oppose this type of state-supervised timber harvesting.

We need to be realistic about what is best for the people of the Adirondacks. People, no matter how easy-going, will only be pushed aside and ignored for so long. Then they will make themselves heard. Some of us wonder if the 130,000 year-round residents are not in some way being discriminated against. Think about it for a moment. No other people in the state fall under state-mandated zoning regulations. Do you think this type of policy could exist anywhere else in the state to the degree it exists here? I think not. So, you can understand how people who believe so much in their country and state can question why their own private lands can be regulated by the state, unlike anywhere else. We, as Adirondack residents, need to know that we have not been overlooked when people outside the Adirondacks discuss the park's future. When the Adirondacks are discussed, it is the mountains, lakes, and rivers, and how important and valuable they are to all. Far too often the people are forgotten among those beautiful mountains, lakes, and rivers.

# 29

## The Adirondack North Country Association
*Strategies in Economic Development*

TERRY DEFRANCO MARTINO

In 1992 the Adirondack Park Centennial was a historic footnote to a century of an Adirondack Park experience that played tribute to "a place of people and natural wonder." The understanding of the Adirondack Park as a special place was often limited to the park as an "experiment" in land conservation and economic and community life. For Adirondackers the experiment can be viewed through the lens of organizations that have been on the front lines of addressing public policy, advocacy, the role of government, and citizen involvement. From the beginning the message has been recognition of how people and their actions are vital to the definition of what is special.

One organization in particular provides a perspective on the coexistence of community needs and human aspirations about "place" within a natural environment that is noted for its specialness. This organization is known today as the Adirondack North Country Association, and was known through its formative years as the Adirondack Park Association. The 55-year history, beginning in 1954, provides insights into how people thought about their home communities, their relationship to the land, and their reactions to the development of an Adirondack Park Study Commission, Adirondack Park Agency, and private and public land-use plans.

As people settled throughout the Adirondacks and lived in the various hamlets, towns, and villages, they did what people do everywhere in community—discuss the meaning of their lives in community while exploring questions of how to work collectively to improve their social and economic standing. In the mid–twentieth century the Adirondack North Country Association grew from these beginnings and represented a voice of people who came together on a snowy day in Tupper Lake, New York, in December 1953. During the initial organizational meeting, 60 representatives from through-out the Adirondack Park met at the old Iroquois Hotel to discuss the need for an "Adirondack Development Commission." In December of the same year, they met again with more than 100 representatives from throughout the Adirondack Park who were unanimous in their opinion that "the region can develop its true potential only through cooperation." They agreed to refer to their efforts as an "Adirondack Association."

On May 5, 1954, the founding meeting for the Adirondack Association was held in Lake Placid, with more than 300 Adirondack citizens attending. Participants agreed "to unite the communities within the blue line of the Park, and other nearby communities to foster, to protect, and to publicize in every way the recreational, commercial, industrial and civic interests beneficial to the territory defined." Following the meeting, the May 25, 1954, press release noted that:

> high priority was given to the problem of improving highways in the area. Among the other objectives are better publicity for the entire area, to promote the establishment of industries in those communities which desire them, in order to establish a more sta-ble economy; to work with railroads, air lines, bus lines and others to provide adequate means of travel; to represent the Adirondack people before governing bodies and policy-making groups; to encourage ethical standards for the conduct of recreational, busi-ness and other industries; to study surveys and zoning plans to make highways and villages more attractive; and to maintain and conserve the outstanding natural resources of the Adirondacks, including forest, water, fish and game.[1]

A 17-member Executive Committee was established that included representation from the entire Adirondack Park region. Members followed up with incorporation as the Adirondack Park Association (APA). The early beginnings provided the organizational capacity and depth to respond to a wide range of issues and opportunities that affected the Adirondack Park region and members conducted an early survey of "Adirondack resources and needs." The original leaders of the association, most prominently Roy Higby and Roger Tubby, the group's first president and secretary, respectively, addressed questions such as: How to conserve what is important about our land base? What are the steps we can take to ensure positive gains in both areas? How do we work toward balance?

Tubby brought a vision to the North Country from years of national and international work. Credited in the mid-1980s by the board of directors as the founding director of the association, Tubby had a long and illustrious career. After serving as press secretary to President Harry S. Truman in the early 1950s, Tubby first moved to the Adirondack region in 1953 and settled in Saranac Lake with his wife and family. Shortly thereafter he became copublisher with Jim Loeb of the *Adirondack Daily Enterprise*. A graduate of Yale University, Tubby soon became an avid spokesperson for the Adirondack region. His love of the Adirondacks translated into a broad spectrum of thought about how people could work collectively to address adversity and build community.

Tubby's vision for the association was during a time of social change for his beloved Saranac Lake community. The advent of antibiotics had a direct impact on Saranac Lake's ability to market itself as a healing place for people seeking a tuberculosis cure. In a December 1954 editorial in the *Adirondack Daily Enterprise*, Tubby addressed the need for "Lifting Ourselves Up by Our Bootstraps." He commented that the "Trudeau Sanatorium discharges its last patient tomorrow. What its closing will mean to Saranac Lake will become apparent as the weeks and months go by. . . . Take a big payroll out of town and it hurts nearly everybody." Through the experience of economic change, Tubby saw a vision for the community's economic future. He wrote, "One way we can do this is to boost our town and our area as an ideal place in which to work, live and play. We need a far bigger job of promotion than ever before. We need to cooperate with other Adirondack communities because we cannot afford to do an effective job alone." Within cooperation Tubby saw the potential for economic renewal. He noted,

> We need to cooperate with them not only on promotion and advertising in metropolitan papers and national magazines, but we need to cooperate with them also in working for better roads and in stimulating better conditions for businesses, for the sportsman and for recreation generally. We can cooperate with other Adirondack towns through the Adirondack Park Association which was founded last May and which includes representatives from 32 towns and 17 villages of more than 500 population.[2]

It is striking to see the early focus Tubby and the association had on a regional approach to the North Country community and the need for people to be advocates and directly involved in planning their future. The emphasis on collaborative decision making and local dialogue was tested early on in the association's response to the potential for an Adirondack National Park in 1968. The association members, like many of the North Country citizens, were suspicious of federal involvement and control of the Adirondack Park region. This suspicion of federal involvement in the Adirondack Park mirrored the concerns of local citizens and elected representatives. The interplay of local involvement and the role of local government in land-use planning versus outside influences, public policy, and legislative actions was a strong calling card for the association members. So, the Association's membership opposed the proposed Adirondack National Park.

From its beginning the association was a voice for local involvement. Members were directly involved in a wide range of issues including work for the completion of the Adirondack Northway and promotion of the region's scenic roads through publications such as "Off the Beaten Path." In October 1964 the association's Special

Committee on Adirondack Home Rule met with legislators and prepared a report for the membership and legislators that advocated the board's "stand in favor of Home Rule rather than an Adirondack Park Commission." They reported, "A Commission is unnecessary; its work would be a duplication of various State agencies and a needless expense to the taxpayer."[3] During this period members worked for the maintenance and restoration of the Remsen–Lake Placid Rail Corridor, addressed legislative initiatives, and worked through committees such as Environmental Quality, Conservation, Industrial Development, Historic Sites, Legislative, Publicity, Roads and Highways, and Recreational Development.

The early 1970s was a time for reflecting upon the association's regional approach while also responding to discussions about the future of the Adirondack Park and land-use controls. In his report to the Conservation Committee, Chairman Lilbern Yandon said,

> Most of our activity during 1971 was due to our interest in the Adirondack Study Commission's report on *The Future of the Adirondacks*. Because of the amount of material and recommendations that were involved in the study, the Adirondack Park Association directors voted for a one-year delay in the implementation of the report until the people were made more familiar with it. However, this did not happen and the Agency Bill was passed by the Legislature. The Adirondack Park Agency Act did contain amendments, however, [that] gave some benefit to the landowners and the permanent residents of the Park.

Yandon goes on to state,

> As a result of the [legislation], many towns in the Adirondack Park passed zoning and sub-division regulations. During the period when the proponents of the Agency Bill were discussing its merits, they did state that zoning and sub-division regulations would be good, however now they are being highly critical of those regulations and are discussing the hope that they can have them declared illegal by court or other action. This again

only demonstrates the desire, at higher levels of government, for complete control of the Adirondack Park. Likewise it brings into question their sincerity of wishing local government to participate in local land controls.[4]

It is interesting how the suspicions of federal involvement in the region had come to be concerns about state initiatives.

Throughout the early 1970s, the association worked through its legislative (watchdog) committee to provide input on a variety of bills that were presented during the year. The association sponsored a yearly Adirondack legislators' luncheon during which they honored the North Country legislators. Members and friends were invited to the event. Minutes from 1972 documented their attention to the legislation addressing the work of the Adirondack Park Agency:

> The Adirondack Park Agency will be introducing some important legislation during the pre-file period this year in accordance with Section 805 of the Adirondack Park Agency Act, which states in part: "On or before January first, nineteen hundred seventy-three, the agency, in cooperation and consultation with local governments, shall prepare and submit to the governor and legislature for adoption or modification, in whole or in part, a land use and development plan applicable to the entire area of the Adirondack Park, etc."[5]

The association's 1972 minutes went on to state, "It is very important that members of this organization and local government work closely with the Adirondack Park Agency to insure the legislation introduced will be in the best interest of the people of the Adirondack Park Area."

By September 1973 the president of the association, Paul Stapley, commented in his annual report that the association's members worked unsuccessfully to secure a delay in the park agency legislation and "had hoped for changes and modifications to improve the effectiveness of the Agency and to make for workable controls at the Town level of government." His report also stated that "The

Agency legislation has been passed and the controversy is now history." He mentioned that a committee had been established to consult with the agency following the request of agency chairman Richard Lawrence, Jr.

As time went on, there was a continued focus on how the association could work with the agency. At the annual meeting of the Adirondack Park Association in 1974, board president Nat Oppenheim provided a perspective on the relationship of the association to the agency:

> The Adirondack Park Agency is a fact of life. Your Association maintains an excellent liaison with its Chairman, Mr. Richard Q. Lawrence, Jr. and other members. Our Liaison Committee has been very responsive to our membership's need and wishes in their relationship with the Agency, and makes every effort to present a protective viewpoint. Be assured they will continue to do so.[6]

By October 1975, President Oppenheim commented during the annual meeting, "The Adirondack Park Association has just completed two decades of existence. It has weathered assaults from all areas in defense and protection of the Adirondack Park." He pointed out that areas of activity included work as an "umbrella organization" involved with a broad agenda including: comments to the Army Corps of Engineers over the jurisdiction of New York State waters, especially in the Lake George area; continued work for a state-controlled barge canal system to prevent a takeover by the federal government; voiced concern over the U.S. Air Force's low-altitude training; and worked to ensure the tracks would not be pulled up in the Remsen–Lake Placid rail route of the Penn Central.

By the following year, in October 1976, Oppenheim stated publicly in his annual report that the confusion between the initials of the two organizations—the Adirondack Park Agency and the Adirondack Park Association—had become a problem. He stated, "After twenty-four years of being known for our accomplishments throughout the Adirondacks, the initials of our Association through no fault of ours have become an abomination. Therefore to exist and to continue to grow, we must change our name so that all 'North Country People' can identify with us and we can continue to function effectively."[7] Following his comments the membership voted to change the name of the association, but as Grace Hudowalski pointed out in her 1977 report, the "directors decided to continue with our time-honored name and refer to the Adirondack Park Association as the 'Association.'"[8] It was the same year that newly elected president Paul Meader stated, "Our limited funds are overcome by tremendous People Power." Questions about the association's name continued through the remainder of the decade with an ongoing commitment to doing the "people work" that Meader referenced. In the early 1980s, they referred to themselves as the Adirondack Association.

The early to mid-1980s saw tremendous change in the association. In 1983 the Adirondack Park Association, Inc., filed a certificate with the New York Department of State to change the organization's name to the Adirondack North Country Association, Incorporated (ANCA)—the name that continues to the present. In 1985 ANCA received its status as a not-for-profit 501(c)3 organization. In 1985 the first executive director was hired—Robert Quinn of Sackets Harbor. It was during that time that the members and board effectively lobbied the state legislature for New York State funding. A member item commitment of $500,000, combined with a Department of State grant for crafts marketing, resulted in ANCA having a state-supported operating budget for the first time in the organization's history. Program work began in agriculture and crafts development, including the association's opening of the Adirondack North Country Craft Center Store in Lake Placid in August 1986 with forty participating businesses.

The mid-1980s through early 1990s were a flurry of activity for the association. Within a span of five years, 1986 to 1991, ANCA managed a total of $4.4 million in New York State funding made available as member appropriations through the leadership of Senator Ronald Stafford and the North Country legislative delegation. During this period core program areas included Agriculture, Enterprise and Community Development, Natural Resources, Services and Culture, and Tourism. ANCA staff developed an annual grant application process and solicited applications from throughout the North Country to develop projects that supported ANCA's program and regional economic development goals. ANCA administered funding for hundreds of program initiatives with organizations such as the Adirondack Economic Development Corporation (graduated loan investment fund and marketing); Adirondack Mountain Club (backcountry trail maintenance); Black River RC&D and Greater Adirondack RC&D (wood-products marketing and development); High Peaks Hospice (certificate of need application); Adirondack Scenic Railroad (economic assessment and feasibility study of the Adirondack corridor); Adirondack North Country Crafts Center Store (crafts retail business marketing); Empire State Forest Products Association (wood-products marketing); Jackrabbit Ski Trail (trail improvements); Pendragon Theatre (seating expansion); and Adirondack Farmer's Market (tents and marketing), among others.

In 1991, the association was confronted once again with a study and a follow-up legislative initiative based on the work of the state's Commission on the Adirondacks in the Twenty-First Century. Following Tom Tobin's five-year record as executive director, I was appointed executive director in September after five years of directing ANCA's program activities. I worked with then president Dan Palm and the board to invite Governor Mario Cuomo to ANCA's fall annual meeting. The governor's presentation at ANCA's meeting provided an interesting footnote to the six-year record the association had developed in providing economic development services and programs in a partnership with New York State. Following the strong and negative response to the Twenty-First Century Report that he had called for, the governor used the meeting to speak directly about the future he envisioned for the Adirondacks. At the meeting he stated, "Our obligation is to preserve our commitment to the Adirondack region as a unique, natural treasure, and as the home of 130,000 New Yorkers. In recognition of this responsibility, nearly three years ago I asked my Advisory Committee on the Adirondack Park in the Twenty-first Century to evaluate the effectiveness of current state policies." He went on to discuss the reactions to the report, the ensuing controversies, and his outreach to local government officials in Plattsburgh in 1990. He presented the overarching Adirondack issues with which he believed the commission members had wrestled: "How can we best preserve both public and private lands of the magnificent region that we call the Adirondacks for future generations? And, at the same time, provide the 130,000 residents of the Park a useful and fair voice in determining their own future? Now there are obviously competing interests."

Governor Cuomo discussed his desire "to reconcile our needs and our desires reasonably and fairly, if not perfectly." He presented a proposal to have more local representatives on the Adirondack Park Agency with more dialogue with government in Albany. In addition he presented what some saw as the "economic carrot" when he stated, "Adirondackers will have more influence over their own economic future through an Adirondack North Country Authority." He described the authority as a public benefit corporation that would be responsible for a number of development projects in areas he described as, "industrial and commercial facilities farming, tourism, commercial forestry, secondary wood products manufacturing and community facilities." He charged the authority "with developing a comprehensive economic development plan which on adoption will guide Adirondack Park Agency's decision making." He also said the authority will administer what he called an "Adirondack Economic Opportunity Zones Program."

At ANCA's annual meeting, the governor concluded his presentation by stating,

> To sum up, this is the Adirondack covenant I propose very briefly. The most critical of the private lands to the Park, rural use and resource management lands as well as critical environmental areas will be protected by an agency on which Adirondackers have a real voice and the state will assist the local Adirondack North Country Authority in promoting appropriate economic development in appropriate parts of the Adirondacks in every way we can.

While ANCA staff had been involved in discussions with the governor's staff about the need for regional economic planning, the role of the authority and its relationship to ANCA were discussed in the early part of 1991 prior to the release of the legislative package. There was the potential for the association to be the not-for-profit that would take on many of the program activities that would not be directed by the authority, but the lines of communication and organizational responsibilities were not defined.

Prior to the October 1991 release of the Adirondack Park legislation, correspondence from the Department of Economic Development in January 1991 proposed a restructuring of ANCA as a regional economic development entity for the Adirondack Park. On January 10, 1991, Dr. Dan Palm, ANCA board president, attended the Adirondack Planning Commission meeting to discuss the department's proposal. He had two questions in his discussion with local representatives: (1) Were they in favor of such an entity? and (2) Should ANCA be that entity? In calling a special meeting of the ANCA Board of Directors for January 25, 1991, Palm noted that the "Commission passed a resolution supporting ANCA as the entity and requesting that ANCA proceed to explore the subject with NYS representatives." He pointed out that discussions with the governor's staff led him to believe the proposal was serious.

The association members certainly saw the potential confusion of their name, once again, with a potential new state agency—the Adirondack North Country Authority that was planned as a public benefit corporation "to serve as the regional catalyst and support arm for economic development within the Blue Line." On a regional level there continued to be concern about a top-down strategy to define and support economic development and comprehensive planning, particularly when the economic plan would have to be submitted to the Adirondack Park Agency for review to see if the economic planning was consistent with the Adirondack Park Land Use and Development Plan. Following the release of the governor's legislative package at the ANCA annual meeting, coupled with long-standing concerns about the Twenty-First Century

Commission Report, it became obvious over time that these concerns defeated any potential changes.

Throughout 1992, the year of the Adirondack Park Centennial, the association witnessed regional and international change and a tremendous interest in the North Country. ANCA experienced the impact of international change through a meeting with Adirondack Park Agency representatives and Vladimir B. Saganov from the Russia Council of Ministers of Buryatia. At the time Mr. Saganov was intrigued by ANCA's role as a private association that worked to strengthen the economy and provide programs throughout the Adirondack Park. He had many questions about how to achieve economic prosperity in his homeland that centered on the future of privatization, the need for investment capital, land, and economic reform that were all very interesting evolutions away from total state control. He was particularly interested in the role of the not-for-profit organization and questioned why the state of New York did not have a state agency responsible for economic development services in the park.

The questions the Russian minister asked mirrored the types of questions that had long surfaced about Adirondack Park Agency Act Section 801, which acknowledged the need for open space and a vibrant economic base: "In support of the essential interdependence of these needs, the plan represents a sensibly balanced apportionment of land to each." While the association certainly benefited from a New York State funding commitment, the Senate member-item funding clearly fluctuated. There continued to be the question of how to sustain economic development services throughout the Adirondack Park.

The association received word in January 1992 that the organization had been included in the governor's budget. Between 1992 and 2002 staff were able to work directly with the New York State Division of Budget, with funding that continued to be contracted through the Department of Economic Development. The funding spanned the administrations of both Governor Mario Cuomo and Governor George Pataki. While significantly reduced from the funding levels of the late 1980, the governors' budget allocations provided a secure home for the association, permitting a foundation through which the association could compete for grant funding for wood-products development, agriculture marketing, tourism, and community planning and promotion. It was the competitive core of the programs developed in the mid-1980s and early 1990s that made the association successful in securing other public funding from the Empire State Development Corporation, the USDA Grazing Lands Conservation Initiative, the USDA Forest Service, the Federal Highway Administration and NYS Department of Transportation, the NYS Division of Housing and Community Renewal, the NYS Department of Labor, the NYS Empire State Development Environmental Assessment Program, and the USDA Rural Business Enterprise Grant Program to administer program funding, among others. ANCA generated millions of dollars in public funding through competitive grant applications to leverage New York State's investment. The public funding was matched by private contributions solicited through an annual fund appeal and project partnerships with corporations such as the Northern Forest Canoe Trail, the Niagara Mohawk Power Corporation (National Grid), and International Paper, among others. Total annual program expenses through the early part of the twenty-first century fluctuated between $300,000 to a high of $2.6 million.

Throughout this period the association remained committed to providing services and programs while maintaining a small program and administrative staff from headquarters in Saranac Lake. The association redefined how economic development takes place in a rural region, and how an interdisciplinary, community-based model holds merit for building sustainable communities and healthy environments. In addition, the association fostered an economic development model that included community planning; recreational planning with resource linkages of waterway, bikeways, and trails; product development, branding, and marketing; community infrastructure, including our roads, byways, and telecommunications; and entrepreneurial networking and support.

In the early 1990s, ANCA staff participated on the Advisory Committee to the Northern Forest Lands Council. The resulting report, *Finding Common Ground: Conserving the Northern Forest,* provided a unique perspective on the regional status of the Northern Forest. Ten years later ANCA staff provided a community perspective to the council's *Tenth Anniversary Forum* report. The review process paralleled a number of discussions across the Northern Forest, particularly ANCA's ongoing work with the Northern Forest Center in Concord, New Hampshire, that addressed the need for increased economic development and community planning. There was recognition that progress had been made with many of the strategies proposed in the *Common Ground* report for land conservation and stewardship but there was still much work to be done to support comprehensive economic and community planning.

Through these various regional dialogues, ANCA's work in providing programs and services traveled full circle back to the main overriding questions. Federal and state resources were committed on an ongoing basis to the goals of land conservation and stewardship, with various tracts totaling in excess of 600,000 acres being added to state ownership during Governor Pataki's tenure. What were the companion strategies that had to be developed and sustained to ensure that our communities remain healthy and thrive within the bounds of their surrounding special landscape? What type of economic development planning needed to be institutionalized to best integrate the work of the range of organizations committed to the region and its communities?

Many other organizations committed to a range of economic development services emerged to address a wide range of topics including business planning, financing, community planning, and infrastructure. These included the Adirondack Economic Development Corporation, Friends of the North Country, ComLinks, and the North Country Alliance. Other organizations such as Historic Saranac Lake, Adirondack Architectural Heritage, and Traditional Arts in Upstate New York began effectively to blend historic preservation and community interests. Organizations such as the

Adirondack Regional Tourism Council developed new strategies to promote the Adirondack region, including waterways, historic tours, and byways. The Wildlife Conservation Society brought its expertise to the region with an important focus on environmental stewardship and conservation in combination with community outreach. Through the years, ANCA welcomed the many opportunities to partner with many of these organizations.

The various successes that ANCA achieved in providing economic programs and services through New York State's investment of more than $8 million (1986–2005) and leveraged public and private funding point to the work that still needs to be done. The discussions within the association that have taken place over the decades all point to how the association has held economic improvement and quality of life as the bull's-eye target. In 2005, ANCA's two-year loss of a higher level of New York State funding that began in 2003 necessitated that ANCA look to secure its operations. While any of these changes caused the association and its members to pause, it brought reflection about innovative approaches to plan and adapt. The regional rhetoric about the need for economic development services and programs remained focused on how best to sustain these services throughout the Adirondack Park. The association continued to sustain services and build recognition for its commitment to economically viable communities and a rural quality of life. The needs of communities would become aligned with and equal to the conservation interests.

The association's fifty-plus-year history of providing services and programs throughout the Adirondack North Country has been built from the tremendous volunteer contributions of countless members who have been committed to a vision of working together to build economic prosperity and quality communities. Their vision and commitment has been strengthened over the years through New York State's funding support. In today's economic climate our communities are at the forefront of being affected by economic, social, and cultural change. Changes in land ownership, combined with the loss of manufacturing jobs, point to the need for bold new strategies, and the personnel and fiscal resources that are necessary in planning for our future. The community and economic development needs of the region are as important today, if not more so, as they were on that snowy day in December 1953 when people from around the Adirondack North Country identified a need for an association of members to address advocacy and community needs.

More than thirty years after the development of the Adirondack Park Agency and the State Land Master Plan, the region continues to experience the benefits of land conservation, stewardship, open space, large forested tracts of land, and the scenic and recreational qualities of the unique public and private mix of the Adirondack Park. Community and economic development presents a host of opportunities and questions about how we can most effectively work to build attractive and quality communities. In recognition of the dialogues taking place across the four Northern Forest states of New York, Vermont, New Hampshire and Maine, the association's history has contributed to a newer understanding of regional linkages while remaining focused on the unique needs of a fourteen-county region in Northern New York that has the Adirondack Park at the core of the association's service area.

All of the association's work over the past fifty-plus years has been to bring the economic concerns of residents and businesses to the forefront, seek solutions, and provide services and programs that support economic development and quality of life. The Adirondack North Country Association's history and work points to the continued need to address the economic and community part of the regional equation to ensure that we achieve what the APA Act promises, the "complementary needs of all the people of the state for the preservation of the park's resources and open space character and of the park's permanent, seasonal and transient populations for growth and service areas, employment, and a strong economic base, as well." In recognition of the substantial state regulatory impact on the Adirondack Park, there continues to be a need to better institutionalize and sustain an ongoing economic development delivery system. There are significant opportunities to further support the economic renewal and vitality of the park's population centers and resources. The association believes the economy and communities must remain an important part of the formula in the future of the Adirondack Park. Now is the time to balance the equation between a healthy environment and a healthy economy.

# 30

## The Adirondack Environmental Nongovernmental Organizations

*Strategies in Conservation*

GRAHAM L. COX

A dozen land conservation nongovernmental organizations (NGOs) have operated successfully in the Adirondack Park for many decades. One NGO, the Association for the Protection of the Adirondacks, can trace its history almost back to the origins of the park and Forest Preserve; another, the Adirondack Mountain Club (ADK) owes its existence to the early state Conservation Department and its need for help in trail creation and maintenance. Most of the others have come into existence and of age since the major changes of the 1960s, each in response to emerging needs and opportunities.

Each NGO seems to occupy its own "ecological niche" in the park history and political structure, most often emerging from a crisis or perception of such. What is apparent today is that, though each came about to serve a need and a particular constituency, together they are forging a way forward. They work together in a number of loose, sometimes shifting, alliances and coalitions, and they have learned that forming partnerships with other related interests is in their collective best interests. But it has been and continues to be a tough learning experience. According to one NGO leader, the groups "are process-challenged." In other words, they can make progress together by collaborating and coordinating, competing or consolidating.

One fact keeps most of them energized and together: their concern that the government agencies entrusted with the care and management of the Forest Preserve and the Adirondack Park cannot be fully trusted to do the job without oversight from the NGOs. Often this oversight takes the form of friendly support and advice; often it takes the form of advocacy and political pressure on the governor's office and state legislature. But on many occasions in the history of the park this oversight has turned antagonistic and adversarial, with lawsuits, threats of lawsuits, and inveighing of strong political pressure.

Among their common challenges is their quest to find adequate funds. First, they need to finance their group and carry out their mission, which is difficult when, as one NGO leader puts it, "we are all fishing in the same pond." Second, and more important for the park itself, they advocate for adequate funds in the state and federal budgets and from private sources to meet their collective goals for the park. These goals include the judicious expansion of the Forest Preserve, purchase of conservation easements to support the continued profitable operation of commercial forest management, and day-to-day management and enforcement of the complex regulations on both the public and private lands.

We can describe the NGOs as organizations, but what has driven their creation, operation, and missions has been a handful of creative, committed, and visionary leaders. For example, several credit their inspiration to the vision and energy of Paul Schaefer (1908–1996), but he and many others mentored modern environmental leaders, including David Sive, David Newhouse, Barbara McMartin, Gary Randorf, Arthur Crocker, George Davis, and others. In turn, behind these visionary leaders have been people and foundations of great wealth and influence, prepared to invest their private funds to support the NGOs and their leadership and step in with land acquisition funds at crucial moments, with no expected return but the satisfaction of seeing the park maintained as a unique ecological and human experiment.

What follows are some observations on the recent history, mission and lessons from some, but not all, of the NGOs active in the park and in the state based on interviews with their respective leaders. Each NGO and their own defined mission are introduced in the order they appeared in the political landscape through the twentieth century. Discussion includes examination of how they have dealt with some of the major issues and the roles they have played, as well as the lessons learned and their individual visions for the park. Later in the chapter the discussion leads to the emergence of a collective vision for the park. Finally some lessons are offered that could be applied in other regions of the world, where a park is also home to many thousands of permanent residents and the focus for many thousands more for recreation and even second-home development.

Peter Bauer, for many years the executive director of the Residents' Committee to Protect the Adirondacks, provides a long-term perspective on issues and groups that have formed in and around the park to fight for its conservation over the last century. He states, "We can argue that it has been public advocacy that has pushed New York to act. Since 1864, every action by the state has been a response to public outcry, organized by individuals, or by reporters' articles and editorials in the *New York Times*."

There was no formal citizen organization until the Association for the Protection of the Adirondacks was formed in 1901. However, there were informal NGOs in the 1880s. They advocated for creation of the Adirondack Park and the Forest Preserve, and they organized to fight the effort to bring timber management to the Forest Preserve. After World War I, they formed citizen organizations advocating for a vision for the park. The state lacked a clear vision for the park in these early days. Somehow, the state's vision was often at cross-purposes with how it managed the park. For example, the state kept expanding the Blue Line but had no funds to buy land inside the expanding boundary, even though the original idea was for the state to buy all the land inside the Blue Line for the park.

Bauer credits Paul Schaefer for his organizational abilities to protect the park through its early decades. Schaefer organized many groups, depending on the issues. He would work on one issue with the Association for the Protection of the Adirondacks and the

Adirondack Mountain Club, organizations for whom much of his efforts were focused in the early years. However, if the association moved too slowly, as it did in 1946 concerning the threat posed by large hydropower dams on the South Branch of the Moose River, he would form his own group, such as the Moose River Committee. Ultimately, the association joined Schaefer's coalition in 1947 and elected him vice president. Schaefer is credited with forming a dozen organizations to fight various battles or address critical issues, such as the urgency to protect more land in the park. For that reason, he helped to create the Adirondack Nature Conservancy in 1972. The history of advocacy groups to monitor and intervene on park management goes hand-in-hand with the history of the park.

The pace quickened starting in 1970 with the publication of the Temporary Study Commission report and the subsequent organization of the Adirondack Park Agency. These events ushered in the modern age of how the Forest Preserve and the park were to be managed. As Bauer recalls, "We got the Wilderness and Wild Forest classifications on the public lands, the Unit Management Plans and the State Land Master Plan. This greater focus of the state resulted in a much greater focus from NGOs to oversee the state actions and management."

## The Association for the Protection of the Adirondacks

The history of the Association for the Protection of the Adirondacks goes back almost to the formation of the Forest Preserve and Adirondack and Catskill Parks, back to 1901. It advocates for and defends the ideals expressed in Article 14 of the state constitution, the Forever Wild clause, and is trying to promote the ideals more broadly, extending their reach to all state agencies that operate there, including the Adirondack Park Agency and transportation, energy, and river regulating agencies. In this capacity, the association has for a century harnessed the power of citizen action against the many threats to the park. These threats have included illegal logging of the Forest Preserve, which was widespread in the early years; proposed dams that threatened to flood the park's finest river valleys and the settlements within them; and the support of state officials for commercial development on the Forest Preserve, with roads driven deep into the backcountry.

From the beginning, the association distrusted the state's administration of the Forest Preserve. In the 1915 Constitutional Convention, state officials tried to allow logging on the public's Forever Wild lands. They were foiled by the great conservationist Louis Marshall, father of Bob Marshall and a trustee of the association. In 1927, voters approved a constitutional amendment to construct a highway to the top of Whiteface Mountain despite opposition from conservationists. However, efforts to light a permanent torch on top of the mountain were nixed by the association and other advocates of "Forever Wild." Then came efforts to build truck trails and a bobsled run on state land for the 1932 Winter Olympics. The association's successful lawsuit in 1930, *McDonald v. Association for the Protection of the Adirondacks,* blocked that development, forcing the bobsled run to be built on non–Forest Preserve land and thereby establishing the constitutional tests for compatible recreation on the Forest Preserve that are still applied to this day. The 1938 Constitutional Convention saw serious assaults on the park but, in the end, only the number of the famous Forever Wild article was changed, from Article 7 to Article 14. In the 1967 Constitutional Convention there was another push to alter Article 14. A new coalition, the Constitutional Council for the Forest Preserve, was established out of the Sierra Club, Association for the Protection of the Adirondacks, and the Adirondack Mountain Club to stop these changes.

In its long history, the association has adapted to new threats and found new priorities. Starting in 1945, the threat of dams and reservoirs for water power and canal diversions persisted. Schaefer organized coalitions to stop this assault. In 1956 Congress passed the Interstate Highway Act, and in 1959 New York voters approved a constitutional amendment to remove 300 acres of the Forest Preserve for what is now I-87, the Adirondack Northway. Serious conservationists split not over whether to build the highway, but where it should be routed and whether any Forest Preserve land should be impacted.

In its second century of work, says David Gibson, the association's board and staff have renewed the activism of old:

> We are flexing our muscles at 106 years and learning to market our vision better, and to broaden the membership, including people from minority communities. We act on a vision of the Adirondacks as a model of integrated conservation in both wild and lived-in landscapes. For the association the key lesson for the future is simple: Our Forest Preserve, as large and magnificent as it is, will not save the Adirondack Park. People living in and owning land in the park, and the park's young people, are the keys to the park's current and future stewardship. We must build on programs that encourage private land stewardship and sustainable community development. And the state agencies need very close oversight and coordination.

## Adirondack Mountain Club (ADK)

The Adirondack Mountain Club was founded in 1922 in part to help the early state Conservation Department develop and maintain trails in the High Peaks. Its mission is to protect and make responsible recreational use not only of the Forest Preserve, but also of state parks, wildlands, and waters. ADK also involves itself with private land development issues that impact the Forest Preserve. It works through outdoor recreation, advocacy, environmental education, and natural resource conservation. Its most widely recognized products and services are the comprehensive trail guides and maps, the operation of the Adirondack and Johns Brook hiker's "lojs," and the hard work of its trail crews and mountain-summit stewards. ADK, alone of the Adirondack NGOs, has sued in the federal courts, all the way up to the United States Supreme Court, to enforce the provisions of the Clean Air Act that were intended by Congress to eliminate the scourge of acid rain and mercury by compelling midwestern coal-burning utilities to install flue gas scrubbers.

ADK's recreation interests are pedestrian, not motorized. It has 35,000 dedicated members, mostly in New York and New Jersey, who are a highly motivated group of advocates. No matter what the issue or the hearing venue, ADK members turn out. "They have a deep attachment to the park; they ski, hike and canoe in the park constantly," says executive director Neil Woodworth. "We were able to turn out hundreds of people to the Whitney hearings in 1999, for example, because our members know the park. We did the same on the DEC's snowmobile trail plan in 2004."

A constant concern of ADK, Woodworth says, is that the Forest Preserve "cannot be infinitely changed to suit every recreational whim and gadget that comes along." He cites the principle of the Appellate Division Third Department decision of 1930, upheld by the Court of Appeals that same year on the Forest Preserve:

> it must be a wild resort in which nature is given free rein. Its uses for health and pleasure must not be inconsistent with its preservation as forest lands in a wild state. It must always retain the character of a wilderness. Hunting, fishing, trapping, mountain climbing, snowshoeing, skiing or skating find ideal setting in nature's wilderness. No artificial setting is required for any of these purposes. Sports which require a setting which is man-made are unmistakably inconsistent with the preservation of these forest lands in the wild and natural state in which Providence has developed them.[1]

The conservation community fought hard in the days of the Temporary Study Commission to limit snowmobile access. "The snowmobile people wanted to have complete access and they were going to sue the state for it. ADK and the Association sued, based on the MacDonald language, and this resulted in the compromise which allows snowmobile trails in Wild Forest only on trails built for hikers, unlike other parts of the U.S."

ADK's greatest concern today is the intrusion of motorized uses on the Forest Preserve. These uses include ATVs, trail bikes, and motocross dirt bikes with tractor-style tires that can go up most hiking trails. The State Land Master Plan prohibits material increase in motorized uses on the Forest Preserve, but Woodworth notes, "The state has been getting around that recently by substituting Conservation Easement purchase rather than fee purchase. Our fear is that Conservation Easement lands will be honeycombed with motorized access trails and this will impact the Forest Preserve and wild character of the park."

## The Adirondack Chapter of the Nature Conservancy/ Adirondack Land Trust (ANC/ALT)

The ANC/ALT is a private conservation group that is best known for protecting and acquiring land, alone or for the state; it also supports private efforts to conserve land and species. They have a massive land-protection program.

The Temporary Study Commission in 1970 called for the formation of something like the ANC/ALT, an organization to work with the New York State DEC to help protect land, and since then they have protected over 600,000 acres in the Adirondack Park in close to 200 projects. This is about 20 percent of all the protected land in the park. The protection includes conservation easements (they still hold 70 of these as a land trust responsible for annual monitoring), nature preserve, and significant transfers to the state to be included in the Forest Preserve. But in the beginning their course and their modus operandi were not so clear. Their early mandate was to identify and protect rare and endangered species and to protect biodiversity. According to Tim Barnett, the first executive director, "In the Adirondacks initially we did not understand what was rare about the park environment, so we, more by accident than design, operated at the landscape scale. An early definition of our mission was to 'save the last of the least and best of the rest' but we discovered in the park that the common and ordinary has become rare, from species to communities to landscapes. What existed in the Adirondacks rose to the top of the list as rare examples of land and eco-regional types in the world as well as the Northeast U.S.A."

Barnett credits George Davis through the creation of his *2020 Vision* reports. Davis prepared them for the Adirondack Council and then formed the Adirondack Land Trust, which became a partner of the Adirondack Nature Conservancy in 1988. ANC/ALT has very delicate relations with the DEC because the DEC has its own conservation agenda. "We do not want to get ahead of the agendas of the local regional office and the Albany office," Barnett explains. ANC/ALT steers clear of other organizations because they are primarily advocacy groups. ANC/ALT does not do advocacy in the same manner as other groups but does benefit from the advocacy efforts of the Nature Conservancy's state office in Albany. "They do advocate for climate change issues, funding, good conservation laws and more, but in the Adirondack Park we walk a fine line and keep a low profile, so we are trusted by all sides. You could say that we are a safe date," Barnett says.

Their operation today is to preserve the function of life at a landscape level. ANC/ALT maps ecosystems and ecological land units using Geographic Information System (GIS) technology. They target key pieces so far not protected by some means, rather than simply buying pieces as they become available. They work through a strategic planning process, identifying threats and developing strategies for each of 24 target ecological land units and target species in the park and maintain connection with areas adjacent to the park fringes to provide wildlife access to other natural areas.

Barnett is now also thinking about the smaller pieces and the trail connections for recreational use, adapting their thinking through time. "It's interesting now to see how the land trusts fit in the Adirondacks. Land trusts should look at creating recreational trails; for example, creating opportunities to stay in Westport to hike and bike. We should not just focus on acquiring large or key parcels for open space protection. There should be room for both protection and opening up recreation opportunities."

Barnett concludes: "We have done more to protect the real Adirondack Park in recent times than all of these other advocates. Remember we are investing millions of dollars to purchase land with no firm guarantee of recovering our investment." He cites the example of the Bob Marshall or Great Oswegatchie Wilderness. "Our recent purchases have gone a long way toward completing the protection of that wilderness tract, but we too often do not get the credit for actually doing the work."

## The Adirondack Council

The Adirondack Council, formed in 1975, was initially an umbrella coalition that included several national environmental groups, including the Natural Resource Defense Council, the Wilderness Society, the Association for the Protection of the Adirondacks, the Sierra Club, and the National Audubon Society. The council formed as the watchdog over the Adirondack Park Agency Act and the park agency itself. Basic policy differences on several issues, notably the construction of ski jumps at Lake Placid for the 1980 Olympics, led to defections. Today the council is a member-based organization. Its wide scope of interests has stayed constant, including anything affecting the ecological integrity or wild character of the park. But the council's thinking and strategies have changed.

"The council needs to be an advocate for the park and its people," says Brian Houseal, executive director. "There are not many places left in this world where you can draw a line around six million acres without taking account of local residents' basic needs and economic aspirations."

The council's working vision is largely based on pioneering work by George Davis in the three-volume *2020 Vision* reports on the Forest Preserve published in 1988. These booklets identify key areas to protect biodiversity, by expanding the Wilderness and Wild Forest designated areas, and plan for eco-friendly recreation. Based on these reports, the council says: "We envision an Adirondack Park composed of large core wilderness areas, connected to working farms and forests, and augmented by vibrant local communities, all within a diverse mosaic of biologically intact landscapes."

To achieve this vision, the council has four objectives: protect and expand the wilderness, restore habitat on private lands, improve water quality on a watershed scale, and tackle the problems of atmospheric deposition, acid rain, climate change and their devastating impacts on all life in the park. Houseal, who has extensive experience in the private sector (in a landscape architecture consulting firm) and in other eco-regions throughout Latin America and the Caribbean, offers an outsider's perspective: "The park is one of the largest patches of temperate forest remaining. There are not many big blocks of forested landscape in this hemisphere outside of the Amazon basin. The park is therefore important for the future of conservation."

In its early years, the Adirondack Council rarely reached out to the Adirondack communities. Now it recognizes them as vital partners in the decisions that are made in the park. This communication is going both ways, Houseal says. He goes to town supervisors and they come to him. "We are now getting town boards coming to the council to work jointly on land problems," citing council-town-citizen cooperation on issues such as pollution of Wilmington's town beach and proposals for unsightly and unpopular communications towers overlooking Lake George and above the Sacandaga Reservoir. More recently, the council served as a core member of the Common Ground Alliance, a diverse group of local elected officials, environmental nonprofits, and economic development nonprofits that are identifying solutions that benefit the park's communities, their economies, and the environment.

"We have to think about people and economic development of the park. But there is a huge risk in it, for them talking to the 'greens' and the conservation groups talking to the towns. We must get to know the supervisors, we must listen and learn about their issues. We are in the radical middle; we try to be a reasoned and moderate voice for environmental issues across the park.

"We see a change in attitudes in the park. We are no longer at loggerheads. This is also partly because there is a change in who is getting elected. Local people say, 'We would like the community to stay the way it is.' It is outside developers who are challenging the park as they know it." Commenting on trends in vacation-home building and escalating housing costs, Houseal explains, "This is unsustainable for local residents, so affordable housing is a big issue for all of us."

A top priority for the council is the establishment of what has come to be called the Bob Marshall Wilderness (to some it is the Great Oswegatchie Canoe Wilderness). The council defines it as a 408,000-acre complex of public and private lands, the largest road-less wilderness remaining in the East. The key to creating this wilderness, says Houseal, is helping local communities get the benefits and economic opportunities of being visitor gateway communities to a huge intact wilderness: year-round B&Bs, guide services, canoe and kayak sales and rentals, ski touring centers and much more. The council is working with local economic development specialists to go after federal funds to develop this gateway concept.

Atmospheric deposition remains one of their core issues, with climate change, acid rain, and mercury contamination as widespread and damaging problems. Among other priorities are concerns over the impact of motorized off-road recreation vehicles, development pressures on private land, the threat of invasive species to park flora and fauna, and what it terms the Conservation Easement frenzy. Easement stewardship is at issue, and one alternative has been to shift motorized vehicle traffic to the easement lands, taking the pressure off the Forest Preserve. Like the ADK, the council sees many of the park stewardship problems stemming from the fragmented park administration. Land management is split between state agencies, and even within the principle agency, the DEC, the park is split between two regions.

In summary, Houseal offers the following observations on the perspective role of government agencies and NGOs: "The job of government agencies is to regulate; they react to events and pressures, they are not necessarily proactive. The NGOs have a responsibility to monitor what the agencies do. But they also have a responsibility to be proactive, to innovate. The agencies have to play by the rules, for example, preparing Unit Management Plans for units that are far too small from an ecological viewpoint. Planners have to think on a bigger scale and include the conservation easement lands and whole watersheds in the planning process. To make sense, the NGOs have to change the rules and bring this larger perspective to the planning and management decisions."

## Residents' Committee to Protect the Adirondacks (RCPA)

RCPA's mission is to bring to the public debate the voices of the park residents who support the Forest Preserve, the APA, and regional development controls. RCPA's long-serving and first executive director, Peter Bauer, was a staff member of the Commission on the Adirondacks in the Twenty-First Century. After the report was finished in May 1990 he and other full-time park residents formed the organization to fill what they saw as a vacuum.

"Many people in the park have chosen to live here or stay here through many generations because of the Forest Preserve and the protected landscape," says Bauer. "RCPA's interests are not represented by existing statewide environmental or property rights groups operating in the park."

The RCPA focuses on private land development issues and on management of the Forest Preserve. It has broadened its reach to include research on land uses, lake water quality, problems with septic systems and on the number and patterns of building permits issued by the APA and the towns during the last three decades. It has helped communities develop local laws to curb jet-ski use, improve water quality management, and help small private forest landowners be part of sustainable certified forest programs, with more than 30 owners of small private forest properties totaling over 12,500 acres participating.

As a measure of its success, says Bauer, "We formed in 1990 and we are still here. We are bigger, better, with more funds. We have found a lot of support within the park for serious on-the-ground work. We do the things we do by organizing a strong volunteer network. We see our job as to provide leadership, bring good research to the public debate, and expose our research in order to change public policy. We work in coalitions—with local governments, with the Adirondack Council and other NGOs."

Bauer notes that the RCPA has adapted through time: "First, in the 1990–94 years, we tried to pass the Berle Commission report[2] recommendations with variations as state legislation. This passed the Assembly for four years but not the Senate. In 1994 we started to work with groups who wanted specific action on specific issues— for example, on the Essex County landfill, on the Unit Management Plan process, on jet skis, on ATVs, and on development issues. Today, 90 lakes are being monitored for basic parameters. We are aiming for 100 lakes, doing this in partnership with the Adirondack Watershed Institute at Paul Smith's College."

In hindsight, says Bauer, RCPA could have developed a proactive economic development assistance program: "We did not spend enough time on economic development. We paid just sporadic attention. Similarly on community infrastructure needs, it was just not enough of a focus for us."

Looking to the future, Bauer is somewhat pessimistic: "We are at a point in the park, because of outrageous land prices and climbing property taxes, you can no longer grow trees and make a profit. The same goes for farming in the Champlain Valley. Residential development is the only option for many. Change in the basic economics must bring about major changes in the way we plan for its future."

## The Sierra Club

The Sierra Club was a founding member of the Adirondack Council and has been a significant player in park issues, but in a very different way than the other NGOs. The club works primarily in the park through volunteers, puts money into political action, and takes positions that are often unpopular with other NGOs as well as local communities.

"Other groups have staff working the inside game. The Sierra Club plays the outside game with the public," says Chris Ballantyne who managed club activities in the Northeast and Mid-Atlantic states from his office in Saratoga Springs. "The club drives the arguments to the left of mainstream. Our outsider reputation serves us well. It is easier for the mainstream groups if we take a position out in left field. We catch a lot of heat but it makes them seem more moderate, more reasonable."

When the report of the Commission for the Adirondacks in the Twenty-First Century was issued in 1990, the Sierra Club gave its wholehearted support, only to find itself out on a limb. "We were frustrated in seeing so much opposition to many of the commission recommendations from other NGOs and from the property-rights groups," Ballantyne says. "This was a big missed opportunity for the state to strengthen the park, the Forest Preserve, and the APA Act. Now the politics have changed. It just shows what a difference a governor makes. Governor George Pataki has shown much more interest than Governor Cuomo in protecting land using both fee acquisitions and conservation easements."

## Audubon New York/National Audubon Society

Audubon New York's mission is the protection of birds, wildlife, and their habitat. As the state office of a national organization with a 100-year history, Audubon New York has a statewide perspective, yet much that it does relates to the park and the larger Northern Forest. In 1987 the National Audubon leadership and its regional vice president, David Miller, opened a regional office in Albany, and took an active role in Northern Forest issues.

Then president of the society Peter A. A. Berle had been involved as an Assembly member in the creation of the APA, in drafting the State Land Master Plan language with Peter Paine, and in supporting the Adirondack Park Land Use and Development Plan. As DEC commissioner from 1976 to 1980, Berle was involved in implementing the new APA law to protect the park. In 1988, he agreed to chair the Commission on the Adirondack Park in the Twenty-First Century.

Audubon's subsequent involvement was closely tied to the work and report of the commission, starting in 1990. Berle created a special Adirondack Unit within the regional office to carry the commission's legislative package forward. The Assembly did so for four years in a row, but not the Senate. Meanwhile Governor Mario Cuomo distanced himself from his own commission after the wise use/property rights advocates opened fire on the report, Berle, the governor, and the APA. When that happened the Audubon focus shifted from park issues to statewide bird conservation issues. Audubon's regional director/regional office structure was changed to a state office in 1996, after Berle left the society. In due course, Audubon became something of an insider player in Governor Pataki's office, advocating for specific land acquisitions, and it also broadened its interest to the Northern Forest.

Looking to the future, Audubon is trying to introduce biodiversity and bird conservation concepts to support conservation of wildland core areas and creation of sustainable forest buffers and connections. It is also working to connect nature protection and eco-friendly recreation to the economic benefits for communities and for the park as a whole.

## The Northern Forest Alliance

The Northern Forest Alliance (NFA) organized as a coalition in 1994 partly as a reaction to, and in support of, the recommendations of the Northern Forest Lands Council study, *Finding Common Ground*. The alliance encourages its 50 member groups to work with others across four states. It was formed to advance three basic ideas: protect core wildlands; identify and create sustainable working forest buffers; and stimulate local community economies, with emphasis on supporting and promoting recreation, resource-based businesses, and cultural heritage.

The alliance has become very effective over time, with an annual publication laying out an agenda of Forest Legacy easement purchases and fee acquisitions. A spin-off publication developed by the alliance's New York Caucus prepared a New York acquisition and easement list, complete with a map based on the 1997 priority list developed by the New York NGOs. Each year NFA sends to Congress an updated description of its priorities for Forest Legacy funding.

The alliance believes that the key action for federal funds lies in the congressional appropriations process, that the best hope for working-forest conservation lies in the Forest Legacy program, and that an even broader coalition may be needed to make progress. The alliance is now joining with economic development groups to push for community economic development programs and funds, and joining with sports groups to broaden the base for protecting habitat and biodiversity. The alliance is also pushing hard with the Northern Forest Center for specific Northern Forest legislation to bring additional federal dollars to all aspects of the region's economy and communities, to complement the land conservation work. The alliance is also developing a sharper message on the trends in land exchanges, and in explaining "globalizing" economic forces affecting the region.

## Open Space Institute

The Open Space Institute (OSI) has been quietly operating in the Adirondack Park for more than a decade. In one sense they can be considered as playing a supporting role to the bigger and better-known Nature Conservancy; however their accomplishments and their means are impressive in their own right.

For a long time OSI operated only in the lower Hudson Valley using funds from the Lila Acheson and DeWitt Wallace Fund for the Hudson Highlands to purchase fee and easement properties. But in 1995 they took a bold step out of the Hudson Valley to help conserve a major property on the west shore of Lake Champlain, the Split Rock tract. OSI pulled a small handful of funding sources together and risked $1.65 million to buy this 2,100-acre tract just before it was sold at auction.

OSI spent more than 10 years in on-again-off-again negotiations with the industrial owner of the 11,000-acre Tahawus property in the heart of the Adirondacks. Although the Wallace Fund agreed to the purchase as early as 1995, OSI did not reach an agreement with NL Industries until the spring of 2003 at a historic meeting in Houston, Texas. NL operated a titanium mine on the southern end of the property from 1941 until 1984. The outlet of Henderson Lake, the centerpiece of the property, is the beginning of the

Hudson River, and OSI had a long-time interest in this site because of its rich mix of natural and historic features. The Wallace Fund provided OSI with the $8.5-million purchase price, and OSI held this money from 1995 to 2003, when the sale was at long last closed. They agreed on a two-lot subdivision. NL would keep the industrial site, and OSI would purchase the spectacular forested area, including the long abandoned Village of Adirondac, a nineteenth-century iron-mining town, an intact blast furnace built in 1854, and a stunning mix of mountains, lakes, rivers, streams, and wetlands.

"There is so much history on this site," says Joe Martens, OSI's president. "OSI deliberately kept the historic sites out of the land that will in due course go into the state Forest Preserve."

Another significant contribution to conservation was OSI's creation of a $12.6-million Northern Forest Protection Fund, endowed by the Duke and Surdna Foundations. The fund, administered by OSI, provides grants and loans to land trusts and conservation organizations to promote cutting-edge conservation in the northern reaches of Maine, New Hampshire, Vermont, and New York. The fund has helped protect more than a million acres of land in the region.

## The Emergence of an Environmental NGO Consensus for the Future of the Adirondack Park

A consensus seems to be emerging that to play their role more effectively in the future, the NGOs need to get their act together, and maybe even consolidate. "They do their best to keep up with the day-to-day issues and they have been effective as watchdogs, on the APA and the DEC," Martens acknowledges. But, he adds, there has been little effective coalition around the Adirondack Council's seminal *2020 Vision* reports, for example. Martens and others echoed the view that if consolidation is politically impossible, then NGOs can at least come up with a central list of priorities and threats. Houseal stressed the importance of creativity and innovation within the NGO community, stating that every seven to ten years "we need to re-pot ourselves."

Houseal continued, "We have environmental knowledge and science galore to support management decisions, but we are process-challenged. . . . We can collaborate and coordinate, compete or consolidate." In the long run, Martens concludes, the future of the Adirondack Park depends on the vision and work of the NGOs. "It is their ideas that count."

What lessons emerge from the experiences of the conservation NGOs operating in and on behalf of the Adirondack Park? From interviews with their leaders we can identify five themes:

*Exercise constant vigilance:* This is necessary to monitor the government agencies responsible for park planning and management. By all means support the responsible government agencies; they need the human and material resources to do their jobs. Encourage them, help them, but always be ready to challenge policy and management decisions and to wield a big stick—political or legal action—to challenge decisions the agencies make.

*Funding drives decisions:* NGOs must have the ability to raise funds for their own organization's purposes. This can be for advocacy, for science, and probably most important, for their own land conservation efforts. But funding for the government agencies is always crucial, so NGOs must advocate for funds for the government agencies responsible for planning and management in the park.

*Vision is imperative:* Each NGO has developed its own mission, its own statement of priorities, and its own agenda. But to be effective there must be a joint vision that guides their long-term combined actions. They really must have a vision that all parties can agree to, promote, and translate to legislation or to specific actions.

*Understand and forge links:* For ecosystems, human communities, and economic systems there are links within and between each. Internally, the vision and actions should link these three big systems together, connecting the ecological, economic, and social bottom lines.

*Provide leadership:* It certainly helps to have leaders with broad experience and vision gained from working and observing in the national or global context. But the NGO leaders cannot be seen by the park residents as outsiders or as representing an elitist interest. Local leadership and involvement is also imperative.

The NGOs described here have come by these lessons the hard way. They know that constant vigilance means just that—constant, not letting their guard down. Funding is a difficult issue for all of them "fishing in the same pond," as one leader put it, for support for their own agendas and securing public funds for the public agencies when there are many competing public needs. Creating a joint vision has proven difficult, but they have strong building blocks, namely the state master plans for the public and private lands and the vision of the *2020* reports. Seeing and making links of all kinds is imperative, but only recently have the conservation NGOs seen the value of linking with economic and local community interests in a common agenda. And finally, providing leadership is crucial for all of these items.

# 31

## Envisioning the Future of Wilderness

*Public Demands and Private Lands*

ELIZABETH THORNDIKE

Wilderness and wildlands—landscapes where natural systems pre-dominate and are of sufficient size to permit those systems to flour-ish over time—are rapidly vanishing in the United States east of the Rockies. They are the scarcest and most endangered natural resource in the 37 states where three-fourths of the U.S. population resides, an area that comprises 60 percent of the land mass of the contiguous United States and stretches from the Rocky Mountains front to the Atlantic coast, and from the Great Lakes to the Gulf of Mexico. Their accelerating disappearance is the result of consump-tion, fragmentation, and widespread lack of understanding about what is at stake.

Wilderness and wildlands are of value for their own existence, as relatively undisturbed portions of the earth's natural capital. They also provide a number of critically important benefits for humans and represent values deeply ingrained in American culture. These benefits and values include: protection of ecological functions and services, plant and wildlife habitat, genetic pools, freshwater

The author thanks Cornell colleagues David J. Allee (deceased), Richard S. Booth, Timothy J. Fahey, Charles C. Geisler, Theodore L. Hullar, and Peter L. Marks for their active participation in the working group to devise an Eastern Wildlands Society Research Network in 1999–2000. Their ideas and expertise stimulated much of the thinking embodied in this chapter.

supplies, flood control, soil erosion, air quality, and renewable resources. Wildlands preserve historical landscape heritage, serve as laboratories for scientific research and as classrooms for environmental education, are settings for outdoor recreation for millions, afford unparalleled opportunities for scenic vistas and solitude, and enhance property values.

New York State's Adirondack Park, at nearly 6 million acres, is the largest designated park in the contiguous 48 states. The park is as large or larger than each of seven states. It includes 2.8 million acres of public lands (Forest Preserve) and waters, of which about 1.1 million acres are designated Wilderness, where motorized use is prohibited. The park has the largest area of designated (motorless) Wilderness in the 37 United States east of the Rockies.[1] The park also includes over 3 million acres of private land, much of it owned in large tracts, interspersed in a mosaic pattern among the public lands and waters, including some 103 towns and villages and over 130,000 year-round residents.

The designated Wilderness acreage in the Adirondack Park is about 25 percent of all designated Wilderness in the 37 states east of the Rockies and 85 percent of Wilderness in the densely populated Northeast. Adirondack Park Wilderness designation criteria are nearly identical to those in the National Wilderness Preservation Act of 1964, except that minimum size of Adirondack Wilderness units must be 10,000 acres, as compared to 5,000 acres on federal lands. Only 10 contiguous western states have more designated Wilderness (Utah has less) than New York State. The Forest Preserve is the core protected area of the Champlain-Adirondack Biosphere Reserve, a UNESCO and National Park Service designation.

What, then, is unique about the Adirondack Park, its Forest Preserve, and its designated Wilderness? What is it about these lands that over the years has spawned protection under the New York State Constitution; a constituency of hundreds of thousands of individuals; dozens of associations and organizations dedicated to protection, conservation, education and research of the park's public lands and waters; a parkwide zoning code and regulatory system; extensive library collections, volumes of books written about the park and its Forest Preserve; museums; visitor centers; untold numbers of conferences and symposia; millions of annual visitors; and over 250,000 year-round and seasonal residents?

What is unique about the park is not the vast open space, not the special natural areas, not the mountains, or the lakes, or the rivers and streams, nor the wetlands, nor the fields, nor the forest; not the vistas, not the harmony of human settlements intermingled with the public lands. What is unique is the combination of all these interlocking ecosystems. What is unique is a wilderness resource and a wild forest atmosphere of such size and such diversity amid the largest concentration of people on the North American continent.

## The Future of Adirondack Wilderness Lies in Private Hands

The park's designated Wilderness in the Forest Preserve is owned in common by nearly 20 million New Yorkers and protects significant public values. There is a critical need to protect a reservoir of remaining wilderness/wildland ecosystems, whether public, private, or mixed ownership such as easements. The opportunity to protect wildlands and wilderness in the Adirondack Park has no parallel in the eastern United States. The park's overlapping ecosystems do not respect public/private boundaries. What happens on public lands affects private land values, and what happens to the private lands affects the value of public land. Avoiding consumption and fragmentation of all existing park wildlands and wilderness is the single greatest imperative for the park to insure that the lands and waters are protected so that their ability to let natural processes prevail over time continues in perpetuity. Why should private landholdings not remain Forever Wild?

About 1.3 million acres of private land in the park are owned by the 30 largest landowners. Topping the list, at a total of 900,000 acres, are six forest-products companies, most of whose lands are now covered by easements that prevent development and promote sustainable forestry.[2] Studies in 1988 showed that a little over 2 million acres of private lands were held by 564 owners of large (tracts over 500 acres) landholdings. Of these, about 100 landowners had holdings over 2,500 acres. Ownership types comprised 336 individuals and 228 corporate or other collective owners. Over time, the number of large landholdings has decreased, and the acreage per landholding has increased.[3]

These large landholdings are key to the wildlands stewardship of the park. The long-term tenure of their holdings should be the principal focus of public policies and private initiatives, if wilderness and wildlands are to have a future in the park commensurate with the demand for their benefits and the pressures (often unwitting) to extinguish their values. No major proposal for the park in modern times has ever called for the public lands of the park to constitute more than about 50 percent of the area. The Temporary Study Commission in 1970 recommended fee acquisition and easements for 600,000 acres. The report of the governor's Commission on the Adirondacks in the Twenty-First Century in 1990 recommended acquisition of 650,000 acres, along with use of easements and transfer of development rights for private lands. It is unlikely that sufficient public assets will ever be secured to protect all sensitive natural resources in fee, or insure retention of all open space in public hands. Nor is it likely that the taxpayers will support resources to manage the entire park in public ownership. The use of easements, which retain private rights but require stewardship responsibilities, has accelerated dramatically in the past decade and promises to become the single most effective tool for wildlands/wilderness protection.

Private landowners, along with local governments, which control over 50 percent of new development in the park, have an enormously important role to play. The large landowners can, through the exercise of wilderness stewardship, insure not only the sustainability of their forest, but the protection of the many wildland benefits. Small landowners have equal responsibility to insure that wildlands remain the hallmark of the park. Death by a thousand cuts, the cumulative impact of countless local decisions about how land is used, can have a major effect. And local governments need to increase their capacity to support goals for private land stewardship.

With private rights, which all Americans hold dear, come responsibilities for the effects of private action on the neighboring public properties owned in common by the people of the state of New York, the "life tenants" who own the public lands and waters of the park. Private land protection can help conserve public values; in the Adirondacks, where the state makes payments in lieu of taxes, Forest Preserve Wilderness benefits local communities.

Over 90 percent of potential designated Wilderness east of the Rockies is now privately owned. In the 27 states east of the Mississippi, there are 27 million acres of federal public lands in 270 units. Together with state lands, they constitute about 5 percent of the land area of these 27 states. Of that, 14 percent (3,832,856 acres) are designated Wilderness. Including all 37 contiguous states east of the Rockies, there are 4,312,744 acres of designated Wilderness, or about 4 percent of the total acreage in the National Wilderness Preservation System. The remaining U.S. Wilderness, 101,382,432 acres, is in the eleven western states, Alaska, and Hawaii, where less than 25 percent of the population resides and where public lands constitute about 57 percent of the land area. In the West, vast reservoirs of Bureau of Land Management (BLM) lands serve as potential Wilderness. There are almost no BLM lands east of the Rockies and none in the Adirondacks.

In New York, it is state laws and state agencies that are the protectors of wilderness. The people of the state of New York have shown a deep and abiding concern for management and use of state lands, evidenced by the passage of Article 14, Section 1 of the New York State Constitution in 1894, the wording of which has not been changed since then. Of more than 130 proposed amendments introduced in the state legislature to change Article 14, only 22 have succeeded and they have all (with one exception) involved small acreage.

With enactment of the State Land Master Plan (SLMP) in 1972, drafted by the Adirondack Park Agency, Wilderness was defined as in the 1964 National Wilderness Preservation Act, whose architect, Howard Zahniser, had composed much of this legislation during summer residence in the Adirondacks. The SLMP also includes guidelines and criteria for management and use of state lands other than Wilderness, but the chief distinction is availability of motorized access, which is not permitted in Wilderness. However, the unifying theme governing all Forest Preserve lands is that protection and preservation of the natural resources of state lands in the park are paramount, in contrast to human use and recreation.

With adoption of the APA Act in 1971, the state legislature established a two-tiered structure regarding policy and management of state lands in the park. The APA, as administrator of the State Land Master Plan, is responsible for long-range planning and policy, including classification of state lands according to "their characteristics and capacity to withstand use" and for interpretation and revision of the plan, in consultation with the Department of Environmental Conservation. The DEC, and other state agencies with respect to the more modest acreage of land under their jurisdictions, have responsibility for management of those lands in compliance with the guidelines and criteria in the plan. DEC is responsible for acquisition of lands from willing sellers and also for preparing management plans for the units of land classified in the plan, in consultation with the APA, which must find them in compliance with the general guidelines and criteria set forth in the SLMP.

The SLMP has not been revised since 1987, although the statute calls for revision of unit management plans every five years. Since its enactment in 1972, the plan was reviewed and officially revised in 1979 and again in 1987. The combination of inadequate resources for the agency to undertake the complex revision process and the environmental community's reluctance to support opening up the plan for examination and discussion are the reasons for this inaction.

The SLMP takes both a biocentric (nature's perspective) and anthropocentric (human perspective) approach as the legal instrument that classifies state lands and establishes policies, guidelines, and criteria for the management actions carried out by the state Department of Environmental Conservation. The SLMP has withstood the test of time since its enactment as part of the APA Act in

1973. From its initial adoption in 1972, it has been much less contro-versial than the Adirondack Park Land Use and Development Plan.

The DEC has never had sufficient resources to insure vigilant management of the Forest Preserve. Convincing the department to present a consistent wilderness stewardship face to the public in designated Wilderness will not be easy. While the wilderness-as-paradise purist may be content with "a loaf of bread, a jug of wine, and thou," sportsmen and other users also value wildlands. And they represent a significant segment of the public that prefers motorized access in all seasons as their means of enjoying the lands. That is what sets up the conflict and the two camps. DEC personnel, as public representatives, also line up on different sides of the motorized access issue, often closely aligned with their heritage, in this respect.

## Trends, Challenges, and Goals

Many diverse trends in the early twenty-first century will have an impact on the sustainability of wilderness and wildlands.[4] This chap-ter has taken the position that our goal must be to protect wilderness quality lands and landscapes, not only through state actions, but also through local communities and private landowners. Avoiding death by a thousand cuts and retaining the essential component of security of tenure as the means to sustainability will be influenced, for better or worse, by the actions of all three sectors.

I make the following assumptions. Sustainability of the park's wilderness and wildlands (with a small "w") is ecologically as important as adding Wilderness (with a capital "W") to the Forest Preserve. We will cope better from positions of foresight rather than hindsight. Collaborative rather than adversarial processes will result in more joint gains as challenges are faced. A flexible approach in regulatory matters should be applied—fairly, equitably, and consist-ently, but cognizant of highly varying circumstances in different geographical areas of the park.

I briefly address three trends that will affect sustainability of wildland resources. I predict they will be at the center of considera-tion during the first half of the twenty-first century.

*Demand for wilderness will accelerate at the same time that wilderness and wildlands continue to diminish or disappear, especially east of the Rockies.* The Adirondack Park will remain an oasis in the eastern United States. More and more people, at an earlier age and at a later age, will want to use wilderness resources. If we are able to protect these resources, holistically as overlapping ecosystems on the public and private lands of the park, and prevent degradation of their physical and biological contexts, as well as their social or psychological aspects, we will sustain the wilderness resource. If not, the reverse will happen.

*Economic vitality of park communities is inextricably linked with the wildlands of the park.* The environment is the economy, based on tourism, recreation, and second-home amenities in the settled areas. Building the capacity of local governments to recognize and take advantages of proximate wilderness as a benefit to their community will continue to require resources.

*Motorized access on Wilderness and wildlands will remain controversial.* Snowmobiles, motorized watercraft, all-terrain vehicles, and perhaps yet-to-be-invented other means of motorized transport on the interior roads, trails, and waterways of the park will continue to have supporters and opponents. Zoning is one way to deal with noise and speed and public safety concerns. But ecological issues will become even more prominent as wildlands become scarcer, and this will remain the most divisive issue in the park.

The following eight recommendations are offered as means to achieving wilderness and wildlands sustainability in the Adirondack Park.

*Governor's task force on security of tenure.* As noted, there are approximately 500 landowners who collectively are key to retention of the wilderness/wildlands values that are synonymous with the park. A governor-appointed task force/commission needs to focus on, examine, assess, and recommend the best fiscal and tax policies to insure that the large private landholdings are not consumed or fragmented so as to make impossible their retention over time. State legislators representing the single largest landowner (the people of the state of New York), local elected officials, economists and other fiscal experts, and representatives of the large landholders should constitute the membership of the task force. They should look at impediments and devise incentives, able to be implemented at the state level, to sustain these large private resources that, together with the Forest Preserve, represent the crown jewels of New York State.[5]

*Eliminate the double standard.* If the state is ever to assume its appropriate role as guardian of the park and the Forest Preserve, it must first have a consistent message through its many agencies operating in the park. The APA is responsible for restrictions on the uses of private land, but it has only an advisory role with regard to state agency actions, other than those in wetlands. The state is the major developer in the park, and that development directly affects the Forest Preserve wildlands and also the wildland sustainability of private land. State agencies, by legislation, should be held to the same standards of permit review as private actions, subject to the governor's discretion, so as to have a system of uniform and comprehensive land-use controls. There is also a need to examine conflicting agendas and policies of state agencies that are involved in the park and make some attempt at consistency as has been accomplished with the Department of State coastal resource management program. An interagency task force, led by the APA chairman, should undertake this task simultaneous to legislative action to require permit review by the APA for state agency actions.

*Restore sufficient land-use planning funds for local governments.* The Adirondack Park, because of its special nature, has special restrictions about land use and development. Adirondack communities need to build the capacity to be true partners with the state in channeling land use and development where it is most appropriate and in addressing issues of economic vitality that affect large rural areas. The state has the responsibility to fund local government planning efforts that attempt to achieve those goals.

*Develop, resolve, and assess criteria, monitoring, and enforcement for conservation easements.* Along with public and private lands in the park, easements have become a significant category of mixed ownership for more than half a million acres. Easements retain benefits of private ownership, while simultaneously protecting wilderness and wildland values and public benefits. Lack of consistency in defining criteria for easements, issues of public access for state-acquired easements, and property-tax abatement for conservation organization acquisitions need to be resolved in order not to constrain their cost-effective use.

*Revise the Adirondack Park Land Use and Development Plan to incorporate modern ecological concepts as criteria for determining adverse impacts of development.* When the APA Act was written in the early 1970s, holistic ecological concepts, a routine part of contemporary environmental planning and management, were at the time in their infancy and not incorporated into reviews of environmental impacts required by the APA Act. Ecosystems, whole watershed planning, biodiversity, cumulative environmental impact, and carrying capacity of lakes, rivers, wetlands, forest tracts or watersheds were not part of the 1973 Act's language or assessment. That needs to happen.

*Create a single Forest Preserve management system.* The need to consolidate the administrative boundaries of the state agencies in New York so they are the same for each agency is imperative. This may yet be a long time in coming. The present system of overlapping state agency administrative boundaries creates frustration, inefficiency, and confusion both in and out of government. There have been previous calls for an Adirondack Park Service. However, in the short term, an administrative order to combine DEC Regions 5 and 6 under a single regional director would go a long way toward creating more consistent state administration of the Forest Preserve Wilderness and Wild Forest areas and their resulting intersection with the private lands of the park. This order would require no change in boundaries of the buffer areas outside the park in the North Country, no change in facilities, and no change in total personnel, in addition to a single regional director, a single chief ranger, chief permit administrator, and chief forester. The Wilderness lands in the Forest Preserve are guided by a single APA-administered State

Land Master Plan, but management actions are subject to different interpretation in the two regions. If the DEC were to treat the park as a single entity, instead of two, it would go a long way toward consistent management of the Forest Preserve and its abiding wilderness resources.

*Focus on assembling the Greater Oswegatchie/Bob Marshall Wilderness as the premier contiguous Wilderness/wildland area in the eastern United States.* The Adirondack Council and the Sierra Club have taken leading roles in efforts to call public attention to the potential for creating this magnificent wilderness, which is already largely in public ownership and with protected easement lands. For canoeing, for hiking, for skiing and snowshoeing, and just for its own sake as an ecological treasure house, this is a wildland area that deserves the strongest support from all concerned with its special resources and ownership patterns. Finding common ground to keep the area Forever Wild, over time, should be a major initiative.

*Foresight capability should be nurtured at every opportunity.* Hindsight offers many valuable lessons. But foresight enables the avoidance of adverse actions or consequences that could have been avoided if they had been addressed at the earliest possible time and as part of an ingrained perspective that looks at the forest (which is what is being preserved), not just the trees. Foresight is a cost-effective, time-efficient way of applying public policies and private investments.

It is noteworthy that wilderness users make up a much larger part of the populations than might appear from their numbers in the back country. Norm Van Valkenburg, former director of Lands and Forests for the Department of Environmental Conservation, ranked five classes of wilderness users. The first three classes ranged from party and play, to preference for nonmotorized recreation with facilities, to self-sufficient backpackers. Those who never enter into the back country, but prefer to view it from the periphery, and those who will never visit wilderness but are glad it is there, make up the largest number of wilderness constituents.

In closing, as Justice William O. Douglas noted in *A Wilderness Bill of Rights,*

Wilderness values may not appeal to all Americans but they make up a passionate cause for millions. They are indeed so basic to our national well-being that they must be honored by any free society that respects diversity. We deal not with transitory matters but with the very earth itself. We who come this way are merely short-term tenants. Our power in wilderness terms is only the power to destroy, not to create. Those who oppose wilderness values today may have sons and daughters who will honor wilderness values tomorrow. Our responsibility, as life tenants is to make certain that there are wilderness values to honor after we have gone.[6]

# 32

## Toward a New Wilderness Paradigm for Adirondack Park

*The View from Bear Mountain*

RAINER H. BROCKE

Climbing this modest mountain is easy, my students attest; I agree—
helped along by frequent "educational" stops. We emerge from
shrouding forest onto a summit ledge, and suddenly Cranberry Lake
and its forested environs unfold below us, stretching into the blue
northwest Adirondack horizon. The view is spectacular! Like other
memorable overlooks, this one generates its own share of deeper
thoughts, and grist for them is ample. Immediately obvious—
human intrusion along the shores of this lake, third largest in the
park, is surprisingly minor. Lakeside cottages, largely hidden from
our view, are restricted to just two of the lake's six radiating arms,
namely the northern one reaching into Cranberry Lake village and
the western one terminating in Wanakena. With the exception of
SUNY College of Environmental Science and Forestry's two educational institutions—the Cranberry Lake Biological Station and the
New York Ranger School—the lake's scenic 55-mile-long shoreline is almost uninterrupted state land. The view across Cranberry's
sparkling waters brings back personal memories of morning canoe
trips along the lake's wild periphery—summer trips when I might
spy a beaver swimming lodgeward, hauling bounties of greenery;
a yodeling loon pair herding away their diminutive black chicks; a
naughty whitetail fawn leaving its hiding place and boldly exploring

the beaver-browsed bank, thus making itself a beacon for predators; or a black bear intently digging for small prey among the rocks, oblivious to the blackfly cloud circling its head. Such are the dramas that compete for my attention as I fly-fish for bass, casting a deer hair bug to the far side of a submerged spruce stump—the lair of a capital smallmouth. Ah, what balm for the harried modern—the quintessential wilderness experience—yet, in an area that is not Wilderness by accepted criteria.

Shifting our gaze to the southwest, my students and I can see 10 miles into the Five Ponds Wilderness, an uninterrupted vista of forested lowlands punctuated by low mountains, small lakes, beaver ponds and swamps. Beginning on Cranberry's far shore, this wild tract contains 101,170 acres of state land (Forest Preserve), of which the southern half (45,000 acres) is continuous virgin forest—the largest such area in the Adirondack Park and probably in the northeastern United States. The Five Ponds Wilderness is one of 14 wild areas so designated by the Adirondack Park Agency, defined as:

A Wilderness Area, in contrast with those areas where man and his own works dominate the landscape, is an area where the earth and its community of life are untrammeled by man—where man himself is a visitor who does not remain. A Wilderness Area is further defined to mean an area of state land or water having a primeval character, without significant improvements or permanent human habitation, which is protected and managed so as to preserve, enhance and restore, where necessary, its natural conditions and which (1) generally appears to have been affected primarily by the forces of nature, with the imprint of man's work substantially unnoticeable; (2) has outstanding opportunities for solitude or primitive and unconfined type of recreation; (3) has at least ten thousand acres of land and water or is of sufficient size and character as to make practicable its preservation and use in unimpaired condition; and (4) may also contain ecological, geological or other features of scientific, educational, scenic or historical value.[1]

With this passage in mind, my students and I hike into the heart of the Five Ponds Wilderness on our annual two-day trip, providing us ecological perspectives to compare these wildlands with the APA's Wilderness definition. The students are initially unaware that, with the exception of the interior virgin forest tract, humans have ground a heavy boot into these lands, beginning in the late 1800s when sequential railroad construction, logging camps, and sequels of fire swept these lands. As resources were exhausted, most of the population moved on. Even Cranberry Lake on whose southeastern shores this wilderness begins, is artificial, the product of two earlier logging dams followed by a concrete one built in 1916, raising Cranberry's waters 20 feet above the Oswegatchie River's original Stillwater. Hence, today the lake looks very unlike the original. Most visitors would not recognize it as an impoundment without seeing the dam. Wilderness icons have made it their home—icons such as the loon, bald eagle, and osprey and, in time, moose will again grace its summer shallows.

On our hike, we first encounter logged timberlands now completely reforested, except for the Plains—a clearing that persists today as a frost pocket, occasionally swept by fire. Canada jays, black-backed woodpeckers, hermit thrushes, and boreal chickadees haunt the black spruces and mixed forest nearby. Soon the trail follows an old railroad bed, swallowed by vegetation. Crossing the Oswegatchie River, we traverse snag-dotted beaver flows into virgin forest—its giant spruces and white pines towering overhead. As we cross ecological boundaries of land history, students find it initially difficult to identify differences between logged and virgin forest. Yes, they see the virgin pines, but the large, open-grown pines surrounding the logged Plains—nearly three feet in diameter and only one century old—are satisfyingly similar to the more "ancient" pines. Clearly, the imprint of man's work is now substantially unnoticeable, and it took nature only one century to achieve that. To them this is indeed wilderness—any distinctions between human or natural agents are unnecessary.

Traversing the virgin forest without any imprint of man's work, students are surprised by extensive tracts of recent destruction. Here they see the aftermath of nature's mayhem in patches as large as football fields—sequential destruction by microbursts, ice storms, lightning fires, beaver flows, and insect defoliations. Here they see an alien rationale beyond imagining, where landmark white pines have been leveled helter-skelter by monstrous winds. Here they see new beaver floodings that have snuffed out all previous life—effects fully equivalent to a mall parking lot—sights that give added meaning to the phrase "affected primarily by the forces of nature." Clearly, Mother Nature was doing her own share of trammeling, perhaps tired of her handiwork grown old, but, with death comes new life. Young spruces poke through gray carcasses of their wind-thrown parents, and having waited patiently for decades, white pine saplings make up for lost time. Mature beaver ponds and their snag-filled openings, now surrounded by lush greenery, become fonts of quickened energy, and nutrients flow—magnets for recolonizing and reproducing wildlife. Here, trout, otter, heron, merganser, kingfisher, and osprey hobnob with snowshoe hare, ruffed grouse, kingbird, tree swallow, edge warblers, and broad-winged hawks. Here the whitetail hides its fawns—black bears and fishers seek them out. For my students, there is a big lesson in this eastern virgin forest: it is not the continuous old growth they expected, but rather a vibrant, restless, biotic mosaic, ever freshened by disturbance—itself a very normal occurrence, true too for western forests.[2]

Having opted for my wilderness wildlife conservation course, students hope to see at least some charismatic megafauna here. After all, human exploitation in this remote area is near zero; besides they are used to seeing television programs showing such pristine places packed with wildlife. Not true here—merely seeing a whitetail or occasional bear is unusual, and in the late 1990s deer sightings reached the vanishing point. Poor visibility accentuates perceived deer scarcity, but nature's signs soon tell us this decline is real. Old browsed-out winter deer yards are healing; the few coyote scats we find on the trail are replete with deer hair and fawn hooves; and large expanses of maple and yellow birch seedlings now carpet the forest floor. The recent addition of coyote predation to the whitetail's previously low survival rate owing to severe winter energy burdens reduced deer densities to only a few per square mile. We were witnessing firsthand a return to this area's original ecological carrying capacity[3]—the equilibrium between vegetation, herbivores, and predators that existed here in pre-European times over two centuries ago. Of course, I was the only class participant who had actually witnessed a significant portion of this trend, and given a rare opportunity, I felt especially fortunate to play my professor's role here. Today this ecological trend is reflected widely across the interior Adirondacks, judging from the DEC's published annual buck kill. The coyote, principal large predator in the ecosystem, is a very successful stand-in for the wolf. By 2050 some genetic variant of the wolf will probably roam these forests again, along with moose.

The degree to which ecological carrying capacity is realized in wilderness is a key measure of its biodiversity and stability, pointing to a need in the APA's definition of Wilderness to include statements about the role of ecological processes. More comprehensively, a fundamental statement of philosophy is appropriate concerning desirable goals for processes such as energy flow and nutrient cycling, plant succession, agents of disturbance, ecological equilibria and their interactions with modern civilization in the Adirondack Park. Assuming that American culture is to be an integral part of the natural landscape in appropriate park corridors, compromises are necessary within acceptable limits of physical carrying capacity[4] (the park's ability to withstand esthetically displeasing human-caused damage), and psychological carrying capacity (the impact of crowding on users' perceptions of wildness). These measures reflecting classic concerns in park and wilderness management are addressed in the State Land Master Plan.

Prior to the Five Ponds hike, the view from Bear Mountain reinforced my students' expectations that they were about to experience a real northeastern wilderness. In this panorama, they saw inviting qualities of remoteness, wild beauty, and perfect nature idealized by preservationists, writers, and poets. Steeped in wilderness philosophy and its cultural history, so well explored by Roderick Nash in

*Wilderness and the American Mind* and reinforced by currently prevailing urban thought, most students had a muted perception that our impending intrusion bordered on physical threat to this "fragile" ecosystem.[5] As humans, we would rank just short of being Martians entering this state of natural perfection. However, descending into this wilderness, students soon discovered that its biological realities trumped most idealistic perceptions they had felt as distant onlookers—a change akin to what a naïve tourist might experience first surveying the battlefield at Gettysburg on a beautiful spring morning, then later discovering bloody details of its history. They saw up close that this wildland and its life had recently experienced every conceivable force of natural destruction. Far from being fragile, they saw ample evidence of nature as a resurrecting phoenix, reinventing itself through every succeeding episode of storm, rain, snow, ice, flood, fire, bright sun, and dark shade. They saw that man's brief tenure had been just one of these episodes, barely recognizable with the passage of a century. They began to understand that Adirondack pioneers must have led a supremely harsh life, trying to eke out a living from such infertile lands. In their ecological struggles these people must have resembled the wildlife around them—merely top-predators living in larger "beaver houses," overlooking their temporary "human meadows" in the forest. Unlike pioneers, we hikers were freed from toil to enjoy the beauties of this wildland, fortified with canned food, portable shelter, and warm bedding. And, students reminded me, we would soon have bug-free housing, steak, and ice cream, merely one day's hike away. But, beyond our modern veneer, we were still those original, very vulnerable humans, no less natural than other beings in these surrounding wilds.

The perception of man as an alien being—an unnatural intruder in wilderness, his mere presence at odds with nature—is quite recent and peculiarly American in origin. It was born of our unique history and the rapid settlement of a vast new continent. Conquest of indigenous peoples in the 1700s and early 1800s was followed by enforced removal of their survivors to reservations, thus leaving their homelands depopulated—lands now open to settlement or to rediscovery as wildlands, particularly in the West, by naturalists, artists, and preservationists. While they knew that Indians had once roamed these lands, evidence of their presence was now muted. Even forestlands periodically opened up by native fires soon showed little evidence of past burns. For these new explorers, if humans had ever been present previously, they must have been temporary visitors to have had so small an impact on the land—a perception reinforced by scenes of freshly human-trammeled nature common in the settler's wake. Into this perceptual mix, transcendentalists like Thoreau, Muir, and Olson injected their belief that these pristine wildlands reflected the perfection of God-created nature, unsullied by (non-natural) humans, indeed that natural objects were manifestations of the Christian God.

In the waning years of the industrial 1800s, urbanites were disenchanted by their crowded cities, rampant pollution, and land greatly changed by agriculture, even as wildlands were subdued and fast disappearing. Protagonists for conservation fought valiantly for their cause, each in his own way.[6] Indigenous people had long since been removed from American lands in the aftermath of conquest, and these conservationists personally encountered few ethical conflicts in abridgment of native ownership rights or in their proposals to have wildlands set aside for preservation. Similarly, national and state politics proceeded with minimal impediment as governmental actions declared vast acreages as national parks, reserves, and public timberlands, the most outstanding case being Theodore Roosevelt's set-asides totaling 150 million acres between 1901 and 1909, including 5 national parks and 51 wildlife refuges. Given a different American history, such grand acts of preservation might have been impossible. One wonders what the cliff-dwelling Indians along New Mexico's Gila River, and the warring tribes around them, might have thought about forester Aldo Leopold's designation of their lands as wilderness, had they been alive and present in 1924! Of course, these actions of wildland preservation were hailed across the country, especially by urbanites—quite obviously a fine thing to do with "empty" unproductive mountainous lands, some displaying wonders of nature like geysers, mud boils, colorful cliffs, falls, giant trees, and spectacular wildlife. From this cultural stew of history and geography laced with legal strategies was born the 1964 Wilderness Act and APA's wildland definitions, containing passages stating or implying that humans are destructive, unnatural beings in wilderness—aliens whose presence must be severely restricted to preserve pristine nature.

Along with other things American, the concepts of wilderness, national parks, game reserves, and nature sanctuaries were embraced abroad, their export enthusiastically encouraged and abetted by conservation organizations in the United States and Europe. Third-world regions, including India, Africa, and Southeast Asia were particular targets because they still contained large tracts of nature in the raw. But there was a problem—the fundamental premise of American wilderness philosophy is that humans are only visitors in wilderness, not residents, a wildland condition almost unknown in non-American wilds, nor easily imagined abroad. Elsewhere people had always been an integral part of wilderness, living there at low densities, even in the remotest regions. What to do? Of course, the solution of choice was to evacuate residents from the incipient park abroad thus conforming to the American wilderness paradigm—shades of moving "Indians" to reservations all over again!

A friend attending an international conservation congress in Africa related the following experience: Officials from Botswana were in the process of establishing the Central Kalahari Game Pre-serve (12.8 million acres), and they needed advice—how should they classify the Bushmen (Juwase), the region's indigenous people for millennia?[7] Were they people or were they wildlife? If wildlife, they could remain in the park consistent with the wilderness paradigm. They eventually decided they were people after all, badly in need of civilization—and hence had to be removed. To date more than 2,000 bushmen have been evacuated to villages outside the game reserve.[8] Reports of government brutality are common, and the issue has become highly confrontational, involving an indigenous-rights group, nongovernmental agencies (NGOs), and the United

Nations. This is not an isolated incident. Indeed it is the norm across third-world countries where indigenous people have been evicted from newly established parks, leaving behind their means of traditional livelihood (living off the land).

Currently, 49,000 protected wildland areas are spread across the planet, comprising 6 percent of its total land area, and in India, nearly 4 million people face eviction following new protected-area policies. Brockington and Schmidt-Solton write, "One of conservation's severest forthcoming challenges is how to deal with this portending displacement, to be carried out in nature's name."[9] Budiansky, quoted by Brown, observes, "Excluding people from protected landscapes has become an end in itself—despite the rising rhetoric to the contrary."[10] And so we have well-intentioned Western conservationists—elites working top-down with local governments—applying the Wilderness paradigm, effectively dispossessing native residents to benefit recreation of the foreign wealthy. In Africa, a backlash is already underway. Burgeoning populations of the poor surrounding national parks and game preserves, deriving little or no benefit from tourism and lucrative sport-hunting venues (largely siphoned off by governments), have taken to large-scale poaching, resulting in widespread wildlife depopulation.[11]

The reader may ask what this discussion has to do with wildlife conservation in the Adirondack Park: in a word, everything. On a lesser scale, conservation conflicts in the Adirondack Park are cut out of the same cloth as such conflicts elsewhere between rural residents and urban wilderness interests in the United States (e.g., within the Yellowstone ecosystem) and the world. Here, the wilderness paradigm was used as a political and legal tool in affecting restrictive zoning by conservation elites, New York State, and the APA—zoning that would protect this wildland from development, primarily benefiting downstate and eastern urbanite recreationists, but thereby dispossessing park residents of various rights. And so we have a wildland assembled by bits and pieces—a park about which McMartin observed, "It was never a park like Yosemite, a pristine place to be preserved,"[12] yet has willy-nilly acquired trappings of a western wilderness park in its perceived management philosophy, political battles, and legalities describing its wild places.[13]

It is not surprising then that park residents and their village governments, who lost the political battles establishing the Adirondack Park Agency in 1971, feel themselves pitted against the APA, New York State government in Albany, and downstate wilderness preservationists—circumstances that have conferred an us-versus-them attitude among park residents. It should not be surprising that conservation initiatives fostered by perceived outsiders will be opposed by residents—simply seen as a new form of "taking." It should not be surprising that residents would oppose additional state acquisitions of commercial forestlands, merely to round out designated wilderness areas or to establish some politician's conservation heritage, thus reducing the local economic base and restricting access. It should not be surprising that additional acquisition of lands supporting rare and threatened wildlife or plant communities will receive little if any resident support. It should not be surprising if a newly acquired lake harboring a rare trout strain should be immediately compromised by perch or bass fry dumped there by a disgruntled resident (as happened at Little Tupper Lake). It should not be surprising that newly colonizing wolves, by designed program or natural expansion, might be poached to extinction under a "shoot, shovel, and shut up" dictum, as occurred in the West, or that the occasional disgruntled resident levels a colonizing moose.

The solution lies in identifying and defining a new paradigm for the Adirondack Park—a paradigm that leaves behind a wildland myth born of our historical past, denying humans a natural place in wilderness—a paradigm that builds on the recent explosion in scientific information about natural processes and wildlife ecology—and a paradigm that recognizes the legitimacy and equal role of all stakeholders in making political decisions. Such a paradigm would not discard the fruits and successes of the park's past conservation battles. Rather, it would build upon them toward more effective conservation and towards greater realization of democratic ideals befitting the twenty-first century. The essence of such a paradigm can be approximately described by a logo, "Adirondack Park—The New Wilderness—Integrating Responsible Conservation with Community Values."

Whatever new paradigm and new set of principles are considered to redefine wildland resource conservation and associated human affairs in the Adirondack Park, their attainment will be a challenge. The track record of a recent effort involving the four northeastern states is not encouraging. In 1988, the governors of Maine, New Hampshire, New York, and Vermont established the (temporary) Northern Forest Lands Council to recommend strategies to reverse current development threats to the region's rural life, open space, and forest resources—this area including Adirondack Park. Their report, a voluminous effort incorporating the work of many dedicated people, was submitted in 1994 without appreciable results in any of the four states. This report still stands as a useful compendium of information for future use.

Experiences from the Northwest Forest Plan (NFP), introduced in the early 1990s, have much to inform conservation in Adirondack Park. The plan, resulting from a legal challenge to a federal plan protecting the spotted owl (*Strix occidentalis*) under the Endangered Species Act, precipitated a massive regional shift from timber management to conserving biodiversity. The plan was implemented on a strip of Pacific coastland, stretching from northern Washington to northern California, encompassing 25 million acres of wild federal lands, interspersed with private lands, highways, towns, and cities.[14] Space will not permit more than a passing commentary on this bitter and complicated conflict between preservationists seeking to close down timber harvesting, private timber producers, federal agencies with diverse management goals, and local residents dependent on a wood-producing economy.

The spotted owl, trigger for the legal conflict, does best in old-growth forest. But research has also shown that it survives in logged forests, and cessation of logging in federal forests has in many cases not slowed its population decline. Apparently, a major cause of its continuing decline is widespread invasion of its habitat by the barred owl (*Strix varia*), a closely related species.[15] The barred owl not only competes for food but aggressively displaces it or even hybridizes with it. Old-growth forests are now widely valued for more than their economic values or biological functions—namely for their large and beautiful trees, invariably rare and comparable to "cathedrals," as John Muir noted long ago. Hence, any cutting of such old growth in the NFP area is very unlikely in the future. Recent studies have shown high species diversity in successional forests produced within old growth following natural disturbances including fire,[16] diversity that can also be produced by good silvicultural practices, as in the Adirondacks.[17] In their conclusions, Thomas and co-authors state: "it is time . . . to recognize that timber harvest, in certain conditions and done in certain ways is compatible with and essential for conservation of some types of forests and species in them."[18]

Implementation of the Northwest Forest Plan had immediate and drastic social and economic consequences in the region. Between 1990 and 2000, about 30,000 jobs in the wood products industry were lost.[19] Some communities were heavily hit and have yet to recover. Others gained economically from tourism and an influx of retirees, second-home owners, self-employed workers, and immigrants. Political reactions to economic impacts and reassessments by federal agencies to their ineffective implementation of agency mandates have led to modified and streamlined regulations, facilitating timber harvests on federal lands.[20] Writing about social perspectives in the Northwest experience, Charnley writes: "To be a successful model for broad-scaled ecosystem management by today's standards, a management plan should address the social, economic and ecological components of sustainability. . . . Broad-scale ecosystem management plans should seek to implement conservation strategies that contribute to healthy communities while fostering engagement of those communities in ecosystem management."[21]

A wildlife conservation study by Peterson and coworkers sheds much light on why deep-rooted feelings of alienation remain between Adirondack Park residents and environmental interests residing largely outside the park.[22] Peterson and colleagues sought to learn why two attempts to implement the Endangered Species Act through Habitat Conservation Plans failed, respectively, for Florida's key deer (a small subspecies of the whitetail, popularized as "toy deer") and the Houston toad in Texas. The efforts began well enough, with positive feelings on all sides. Stakeholders and players in the conflict were state and federal agencies, state and county legislators, national and state environmental groups, local landowners, and planners. As in the case of Adirondack Park, these conflicts collided head-on with the paradox of liberal democracy—namely facilitating a balance between the right of liberty (property rights of the individual) and equality (popular sovereignty of the people at large). The authors summarize their conclusions as follows:

> In both cases, the process was framed as a search for the optimum solution through collaboration and consensus building, and in neither case was the solution achieved. The paradoxical nature of liberal democracy precluded the possibility of a single, ideal solution. Failing to find the optimal solution led to disillusionment and pessimism with the process among HCP participants. We suggest that within democratic political contexts, approaches to conservation planning that center around bounded conflict, which is rooted in the paradox inherent in the ideals of liberty and equality, are more likely to produce satisfactory results than are consensus-based approaches.[23]

In short, the first step is to acknowledge to the participants the reality of these two equally legitimate freedoms, and to recognize the need for both sides to compromise.

## Looking to the Future

If the fauna of the Adirondack Park is to attain the "Hallmark of Quality" proposed by C. H. D. Clarke 35 years ago,[24] it is essential that stakeholders, particularly Adirondack residents, be given a vested interest in the restoration and survival of the park's present and potential wildlife complex. Toward that end, much needs to be done. We can begin by drafting a collective vision—a paradigm of inclusiveness, integrating responsible conservation with human values, thus conferring on all a stake in the welfare of Adirondack wildlife, followed by a steady, long-term effort to implement it.

At the dawn of this millennium we survey a world of possibilities beyond imagining—a world where humans stand at the controls of life itself; where each can communicate instantly with any other anywhere; where basic human needs can be met everywhere, if we but have the political will; where the sun's energy can be ingeniously captured to make anyone a superman; and where a trip to another planet is entirely possible. We also face unprecedented pressure on our wild places, which must serve us more effectively if they are to survive. For the Adirondack Park, we stand at the threshold of exciting possibilities toward making this a better wildland, biologically and culturally, and perhaps its checkered history and ecological imperfections will prove to be an asset in this process.

Suggesting details in wildlife conservation for the park is beyond my purview here. These can be worked out with honest compromises, by all stakeholders and participants, including interested citizens, professionals, researchers, community representatives, environmental organizations, and the DEC. Within the biological limitations of individual species and the park's ecological shortcomings, much is possible in wildlife management today, given the field's great advances in the last century. General guidance for wildlife management in wilderness is provided by The Wildlife Society and in other scientific publications.[25] Summarizing information in this chapter and drawing on my own experience as a wildlife biologist formerly residing in the park, I offer some considerations addressing ecological and cultural contexts toward enhancing wildlife conservation in the Adirondack Park.

The park is not distinctive in fielding its own unique species of wildlife. Rather, the region serves as a dynamic meeting ground for juxtaposed northern and southern wildlife, coexisting like interlocking fingers of clasped hands. Here characteristically southern species like the whitetail, bobcat, eastern cottontail, southern flying squirrel, red-shouldered hawk, wood thrush, cardinal, blue jay, and turkey hobnob with northerners like the moose, fisher, snowshoe hare, northern flying squirrel, goshawk, Bicknell's thrush, red cross-bill, gray jay, and spruce grouse. Such diversity is possible not only because of latitude, but also because of locally wide variations in altitude and drainage within the park. The Adirondack region is one of those few beautiful places on earth where substantial mountain-ous terrains coexist with large rivers, lakes, and swamps—mutually exclusive in most places.

The park's natural wildlife diversity is enhanced by forest rejuve-nation on privately managed timberlands, mimicking areas of natu-ral disturbance. Research has shown that wildlife diversity is highest on logged lands. Recent studies have also shown that amphibian and reptile populations, often most susceptible to human impacts, are not harmed by normal forest management practices in the Adiron-dacks.[26] Natural fires have not normally been a factor rejuvenating forest succession in the park (extensive fires of the late 1800s were caused by the period's unusual logging slash leavings). While early succession on private timberlands tends to compensate for the state's policy of fire suppression in the park, the latter might be reexamined for a few limited areas like the Moose River Plains and Five Ponds Plains, where management by fire may benefit species such as spruce grouse and golden eagle.

Private timberlands play two important ecosystem-wide roles for the park's wildlife conservation. First, on a landscape level, they provide broad habitat connections of relatively undeveloped space between Forest Preserve tracts. Contrary to popular opinion, man-aged timberlands *are usually not* barriers to wildlife movements in the Northeast; they usually *do not* create habitat islands, isolating wild-life subpopulations. In the Adirondack Park, managed timberlands and Forest Preserve lands essentially function as a single ecological unit in supporting wildlife.

Second, managed timberlands provide habitats of enhanced productivity, thus playing a potentially important role in support-ing metapopulations of large, wide-ranging mammals. As discussed previously, extensive space requirements of large wild mammals tell us that from a comprehensive perspective, the park's ecosystem is small. There is no appreciable buffer zone of public wildlands or sparsely populated private lands surrounding the park as in the Greater Yellowstone Ecosystem. Hence, it lacks a buffer between it and civilization, and thus the park's ecosystem boundaries coincide with its political boundaries. In contrast, Yellowstone Park's area comprises merely 12 percent of the GYE's area totaling 18 million acres. Consequently, resident wildlife populations in Adirondack Park must meet all their survival needs within the park's limited space. Far-ranging animals wandering outside the park risk potential conflicts with humans and, at worst, quick death, thus impoverishing the breeding population. As the park is essentially an ecological island, immigration to sustain its wildlife populations is minimal.

In view of the park's characteristics of small ecological size and discontinuous public ownership, private timberlands assume an unusual and important role as productive successional lands, where the rejuvenated forest enhances survival of large ungulates and their predators, potentially maintaining their populations at locally higher densities—species including whitetails, moose, bobcats, fishers, black bears, and, potentially, restored wolves. This unique role of the park's managed forest cannot be overstated. Clearly, it is not in the interests of wildlife conservation in Adirondack Park to continue the state's practice of buying up these timberlands, with their subsequent conversion to lower productivity (old-growth) Forest Preserve lands. Indeed, this conversion process may have already gone too far. Every effort should now be made to encourage and sustain forest management on private lands by conservation easements, tax incentives, and other means. This is a way we might achieve a "big park" wildlife complex, while having only a "small park" at our disposal—isolated at that.

Aesthetics are currently the driving force behind the APA's land-use classifications. Although it is important for some of them, there must be an ecological basis for others if they are to be useful for biotic decisions. Solid estimates of ecological carrying capacity or other biological parameters expressed as bracketed ranges for Resource Management lands can delineate those areas where timber management is to be encouraged. Conversely, unusual habitats and areas of low carrying capacity (e.g., mountaintops, ridges, bogs, and boreal habitat) can be identified for possible acquisition as Forest Preserve. Areas where management by fire is appropriate (e.g., Moose River Plains, Five Ponds Plains and other areas) need to be delineated along with development of legal processes to implement such management in selected areas. These measures may help to regenerate habitats fostering survival of spruce grouse, golden eagles, and other species.

There is no good reason, in my opinion, to maintain the Wild Forest category, as it is ecologically largely indistinguishable from Wilderness; Wild Forest lands should be reclassified as Wilderness—a category conversion that would confer greater public respect for the wild resources of these lands. Assuming such reclassification, decisions about appropriate public recreational access can be rethought and relaxed for some of the Wilderness category as a whole. Likewise, most of the Resource Management category might best be renamed Wildland Management or Forest Management for privately managed timberlands offering the owner opportunities for pride in good management. In my opinion, these changes are more in keeping with the park's goal of providing the magical "wilderness experience," with all that this phrase means to each individual.

Wild animals are a universal measure of a land's wildness. But as natural reforestation reclaims the once-denuded Northeast, and as enlightened management fosters wildlife abundance beyond imagining merely one century ago, Mr. and Ms. Citizen may well ask, "Why do I need wilderness when whitetails ate my peonies, a black bear hibernated under my neighbor's house last winter, and peregrine falcons nest in my city?" Good question—and each will have an answer. Many a naturalist, hiker, and hunter will go to great expense and exert great effort seeking out wildlife in wilderness. They have learned that wilderness provides a setting for wild animals akin to that of velvet displaying a gem. Encountering a wild creature in silence, framed by wild beauty, is like no other happening. It is often a rare event, and therefore precious; it is spying a wild creature ever alert for the predator; it is witnessing living camouflage, perfectly matching its surroundings; it is watching the predator, the ultimate wild hunter at work, or finding mute signs of past drama in the snow; it is the beauty of wild form and function, silhouetted against the blazing sky, experiences that are the elixir of wilderness.

It has always puzzled me why we Americans are so reluctant to assign economic value to aesthetic qualities, of which wildness is one. It seems that to Americans, nature's bounty merits dollar equivalents only when measured in pounds, bushels, acres, or board feet. American wilderness is such a value orphan. In the Swiss Alps, farmers are handsomely remunerated for producing sheep and milk cows the old way—sparsely herded on verdant hillsides near picturesque Alpine farmsteads. They are paid by a grateful government not for producing wool, meat, or milk, but for their visual contribution to some of the most breathtaking pastoral scenery on earth, attracting armies of tourists yearly. This scenery did not just happen. Planners use computer-generated landscapes to produce the most scenic combination of rocky cliffs, forests, and contrasting grassland pastures.

In the Adirondacks, we are barely beyond the exploitation stage in terms of New York State's economic responsibility to private timberland owners. What does the public owe the timberland owner who maintains beautiful forested roadside vistas for 40 of 50 years between cutting cycles, without profit from timber? To the motoring or hiking public of the Adirondack Park, what is the worth of a spectacular forest landscape or loon-tenanted lake, both in private ownership? What is private forestland worth where it plays an ecosystem function of providing biological services and supporting the public's far-ranging wildlife? Today, these questions are not even asked, let alone addressed to remunerate timberland owners. By any measure, private timberlands are indeed sparsely compensated for the public services they provide in the Adirondack Park.

On another front, a conservation problem second to none is that of chemical pollutants and invading organisms. Day and night, during all seasons, they compromise the Adirondack ecosystem, their destructive impact usually profound when it is finally discovered. Both problems have mostly distant origins. Chemical pollutants are generated by midwestern factories or auto corridors to the south. Invasive organisms hitchhike in ships' cargo holds, on airplanes, or are simply blown across oceans in giant storms. The Adirondack ecosystem is particularly vulnerable to airborne pollutants, including acids and mercury due to its geologic characteristics.

Shopping at Wal-mart is actually very expensive if all its ecological costs via invasions by foreign organisms are tallied. We have already lost the elm and chestnut to exotic diseases, and the beech is not far behind; gray patches of dead and dying beech infected by beech scale disease now dot the Adirondack forests. Final loss of the beech, a key provider of fattening mast, would be catastrophic for many animals, especially because it is the only nut producer remaining in the central Adirondacks. Around the park, aquatic invaders are legion, and penetration from the periphery is only a matter of time.

Lakes and ponds acidified by aerial pollution are scattered throughout the park,[27] concentrated in the western Adirondacks with its acid soils and rock. Approximately 240 Adirondack lakes are known to be fishless. They no longer support top-predators like otters, loons, ospreys, mergansers, great blue herons, and kingfishers. We can only guess what wildlife once frequented these now-silent waters—life whose presence was not even documented before it disappeared without a trace. If I were to prioritize measures to foster wildlife conservation in the Adirondack Park, solutions to these problems would rank near the top. Measures to combat pollution and invading organisms are national problems with worldwide scope—their implementation must be vigorously addressed at the continental level without delay.

The last summer tourists leave the park by Labor Day and the locals quietly rejoice: "September is our month and bullhead is our meat." A collective sigh of relief can almost be heard beyond the mountains, now touched by the first leafy flames of autumn, as

Adirondackers roll up the sidewalks, pack the bars, and fire up their boats nightly to go bullheading; no Royal Coachman for them—trout, bass, and pike are for the tourists. The outsiders are leaving and mostly good riddance for eight months! Yes, there are invasive tourist blips on some weekends, weather permitting—tourists seeking fall color, snowmobiling, skiing, and snowshoeing. But mostly, the quiet of winter snow land dominates. "What do you guys do here all winter?" so many ask, as with a tinge of relief they head back to their frantic lives in noisy cities.

And so, another year cycles through an unspoken truce. Oh, the "natives" have close friends among the outsiders, and they know where their bread is buttered. They can even dimly understand the downstater's "strange" views about nature, given his green-starved city environs. But they cannot get over the hypocrisy of externally inflicted (state) zoning regulations for park residents; if downstaters think these regulations are exemplary, why do they not apply them in their own backyards? Why did the concept of Catskill State Park die on the political vine following its own study commission report? Perhaps such a park was too close for comfort for politically powerful landowners.

And so the muted schism persists—a classic conflict embodying the paradox of liberal democracy, namely the individual's freedom to control his own property, pitted against the right of popular sovereignty—the public's striving for the common good. To Adirondackers, the state's abridgement of property rights over an area as large as Vermont goes beyond the pale.

The relevance of this schism for wildlife conservation in the park has been discussed. Adirondackers live closely with their wild animals year-round; they attract little attention, unless they are large predators. Park residents were first in the state to learn that their pet cats and dogs are preferred coyote food. During our lynx restoration effort, we were surprised to discover an undercurrent of concern among some residents, especially parents, about a possible backyard visit by a lynx. The prospect of reintroducing predators, an idea usually championed by outsiders, is understandably unsettling. Again, their reaction: "Why don't you do it in your own backyard?"

Education programs planned by both residents and nonresidents are one long-term answer towards reconciling this schism—science-based programs addressing the park's natural history and resource conservation in a unique wildland setting. Several are already in progress, including SUNY-ESF's "Stalking Science Education in the Adirondacks" for teachers, led by Andrew Saunders; and the APA's interpretive program with nature centers at Newcomb and Paul Smiths. The Adirondack Museum at Blue Mountain Lake, focusing on cultural history, was complemented in 2006 by completion of the Natural History Museum of the Adirondacks at Tupper Lake. This distinctive museum, an effort conceived and implemented by Elizabeth Lowe, was planned at the outset to involve Tupper residents as active partners, giving the village community a vested interest in nature education and wildland stewardship. As a year-round program, it clearly benefits the community's own youth.

In the short term, there will be important opportunities to involve year-round community residents as equal partners in decision making, especially about the park's development and economy. I have briefly made the case for a new Adirondack Park paradigm— call it the New Wilderness, or some such equivalent—emphasizing inclusiveness and shucking out-of-date wilderness ideas born of our colonial past, specifically that humans are alien to, and not compatible with, wilderness. Discussions or attempted collaborations seeking quick consensus about conflicting views will *not* be successful. As research has shown, solutions for the long term are possible only if such efforts are treated as bounded conflicts, requiring both sides truly to compromise, an effort requiring good planning, care, and patience. If an improved economy can be achieved in the Adirondack Park, accompanied by a strong perception among residents that they have an equal voice in the park's development and its wildland conservation, the future integrity of this culture-rich wilderness and its wildlife is bright.

As a conservationist, I have found the word "Adirondack" of inestimable value in raising wildlife research funds or simply communicating with the public. It is a brand name with cachet, its instant recognition peculiarly fitting for our cyberspace times. Today, economic products in the United States have become predominantly conceptual, reflecting the reality that ideas and innovations are the most important national resource, replacing land, energy, and raw materials. For the Adirondacks, long gone is the era of mining, irresponsible timber extraction, commercial hunting, and subsistence agriculture. Yet, through these epic changes, the word "Adirondack" has prevailed, ever fresh, ever beckoning with reinvented magic. This single word has helped to lift the park, its nature, and its culture out of the ordinary, truly a conceptual resource for our age. Used wisely, this single word promises timeless service in conserving the park and its wildlife for the future.

# 33

## Can Such a Noble Endeavor Succeed?

*Alaska and the Adirondack Park*

DONALD BEHREND

The saga of Alaska began long ago, but the name that still captures the American imagination dates from 1867. That summer Senator Charles Sumner, chairman of the Senate Foreign Relations Committee, named this land Alaska as he argued for its purchase from Russia. Derived from the Aleut "aleyeska," meaning great land, Alaska thus became part of a young nation and soon captivated Americans with visions of a great northern wilderness rich with gold, furs, fish, minerals, and adventure. This great land became a territory of the United States in 1912, and a state of the union on January 3, 1959.

Closer to home for most Americans, another wilderness was being rediscovered in the mid-1800s. Tiny compared to Alaska, but soon to become large on the nation's stage, the Adirondack region of northern New York was rich with great forests, lakes, streams, and mountains. Close to the increasingly crowded cities of the Northeast, the region would soon be accessible through improvements in transportation for those seeking escape from the summer heat of the bustling cities. Lumbermen were also attracted by the rich forests, where heavy logging would soon generate much concern for the region's watersheds. So great was the attractiveness of the Adirondacks and the concerns for its watersheds by the late 1800s, that a series of statutes and constitutional amendments were enacted, including the establishment of the Adirondack Park.

At a glance, it seems unlikely that the Adirondack Park and Alaska have much in common. Differences in size, latitude, climate, ecosystems, population, and land ownership are pronounced. Yet one characteristic is common to both wildernesses. The wilderness character of both places consists of formally established wilderness areas, other public lands, and the communities they contain. What follows is thus about the wilderness characters of the park and the great land, their recent pasts, and their possible futures. It is offered with the hope that it may bring some additional perspective to the quest for maintaining the wilderness character of the Adirondack Park.

While Alaska is indeed a great land, its size is seldom fully appreciated. Stephen Haycox contends that "Alaska is so large its size almost defies comprehension."[1] Were it a nation, the great land would rank nineteenth in size. It is about half the size of India; one-fifth that of the contiguous 48 states combined; over twice the size of Texas; approaching twice the area of California, Oregon, and Washington together; more than five times larger than the New England states and New York combined; and roughly sixty-one times larger than the Adirondack Park. And, the great land's coastline of 6,640 statute miles constitutes almost 54 percent of the nation's total.[2] Distances over Alaska are correspondingly great. With the Aleutians included, corner-to-corner distances exceed 2,000 miles; sans the Aleutians, 1,200 to 1,500 miles. Approximately 1,340 miles separate Barrow on the Arctic Ocean and Ketchikan in the far southeast. Roads do not connect these communities or many others that can only be reached by air, water, or over snow. The road system connecting communities is largely restricted to the area reaching from the tip of the Kenai Peninsula to Fairbanks, to Valdez, plus links to Canada's Yukon Territory. Additionally a "haul road" links Fairbanks and Prudoe Bay.

Alaska is as diverse as it is vast. Major ecosystems include 4 climatic and 6 geological zones, 4 permafrost and 3 physiographic divisions, 6 hydrologic regions, and 7 marine and 12 terrestrial ecosystems. A trip from Ketchikan to Barrow begins in temperate coastal rain forest with up to 300 inches of annual precipitation and ends in arctic tundra with as little as 4. Maximum and minimum temperatures over four climatic zones—artic, continental, transitional, and maritime—vary greatly over the seasons with the greatest range in the continental (100°F to -75°F) and least in the maritime (92°F to -42°F).[3]

The population of the great land is much changed since 1880, when a total of 33,462 included only 426 non-Alaska Natives.[4] By 1960 the year following statehood, the population was 226,167. The oil boom of the 1970s and early 1980s brought more growth, and by 1990 the population had reached 550,043. Thirteen years later, a total 648,818 was constituted as follows: 69.3 percent white, 15.6 Native American, 4.0 Asian, 0.5 Hawaiian/Pacific Islander, 5.4 multiracial, 1.6 other, and 5.1 percent Hispanics of any race. Alaska Natives constitute the majority of 101,215 Native Americans, the major groups being Inuit, Yupik, Aleut, Athabascan, Tlingit, and Haida. Haycox states that many Native Alaskans reside in 225 villages, with 20,000 living in Anchorage.[5] Overall, roughly half of the state's population resides in Anchorage, Eagle River, and the nearby communities of the Matanuska-Susitna Valley.

Distribution of employment for May 2004 is listed as follows: 27.1 percent government; 20.6 trade/transportation /utilities; 3.1 manufacturing; 11.3 education/health services; 7.7 professional/business services; 10.2 leisure/hospitality; 4.8 finance; 5.8 construction; and 2.3 information. Unemployment for 2003 was 8 percent.[6] It is not clear how or if those figures account for residents who are primarily or solely engaged in subsistence hunting, fishing, and gathering. Irrespective of employment status, however, many Alaskans harvest fish and game for family fare.

The level of employment in government is of particular note. Statistics from the *Anchorage Daily News* (*ADN*) editorial of September 3, 2005, show the uniformed military and the federal civil service as ranking one and two, respectively, among Alaska's five largest governmental employers. Moreover, the state's five largest employers are all governmental entities, employing 67,760 people. The *ADN* thus projected it would take a hundred of Alaska's largest private employers to roughly equal the jobs provided by the state's five largest governmental entities.

Alaska's dramatic growth is clearly attributable to the oil boom and the attendant growth in government plus the assignment of military personnel. The prosperity accompanying this growth has brought significant change in the environment, some welcomed and some disliked by those who came seeking the old Alaskan wilderness character. Thus, as many have prospered some have lost, or perhaps others have never found the environment they originally sought.

What does this bode for the great land's future? And what, if anything, can Alaska's experience bring to the divining of the future of the Adirondack Park? The questions seem clear enough, the answers far from it.

By the end of the twentieth century, the respective roles of the Adirondack Park and Alaska in wilderness preservation were well-established: Alaska leading the nation in federally designated wilderness comprising 57,522,294 acres, and the park leading in state-designated wilderness totaling more than one million acres, with Alaska a close second with 922,700 acres of state-designated wilderness.[7] Despite huge differences in scale, these designated wilderness areas provide anchoring points for the wilderness characters of both places and should continue to so serve for the foreseeable future.

Other differences, however, abound. These include a huge federal presence in Alaska; the long-established role of state government in the Adirondack Park; significant native populations and institutions in Alaska; widespread extraction of nonrenewable energy resources in Alaska; the continuing presence of the great land on the nation's agenda; the tendency of Alaskans to view themselves as the owners and direct financial beneficiaries of their state's natural resources; an increasing tendency of Alaskans to view themselves as either urban or rural residents; and the absence of zoning over most of Alaska. And the list could go on.

Nonetheless, important similarities exist: sources of capital for investment lie outside the boundaries of both places; Adirondackers and Alaskans alike strongly resent what they see as attempts by outsiders to impose their agendas; residents balk at the imposition of restrictions on the development of private lands; the visitor industry is increasingly seen as a desirable source of income; wilderness character is viewed as both a desirable part of the residents' environment and as an attraction for visitors; and a majority of residents of both places would likely find the establishment of more large, designated wilderness areas unacceptable. While the exact roles these differences and similarities may play in the futures of Alaska and the park are debatable, two things seem clear: the maintenance or loss of wilderness character will be defining, and the uses of private lands will largely determine whether wilderness character waxes or wanes.

Roderick Nash, in *Wilderness and the American Mind,* claimed that although definitions differed, more than 95 percent of Alaska could be called Wilderness in 1959, when statehood was granted.[8] This wilderness was virtually all federal land that was subsequently apportioned between the state, Alaska Native corporations, and the federal government. In 1970 the state's wilderness program was initiated with the designation of three areas totaling 922,700 acres. Ten years later, President Carter signed the Alaska National Interest Lands Conservation Act, providing protection for roughly 104 million acres of federal land, or 28 percent of the state, an area larger than California. To this day, the strokes of President Jimmy Carter's signing pens are celebrated by preservationists and cursed by some Alaskans, who perceived promises broken and the state shortchanged. Differences not withstanding, the centerpiece of Alaska's designated wilderness was thus writ large on the map of the great land.

But the transformation of Alaska had been underway since 1974 when the oil and gas discoveries of the 1960s were acted upon and the buildup for construction of the Trans Alaska Pipeline (TAP) begun. By 1975 the states population and labor sources were soaring as Alaska's gross product hit 5.8 billion—double the 1973 figure. Completion of the TAP in 1977 brought the first "black gold" to Valdez for shipment to Puget Sound and the first batch of "greenbacks" to Juneau for the state's coffers. In 1980 the legislature repealed the state income tax, refunded the 1979 tax payments, and established a permanent fund for one-quarter of all oil-generated revenues. Annual dividends payable to all legal residents of all ages were initiated and maintained. State government to administer to a burgeoning population and funding for construction of public facilities mushroomed. Overall, about 85 percent of the state's expenditures were and are still funded by royalties from oil production. Whatever the future holds, the changes of the past 30 to 35 years have led some to conclude that the great land's wilderness character has been and continue to be degraded. John Strohmeyer addresses this in the preface of *Extreme Conditions: Big Oil and the Transformation of Alaska*, stating, "this is a book about the more significant perils confronting the great land today—specifically the threats to the face and character of Alaska."[9] Haycox contends that while Alaska stands as an icon of wilderness, "the reality . . . has seldom matched the Alaska of the imagination."[10] Terrance Cole, reviewing another of Haycox's books, entitled *Frigid Embrace: Politics, Economics, and Environment in Alaska*, sums up, stating:

> The unresolved issue appears to be Haycox's charge that commodifying nature necessarily leads to the destruction of nature. But the question that remains is how does one have any level of sustainable economic development in the cities or villages of Alaska without a degree of commodifying nature. In this world it is the buying and selling of commodities that enables us to afford not only food, clothing and shelter but also colleges, books and history professors.[11]

Scholarly differences aside, the great majority of Alaska's residents and visitors alike apparently continue to view most of Alaska as retaining sufficient wilderness character to satisfy for now. Yet the world's quest for energy resources continues to grow and will somehow continue to involve Alaska. The recent battles in the U.S. Congress over proposed drilling in the Artic National Wildlife Refuge (ANWR) was simply one more engagement in a continuing struggle that is far from over. Moreover, if drilling never occurs in ANWR, gas and oil and other energy resources will be pursued elsewhere in the great land as demand increases at home and abroad. The next efforts will likely include the rescue of Alaska's long-stranded natural gas on its north slope. And while oil production from Prudoe Bay continues to decline, new sources will continue to be found and developed. In short, it seems virtually certain that petroleum and natural gas will remain an important part of this country's energy supplies throughout its transition to a mix of new fuels and technologies. This, coupled with burgeoning demand for energy in China, India, and elsewhere, plus the tenuous stability of many oil-producing nations, may well require increases in U.S. production. Should that occur, the development of new sites for the extraction and transport of oil would clearly affect more of the great land's wilderness character. The overall impact would depend on the exact locations of new sites, the increases in new Alaskans attracted by expanded opportunities for employment, and the provision or lack of lead time for new developments.

Other sources of energy being considered for increased attention include coal, coal-bed methane, and wind. (Coal is currently exported.) Additional sectors for further development include the transshipment of cargo by air, processing of fish and wood products, and the visitor industry. With the exception of wind, most of these developments will likely occur on or near already developed sites and will have relatively little impact on wilderness character.

In sum, the greatest impacts on Alaska's wilderness character began with the oil boom of the 1970s and 1980s and has yet to run its full course. These years brought great changes to the great land's wilderness character even as huge areas of wilderness were protected. What is in store for Alaska over the next 40 years when its resources may be sought by so many?

Whatever comes will come to a state with a vastly different pattern of ownership than the old, pre-oil-boom Alaska. Any attempt to define its present wilderness character or to divine its future must begin with an understanding of these patterns, plus existing and likely future uses. In 1960, immediately following statehood, about 99.6 percent of the great land was in federal ownership. Forty years later federal lands had been reduced to 65 percent, and state and private holdings were 24 and 11 percent, respectively (table 33.1). Of these private lands, 37.5 million acres were owned by Alaska Native corporations, leaving but 2.69 million acres in other private ownerships. Looking ahead, Hull and Leask estimated that: (1) federal public domain would likely decline by about 20 million acres through transfers of another 13 million to state government and 7 million to native corporations; (2) municipal land will increase through transfers of more state and native corporation lands; and (3) private ownership will increase through state, municipal, university, and other land sales and as individuals receive more acreage through the Native Allotment Program. Alaska is clearly still a work in progress.

Yet, mid-twenty-first century Alaska will likely resemble that of the current decade. Despite the changes of the 1970s, 1980s, and

TABLE 33.1. **Alaska land ownership in 1960 and 2000 in millions of acres and percentage of total**

| Year | Federal[a] | State[b] | Private[c] | Total[d] |
|---|---|---|---|---|
| 1960 | 374.00 (99%) | 1.15 (<1%) | 0.50 (<1%) | 374.50 (100%) |
| 2000 | 242.00 (65%) | 89.50 (24%) | 40.09 (11%) | 371.59 (100%) |
| Change | -132.00 | +89.50 | +39.59 | |

*Source:* Adapted from T. Hull and L. Leask, 2000. "Dividing Alaska, 1867–2000: Changing Land Ownership and Management," *Alaska Review of Social and Economic Conditions* 32 (2001): 1–12.

[a]Federal statistics include public domain, national parks, wildlife refuges, forests, monuments, various reserves.

[b]State statistics include legislatively designated areas, parks, refuges, forests, etc., plus Mental Health Trust, Univ. of Alaska, and municipal lands.

[c]Private lands include Alaska Native Corporation lands, federal and state land programs, and municipal land sales.

[d]Total acreage figures differ slightly as some agencies count submerged land while others do not, thus totals differ from the 375 million acres most commonly cited for Alaska.

1990s, the great land will still dwarf the rest of the nation in designated Wilderness areas and overall wilderness character. This should maintain, or be little diminished largely because of the size of the state, the remoteness of large tracts of land, the continuing prominence of public lands, and the growing recognition by Alaskans that wilderness character is not only of great value to them, but to visitors and the local businesses they support.

Important questions remain, however. Most prominent are the future uses of the Native Corporation and state lands. As further land transfers occur, the combined area of these lands may exceed 140 million acres, about two-thirds and one-third in state and Native Corporation ownerships, respectively. The future uses of and changes in these lands will largely be determined by the global demand for energy, minerals, wood and wood products, fish and fish products, and tourism, including ecotourism and wilderness visits.

What can this glimpse of Alaska's past and present bring to an expanded understanding of the Adirondack Park today, next year, or for the rest of the twenty-first century? The report of the Commission on the Adirondacks in the Twenty-First Century provides a convenient and cogent point of departure for the pursuit of an answer. *The Adirondack Park in the Twenty-First Century,* dated April 1, 1990, makes clear what the commission saw as threats to the park and what steps were needed to address them: in essence, what actions were required to maintain the rural and wilderness character of the Adirondack Park, to maintain affordable communities for full-time residents, and to provide increased opportunities for gainful employment.

The commission's own words on open space are instructive:

> It is vital to the economy of the State and the Park that these spaces, both publicly owned (the Forest Preserve) and privately held (more than half the land within the Park boundary), remain open. It is vital to the quality of life of those who live in the Park and those who visit it. It is vital—it is paramount—in any responsible vision of the Park in the 21st century. Yet this open

space is by no means guaranteed for future generations. This is the premise for this commission, as it was 20 years ago for the Temporary Study Commission on the Future of the Adirondacks.[12]

While few would question this premise, few would disagree that the 38 years since the Temporary Commissions report or the 19 years since the 1990 report have yet to bring the guarantee of open space for future generations. Some might even contend that over these years, while Alaska was being transformed by its oil boom, the Adirondack region has been enjoying or suffering a boom of its own—the burgeoning real estate market with its subdivision of private open land and attendant construction of second homes and recreational properties. This boom, created and fueled by a soaring real property market and a declining market for many traditional forest products from industrial lands, remains the chief threat to the park's open space, which the Twenty-First Century Commission identifies as "The Essence of the Park."[13]

The 245 recommendations in the 1990 report deal with park administration, quality of life, revitalizing hamlets, open space, compatible uses, performance standards, creating greenways, and extending the park boundary. It is an impressive work, comprehensive, detailed, and visionary, as might be expected for a 6-million-acre park nearing its one hundredth birthday. While many of the topics covered also apply to specific locales in Alaska, most comparisons would be of little use at this point in an old park's and a young state's development. Two areas, however, warrant discussion: open space and the quality of life, especially opportunities for employment.

If open space equates to underdeveloped land, the questions are clear: How much, where, and what kinds of development on private lands can the park sustain while retaining sufficient open space to guarantee its overall wilderness character?

Peter Bauer, reporting in another chapter of this book (chapter 12), describes the rates and patterns of development in the park from 1990 through 2006. He found that from 1990 through 2004 more than 13,500 new homes were permitted across the Adirondacks, and another 1,500 were added in 2005–6. Distribution was uneven with the 10 most active towns accounting for 30 percent of the total with just under 4,000 new homes. Numbers in 1990 and 2004 were 1,150 and 1,200 new dwellings, respectively. Other indicators of growth such as property transfers and values, new subdivisions, and population all trended upward. Over the entire 17 years, the Adirondack Park Agency regulated 34 percent of these developments, towns and villages the remainder.

Although these findings are clear, opinions on whether or not they constitute an uncontrolled and undesirable boom in development vary. Bauer contends that even as we face the challenges of global climate change that could alter the park's flora and fauna, it is residential development that will determine whether or not a "truly wild landscape will exist at all." He sees development as threatening not only the ecological integrity and wild character of the park, but also its social fabric and culture, which has already made some communities unaffordable to many who have grown up there as well as others desiring to move in.

Bauer closes by enumerating the challenges of the next 25 years as: the protection of the park's great northern forest through increases in the Forest Preserve; increasing purchases of conservation easements; mounting more effective programs for open-space stewardship on private lands; increasing preservation of communities through better planning; mounting programs for affordable housing; and investing in and building community infrastructure and capacity to support local economies based on tourism, small businesses, and forest products.

Bauer and doubtless many others thus see the Adirondack Park's open space and wilderness character as under attack by a coalition of both outside and inside forces known as the real estate market. Many of these threats and challenges are common to other areas of the nation and beyond, but few are likely to face the same level of threat to open space and wilderness character as will the park. Still, the common pattern is clear: an abundance of capital for investment and the desires of more and more people for more homes in high-quality environments.

How can the Adirondack Park's open space, wilderness character and human community structure be perpetuated in the face of such market pressures? Definitive answers are far beyond the scope of this work, which can only offer some thoughts shaped by experience in the park and in Alaska.

Why do people choose to live in the Adirondack Park and in Alaska? With the exception of those who came to the great land to strike it rich, the reasons of others seem essentially alike. Most probably came to either place seeking an environment with less apparent day-to-day regulation, less hassle, more sense of community, a place where they would be more self-reliant and more directly involved with decisions concerning the future of their communities. And most sought to enjoy more open space, more natural beauty and more access to a variety of outdoor recreation.

The populations that resulted have turned out to be similar in size, but very different in density. In 2003, the Adirondack counties and the state of Alaska recorded 770,308 and 648,818 residents, respectively. Overall population per square mile was 52.8 for the Adirondack counties and 1.1 for Alaska. Even Hamilton County, with the lowest density in the park, that is, 3.1 per square mile, was three times more densely populated than the state of Alaska. Population densities for the 12 counties wholly or partially within the Adirondack Park and for 27 Alaska census divisions are shown in table 33.2. These comparisons make clear that the great land is indeed a vast land with a sparse population. It follows that Alaska is rich with open space that constitutes the core of its wilderness character. Even in Anchorage, with nearly 160 people per square mile, most residents and visitors view open spaces every day. This engenders the feeling that Alaska is nearly replete with open space, that it needs no more and perhaps could do well with less. Most important is that the sense of open space, hence wilderness character, that is so common among Alaskans and so impressive to residents and visitors alike.

TABLE 33.2. **Population per square mile for Adirondack Park counties and Alaska Census Divisions, 2003**

| Adirondack Park Region Counties | | Alaska Census Divisions | |
|---|---|---|---|
| Saratoga | 258 | Anchorage | 160 |
| Oneida | 193 | Fairbanks | 12 |
| Fulton | 111 | Juneau | 11 |
| Clinton | 78 | Ketchikan | 11 |
| Warren | 74 | Kenai Peninsula | 3 |
| Washington | 74 | Matanuska–Susitna | 3 |
| Herkimer | 45 | Bristol Bay | 2 |
| St. Lawrence | 41 | Kodiak Island | 2 |
| Franklin | 31 | Aleutians West | 1 |
| Essex | 22 | Wrangell–Petersburg | 1 |
| Lewis | 20 | Haines | 1 |
| Hamilton | 3 | Remaining 16 each | 1 |

*Source:* World Almanac Education Group, *The World Almanac and Book of Facts 2005* (New York: St. Martins Press, 2005).

Might these thoughts on open space and wilderness character be focused on the Adirondack Park with its smaller size, different physiography, and much different history? As always, the Adirondack region defies easy answers. Paul Schneider captures the sense of the problem in *The Adirondacks: A History of America's First Wilderness:*

> The story of this century has been the struggle to transform the initial romantic infatuation of the Adirondacks into a sustainable marriage—to find an acceptable definition of wilderness that can survive our culture's seemingly insatiable desires. Depending on whom you ask, the park today is either an important, albeit seriously flawed model of peaceful coexistence between civilization and the wild, or a dysfunctional pipe dream. The proper meanings and uses of wilderness are not yet settled. [14]

He continues, "If there is one thing the history of the Adirondacks teaches it is that the meaning of wilderness, like love, changes as soon as it is defined."[15] This lesson certainly transcends the Adirondacks in the twenty-first century. *Roget's Thesaurus* includes wilderness in four places, including "open space" and "complexity," the latter listing "jungle," "morass," and "quagmire."[16] It seems that wilderness has long had many meanings, perhaps too many. But definitions and usage have always been up for change, and still are as witnessed by current events. As the meaning of wilderness thus varies, perhaps the broader term—wilderness character—may prove more useful than wilderness alone in understanding how most people probably view Alaska and the Adirondack Park. The wilderness character of the park would include close-up and distant views of undeveloped land including designated Wilderness areas, abandoned lands reverting from developed to the wild, managed forests, active and abandoned farms, and other designations. Developments on private lands might even be planned, designed, sited, and constructed with components of wilderness character in mind. This would obviously require an unusually bold stroke of public and private sector cooperation, difficult to envision for the young state of Alaska but perhaps not quite as difficult for the Adirondack Park.

While wilderness character provides the stage for acting out the drama of the Adirondacks, it alone will not provide gainful employment for the park's residents. The report of the Commission on the Adirondacks in the Twenty-First Century speaks about this problem in the opening of chapter 3:

> The advantages of living in the Adirondack Park are apparent: a high quality environment and ready access to wildland experiences. The disadvantages are less evident. Unemployment in the Park is usually one or two percentage points above state averages; in some counties the gap is much wider, particularly in winter. Per capita income is below state levels; in 1985, the last available benchmark, it was $8,429 in the Adirondack Park, $9,009 in rural counties elsewhere in New York and $11,765 statewide.[17]

The listing of difficulties continues with the sudden loss of a large employer, the steady loss of farming, and soaring demand for recreational homes putting the cost of land and housing beyond the reach of full-time residents. It goes on to cite "the uneasy balance of economic forces in the Park . . . the Park's immense contribution to the local economy," and "the potential of the regions amenities for future employment and income growth."[18] Major industries are identified as forest-products and tourism, which offer great potential yet are presently beset by difficulties: namely lack of value-added products and relatively high real property taxes for the former, and less than adequate facilities and united education and marketing programs for the latter. Recommendations are offered covering: state development and marketing policies and programs; consolidation and restructuring; planning; local programs; publication of sites for commercial and industrial use; direct marketing for the forest-products industry; improvement of roads and bridges; creation of a single Department of Economic Development tourism region; a park-wide tourism board; and promotion of Adirondack crafts and products.

These and other recommendations were forwarded to then governor Mario Cuomo on April 1, 1990. Why have so few been accepted and acted upon over 19 years later? That is not to say there has been no progress since 1990, for example, in increasing the Forest Preserve and conservation easements, but to ask why virtually nothing has been put in place to promote the tourism and forest-products industries or to offer the owners of private lands attractive alternatives to the business-as-usual approach to the subdivision and sale of land for residential development?

Some contend that the Twenty-First Century Commission's proposed one-year moratorium on further subdivision and development on Resource Management and Rural Use classifications not only failed to be enacted, but was more than any other recommendation the cause for rebellion against the entire report. Worse, perhaps, some might contend that the commission thus further hardened the divisions between the environmental community and many citizens of the Adirondacks. Whatever the reasons, as ever, good intentions alone have not paved the high road to success.

So the question remains. Is there really any grist from the great land to aid in the quest for a more secure future for the Adirondack

Park? Is there a future that is firmly based on the preservation of its wilderness character and a strong, sustainable economy? The best answer is probably one heard each morning for a week at a Canadian fishing camp from an elderly boat tender who, when asked if it would rain that day, always answered in three words: "Maybe, maybe not." This seemed to bring him great satisfaction and a touch of wry amusement. And contrary to first impressions, his three words were invaluable to the fishermen who never again forgot their rain gear after their first soaking.

What follows, thus, is some grist from Alaska that may be or may not be helpful in securing the future of the Adirondack Park in the second decade of the twenty-first century. This future can occur if, and only if, those who actively seek to secure the park's future can somehow make a bold break with the past.

Consider the transformation of Alaska over the past 50 years, which was fueled by a perceived national need for more domestic oil production, by the possibility of creating many, many well-paying jobs, and by the investment opportunities seen by the oil industry and others. The following account is from "Going Up in Flames: The Promises and Pledges of Alaska Statehood under Attack":

> The National Environmental Policy Act (NEPA), which had passed in December 1969, ushered in a new world of regulations and procedures. Additionally, once the Permafrost and other engineering issues were resolved, opponents to development of any kind filed a lawsuit to stop the entire project.
>
> Some Alaska business groups lobbied Congress but had little effect. Finally in 1973, three critical events took place. The Arabs embargoed oil destined for the U.S. market. This created a national groundswell in support of domestic oil production and the trans-Alaska pipeline. Secondly, Hickel, then a private citizen, convinced AFL–CIO President George Meany and his 36 international presidents to throw their considerable weight behind the passage of an act to expedite the construction of an Alaska pipeline. And finally, Senator Mike Gravel of Alaska introduced a

bold amendment to the bill which stated that the environmental impact statement met NEPA's requirements and placed a short time frame on pipeline litigations. This controversial amendment was adopted, and the pipeline bill passed the Senate by the narrowest of margins with Vice President Spiro Agnew casting the deciding vote, breaking a tie.[19]

Irrespective of specifics, controversial and otherwise, the foregoing suggests some potentially pivotal question about the future of the Adirondacks: might such a cast of actors ever trod a single stage in the drama of the Adirondack Park, each somehow including in their respective roles the commitment to work for the perpetuation of the wilderness character of the park and for increased employment opportunities for its residents? And could such a case include the real estate industry, the tourist industry, small business development centers, or public and private education institutions? It would be a bold step, risky for some, transcending territorial imperatives with no guarantee of success. But unlike many other endeavors, it would be focused on the two fundamental goals for the Adirondack Park in the twenty-first century: perpetuation of wilderness character and attainment of improved employment opportunities for residents. And, it would be centered on the park's most marketable resource—an attractive environment.

Could such a noble endeavor succeed? Maybe, maybe not. If not, what would be lost but a little more time? If so, then the future of the Adirondack Park would not only be secured but would provide a model for parks across the world by incorporating public and private lands. Who among us would opt for anything less or require anything more?

# 34

## The Adirondack Park in Global Perspective

BILL WEBER AND AMY VEDDER

Across the less-developed regions of the world, a common scenario unfolds.

> *A pristine forest is being cleared and degraded. First the ancient giants are felled. Then any pretense of forestry gives way to uncontrolled logging, as clear-cuts spread across the landscape. Hunters and trappers have already seen the forest's wildlife decline and disappear. The elders say the forest used to be more bountiful; but many recognize their own role in overexploiting nature's bounty.*
>
> *Conservationists decry the loss, but offer a solution: protect what's left of the forest as parkland, drop destructive uses, and adopt more sustainable practices. One such use is to provide guide and other services to wealthy visitors, most of whom come from urban areas where untouched nature is rare—and therefore highly valued.*

It is a story that could be told from hundreds of forests now under threat around the world, and especially across the tropics. It is also the much older story of New York's Adirondack Forest in the late 1800s. This long, parallel history is but one of several reasons the Adirondack experience is held up as a model for effective conservation of other forested sites around the world.

There is no question that the Adirondack Mountains qualify as a conservation area of global importance. Covering almost 9,300 square miles, the Adirondack Park is larger than the Yellowstone, Yosemite, and Grand Canyon parks combined. It is comparable to all but the largest of Alaska's reserves, and stands in the top 5 percent of international protected areas ranked by size. With size comes a scale at which natural phenomena—wind storms, ice storms, and even extinction—can occur and their effects reverberate throughout the ecosystem. With size comes sufficient habitat to support more than 90 percent of the species found across the Northern Forest. And with size comes the ability to support a significant resident human population dispersed in settlements across the park. As further proof of its global significance, these and other reasons combine to justify the designation of the Adirondack Park as an International Biosphere Reserve.

Global significance, however, does not guarantee relevance as a model. This chapter takes a critical look at that claim of Adirondack relevance and comes to some surprising conclusions.

## The Adirondacks as Anomaly

Any assessment of the Adirondacks as a model needs to begin with recognition of its potential limits. These include such fundamental elements as its origins, evolution, current form, and finances, as well as some lesser idiosyncrasies.

*Origins.* The first American parks were created to preserve sites of great natural beauty and wonder. In the visionary mind of John Muir, they were to be unspoiled sanctuaries where the increasingly urbanized human spirit could be uplifted and restored through the direct experience of untrammeled nature. Yellowstone's geothermal wonders and Yosemite's rugged peaks and cascading waterfalls were classic early examples of this model. More recently, especially in the international sphere, the emphasis has shifted to preservation of wildlife communities and endangered species. The great African parks are striking examples of this trend and were some of the first created expressly for wildlife conservation. The Virunga National Park of Congo/Rwanda was established "to make the world safe for mountain gorillas" in 1925, followed by Kruger, Serengeti, and others to protect the savanna spectacles of their still-vast herds of large mammals.

Contrary to either of these trends, the Adirondack Park was created almost entirely from degraded lands and a depleted fauna. Most of the land had not only been logged, but had also been cleared of all forest cover. Its denuded mountain soils were so exposed that the threat of catastrophic erosion and sedimentation were widely cited to justify its formal protection in 1892. Much of the early park, in fact, was acquired when logging companies failed to pay taxes, usually following a terminal clear-cutting phase. At best, no more than 10 percent of current parkland forest escaped the ax and the blade.

The native Adirondack wildlife, too, was decimated by the time of the park's creation. Market forces had driven the once-ubiquitous beaver to local extinction more than a century earlier. The wolf, cougar, lynx, and moose would all follow, with black bear, otter, and marten precariously close to the edge. A growing network of dams diminished natural trout habitat, while native fish in general were replaced by human-favored species. A few species, like deer, probably benefited from the secondary vegetation that followed logging, but the natural diversity of the wildlife once supported by Adirondack forests, marshes, lakes, and rivers was in serious decline by the end of the nineteenth century.

To this point, the global trend in park creation has overwhelmingly followed the preservationist model of Yellowstone, and more recently, the wildlife focus exemplified by the Serengeti. Whether this trend continues, however, is an open—and contentious—question in modern conservation. Should conditions change dramatically, the Adirondack experience may take on added relevance.

*Restoration.* Where preservation of intact ecosystems and wildlife populations is the starting point for conservation, restoration is generally a minor concern. The exception to this rule usually arises when the original size of a protected area is too small to sustain certain species or ecological interactions. For the reasons noted above, however, the Adirondack experience can again be seen as not only outside of, but contrary to, that of most of the world's protected areas.

Given that such a great proportion of the Adirondack forest was cleared, it is difficult to view its recovery as a model for other protected areas set aside for their intact flora and fauna. One can be encouraged by the fact that much of the original forest cover has returned. However, the relatively favorable conditions of the Adirondacks are not replicated in most forested areas of the world. In the harsh conditions of more northerly latitudes, short growing seasons may extend the recovery timeframe to centuries for the boreal forests of Russia and Canada. In the tropics, generally poor soils inhibit rainforest regeneration, while overall ecosystem complexity greatly complicates species recovery. Thus in each of these vast realms, effective conservation requires protection prior to any significant degradation.

*Park structure.* A close friend and colleague, Marcio Ayres, dedicated his too-short life to the creation of one of the world's most dynamic multiple-use reserves, in the flooded Amazonian forest of his native Brazil. The Mamiraua Sustainable Use Reserve ultimately covered more than 7,700 square miles within a variety of management zones, from pure wilderness to areas designated for sustainable hunting, fishing, and logging. While visiting New York one time, we showed Marcio a map of the official Adirondack Park zonation scheme and said, "this is what Mamiraua will look like after a century." We were joking, but Marcio stared hard, trying to make sense of the incomprehensible patchwork before him. After a few minutes he cringed and withdrew, shaking his head.

The fact is, no one in his right mind would design a protected area that looks like the current Adirondack Park. Its cheek-to-jowl juxtaposition of public and private lands, its lack of a solid core Wilderness area, and its lack of designated connectivity among multiple scattered Wilderness areas all attest to a lack of initial design—and a lack of subsequent strategic action during its first 80 years of existence. In fact, much of the land in the Forest Preserve—the fully protected part of the park—was acquired simply on the basis of its availability. It is far from the typical plan often described as the "biosphere model," characterized by a core protected area surrounded neatly by a wide buffer zone of restricted human use. Since the 1970s, far more attention has been given to strategic planning and acquisitions, with particular weight to biological and ecological factors. Private lands, too, are better managed today. But the Adirondack Park is still a better model of what not to do in reserve creation.

*Financing.* Where's the gate? The Adirondack Park has nothing like the dramatic arch outside of Gardiner, Montana, that proclaims one's entry into Yellowstone National Park. Nor are there any other forms of controlled entry. The Adirondack Park can be accessed by road at no fewer than 33 major points, none of which collect a fee or even keep entry statistics. With annual visitation nonetheless estimated at between 5 and 10 million tourists, this represents a significant failure to derive revenues from wilderness, wildlife, and amenity values.

Park services around the world share a common interest in paying for their operations. Among the many strategies pursued toward this end, the collection of entry fees is probably the most widespread practice. These may range from a few dollars a day to $375 for a one-hour visit among Rwanda's remarkable mountain gorillas. But the Adirondack Park is among a very small group of sites that charge no entry fee whatsoever. This is partially compensated for by some very creative financing mechanisms, as discussed below, but it remains an anomaly.

Thus, it is possible to argue that the Adirondack Park has too many unique and distinctive characteristics to serve as a model for most protected areas around the world. Its degraded origins, subsequent recovery, chaotic management structure, and failure to capture significant user revenues all support this line of argument. It is perhaps least appropriate for those areas where the preservationist model still prevails. However, as multiple use emerges as the dominant management mode for new protected areas, the Adirondack experience is increasingly relevant. This is true for both its successes and failures.

## The Adirondacks as Model

The anomalies noted above may challenge conventional views of the Adirondacks as a model; however, they hardly undermine the case. Scale alone would argue for consideration of any region of this size and natural condition. Add a long, rich history of conservation effort and you have a primary subject for close study. We would argue further that the following points truly make the Adirondacks an indispensable model for twenty-first-century conservation.

*Wildlife recovery.* The Adirondack experience has shown that the return of forest cover and the regulation of hunting have allowed most native animal populations to increase once again, including some that were locally extinct. The beaver, otter, peregrine falcon, and bald eagle needed government assistance in this effort; the moose, marten, and fisher repopulated on their own. Even a planned reintroduction failed to help the lynx, but many think the cougar has come back on its own. The wolf is certainly the most significant species missing from the original mix. Overall, this is a great conservation success story. And—with the notable exception of most rainforests—it is a story of great relevance to many parks and wild areas around the world.

Sadly, many official protected areas around the world are no more than "paper parks," with no effective protection. For some, where human pressures are minimal, this lack has little effect on their conservation value. Still others pay a heavy price for neglect. Such costs are especially high for wildlife at times of civil war. Two notable examples are Uganda's Queen Elizabeth Park and Mozambique's Gorongosa Park: world-class reserves with great herds of elephants, buffalo, zebra, and other large mammals, whose large animal faunas were almost completely annihilated for food and revenue to sustain the combatants during extended periods of war. Absent combat, wildlife can still suffer if hunting and other uses are not controlled. Many modern forest reserves are managed for multiple use, including both logging and hunting. Commercial logging is valued as a source of government revenue and local employment; hunting is intended to meet local subsistence needs. Yet opening the forest to logging trucks requires a network of roads which exposes traditional subsistence cultures to distant market forces, while also providing direct transportation to those markets. If not controlled, the inevitable result is over-exploitation of native wildlife for the commercial meat trade; and the forest grows silent. This is the story throughout much of forested Asia, Latin America, and Africa.

The need for restoration and recovery within established protected areas is thus very real and almost certain to get worse. Yet the global experience with restoration and recovery is quite limited, with conservationists more concerned with reserve creation and protection. Enter the Adirondacks: not as model of planned protection, nor even of planned recovery or management, but one that stands as an inspirational example of people recognizing mistakes, correcting behavior, and creating the conditions for wildlife recovery. This experience is especially relevant to those areas where wildlife depletion has not been accompanied by significant habitat loss and where human behaviors can be changed. Such areas would include a long list of African parks in post-conflict zones; forest reserves where minimal direct logging impacts nevertheless led to commercial over-hunting; and marine reserves affected by comparable over-fishing. If any single action could be emulated, it is the recognition by individuals that hunting regulations first imposed by the state ultimately benefit the whole community by assuring a steady supply of bountiful wildlife—for hunters, viewers, and the animals themselves. Finally, for those protected areas that still sustain their original faunas, perhaps the Adirondacks can provide another very important lesson: it is far less expensive to preserve wilderness and wildlife values than it is to restore them.

*Salvage conservation.* The Adirondack experience is one that instills hope for conservation of even badly damaged natural systems. As the era of protecting large wild areas ebbs, the promise of significant conservation benefits through recovery of already degraded lands could gain great power and impact. Such "salvage conservation" efforts would seem especially effective in areas where the cause of degradation—such as logging or mining—is transient, and where the habitat and most species indicate potential for natural recovery or restoration. While excluding sensitive tropical rainforest environments, a broad array of more robust systems could be covered.

It is no accident that Italy's Abruzzo National Park is formally twinned with the Adirondack Park. Each combines large natural areas within a landscape mosaic that sustains both human settlements and recovering wildlife populations. In Abruzzo, the latter even include wolves and brown bears. Elsewhere in Europe, popular sentiment in favor of wildlife recovery is encountering a serious problem: a lack of natural habitats to sustain the target species in the wild.

No country on earth offers greater potential—or more serious constraints—for restoration conservation than China. Its natural areas few and degraded, its wildlife resources depleted, China now faces the twin threats of expanding rural poverty and rapid industrialization fueled by resource utilization. A nascent environmental movement has risked government censure in calling attention to the human impacts of further degradation, but wildlife conservation is considered less politically charged. In this case, no better source of hard-earned experience could be found than the comparably temperate Adirondacks.

*Sustainable use.* The early history of the Adirondacks seems an unlikely place to look for examples of sustainable use. In fact, the massive clear-cutting of its forests made the Adirondack region a "poster child" for resource abuse. Yet even before the park was created, those areas that were spared the ax were touted for their restorative powers for the human spirit. It would be another century before someone coined the term ecotourism: but its forerunners—nature and adventure tourism—cut their teeth in the Adirondacks. And like most ecotourists, those who first came to the North Woods were generally wealthy city-dwellers, willing to pay a premium for untouched nature. Later, driven by popular accounts of the region and its attractions, middle-class tourists would make their way north in even greater numbers. Once there, they would first stay at local inns and hostels, then head into the woods in the care of local guides. It is impossible to calculate the economic impact of these early visitors; their total contribution was no doubt a small percentage of what they spent in their home cities. Yet the seasonal flush of revenue and employment certainly contributed in appreciable ways to the well-being of many Adirondackers living on the margins of the mainstream economy.

In 1978, we went to Rwanda to understand and address the problems confronting that nation's highly endangered mountain gorillas. Habitat loss and trophy hunting were key factors in the gorillas' population crash, from almost 500 in 1960 to barely 260 in our 1978 census. Yet behind these direct threats was a set of more fundamental driving factors. Rwanda at that time was one of the world's most densely populated countries; 90 percent of its people depended for their survival on subsistence farming; the national land base was fully exploited—except for the national parks and reserves; and the parks were seen as a colonial legacy that contributed nothing to local human welfare. In this context, we saw the development of tourism as a way to generate revenue, employment, and political support for conservation. Almost thirty years later, despite intervening conflict and genocide, the Rwandan program is seen as a model for ecotourism; and the gorilla population has rebounded to more than 400 individuals.

Ecotourism is not a universal salve. It is easier in open environments like savannas and mountains, where visitors are rewarded by views of spectacular wildlife in striking landscapes. Yet wherever ecotourism is to be developed, managers and decision makers would do well to study the Adirondack experience. It is a rich history; one that spans a long and often difficult transition from an underdeveloped, overexploited frontier condition, through several intermediate stages, to the present period in which tourism and related services now drive the regional economy. Most developing countries will go through comparable transitions. If there is a single lesson for them to learn from the Adirondacks, it is the role of the private sector in assuring a more diversified economic base, with a greater percentage of benefits staying in local hands within the regional economy. In most countries, government agencies and interests dominate the tourism sector.

Forestry is another form of sustainable use. It came much later to the Adirondacks, and some still question if it has truly arrived.

Approximately 20 percent of the Adirondack land base remains in some form of commercial forestry, much of it subject to sustainability criteria. Formal regulation in the form of Forest Stewardship or Smartwood certification programs is on the rise, led by the example of Paul Smith's College. Working forest conservation easements are also on the rise, with management criteria negotiated between private owners, land trusts, and state agencies. Certification and easements are relatively new management tools: each suffers from light enforcement of uncertain standards. Yet both systems are a great improvement on past uncontrolled practices and, in the long run, are intended to promote more sustainable forestry.

Sustainable forestry and certification are on the rise across the forested world, beginning first in Latin America and Asia, with operations in Africa slowly following suit. With its head start in these efforts, a significant portion of its land area in forestry practice, and a major forestry college at Paul Smith's, the Adirondacks should be a global leader in this field. That it has not yet achieved this stature will be addressed in the final section below.

*Land-use planning and stewardship.* As noted above, planning initially played little role in the acquisition and management of public lands in the Forest Preserve. It played none on private lands. For most of its history, the park was dependent on a single extraordinary clause in the New York State constitution that protected its Reserve lands as "Forever Wild." By 1970, the DEC was created to manage state lands, including the publicly held lands of the Adirondack Park. Only in 1971 was the Adirondack Park Agency (APA) established with a mandate to regulate private land uses. This action reflected a growing perception that the park, despite its protected wild areas, would lose its essential character if it were infected by the rapidly spreading disease of suburban sprawl.

The Forever Wild clause, the creation of the park, and the establishment of the DEC and APA reflect a recognition of important values and benefits, declared for the common good of society at large, and held for future generations. They have also engendered considerable hostility on the part of some longtime residents who resent any such government intrusion. Regulation prevailed, though imperfectly and at considerable social cost. From outside the Blue Line, the regulatory environment of the Adirondacks looks increasingly attractive. Much as most residents of New Hampshire would have fought any regulatory efforts a quarter century ago, today they feel helpless as Boston sprawls inexorably northward, into its forests, lakes, and mountains.

Residents of New Hampshire, Greater Yellowstone, the southern Appalachians, and other high-amenity areas know the threat posed by sprawl, even if their political philosophies keep them from agreeing on a common course to avoid its ills. That is not the case for residents of many foreign countries. In much of southeast Asia and parts of Latin America, the combination of expanding economies, human populations, and "quality of life" aspirations is placing great pressure on existing protected areas. Sitting on the shores of Garnet Lake in 2005, the director of Malaysia's Wildlife Department, Dr. Melvin Gumal, listened to the silence, punctuated by the raucous cries of the loon. Deeply moved, he lamented his nation's rush to build hotels, restaurants, and stores, and to accommodate all forms of use within their protected areas. For him conservation was all about managing people, not wildlife. And he envied the regulatory structure available to Adirondack authorities. If it is too late to help Malaysia, there remain many other countries on the cusp of development, whose leaders could learn important lessons from the Adirondack experience with regulation and zoning.

The alternative to regulation is effective private stewardship. Here, too, the Adirondack experience has much to offer. From an early history of great abuse at the hands of private owners, an ethic of responsible management has evolved among a high percentage of private landowners within the park. For some, this ethic seems as much a result of their economic comfort and reduced need to exploit, or the need to conform to regulations, as it is a result of any changed attitudes toward the natural world. But there is no question that sound stewardship is on the rise. This, too, could offer inspiration to others in comparable situations. Even in the world's poorest countries, there is no shortage of wealthy people, many of whom transform their wealth into large landholdings. Demonstrating a concern for the responsible management of those lands and sustainable resource use could go a long way toward limiting some of the worst abuses seen in the early Adirondacks. Demonstrating ways for less-advantaged landowners to care for their much smaller holdings could be an even greater, if more elusive, achievement.

*Human communities.* Most of the regulations referred to above would not be needed if there were no people, if the Adirondack Mountains were like the ideal, traditional park. But, ideal or not, a growing percentage of the world's parks contain human communities, often of people marginalized economically and politically. In some instances, these reserves protect not only wildlife, but indigenous cultures practicing traditional lifestyles little changed for millennia. Yet change is a constant in the modern world.

Over the past century, Adirondack human communities have undergone a recurrent cycle of economic boom, bust, and recovery as the extractive industries of mining and logging have given way to service economies, including tourism. There is every reason to believe that communities living in and around protected areas in other countries and cultures will be forced to undergo comparable transitions. If the Adirondack experience holds true, many in these communities will feel marginalized by the process, angered at government authorities they hold responsible for undermining resource-dependent livelihoods. Yet Adirondackers have also demonstrated great resilience in the face of change, with a growing recognition that global markets have as much impact on their local economy as do wilderness protection and land-use regulation.

Conflict is inherent in conservation, as humans react to prohibitions and limits on wildlife and other resource use. Effective conservation requires management of this conflict. Adirondack history contains many examples of successful conflict management, as well as some spectacular failures. This history is worthy of close study not only by those in other nations, but also by American conservationists hoping to improve their effectiveness. If there is a fundamental lesson from the Adirondacks, it is that conflicts never go away; they just change with time and require constant learning and adaptation.

*Conservation finance.* The failure of the Adirondack Park to derive direct revenues from entry fees was noted above. Yet this striking departure from standard practice is perhaps more than offset by other innovative sources of indirect revenue. The most important of these is triggered when the state acquires land from a private owner. In most comparable situations, tax revenues from the acquired property are lost to local communities, in addition to any private use values. In New York, taxes from the entire state population are instead used to cover any potential local tax losses, assuring continued support for local schools and other services. While many Adirondack communities decry their dependency on government, this is an arrangement to be envied by any community bordering protected areas around the world.

Two other conservation finance tools are not limited to the Adirondacks, but are rarely seen outside the United States. The first is the significant role of private funding in land acquisitions. Land trusts and conservancies not only help to identify key lands for acquisition, they also contribute funding and, in many instances, play a longer-term role in management. The second tool, the conservation easement, has become even more important over the past decade. As discussed above, easements permit lands to remain in private hands, while requiring the landowner to bear the opportunity costs of foregone exploitation. They also impose even greater management costs on the conservancies charged with their oversight. The benefits accrue to society at large in the form of protected landscapes and healthy wildlife populations. This model is currently of limited value to much of the world but is beginning to prove helpful in more developed countries such Argentina, where significant lands are in private hands.

## Beyond the Blue Line

No park is an island. The Adirondack region suffers severe effects of acid rain and growing effects of global warming, two threats whose origins lie far beyond the park's boundary. Adirondack lakes tell the tale of acid deposition in the form of depleted fish stocks and methyl-mercury contamination. This contamination is occurring decades after the problem's source was first identified in uncontrolled emissions from midwestern power plants. Similarly, the record from dozens of meteorological stations reveals the same hot truth: average winter temperatures in the Adirondacks have risen nearly four degrees Fahrenheit over the past century, more than any other region in the northeastern United States. Again, the cause lies outside the Adirondack system, in our collective use and abuse of carbon-based energy resources. Thus, regardless of the large scale, richness, and recovery of such an extraordinary forest ecosystem, complacency is not an option for conservationists, who must constantly adapt to new and often unforeseen challenges.

No park is an island. More than ever, this truth applies regardless of location around the world, forcing changes in the way we do conservation. Lessons learned today in the Adirondacks may help others to adapt to this overarching reality.

## Conclusions

The Adirondack Park offers more than a century of important lessons for conservation. Some are certainly of the "what not to do" variety. Foremost among these is the region's fragmentation and lack of connectivity between wilderness areas. But many other experiences offer lessons of great global importance. These include the potential for wildlife recovery, and perhaps even "salvage" restoration; the development of sustainable forms of wildlife and forest utilization; the evolution of adaptable community responses to economic change; and the creation of dynamic new mechanisms to finance conservation action.

Other lessons are still imperfectly learned works in progress, and therefore more difficult to pass on. Especially problematic is the fact that the Adirondack region is exploited as a primary source by researchers and other outsiders—most of whom return little, if anything, to the source in the form of publications or even reports. In this regard, the region is no better off than the less-developed countries for which it aspires to be a model. Thus, an immediate need is to capture existing information and analyses; to curate this information in a centralized, accessible location; and to make it available to the largest possible audience.

A model is only valuable to the extent that it is visible. At this time, the Adirondack experience is not sufficiently well known. Once the wealth of Adirondack information is compiled, demand for this information must be stimulated through strategic publications and publicity. To capture this demand, a regional training center or program should be created to foster applied research, offer courses and practical experience, draw lessons, and share these with new and experienced partners. If successful, then foreign managers and decision makers, who now go to Yellowstone or Yosemite, will instead come to the Adirondack Park to learn at a global crucible of conservation.

# Conclusion

*The Adirondack Experiment in a Full World*

JON D. ERICKSON, WILLIAM F. PORTER,
AND ROSS S. WHALEY

What are the lessons of conservation and development from the Adirondack experiment? It is evident from the voices we have heard that the lessons occur at several levels. When we ask once again, "why is it still here?" we have to acknowledge that the Adirondack region is like many of the wilderness areas designated elsewhere: it was passed by in the settlement of North America by Native Americans and then European colonists because it simply was not hospitable. To attract settlement and sustain communities required support for an agricultural economy, and the poor soils, short growing season, and difficult terrain of the Adirondacks would not support such an economy. With improving transportation infrastructure, the natural resources of the Adirondacks became valuable to burgeoning markets throughout New York, New England, and southern Canada. Reflecting back to our original organizing concept for the book of the *ultimate means to ultimate ends spectrum,* the Adirondacks could not provide the means for an agrarian economy, but eventually the region was opened to resource exploitation by water, rail, and road.

The ax of the logger, the pick of the miner, and the hammer of the track layer would eventually find the Adirondacks. But what sets this region apart from other heavily exploited environments is that the ecosystem largely recovered from early exploitation and already had significant land protections in place before twentieth-century modernity really took hold. Good fortune surely played a role because at several pivotal moments, shifts in economic or environmental conditions prevented exploitation from being even greater. However, the lesson of the political response to this exploitation is that society began to recognize a different set of resources. The forests of the Adirondacks could provide a sustainable source of water to meet the needs of powerful economic interests. Open space provided a sustaining source of health and sense of well-being to meet the needs of a growing wealthy class. And with rail and then road came a democratization of recreation for the masses. The means of the Adirondack experiment began to be seen more broadly, and as such the ends began to change.

Implementing a change of this magnitude required a political context that permitted bold action and strong political leaders who knew how to use power to take big steps. The end of the nineteenth century and the middle of the twentieth century produced both the opportunities and the leaders. The result was a Forest Preserve guided by a societal goal of setting aside large areas of land as Forever Wild and later a set of land-use regulations guided by a goal of sustaining both a wilderness ecosystem and human economy. Political leaders of the caliber of Theodore Roosevelt and Nelson Rockefeller were in position to wield power and effect change.

What we have witnessed over the past 40 years, and the larger focus of this book, is the playing out of the hand that was dealt by previous generations. The Adirondack experiment is still a work in progress instead of a distant memory because of the decisions made by these generations. The current generation at times seems as if it would rather fight than win because the past 40 years have been filled with acrimony. Establishing the Forest Preserve and Adirondack Park were certainly bold decisions, with little input from those towns and villages within the Blue Line, and these decisions were bound to generate debate. The process has done what open debate in democracy does well: clarify the issues and examine the successes and failures arising from experience. Society must draw on the lessons from which to make the decisions that will affect future generations.

As the editors of this book, we have sought to identify the emergent lessons. We see five central ideas that, while not necessarily new, may clarify the fundamental issues.

1. The heart of the debate, and the reason for heat, is a long-standing divide between those who see the world as too full, and running out of resources, and those who see the world as empty, with limitless resources yet to exploit. This difference in mindset often materializes in debates over the equitable distribution of private and public property rights.

2. The principal effect of Article 14, the Adirondack Park Agency Act, the State Land Master Plan and the Adirondack Park Land Use and Development Plan is clustering of development. Clustering has been and will continue to be the primary driver of the ecological and economic change in the park.

3. Where the economic vitality of the Adirondacks was once limited by the challenges of transportation in a manufacturing economy, the economic conditions of the future will be driven by communication in a service economy. Ironically, the biggest future challenge to the Adirondacks may be the wealth coming into the region because of this change in the economy.

4. The remote character and quality of life in communities that are limited in size will draw a new segment of society to the Adirondacks, a demography whose preferences for preservation and development are as yet unclear.

5. The important environmental challenges likely to face the Adirondacks in the near future are likely to be more about decisions made outside the Blue Line than within.

Let's begin with the 800-pound gorilla in the room: property rights. The experience of the Adirondacks is one tied closely to the ongoing, worldwide struggle to distribute the benefits from property ownership between individuals and the public, between current and future generations, and between humanity and the rest of nature. In the modern economy, every economic decision depends on the assignment of property rights between each of these domains. Without rights established through formal means such as legal institutions, or informally through norms and custom, social cooperation toward individual or common goals is impossible. The assignment of property rights is at the core of basic obligations and responsibilities of individuals, communities, states, and global institutions. As such, the goals of society shape, and are shaped by, the societal choice of property rights regimes.

In the Adirondacks these choices resulted in the allocation of some rights to the public at large (current and future generations) through the creation of the Forest Preserve, and a more complicated allocation of certain property rights through the creation of the Adirondack Park. The choices of how and for whom to assign property rights in a democracy are made by the people. Even in democracies where property rights are tilted more toward the individual than the state, this assignment is ultimately a product of the collective voice of the people as embodied by the state. Strict private property regimes should not be confused as a prerequisite for a free society, nor should pure public property regimes be confused with totalitarian rule. Both extremes, and every variation in between, are all possible choices within a democracy.

Critical to this choice is the relative abundance of natural resources and knowledge of their characteristics and function. When resources are abundant, a social system where the individual is assigned the rights to do as they please with property, but not the responsibility of their actions, is one among many logical outcomes. When uncertainty or ignorance of the consequences of individual decisions is high, then again a democratic process might favor a regime where the individual exercises their rights in a vacuum, without knowledge of or care for the impacts of their actions on others. We might call this the "empty-world" mindset, where resources seem unlimited and economies are thought to grow without bounds.

However, in a world of increasing scarcity and improving knowledge, society at large may choose to reassign portions of property rights away from the individual and to the larger community.

We might call this the "full-world" mindset. The exponential rise of the human population set against the hard realities of declining nonrenewable resource stocks and degraded renewable service flows from nature may lead to social systems that recognize limits to growth. Viewed from this perspective, the action of the citizens of New York in establishing the Adirondack Park Agency was a reaction to the anticipated pressures of a full-world experience. In an empty world, quantity is often equated with quality. The more we have, the better off we are. In a full world, thresholds are reached where quantity takes away from quality, and genuine economic development finds its source in balance and resilience over growth and fragility. Whether the world is empty or full, however, may not be uniformly perceived, and therefore the amount and kind of public remedies is likely to be controversial.

Coming to terms with limits and redefining the meaning and measures of progress is perhaps the greatest lesson from the Adirondack experiment. The New York Forest Preserve and the Adirondack Park were created in a time when the northeastern United States was beginning to realize the limits of industrialization. New York was home to the Rockefellers, Vanderbilts, and other oil, rail, and industrial empires that became synonymous with a late nineteenth-century free-market ideology never before experienced. The Adirondacks represented the last frontier for exploitation in the northeastern United States. What timber could be cut and hauled by river was taken early in the nineteenth century. Then came the appetite for hemlock for the tanneries and charcoal to fuel the iron smelters and wood fiber for pulp and paper. In this mountainous terrain with its harsh climate, there were many biological and physical limits that slowed the advance of resource exploitation. And much of the land hammered the hardest often fell back to the state when taxes were not paid. Just at the time when many of those biological and physical limits were giving way to technology, rail, and road, New York's citizens found themselves as owners by default of over half a million Adirondack acres.

The Adirondack region was a large, fairly intact ecosystem before the tidal wave of twentieth-century technology and economic growth. Ultimately the legislators' pen was quicker than the rail and mightier than the lumberman's ax. It anticipated a public demand for a different set of resource values. Article 14 of the New York State Constitution, while visionary, was born of a pragmatism to protect the watershed of New York's burgeoning canal system, the very economic blood of New York's commercial power, and a call for strategic assets of timber shepherded by the original wise-use movement, with Theodore Roosevelt at the helm. It was also born of romanticism by an urbanizing public desperate for escape from the ills of large cities for the rejuvenation of nature's beauty. When the rails and roads penetrated the interior of the Adirondacks, Article 14 had already declared the public lands of the park "be forever kept as wild forest lands." Together with the political prowess of the Great Camp elite and the thousands of tourists who demanded forest vistas and quiet waters for their escape from city life, the Forever Wild clause would shape an American environmental ethic. The Adirondack experiment at the turn of the nineteenth century would be the touchstone for defining public land stewardship in the United States. Roosevelt would articulate this new ethic in terms of a public responsibility for wise management of all natural resources and would simultaneously pull back, ever so slightly, on the reins of privatization and free-market economics.

The Adirondack experiment is in many ways a microcosm of the evolution from private property to liability rules and then inalienable rights that define the individual's rights and responsibilities in democratic societies worldwide. With rights defined only by private property rules—when an individual is free to interfere with or prevent interference from another—a person is not obligated to limit the impact of their decisions on others. Excludability (e.g., no-trespassing laws) directs the benefits of ownership to the individual under private property rule. "No trespassing" signs first appeared around the time the state was defining its holdings as Forest Preserve. Within a period of a few years the advent of private property rules would transform the Adirondack landscape from a vast, open-access resource for local hunter and downstate explorer alike, to a patchwork quilt of ownership. Use and development of the inter-mingled private property remained subject to the whim of indi-vidual landowners.

However, when society deems a narrow assignment of rights to the individual to be harmful and unfair to others, liability rules can be added that restrict activities on private interests. Hunting regulations, pollution standards, and legal mechanisms that provide for damage compensation are each examples of liability rules. In the Adirondacks, game laws were the first such rules to evolve, creat-ing legal excludability on a previously open-access resource—the beginning of drawing individual rights (i.e., unregulated hunting and fishing) into the public domain (i.e., hunt and fish according to public law). Restrictions on recreation intensity on public land, and cutting practices and residential density on private land, were to follow.

The environmental movement of the 1960s brought a broad societal recognition of the implications of a full world and a mix of inalienable rights to protect the remaining open spaces and natural environments for current and future generations. The Wilderness Act and the Endangered Species Act were obvious manifestations of this shift in ethic. So, too, were the National Environmental Policy Act and National Forest Management Act because while not directly seeking to protect open spaces, they demonstrated a public interest in how lands were managed, and thus a desire for societal oversight. This new recognition of the full world went beyond oversight of public resources to seeking input for the management of private lands through zoning laws. Viewed in this larger context, it is not surprising that the Temporary Study Commission on the Future of the Adirondacks arrived at a prescient, or strident, imposition of public voice to all lands within the region. This sweeping legisla-tion codified the intent of "wildness" of Article 14 by classifying public lands along a spectrum of recreation intensity. But it also extended the concept to private land. There it centralized develop-ment density restrictions and enforcement to create an Adirondack Park as an integrated model of public and private land management.

As did Article 14 with public land, the Adirondack Park Agency Act retracted private land from the sphere of indiscriminate use.

The work of the Temporary Study Commission was a direct translation of the larger societal vision. The Adirondack Park Agency Act, the State Land Master Plan, and the Adirondack Park Land Use and Development Plan were the first to lay out a full complement of private, liability, and inalienable rules to achieve regional protection of a wilderness already occupied by a sizable population. By defining this mix of rules for land use, these documents laid the foundation for a vision of sustainability of economic vitality in the context of a wilderness character.

The Adirondack Park of today is the product of a natural endowment that included harsh weather and a mountainous terrain, visionary advocates, and compromise between those who wanted as much of the natural environment protected as possible and those who were more concerned about economic prosperity (or some would say economic survival) for local residents. If one views the Adirondack region from an airplane or from one of its highest peaks, it does appear as one of the truly wild places in the United States. Up close, however, an expanding development of second homes is ever-present. Waterfront property has become sufficiently scarce that wealthy individuals are purchasing motels and other commercial establishments located adjacent to lakes and razing them to construct private residents. Change is evident.

In addition to public lands (the Forest Preserve) in the park, large tracks owned by the forest-products industry have helped maintain the forested landscape of the Adirondacks. That, too, is changing dramatically. In the past decade Champion International, Domtar, International Paper, and Finch Pruyn have each sold their timber holdings in the park. Some of that land has been sold to the state and some to timber investment management organizations (TIMOS) and real estate investment trusts (REITS). Much of the land sold to other kinds of private-sector investors has included the sale of conservation easements to the state as a means of further protecting the land from development. The conservation easement has become a refined tool for managing lands in a way that partitions property rights between semiprivate means and semipublic ends.

Is there an advantage to shifting our focus on the Adirondack Park from one of simply protecting the natural environment (not that that is a simple proposition) to using the metaphor of sustainable development? We are aware of the controversy over whether there is real substance to the notion of sustainable development. Still, the words of the World Commission on Environment and Development that defined sustainable development as that which "meets the needs of the present without compromising the ability of future generations to meet their own needs"[1] appear to have meaning here in the Adirondack Park. Sustainable development in the context of the Adirondack Park would include at least five goals:

1. Protect the wild character and ecological integrity of the public lands in the park.

2. Assist each hamlet to develop its own personality both esthetically and culturally so that its residents want to live there because of the quality of the experience.

3. Protect and improve where necessary the infrastructure in the park.

4. Promote and enable appropriate development that neither destroys nor impoverishes the natural resources on which that or other development depends.

5. Promote a shared vision with shared responsibility for the park.

Many people will agree that these are important goals. Even the most vocal critics of the Forest Preserve and the Adirondack Park Agency will point to wilderness as an asset. Whether we understand the science in depth or not, it seems intuitive that ecological integrity involves the protection of the function and structure of natural ecosystems on the public lands and a smooth transition between public and private lands. It seems obvious as well that we want to avoid public beautiful here and private ugly there. And many of the strongest advocates for wilderness will agree that community identity is important. All people want to brag about their community— their neighbors, churches, schools, and villagescape.

One of the cornerstones to quality of life is the infrastructure to support basic needs. Water is possibly the single biggest short-term environmental problem facing the world. The water quality and quantity of the Adirondacks is superb; therefore there is a temptation to ignore it (the empty-world mindset!). That would be the demise of sustainable development in the park. Maintaining water quality calls for particular attention to the appropriate disposal of commercial and household waste, adequate filtration of surface water run-off prior to entry to water bodies, protection of wetlands, and protection from invasive species. Similarly, promoting quality schools and building better communication systems are crucial.

These goals, of course, become irrelevant without an ability to keep the economy intact. The park is based on a rural economy. It is not the big projects with outside capital that will build an enduring economy, but the small actions that involve all sorts of people at the local level. It is the local real-estate broker, the banker, and the lawyer, rather than the Wall Street brokers and the big construction firms that bring vitality to communities. But the issue is not just about local decisions. The park's historic economy was sustained only because of close ties to the larger regional and global economy. Our failures all relate to our inability, still, to understand sustainability at multiple scales. Most recently, our failures to understand the cumulative impact of decades of deregulation and poor land-use planning, which created a "housing bubble" in the United States, led in large part to the global financial collapse of 2008. And unlike other recent economic woes such as the bursting of the dot-com bubble, the housing fiasco was not isolated to just a few economic sectors. We are all connected now.

It is the goal of achieving a shared vision that perhaps stirs the most controversy. The majority of New Yorkers live in full-world environments where human impact is pervasive and where they cope with crime, pollution, and traffic. To them, the Adirondack Park represents a place where the environment is safe, unblemished, and empty. To them, more acquisition of land for wilderness—land that would remain empty—is important because their world is full.

To those living in the Adirondacks, the world is anything but full. What many local residents see everyday when they walk out the door is an overabundance of land sitting idle. Many cannot conceive of a reason to set aside more wilderness.

The focal point for the debate is the land-use classification. At the heart of the classification system is an intention to cluster human impacts. Heavier human impact is limited to Rural, Hamlet, Low Intensity, Moderate Intensity, and Industrial areas. The clustering occurs because these classes represent less than 15 percent of the park. To the town supervisors seeking to promote economic vitality in their communities, this limit to growth is *the* reality of living in the Adirondack Park. To environmental advocates, the clustering is not stringent enough.

On the whole, though, it is the clustering that is largely responsible for the rise in both the environmental condition and the economic value of land in the Adirondacks. Land-use classification and economic disincentives to develop lands owned by timber industries limited fragmentation of the region. Measures of ecological integrity show that large portions of the park have returned to natural conditions akin to those of the sixteenth century. The presence of exotic species and the loss of native species, the key indicators of ecosystem decline, occur primarily in those areas designated for human development. Recent sales of development rights through establishment of conservation easements on large areas of industrial forestlands mean that fragmentation is unlikely to become ubiquitous. At the same time, economic value is increasing as limits to the amount of available land combine with changing economic and demographic conditions to drive up the cost of real estate. The retirement of the baby boomers and their unprecedented wealth, and the appeal of a second home or permanent move away from crime, pollution, and traffic to the slower pace of the Adirondacks have focused demand on the little land that is available for development. And the developable land is more valuable precisely because 85 percent of the surrounding landscape is protected. U.S. communities that suffered the most dramatic declines in real estate values in the 2008 collapse were precisely the communities with the least amount of planning and growth controls.

The debates about property rights in the future will be shaped by the questions about the limits to available space for development and, in particular, clustering. Some have argued that the density criteria for buildings in Resource Management areas are too general and that we are now reaping the consequences in the form of local fragmentation. The law allows one building for 42.7 acres, which translates into a potential 15 buildings per square mile. With dispersion of the buildings come more roads and other infrastructure. Would tighter clustering of development reduce environmental degradation? Others have argued that the boundaries of hamlets should be expanded to allow at least modest development of local economies. Can the restrictions on the periphery of hamlets be relaxed without incurring a large ecological cost? Are there thresholds to expansion of development and attendant human impact on surrounding lands beyond which the resilience of the natural ecosystem is no longer able to cope? If so, where are those thresholds? The science available to date does not provide any clear answers. Until science can provide good answers, decision makers will be faced with economic pressures and diverse opinions about change that challenge the legal precedents of land-use regulation.

Perhaps the greatest economic pressure will arise not from the desire for second homes, but the emergence of infrastructure and what might be called the Emerson Effect. In 1858, Ralph Waldo Emerson and the small group of people who would pioneer philosophy in America convened a Philosophers' Camp near Follensby Pond in the central Adirondacks. Emerson left the camp motivated by a desire to get back to Boston to learn of the news of the first transatlantic cable. What would have happened if Emerson were in the middle of the Adirondacks with immediate connection to society? Would he have been as anxious to leave? We appear to be at the leading edge of the Emerson Effect today, where our desire to be connected to society is promoting penetration of high-speed telecommunication. Reliable telephone, fax, high-speed internet, and overnight package delivery is slowly reaching to even the most remote communities of the Adirondacks. The perception of a higher quality of life associated with small communities and the aesthetics of the surrounding wilderness, coupled with good communication, is fostering a new migration of Americans from the suburbs back to rural environments. Will the Emerson Effect prove to be a metaphor for the Adirondacks of the next generation?

As we look to the future, we ask once again, did the succession of laws and policies from 1885 to 1972 meet the lofty goals of the authors who wrote them and the legislators who gave them the status of law? John Davis, conservation director for the Adirondack Council, answers this question with a still deeper one: "This is perhaps the best-protected landscape in the country, but is it protected well enough?" The Adirondack Park was created through an extraordinary confluence of societal will and political savvy. Once put in place, the park has sustained itself in the face of substantial challenges. Both politically and ecologically, the park has demonstrated remarkable resistance to outside forces. To some people, the ultimate measure of that resistance is evident in the decisions of the forest industry to pull out, ceding its lands to be part of the wilderness. For many of these advocates, the debate now shifts to housing subdivisions. For still others, the debate will focus on whether economic vitality and ecological integrity is an either-or question, and if science can provide an avenue to sustainability of both. Yet to others, the debate over property rights and how best to define sustainability has only begun. The enabling legislation of the Adirondack Park Agency sought nothing less than to codify a distribution of the benefits from property ownership between individuals and the public, between current and future generations, and between humanity and the rest of nature. Much of the past 38 years of the Adirondack Park Agency has been spent firming up the legal foundation for this approach and refining the process by which the distribution of rights is implemented day to day. As such, the park reflects the societal choice from the full spectrum of property-rights regimes.

On the horizon may be new societal choices, as indicated by observations that young people have less affinity for nature than previous generations. In question is a fundamental issue: is wilderness an important asset to the human condition, and therefore is conservation of the resources of a region a reasonable goal? Is sustainability through preservation of a wilderness environment possible? In concrete terms, what is the societal cost of wind turbines in a wilderness? What is the value of wild rivers in the face of the need for hydropower? And ultimately, how should we consider a forest that could be harvested to provide resources for cellulose-based biofuels or wood-fired electricity generation? The Adirondack region is located within 500 miles of over 90 million people, so the immediacy of the issues like energy is obvious. Less obvious are the broader issues that could drive the debate about wilderness.

The future the Adirondacks will play in society's thinking about the sustainability of the combination of wilderness and human economies is likely to be predicated on three remarkable ironies. The first is that the biggest threat facing the Adirondacks is the risk that wealth will flow into the Adirondacks. Local governments have railed against the Adirondack Park Agency for limiting their ability to bring economic vitality to their communities. The challenge they face is certainly affected by land-use regulation. However, for much of the past 40 years, the goal was to bring manufacturing jobs into the region. The challenges of transportation plagued the economic development of all of the northern forest from Minnesota to Maine. The forest industry is the common denominator in all these states, and even in the absence of the Adirondack Park Agency, northern Wisconsin and northern Michigan faired little better that northern New York. Yet the Emerson Effect may accomplish what forest industry could not, drawing high-paying jobs to the region that are generated by small entrepreneurs and digital connections to corporate America. The service-based economy is highly mobile and quality of life drives the decisions about where people choose to live. As high-speed internet service becomes standard in the Adirondacks, the software companies around Boston and the financial corporations of New York City may begin to see strategic advantage in locating in the Adirondacks because doing so enables them to compete more successfully for talented employees. And in a post-AIG and post–Big Three auto era, where even the most dogmatic deregulators are questioning the mantra "too big to fail," might an economic model of small and local make a comeback?

Ultimately, however, human economies need energy and materials to survive. In the end, can the Adirondacks be held to a standard of sustainability if environmental protection and quality of life are sustained within the Blue Line at the expense of degrading environments elsewhere? A planning ethic of "not in my backyard" no longer applies when scaled up to the level of the whole earth's sustaining and containing ecosystem. As goes the planetary experiment, so goes the Adirondack experiment.

The power of wealth and values of society a century ago put the Adirondack experiment in motion. The power of wealth today may cast the old issues in a new light. Once again, property rights will be central. The limited land available for development will exacerbate issues of affordable housing to the point that it may produce a demographic shift. Gone will be the society of self reliance that has been pervasive for at least six generations. Ushered in will be a society with a desire for government to provide greater service. Yesterday, local governments were challenged by people who viewed the lack of cell-phone coverage as inconvenient. Today, they are faced with a society that sees it as dangerous. And today, local governments are challenged by the emergence of large numbers of seasonal residents who see the lack of shopping malls as inconvenient. Tomorrow, they may be facing the implications of rapidly growing population of year-round residents who demand all the conveniences of the suburbs.

The second remarkable irony is that Adirondack residents of today may be the last generation really to understand the nature of the region. As much as residents saw the park agency as limiting what they could do with a wilderness, they were at home *within* it. If Richard Louv has it right in *Last Child in the Woods,* American society is moving away from outdoor experiences, and the future residents of the park may only live *beside* it.[2] If the demand of economic wealth combines with a societal shift in the perception of the value of wilderness, then redrawing of the lines and perhaps reconsideration of the entire classification system are likely. Article 14, the Adirondack Park Agency, the State Land Master Plan, and the Adirondack Park Land Use and Development Plan are political constructs that can be undone.

The third irony is that what happens outside of the Blue Line may be more important to the Adirondack environment than the decisions made within. The ecological resilience of the Adirondack Park is evident by the return of wilderness species such as the moose. The moose became reestablished after more than a century of absence because the Adirondack region remains ecologically connected to wild ecosystems of northern Vermont, New Hampshire, Maine, and southern Ontario and Quebec. That connection is tenuous and may eventually be broken by intense human development in the St. Lawrence River, Lake Champlain, and Mohawk River valleys. Moose are able to cross this ring of development today because what was once open farmland has been abandoned in the past century and reverted to forest, even if fragmented. That forest, though, is in transition to residential and commercial development with the attendant multilane highways. The "rooftop" highway under consideration for the St. Lawrence River valley from Watertown to Plattsburgh illustrates the immediacy of this vision of the future. Once the intensity of development truly isolates the Adirondack Park, 6 million acres may not be sufficient to retain the communities of species and the natural processes of the wilderness ecosystem.

Even regional connectivity may not be the most crucial issue. As is evident from three decades of scientific study, acidic deposition and atmospheric inputs such as mercury have been detrimental to the Adirondack ecosystems and potentially to the health of people living in the region. The long-term measurements show that the ecosystem remains resilient as exemplified by the signs of natural recovery during the years of stringent federal air-quality standards.

However, if current trends in degradation continue, there is an ultimate threshold beyond which recovery is not likely to occur. Of course, the specter of global climate change overshadows all. Already there are signs of shifts of songbird communities, with the southern edges of northern bird species shrinking, and the northern edges of southern species expanding. With changes in length of the warmer seasons will come new diseases and insect pests resulting in a decline of many of the tree species that are hallmarks of the Adirondacks: maple, birch, spruce, and hemlock.

The future of the Adirondacks is certain to include significant change. Economic and ecological characteristics of the region today that influence so many of the decisions we make are unlikely to be the only considerations that shape future concerns. Yet while society in general, and Adirondack residents in particular, face the challenges of moving forward in a context of broad uncertainty, and certainly an absence of complete understanding of how to achieve sustainability, there is nevertheless a need to make decisions. We can continue to debate decisions regarding hamlet boundaries and lakeshore setbacks for construction, and we should, but we must also cast an eye to the gathering clouds on the horizon. If we are to find a means of sustaining a vibrant economy amidst a wilderness ecosystem, we will need to forge a new consensus for a shared vision not just within the Adirondacks, but within our larger society.

We return to the lessons of this book with the hope that they may offer insight to help us come together in a shared vision for not just the Adirondacks but other areas facing similar decisions. While the central insight is not novel, it is fundamental: whether we speak of the Adirondacks, Alaska, or the developing world, philosophical agreement is the first step to moving forward. The Adirondack wilderness persists today because earlier generations came to broad philosophical accord and then political agreement on a vision for a Forest Preserve and the Adirondack Park. We will need to achieve that political accord once again. To do so, we will need to recognize the difference in perceptions between those who experience the full world and those who experience the empty world. That difference created the wedge issues of the past 40 years and is likely to be the cause of great change in the decades ahead. The shift in geography of economic activity and footloose income to rural environments, and the decreasing societal affinity for the natural environment, will precipitate a new debate about the value of wilderness. A new demographic group will inhabit the Adirondacks, and it is likely they will share the philosophical position of neither the contemporary environmentalist nor developer. Rather, a new philosophy will emerge.

The other insight pertains to the mechanism for implementing a shared vision. The implementation of a vision of sustainability will be inherently messy because we live in a democracy, and because we must make so many decisions without a complete understanding of either their economic or ecological implications. We will need a mechanism for synthesizing what is known and identifying what is not, objectively evaluating pros and cons in light of this knowledge and then moving forward with the best possible decisions. Ideally, we will need a means for testing some of the underlying assumptions to the decisions made, monitoring the outcomes of those tests, and improving the decisions with each cycle. The Adirondack Park Agency Act offers one model, among probably many, for implementing a vision of land use over a large area. Many people continue to disagree with the decisions made by the park agency over the years, and many object to the time often required to reach a decision, but decisions are made. In the process, the agency provides a forum for debate, clarifies and documents the issues, attempts various solutions, and finally integrates new knowledge to improve the decisions it makes. We can argue about the execution, but there is much to be said for the model.

The lesson about mechanism is also one of limitations. It is likely that a mechanism such as the Adirondack Park Agency Act can serve to move the park, and society, closer to the goal of a sustainable environment. To do so, though, means that the agency must find ways to integrate a complicated economic system and, one could argue, an even more complex ecosystem. If that is not daunting enough, the Adirondack Park Agency faces outside influences to these economic and ecological systems that it cannot affect. Like all government agencies, it is vulnerable to political pressures, or interference, and that risk grows as economic stakes get larger. And, like all agencies, it lacks the authority necessary to control the destiny of the resources it is charged with overseeing. In this case, that is because the Adirondack region can be isolated, to its detriment, from the surrounding ecosystems and also because it is attached, again to its detriment, to the regional weather patterns and global climate. Thus, as much as the Adirondack economy seems at the whim of outside forces, so too is the health of the natural ecosystem.

As we said at the outset, the Adirondack region was the crucible of the American conservation ethic at the turn of the twentieth century. So it appears to be poised to serve that role again. Both philosophically and mechanistically, the fact that wilderness protection and at least modest economic development has worked in the past creates an enormous inertia going forward. It is likely that the Adirondacks will be the place where the debates of how to define, measure, and manage for sustainability will be vigorous. Once again, the decisions arising from the Adirondack experience are likely to shape, as much as be shaped by, new societal paradigms.

We end with an expression of deep respect for the prescience of earlier generations and key leaders in creating an opportunity for this generation, and those to come, to test the idea that sustainability is possible. The wisdom gained by the generation now beginning to pass from the scene and captured, in part, by the many voices of this book, is remarkable. We hope future generations can learn from it. Yet our guiding question—"Why does the Adirondack experiment still persist?"—is never fully answered because at the core of sustainability is the hope, and indeed the expectation, that generations from now, people will be asking the same question.

# Afterword

*Living Within Limits*

BILL MCKIBBEN

The hand of man has been (relatively) light on the Adirondacks in the past. Yes, most of it has been cut over at one time or another, but in many cases just once. (And as historian Barbara McMartin has argued, even that was a light brush across hundreds of thousands of acres.) There are relatively few places on this continent that can point to a single encounter with human enterprise—certainly not the vast swatches of the American West perennially retransformed by cow and sheep, nor the plains plowed each spring, nor the off-shore sea bottoms trawled with depressing regularity.

That relative wildness and pristinity are the key defining features of the park; the Blue Line is a psychological circle of a sort. It demarks a series of historical choices that have limited human impact on the landscape. Humans have reduced their demands on this place. Not entirely, of course, and perhaps not enough, as the current second-home development boom demonstrates. But *relatively*. To stand in the Pepperbox Wilderness or the Wilcox Lakes Wild Forest (and to know that you are one of maybe a dozen people standing in those places on that day), and to see that they have been saved not for their Yosemite-quality splendor but just *because,* is to understand the heart of the Adirondack experiment. Especially if you have stood that same day in North Creek or Old Forge and understood that the distance from the human world is neither great nor artificial. A sweeping (if relative) wildness, a recovered (if relative) wildness, a wildness juxtaposed with the human—these are the hallmarks of this place.

But what will they mean a half-century hence? I think the Adirondack region is better equipped than most places to its mix of uses—some combination of enlightened government and enlightened philanthropy may be able to figure out some of the conundrums (high housing prices especially) that threaten this experiment. But it is no better equipped than any other place to survive the large-scale human impacts that will come as we rapidly warm the planet.

That approaching warming is by now conceded by all credible climatologists, who differ only on the degrees and rates with which it will manifest. Although there is an enormous amount of work to be done to slow global warming (obvious work—raising automobile efficiency, taxing carbon, building renewable sources of power), none of it will be enough to prevent large-scale climate change. The best estimate (not by any means the worst-case scenario) of the world's scientific establishment is that this century will see a temperature increase on the order of 5 degrees Fahrenheit globally averaged, a number that may well be somewhat higher at this latitude. That is a very, very large shift—the world would be warmer, should that happen, than at any time since before the start of primate evolution. We literally can barely imagine what such a world would be like.

Given a limited area like the Adirondacks, however, it is becoming easier for the computer modelers to make predictions. A team centered at the University of New Hampshire published in the fall of 2001 the most detailed forecast yet for northern New England and northern New York. Barring some strange surprise—say, a slowdown of the Gulf Stream from Arctic melting that paradoxically cools parts of the Atlantic coasts of North America and Europe—the picture of a superheated Adirondacks begins to emerge. It would not resemble the park that we know today. For one thing, the tree species that dominate our slopes would disappear. Hemlocks would no longer shade and cool our streams. The upland forests would no longer be dominated by birch, beech, and maple with their magnificent autumn show. Instead, some mix of oak and hickory would likely move in from the south, an event that would among a thousand other consequences end that rite of spring, the sugar season. (A rite of spring that has already become a rite of late winter in recent decades; in fact, at this latitude spring already arrives about 7 days earlier on average than it did in 1970.)

Even more stunning, the season that we know as winter would essentially disappear. When it gets that warm it is far more likely to rain than snow, and what snow there is melts away fast. Lakes do not freeze, except ephemerally and at altitude. (Already the great low lake of the region, Champlain, has experienced unprecedented stretches of years when it fails to ice-over totally in the course of a winter.) The report concluded that although some kind of short alpine ski season might be eked out on manmade snow, both snow-mobiling and cross-country skiing would become extinct.

The economic effects of such a huge shift would be large, of course—if winter becomes one long mud season, and the fall foliage turns a drab brown, who knows what will happen to the tourist economy. Too, the biological effects are likely to be enormous—how will trout populations survive heating waters? The most likely answer is, they will not, and similar stresses will be felt across the entire flora and fauna. But in this context I will leave those questions for others. (I have tried to answer some of them in a cover article for *Adirondack Life* magazine dated April 2002.)

What concerns me more here is how the *meaning* of the Adirondacks will change. To the extent that its meaning derives from a sense that it is pristine, Forever Wild, largely untouched by man at least in the Forest Preserve, then that meaning may be in for as rough a ride as the trout. The Blue Line is, obviously, no defense against climate change; in fact, it will be felt far more powerfully in the Adirondacks than in, say, Clifton Park precisely because people here pay attention to the "natural" world. Winter is a far more palpable concept in Saranac Lake than in Shenendehowa, and so its absence will be more profoundly felt. The American suburb, where most of our countrymen now live, is a device for making the physical world disappear—who knows where its rivers run, or what its native species are? Only places like the Adirondacks still have a deep connection to the physical, and so the damage will be more blatant there.

Just as winter and fall are eliminated, so also may the sense of living someplace apart be eroded. If smog was the great environmental metaphor of the last century, you could escape it by leaving the city; this greenhouse smog will blanket everything. Thoreau wrote once that he could walk half an hour from his Concord cabin and come to a place where no man stood from one year to the next, "and there consequently politics are not, for politics are but the cigar smoke of man." In some ways it will no longer make much sense to talk about the Adirondacks as "wild."

But in such a world, paradoxically, wild will become more important than ever. *Relative* wild. It is true that the park will be heating up. But it is also true, barring hideous folly by the voters of New York, that the 3 million acres of Forest Preserve will still be free of development, and that the APA will, I hope, manage development in the rest of the park in exemplary ways. By contrast to the rest of the East, and indeed to most of the lower 48, it will remain an island of wildness, and that island will be all the more important, *if only to prove that we as a species are in fact capable of leaving something alone.* There will be great practical value in the unbroken forest, too, of course—as plants and animals stream northward against the rising heat it will be an invaluable refugium, and a stop on the underground railroad fighting extinction as it was once a stop on the underground railroad battling slavery. But in a world far more tinged even than our own with a sense of how badly humans have overrun their wise and proper bounds, the example of the Blue Line will speak volumes. It is not hard to imagine the bicentennial of the park's founding, in the 2090s, in a world much chastened by the example of endless human overreach—the park will be one of those places of which we can still be proud, and from which we can take some clues about how to proceed on the other side of the environmental crises that mark our century.

The human communities of the park will also offer valuable lessons to the world around us, I think. It is at least possible that in a carbon-constrained world (or the post-fossil-fuel age envisioned by an increasing number of researchers focusing on "peak oil"), we will need examples of places less tied into the global economy, more able to fend for themselves. The Adirondack Mountains possess certain of these characteristics—some of its energy is locally derived from wood, for instance. Combined regionally with the Champlain Valley, the possibility for a more self-sufficient food and energy economy grows. Maybe more to the point, many of its residents manage still to take a great part of their satisfaction from contact with the world around them instead of from material acquisition. This trick—which Adirondack guides helped teach city swells a century ago in the first heyday of "ecotourism"—may be equally important in the world now dawning. Intact communities, relatively low consumption lifestyles, homegrown entertainment—these are distinctions that may seem more significant in a more stressed world. If the suburban dream begins to tarnish, we will need some other dreams to replace it. This could be one.

Global warming changes everything, obviously. It is the most pronounced change humans have made to the planet since we crawled down from the trees, and it is vanity to try and predict exactly how we will react. But those things that already distinguish the Adirondacks—a sense of wildness, and human communities embedded within that wildness—may become even more precious in the scary days ahead. At the least, it is crucial now more than ever to keep these mountains and these hamlets as intact as possible. They may be touchstones in the chaos—ecological and human—now heading our way.

ADIRONDACK CHRONOLOGY

NOTES

BIBLIOGRAPHY

INDEX

# Adirondack Chronology

This chronology is intended to capture the key events that shaped the Adirondack region and the evolution of the Adirondack Park. Our intent is to describe in a concise manner the ecological, economic, and political changes in the Adirondacks, especially since the arrival of Europeans. Our goal is not a comprehensive listing of events. Rather, we hope to provide a sketch of Adirondack history as a progression from ultimate means to ultimate ends. To construct this chronology, we began with a rich summary of events created by Gary Chilson for the Association for the Protection of the Adirondacks, pared down the entries, and then supplemented this listing with the dates presented throughout this book. Other people might have chosen different events, but we find this summary helpful as a context for discussing the more complex issues presented throughout the book. Interested readers may also want to consult *The Adirondack Atlas,* by Jerry Jenkins and Andy Keal (2004), and *The Great Forest of the Adirondacks,* by Barbara McMartin (1994).

| | |
|---|---|
| 12,700 BP | Glacial ice sheet is in active recession from Adirondacks and Catskills. |
| 12,600 BP | Glacial Lake Iroquois begins drainage of melt waters through the Mohawk Valley. |
| 11,000 BP | Glacial melting exposes the Lake George graben and Lake George fills. |
| 10,200 BP | Tundra declines and a spruce-rich boreal forest emerges in northern New York. |
| 9,600 BP | Boreal forest declines and pine-rich forest emerges in Hamilton County. |
| 4,800 BP | Eastern hemlock shows an extensive decline in dominance as birch, maple, beech, and pine begin to increase. |

4,000 BP    Birch, beech, maple, and pine are invaded by spruce and fir.

1000    Late Woodland Period of human culture prevails in north-eastern North America.

1600    Human global population is estimated at 500 million.

1609    Samuel de Champlain enters the lake now bearing his name.

1620    Harvest of beaver pelts supports establishment of trading posts at Montreal and Beverwyck (later known as Albany).

1630–50    Beaver populations are largely eliminated from the Adirondacks.

1741    New York State implements hunting season to limit harvest of deer.

1755–60    The diary of Major Roberts indicates scarcity of deer in the eastern Adirondacks.

1763    First of many lumber mills is built in Glens Falls.

1771    1,150,000 acres of Adirondack land purchased from the Mohawks (Totten and Crossfield purchase).

1777    New York State Constitution is ratified at Kingston.

1779    New York State Act of Attainder assigns British Crown lands (9 million acres) to people.
New York State Land Commission is established to sell off excess property.

1784    Simeon DeWitt, surveyor general, begins major Adirondack surveys.

1785    The 1784 law fostering sale of "waste" and "unassigned lands" is repealed.
New York State law fosters settlement of public lands through auction.

1786    Not one soldier of the Revolutionary Army accepts lands in the Adirondack Military Tract.

1790    New York State population is 340,000, with a density of 7.1 persons per square mile, and 89 percent rural.

1792    Alexander Malcomb purchases 3.9 million acres of Adirondack land from New York State.

1804    Successful iron-ore mining begins at Mineville near Port Henry in eastern Essex County.

1808    New York State law prohibits cutting of public woods in Essex County.

| | |
|---|---|
| 1811 | Hamilton County institutes a bounty on wolves. |
| 1825 | Erie Canal opens and draws pioneers west. |
| 1830 | Extensive harvest of large spruce begins. |
| 1836 | New York State begins the Natural History Survey with Professor Ebenezer Emmons as geologist. |
| 1837 | W. C. Redfield, E. Emmons, and others ascend Mt. Marcy. E. Emmons names Mt. Marcy in honor of the governor. |
| 1838 | E. Emmons uses the name "Adirondack group" in New York State Geologic Survey. |
| 1849 | Rev. Joel T. Headley publishes *The Adirondack: or, Life in the Woods.* |
| 1850 | New York State leads the nation in lumber production. New York State population is 3,097,000, with a density of 65.0 persons per square mile. Commercial white pine resource of the Adirondacks is exhausted. |
| 1851 | Henry David Thoreau observes that "in wildness is the preservation of the world." |
| 1854 | McIntyre blast furnace is completed at Tahawus. |
| 1857 | McIntyre blast furnaces ceases operation because of low production, lack of transportation of iron, and economic downturn. |
| 1858 | "Philosophers Camp" occurs at Follensby Pond; notable attendees include Ralph Waldo Emerson, James Russell Lowell, Louis Agassiz, and Oliver Wendell Holmes. Ralph Waldo Emerson writes his poem "The Adirondacks." |
| 1861 | Last three documented moose kills in the Adirondacks; the species was described as abundant in 1840. |
| 1864 | George Perkins Marsh publishes *Man and Nature; or Physical Geography as Modified by Human Action.* |
| 1868 | Verplanck Colvin lectures at Lake Pleasant, calling for an Adirondack state park and forest preserve. |
| 1869 | W. H. H. Murray publishes his best-selling *Adventures in the Wilderness.* |
| 1870 | New York State population is 4,383,000, with a density of 92.0 persons per square mile, and 50 percent rural. |
| 1870s | 60 logging companies maintain offices in Glens Falls. |

1871    New York State begins acquisition of Adirondack forest-
        land through tax title claims.
        New York State begins offering bounties on predators and
        pays 46 cougar and 45 wolf bounties in the subsequent 11
        years.

1872    Verplanck Colvin is appointed to survey and map the
        Adirondacks.

1873    Commission of State Parks recommends a state park in the
        Adirondacks.

1875    More than 200 hotels operate in the Adirondack region.

1877    Camp Pine Knot is constructed by W. W. Durant, estab-
        lishing the Adirondack Great Camp tradition of outwardly
        rustic construction appointed to provide for gracious living
        by the wealthy elite.

1883    New York State Legislature forbids the resale of Adiron-
        dack lands acquired in tax sales.

1884    First tuberculosis sanatorium in the United States is estab-
        lished at Saranac Lake.
        Francis Trudeau founds TB research laboratory at Saranac
        Lake.
        Sargent Commission is established by New York State to study
        forest preservation and calls for a map of the Adirondacks.

1885    Sargent Commission recommends formulation of a law
        creating New York State's forest preserve.
        New York State Legislature passes Forest Preserve bill.
        Governor David Hill signs an act establishing the New
        York State Forest Preserve.

1886    New York State accepts taxation of Forest Preserve lands,
        directing that "state lands subject to taxation shall be val-
        ued as if privately owned."

1890    Adirondack League Club is established with 104,000 acres
        in the southwestern Adirondacks.
        Harvest of large spruce peaks, and harvest of hemlock
        declines rapidly as the tannery industry moves to southern
        New York and Pennsylvania.
        Beech bark insect is inadvertently introduced into Nova
        Scotia from Europe.

1892    Governor Roswell P. Flower signs the Adirondack Park Enabling Act.

Adirondack Park of 2.8 million acres is delineated by the "Blue Line."

1894    New York State Constitution amended (Article 7) to prohibit all timber sales on the Forest Preserve: "The lands of the state, now owned or hereafter acquired, constituting the forest preserve as now fixed by law, shall be forever kept as wild forest lands. They shall not be leased, sold, or exchanged, or be taken by any corporation, public or private, nor shall the timber thereon be sold, removed, or destroyed."

New York State pays last mountain lion bounty.

1898    Seventeen mills join to form the International Paper Company headquartered at Corinth.

1899    Last documented wolf kill in New York State in St. Lawrence County.

1899    G. E. Dodge, T. M. Meigs, and F. J. Meigs establish the St. Regis Paper Company.

1900    Louis Marshall and friend establish Knollwood Great Camp at Lower Saranac Lake.

Adirondack region leads the nation in paper production.

1902    First meeting of Association for the Protection of the Adirondacks board of trustees is held, Judge W. Higley presiding.

1902–9    Beavers are translocated from Yellowstone Park into the Adirondacks.

1903    New York State Forest, Fish, and Game Commission declares the black bear in danger of extirpation and calls for protection.

1903–8    Extensive fires burn throughout the Adirondack region as a result of drought, accumulating slash from logging, and sparks from steam engines.

1905    Adirondack timber harvest peaks at 3.5 million trees. Railroads extending into the interior of the region permit harvest of hardwoods.

1910    New York State population is 9,114,000, with a density of 191 persons per square mile, and 21.2 percent rural.

1912    Hunting of deer is regulated and restricted to taking bucks only.

1920    Timber industry in the Adirondacks experiences a sharp contraction.

1922    Meade Dobson, G. D. Pratt, and William G. Howard found Adirondack Mountain Club.

1923    Northville–Lake Placid Trail is completed.

1928    Adirondacks are again opened to beaver harvest, and nearly 5,000 are trapped.

1930    New York State population is 12,588,000, with a density of 262.6 persons per square mile.

1931    Blue Line is enlarged to 5.6 million acres to include parts of Lake Champlain.

1932    Governor Franklin D. Roosevelt opens the Third Olympic Winter Games at Lake Placid.

1935    Attempts to amend constitution to permit logging on Forest Preserve lands are thwarted by Louis Marshall Constitutional Convention recodifies Article 7 to Article 14.

1941    National Lead (later NL Industries) purchases Tahawus property and begins mining for titanium.
        Amendment to Article 14 allows development of ski trails at Whiteface Mountain.

1944    Last railroad tracks laid in the Adirondacks, connecting the D&H main line in North Creek to the National Lead titanium mine at Tahawus.

1946    Moose River Committee is formed in response to proposal to construct large hydroelectric power dam on the South Branch of the Moose River.

1947    Amendment to Article 14 allows development of ski trails at Gore Mountain.

1950    New York State population is 14,830,000, with a density of 309.3 persons per square mile, and 14.5 percent rural.
        Last large log drive on the Hudson River.

Mid-    New process allows use of hardwoods as a source for pulp
1950s   in the manufacture of paper.

1953    Article 14 amended to revoke power of legislature to authorize construction of reservoirs in the Forest Preserve.

1954    Adirondack Park Association (Adirondack North Country Association) is established.

1955    Total production from Adirondack mines reaches all-time high.

1956    Blue Line is extended, enlarging the Adirondack Park to 5,693,500 acres.

1957    Adirondack Historical Association opens the Adirondack Museum at Blue Mountain Lake.

1959    Amendment to Article 14 allows construction of I-87.

1960–70  Hardwoods become dominant source of pulp for manufacture of paper in the region.

1963    Commissioner Wilm allows snowmobiles on snow-covered trails of the Forest Preserve.

1964    Conservation Department restricts snowmobiles to signed roads and trails in response to a challenge by the Association for the Protection of the Adirondacks.
        Federal Wilderness Act is signed into law.

1965    Beech bark disease arrives in the Adirondacks.

1967    Laurance Rockefeller's proposal for an Adirondack Mountains National Park is defeated.

1968    Governor Nelson Rockefeller appoints the Temporary Study Commission on the Future of the Adirondacks.

1970    National Environmental Policy Act is signed into law.
        Conservation Department is reorganized as the Department of Environmental Conservation (DEC).
        Temporary Study Commission publishes *The Future of the Adirondacks* and proposes creation of Adirondack Park Agency.
        New York State population is 18,237,000, with a density of 381.0 persons per square mile, and 14.4 percent rural.

1971    Governor Nelson Rockefeller signs a bill creating the Adirondack Park Agency.
        International Paper Company opens its $76-million kraft paper process plant at Ticonderoga.

1972    Governor Nelson Rockefeller signs State Land Master Plan.

1973    Adirondack Park Agency completes Adirondack Park Land Use and Development Plan.

Federal Endangered Species Act is signed into law.

1974    Federal Forest and Rangeland Renewable Resources Planning Act is signed into law.

National Forest Management Act is signed into law.

1975    Adirondack Council is established in Elizabethtown.

1976    Adirondack legislators introduce a bill to abolish the Adirondack Park Agency, but the bill fails.

1980    Lake Placid hosts the Thirteenth Winter Olympic Games.

1984    George Davis and others found the Adirondack Land Trust.

1989    Governor Mario Cuomo appoints second temporary study commission (Commission on the Adirondacks in the Twenty-First Century).

NL Industries ceases mining operations for titanium at Tahawus.

New York State Adirondack Park Agency Visitor Interpretive Center opens at Paul Smiths.

1990    Commission on the Adirondacks in the Twenty-First Century issues its report.

Adirondack Fairness Coalition is formed in opposition to the Twenty-First Century Commission Report.

Citizen's Council and Adirondack Fairness Coalition stage rally protesting Twenty-First Century Commission Report.

Major road rally on Northway led by Adirondack Solidarity Alliance immobilizes traffic.

Senator Stafford leads second protest rally of 400 slow-moving vehicles on Northway.

Adirondack Solidarity Alliance stage third motorcade rally ending at the Capitol in Albany.

Blue Line Council forms as coalition of state officials, educators, landowners, and health care professionals to seek a balance between preservation and development in reaction to the Twenty-First Century Commission Report.

Residents' Committee to Protect the Adirondacks is founded in North Creek in reaction to the Twenty-First Century Commission report.

Adirondack Landowners Association is established in reaction to the Twenty-First Century Commission report.

New York State Adirondack Park Agency Visitor Interpretive Center opens in Newcomb.

New York State population is 17,990,455, with a density of 381 persons per square mile.

1992 Adirondack town supervisors, mayors, and town councils form the Adirondack Association of Towns and Villages.

Northern Forest Lands study, *Finding Common Ground,* is published.

1994 Northern Forest Alliance formed.

Adirondack Research Consortium formed.

1995 A wind event (derecho) of exceptional scale and severity blows down 130,000 acres of Adirondack forest in 30 minutes and damages another 150,000 acres.

Survey tallies 67 moose inhabiting the Adirondacks.

A January ice storm causes more than 3 inches of ice to accumulate affecting more than 4 million acres of forest-land in New York. Hardwoods show greater damage than softwoods. Average loss of crown branches is estimated to be 22 percent.

2000 An estimated 90 percent of all beech trees larger than 6 inches in diameter are infected with beech bark disease.

2002 Adirondack Park Agency Policy on Telecommunication Towers and Other Tall Structures introduces a new standard: "substantially invisible."

2000– The largest remaining industrial forest owners (Champion
2007 International, International Paper, Whitney, Domtar, and Finch-Pruyn) sell their holdings of more than 600,000 acres through a combination of state and land trust acquisitions, and conservation easements.

2007 More than 100 individuals representing a diverse array of stakeholders hold the first meeting of the Common Ground Alliance in Long Lake. The meeting results in a document, "Blueprint for the Blue Line."

# Notes

## Part One. Introduction: A Dark Spot in a Sea of Lights

1. J. S. Thaler, *Adirondack Weather* (Yorktown Heights, N.Y.: Hudson Valley Climate Service, 2004), 7.

2. Ibid., 78–79.

3. Ibid., 81–82.

4. H. Kaiser, *Great Camps of the Adirondacks* (Boston: David R. Godine, 1982), 1.

## 1. Geology of the Adirondack Mountains: Like an Egg with Its Major Axis to the North

1. E. Emmons, 1842, *Survey of the Second Geological District* (Albany: Appleton, Wiley and Putnam, 1842), 11, 12.

## 2. Water Resources: The Unique Adirondack Aquascape

1. R. M. Newton and C. T. Driscoll, "Classification of ALSC Lakes," in *Adirondack Lakes Survey: An Interpretive Analysis of Fish Communities and Water Chemistry, 1984–1987,* ed. J. P. Baker et al., 2–70-2–91 (Ray Brook, N.Y.: Adirondack Lakes Survey Corp., 1990).

## 5. Fish and Wildlife Communities of the Adirondacks

1. J. Jenkins and A. Keal, *Adirondack Atlas: A Geographic Portrait of the Adirondack Park* (Syracuse: Syracuse Univ. Press, 2004).

2. M. J. Glennon and W. F. Porter, "Effects of Land-Use Management on Biotic Integrity: An Investigation of Bird Communities," *Biological Conservation* 126 (2005): 499–511.

3. N. Schoch and D. C. Evers, *Monitoring Mercury in Common Loons: New York Field Report, 1998–2000* (Falmouth, Me.: BioDiversity Research Institute, 2002).

4. B. A. Louks, "Peregrine Falcon: *Falco peregrinus,*" in *Bull's Birds of New York State,* ed. E. Levine (Ithaca, N.Y: Cornell Univ. Press, 1998), 203–6; P. Nye, "Bald Eagle: *Haliaeetus leucocephalus,*" in *Bull's Birds of New York State,* ed. E. Levine (Ithaca, N.Y.: Cornell Univ. Press, 1998), 182–85; P. Nye, "Golden Eagle: *Aquila chrysaetos,*" in *Bull's Birds of New York State,* ed. E. Levine (Ithaca, N.Y.: Cornell Univ. Press, 1998), 198–200.

5. J. E. DeKay, *Natural History of New York—Zoology* (New York: Appleton, Wiley and Putnam, 1842).

6. C. H. Merriam, *The Mammals of the Adirondack Region, Northeastern New York* (New York: Press of L. S. Foster, 1884).

7. Ibid; P. G. Terrie, *Wildlife and Wilderness: A History of Adirondack Mammals* (Fleischmanns, N.Y.: Purple Mountain Press, 1993).

8. P. C. Paquet, J. R. Strittholt, and N. L. Staus, *Wolf Reintroduction Feasibility in the Adirondack Park: Prepared for the Adirondack Citizens Advisory Committee on the Feasibility of Wolf Reintroduction* (Corvallis, Ore.: Conservation Biology Institute, 1999).

9. H. M. Fener, J. R. Ginsberg, E. Sanderson, and M. E. Gompper, "Chronology of Range Expansion of the Coyote, *Canis latrans,* in New York," *Canadian Field Naturalist* 119 (2005): 1–5.

10. M. E. Gompper, "Top Carnivores in the Suburbs? Ecological and Conservation Issues Raised by Colonization of Northeastern North America by Coyotes," *Bioscience* 52 (2002): 185–90; P. J. Wilson, W. J. Jakubas, and S. Mullen, *Genetic Status and Morphological Characteristics of Maine Coyotes as Related to Neighboring Coyote and Wolf Populations,* Final report to the Maine Outdoor Heritage Fund Board, Grant #011-3-7 (Bangor: Maine Department of Inland Fisheries and Wildlife, 2004).

11. H. Kruuk, *Hunter and Hunted: Relationships Between Carnivores and People* (New York: Cambridge Univ. Press, 2002).

12. W. Stone, *Puma concolor Necropsy Report* (Albany: NYSDEC Wildlife Pathology Laboratory, 1993).

13. K. L. Kogut, "A Look at Fish and Wildlife Resources in the Adirondack Park in the Twenty-First Century," *The Adirondack Park in the Twenty-First Century, Technical Reports,* vol. 1 (Albany: State of New York, 1990), 462–519.

14. D. M. Carlson and R. A. Daniels, "Status of Fishes in New York: Increases, Declines, and Homogenization of Watersheds," *American Midland Naturalist* 152 (2004):104–39.

15. D. M. Carlson, *Species Accounts of the Rare Fishes of New York* (Albany: NYS Department of Environmental Conservation, 2001).

16. F. Mather, "Memoranda Relating to Adirondack Fishes with Descriptions of New Species from Researches Made in 1882," appendix to the 12th report (Albany: State of New York Adirondack Survey, 1886).

17. R. A. Daniels and D. M. Peteet, "Fish Scale Evidence for Rapid Post-Glacial Colonization of an Atlantic Coastal Pond," *Global Ecology and Zoogeography Letters* 7 (1998): 467–76.

18. Kogut, "A Look at Fish and Wildlife Resources."

19. C. J. George, *The Fishes of the Adirondack Park,* Lake Monograph Program (Albany: NYS Department of Environmental Conservation, 1981).

20. E. Moore, Biological surveys of the Champlain (1929), Oswegatchie and Black River systems (1931), Upper Hudson Watershed (1932), Raquette Watershed (1933), and Mohawk-Hudson Watershed (1934), supplements to the annual reports of the New York State Conservation Department (Albany: NYS Conservation Dept., 1930–35).

21. J. Gallagher and J. Baker, "Current Status of Fish Communities in Adirondack Lakes," in *Adirondack Lakes Survey: An Interpretive Analysis of Fish Communities and Water Chemistry, 1984–87,* 3–11–3–48 (Ray Brook, N.Y.: Adirondack Lake Survey Corporation, 1990).

22. T. R. Whittier and T. M. Kincaid, "Introduced Fish in Northeastern USA Lakes: Regional Extent, Dominance, and Effect on Native Species Richness," *Transactions of the American Fisheries Society* 128 (1999): 769–83; T. R. Whittier, D. B. Halliwell, and R. A. Daniels, "Distribution of Lake Fishes in the Northeast—II: The Minnows (Cyprinidae)," *Northeastern Naturalist* 7 (2000): 131–56.

23. W. T. Keller, *Management of Wild and Hybrid Brook Trout in New York Lakes, Ponds, and Coastal Streams* (Albany: Bureau of Fisheries, NYS Department of Environmental Conservation, 1979), 1–40.

24. Carlson, *Species Accounts of the Rare Fishes of New York.*

25. B. Czech and P. R. Krausman, "Distribution and Causation of Species Endangerment in the United States," *Science* 277 (1997): 1116–17.

26. R. Carson, *Silent Spring* (Boston: Houghton, 1962).

## 6. Wildlife Exploitation in the Adirondacks:
## From Beavers to Biodiversity

1. R. M. DeGraaf and M. Yamasaki, *New England Wildlife* (Hanover, N.H.: Univ. Press of New England, 2001).

2. DeGraaf and Yamasaki, *New England Wildlife*, 11.

3. Terrie, *Wildlife and Wilderness*, 41.

4. Ibid., 58, 79.

5. P. J. Wilson, S. Grewal, T. McFadden, R. C. Chambers, and B. N. White, "Mitochondrial DNA Extracted from Eastern North American Wolves Killed in the 1800s Is Not of Gray Wolf Origin," *Canadian Journal of Zoology* 81 (2003): 936–40.

6. Jenkins and Keal, *Adirondack Atlas*, 42.

7. Terrie, *Wildlife and Wilderness*, 129.

8. W. Severinghaus and C. P. Brown, "History of White-tailed Deer in New York," *New York Fish and Game Journal* 3, no. 2 (1956): 129–67.

9. R. F. Andrle and J. R. Carroll, *The Atlas of Breeding Birds in New York State* (Ithaca, N.Y.: Cornell Univ. Press, 1988); J. K. Mcgowan and K. Corwin, eds., *The Second Atlas of Breeding Birds in New York* (Ithaca, N.Y.: Comstock, 2008).

10. C. Spilman, "The Effects of Lakeshore Development on Common Loon Productivity in the Adirondack Park, New York" (master's thesis, SUNY College of Environmental Science and Forestry, 2006).

11. D. L. Garner, "Ecology of the Moose and the Feasibility for Translocation into the Greater Adirondack Ecosystem" (master's thesis, SUNY College of Environmental Science and Forestry, 1989).

## 10. Recreation and Tourism in the Adirondacks

1. P. G. Terrie, *Contested Terrain: A New History of Nature and People in the Adirondacks* (Blue Mountain Lake, N.Y./Syracuse: Adirondack Museum/Syracuse Univ. Press, 1997), 223.

2. H. D. Thoreau, *The Maine Woods* (Princeton: Princeton Univ. Press, 1972), 82.

3. K. Durant and H. Durant, *The Adirondack Guide Boat* (Blue Mountain Lake, N.Y.: Adirondack Museum, 1980).

4. Jenkins and Keal, *Adirondack Atlas*

5. C. Brumley, *Guides of the Adirondacks: A History* (Utica, N.Y.: North Country Books, 1994).

6. P. Jamieson, *The Adirondack Reader* (Glens Falls, N.Y.: Adirondack Mountain Club, 1983), 525; P. Schneider, *The Adirondacks: A History of America's First Wilderness* (New York: Henry Holt, 1997), 368.

7. P. Schaefer, *Adirondack Explorations: Nature Writings of Verplanck Colvin* (Syracuse: Syracuse Univ. Press, 1997), 160–61.

8. Ibid., 162.

9. C. A. Gilborn, *Adirondack Camps: Homes Away from Home, 1850–1950* (Syracuse: Syracuse Univ. Press, 2000).

10. Schaefer, *Adirondack Explorations*.

11. Schaefer, *Adirondack Explorations;* J. M. Glover, *A Wilderness Original: The Life of Bob Marshall* (Seattle: Mountaineers Press, 1986).

12. H. Zahniser, *Where Wilderness Preservation Began: Adirondack Writings of Howard Zahniser* (Utica, N.Y.: North Country Books, 1992).

13. E. Brown, *The Forest Preserve of New York State: A Handbook for Conservationists* (Glens Falls, N.Y.: Adirondack Mountain Club, 1985), 269.

14. Ibid.

15. Ibid.

16. Judge H. J. Hinman, in *Association for the Protection of the Adirondacks v. MacDonald,* 253 N.Y. 234 (1930).

## 11. Great Camps and Conservation

1. Roger C. Thompson, "The Doctrine of Wilderness: A Study of the Policy and Politics of the Adirondack Preserve-Park" (Ph.D. diss., State Univ. College of Forestry at Syracuse Univ., 1962), 77.

2. C. Gilborn, *Durant: The Fortunes and Woodland Camps of a Family in the Adirondacks* (Utica/Blue Mountain Lake, N.Y.: North Country Books/Adirondack Museum, 1981), 12.

3. W. W. Durant, letter to A. G. Vanderbilt, 1901, Durant Letter Book, Adirondack Museum Library MS65–26, box 2.

4. In reminiscences of Kamp Kill Kare by Dr. Garvan at a meeting of historic preservationists I attended.

5. J. B. Jackson, *Discovering the Vernacular Landscape* (New Haven: Yale Univ. Press, 1984).

## 13. Wildlife for a Wilderness: Restoring Large Predators in the Adirondacks

1. DeKay, *Natural History,* pt. 1, 51

2. G. S. Miller, Jr., "Preliminary List of the Mammals of New York," *Bulletin of the New York State Museum* 6 (1899): 339–40.

3. J. H. Vashon, A. L. Meehan, W. J. Jakubas, J. F. Organ, A. D. Vashon, C. R. McLaughlin, G. J. Matula, Jr., and S. M. Crowley, "Spatial Ecology of a Lynx Population in Northern Maine," *Journal of Wildlife Management* 72 (2008): 1479–87.

4. H. R. Siegler, "The Status of Wildcats in New Hampshire," in *Proceedings of a Symposium of Native Cats of North America: Their Status and Management,* ed. S. E. Jorgensen and L. D. Mech (St. Paul, Minn.: USDI Bureau of Sport Fisheries and Wildlife, 1971); C. L. Hoving, "Historical Occurrence and Habitat Ecology of Canada Lynx (*Lynx canadensis*) in Eastern North America" (master's thesis, Univ. of Maine, 2001).

5. L. B. Fox, "Ecology and Population Biology of the Bobcat (*Felix rufus*) in New York" (Ph.D. diss., SUNY College of Environmental Science and Forestry, 1990).

6. B. Slough, unpublished data from the Yukon Territory, Canada, personal communication, 1991. Slough is biologist for the Yukon Environmental Department. G. M. Koehler, "Population and Habitat Characteristics of Lynx and Snowshoe Hares in North-Central Washington," *Canadian Journal of Zoology* 68 (1990): 845–51; L. D. Mech, "Age, Sex, Reproduction, and Spatial Organization of Lynxes Colonizing Northeastern Minnesota," *Journal of Mammalogy* 61 (1980): 261–67.

7. Additional perspectives on lynx restoration and survival are given in R. H. Brocke, K. A. Gustafson, and L. B. Fox, "Restoration of Large Predators: Potentials and Problems," in *Challenges in the Conservation of Biological Resources: A Practitioners Guide,* ed. D. J. Decker, M. E.Krasny, G. R. Goff, C. R. Smith, and D. W. Gross, 303–15 (Boulder, Co.: Westview Press, 1991).

8. Details on procedures and political perspectives are given in R. H. Brocke, K. A. Gustafson, and A. R. Major, "Restoration of the Lynx in New York: Biopolitical Lessons," in *Transactions of the 55th North American Wildlife and Natural Resources Conference,* 590–98 (Washington, D.C.: Wildlife Management Institute, 1990):

9. D. C. Stoner, M. L. Wolfe, and D. M. Choate, "Cougar Exploitation Levels in Utah: Implications for Demographic Structure, Population Recovery and Metapopulation Dynamics," *Journal of Wildlife Management* 70 (2006): 1588–1600.

10. L. D. Mech, "Managing Minnesota's Recovered Wolves," *Wildlife Society Bulletin* 29 (2001): 70–77.

11. Stoner et al., "Cougar Exploitation Levels."

12. D. S. Maehr, E. D. Land, and M. E. Roelke, "Mortality Patterns of Panthers in Southwest Florida," *Proceedings of Annual Conference of Southeastern Fish and Wildlife Agencies* 45 (1991): 201–7.

13. Stoner et al., "Cougar Exploitation Levels."

14. S. R. Kendrot, "The Effects of Roads and Land Use on Home Range Use, Behavior, and Mortality of Eastern Coyotes (*Canis latrans var.*) in Northern New York" (master's thesis, SUNY College of Environmental Science and Forestry, 1998).

15. R. H. Brocke, J. P. O'Pezio, and K. A. Gustafson, "A Forest Management Scheme Mitigating Impact of Road Networks on Sensitive Wildlife Species," in *Is Forest Fragmentation a Management Issue in the Northeast?* Northeastern Forest Experiment Station General Technical Report NE-140 (1988): 13–17.

16. D. L. Garner, "Ecology of the Moose and the Feasibility for Translocation into the Greater Adirondack Ecosystem" (Ph.D. diss., SUNY College of Environmental Science and Forestry, 1989).

17. E. K. Harper, W. J. Paul, and L. D. Mech, "Causes of Wolf Depredation Increase in Minnesota from 1979–1998," *Wildlife Society Bulletin* 33 (2005): 888–96; A. S. Chavez and E. M. Gese, "Landscape Use and Movements of Wolves in Relation to Livestock in a Wildland-Agricultural Matrix," *Journal of Wildlife Management* 70 (2006): 1079–86.

18. S. K. Grewal, P. J. Wilson, T. K. Kung, K. Shami, M. T. Theberge, J. B. Theberge, and B. N. White, "A Genetic Assessment of the Eastern Wolf (*Canis lycaon*) in Algonquin Provincial Park," *Journal of Mammalogy* 85 (2004): 625–32.

## Part Two. Introduction: The Park in Perspective

1. J. D. Erickson, "In Search of Sustainable Development: Lessons in Application from the Adirondack Park," in *Sustainability in Action: Sectoral and Regional Case Studies,* ed. J. Köhn, J. Gowdy, and J. van der Straaten (Cheltenham, U.K.: Edward Elgar, 2001), 261–80.

2. For a thorough analysis based on tax and other land records throughout the Park, see B. McMartin, *The Great Forest of the Adirondacks* (Utica, N.Y.: North Country Books, 1994), 76–91.

3. McMartin, *Great Forest of the Adirondacks,* 149.

4. The legislative and court room battles of these industrial challenges to the Forest Preserve are detailed from a front-row seat in P. Schaefer, *Defending the Wilderness: the Adirondack Writings of Paul Schaefer* (Syracuse: Syracuse Univ. Press, 1989).

5. World Commission on Environment and Development, *Our Common Future* (New York: Oxford Univ. Press, 1987).

6. I. L. McHarg, *Design with Nature* (Garden City, N.Y.: Natural History Press, 1969).

7. Originally proposed in J. D. Erickson, "Sustainable Development and the Adirondack Park Experience," *Adirondack Journal of Environmental Studies* 5 (1998): 24–32.

8. R. F. Noss, "A Regional Landscape Approach to Maintain Biodiversity," *Bioscience* 33 (1983): 700–706; L. D. Harris, *The Fragmented Forest: Island Biogeography Theory and the Preservation of Biotic Diversity* (Chicago: Univ. of Chicago Press, 1984).

9. R. F. Noss, "The Wildlands Project: Land Conservation Strategy," in *Environmental Policy and Biodiversity,* ed. R. Edward Grumbine (Washington, D.C.: Island Press, 1994).

10. Adirondack Park Agency Act (1998), sec. 801. The full text of the act is available at http://www.apa.state.ny.us/Documents/Laws _Regs/APAACT.PDF.

11. This theme is addressed more fully in: J. D. Erickson and S. O'Hara, "From Top-Down to Participatory Planning: Conservation Lessons from the Adirondack Park, NY, USA," in *Biodiversity and Ecological Economics: Participation, Values, and Resource Management,* ed. L. Tacconi (London: Earthscan, 2000), 146–61.

12. The most recent open space plan was approved in 2006. See http://www.dec.ny.gov/lands/26433.html.

## 14. Cultural History of the Adirondack Park:
## From Conservation to Environmentalism

1. J. F. Sears, *Sacred Places: American Tourist Attractions in the Nineteenth Century* (New York: Oxford Univ. Press, 1989).

2. R. Nash, *Wilderness and the American Mind,* 4th ed. (New Haven: Yale Univ. Press, 2001), 67–83; P. G. Terrie, "Urban Man Confronts the

Wilderness: The Nineteenth-Century Sportsman in the Adirondacks," *Journal of Sport History* 5 (Winter 1978): 7–20.

3. Terrie, *Contested Terrain,* 44–82.

4. J. T. Headley, *The Adirondack; or, Life in the Woods* (New York: Baker and Scribner, 1849). Other examples of this genre are C. Fenno Hoffman, *Wild Scenes in the Forest and Prairie* (New York: W. H. Colyer, 1843); S. H. Hammond, *Hills, Lakes, and Forest Streams* (New York: J. C. Derby, 1854); and A. B. Street, *Woods and Waters; or, the Saranacs and Racket* (New York: M. Doolady, 1860).

5. McMartin, *Great Forest of the Adirondacks,* 29–72.

6. S. H. Hammond, *Wild Northern Scenes: or Sporting Adventures with the Rifle and the Rod* (New York: Derby and Jackson, 1860), 83.

7. G. P. Marsh, *Man and Nature; or, Physical Geography as Modified by Human Action* (New York: Scribner, 1864; reprint, ed. D. Lowenthal, Cambridge, Mass.: Belknap Press of Harvard Univ. Press, 1965). The importance of Marsh to the environmental movement has been much discussed by environmental historians; see, e.g., L. C. Mitchell, *Witnesses to a Vanishing America: The Nineteenth-Century Response* (Princeton, N.J.: Princeton Univ. Press, 1981), 59–61, and M. Oelschlaeger, *The Idea of Wilderness: From Prehistory to the Age of Ecology* (New Haven, Conn.: Yale Univ. Press, 1991), 106–8.

8. *First Annual Report of the Commissioners of State Parks of the State of New York,* Senate Document 102, 1873 (Albany, N.Y.: Weed Parsons, 1874), 5.

9. M. W. Kranz, "Pioneering in Conservation: A History of the Conservation Movement in New York State, 1865–1903" (Ph.D. diss., Syracuse Univ., 1961), 147–48.

10. Terrie, *Contested Terrain,* 95–96.

11. F. Graham, Jr., *The Adirondack Park: A Political History* (New York: Knopf, 1978), 108.

12. *First Annual Report of the Commissioners of State Parks of the State of New York,* 19.

13. New York State Forest Commission, *Annual Report . . . for 1890* (Assembly Document 84, 1891), 57, 77, 87–88. On the great clubs and preserves, see, e.g., E. Comstock, Jr., ed., *The Adirondack League Club, 1890–1990* (Old Forge, N.Y.: Adirondack League Club, 1990).

14. Terrie, *Contested Terrain,* 99.

15. *Laws of the State of New York, 1892,* chap. 707, 459–60.

16. T. L. Cobb, "The Adirondack Park and the Evolution of Its Current Boundary," *The Adirondack Park in the Twenty-First Century, Technical Reports,* vol. 1 (Albany: State of New York, 1990), 24.

17. Graham, *Adirondack Park,* 107–12, 126–30.

18. Article 7, section 7, of New York State Constitution, approved Nov. 1894, becoming effective Jan. 1, 1895.

19. The constitution of 1967 reincorporated this exact language, but because of provisions involving state funding of parochial schools, it was rejected by the voters. The current New York constitution was approved in 1938, when the Forever Wild provision was renumbered as Article 14. See Graham, *Adirondack Park,* 213–18. The New York State Constitution is accessible online at http://www.senate.state.ny.us/lbdcinfo/senconstitution.html.

20. New York Forest, Fish, and Game Commission, *Eighth and Ninth Annual Reports* (Albany: J. B. Lyon, 1904), 36.

21. K. Jacoby, *Crimes Against Nature: Squatters, Poachers, Thieves, and the Hidden History of American Conservation* (Berkeley: Univ. of California Press, 2001), 29–47.

22. Graham, *Adirondack Park,* 164–71, 184–207.

23. New York State Conservation Commission, *Ninth Annual Report for the Year 1919* (Albany: J. B. Lyon, 1920), 101. According to Edith Pilcher, *Up the Lake Road: The First Hundred Years of the Adirondack Mountain Reserve* (Keene Valley, N.Y.: Adirondack Mountain Reserve, 1987), 53, the purchase was not finalized until 1923.

24. Terrie, *Contested Terrain,* 113–15.

25. Kaiser, *Great Camps of the Adirondacks;* Gilborn, *Durant.*

26. Terrie, *Contested Terrain,* 143–46

27. R. Gottlieb, *Forcing the Spring: The Transformation of the American Environmental Movement* (Washington, D.C.: Island Press, 1993), 105–14.

28. J. Sax, "The Public Trust Doctrine in Natural Resource Law: Effective Judicial Intervention," *Michigan Law Review,* 1970, quoted in Mark Dowie, "In Law We Trust," *Orion,* 22 (July–Aug., 2003): 18–25.

29. Graham, *Adirondack Park,* 236.

30. Temporary Study Commission on the Future of the Adirondacks, *The Future of the Adirondacks,* 2 vols. (Blue Mountain Lake, N.Y.: Adirondack Museum, 1971), vol. 1, 32; A. Rome, *The Bulldozer in the Countryside: Suburban Sprawl and the Rise of American Environmentalism* (Cambridge: Cambridge Univ. Press, 2001), 15–43.

31. F. J. Popper, "Understanding American Land Use Regulation since 1970," *Journal of the American Planning Association* 54 (Summer 1988): 291–301.

32. R. H. Platt, *Land Use and Society: Geography, Law, and Public Policy* (Washington, D.C.: Island Press, 1996), 347–50; Rome, *Bulldozer in the Countryside,* 221–53.

33. The following section is indebted to F. Bosselman and D. Callies, *The Quiet Revolution in Land Use Control* (Washington, D.C.: Council on Environmental Quality, 1972), and their discussion of the key issues that came to define the "Quiet Revolution," 314–26.

34. D. Worster, *Nature's Economy: A History of Ecological Ideas* (New York: Cambridge Univ. Press, 1985).

35. D. Potter, *People of Plenty: Economic Abundance and the American Character* (Chicago: Univ. of Chicago Press, 1954).

36. Temporary Study Commission, *Future of the Adirondacks,* vol. 1 (1971), 26.

37. Ibid., emphasis in original.

## 15. Legal Structure and Defense of the Adirondack Park

1. W. R. Ginsberg and P. Weinberg, *Environmental Law and Regulation in New York* (St. Paul, Minn.: West Publishing Co., 1996), §12.3.4.

2. *Balsam Lake Anglers Club v. DEC,* 583 N.Y.S.2d 119, 123 (1991).

## 16. Public and Private Land-Use Regulation of the Adirondack Park

1. Temporary Study Commission, *Future of the Adirondacks.*

2. From Adirondack Park Agency, *Adirondack Park State Land Master Plan* (Ray Brook, N.Y.: Adirondack Park Agency, 2001); available at http://www.apa.state.ny.us/.

3. All definitions of land-use classes are paraphrased from the Adirondack Park State Land Master Plan.

4. Area figures of wilderness are from Jenkins and Keal, *Adirondack Atlas.* Estimates of proportion of wilderness contained within the Adirondack Park are taken from the State Land Master Plan.

5. Jenkins and Keal, *Adirondack Atlas.*

6. R. Glennon, "Non-forest Preserves: Inconsistent Use," *The Adirondack Park in the Twenty-First Century, Technical Report 5,* vol. 1 (Albany: State of New York, 1990), 74–111.

7. From the *Citizen's Guide to the Adirondack Park Agency Land Use Regulations* (Ray Brook, N.Y.: Adirondack Park Agency, n.d.). See http://www.apa.state.ny.us/documents/guidelines/citizensguide.pdf.

8. Percentage values for land-use classes are from Jenkins and Keal, *Adirondack Atlas*, 25. Some descriptive material, especially pertaining to intentions of APA in designating private land classes are from R. Glennon, *The Adirondack Park in the Twenty-First Century, Technical Report 32,* vol. 2 (Albany: State of New York, 1990), 136–83.

9. R. Glennon, "The Ability of the Adirondack Park Agency Act to Achieve Its Objectives," *The Adirondack Park in the Twenty-First Century, Technical Reports,* vol. 2, 152.

10. Ibid., 158–59.

## 19. A Land Not Saved

1. R. Glennon, "The Ability of the Adirondack Park Agency Act to Achieve Its Objectives," 190.

2. *Wambat Realty Corp v. State of New York,* 41 NY2d 490 (1977), 491.

3. Ibid., 494–95.

4. Ibid., 495.

5. Ibid., 497–98.

6. J. A. McNeely et al., *Conserving the World's Biological Diversity* (Gland, Switzerland, and Washington, D.C.: IUCN, WRI, CI, WWF-US and World Bank, 1990), 60–61).

7. M. Hunter, *Fundamentals of Conservation Biology* (Malden, Mass.: Blackwell Science, 2002), 255.

8. J. M. Gowdy and C. N. McDaniel, "One World, One Experiment: Addressing the Biodiversity-Economics Conflict," *Ecological Economics* 15 (1995): 188.

9. J. F. Franklin, "Structural and Functional Diversity in Temperate Forests," in *Biodiversity,* ed. E. O. Wilson (Washington, D.C.: National Academies Press, 1988), 173.

## 21. Lessons from the Commission on the Adirondacks in the Twenty-First Century

1. I served on the Governor's Commission on the Adirondacks in the Twenty-First Century. In this chapter I attempt to both describe the workings and conclusions of the commission and to offer my own

personal critique. In so doing I attempted to report the workings and conclusions as accurately as possible. The critique, however, is my own, and my opinions certainly may differ from those of any other commission member.

2. New York State Commission on the Adirondacks in the Twenty-First Century. *The Adirondack Park in the Twenty-First Century* (Albany, N.Y.: State of New York, 1990), 29.

3. Ibid., 47.

4. Ibid., 51.

5. Ibid., 52.

## 23. Reflections on the Adirondack Park Agency in the Current Era

1. In this chapter, my recollection of some of the events that occurred during the time I was at the agency is intended to bring attention to the fact that there is a huge political influence on the Adirondack Park. As I see it, the people and politics of the park are no less a factor in defining the Adirondack Park than the clean water, wildlands, geology, and beautiful view sheds. Politics, when filtered through the Adirondack prism, is an important factor in defining and identifying the Adirondack Park.

2. P. Drucker, *The Practice of Management* (New York: Harper and Row, 1954).

3. G. A. Steiner, *Strategic Planning* (New York: Free Press, 1997).

4. J. Howe, E. McMahon, and L. Propst, *Balancing Nature and Commerce in Gateway Communities* (Covelo, Calif.: Island Press, 1997).

5. Additional information can be found at http://www.parcoabruzzo.it.

## Part Three. Introduction: Visions for the Adirondacks and Beyond

1. J. Diamond, *Collapse: How Societies Choose to Fail or Succeed* (New York: Viking Press, 2005), 30.

2. Ibid., 33.

3. This contrast draws on Erickson, "Sustainable Development and the Adirondack Park Experience," 24–32.

4. These metrics are drawn from J. Northrup, *The Adirondack Condition: Economic, Environmental, and Social Well-Being* (Albany: Environmental Advocates, 1997).

5. The following draws again on Erickson, "Sustainable Development and the Adirondack Park Experience."

## 24. Compromise, Continuity, and Crisis in the Adirondack Park: Shortcomings and Opportunities in Environmental Protection

1. Graham, *Adirondack Park,* 253.

2. R. S. Booth and T. L. Hullar, "Has the Adirondack Park Agency Made a Difference?," *Amicus Journal* (Summer 1980): 14, 15.

3. The following discussion of problems with the Adirondack Park Land Use and Development Plan depends, in addition to the print sources cited, on conversations with Peter Bauer, Aug. 20, 2003; Richard Beamish, Sept. 3, 2003; David Skovron, Sept. 24, 2003; and John Collins, Peter Bauer, and Brian Houseal, Sept. 25, 2003.

4. R. A. Liroff and G. G. Davis, *Protecting Open Space: Land Use Control in the Adirondack Park* (Cambridge, Mass.: Ballinger, 1981).

5. Popper, "Understanding American Land Use Regulation since 1970," 291–301.

6. The best account of the legislative debate is Graham, *Adirondack Park,* 248–53.

7. Liroff and Davis, *Protecting Open Space,* 30.

8. Adirondack Park Agency, *Adirondack Park Land Use and Development Plan and Recommendations for Implementation* (Ray Brook, N.Y.: Adirondack Park Agency, 1973), 7; Liroff and Davis, *Protecting Open Space,* 37.

9. Residents' Committee to Protect the Adirondacks, *The Park Report* 9 (Mar. 2004): 3.

10. P. Brown, "The Downside of Upland Development," *Adirondack Explorer* 6 (Jan.–Feb. 2004): 6–7, 44–45.

11. A. Bates, "APA Board Backs Recommendation for Spiegels to Move Hillside House," *Adirondack Daily Enterprise,* Aug. 13–14, 2005. See also an editorial by Dick Beamish in *Adirondack Daily Enterprise,* Aug. 2, 2005.

12. Residents' Committee to Protect the Adirondacks, *Growth in the Adirondack Park: Analysis of Rates and Patterns of Development,* 8, 123–25.

13. B. L. Bedford and E. M. Preston, "Developing the Scientific Basis for Assessing Cumulative Effects of Wetland Loss and Degradation on Landscape Functions: Status, Perspectives, and Prospects," *Environmental Management* 12 (1978): 752.

14. Presentation by Dr. Barbara L. Bedford, Department of Natural Resources, Cornell Univ., "Cumulative Impact Assessment," typescript,

reference #2038, Adirondack Park Agency files, Raybrook, N.Y., May 10, 1991, 5, 10.

15. "Over 1,500 New Houses Permitted in 2000–2001," *The Park Report: Newsletter of the Residents' Committee to Protect the Adirondacks* 8 (Dec. 2002–Jan. 2003): 3. For the development figures for the decade of the 1990s, see Residents' Committee to Protect the Adirondacks, *Growth in the Adirondack Park*.

16. Jenkins and Keal, *Adirondack Atlas,* 3.

17. P. Brown, "Pataki Forging Legacy in Land," *Adirondack Explorer* 6 (July–Aug. 2004): 42. See also Mary Thill, "Acres and Pains," *Adirondack Life* 36 (Sept.–Oct. 2005): 63–65, 76–77.

18. A. DePalma, "A Deal Is Reached to Preserve Land and the Economy in the Adirondacks," *New York Times,* Apr. 22, 2004, A24.

19. A. DePalma, "A Template for Conservation," *New York Times,* May 1, 2004.

20. M. K. Heiman, *The Quiet Evolution: Power, Planning, and Profits in New York State* (New York: Praeger, 1988); see especially the article "Critical Area Protection and the Ideology of Nature," 187–237.

21. Adirondack Council, *Newsletter* (Summer 2003).

22. P. Bauer, *Bottom of the Class: The Case for Reform of New York State's Septic System Regulations* (North Creek, N.Y.: Residents' Committee to Protect the Adirondacks, 2004), 3, 8.

23. See Pete Klein, "Bill Would Obstruct Most Development," *Hamilton County News,* Apr. 13, 2004.

24. NYS Department of Environmental Conservation, "Draft Comprehensive Snowmobile Plan for the Adirondack Park/Draft Generic Environmental Impact Statement," http://www.dec.state.ny.us/website/dlf/publands/snow/index.html, accessed Mar. 27, 2004, but no longer available online.

25. Residents' Committee to Protect the Adirondacks, "RCPA Opposes Draft Comprehensive Adirondack Snowmobile Plan," news release, Feb. 9, 2004, http://www.adirondackresidents.org/, accessed Mar. 27, 2004.

26. See, for example, "Champion of 'Balanced Use,'" *Adirondack Explorer,* 7 (July–Aug. 2005): 25, 68, where Hank Ford, supervisor of the Town of Colton, argues for the construction of a bridge over the Raquette River in his town to facilitate snowmobile access to existing logging roads.

27. P. Bauer, *Rutted and Ruined: ATV Damage on the Adirondack Forest Preserve* (North Creek, N.Y.: Residents' Committee to Protect the Adirondacks, 2003).

28. "State to Ban ATVs in Preserve," *Adirondack Explorer* 6 (July–Aug. 2004): 4.

29. H. Oles, "Monitoring the Pulse of Invasive Plants in the Adirondack Park: A Coordinated Approach to Regional Invasive Plant Management," *Adirondack Journal of Environmental Studies* 11 (Spring/Summer 2004): 14.

30. W. Hu, "Use of Herbicide Is Proposed in Weed-Choked Lake George," *New York Times,* Apr. 29, 2001.

31. Association for the Protection of the Adirondacks, *Newsletter* (Fall 2003).

32. "APA Watch," *The Park Report: Newsletter of the Residents' Committee to Protect the Adirondacks* 8 (Dec. 2002–Jan. 2003): 28–29.

33. Oles, "Monitoring the Pulse of Invasive Plants in the Adirondack Park," 19.

34. Association for the Protection of the Adirondacks, *Newsletter;* Oles, "Monitoring the Pulse of Invasive Plants," 19.

35. This quotation is from, and this paragraph is based on, K. Roy, W. Kretser, H. Simonin, and E. Bennet, "Acid Rain in the Adirondacks: A Time of Change!" *Adirondack Journal of Environmental Studies* 7 (Spring/Summer 2000): 26–32.

36. Jenkins and Keal, *Adirondack Atlas,* 107.

37. "Try Not to Breathe," *Adirondack Explorer* 4 (July–Aug., 2002): 4.

38. New England Regional Assessment Group, *Preparing for a Changing Climate: The Potential Consequences of Climate Variability and Change* (Durham: Univ. of New Hampshire, 2001), 33. Available online at http://www.necci.sr.unh.edu/2001-NERA-report.html, accessed June 28, 2004.

39. P. Brown, "Please Don't Eat the Fish: 15 Lakes on Mercury Blacklist." *Adirondack Explorer* 3 (June 2001): 7.

40. http://www.health.state.ny.us/nysdoh/commish/2003/fish/adv_06-04-2003.htm, accessed Apr. 10, 2004; N. Schoch and D. C. Evers, "Monitoring Mercury in Common Loons," Report BRI 2001–01, submitted to U. S. Fish and Wildlife Service and New York State of Environmental Conservation, 2002, iii, 1; available at http://www.adkscience.org/loons/publications.htm.

41. New England Regional Assessment Group, *Preparing for a Changing Climate,* iii.

42. Jenkins and Keal, *Adirondack Atlas,* 23.

43. Ibid., 39.

44. New England Regional Assessment Group, *Preparing for a Changing Climate,* iii.

45. Jenkins and Keal, *Adirondack Atlas,* 244.

46. With the term "land ethic" I am referring to the famous expression of such an ethic by ecologist Aldo Leopold: "A thing is right when it tends to preserve the integrity, stability, and beauty of the biotic community. It is wrong when it tends otherwise." A. Leopold, "The Land Ethic," *A Sand County Almanac: And Sketches Here and There* (New York: Oxford Univ. Press, 1949), 201–26.

47. H. Seely, "How Much Development Is Too Much?," *Syracuse Post Standard,* Aug. 10, 2003.

48. Graham, *Adirondack Park,* 248–50.

## 25. Renewing Adirondack Park Mission Through an Educational Forest Preserve: Shortcomings and Opportunities in Wilderness Preservation

1. From Ketchledge's address to the Celebrating the Constitutional Protection of the Forest Preserve, 1894–1994, conference, Silver Bay Conference Center, Sept. 30, 1994, sponsored by the Association for the Protection of the Adirondacks et al.

2. Draft St. Regis Canoe Area UMP, Aug. 2005, NYS Department of Environmental Conservation, Albany, N.Y.

3. Schaefer, *Defending the Wilderness,* 208.

4. *Adirondack Park State Land Master Plan,* updated 2001, Wild Forest Guidelines, Recreational Use and Overuse, 38.

5. From Woodley's address to the Discover Life in the Adirondacks conference, Sept. 21–22, 2001, Lake Placid, N.Y., sponsored by the Association for the Protection of the Adirondacks et. al.

## 26. The Role of the People in Wilderness Preservation: Shortcomings and Opportunities in Governance

1. R. Benedict, interview with author, Feb. 7, 2000.

2. The section starting on page 387 ("[E]veryone") is inserted from B. McMartin, *Perspectives on the Adirondacks,* 333–35.

3. This paragraph is inserted from B. McMartin, *Perspectives on the Adirondacks,* 8.

## 27. Public Opinion and Public Representation: Strategies in Bio-Regional Development

1. This section is adapted from Erickson and O'Hara, "From Top-Down to Participatory Planning."

2. Adirondack Park Agency Act, sec. 801.

3. Ibid., sec. 803.

4. Ibid., sec. 803a.

5. Ibid., sec. 807.

6. D. Dobbs and R. Ober, *The Northern Forest* (White River Junction, Vt.: Chelsea Green, 1995).

7. See chapter 28 of this book, as well as http://aatvny.org/content.

8. See http://www.adkresearch.org.

9. See the WCS Adirondack Communities and Conservation Program at http://www.wcs.org/international/northamerica/Adirondacks/adirondackcommunities.

10. This section is adapted from: G. L. Cox, J. D. Erickson, W. F. Porter, and A. M. Woods, "How Would You Invest in a Sustainable Future for Your Community? North Country Respondents Make Their Choices Clear in Research Conducted by SUNY ESF and UVM," *Adirondack Journal of Environmental Studies* 14 (2007): 32–40.

## 29. The Adirondack North Country Association: Strategies in Economic Development

1. Adirondack Park Association, *Founding Meeting Report,* 1954.

2. Roger Tubby, "Lifting Ourselves Up by Our Bootstraps," *Adirondack Daily Enterprise,* Dec. 1, 1954.

3. Adirondack Park Association, *Special Committee Report,* 1964.

4. Adirondack Park Association, *Conservation Committee Report,* 1971.

5. Adirondack Park Association, *Adirondack Legislators' Luncheon Report,* 1972.

6. Adirondack Park Association, *Annual Meeting Report,* 1974.

7. Adirondack Park Association, *Annual Meeting Report,* 1977.

8. Adirondack Park Association, *Annual Meeting Report,* 1977.

## 30. The Adirondack Environmental Nongovernmental Organizations: Strategies in Conservation

1. *The Association for the Protection of the Adirondacks v. MacDonald,* 228 App. Div. 73, 3d Dept., affirmed 253 N.Y. 234, 1930.

2. New York State Commission on the Adirondacks in the Twenty-First Century. *The Adirondack Park in the Twenty-First Century.*

## 31. Envisioning the Future of Wilderness: Public Demands and Private Lands

1. Everglades National Park in Florida has 1,296,500 acres of designated Wilderness, of which about 40 percent (an estimated 500,000 acres) are open to motorboat use on surface waters above the submerged marine lands designated Wilderness. Personal communication from Bob Howard, Everglades Nation Park.

2. Jenkins and Keal, *Adirondack Atlas,* 31.

3. New York State Commission, *The Adirondack Park in the Twenty-First Century,* 288.

4. This section builds upon and adapts recommendations originally made by the author in a two-part series of articles, *The Adirondack Park in the 21st Century,* which appeared in the *Adirondack Journal of Environmental Studies* 4, no. 2 (Fall/Winter 1997) and 5, no. 1 (Spring/Summer 1998).

5. The 2007 sale of Finch-Pruyn lands to the Nature Conservancy, following similar recent action of other paper companies, and the 2007 publication of *Private Land Stewardship,* vol. 4 of *2020 Vision: Fulfilling the Vision of the Adirondack Park,* by the Adirondack Council underscore the timeliness of the need for this task force.

6. Douglas, William O. *A Wilderness Bill of Rights* (Boston: Little, Brown, 1965).

## 32. Toward a New Wilderness Paradigm for Adirondack Park: The View from Bear Mountain

1. *Adirondack Park State Land Master Plan* (Ray Brook, N.Y.: Adirondack Park Agency, 1972).

2. T. A. Spies, M. A. Hemstrom, A. Youngblood, and S. Hummel, "Conserving Old-Growth Forest Diversity in Disturbance-Prone Landscapes," *Conservation Biology,* 20 (2006): 351–62.

3. G. Caughley, "What Is This Thing Called Carrying Capacity?" *North American Elk: Ecology, Behavior, and Management,* ed. M. S. Boyce and L. D. Hayden-Wing (Laramie: Univ. of Wyoming, 1979).

4. Nash, *Wilderness and the American Mind.*

5. Ibid.

6. Graham, *Adirondack Park;* Nash, *Wilderness and the American Mind.*

7. E. M. Thomas, *The Old Way: A Story of the First People* (New York: Farrar, Straus, Giroux, 2006).

8. "The Row about the Bushmen," *Economist* 378 (Feb. 18, 2006): 47.

9. D. Brockington, J. Igoe, and K. Schmidt-Soltan, "Conservation, Human Rights, and Poverty Reduction," *Conservation Biology* 20 (2006): 250–52.

10. K. Brown, "The Political Ecology of Biodiversity, Conservation, and Development in Nepal's Terai: Confused Meanings, Means and Ends," *Ecological Economics* 24 (1998): 73–87.

11. R. Thomson, "Solving Africa's Commercial Poaching Pandemic," *African Sporting Gazette* 11 (2006) 16–18; Brockington, Igoe, and Schmidt-Soltan, "Conservation, Human Rights, and Poverty Reduction."

12. B. McMartin, *Citizen's Guide to the Adirondack Forest Preserve* (Ray Brook, N.Y.: Adirondack Park Agency, 1985).

13. *Adirondack Park State Land Master Plan.*

14. J. W. Thomas, J. F. Franklin, J. Gordon, and K. N. Johnson, "The Northeast Forest Plan: Origins, Components, Implementation Experiences, and Suggestions for Change," *Conservation Biology* 20 (2006): 277–87.

15. B. Noon and J. A. Blakely, "Conservation of the Northern Spotted Owl under the Northern Forest Plan," *Conservation Biology* 20 (2006): 288–96.

16. Spies, Hemstrom, Youngblood, and Hummel, "Conserving Old-Growth Forest Diversity," 351–62.

17. M. S. Deisch and R. W. Sage, Jr., "Songbird Diversity Following Shelterwood Cutting in Two Northern Hardwood Stands in the Central Adirondacks," Abstract, Northeast Fish and Wildlife Conference, Nashua, N.H. Apr. 1990, 9–11; Z. Wang and R. D. Nyland, "Tree Species

Richness Increased by Clearcutting of Northern Hardwoods in Central New York," *Forest Ecology and Management* 57 (1993): 71–84.

18. Thomas, Franklin, Gordon, and Johnson, "The Northeast Forest Plan."

19. S. Charnley, "The Northwest Forest Plan as a Model for Broad-Scale Ecosystem Management: A Social Perspective," *Conservation Biology* 20 (2006): 330–40.

20. Thomas, Franklin, Gordon, and Johnson, "The Northeast Forest Plan"; R. Molina, B. G. Marcot, and R. Lesher, "Protecting Rare, Old-Growth Forest-Associated Species under the Survey and Manage Program Guidelines of the Northwest Forest Plan," *Conservation Biology* 20 (2006): 306–18.

21. Charnley, "Northwest Forest Plan as a Model for Broad-Scale Ecosystem Management."

22. M. N. Peterson, S. A. Allison, M. J. Peterson, T. R. Peterson, and R. R. Lopez, "A Tale of Two Species: Habitat Conservation Plans as Bounded Conflicts," *Journal of Wildlife Management* 68 (2004): 743–61.

23. Ibid.

24. C. H. D. Clarke, *The Future of the Adirondacks, Technical Reports,* vol. 2, *Wildlife* (Albany: Temporary Study Commission on the Future of the Adirondacks, 1974).

25. J. B Haufler, L. G. Adams, J. Bailey, R. H. Brocke, M. J. Conroy, G. J. Joslin, and K. G. Smith, *Wildlife Management in North American Wilderness,* Wildlife Society Technical Review 96–1 (Washington, D.C.: The Wildlife Society, 1996).

26. J. P. Gibbs, A. R. Breisch, P. K. Ducey, G. Johnson, J. L. Behler, and R. C. Bothner, *Amphibians and Reptiles of New York State* (New York: Oxford Univ. Press, 2007).

27. Jenkins and Keal, *Adirondack Atlas.*

## 33. Can Such a Noble Endeavor Succeed?
## Alaska and the Adirondack Park

1. S. Haycox, *Alaska: An American Colony* (Seattle: Univ. of Washington Press, 2002), 1.

2. World Almanac Education Group, *The World Almanac and Book of Facts 2005* (New York: St. Martins Press, 2005).

3. Joint Federal-State Land Use Planning Commission for Alaska, *Major Ecosystems of Alaska* (Fairbanks, Alaska: U.S. Geological Survey, 1973).

4. *World Almanac and Book of Facts 2005.*

5. Haycox, *Alaska.*

6. *World Almanac and Book of Facts 2005.*

7. C. P. Dawson and P. Thorndike, "State-Designated Wilderness Programs in the United States," *International Journal of Wilderness* 8 (2002): 21–26.

8. Nash, *Wilderness and the American Mind.*

9. J. Strohmeyer, *Extreme Conditions: Big Oil and the Transformation of Alaska* (New York: Simon and Schuster, 1993), 9.

10. Haycox, *Alaska: An American Colony,* x.

11. T. Cole, "Book Review of Stephen Haycox, *Frigid Embrace: Politics, Economics, and Environment,*" *Pacific Northwest Quarterly* 94 (2003), 208.

12. New York State Commission, *The Adirondack Park in the Twenty-First Century,* 11.

13. Ibid., 45.

14. Schneider, *The Adirondacks: A History of America's First Wilderness,* xii.

15. Ibid., xiii.

16. R. L. Chapman, ed., *Roget's International Thesaurus, 5th Edition* (New York: Harper Collins, 1992).

17. New York State Commission, *The Adirondack Park in the Twenty-First Century,* 29.

18. Ibid.

19. R. B. Atwood et al., "Going Up in Flames: The Promises and Pledges of Alaska Statehood under Attack," in *Commonwealth North,* ed. M. B. Roberts, 45 (Anchorage: Alaska Pacific Univ. Press, 1990).

## Conclusion: The Adirondack Experiment in a Full World

1. World Commission on Environment and Development, *Our Common Future.*

2. R. Louv, *Last Child in the Woods: Saving Our Children from Nature-Deficit Disorder* (Chapel Hill, N.C.: Algonquin Books, 2005).

# Bibliography

Adirondack Council. *Newsletter* (Summer 2003).

Andrle, R. F., and J. R. Carroll. *The Atlas of Breeding Birds in New York State.* Ithaca, N.Y.: Cornell Univ. Press, 1988.

"APA Watch." *The Park Report: Newsletter of the Residents' Committee to Protect the Adirondacks* 8 (Dec. 2002–Jan. 2003): 28–29.

Association for the Protection of the Adirondacks, *Newsletter,* Fall 2003.

Atwood, R. B. et al. "Going Up in Flames: The Promises and Pledges of Alaska Statehood under Attack." In *Commonwealth North,* edited by M. B. Roberts. Anchorage: Alaska Pacific Univ. Press, 1990.

Bates, A. "APA Board Backs Recommendation for Spiegels to Move Hillside House." *Adirondack Daily Enterprise,* Aug. 13–14, 2005.

Bauer, P. *Bottom of the Class: The Case for Reform of New York State's Septic System Regulations.* North Creek, N.Y.: Residents' Committee to Protect the Adirondacks, 2004.

———. *Rutted and Ruined: ATV Damage on the Adirondack Forest Preserve.* North Creek, N.Y.: Residents' Committee to Protect the Adirondacks, 2003.

Bedford, B. L. "Cumulative Impact Assessment." Typescript, Reference #2038, Adirondack Park Agency files, Raybrook, N.Y., May 10, 1991.

Bedford, B. L., and E. M. Preston. "Developing the Scientific Basis for Assessing Cumulative Effects of Wetland Loss and Degradation on Landscape Functions: Status, Perspectives, and Prospects." *Environmental Management* 12 (1978): 752.

Booth, R. S., and T. L. Hullar. "Has the Adirondack Park Agency Made a Difference?" *Amicus Journal* (Summer 1980): 14–15.

Bosselman, F., and D. Callies. *The Quiet Revolution in Land Use Control.* Washington, D.C.: Council on Environmental Quality, 1972.

Boyce, M. "Natural Regulation or Control of Nature." In *The Greater Yellowstone Ecosystem,* edited by R. B. Keiter and M. S. Boyce. New Haven, Conn.: Yale Univ. Press, 1991.

Brocke, R. H., K. A. Gustafson, and L. B. Fox. "Restoration of Large Predators: Potentials and Problems." In *Challenges in the Conservation of Biological Resources: A Practitioners Guide,* ed. D. J. Decker, M. E.Krasny, G. R. Goff, C. R. Smith, and D. W. Gross, 303–15. Boulder, Co.: Westview Press, 1991.

Brocke, R. H., K. A. Gustafson, and A. R. Major. "Restoration of the Lynx in New York: Biopolitical Lessons." In *Transactions of the 55th North American Wildlife and Natural Resources Conference,* 590–98. Washington, D.C.: Wildlife Management Institute, 1990.

Brocke, R. H., J. P. O'Pezio, and K. A. Gustafson. "A Forest Management Scheme Mitigating Impact of Road Networks on Sensitive Wildlife Species." In *Is Forest Fragmentation a Management Issue in the Northeast?* Northeastern Forest Experiment Station General Technical Report NE-140 (1988): 13–17.

Brockington, D., J. Igoe, and K. Schmidt-Soltan. "Conservation, Human Rights, and Poverty Reduction." *Conservation Biology* 20 (2006): 250–52.

Brown, E. *The Forest Preserve of New York State: A Handbook for Conservationists.* Glens Falls, N.Y.: Adirondack Mountain Club, 1985.

Brown, K. "The Political Ecology of Biodiversity, Conservation, and Development in Nepal's Terai: Confused Meanings, Means and Ends." *Ecological Economics* 24 (1998): 73–87.

Brown, P. "The Downside of Upland Development." *Adirondack Explorer* 6 (Jan.–Feb. 2004): 6–7, 44–45.

———. "Pataki Forging Legacy in Land." *Adirondack Explorer* 6 (July–Aug. 2004): 42.

———. "Please Don't Eat the Fish: 15 Lakes on Mercury Blacklist." *Adirondack Explorer* 3 (June 2001): 7.

Brumley, C. *Guides of the Adirondacks: A History.* Utica, N.Y.: North Country Books, 1994.

Carlson, D. M. *Species Accounts of the Rare Fishes of New York.* Albany: NYS Department of Environmental Conservation, 2001.

Carlson, D. M., and R. A. Daniels. "Status of Fishes in New York: Increases, Declines, and Homogenization of Watersheds." *American Midland Naturalist* 152 (2004): 104–39.

Carson, R. *Silent Spring.* Boston: Houghton, 1962.

Caughley, G. "What Is This Thing Called Carrying Capacity?" In *North American Elk: Ecology, Behavior, and Management,* edited by M. S. Boyce and L. D. Hayden–Wing. Laramie: Univ. of Wyoming Press, 1979.

"Champion of 'Balanced Use.'" *Adirondack Explorer* 7 (July–Aug. 2005): 25, 68.

Charnley, S. "The Northwest Forest Plan as a Model for Broad-Scale Ecosystem Management: A Social Perspective." *Conservation Biology* 20 (2006): 330–40.

Chavez, A. S., and E. M. Gese. "Landscape Use and Movements of Wolves in Relation to Livestock in a Wildland-Agricultural Matrix." *Journal of Wildlife Management* 70 (2006): 1079–86.

*Citizen's Guide to the Adirondack Park Agency Land Use Regulations.* Ray Brook, N.Y.: Adirondack Park Agency. http://www.apa.state.ny.us/documents/guidelines/citizensguide.pdf.

Clarke, C. H. D. *The Future of the Adirondacks, Technical Reports,* vol. 2, *Wildlife.* Albany: Temporary Study Commission on the Future of the Adirondacks, 1974.

Cobb, T. L. "The Adirondack Park and the Evolution of Its Current Boundary." *The Adirondack Park in the Twenty-First Century, Technical Reports,* vol. 1. Albany: State of New York, 1990.

Cole, T. "Book Review of Stephen Haycox: *Frigid Embrace: Politics, Economics, and Environment.*" *Pacific Northwest Quarterly* 94 (2003).

Comstock, E., Jr., ed. *The Adirondack League Club, 1890–1990.* Old Forge, N.Y.: Adirondack League Club, 1990.

Cox, G. L., J. D. Erickson, W. F. Porter, and A. M. Woods. "How Would You Invest in a Sustainable Future for Your Community? North Country Respondents Make Their Choices Clear in Research Conducted by SUNY ESF and UVM." *Adirondack Journal of Environmental Studies* 14 (2007): 32–40.

Czech, B., and P. R. Krausman. "Distribution and Causation of Species Endangerment in the United States." *Science* 277(1997): 1116–17.

Daniels, R. A., and D. M. Peteet. "Fish Scale Evidence for Rapid Post-Glacial Colonization of an Atlantic Coastal Pond." *Global Ecology and Zoogeography Letters* 7 (1998): 467–76.

Dawson, C. P., and P. Thorndike. "State-Designated Wilderness Programs in the United States." *International Journal of Wilderness* 8 (2002): 21–26.

DeGraaf, R. M., and M. Yamasaki. *New England Wildlife.* Hanover, N.H.: Univ. Press of New England, 2001.

Deisch, M. S., and R. W. Sage, Jr. "Songbird Diversity Following Shelterwood Cutting in Two Northern Hardwood Stands in the Central Adirondacks." Abstract. Northeast Fish and Wildlife Conference, Nashua, N.H., Apr., 1990.

DeKay, J. E. *Natural History of New York—Zoology.* New York: Appleton, Wiley and Putnam, 1842.

DePalma, A. "A Deal Is Reached to Preserve Land and the Economy in the Adirondacks." *New York Times,* Apr. 22, 2004, A24.

———. "A Template for Conservation." *New York Times,* May 1, 2004.

Diamond, J. *Collapse: How Societies Choose to Fail or Succeed.* 2005. New York: Viking Press, 2005.

Dobbs, D., and R. Ober. *The Northern Forest.* White River Junction, Vt.: Chelsea Green, 1995.

Drucker, P. *The Practice of Management.* New York: Harper and Row, 1954.

Durant, K., and H. Durant. *The Adirondack Guide Boat.* Blue Mountain Lake, N.Y.: Adirondack Museum,1980.

Emmons, E. *Survey of the Second Geological District.* Albany: Appleton, Wiley and Putnam, 1942.

Erickson, J. D. "In Search of Sustainable Development: Lessons in Application from the Adirondack Park." In *Sustainability in Action: Sectoral and Regional Case Studies,* edited by J. Köhn, J. Gowdy, and J. van der Straaten, 261–80. Cheltenham, U.K.: Edward Elgar, 2001.

———. "Sustainable Development and the Adirondack Park Experience," *Adirondack Journal of Environmental Studies* 5 (1998): 24–32.

Erickson, J. D., and S. O'Hara, "From Top-Down to Participatory Planning: Conservation Lessons from the Adirondack Park, NY, USA." In *Biodiversity and Ecological Economics: Participation, Values, and Resource Management,* edited by L. Tacconi, 146–61. London: Earthscan, 2000.

Fener, H. M., J. R. Ginsberg, E. Sanderson, and M. E. Gompper. "Chronology of Range Expansion of the Coyote, *Canis latrans,* in New York." *Canadian Field Naturalist* 119 (2002): 1–5.

*First Annual Report of the Commissioners of State Parks of the State of New York.* Senate Document 102, 1873; Albany: Weed Parsons, 1874.

Franklin, J. F. "Structural and Functional Diversity in Temperate Forests." In *Biodiversity,* ed. E. O. Wilson. Washington, D.C.: National Academies Press, 1988.

Gallagher, J., and J. Baker. "Current Status of Fish Communities in Adirondack Lakes." In *Adirondack Lakes Survey: An Interpretive Analysis of Fish Communities and Water Chemistry, 1984–87,* 3–11–3–48. Ray Brook, N.Y.: Adirondack Lake Survey Corporation, 1990.

Garner, D. L. "Ecology of the Moose and the Feasibility for Translocation into the Greater Adirondack Ecosystem." Master's thesis, SUNY College of Environmental Science and Forestry, 1989.

George, C. J. *The Fishes of the Adirondack Park.* Lake Monograph Program. Albany: NYS Department of Environmental Conservation, 1981.

Gibbs, J. P., A. R. Breisch, P. K. Ducey, G. Johnson, J. L. Behler, and R. C. Bothner. *Amphibians and Reptiles of New York State.* New York: Oxford Univ. Press, 2007.

Gilborn, C. *Adirondack Camps: Homes Away from Home, 1850–1950.* Blue Mountain Lake, N.Y./Syracuse: Adirondack Museum/Syracuse Univ. Press, 2000.

———. *Durant: The Fortunes and Woodland Camps of a Family in the Adirondacks.* Utica: North Country Books, 1981.

Ginsberg, W. R., and P. Weinberg. *Environmental Law and Regulation in New York.* St. Paul, Minn.: West Publishing Co., 1996.

Glennon, M. J., and W. F. Porter. "Effects of Land Use Management on Biotic Integrity: An Investigation of Bird Communities." *Biological Conservation* 126 (2005): 499–511.

Glennon, R. "The Ability of the Adirondack Park Agency Act to Achieve Its Objectives." *The Adirondack Park in the Twenty-First Century, Technical Reports,* vol. 2. Albany: State of New York, 1990.

———. "Non-forest Preserves: Inconsistent Use." *The Adirondack Park in the Twenty-First Century, Technical Report 5,* vol. 1. Albany: State of New York, 1990.

Gompper, M. E. "Top Carnivores in the Suburbs? Ecological and Conservation Issues Raised by Colonization of Northeastern North America by Coyotes." *Bioscience* 52 (2002): 185–90.

Gottlieb, R. *Forcing the Spring: The Transformation of the American Environmental Movement.* Washington, D.C.: Island Press, 1993.

Gowdy, J. M., and C. N. McDaniel. "One World, One Experiment: Addressing the Biodiversity-Economics Conflict," *Ecological Economics* 15 (1995): 181–92.

Graham, F., Jr. *The Adirondack Park: A Political History.* New York: Knopf, 1978.

Grewal, S. K., P. J. Wilson, T. K. Kung, K. Shami, M. T. Theberge, J. B. Theberge, and B. N. White. "A Genetic Assessment of the Eastern Wolf (*Canis lycaon*) in Algonquin Provincial Park." *Journal of Mammalogy* 85 (2004): 625–32.

Hammond, S. H. *Hills, Lakes, and Forest Streams.* New York: J. C. Derby, 1854.

———. *Wild Northern Scenes: Or Sporting Adventures with the Rifle and the Rod.* New York: Derby and Jackson, 1860.

Harper, E. K., W. J. Paul, and L. D. Mech. "Causes of Wolf Depredation Increase in Minnesota from 1979–1998." *Wildlife Society Bulletin* 33 (2005): 888–96.

Harris, L. D. *The Fragmented Forest: Island Biogeography Theory and the Preservation of Biotic Diversity.* Chicago: Univ. of Chicago Press, 1984.

Haufler, J. B., L. G. Adams, J. Bailey, R. H. Brocke, M. J. Conroy, G. J. Joslin, and K. G. Smith. *Wildlife Management in North American Wilderness,* Wildlife Society Technical Review 96–1. Washington, D.C.: The Wildlife Society, 1996.

Haycox, S. *Alaska: An American Colony.* Seattle: Univ. of Washington Press, 2002.

Headley, J. T. *The Adirondack; or, Life in the Woods.* New York: Baker and Scribner, 1849.

Heiman, M. K. *The Quiet Evolution: Power, Planning, and Profits in New York State.* New York: Praeger, 1988.

Hoffman, C. F. *Wild Scenes in the Forest and Prairie.* New York: W. H. Colyer, 1843.

Hoving, C. L. "Historical Occurrence and Habitat Ecology of Canada Lynx (*Lynx canadensis*) in Eastern North America." Master's thesis, Univ. of Maine, 2001.

Howe, J., E. McMahon, and L. Propst. *Balancing Nature and Commerce in Gateway Communities.* Covelo, Calif.: Island Press, 1997.

Hu, W. "Use of Herbicide Is Proposed in Weed-Choked Lake George." *New York Times* Apr. 29, 2001.

Hull, T., and L. Leask. "Dividing Alaska, 1867–2000: Changing Land Ownership and Management." *Alaska Review of Social and Economic Conditions* 32 (2001): 1–12.

Hunter, M. *Fundamentals of Conservation Biology.* Malden, Mass.: Blackwell Science, 2002, 255.

Jackson, J. B. *Discovering the Vernacular Landscape.* New Haven: Yale Univ. Press, 1984.

Jacoby, K. *Crimes Against Nature: Squatters, Poachers, Thieves, and the Hidden History of American Conservation.* Berkeley: Univ. of California Press, 2001.

Jamieson, P. *The Adirondack Reader.* Glens Falls, N.Y.: Adirondack Mountain Club, 1983.

Jenkins, J., and A. Keal. *The Adirondack Atlas.* Syracuse: Syracuse Univ. Press, 2004.

Jerry, H. *A Museum Memoir.* Chicago: Blueline Press, 2007.

Joint Federal-State Land Use Planning Commission for Alaska. *Major Ecosystems of Alaska.* Fairbanks, Alaska: U.S. Geological Survey, Fairbanks, 1973.

Kaiser, H. *Great Camps of the Adirondacks.* Boston: David R. Godine, 1982.

Keller, W. T. *Management of Wild and Hybrid Brook Trout in New York Lakes, Ponds, and Coastal Streams.* Albany: Bureau of Fisheries, NYS Department of Environmental Conservation, 1979.

Kendrot, S. R. "The Effects of Roads and Land Use on Home Range Use, Behavior and Mortality of Eastern Coyotes (*Canis latrans* var.) in Northern New York." Master's thesis, SUNY College of Environmental Science and Forestry, 1998.

Klein, P. "Bill Would Obstruct Most Development." *Hamilton County News,* Apr. 13, 2004.

Knott, C. H. *Living with the Adirondack Forest—Local Perspective on Land Use Conflicts.* Ithaca, N. Y.: Cornell Univ. Press, 1998.

Koehler, G. M. "Population and Habitat Characteristics of Lynx and Snowshoe Hares in North-Central Washington." *Canadian Journal of Zoology* 68 (1990): 845–51.

Kogut, K. L. "A Look at Fish and Wildlife Resources in the Adirondack Park in the Twenty-First Century." *The Adirondack Park in the Twenty-First Century, Technical Reports,* vol. 1. Albany: State of New York, 1990.

Kranz, M. W. "Pioneering in Conservation: A History of the Conservation Movement in New York State, 1865–1903." Ph.D. diss., Syracuse Univ., 1961.

Kruuk, H. *Hunter and Hunted: Relationships Between Carnivores and People.* New York: Cambridge Univ. Press, 2002.

LeFebvre, D. "A.A.T.V.–A Definition, a Direction." *Adirondack Journal of Environmental Studies* 1 (1994):13–19.

Leopold, A. "Land Ethic." *A Sand County Almanac: And Sketches Here and There.* New York: Oxford Univ. Press, 1949.

Liroff, R. A., and G. Davis. *Protecting Open Space: Land Use Control in the Adirondack Park.* Cambridge, Mass.: Ballinger, 1981.

Louks, B. A. "Peregrine Falcon: *Falco peregrinus.*" In *Bull's Birds of New York State,* edited by E. Levine. Ithaca, N.Y.: Cornell Univ. Press, 1998.

Louv, R. *Last Child in the Woods: Saving Our Children from Nature-Deficit Disorder.* Chapel Hill, N.C.: Algonquin Books, 2005.

Maehr, D. S., E. D. Land, and M. E. Roelke. "Mortality Patterns of Panthers in Southwest Florida." *Proceedings of Annual Conference of Southeastern Fish and Wildlife Agencies* 45 (1991): 201–7.

Marsh, G. P. *Man and Nature; or, Physical Geography as Modified by Human Action.* New York: Scribner, 1864; reprint, edited by D. Lowenthal. Cambridge, Mass.: Belknap Press of Harvard Univ. Press, 1965.

Mather, F. "Memoranda Relating to Adirondack Fishes with Descriptions of New Species from Researches Made in 1882." Appendix to the 12th report. Albany: State of New York Adirondack Survey, 1886.

Mcgowan, K. J., and K. Corwin, eds. *The Second Atlas of Breeding Birds in New York.* Ithaca, N.Y.: Comstock, 2008.

McHarg, I. L. *Design with Nature.* Garden City, N.Y.: Natural History Press, 1969.

McMartin, B. *The Great Forest of the Adirondacks.* Utica, N.Y.: North Country Books, 1994.

———. *Perspectives on the Adirondacks: A Thirty-Year Struggle by People Protecting Their Treasure.* Syracuse: Syracuse Univ. Press, 2002.

McNeely, J. A., et al. *Conserving the World's Biological Diversity.* Gland, Switzerland, and Washington, D.C.: IUCN, WRI, CI, WWF-US and World Bank, 1990.

Mech, L. D. "Age, Sex, Reproduction, and Spatial Organization of Lynxes Colonizing Northeastern Minnesota." *Journal of Mammalogy* 61 (1980): 261–67.

Merriam, C. H. *The Mammals of the Adirondack Region, Northeastern New York.* New York: Press of L. S. Foster, 1884.

Miller, G. S., Jr. "Preliminary List of the Mammals of New York." *Bulletin of the New York State Museum* 6 (1899): 339–40.

Mitchell, L. C. *Witnesses to a Vanishing America: The Nineteenth-Century Response.* Princeton, N.J.: Princeton Univ. Press, 1981.

Molina, R., B. G. Marcot, and R. Lesher. "Protecting Rare, Old-Growth Forest-Associated Species under the Survey and Management Guidelines of the Northwest Forest Plan." *Conservation Biology* 20 (2006): 306–18.

E. Moore, E. "A Biological Survey of the Champlain Watershed." Supplement to the 19th Annual Report of the New York State Conservation Department (1929). Albany: New York State Conservation Department, 1930.

————. "A Biological Survey of the Oswegatchie and Black River Systems." Supplement to the 21st Annual Report of the New York State Conservation Department (1931). Albany: New York State Conservation Department, 1932.

————. "A Biological Survey of the Upper Hudson Watershed." Supplement to the 22d Annual Report of the New York State Conservation Department (1932). Albany: New York State Conservation Department, 1933.

————. "A Biological Survey of the Raquette Watershed." Supplement to the 23d Annual Report of the New York State Conservation Department (1933). Albany: New York State Conservation Department, 1934.

————. "A Biological Survey of the Mohawk-Hudson Watershed." Supplement to the 24th Annual Report of the New York State Conservation Department (1934). Albany: New York State Conservation Department, 1935.

Nash, R. *Wilderness and the American Mind.* 4th ed. New Haven: Yale Univ. Press, 2001.

New England Regional Assessment Group. *Preparing for a Changing Climate: The Potential Consequences of Climate Variability and Change.*

Durham: Univ. of New Hampshire, 2001. http://www.necci.sr.unh
.edu/2001-NERA-report.html, accessed June 28, 2004.

Newton, R. M., and C. T. Driscoll. "Classification of ALSC Lakes." In
*Adirondack Lakes Survey: An Interpretive Analysis of Fish Communities and
Water Chemistry, 1984–1987,* ed. J. P. Baker, 2–70-2–91. Ray Brook,
N.Y.: Adirondack Lakes Survey Corp., 1990.

New York Forest, Fish, and Game Commission. *Eighth and Ninth Annual
Reports.* Albany: J. B. Lyon, 1904.

New York State. *Adirondack Park State Land Master Plan.* Ray Brook, N.Y.:
Adirondack Park Agency, 1972.

———. *Adirondack Park State Land Master Plan.* Approved Nov. 1987,
updated 2001. http://www.apa.state.ny.us/.

New York State Commission on the Adirondacks in the Twenty-First
Century. *The Adirondack Park in the Twenty-First Century.* Albany: State
of New York. 1990.

New York State Conservation Commission. *Ninth Annual Report for the
Year 1919.* Albany, N.Y.: J. B. Lyon, 1920.

New York State Department of Environmental Conservation. "Draft
Comprehensive Snowmobile Plan for the Adirondack Park/Draft
Generic Environmental Impact Statement." http://www.dec.state
.ny.us/website/dlf/publands/snow/index.html, accessed Mar. 27,
2004, but no longer available online.

New York State Forest Commission. *Annual Report for 1890.* Albany:
Assembly Document 84, 1891.

Noon, B., and J. A. Blakely. "Conservation of the Northern Spotted
Owl under the Northern Forest Plan." *Conservation Biology* 20 (2006):
288–96.

Northrup, J. *The Adirondack Condition: Economic, Environmental, and Social
Well-Being.* Albany: Environmental Advocates, 1997.

Noss, R. F. "A Regional Landscape Approach to Maintain Biodiversity."
*Bioscience* 33 (1983): 700–706.

———. "The Wildlands Project: Land Conservation Strategy." In *Environmental Policy and Biodiversity,* edited by R. E. Grumbine. Washington, D.C.: Island Press, 1994.

Nye, P. "Bald Eagle: *Haliaeetus leucocephalus.*" In *Bull's Birds of New York
State,* edited by E. Levine, 182–85. Ithaca, N.Y.: Cornell Univ. Press,
1998

———. "Golden Eagle: *Aquila chrysaetos*." In *Bull's Birds of New York State,* edited by E. Levine, 198–200. Ithaca, N.Y.: Cornell Univ. Press, 1998.

Oelschlaeger, M. *The Idea of Wilderness: From Prehistory to the Age of Ecology.* New Haven, Conn.: Yale Univ. Press, 1991.

Oles, H. "Monitoring the Pulse of Invasive Plants in the Adirondack Park: A Coordinated Approach to Regional Invasive Plant Management." *Adirondack Journal of Environmental Studies* 11 (Spring/Summer 2004): 14.

Paquet, P. C., J. R. Strittholt, and N. L. Staus. *Wolf Reintroduction Feasibility in the Adirondack Park: Prepared for the Adirondack Citizens Advisory Committee on the Feasibility of Wolf Reintroduction.* Corvallis, Ore.: Conservation Biology Institute, 1999.

Penney, J. "My View." *Adirondack Journal of Environmental Studies* 4 (1997): 24–26.

Peterson, M. N., S. A. Allison, M. J. Peterson, T. R. Peterson, and R. R. Lopez. "A Tale of Two Species: Habitat Conservation Plans as Bounded Conflicts." *Journal of Wildlife Management* 68 (2004): 743–61.

Pilcher, E. *Up the Lake Road: The First Hundred Years of the Adirondack Mountain Reserve.* Keene Valley, N.Y.: Adirondack Mountain Reserve, 1987.

Platt, R. H. *Land Use and Society: Geography, Law, and Public Policy.* Washington, D.C.: Island Press, 1996.

Popper, F. J. "Understanding American Land Use Regulation since 1970." *Journal of the American Planning Association* 54 (Summer 1988): 291–301.

Potter, D. *People of Plenty: Economic Abundance and the American Character.* Chicago: Univ. of Chicago Press, 1954.

Residents' Committee to Protect the Adirondacks. *Growth in the Adirondack Park: Analysis of Rates and Patterns of Development.* North Creek, N.Y.: The Residents' Committee to Protect the Adirondacks, 2001.

———. *The Park Report* 9 (Mar. 2004): 3.

———. "RCPA Opposes Draft Comprehensive Adirondack Snowmobile Plan," news release, Feb. 9, 2004, http://www.adirondackresidents.org/.

Rome, A. *The Bulldozer in the Countryside: Suburban Sprawl and the Rise of American Environmentalism.* Cambridge: Cambridge Univ. Press, 2001.

Roy, K., W. Kretser, H. Simonin, and E. Bennet. "Acid Rain in the Adirondacks: A Time of Change!" *Adirondack Journal of Environmental Studies* 7 (Spring/Summer 2000): 26–32.

Sax, J. "The Public Trust Doctrine in Natural Resource Law: Effective Judicial Intervention." *Michigan Law Review,* 1970, quoted in M. Dowie, "In Law We Trust," *Orion* 22 (July/August, 2003): 18–25.

Schaefer, P. *Adirondack Explorations: Nature Writings of Verplanck Colvin.* Syracuse: Syracuse Univ. Press, 1997.

———. *Defending the Wilderness: The Adirondack Writings of Paul Schaefer.* Syracuse: Syracuse Univ. Press, 1989.

Schneider, P. *The Adirondacks: A History of America's First Wilderness.* New York: Henry Holt, 1997.

Schoch, N., and D. C. Evers. *Monitoring Mercury in Common Loons: New York Field Report, 1998–2000.* Falmouth, Me.: BioDiversity Research Institute, 2002.

Sears, J. F. *Sacred Places: American Tourist Attractions in the Nineteenth Century.* New York: Oxford Univ. Press, 1989.

Seely, H. "How Much Development Is Too Much?" *Syracuse Post Standard,* Aug. 10, 2003.

Severinghaus, W., and C. P. Brown. "History of White-tailed Deer in New York." *New York Fish and Game Journal* 3, no. 2 (1956): 129–67.

Siegler, H. R. "The Status of Wildcats in New Hampshire." In *Proceedings of a Symposium on the Native Cats of North America—Their Status and Management,* edited by S. E. Jorgensen and L. D. Mech. St. Paul, Minn.: USDI Bureau of Sport Fisheries and Wildlife, 1971.

Spies, T. A., M. A. Hemstrom, A. Youngblood, and S. Hummel. "Conserving Old-growth Forest Diversity in Disturbance-prone Landscapes." *Conservation Biology* 20 (2006): 351–62.

Spilman, C. "The Effects of Lakeshore Development on Common Loon Productivity in the Adirondack Park, New York." Master's thesis, SUNY College of Environmental Science and Forestry, 2006.

"State to Ban ATVs in Preserve." *Adirondack Explorer* 6 (July–Aug. 2004): 4.

Steiner, G. A. *Strategic Planning.* New York: Free Press, 1997.

Stone, W. *Puma concolor Necropsy Report.* Albany: NYSDEC Wildlife Pathology Laboratory, 1993.

Stoner, D. C., M. L. Wolfe, and D. M. Choate. "Cougar Exploitation Levels in Utah: Implications for Demographic Structure, Population

Recovery, and Metapopulation Dynamics." *Journal of Wildlife Management* 70 (2006): 1588–1600.

Street, A. B. *Woods and Waters; or, the Saranacs and Racket.* New York: M. Doolady, 1860.

Strohmeyer, J. *Extreme Conditions: Big Oil and the Transformation of Alaska.* Simon and Schuster, 1993.

Temporary Study Commission on the Future of the Adirondacks. *The Future of the Adirondacks,* 2 vols. Blue Mountain Lake, N.Y.: Adirondack Museum, 1971.

Terrie, P. G. *Contested Terrain: A New History of Nature and People in the Adirondacks.* Blue Mountain Lake, N.Y./Syracuse: Adirondack Museum/ Syracuse Univ. Press, 1997.

———. "Urban Man Confronts the Wilderness: The Nineteenth-Century Sportsman in the Adirondacks." *Journal of Sport History* 5 (Winter 1978): 7–20.

———. *Wildlife and Wilderness: A History of Adirondack Mammals.* Fleischmanns, N.Y.: Purple Mountain Press, 1993

Thaler, J. S. *Adirondack Weather.* Yorktown Heights, N.Y.: Hudson Valley Climate Service, 2004.

Thill, M. "Acres and Pains." *Adirondack Life* 36 (Sept.–Oct. 2005): 63–65, 76–77.

Thomas, E. M. *The Old Way, a Story of the First People.* New York: Farrar, Straus, and Giroux, 2006.

Thomas, J. W., J. F. Franklin, J. Gordon, and K. N. Johnson. "The Northeast Forest Plan: Origins, Components, Implementation Experiences, and Suggestions for Change." *Conservation Biology* 20 (2006): 277–87.

Thompson, R. C. "The Doctrine of Wilderness: A Study of the Policy and Politics of the Adirondack Preserve-Park." Ph.D. diss., State Univ. College of Forestry at Syracuse Univ., 1962.

Thomson, R. "Solving Africa's Commercial Poaching Pandemic." *African Sporting Gazette* 11 (2006): 16–18.

Thoreau, H. D. *The Maine Woods.* Princeton, N.J.: Princeton Univ. Press, 1972.

Thorndike, Elizabeth. "The Adirondack Park in the 21st Century." *Adirondack Journal of Environmental Studies* 4, no. 2 (Fall/Winter 1997) and 5, no. 1 (Spring/Summer 1998).

"Try Not to Breathe." *Adirondack Explorer* 4 (July–Aug., 2002): 4.

Vashon, J. H., et al. "Spatial Ecology of a Lynx Population in Northern Maine." *Journal of Wildlife Management* 72 (2008): 1479–87.

Wang, Z., and R. D. Nyland. "Tree Species Richness Increased by Clearcutting of Northern Hardwoods in Central New York." *Forest Ecology and Management* 57 (1993):71–84.

Whittier, T. R., D. B. Halliwell, and R. A. Daniels. "Distribution of Lake Fishes in the Northeast—II: The Minnows (Cyprinidae)." *Northeastern Naturalist* 7 (2000): 131–56.

Whittier, T. R., and T. M. Kincaid. "Introduced Fish in Northeastern USA Lakes: Regional Extent, Dominance, and Effect on Native Species Richness." *Transactions of the American Fisheries Society* 128 (1999): 769–83

Wilson, P. J., S. Grewal, T. McFadden, R. C. Chambers, and B. N. White. "Mitochondrial DNA Extracted from Eastern North American Wolves Killed in the 1800s Is Not of Gray Wolf Origin." *Canadian Journal of Zoology* 81 (2003): 936–40.

Wilson, P. J., W. J. Jakubas, and S. Mullen. *Genetic Status and Morphological Characteristics of Maine Coyotes as Related to Neighboring Coyote and World Populations.* Final Report to the Maine Outdooor Heritage Fund Board, Grant #011-3-7. Maine Department of Inland Fisheries and Wildlife, 2004.

World Almanac Education Group. *The World Almanac and Book of Facts 2005.* New York: St. Martins Press, 2005.

World Commission on Environment and Development. *Our Common Future.* New York: Oxford Univ. Press, 1987.

Worster, E. *Nature's Economy: A History of Ecological Ideas.* New York: Cambridge Univ. Press, 1985.

Zahniser, H. *Where Wilderness Preservation Began: Adirondack Writings of Howard Zahniser.* Utica, N.Y.: North Country Books, 1992.

# Index